THE
FOREIGN POLICY
OF
RUSSIA

THE FOREIGN POLICY OF RUSSIA

CHANGING SYSTEMS, ENDURING INTERESTS

THIRD EDITION

ROBERT H. DONALDSON AND **JOSEPH L. NOGEE**

M.E.Sharpe
Armonk, New York
London, England

Library of Congress Cataloging-in-Publication Data

Donaldson, Robert H.
 The foreign policy of Russia : changing systems, enduring interests / Robert H.
Donaldson, Joseph L. Nogee.—3rd ed.
  p. cm.
 Includes bibliographical references and index.
 ISBN 0-7656-1567-3 (hardcover: alk. paper) — ISBN 0-7656-1568-1 (pbk.: alk. paper)
  1. Soviet Union—Foreign relations. 2. Russia (Federation)—Foreign relations.
 I. Nogee, Joseph L. II. Title.

DK266.45.D66 2005
327.47′009′04—dc22   2004023134

Printed in the United States of America

The paper used in this publication meets the minimum requirements of
American National Standard for Information Sciences
Permanence of Paper for Printed Library Materials,
ANSI Z 39.48-1984.

BM (c) 10   9   8   7   6   5   4   3   2   1
BM (p) 10   9   8   7   6   5   4   3   2

Contents

List of Maps

—— Acronyms and Abbreviations ——

ABM	Anti-ballistic Missile
ANC	African National Congress
APEC	Asian and Pacific Economic Council
ASEAN	Association of Southeast Asian Nations
CACO	Central Asian Cooperation Organization
CCP	Chinese Communist Party
CFE	Conventional Forces in Europe
CIA	Central Intelligence Agency (U.S.)
CIS	Commonwealth of Independent States
CMEA	Council for Mutual Economic Assistance
CPSU	Communist Party of the Soviet Union
CSCE	Conference on Security and Cooperation in Europe
CSS	Commonwealth of Slavic States
CSTO	Collective Security Treaty Organization
CTBT	Comprehensive Nuclear Test Ban Treaty
CTR	Cooperative Threat Reduction
DPRK	Democratic People's Republic of Korea
EBRD	European Bank for Reconstruction and Development
EU	European Union
EURASEC	Eurasian Economic Community
FAPSI	Federal Agency for Government Communications and Information
FPS	Federal Border Service
FSB	Federal Security Service
G8	Group of 8 Industrial Nations (Canada, France, Italy, Germany, United Kingdom, United States, Japan, Russia)
GATT	General Agreement on Tariffs and Trade
GDR	German Democratic Republic (East Germany)
GNP	Gross National Product
GPALS	Global Protection Against Limited Strikes
GRU	Soviet Military Intelligence Agency

GUUAM	Georgia, Ukraine, Uzbekistan, Azerbaijan, Moldova
IAEA	International Atomic Energy Agency
ICBM	Intercontinental Ballistic Missile
IFOR	Implementation Force
IMF	International Monetary Fund
INF	Intermediate Nuclear Forces
KFOR	Kosovo Force
KGB	Committee for State Security
KLA	Kosovo Liberation Army
KPD	Communist Party of Germany
MFN	Most Favored Nation
MIRV	Multiple Independently Targeted Reentry Vehicles
MPLA	Movement for the People's Liberation of Angola
NACC	North Atlantic Cooperation Council
NATO	North Atlantic Treaty Organization
NIS	Newly Independent States
NMD	National Missile Defense
NPT	Non-proliferation Treaty
NTV	Independent Television
ORT	Public Radio and Television Broadcasting
OSCE	Organization for Security and Cooperation in Europe
PFP	Partnership for Peace
PLO	Palestine Liberation Organization
PSI	Proliferation Security Initiative
RSDLP	Russian Social-Democratic Labor Party
SALT	Strategic Arms Limitation Talks
SORT	Strategic Offensive Reductions Treaty
SCO	Shanghai Cooperation Organization
SDI	Strategic Defense Initiative
SPD	Social Democratic Party (Germany)
SMF	Strategic Missile Forces
START	Strategic Arms Reduction Talks
SVR	Foreign Intelligence Service
UN	United Nations
UNMOVIC	United Nations Monitoring, Verification and Inspection Commission
USSR	Union of Soviet Socialist Republics
WTO	World Trade Organization

Acknowledgments

We thank Daniel S. Papp, who read our original manuscript and made helpful suggestions. We alone are responsible for errors of fact or interpretation.

We also thank our respective institutions, the University of Tulsa and the University of Houston, for their support of our work.

Finally, we are grateful to our families for their encouragement and support, and for their tolerance of the many distractions from family life that writing a book entails.

THE
FOREIGN POLICY
OF
RUSSIA

1

Introduction

We attempt in this book to provide both a description and an explanation of the foreign policy of Russia. Our time frame is largely the twentieth century, although we include the latter part of the nineteenth century and the early years of the twenty-first century. Especially over such a broad expanse of time, it is easier to describe policy than to explain it, because causality in politics involves multiple factors that are constantly changing in value.

For that period of Russian politics dominated by the Soviet system, the basic character of foreign policy seemed simple. Marxist-Leninist doctrine appeared to dictate confrontation with the noncommunist world. In fact, however, foreign policy during the Soviet period was never so clear as it appeared to most contemporaries. Nonideological factors produced complex relations between the Union of Soviet Socialist Republics (USSR) and other great powers: at times, cooperation with the West (détente), and at times, hostility to other communist regimes (Yugoslavia and China, for example).

The factors that shape foreign policy are multiple. Some are internal, such as the government and its political elites, the culture, economy, geography, and demography of a country. Others are external, such as foreign threats, political vacuums, and changes in the balance of power. These different factors are always changing in substance and weight, thus making it impossible to come up with a formula or model to explain or predict foreign policy. In short, foreign policy, like all politics, is dynamic.

One broad generalization about Russian foreign policy that we believe to be valid is that there are elements of both continuity and change always at work. Over the course of time, Russian foreign policy has exhibited many profound shifts in direction. Perhaps less obvious has been the continuity in behavior of governments headed by tsars, commissars, and presidents. In many respects, Russian foreign policy has been similar to that of other great powers, and in other respects it has been unique. We begin this survey of Russian foreign policy with a preliminary analysis of the continuity and change we will be describing in Russia's relations with the world, and of the degree to which that policy can be deemed distinctive.

Continuity and the International System

To begin with the continuities and similarities, we note that as a general rule of statecraft, Russia has pursued balance-of-power policies. (Admittedly, it has not always fared well in these, as evidenced by the disaster of the 1939 Nazi-Soviet Pact,[1] but in that respect also, Russia has shared a characteristic with the other great powers in the world.) In principle, *balance-of-power policies* are the measures taken by governments whose interests or security is threatened, to enhance their power by whatever means are available.[2] The most common technique associated with the balance of power is forming or joining military alliances, but the balance of power may also entail, among other things, military buildups, intervention in weaker countries, or resort to war. Essentially it involves the mobilization of power to countervail the power of an enemy or a potential adversary. Thus, tsarist Russia was a member of the Triple Entente (with Great Britain and France) in the period leading up to World War I, as a counter to the Triple Alliance headed by imperial Germany. In the Soviet period the Warsaw Pact served as a military counterpart to the North Atlantic Treaty Organization (NATO).

The Russian Federation differs from preceding regimes in not being a member of any military alliance. This is because post-Soviet Russia, unlike preceding regimes, has no major enemies. Nevertheless, it does have rivals and competitors—for example, Iran and Turkey, to the south. Some aspects of Russia's foreign policy in Central Asia are strikingly reminiscent of the "great game" of power politics played by European powers in that region in the nineteenth century.[3] In Europe, an example of Moscow's continuing pursuit of balance-of-power policies is Russia's opposition to NATO expansion.

The enduring goals pursued by Russia through its foreign policy have placed primary emphasis on ensuring national security, promoting the economic well-being of the country, and enhancing national prestige. In this respect, Russia's behavior is not markedly different from that of most great powers, but how these goals have been interpreted and achieved has changed with time and circumstances.

We can explain the similarities and continuities of Russian behavior in large part as a consequence of the *international system*, which conditions the foreign policies of all states. As the primary units or actors in international politics, states—though in some respects interdependent—operate from the premise that they are sovereign and independent entities. Their independence stems from the lack of a global political authority to govern all states. Thus, the international system is decentralized; each nation is free in principle to determine the range of policies it will pursue for itself, including at times the use of force. Sometimes the term "anarchic" is used to describe this feature of the international system.[4]

In reality, foreign policy rarely expresses the principle of national sovereignty (or anarchy) in absolute terms. Just as states are not fully constrained by international norms, economic interdependence, or the power of other states, so they are never totally free of such constraints. But the larger and more powerful a state is, the greater is its freedom of action; small and weak states are more limited. Precisely because there is no world government or protective mechanism for nation-states, each must constantly be on guard to protect its security and interests from those states that periodically emerge on the world scene as a threat to others. In the words of Kenneth N. Waltz:

> Each state pursues its own interests, however defined, in ways that it judges best. Force is a means of achieving the external ends of states because there exists no consistent, reliable process of reconciling the conflicts of interest that inevitably arise among similar units in a condition of anarchy.[5]

Of the many interests pursued by states, none is more important than survival—maintaining territorial integrity and political independence. Unlike the individual in domestic society, the sovereign state is unprotected by legal institutions (police, courts, militias, and so on) and must look instead to the tools of statecraft—diplomacy, armaments, and political and military alignments—for self-protection.

Explaining Variability in Foreign Policy Behavior

The international system defines the broad parameters of foreign policy behavior, but obviously it cannot explain the specific decisions that determine the behavior of states in the realm of international politics. While theory might have predicted that Moscow in 1939 would seek an alliance with some European power, it could not account for Stalin's choice of Germany over Great Britain and France. Exactly a half-century later, theory also could not have predicted that the leaders of the Soviet Union would simply stand aside as the Warsaw Pact disintegrated before their eyes. Foreign policy cannot be predicted because it is the outcome of a large number of constantly changing variables.

Thus, for example, Soviet policy during the Cold War exhibited considerable variability, notwithstanding the fundamental antagonism between the communist world and the West. East-West relations were at times close to military confrontation, and at times cooperative. The arms race was interspersed with arms control agreements. Former friends became enemies, and intervention gave way to "new thinking." In a word, throughout the Soviet period there were multiple forces at play that constantly pushed Moscow in new directions.

In a study of Soviet foreign policy after World War II, the authors of this text identified seven general variables that we believe influenced the changing direction of Soviet foreign policy.[6] These were not the only factors influencing Moscow, but they were among the most important. These variables are:

1. The change in the structure of the international system from multipolarity to bipolarity;
2. The growth of polycentrism in the international communist movement, followed by the collapse of the movement altogether;
3. The development of a military technology that makes possible the total destruction of an adversary;
4. The achievement of military parity between the Soviet Union and the United States, followed by the collapse of the USSR as a superpower;
5. The transition of the Soviet regime from a totalitarian system to an authoritarian oligarchy and then to a fragmented polity;
6. The failure of the command economy;
7. The differences reflected in the leadership of different personalities, from Stalin to Khrushchev to Brezhnev to Gorbachev.

Some of these variables were of an external nature, reflecting changes in the international environment, and others were domestic or internal in nature. Together they reflect the fact that foreign policy has its roots in both domestic and foreign forces.

As we survey Russian foreign policy in the post-Soviet period, we can identify five broad underlying factors that collectively explain much of the change and variability in Russian foreign policy. These observations are necessarily preliminary; independent Russia has existed for slightly more than a dozen years, and it can be expected that over a longer period of time new determining forces will become evident. We consider the following particularly critical in explaining Russian foreign policy:

1. The change in the structure of the international system away from bipolarity;
2. The decline in Russian military capability;
3. Russia's transformation from a command economy to a market economy;
4. Russia's integration into the global economy and its increasing reliance on the global market;
5. Russia's political leadership and domestic politics, especially as manifested in the struggle between Yeltsin and Russian nationalists, followed by Putin's efforts to restore the power of the state and its central control.

We have noted above the general impact of the international system on foreign policy. But clearly, the international system does not possess a fixed or unchanging structure; the number and hierarchy of great powers changes over time. The term *polarity* is commonly used to describe the structure of the international system. A universe dominated by one great power would be designated "unipolar"; one dominated by two powers (or blocs) is "bipolar"; and one characterized by several powers (usually five or more) is "multipolar." What impact does the structure of the international system have upon foreign policy and international politics? While political scientists are in disagreement about the precise impact of polarity on international politics, most would agree that there is a connection.[7]

A bipolar system is characterized as one in which the two dominating powers are juxtaposed against each other in an unceasing struggle for power. Each side sees the other as a deadly adversary, and both view international politics as a "zero-sum game." That is, each adversary views any gain for the other as a loss for itself. International politics in a bipolar system is characterized by continuous tension and frequent crisis. There are occasional military clashes, but more commonly (because of the power of the adversary) the struggle is fought by means of economic competition, propaganda, and subversion.

By contrast a multipolar system is more benign. There is a competitive feature to international politics, but the competition is moderated by the fact that each state views the others as potential allies as well as adversaries. Relations between states in a multipolar system are thus more fluid and less antagonistic.[8] Most political scientists consider multipolarity to be more stable than bipolarity.[9]

"Bipolar world" comes closer to describing the Cold War between the Soviet bloc and the Western bloc (1945–90). There was no Cold War between the Soviet Union and the West before 1945 for the basic reason that international politics was multipolar and not bipolar. Indeed, bipolarity on a global scale had never existed until the end of World War II. The only examples of bipolarity prior to the twentieth century were within geographic regions.[10]

With the collapse of the Warsaw Pact and the disintegration of the Soviet Union, the international system was no longer bipolar. Though the United States became the most powerful state in the world, with unrivaled military strength and a defense budget larger than that of all of its potential competitors combined, it did not—despite complaints to the contrary from Moscow, Paris, Beijing, and other capitals—dominate world politics in a way that would create a "unipolar" world. Especially in the realms of diplomacy, economics, and transnational relations, the patterns of interactions, involving both states and non-state actors, quickly began to resemble those of a multipolar world.

In 1992 there was marked improvement in Moscow's most important relationship in the West—that with the United States—with a new round of Strategic Arms Reduction Talks (START II) and American support for Russia's domestic reform. But Russia no longer treated the West as a monolith. Yeltsin moved to develop a differentiated relationship with the countries of Europe. Annual summits were planned between the presidents of Russia, Germany, and France, independently of those between Yeltsin and Clinton. Annual summits were also agreed upon between Yeltsin and China's Jiang Zemin. At one of these summits in the spring of 1997, Yeltsin and Jiang signed the Joint Declaration on a Multipolar World and the Formation of a New International Order, in which the two presidents explicitly declared:

> The cold war has ended. The bipolar system has disappeared. Positive trends toward the formation of a multipolar world are developing at an accelerated pace, and relations are changing among the major states, including former cold war adversaries. Regional organizations for economic cooperation are showing significant vitality. Diversity in the political, economic, and cultural development of all countries is becoming firmly established, and the role of forces that favor peace and broad international cooperation is growing.[11]

In the new, more complex world of the 1990s, Russia could and did pursue a more flexible policy toward its friends and enemies.

Whatever the international structure, the ability of a state to play an active role in world politics is linked to its *military capability*. Military power is traditionally assumed to be a prime shaper of foreign policy because it is the most immediately employable power asset for protecting populations, controlling territory, and coercing others. To a degree, economic power can compensate for military weakness—Japan is a case in point—but traditionally a state's capacity to project force abroad has been a vital element in defining its status as a great power. There would have been no Cold War without the power of the Red Army backed by a nuclear capability. That explains why the Soviet Union between 1917 and 1945 was not a superpower and why there was no Cold War until the USSR emerged, following the defeat of Nazi Germany, as the strongest military power in Europe.

Eventually the Soviet Union achieved an overall relative military parity with the West. With combat forces numbering in excess of 4 million, the Red Army was twice the size of the U.S. army. By most quantitative measures, the Warsaw Pact had more weapons than NATO, though qualitatively the West was superior. Since exact comparisons of capability are difficult to measure, it was assumed on both sides that a rough parity existed. Soviet military strength—both conventional and nuclear—continued to grow well into the Gorbachev era.

Militarily, the Russian Federation is another story. Following the collapse of the Warsaw Pact in 1991, Soviet and then Russian military capability steadily declined. The Russian army is a hollow shell of its Soviet counterpart. At the heart of the problem is Russia's inability to finance a powerful fighting machine. Soldiers brought home from Eastern Europe were inadequately housed. The government's severe cash shortage led to the nonpayment of soldiers' wages. Equipment has not been maintained adequately. Russia's pilots and naval personnel have not been able to train adequately. Research and development of weapons have been sacrificed. As a consequence, morale has plummeted. Among Russian conscripts life has been so bleak that many have resorted to desertion or even suicide. If there were any doubt about the military collapse, the performance of Russian forces in Chechnya in 1994–96 removed it. A ragtag army of Chechen guerrillas and combat forces defeated the armed forces of a country enormously larger and richer. Even when Chechen guerrillas invaded Russia twice in 1995, Russian forces were unable to prevent the escape of their leaders. Further demonstration of the decline of Russia's military power came in the summer of 2000, with the sinking of the Russian submarine *Kursk*.

Yeltsin was bitterly condemned for the decline of the armed forces—of which he was constantly reminded. In the spring of 1997, when he fired Igor Rodionov as minister of defense, he exclaimed: "I am not merely dissatisfied. I am outraged . . . over the condition of the armed forces."[12] Yeltsin's proposed military reform contemplated substantial reductions in troop strength and ultimately the creation of a professional army without conscription. But at its root, the problem of military reform was economic. The president had been convinced of the need to reduce spending on defense, while many of his officers wanted an increase in military spending. Vladimir Putin, though he has increased spending, has made building a smaller but more effective military a high priority.

Russia's size, skilled population, resources, and nuclear weapons guarantee its ongoing status as a great power, but its military weakness, so long as it persists, will limit Russia's influence in world affairs. In relations with states of the former Soviet Union, Russian influence will be paramount, because these states are even weaker; but in Europe, Russia will have to concede when the West is united on political or security issues (as it was on NATO expansion and ultimately on Bosnia and Kosovo). From the perspective of its neighbors, Russia's military weakness can even create special problems. Russia's borders have become so porous that smuggling is widespread, and there is even a concern that nuclear materials may be illegally dispersed from military stockpiles. There is, in addition, the danger that dissatisfaction with the regime by the military may lead to efforts to topple or destabilize the constitutionally elected government.

Another variable is Russia's *transition from a command economy to a market economy*. Although that transformation has been mired in controversy in both Russia and the West, there is a general consensus that the old system has now been replaced by the new, though Russians disagree regarding the pace and scope of change. Economic production is now in private hands, the ruble is fully convertible, and prices are free to fluctuate with supply and demand.[13]

From the beginning Yeltsin recognized that Russia needed both Western assistance and Western investment. His government solicited the advice of Western economists such as Jeffrey Sachs of Harvard University and Anders Aslund of Sweden. Indeed, reformist members of the Russian government, such as Egor Gaidar, Anatolii Chubais, and Boris Nemtsov, maintained close relations with Western advisors, to the great suspicion of their critics in the Russian parliament.

U.S. economic aid for Russian reform began in 1992 with the passage of the Freedom Support Act. It continued throughout the 1990s and (in declining amounts) into the first decade of the twenty-first century, amounting to more than $2.5 billion. This aid was defended in the U.S. Congress on the following grounds: "The primary U.S. interest in Russia and the NIS [newly independent states] is to prevent their reemergence as a security threat to the West. This can be best achieved if these states make a transition to market economies and democratic systems of government."[14] In the immediate aftermath of the Soviet collapse, with Russia's economy in virtual free fall, the volume of Western aid was especially large; total assistance to Russia from all sources in 1992–93 was around $60 billion. In direct foreign investment, Russia received $1.554 billion in 1992, $2.956 billion in 1993, and $3.558 billion in the first half of 1994.[15] According to the UN Economic Commission for Europe, cumulative foreign direct investment in Russia from 1988 to 1999 amounted to $19.9 billion, approximately $135 per capita.[16] Both aid and investment from the West declined sharply following Russia's 1998 economic crisis, and the country endured several years of net capital outflow.

As Russia's economy began to grow again in the early years of the new century, it became a more attractive target for foreign investment. In the first six months of 2004, total foreign investment was reported to have grown 50 percent over the same period in 2003, to a level of $19 billion, and the net inflow into Russia was said to have reached $3.7 billion. If Russia's economic reform succeeds in raising productivity and the country's standard of living, it seems clear that the economic linkages to the developed countries of the West will tend to promote cooperative relations with these countries. Increasingly, the resort to war for whatever reasons will be counterproductive to the larger goals of the regime.

Related to Russia's transformation from a command to a market economy is the growing linkage of Russia's economy to the *global economy*. The extent of that linkage should not be exaggerated, because Russia continues to impose significant barriers to the free flow of goods and capital between itself and the world. However, compared to the autarchic policies of the Soviet period, democratizing Russia has gone a long way toward joining the global economy. The ruble is now a convertible currency and is thus subject to the influence of capital flows throughout the world. Russia now sells stocks on the international market as well as domestically. Legislation has been enacted to encourage foreign investment. And Russia has joined international institutions like the International Monetary Fund (IMF) and the World Bank as a means for promoting macroeconomic stabilization.

Economists differ on the full significance for national economies of the growing integration of the world economy; but at the least, that integration limits governments in their freedom of action in the pursuit of domestic economic policies. Boris Yeltsin conveyed his desire for Russia to coordinate its macroeconomic policies with those of the major industrial states by joining the G-7 group of developed states. Russia is also trying to gain admission to the World Trade Organization (WTO).

The clearest evidence of international influence over the economic transformation of Russia was the reliance of the Yeltsin administration on the IMF for assistance in macroeconomic stabilization. As of August 2000 the IMF had approved loans of around $37 billion for Russia, of which $22 billion had been disbursed. The objective of these loans has been to stabilize the country's currency, stop inflation, and strengthen the conditions for fiscal stability with economic growth. IMF credits are always given conditionally and involve intrusive measures, many of which are politically controversial. Among the conditions imposed on the Russian government were the termination of export duties, improvement in tax collection, reduction of state subsidies, reduction of budget deficits, and reduction of credit through the banking system.[17] The dependence on foreign loans has an obvious downside, however. By the end of 1999, Russia's total foreign debt exceeded $146 billion (including about $100 billion incurred during the late Soviet period), and the scheduled repayment burden for the early years of the twenty-first century seemed truly staggering.[18] However, with the resumption of economic growth, under the impetus of sharply rising oil prices, Russia has managed to pay down its external debt, cutting it from $139 billion in 2000 to $120 billion by the beginning of 2004.[19] Looked at in another way, Russia's total public debt in 1998 was 145.6 percent of its gross domestic product (GDP), and was on course to drop to 26.5 percent of GDP by the end of 2004.[20]

The foreign policy implications of economic globalization are clear. War becomes more costly, particularly if it involves states on whose assistance

Russia relies. So long as membership in international institutions is important to Russia, Moscow can be expected to make every effort to resolve its difference with the members of those institutions by peaceful means.

Political Leadership and the Impact of Domestic Politics

Finally, there is the role of *political leadership* in guiding Russian relations with the world. The study of leadership, personality, and politics has been a preoccupation of social scientists for many decades, and there is a rich literature drawn from observations of a variety of political environments, from democratic to totalitarian.[21] The theory that best frames our analysis is that of Fred Greenstein in his classic *Personality and Politics*. Of particular relevance is Greenstein's summary discussion of the circumstances in which individual actions affect events: "The likelihood of personal impact varies with (1) the degree to which the actions take place in an environment which admits of restructuring; (2) the location of the actor in the environment; (3) the actor's peculiar strengths or weaknesses." The latter two conditions are self-explanatory, but the first requires some further elaboration. Political environments that "admit of restructuring," Greenstein explains, are "unstable" or in a state of "precarious equilibrium," whereas a situation that does not admit of restructuring would be one in which the outcome "can be expected to occur even if some of the contributing factors are eliminated."[22]

In the context of the foreign policy of the Russian Federation (or of the USSR before it), it is not difficult to determine which leaders were strategically placed so that their peculiar strengths or weaknesses could be brought to bear on the content of policy. In the Soviet period, since the time of Stalin the general secretary of the Communist Party occupied the strategic leadership position, whereas in the post-Soviet period—and especially after the passage of the 1993 Constitution—the president of the Russian Federation is positioned to dominate the policy process. Under what circumstances, then—that is, at which times or in which issue areas—might we expect the occupants of these positions to have impact on policy? Guided by Greenstein's first proposition, we might hypothesize that a leader's impact would be greater in times of political transition or internal instability. It would also be greater in times when an unrestrained individual dictatorship (a "cult of personality," in Soviet parlance) overrode the norms of collective leadership in the top councils of the party or state. Conversely, it would be unlikely that a leader would have much impact at relatively settled times, when the distribution of influence among interest groups and institutions is fairly static and shared governance (or "collective leadership") prevails. Similarly, opportunities for an individual leader to restructure the political environment are limited at times (or in particular issue areas) when doctrine or ideology is rigidly adhered to and leaves little room for maneuver.

Looking at Moscow's foreign policy since World War II, we can easily discern occasions when Stalin's power was unrestrained and his personality traits had significant impact on policy. The opposite case—relatively little impact of the leader's personality on foreign policy—is well illustrated in the study of the Brezhnev era. Termed by his successor Gorbachev the "era of stagnation," the Brezhnev period in Soviet history was characterized by the collective rule of relatively colorless politicians who represented strong interests and institutions; it was also a time of doctrinal rigidity and established routine. Policy outcomes during this period could usually be expected without regard to the particular personalities at the helm of the Communist Party. Not until Gorbachev began to consolidate his power as general secretary in the late 1980s did the Soviet political environment again admit of *perestroika* (restructuring)—indeed, perestroika was Gorbachev's preferred slogan. The foreign policy record of his administration fairly clearly demonstrated the impact of his personal leadership, as he guided the choice of key personnel, reduced the role of the party bureaucracy, discarded outdated Marxist-Leninist tenets, and conducted an innovative personal diplomacy.[23]

Gorbachev's experiment in perestroika was an immense failure, resulting in the collapse of the political institutions of the USSR and the breakup of the country itself. Stepping into this precarious environment, which decidedly "admitted of restructuring," Boris Yeltsin clearly occupied the strategic location from which he could exert far-reaching impact on the foreign policy of his newly established realm. In Greenstein's framework, it was the third variable that would prove decisive. On Yeltsin's political skills—the strengths and weaknesses of his personality—would ultimately depend the determination of his personal impact as a leader. He was destined by his situation for greatness; but in Sidney Hook's terms, his personal skills would determine whether he would go down in history as a Great Man or a Great Failure.[24]

Although Gorbachev had set a new direction and forged new relationships, the foreign policy challenges facing Yeltsin demanded considerable leadership skill. His political career has been a shifting one marked by many contradictions. From a communist *apparatchik* (party bureaucrat) he transformed himself into a democratic leader. To him fell the unique opportunity of defining a new national identity for Russia and establishing the basic concept for its national security. Moreover, with the collapse of the long-dominant Communist Party, he would need to build the new institutions that would shape foreign policy. His foreign policy, like Gorbachev's, could help set the direction for economic and social changes in the country and could gain the foreign assistance that might spark its recovery from a long downward slide.

A totally new challenge lay in establishing relationships of trust and mutual assistance with the fourteen other newly independent states that emerged from the Soviet collapse.

Russia's new constructive relationships with the West were not yet solidified, and immediate attention to the "non-West" would be required to reduce threats to the security of the borders of Russia and her new neighbors. Finally, Yeltsin would have to pursue policies that ensured that Russia found a prominent "place at the table," to ensure safeguarding not only of its traditional interests, but of its concerns relating to the new dangers of proliferation of weapons of mass destruction, ethno-religious conflict, and terrorism.

Boris Yeltsin's primary aim in foreign policy, like Mikhail Gorbachev's before him, was to create a non threatening external environment that would be most conducive to his country's internal economic and political development. As in the early decades of Soviet rule, this concentration on domestic development, together with relative shortcomings in military strength, produced a foreign policy of accommodation, retrenchment, and risk avoidance—at least, in Russia's relations with states beyond the borders of the former USSR.

After Yeltsin resigned from the presidency of Russia, historians began to debate which appellation he deserves—Great Man or Great Failure. There is no doubt about Yeltsin's skills as a destroyer, for he clearly played a major role in bringing down the Soviet Communist system and in breaking up the USSR, as well as in clearing away the remnants of Soviet-style political institutions in post-Soviet Russia. It is about his qualities as a builder that the debate rages. His defenders cite his record in advancing the cause of democracy in Russia through his respect for the electoral process, the freedom of speech and press, his efforts to achieve compromise at critical junctures, and his tendency to support the efforts of market reformers. His efforts made possible the first law-governed electoral transfer of power in the thousand-year history of his country. His detractors, however, cite his ego-driven and authoritarian style of rule, the absence of a vision or program for his country, his apparent insecurity and lack of personal discipline, his inconsistency, his willingness to resort to violence against internal enemies, and his penchant for destabilizing Russia's politics.

Our survey of Yeltsin's foreign policy in the chapters that follow will support a judgment that his record in responding to the challenges facing Russia is decidedly a mixture of successes and failures. Each of the challenges he faced in 1991–92 was passed on to his successor unresolved. With respect to the task of defining a new national identity for Russia and a basic concept for its national security, the detractors are undoubtedly right in bemoaning Yeltsin's inability to articulate a vision or a larger sense of purpose behind which his people could unite. The inability to accept Russia's new geopolitical confines and the question of the reconstitution of the Russian Empire in some form is still alive in some political circles in Moscow. Yeltsin's famous quest for a "national idea" came up empty, and popular confusion about Russia's identity has not been quieted. Yeltsin himself confessed in his autobiography to this lack of strategic vision:

> Where is this Yeltsin taking us?
> I think the answer will intrigue many people. I am not presenting people with a global strategic goal. I am not setting my sights on some shining peak that must be scaled. Nor am I trying to wipe out the entire path traversed until now.
> No. The chief goal of this restless president is Russia's tranquillity.[25]

At the root of Yeltsin's failures in foreign policy was this lack of an overarching vision of where he was taking his country. Despite the production of documents solemnly listing "concepts" and "doctrines," policy objectives were not clearly defined, and Yeltsin kept shuffling personnel at such a rate that implementation became impossible. This absence of a guiding philosophy—in Dimitri Simes's words, "this preoccupation with political tactics at the expense of substantive policy"—produced a foreign policy that seemed to lurch from point to point.[26]

Returning to Greenstein's framework, we can conclude by speculating whether the outcomes of Russian foreign policy in the last decade would have been expected to occur even if the critical variable—the personality of Yeltsin—had been absent. Would it have made a difference to Russia's place in the world if the August 1991 coup plotters had succeeded in removing Yeltsin from the political scene, or if his parliamentary opponents had succeeded in ousting Yeltsin in October 1993, or if Gennadii Zyuganov had won the June 1996 presidential elections, or if Yeltsin had died on the operating table the following autumn? The clear answer, for better or for worse, is that Russia's course would not have been the same. Or to frame our speculation in another way: Where would Russia be today had its first president been a committed democrat with a clear vision of where he wanted the country to go and the self-discipline to pursue that vision? The Yeltsin legacy is indeed a mix of success and failure, but there is little doubt that the foreign policy of Russia has received enormous impact from the powerful personality of the man who ruled in the Kremlin in the 1990s.

Since January 2000 Russia has been governed by a new president. When he took power, Vladimir Putin was a relative unknown to the outside world (and to many in Russia). His background in the Soviet secret police, the Committee for State Security (KGB), led some to suspect that he had an orientation toward authoritarianism, while his association with Anatolii Sobchak, the reformist mayor of St. Petersburg, suggested a more liberal bent. Putin insists he is a democrat.[27] Our analysis in chapter 9 suggests that he is a pragmatist. Whether his leadership will make a dramatic difference in Russia's course in the world is yet to be determined.

In post-Soviet Russia a new influential force emerged in politics—public opinion. The shift to the right reflected the growth of a nationalist sentiment far less accommodating to the West. The elections in 1993 brought Vladimir Zhirinovskii's Liberal Democratic Party to the forefront in the legislature. Two years later Zyuganov's Communist Party of the Russian Federation emerged as the largest party in the Duma. Though their views were opposed to Yeltsin's, Yeltsin recognized the political forces that brought these groups to power. From 1993 on, he sought limited accommodation with his rivals. He won election to a second term by moving to the right, even to the point of bringing Aleksandr Lebed, a nationalist rival, into his administration. Vladimir Putin has an important political advantage denied to his predecessor. As a result of the parliamentary elections of 1999 and 2003, the Duma is dominated by political forces sympathetic to his administration. Clearly, domestic politics is now a significant factor in Russian foreign policy, even if we cannot predict the direction Russian politics will take in the future.

Thus, in the first decade of the new millennium, there was a great deal of uncertainty regarding Russia's future. Most of the factors we have examined point toward a period of peace and cooperation with the other great powers. Yet there are contradictions: NATO expansion eastward is premised on a potential Russian threat; the United States is even accelerated Baltic membership in NATO. Russians were opposed. Russia is assisting Iran in the construction of nuclear power facilities; the United States is opposed. Russia, Germany, France, and China opposed the use of force to topple Saddam Hussein; the United States and Great Britain launched the war in Iraq despite their disapproval. Russia, Europe, and the United States are determined competitors for arms sales throughout the world. Nevertheless, these contradictions were relatively small compared to the larger forces at work, which produced more cooperation between Russia and its neighbors than at any previous time in the century just ended.

One of these larger forces was illuminated by the terrorist attack on the United States on September 11, 2001. Vladimir Putin found that his common interest in fighting Islamic extremist terrorism overrode Russia's differences with the United States on a wide range of issues. The "war on terrorism" seemed to displace the last remnants of the Cold War.

2

The Tsarist Roots of Russia's Foreign Policy

Territory and Climate

The foreign policy of Russia—whether in its tsarist, its Soviet, or its democratic form—is an expression in some measure of certain relatively fixed geopolitical realities. As it began to escape the confines of Muscovy—the principality with Moscow at its center—the expanding state soon encompassed vast and often forbidding territories. At its peak size, after more than four centuries of expansion, the Russian Empire (including Poland and Finland) covered just under 9 million square miles—over one-sixth of the earth's land surface. After World War II, the Soviet Union, including portions of prewar Poland, Finland, and other East European states, as well as fragments of prewar Germany and Japan, had an area of about 8.6 million square miles. Today's Russia, the successor to the largest of the USSR's fifteen republics, has an area of 6,592,850 square miles—still the largest of any country in the world and almost twice the size of second-ranked Canada. From east to west, it spans more than 6,000 miles and eleven time zones; from north to south, it extends about 2,800 miles.

However, much of this vast land is inhospitable. Located in the high northern latitudes, with no mountain ranges in the north to shield it from frigid Arctic blasts, Russia experiences climatic extremes of bitter cold during the long winters and intense heat during the brief summers. Compared to North America, Russia extends considerably farther northward, with most of its land area north of 50° latitude. St. Petersburg, at 59.5° north, lies more northerly than Juneau, Alaska. Moscow, at 55.5° north, is situated somewhat more northerly than Edmonton, Alberta. Even the southernmost part of Russia, in the Caucasus, is just at 41° north—the same latitude as Cheyenne, Wyoming; Cleveland, Ohio; or New Haven, Connecticut. About one-half of the country is in the permafrost zone, where the subsoil is permanently frozen; most of Russia's major ports and rivers are frozen for part of the year.

Although Russia is a country rich in natural resources, its harsh climate limits the ability to exploit them. Vast reserves of petroleum, natural gas, coal, gold, bauxite, and iron ore lie far from the most populated areas, and some are virtually inaccessible. Apart from its brutal effects on workers, the extreme cold hinders the operation of equipment, and the summer marshiness and omnipresent mud make transportation extremely difficult.

The largely unfavorable combinations of soil conditions, temperature ranges, and precipitation produce a situation in which less than 15 percent of the land is sown in crops. The northernmost soil and vegetation zone, known as the tundra, is a treeless plain, with poorly developed soils and little precipitation. The zone to the south of the tundra is the taiga, comprising well over half the country's land. Its winters are cold and summers are hot; the soils are leached and not very fertile. Much of this rolling land is covered with coniferous forests. South of the taiga in European Russia is an area of mixed forests, with milder winters and more fertile soils. In the southern part of European Russia and Western Siberia are the steppes—grassy plains, with hot summers and cold winters. The soil is black and fertile (*chernozem*), and crops include wheat and sugar beets. The rest of the land is either semidesert or mountainous.

From west to east, the five geological regions of Russia are: the European Plain, the Ural Mountains, the West Siberian Plain, the Central Siberian Plateau, and the Eastern Siberian Uplands. On the European side of Russia are the Caucasus Mountains, located between the Black and Caspian Seas, and reaching heights up to 18,510 feet (Mount Elbrus, the highest point in Europe). The Ural Mountains, the dividing line between Europe and Asia, are low and rounded, averaging 2,000 feet in height; they are rich in deposits of iron, copper, and other metals. The major Siberian mountain ranges are the Altai, in the southern part of Western Siberia; the Sayan, in Eastern Siberia; and the Verkhoyansk, in Northeast Siberia.

In European Russia, the major rivers flow north to south. In their northern reaches, they are frozen for six months a year; in the south, for about two months. From west to east, the largest river systems cutting across the European Plain are the Dniester, the Dnieper, the Don, the Volga, and the Ural. The first two, largely in Ukraine but with Russian tributaries, empty into the Black Sea; the third flows into the Sea of Azov (which connects to the Black Sea). The latter two empty into the Caspian Sea, which is really a vast inland saltwater lake. The three major river systems in Siberia—the Ob, the Yenisei, and the Lena—flow south to north, to the Arctic Ocean. The Amur River flows easterly along the border with China and empties into the Pacific Ocean.

For over two centuries, Russia has been the most populated among the countries of Europe. (Although the European part of Russia constitutes a relatively small part of Russian territory, the largest proportion of the population lives there.) A combination of territorial expansion and rapid population growth propelled the population of the Russian Empire from 17.5 million in 1700 (second to France among the European states) to 37 million in 1800 (one-third larger than France). By 1914, with 171 million people, Russia was two-and-one-half times larger than Germany, which ranked second in Europe. A combination of territorial loss, war, famine, and political persecution slowed the growth considerably, and in 1940 the Soviet Union had 194 million people. With more than 20 million lost in World War II, the USSR's population had grown to 209 million by 1959. High birthrates among the non-Slavic peoples of the Soviet Union helped drive the population to about 290 million at the time of the dissolution of the USSR. Russia, which had 147.4 million in 1989, the time of the last official Soviet census, declined to about 145.2 million in the 2002 census. Of this total, ethnic Russians—who were barely one-half the population of the USSR at the time of its dissolution — make up more than 80 percent, and the rest is distributed among nearly one hundred minority nationalities. Ten percent of the population in 2002 was reported as Muslim.

The natural decrease in population—attributed to an aging population, a sharp drop in the birthrate, environmental degradation, and poor public health—was partially offset by the migration of almost 8 million people into Russia from other areas of the former Soviet Union. However, this inflow had significantly slowed by the end of the 1990s, and the decline in the country's population was expected to drop by an additional 10 million by 2015. The mortality rate (especially for men) had increased sharply in the 1980s and early 1990s, to the point that the ratio of deaths to births stood at 1.8:1 in 2001. Without significant changes in these trends, Russia's population at the middle of the twenty-first century will decline to 100 million (compared to an anticipated U.S. population almost four times higher)! In his first report as president on the state of his country, Vladimir Putin declared this demographic crisis to be the country's most acute problem, endangering the very survival of the Russian nation.

The Legacy of the Tsars

The origins of Russian foreign policy can be traced to the period (1462–1505) when Ivan III (Ivan the Great) reigned over the Muscovite state. The year 1480 saw the formal collapse of the two-and-one-half-century-long "Tatar yoke," as the dominion of the Mongol warrior Genghis Khan and his successors over Russia is popularly known. Ivan had already begun to undermine Tatar power through his policy of "collecting of the Russian lands." The thriving trade center of Novgorod was subjected to Moscow's rule in the 1470s, and the regions around Perm and Tver were incorporated in the following decade. Ivan's westward conquests embroiled him in wars with Poland, which continued under his son Vasily III (ruled 1505–1533), who brought Smolensk into Moscow's orbit in 1514.

Ivan the Great was the first ruler of Moscow to use the title "tsar." His wife Sophia, niece of the last Byzantine emperor, encouraged him to claim the title, which was derived from "Caesar" and was meant—in the wake of the fall of Constantinople to the infidel Turks—to convey supremacy over both the spiritual and the earthly realms. Tsar Ivan was determined to build a strong central state based on his hegemony over other princely families—a policy that drove him to acquire additional lands with which to reward his followers. This linkage of strong rule at the center and expansionism continued under Ivan IV, who ruled from 1533 to 1584. The reign of "Ivan the Terrible" saw the further strengthening of autocracy, symbolized in the institution of the *Oprichnina* (special realm), which had features of a secret police force as well as a parallel administrative structure subordinate personally to the tsar.

Externally, Ivan IV began the expansion of Muscovite power into non-Russian territories through the conquest in the 1550s of the southern Khanates of Kazan and Astrakhan. Gaining access thereby to the Caspian Sea, Ivan also sought, unsuccessfully, to defeat the last remnant of the Tatar empire, on the Black Sea peninsula of Crimea. Even more bitter failure was experienced on Muscovy's western frontier when the Peace of Yam Zapolie with Poland in 1582, and a treaty with Sweden a year later confirmed the loss of prior territorial gains in Livonia (much of present-day Latvia and Estonia), on the Baltic seacoast. Perhaps the most significant of Ivan IV's expansions, however, was the first stage of the conquest of Siberia, which began in 1581. Experiencing only spotty resistance from nomadic tribes, Moscow's forces reached the Ob and Irtysh rivers by the end of the decade. Moving in a northeasterly direction, the entire Siberian conquest, from the Urals to the Pacific Ocean, was accomplished before the midpoint of the 1600s.

The three decades following Ivan the Terrible's death were turbulent times for the young Muscovite state. Ivan's weak son, Fyodor I, left no heir, and was succeeded by the ruthless boyar Boris Godunov. Boris's demise, in the midst of terrible famine, ushered in the so-called Time of Troubles, climaxed by the occupation of Moscow by Polish forces. With the expulsion of the Poles, a new tsar, Michael I, was elected in 1613, and the dynasty of the Romanovs began its lengthy occupancy of the Russian throne. Michael and his son Alexis (ruled 1645–1676) fought eight more wars with Poland, the fruit of which was the incorporation into the Muscovite state of the eastern part of Ukraine, including its capital, the seat of "old Rus," Kiev.

The full flowering of Russian foreign policy took place under the strong leadership of Alexis's son, Peter I (Peter the Great), who reigned from 1689 to 1725. Not only did Peter transform his country into one of the great powers of Europe, but in 1721 he renamed it the Russian Empire and dubbed himself emperor of Russia. Fascinated by the sea from an early age, Peter dreamed of acquiring ports and building a great navy. Frustrated in his efforts to wrest the fortress of Azov on the Black Sea from the Turks, Peter enjoyed his greatest military successes in the Great Northern War against Sweden (1700–1721), fought in the interests of acquiring a coast and ports on the Baltic Sea, for both military and commercial purposes. As early as 1703, Peter began building a new city on the marshlands near the Baltic Sea, which he named St. Petersburg; in 1713, he made it his capital. Although the ultimately decisive battle against Charles XII of Sweden was fought in 1709 at Poltava, the war was ended only in 1721 by the Treaty of Nystad, which effectively confirmed Sweden's decline and its replacement by Russia as a great European power. The treaty formalized Russia's incorporation of Livonia, Ingria (the area southwest of St. Petersburg), and parts of Finland.

Moving Russia's capital westward was only one way in which Peter the Great brought Russia into a European orbit. He himself made two lengthy journeys to Europe, and he brought back many ideas on how to "Westernize" his country. These changes had a far-reaching impact on the administrative structure, educational system, and economy of Russia.

Peter's forays southward were less enduring. He first acquired and then lost access to the Black Sea in wars with Turkey. A war against Persia in 1722–23 resulted in the acquisition of the western shores of the Caspian Sea, including the town of Baku, but these gains were relinquished by his successors. Nor was there territorial expansion in the Far East during Peter's time. The Treaty of Nerchinsk, concluded with China in the same year Peter assumed power, kept Mongolia in the Chinese sphere of influence and confined Russia's colonization to the area north of the Amur River. Supplemented just after Peter's death by the Treaty of Kyakhta, which established certain trade and diplomatic regulations, the agreement at Nerchinsk effectively delimited Russian and Chinese spheres for the next century and a half.

Six monarchs (three women and three men) ruled the Russian Empire in the thirty-seven years between the death of Peter the Great and the beginning of the next significant period in Russian foreign policy: the reign of Catherine the Great. During this interim, Russia participated in three wars: it fought another war with Turkey (1738–39), at last gaining a Black Sea coast through the Treaty of Belgrade; it fought again with Sweden, gaining the Finnish city of Vyborg in the Peace of Abo (1743); and it participated, from 1757 to

1762, in the Seven Years War in Europe, first on the side of Austria and then as an ally of Prussia.

With the accession of Catherine II in 1762, Russia withdrew into neutrality as the war reached its conclusion. But the empress was soon pursuing an active foreign policy, which resulted in adding significant territories to the Russian Empire. Catherine was a full partner in European continental politics, demonstrating Russia's dominance in its immediate neighborhood through its victory in yet another war with Sweden (1787–90) and through three partitions of Poland (in 1772, 1793, and 1795). The partitions gave Catherine White Russia (Belorussia, or Belarus), Lithuania, and western Ukraine; in all, about two-thirds of former Poland was transferred to the Russian Empire.

Equally impressive expansion in the south was produced by two wars with Turkey (1768–74 and 1787–92). The Treaty of Kuchuk Kainarji (1774) and the Treaty of Jassy (1792) gave Russia much of the northern Black Sea coastline, including Azov and Crimea, and extending as far eastward as the mouth of the Dniester River. As one of the fruits of these victories, the great Black Sea port of Odessa was founded in 1796, the year of Catherine's death. By that time she had added another 200,000 square miles to her realm.

Thanks in part to the relative stability of European military organization and technique, Russia had been able to catch up with its Western neighbors by borrowing expertise from them. Indeed, it now had advantages by virtue of the sheer size of its population and by its willingness to spend about three-fourths of the state's finances on the military. This was clearly demonstrated during the course of the Napoleonic wars, at the end of which Russia's army—with a force of 800,000—was superior to any other on the continent. Not until the Industrial Revolution changed the scale of European warfare during the nineteenth century would Russia fall behind again.[1]

Russia's power gave Alexander I (1801–1825) a major role to play at the Congress of Vienna (1815), which constructed post-Napoleonic Europe. By this time, yet another European land (Finland) had been added to the empire, and wars with Turkey and Persia had led to the incorporation of Bessarabia, Baku, and Georgia. Although his tutors had filled his head with Enlightenment ideas, Alexander's multinational empire gave him a vested interest in suppressing nationalism and preserving the status quo. The Holy Alliance, largely his creation, emerged from Vienna as the embodiment of the principle of legitimism, and Russia began to play its role as the "gendarme of Europe." This policy was even more evident under Alexander's successor, his brother Nicholas I, who ruled with an iron hand from 1825 to 1855. "Autocracy, Orthodoxy, and Nationalism" were the guiding ideas of his regime. In 1849, Nicholas sent 200,000 Russian troops to suppress a revolution in Hungary, thus ensuring that one of the last vestiges of the great revolutionary wave of 1848 in Europe would not spread to the Russian Empire.

The conservatism of Nicholas I did not translate into a purely defensive foreign policy. He and his ministers were devoted to the objective of expanding Russia's realms southward—to capture Constantinople and seize control of the Dardanelles and Bosporus straits, thereby controlling passage from the Black Sea to the Mediterranean. Russia's growing naval base at Sevastopol would have greater strategic significance if the tsar, rather than the Turkish sultan, controlled the passage of warships in and out of Russia's back door. The Ottoman Empire, in Russia's eyes, was the "sick man of Europe," and Russia was eager to make arrangements to inherit his territory before he died.

In the cause of protecting the sultan's Orthodox Christian subjects in Greece, who had been struggling for independence since 1821, the Russians went to war against Turkey in 1828, concluding it the following year in the Peace of Adrianople. Its terms not only declared Greek independence but transferred Turkish possessions in the Caucasus to the tsar, brought Russia's frontier to the southern mouth of the Danube, and gave her a protectorate over the Orthodox Christians inhabiting the Danubian provinces of Moldavia and Walachia.

Apparently, for Nicholas, not only were the principles of legitimism and defense of the status quo to be subordinated when Russian strategic interests dictated, but struggles for national liberation of Christians under Muslim rule were to be treated differently from nationalist revolts within the Muslim family. In 1833 he responded affirmatively to the Ottoman sultan's call for assistance in putting down a revolt by Mohammed Ali, his vassal in Egypt. The tsar's reward was the Treaty of Unkiar Skelessi, which gave Russia the right to use the straits for passage of its warships but denied the right to other nations. Britain and France were disturbed by the strategic import of the concessions thus handed to the tsar. Together with the Austrians and Prussians, they insisted upon a multilateral arrangement (the London Convention of 1841), which reversed the terms of Unkiar Skelessi and closed the straits to all foreign warships in time of peace.

Conflicting ambitions of the Russians, British, and French in the Near East reopened the struggle for strategic advantage in the Ottoman lands. When French president (soon to be emperor) Louis Napoleon won a concession from the sultan for protection of Catholics and Christian holy places in Palestine, Tsar Nicholas demanded similar privileges in defense of Orthodox Christians. Having failed to persuade the British to join in an outright partition of the Ottoman Empire, Nicholas proceeded to demand a Russian protectorate in Turkey. Encouraged by Britain, the Turks declared war on Russia in October 1853, and the British and French joined them six months later.

Neither side distinguished itself militarily in the Crimean War, but the Russian performance was especially dismal. Despite its growth in population (from 51 million in 1816 to 76 million in 1860) and in textile and iron production, Russia was falling far behind in economic strength. While Russian iron production doubled in the first part of the nineteenth century, that of Britain increased thirtyfold. A lack of capital or consumer demand and the absence of a sufficiently large middle class seriously impeded Russia's industrial takeoff. While Russia had little more than 500 miles of railroads in 1850, the United States had 8,500 miles. And none of Russia's railroads extended south of Moscow. The tsar had to rely on horse transport to move his army to the Crimea, taking as much as three months to move troops to the front, whereas the British and French could reach it by sea in three weeks. The army thought to be the strongest in Europe at the time of the Hungarian revolution of 1849 was soon exposed as shockingly backward, with inadequate weaponry and poor leadership, and with many of its large contingents tied down in internal policing duties.[2]

Following the death of Nicholas I, his son Alexander II (1855–1881) agreed to the terms of the Treaty of Paris (1856), which ended the Crimean War and stripped Russia of many of its recent territorial gains. The tsar ceded the mouths of the Danube and part of Bessarabia, and he forfeited some of his conquests in the Caucasus. The Danubian principalities were placed under the joint guarantee of the powers, and the Black Sea was neutralized. Turkey was admitted to the Concert of Europe, and the powers promised to respect its integrity and independence. Russia, thus frustrated in its ambitions toward the south, turned its attention inward, toward reform, and confined its external expansion to Asia, where resistance was weaker.

The need for internal political, economic, and social reform in Russia had long been debated by the intelligentsia, who were roughly divided into two camps: Westernizers and Slavophiles. The former group, ashamed of Russia's past and present and attracted by the ideas of the French Revolution, believed that Russia's great mission could be fulfilled only by advancing further on the road Peter the Great had pioneered—imitation of the West. A tragic fate had been suffered in December 1825, at the time of the accession of Nicholas I, by a group of young officers, students, professionals, and nobles (the Decembrists), who had sought to force Westernization on Russia through revolution. In their wake, writers as diverse as the liberal Granovskii, the romantic Herzen, and the radical realist Belinskii continued to insist that Russia must follow the West.

The Slavophiles did not dispute that Russia was backward and needed change, but they saw its salvation not in servile imitation of the West, with its materialism and its ideas of rationalism and individualism. Rather, they sought a return to what they regarded as Russia's true traditions—the faith of its people and the people's sense of belonging to a community. Russia's faults, the Slavophiles believed, were traceable to Peter's introduction of foreign models and his subordination of the Orthodox Church to the state. According to thinkers such as Karamzin, Kirevskii, and Aksakov, a reformed Russia could fulfill its mission by helping to civilize the West. The most influential book to insist on the uniqueness of Russia and its mission was Nicholas Danilevskii's *Russia and Europe* (1871).

Both sides idealized their models. As the Slavophiles readily pointed out, the real West was a grimmer place than Westernizers claimed; but it was just as true that Russia's traditions were not as happy as the Slavophiles imagined.[3] The debate over the extent of Russia's "special mission," and whether the Western experience was something to imitate or avoid, lasted for much of the nineteenth century. In the twentieth century, it resurfaced in arguments among Russian Marxists as the century opened, and in debates among post-Soviet Russian writers and politicians as it closed.

With Russia's weaknesses so sharply exposed in the Crimean War, Alexander II introduced a series of significant reforms, many of which seem designed to avoid the more radical changes urged by both Westernizers and Slavophiles. The most important of these was the emancipation of the serfs, proclaimed in February 1861. This was followed in the next few years by financial, educational, judicial, and administrative reforms, and by an edict to reduce censorship. The change in the legal status of the peasantry was slow to produce benefits in increased agricultural production, but the reforms did have a more noticeable impact in spurring railway construction and industrialization of the economy under state sponsorship. Although the reforms allowed Russia to close some of the distance between itself and the rest of Europe, in its class structure and in the total absence of constitutional or popular rule, Russia remained a rigid and centralized autocracy.

In the wake of its humiliating defeat in the Crimean War, Russia pursued an especially active policy in Asia and the Far East. Russian incursions into Chinese territory in the Amur River region, in violation of the provisions of the Treaty of Nerchinsk, actually began just prior to the war and were intensified during the conflict, in anticipation of an Anglo-French naval attack. After the war, the annexation of the Amur region was legalized in 1858, but the Russians pressed further into Chinese territory, founding Vladivostok in 1860. The same year, the Treaty of Peking established a new border along the Ussuri River. China thus formally ceded to Russia the territory south to Vladivostok. The Russo-Chinese border in the Central Asian region of Turkestan was also revised, allowing the Russians to shift their attention there.

Over the course of two decades, from the time of the capture of Tashkent in 1865 until the conquest of Merv in 1884, Russia penetrated further into Central Asia and subdued and incorporated Transcaspia and Turkestan. The initial conquests were justified by Russia to the other powers by citing the need to defend its subjects and settlements against raids and robbery by subjects of the ruling khans, with each new expansion of the boundary bringing Russia into contact with new raiders. While securing the frontier may indeed have been the initial aim, these territories possessed mineral wealth and were a source of raw cotton. In light of the simultaneous Anglo-Russian conflicts of interest in the Balkans, Russia's policy of expansion in Central Asia also served to bring useful pressures to bear on the British, who feared that Russia would press all the way into India. These concerns were at least temporarily alleviated in 1885, when the two countries signed an agreement delineating the northern boundary of Afghanistan, effectively making it the terminus of the Russian advance.

In contrast to the steadiness of Russia's expansion on the Eurasian landmass, this period also witnessed an important withdrawal from an area to which Tsar Alexander II apparently felt Russia had overextended itself. Russian fur traders had begun to work in the Aleutian Islands and the southern coast of Alaska as early as the 1760s. The Russian American Company in 1799 was given a monopoly over hunting and commerce southward to the fifty-fifth parallel (the southern tip of present-day Alaska). In 1812 the company established a new base for hunting and food supply at Fort Ross, just seventy miles north of San Francisco. Although pressured by both Spain and Mexico, the Russians did not abandon Fort Ross until 1841. The vulnerability of these North American possessions became evident to Russia during the Crimean War, just as the economic benefits began to disappear. Hostility toward Britain influenced the decision to sell Alaska to the United States instead; this was accomplished in 1867, for a price of $7.2 million.

The hiatus in Russian activity in Turkey and the Balkans came to an end in the 1870s. At the beginning of the decade, Russia seized an opportunity (in the wake of the Franco-Prussian War) unilaterally to abrogate the Black Sea clauses of the Treaty of Paris. This action was supported the following year by a convention recognizing the right of both Russia and Turkey to maintain naval forces in the Black Sea. Russian territorial ambitions stirred again at mid-decade, with the occurrence of uprisings against Turkey in Bulgaria and in Bosnia-Herzegovina, and with the outbreak of war between Turkey and Serbia.

These events further fanned the flames of the burgeoning Pan-Slavist movement, which transformed the Slavophile ideology into a foreign policy. Since the fifteenth century, Russian churchmen had regarded Moscow as the "Third Rome," but the nineteenth century brought the notion that the tsar, as head of the Russian Orthodox Church, had a special mission to protect Orthodox Christians against the excesses of Ottoman rule. Pan-Slavists disagreed on whether "Slavdom" included only those who were Orthodox, or all who spoke a Slavic tongue. They also were divided between the Greater Slav idea (with all Slav nations treated as equals) and the Lesser Slav idea (emphasizing the dominant role of the Russian state and the Orthodox religion). The 1863 revolt of the Poles against Russian rule, suppressed with great fury by the tsar, diminished the appeal of the Greater Slav idea. The foreign policy consequences of the Lesser Slav idea—although it was imperialistic—were distinctly less risky in that the object of Russia's liberating zeal would be the Slavic subjects of the sultan, rather than those who lived under Austro-Hungarian or German rule.[4]

With the eruption of the Balkan conflict, amid great popular excitement, the Russian government allowed the public collection of funds for the anti-Turkish cause and permitted Russian army officers to enlist as volunteers against the Turks. The defeat of the Serbs provoked a rare public speech by the tsar, in which he referred to the sufferings of Christians in the Balkans and the "cause of Slavdom," ending with the prayer: "May God help us to fulfill our sacred mission."[5] A few months later, Russia declared war on Turkey, and in March 1878 it was able to dictate peace terms in the Treaty of San Stefano. By its terms, the independence of Serbia and Montenegro was recognized and both received territory; Romania was declared independent; Bulgaria was granted autonomy under an elected prince and Russian military occupation; and Bulgaria was to be substantially enlarged to include most of Macedonia and an Aegean seacoast. Russia received Ardahan, Kars, Batum, and Bayazid from Turkey.

Like the Treaty of Unkiar Skelessi forty-five years before, the Treaty of San Stefano was distinctly not to the liking of most of the other great powers, and they proceeded to call an international meeting to force Russia to modify its terms. With German Chancellor Bismarck as the "honest broker," the Congress of Berlin (June 1878) left Russian Pan-Slavists furious (especially at Germany and Austria) and left the nationalist aspirations of Serbia and Bulgaria unfulfilled. The size of Bulgaria was significantly reduced, and Serbia and Montenegro also lost territory. Austria was given a mandate to occupy Bosnia and Herzegovina. Russia kept Batum, Kars, and Ardahan and gained southern Bessarabia from Romania (thereby ensuring Romanian hostility).

Aware that a frustrated and isolated Russia could go shopping for allies among Germany's enemies, in the wake of the Congress of Berlin, Bismarck devised a plan whereby Russia could achieve some of its security objectives in the Black Sea in return for alignment with the German powers. Germany and Austria had formed an alliance in 1879, and Bismarck proceeded to revive the idea of the Three Emperors' League (*Dreikaiserbund*). Temporarily delayed by the assassination of Tsar Alexander II, the three-way alliance was finally implemented by his son and heir, Alexander III (1881–1894). The highly secret treaty, signed in June 1881, effectively protected Russia against attack in the Black Sea by stating that if Turkey violated the principle of closure of the straits, the three powers would warn the sultan that he had put himself in a state of war with the aggrieved power (Russia). The three powers also agreed that modifications in the territorial status quo in Turkey should take place only after agreement among them, though Austria reserved the right to annex Bosnia and Herzegovina whenever it saw fit. The treaty was renewed once, in 1884, but was allowed to lapse in 1887 because of the tsar's growing dissatisfaction with Austrian policy.

Determined to keep Russia away from France, Bismarck devised a secret treaty (the "Reinsurance Treaty") in which the two empires promised each other neutrality if either became involved in a war with a third power, with the exception of an aggressive war of Germany against France or of Russia against Austria. In Russia's interests, the treaty once more reaffirmed the principle of closure of the straits, but it also went further, promising German moral and diplomatic support "to the measures which His Majesty may deem it necessary to take to control the key of his empire" (i.e., the entrance to the Black Sea). The Germans also recognized Russia's predominant influence in Bulgaria and promised to aid in reestablishing a pro-Russian government there.

The Reinsurance Treaty came up for renewal in 1890, in the wake of Bismarck's dismissal as chancellor, and the young Kaiser Wilhelm II was persuaded by his new advisors to allow it to lapse. This proved a fatal mistake, as it virtually drove the Russians into the arms of the French, setting the stage for the transformation of the European system into a rigid bipolarity of opposing coalitions. The initial Franco-Russian convention of August 1891 was only a vague agreement that the two states would discuss measures to be taken if the peace were endangered or if either were menaced. The following year the Russians agreed in principle to a draft military convention. The actual formalization occurred only at the end of 1893—and not as a treaty, which would have required legislative ratification in France, but as a highly secret military convention. It provided that if France were attacked by Germany, or by Italy supported by Germany, Russia would employ all available forces against Germany; if Russia were attacked by Germany, or by Austria supported by Germany, France would employ all available forces against

Germany. Specific levels of troop commitments were specified in the agreement. Additionally, if the forces of the Triple Alliance (Germany, Austria, Italy) or any one member of it mobilized, France and Russia committed to mobilize without delay.

With the maintenance of the status quo in the Balkans seemingly ensured for the time being, Russia again turned its attention eastward, with the powerful finance minister, Count Sergei Witte as lead strategist. In 1891, Russia decided to build a 5,000-mile railroad from Moscow to Vladivostok, for both strategic and commercial reasons, but since Vladivostok is not ice-free, Russia also renewed its interest in obtaining such a port, either in Korea (Pusan) or on the Liaotung Peninsula. These ambitions directly conflicted with those of Japan, which feared being cut off from the vast Chinese market. Taking matters into its own hands, Japan launched a war against China in 1894, as a result of which it took from China the offshore islands of Formosa and the Pescadores as well as the Liaotung Peninsula. Determined to drive Japan back off the mainland and prevent the premature partition of China, Count Witte enlisted German and French assistance in pressuring Japan to yield the peninsula.

At the coronation of Tsar Nicholas II in 1896, the Chinese ambassador was induced by a bribe to accept a fifteen-year defensive alliance whereby Russia undertook to defend China from attack and China agreed that a Russian railway could be built across Manchuria to Vladivostok (the Chinese Eastern Railway). Two years later, to the great consternation of the Japanese, China granted Russia a twenty-five-year lease of the Liaotung Peninsula, including Dairen and Port Arthur. Japan sought a conciliatory solution, proposing a division of spoils, in true imperialist fashion, with Japan to be granted predominant influence in Korea in return for recognizing Russia's primacy in Manchuria. Confident of its superior position (though unprepared for war), Russia refused the offer.

Seeking a European partner in its quest to block Russian expansion in the Far East, Japan concluded an alliance with Britain in 1902. The following year, as the first trains passed over his Trans-Siberian Railway, Count Witte was dismissed. In the face of growing internal political unrest, Witte's rival in the tsar's court, V.K. Plehve, counseled an even more aggressive policy, arguing that Russia needed "a little victorious war to stop the revolutionary tide."[6] In February 1904 the Japanese launched a surprise attack on the Russian fleet at Port Arthur. Besieged for most of the year, the city fell to the Japanese in December. Further military reversals followed, as the Russians lost a major land battle at Mukden and suffered the loss of a naval fleet of thirty-two vessels in the Tsushima Straits in May 1905. By this time, fueled by humiliation in the Far East, a revolution had erupted in Russia, and the government was impelled to seek an end to the war with Japan. With U.S. president Theodore Roosevelt serving as mediator, a settlement was reached at Portsmouth, New Hampshire, in September 1905. By its terms, the Russians retained their influence in northern Manchuria and escaped the payment of indemnity, but were forced to recognize Japanese preponderance in Korea and to cede to Japan the southern half of Sakhalin Island as well as their rights in the Liaotung Peninsula and Port Arthur. Two years later Russia signed a convention with Japan explicitly renouncing interest in Korea and southern Manchuria, in return for Japanese recognition of Russia's special interests in northern Manchuria and Outer Mongolia.

Ironically, the forcible limitation placed on St. Petersburg's expansionist ambitions in the Far East removed a point of contention between Russia and Britain and helped open the way to the Anglo-Russian Entente, concluded in August 1907. The two powers settled their remaining imperial differences, with Britain recognizing a Russian sphere of interest in northern Persia, Russia recognizing preponderant British influence in Afghanistan, and both sides recognizing Chinese suzerainty in Tibet. Britain also assured the tsar that it would not obstruct Russia's longstanding desire to open up the Bosporus and Dardanelles straits to Russian warships in the Black Sea, thus facilitating a revival of Russian interests in the Balkans.

More sensitive than ever to public opinion in the wake of the 1905 Revolution, the Russian government again took up the banner of Pan-Slavism. The fervor for liberation of the southern Slavs ultimately halted a possible agreement between Russia and Austria, negotiated secretly between their foreign ministers, Alexander Izvolskii and Count von Aehrenthal, in which Austria would have supported a change in the rules governing passage through the straits in return for Russian approval of Austria's annexation of Bosnia and Herzegovina. When Austria rushed to proclaim the annexation in October 1908, the Pan-Slavist outcry in Russia led Prime Minister Peter Stolypin to direct Izvolskii to condemn the Austrian action and instead champion Serbia's claims on these Slavic lands. The ensuing diplomatic crisis hardened the lines between the Triple Alliance and the Triple Entente in Europe, ruined the prospects for a peaceful accommodation of Russian ambitions in the straits, and strengthened Russia's determination to create a barrier against further Austrian influence in the Balkans.

When war finally broke out in the Balkans in August 1914, sparked by the assassination in Sarajevo of Archduke Franz Ferdinand, heir to the Austro-Hungarian throne, by a Bosnian Serb nationalist, it quickly escalated into a European war and then to a world war that none of the great powers truly wanted. By many indicators, Russia was in a much stronger position for such a war than it had been earlier. Its population was three times that of Germany and four times that of Britain, and Russia's standing army was the largest in Europe, with 1.3 million front-line troops and up to 5 million reserves. Russia's industrial output was growing at an average annual rate of 5 percent between 1860 and 1913, and ranked fourth in the world. Railway construction was proceeding at great speed, and Russia was the world's second largest producer of oil.

However, as Paul Kennedy has noted, Russia was "simultaneously powerful and weak."[7] Much of its industry was devoted to food and textiles, and output per capita amounted to only one-quarter of Germany's and one-sixth of Britain's. Given the population growth, annual real national product was expanding by only 1 percent per capita. Eighty percent of the population worked in the inefficient agricultural sector. The average Russian's income was about one-quarter of the average Englishman's, but the average Russian was forced to part with over half of his income for defense. Industrialization had been carried out with forced savings from the population as well as substantial foreign borrowing; Russia's foreign debt was the largest in the world. Most decisively, Russian strength was further undermined by the weakness and ineptitude of its government, starting with Tsar Nicholas II, "a Potemkin village in person."[8]

His great-grandfather's (and namesake's) war in the Crimea had exposed Russia's weaknesses, as had his own war against the upstart Japanese, and yet the tsar and his advisors missed every opportunity to turn away from the path that ultimately not only devastated the country but destroyed the regime itself, in the process opening the way to communist revolution and to the imposition of the Soviet state on the Russian empire.

Expansionism in Tsarist Foreign Policy

Having sketched the broad outlines of Russian foreign policy under the tsars, we can now turn to a search for patterns in tsarist diplomacy, and for explanations of how these were shaped by peculiarities of Russia's geography, of the organization of the tsarist state, of ideology, and of the prevailing norms and characteristics of the international system.

Not surprisingly, the dominant theme most analysts find in the foreign policy of Russia under the tsars is that of expansionism. This is sometimes expressed in a tendency to fill internal vacuums, and sometimes in a push toward the open sea. There are variations in the explanations given for this four-centuries-long pattern of expanding the boundaries of the Russian state. Some analysts stress factors that portray Russia as an unprovoked aggressor fulfilling some messianic or autocratic urge, and others depict a regime haunted by its vulnerability to invasion and obsessed with the search for security.

Russia's geopolitical situation partially explains several facets of Russian expansionism. The vastness and openness of the Russian landmass, and the absence of natural barriers within or around it, help to account for the obsessive concern by Russia's rulers for its security, as these factors permitted easy invasion by neighboring powers and, alternatively, relatively easy outward expansion of Russian power. On those occasions when invasion has occurred—most notably, by Napoleon in 1812 and by Hitler in 1941–43—Russian military commanders have had the luxury of being able to trade space for time, while enlisting the harsh climate as their ally in defeating the invader. Conversely, long distances have sometimes turned into logistical nightmares for Russian generals seeking to move forces or supplies to the front. This was especially so prior to the development of a network of railways in the country (as in the Crimean War), but it remains true in the absence of an all-weather network of highways, on terrain where mud can be a greater impediment than snow or ice.

Finally, from the time of Peter the Great, when Russia's aspirations for naval power were born, the absence of ice-free ports has often been cited as a motive for Russian expansion toward the Baltic and Black seas and toward the warmer waters of the Pacific Ocean. Of equal importance for enhanced naval maneuverability is Russia's need for ports that provide access to open waters leading to the major oceans. Ships leaving the Baltic Sea ports must pass through narrow straits between Denmark and Sweden to reach the North Sea and the Atlantic Ocean. Naval forces leaving the Black Sea for the Mediterranean must pass through the Bosporus and Dardanelles straits, where the rights of passage were subject to treaty restrictions for long periods. In the Far East, Vladivostok is icebound for part of the year, and ships departing southward toward the Pacific Ocean must pass through Tsushima Strait. Had Russia fulfilled its ambition of acquiring Pusan in Korea, it would have controlled this strait. Only during the period when Port Arthur and Dairen were under Russian control was ice-free passage to the Yellow Sea and the Pacific possible.

Another familiar theory is that Russian expansionism was a product of the particular type of regime—that internal despotism found its outward expression in relentless expansion, and that incorporation of numerous subject nationalities required unusually heavy militarization to maintain central control. No checks and balances existed to question or block the tsars' decisions to devote enormous sums of state revenues to the armed forces. In Henry Kissinger's words:

> The absolute nature of the Tsar's powers enabled Russia's rulers to conduct foreign policy both arbitrarily and idiosyncratically. . . .

To sustain their rule and to surmount tensions among the empire's various populations, all of Russia's rulers invoked the myth of some vast, foreign threat, which, in time, turned into another of the self-fulfilling prophecies that doomed the stability of Europe.[9]

Certainly, both Ivan III and Ivan IV found that the necessities of state building were well served by expansion, as they sought to acquire new lands with which to reward their nobles. The process by which the Muscovite state was transformed into the Russian Empire by Peter I also reveals linkages between perceived internal requirements and external policies. But during the reigns of Catherine II and Alexander I, the Russian regime was not noticeably different in type from others in Europe, and it is difficult to argue that Russian foreign policies departed from the balance-of-power policies that were being pursued elsewhere.

By the time Nicholas I ascended the throne, Russia was already lagging behind the other major European powers in permitting constitutional change and expanding democracy, and this gap grew considerably over the ensuing decades. Henry Kissinger argues that "even when Russia was pursuing legitimacy, its attitudes were more messianic—and therefore imperialistic—than those of the other conservative courts."[10] An alternative view, however, would argue that policies of conservatism and preservation of dynastic legitimacy were better served by a stance of preserving the status quo than by upsetting it through expansion.[11]

Analysts who perceive a connection between regime type and expansionist policy also argue that the strong state bureaucracy and central control in Russia produced a diplomatic style that was at considerable variance with European great power norms. They describe Russian diplomacy as more secretive and suspicious, untrustworthy, and displaying unusual hostility toward the Western powers—characteristics that are said to have carried over to the Soviet period. Lord Palmerston, Britain's Russophobic foreign secretary and prime minister in the mid-nineteenth century, stated the case for Russian untrustworthiness in 1860:

> The Russian government perpetually declares that Russia wants no increases of territory, that the Russian dominions are already too large. But while making these declarations in the most solemn manner, every year [it] adds large tracts of territory to the Russian dominions not for the purpose of adding territory but carefully directed to occupation of certain strategical points, as starting points for further encroachments or as posts from whence some neighboring states may be kept under control or may be threatened with invasion.[12]

Denigrating tsarist diplomacy, Kissinger describes Russia's foreign ministers as "little more than servants of a volatile and easily distracted autocrat, for whose favor they had to compete amidst many overriding domestic concerns."[13] Even when the tsar was a dominant personality, Kissinger observes, the autocratic system of policymaking weighed against coherence in policy, while the tsar's "princely lifestyle" made it difficult for him to concentrate attention on foreign issues over a sustained period.

Russia's greatest fault, in Kissinger's view, lay in the unwillingness of the tsars to abide by the maxims of the prevailing international system—balance-of-power politics—which resulted in a Russian expansionism that proceeded without self-imposed limits.

> But Russia seemed impelled to expand by a rhythm all its own, containable only by the deployment of a superior force, and usually by war. Throughout numerous crises, a reasonable settlement often seemed well within Russia's reach, much better in fact than what ultimately emerged. Yet Russia always preferred the risk of defeat to compromise. . . . Russia on the march rarely exhibited a sense of limits.[14]

In similar fashion, Kissinger and other analysts have commented on Russia's tendency when confronted with superior force or war in Europe to turn toward expansion in Asia, and to return to European objectives when more favorable circumstances prevailed.

Instances in Russian history suggest the existence of a greater sense of prudence—and a greater devotion to pragmatic, balance-of-power politics—than this analysis allows. It is true that Russia's wars were not solely defensive—undertaken out of a search for security alone—and that Russia would attack or take territory from neighboring states which were not currently threatening it. However, Russia's targets were invariably states or tribal entities that its rulers perceived to be weaker than itself, and possibly exposed to the ambitions of other states, if preemptive moves were not taken. Examples are the partitions of Poland in the late eighteenth century, Peter I's war against Persia, various wars against Turkey, and acquisition of territory from a weakened Chinese empire by means of what Beijing has long seen as "unequal treaties."

Prior to the disastrous slide into World War I, when confronted with the possibility of going to war with a stronger state, Russia would pull back. Nicholas I found himself at war with Britain and France in the Crimea only because they came to the defense of the "sick man" on the Ottoman throne. Both Alexander II and Nicholas II had occasion to back away from possible wars with Austria in the Balkans, and Nicholas II, having suffered humiliating defeat at the hands of a Japanese state that had been widely perceived as inferior in strength, sought entente with Britain soon after that war, rather than undertake another costly conflict.

Unlike the successor Soviet regime, imperial Russia's expansionist ambitions were not global; even the expansion into North America was soon regarded as too costly to sustain. As Martin Malia argues, a "pragmatic geopolitical motivation accounts for most of Russia's constant westward expansion from the mid-17th century to Alexander I . . . the Russian imperial regime saw no further than the Vistula, the Straits, Iran, or the Yalau."[15]

If tsarist Russia was not following the maxims of the balance of power system, how did it formulate and justify its expansionist policies? The answer, Kissinger and others believe, is that Russian expansion was largely motivated by ideology—alternatively viewed either as the triad of autocracy, orthodoxy, and nationalism or as a messianic Pan-Slavism. Russia's distinctive approach to foreign policy, it is argued, arises not from a sense of insecurity, but from ideology. In Kissinger's words, Russia for most of its history "has been a cause looking for opportunity."[16] Again stressing the continuity between the tsarist and Soviet periods, Kissinger describes Russian exceptionalism as a paradox:

> Unlike the states of Western Europe, which Russia simultaneously admired, despised, and envied, Russia perceived itself not as a nation but as a cause, beyond geopolitics, impelled by faith, and held together by arms. After the Revolution, the passionate sense of mission was transferred to the Communist International.
>
> The paradox of Russian history lies in the continuing ambivalence between messianic drive and a pervasive sense of insecurity. In its ultimate aberration, this ambivalence generated a fear that, unless the empire expanded, it would implode.[17]

As Kissinger notes, tsarist Russia's attitudes toward the West were ambivalent—a complex mix of hostility and admiration. At least in part, this ambivalence reflects a duality in what "the West" represents. As Bruce Porter has written, there was not only the liberal West of the Enlightenment, so beloved by many Russian "Westernizers," but also the other West—"the militarized, regimented, technological juggernaut" embodied by the armies of Charles XII, Frederick the Great, Napoleon Bonaparte, and Kaiser Wilhelm. Whereas Russia's internal cohesion and the power of the state were threatened whenever it emulated the reforming, democratizing West, the frequent interaction with the military might of the West helped ensure that "this was the West that Russia actually emulated."[18]

However accurate are Kissinger's insights on this point, he nevertheless overstates the extent to which the "passionate sense of mission" was a characteristic of official attitudes, as opposed to an undercurrent in society. As Hugh Seton-Watson demonstrates in his study of the foreign policy of Imperial Russia, occasionally the tsar would permit manifestations of Pan-Slavism to be expressed, when it suited his policy; but he could also turn it off again, if it threatened to get out of hand.[19] Much of Russia's expansion had nothing at all to do with Slavic brotherhood, but resulted from a quite pragmatic quest for gold and other valuable minerals, furs, or trading pathways to the storied markets of the Orient.

Martin Malia, a scholar who argues that Russian exceptionalism was largely confined to the Soviet period, makes the case against ascribing Russian expansionism largely to ideological motives:

> In fact, however, Russian foreign policy under the old regime was no more ideological than that of any other European powers. Like all other powers, Russia was expansionist, but essentially for geopolitical reasons.
>
> Indeed, there was probably more ideology in the Western overseas expression of this expansionism than in its Russian, continental, and Eurasian forms. . . .
>
> Russian foreign policy under the old regime did have an ideological component, but only toward the end. Until the early 20th century, pan-Slav ideology was much more the property of society than of the government, which succumbed to it only in the immediate buildup to 1914. . . . It was with the October Revolution that Russia's international role changed fundamentally to a messianic ideology.[20]

Clearly, no single motive force can be found to explain tsarist Russian expansionism; rather, the influences of geography, regime type, the international system, and ideology all weigh in, though in different proportions at different times. As we will see in chapter 3, there are features of tsarist diplomacy that did carry over to the Soviet period, but there are also characteristics that did not. In evaluating the legacy of the tsars, one can, however, surmise that certain lessons could be drawn from the history of the Russian Empire to help guide the foreign policy of both communist and democratic successors. From the Time of Troubles in the seventeenth century through the Crimean and Russo-Japanese wars until World War I, Russian history teaches the dangers that overextension and war pose for internal stability. Sometimes undertaken to divert popular attention from internal problems, war more often than not exacerbates these problems—ultimately, for the tsars, causing the collapse of an empire once regarded as the mightiest in Europe.

3

Soviet Foreign Policy: From Revolution to Cold War

The Russian Revolutionary Tradition

Emerging in the nineteenth century, movements for revolution in Russia produced political values, beliefs, and symbols that formed part of the political landscape in which the foreign policy of the late tsarist period was devised. The distinctive features of this revolutionary tradition not only helped to shape the foreign policy of the Soviet period of Russian history, but they also live on today by virtue of their importance in the political socialization of the current leadership of democratic Russia. This inheritance includes not only the ideas of Karl Marx, Vladimir Lenin, and others who shaped the Marxist-Leninist ideology, but also the political experiences and traditions of the Russian intelligentsia in the nineteenth century, which formed the distinctive environment from which Lenin's Bolsheviks emerged.

The main feature of this environment was autocracy: unrestrained political power in the hands of the tsar, wielded through a strong centralized bureaucracy and augmented by a secret police, and an economy and social order controlled by the state. The Russian Orthodox Church and strong manifestations of Russian chauvinism were the other pillars of tsarist authority over the vast multinational empire. The nineteenth century witnessed a widening gulf between the regime and Russia's intelligentsia—the educated professionals who sometimes were termed "superfluous people" because they were divorced from practical social activity as well as from any opportunity for political participation. In short, it was an environment that sponsored utopianism rather than pragmatism, impulses toward revolution rather than gradual reform, and the eventual replacement of one autocracy and orthodoxy by another.

The mid-century debates between Westernizers and Slavophiles pointed up a tradition, visible on both sides, of *narodnichestvo*—faith in the simple laboring people, especially the peasantry, as uncorrupted by political power and bourgeois values and capable of delivering Russia onto the path of social justice. In the wake of the disillusion in the circles of the intelligentsia over the incomplete reforms of the 1860s, a populist movement grew up, known as *V narod* ("going to the people"). It envisioned an exodus of intelligentsia from the cities to the villages, where they would provide the peasantry with the education and insights that would lift the scales from their eyes and allow them to see the shortcomings of the regime. The movement was an utter failure. Peasants, not yet devoid of their faith in the tsar, distrusted the citified intellectuals—in some cases, going so far as to turn them over to the police.

Arising from the ashes of the utopian hopes of agrarian socialists like Alexander Herzen and Peter Lavrov was the phoenix of violent revolution. As in the earlier division between Westernizers and Slavophiles, the intelligentsia was again divided—this time, between those who were essentially anarchists ("nihilists") and those who adhered to the more deterministic, rationalistic, and Western-oriented Marxian socialism. Lenin's genius was in synthesizing these two streams.

In the former tradition were Mikhail Bakunin, the anarchist, whose hatred for political authority was so great that he engaged in a long battle with Karl Marx, whom he considered too rational and conservative; and P.N. Tkachev, who stated that a revolutionary minority, utilizing terrorism, must seize power to forestall a middle-class revolution and the development of Russia along capitalist lines. Unlike the utopians, these men demonstrated a will to power and a contempt for the spontaneous development of the masses, in whose name they sought to achieve a "preventive revolution."

The tightly organized, highly disciplined revolutionary party advocated by Tkachev, after a campaign of terrorism in the 1870s, succeeded in 1881 in realizing its fondest wish—the assassination of Tsar Alexander II, liberator of the serfs. The consequence of this terrorism was that the new ruler, Alexander III, guided by his reactionary tutor Konstantin Pobedonostsev, opened up a period of political and social reaction, intensified chauvinism, and suppression of the revolutionaries.

Opposed to the anarchists in Russia were the first of that country's Marxists. The first Russian Marxist organization, the Emancipation of Labor, was formed by G.V. Plekhanov and others in 1883, and by 1887 Marx's *Das Kapital* was the most widely read book among Russian students. Unlike its attitude toward the populist parties, the government did not at first seek to suppress Marxist ideas or study groups, viewing Marxism as an abstruse and harmless doctrine, which in fact performed a useful service by downgrading terrorism and preaching the inevitability of capitalist development. One reason for the growth of Marxism in Russia was that industrialization was indeed proceeding rapidly at the end of the nineteenth century—even if it was proceeding under state auspices rather than through the efforts of native capitalists, and the urban proletariat was still a tiny drop in a sea of peasantry. In Marx's terms, this development was only the transition from feudalism to capitalism, and the revolutionary agenda at this stage was not the proletarian revolution and establishment of socialism but the bourgeois-democratic revolution and further development of capitalism. The dilemma for Russian Marxists was that the "progressive" course for their country seemed to require the very development of bourgeois greed and exploitation that so many Russian intelligentsia had long decried in the West. As Engels confirmed in a letter to Russian Marxists in 1892, historical materialism dictated that only after the completion of the bourgeois-democratic revolution could Russian revolutionaries pass on to the promotion of socialist revolution.

There was little formal disagreement with this principle but much argument about what the tactics of Russian Marxists should be. The viewpoint known as "economism" focused on improving the material condition of the Russian proletariat through trade union organization and peaceful strike movements—a position that gained force when the regime made it clear at the end of the century that it would not tolerate political agitation among the workers. Indeed, the First Conference of the Russian Social-Democratic Labor Party (RSDLP), held in Minsk in 1898, was disrupted by the arrest of some of the delegates by the tsarist police.

For those who were determined that the proletariat should have a political party, and not merely bide its time, the question of tactics arose most sharply at the Second Congress of the RSDLP, held in Brussels and London in 1903. The classical Marxist view of a two-stage revolution, obligating the proletariat at present to support the bourgeoisie in Russia in achieving the bourgeois-democratic revolution, was argued by Plekhanov and Julius Martov. (Although the majority of delegates supported this viewpoint, the loss of a vote on a relatively minor issue led to their being labeled *Mensheviks* [minority men] by Lenin and his *Bolsheviks* [majority men]). A second viewpoint, articulated by Leon Trotsky, insisted that the Russian proletariat could itself seize leadership of the bourgeois-democratic revolution, making it into a "permanent revolution" that would grow into a socialist revolution with the critical assistance of a victorious European proletariat.

Lenin agreed with Trotsky that the Russian bourgeoisie was not worthy or capable of leadership, and that the proletariat must substitute. The first-stage objective, however, was overthrow of the tsarist autocracy and establishment of a "revolutionary-democratic dictatorship of the proletariat and peasantry," which would build the material base for a socialist revolution and dictatorship of the proletariat. By 1917, Lenin had taken over Trotsky's view that this process could be more or less continuous, given outside assistance. Lenin and Trotsky and their followers, impatient with Marxist determinism, were unwilling to see the bourgeoisie seize political power. Strictly speaking, they adhered to Marx's doctrine that the bourgeois revolution must come first, but they now spoke of a revolution that was bourgeois by virtue of the tasks it would perform rather than by virtue of its leadership. Temperamentally, Lenin, more than the Mensheviks, was in keeping with the mood of the intelligentsia and with Tkachev's idea of a preventive revolution. Like Tkachev, he doubted the ability of the masses to make their own revolution. The element of political will would be supplied by the party—a centrally directed core of professional revolutionaries that would act as vanguard of the proletariat.

In effect, this Leninist conception of party as elite vanguard, showing the way to the masses, negates the Marxist notion of the proletariat itself as the revolutionary instrument. But this did not mean that the masses were not important to the revolution. Indeed, the "revolutionary situation"—the moment at which the party could seize power—would be characterized by a wave of spontaneous mass uprisings, on the back of which the party could rise to power. At such moments, it was acceptable to utilize slogans inconsistent with the party platform, if they would help to ensure a mass following. Indeed, in 1917 the Bolsheviks came to power not on the basis of their Marxist promises and programs—of which few of the workers and peasants had ever heard—but on the basis of three slogans: immediate peace, all land to the peasants, and all power to the soviets (the councils of workers' and peasants' deputies that had become half of the dual government that succeeded the tsarist regime). None of these were Marxist demands—the latter two were in fact contrary to Marx's program—but they were slogans that enabled the party to utilize the mass unrest and come to power.

The official principle of organization of the Bolshevik wing of the RSDLP—later the Communist Party of the Soviet Union (CPSU)—was what Lenin called "democratic centralism." All issues were to be fully discussed by all before a decision was reached; but once the majority had decided on a course of action, debate would cease and the party would function as a factionless monolith. The democratic element also extended in theory to the choosing of leaders—each party body was to be elected by the body below; but party practice very quickly metamorphosed into the cooptation of new members of the elite by those already in the leadership. Furthermore, in practice, no policy matter could even be opened for debate unless the leadership declared it a debatable question. The failure of a policy line was not allowed to cast doubt on the prerogative of the leadership to continue to operate in this fashion. Rather, mistakes were blamed on scapegoats; the party itself never erred.

What Lenin did was to synthesize the Marxist dialectic method, theory of economics, and doctrine of proletarian revolution with the temperament and organizational principles of the Russian intelligentsia. However suitable it was to the Russian culture, this Bolshevik principle of democratic centralism became (in 1920, at the Second Congress of the Communist International) a precondition for any party that wished to affiliate with the Leninist movement. In this context, it caused great difficulty for parties operating in cultures where democratic theory and the practice of centralized direction by a self-chosen elite were regarded as incompatible.

Marx and Lenin on Foreign Policy

The writings of Marx and Engels contain very little that pertains to foreign policy—indeed, as little as they contain on the operation of a socialist economy. For Marx, the motivating force in the development of industrial society was internal, and the main conflict was among classes rather than nations. Nevertheless, two themes can be extricated from his writings that have relevance to foreign affairs.

The first of these, internationalism, is expressed in the closing words of the *Communist Manifesto:* "Working men of all countries, unite!"[1] The cosmopolitan character of production and the imposition on the whole world of bourgeois values meant that the distinctiveness of nations was fading. The bourgeoisie of the world was already united; likewise, the working man had no country. National sentiments, in Marx's scheme, belong to the superstructure and will entirely pass away with the demise of capitalism. The second theme relates to the nature and function of the state and the uses of state power. Since the state is the instrument of the ruling class for exploiting other classes, it will wither away with the end of the class struggle. During the transition period of the dictatorship of the proletariat, the role of the state is the repression of the bourgeoisie and the creation of conditions for its own withering away. In Marx's view, nation-states and foreign policies would have no place in the communist era of history, when all peoples would live in harmony.

In Western Europe, Marxism evolved in a different direction than it did in Russia. After the outbreak of World War I, Lenin was prompted to formulate a doctrine on international affairs by developments in international socialist circles—and especially in the Social Democratic Party of Germany (SPD), the largest and best-organized Marxist party in the world. Legalized since 1890 and consistently gaining votes in national elections, the SPD had developed a considerable vested interest in the German state. When Lenin heard that SPD delegates in the German parliament had voted in favor of war credits to the imperial government, he was incredulous. The SPD's leadership had reasoned that since the imperial German state was on the verge of being inherited by the SPD and was under attack by reactionary tsardom, defense of the German state was an act in favor of socialism.

Disappointment with the SPD's stand, and with the attitudes of other parties of the Socialist International that had also supported the war effort, impelled Lenin to publish *Imperialism: The Highest Stage of Capitalism.*[2] A new attempt to justify Marxist internationalism, while at the same time recognizing the revolutionary potential of nationalism in less developed areas, the pamphlet depicted a positive role for international conflict in achieving the new world order. In Lenin's view, war would be the agency to defeat world capitalism, even in countries not yet ripe for socialist revolution. Lenin's theory was based on ideas borrowed from John Hobson and Rudolf Hilferding, to which Lenin added certain practical political conclusions of his own. The theory performed the dual function of explaining why Marx's predictions of the imminent fall of European capitalism had not come to pass, and of justifying the attempt to create the first socialist revolution in Russia, the most backward of major European countries.

Marx had been concerned with the capitalist as an individual entrepreneur, but Lenin sought to show how the system had developed to the point where industrial capital and finance capital had merged—the banks had stepped in as sources of finance for industry. Moreover, capital had been increasingly concentrated through the formation of huge international monopolies, which used their financial power to direct the policies of the bourgeois states. And the policy which they had imposed was imperialism—which Lenin described not merely as a policy but as a stage of capitalist development. In order to stave off the ruin of capitalism, which Marx foresaw as the result of the shrinking of the domestic market, the imperialists had turned to investment in less developed countries, using them not only as a source of raw materials, but more importantly as a market for the investment of surplus finance capital.

Thus whole nations had come to be exploited by the capitalists. Moreover, the system had been further propped up by the device of bribing the proletariat in the imperialist countries—creating a labor aristocracy that acted as partner in the plunder of the colonies, and promoting opportunism and jingoism in the socialist movement. This explained the rise of wages and reduction in class conflict within the major capitalist countries; the class struggle had been transferred to the international arena. The international proletariat now included the oppressed peoples of backward countries, both those that were actually colonies, such as India, and those that were formally independent but economically subservient, such as China.

This stabilization of the capitalist system was inevitably impermanent, for the major imperialist powers had by the beginning of the twentieth century appropriated to themselves the major non-European areas of the world, and they were struggling among themselves for a redivision of these markets. This struggle would inevitably result in a great imperialist war; in fact, World War I was such a war, Lenin wrote. The result of this struggle would be the overthrow of capitalism not only in a few advanced countries, but in the whole imperialist system, which was now interconnected. The revolutionary proletariat in Europe—that part that had not sold out to the capitalists—would form an alliance with the peoples of the oppressed countries. Indeed, given the interconnectedness of the system, Lenin argued that it was now likely that the first spark of the revolution would be touched off at the weakest link of the imperialist chain—in Russia—and would quickly spread to the advanced countries. Overthrow of the capitalist system in a country like Russia—a market for investment of French and other European capital—or in a colony like India would inevitably deprive the home country of major and vital markets and provide the economic spark for the downfall of the imperialist system.

This formulation by Lenin assigned importance to elements Marx did not stress; the principle of national liberation became as valid a revolutionary slogan as class struggle. Lenin shifted weight to what Marx saw as a secondary issue—the national issue. The idea that socialists should strive for independence of the colonies would have horrified Marx, who saw the force of, for example, British capital in India as progressive, because it brought industrialization. Likewise, the idea that revolution in backward countries could precede that in more advanced countries was inconceivable to Marx, because it elevated those countries to a higher plane than that to which their stage of historical development entitled them.

Lenin argued that the national problem was the Achilles' heel of Britain and France, as well as of the Russian Empire, but he maintained that the problem of national exploitation was essentially economic. Once socialism resolved the problem of economic exploitation, the national problem could be resolved by arrangements such as federalism. Thus nationalism was not a completely independent force in world politics, but it was conditioned by the stage of economic development.

After Lenin, Soviet theorists continued to stress the uneven development of capitalism in the international arena and the ongoing struggle for redivision of the world. The seeds of capitalist destruction were said to be sown primarily in the international field. The class struggle continued to be fought in the international arena, and peaceful coexistence between the world proletariat and the capitalist world could only be temporary. As a lasting legacy of Lenin's theory of imperialism, Soviet policymakers continued to demonstrate sensitivity to the common ground between socialist states and underdeveloped countries said to be suffering from imperialist exploitation.

The "Operational Code" and Foreign Policy

In addition to the explicit beliefs and values of Marxism-Leninism, which formed part of the belief system of Soviet (and some post-Soviet) decision makers, certain characteristic patterns of thought and action exhibited by Lenin and other Bolshevik leaders continued as an *operational code* for their successors. This term is defined by Alexander George as a set of general beliefs about issues of history and questions of politics as these bear on the problem of action—a prism influencing an actor's perceptions and diagnoses of political events, shaping estimates and definitions, and providing norms and guidelines. While not determining the decisions of its adherents, the operational code bounds the alternative ways they perceive and assess the external world.[3]

As originally set forth by Nathan Leites, the operational code sensitizes its followers to certain approaches to establishing control over people and institutions, orienting them toward the objective of mastering any situation. These precepts are based on the assumption that the party is working in a hostile environment, surrounded by internal class enemies or encircled by capitalist states, and that difficulty, danger, and conflict are the norms of political life—as opposed to the Western view that harmony is the natural political state.[4]

Given these assumptions, and the resulting unrelenting hostility to the status quo with its attendant threats from omnipresent enemies, the code dictates that its followers strive to dominate their environment. Lenin stressed organization as the means by which this control is achieved, but he also displayed great willingness to employ whatever means are necessary, while at the same time retaining tactical flexibility. Given the goal of remaking a corrupt and evil society, the code prescribes the use of whatever means will most speedily ensure attainment of the goal. In an immoral world, no means is more immoral than another; the goal is betrayed if political actors restrict their choice of means on moral grounds. In Lenin's words, "Bolshevism stands on the point of view of expediency: We shall support [any other group] depending exclusively on whether or not we should then be able better to strike a blow against our enemy."[5] The Leninist must not be obsessed with morality, for the end justifies any means. As Trotsky expressed it: "We know that if there are obstacles on the way, they have to be swept away. If this sweeping away of obstacles increases the ruin [of Russia] for a while, then all of this must be rewarded a hundredfold by the policy of economic creativity which the working class must develop after its seizure of power."[6]

The Leninist faces a constant struggle against the tendency to fall into either of two deviations: opportunism—a readiness to adapt too much to the ephemeral conditions of the moment—and sectarianism or dogmatism—becoming so preoccupied with the final goal that one disregards the material obstacles. Official histories of Soviet foreign policy aver that throughout its history the party has steered the correct middle course. But they also reveal another feature of the Bolshevik belief system: there can be at any one moment only one correct policy. The "scientific" element of Marxism-Leninism demands certitude and intolerance of the suggestion that more than one way might be correct.

Given the assumption of a hostile environment, in which all groups are potential enemies and all means are potentially justifiable, the principle emerges that the only good neighbor is the absolutely controlled neighbor. In establishing that control and in destroying its enemies, the party traditionally seeks to manipulate individuals into conflict with one another, exploiting the contradictions in the enemy camp; or the party may form temporary alliances with those who share a common enemy. These alliances are consciously impermanent, based on wariness and distrust, for ultimately the alliance must be broken. Working on the assumption that the other party is operating by the same principles of expediency, Leninists must be sure to destroy their ally before their ally turns on them.

The party must be ready to make temporary retreats in the name of survival, in order to preserve its forces from total destruction, but it must never let up its pressure, even when the enemy appears to be growing weaker. Above all, the Leninist must realize that there can be no permanent balance of power, no lasting compromises. All situations tend toward total victory or total annihilation; one must overtake the adversary or be wiped out. Appeals to conscience or interests cannot reduce hostility; constant pressure rather than reasoned negotiation is the only way to modify the enemy's conduct. In short, as Leites summarizes the operational code, it demands a constant awareness of the question *Kto–kovo?* (Who is prevailing over whom?)[7]

The Role of Ideology in Soviet Foreign Policy

Just as the tsarist foreign policy tradition is one source of the perceptions and behavior of foreign policy decision makers during the Soviet and post-Soviet periods, so also the set of influences just discussed—the Russian revolutionary traditions, the writings of Marx and Lenin, and the operational code—have had a significant effect on Soviet and post-Soviet policy. Taken together, these influences constitute the ideology known as Marxism-Leninism.

An ideology is a comprehensive and consistent set of beliefs and values that usually begins with a critique of existing reality and a statement of goals, and contains a program for the radical transformation of society and attainment of these goals. As such, ideology consists not merely of an assessment of the situation, but an impulse toward action, toward bringing about the desired change in the situation. An adherent of the Marxist-Leninist ideology is provided both with a set of goals and with a distinctive way of looking at events that, in this case, emphasizes the clash of economic classes as the motive force of historical development.

Analysts of Soviet foreign policy have long debated just how large a role ideology played in decision making.[8] At one extreme are those who argue that on issues of foreign policy the doctrine played no active role in shaping Soviet decisions; it was retained as a rationalization and justification for the rule of the party, but doctrinal pronouncements merely masked calculations based on power considerations or national interest. At the other extreme are those—more often found in the world of statecraft than in scholarship—who see Marxism-Leninism as a blueprint providing explicit guidance to Soviet policy and who argue that Soviet policy was thereby rendered quite distinctive. Some stress that as ideology became less operative and relevant on the domestic level, its salience increased on the foreign policy level.[9] In fact, this debate is highly artificial, since there was no contradiction in the Soviet mind between the demands of ideology and those of national interest. Rather, doctrinal tenets were so long term and flexible that they could usually be made to conform to the policies that also promoted the national strength of the USSR.

Vernon Aspaturian has identified six functions of ideology: It provides (1) transcendent objectives, (2) an image of the world, (3) an action program, (4) a system of communication, (5) a means of rationalization, and (6) a symbol of continuity and legitimacy for its adherents.[10] The latter three are passive or "after-the-fact" functions, and there would be little disagreement that Marxism-Leninism played these roles in the Soviet period, providing language and symbols pervasively used in the analysis of events, a way of rationalizing actions taken in the international arena, and a symbol for the regime of the legitimacy of the continued rule of the CPSU. With respect to the former three, the more active functions, the extent to which Marxism-Leninism has performed them varies with time, with the actor, and with the circumstances. That is, the degree to which the doctrine functioned as an operative element in the belief system of Soviet leaders varied from individual to individual—often assuming a larger role in the belief systems of older members of the elite and of those who were not specialists in foreign policy—and from regime to regime, as well as with the external situation that was being faced at any given time.

With respect to the objectives of world revolution and establishment of a new type of international relations, the fact that Marxism-Leninism prescribed no strict timetable for their achievement and the conviction that history was on their side made it easier for its adherents to lengthen the time frame without feeling that they had thereby abandoned the objectives themselves. With respect to the second function, Marxism-Leninism provides an image of the world that heightens the observer's sensitivity to change and conflict, and increases attention to economic and class factors in the analysis of events. By affecting the way certain events are perceived or understood, it does not necessarily alter behavior in any particular way. As a guide to action—the third of Aspaturian's "active" functions—it follows from the very imprecision of Marx's and Lenin's pronouncements on the subject of international relations that nothing very concrete can be expected here. Indeed, it is better to think of this function as less of an "action program" and more of a push toward activism.

Content analysis of Soviet policy pronouncements has shown a stronger ideological component in the longer-range and more general statements, and far less influence on the day-to-day decisions.[11] Still, there was enough continuity in the programmatic statements of the Soviet elite to suggest that the ideology consisted of an unchanging doctrinal core together with an action program that was subject to revision and sensitive to change. Thus ideology can be seen as being at the same time both "principled" and "expedient," and the "creative interpretation" of Marxism-Leninism by Soviet leaders in the light of changed circumstances need not be viewed as either cynical manipulation or abandonment, but rather as a mark of the importance of the doctrine, impelling the leaders to take great care in revising it.

It is entirely in the Leninist tradition to modify the action program or to discard tactics or instruments that are felt to have outlived their usefulness; flexibility is an inherent component of Leninism. Even so, the Soviet party's leadership reserved to itself the right to restate and reinterpret doctrine, not only for itself, but for the entire world communist movement. The party leader who sought to establish his authority attempted to be seen as a learned ideologist, since a challenge to a leader cloaked in priestly robes was seen as a challenge to the sacred mission of the party itself.

The Establishment of Soviet Power

Chapter 2 has already noted the debilitating effects that World War I and its attendant economic and social dislocations had upon the tsarist regime. The revolution that forced the abdication of Tsar Nicholas II occurred unexpectedly and spontaneously in March 1917 (February by the Julian calendar then used in Russia). Bread riots and strikes broke out in Petrograd (a more Russianized version of the capital's name, used during the war), and these escalated into a full-scale general strike and mutiny of soldiers in the capital garrison. After the fall of the tsar, institutions reflecting the bifurcation between the middle classes and the masses—the so-called dual power of the Duma (parliament) and the Provisional Government on the one hand and the Soviets of Workers' and Soldiers' Deputies on the other—coexisted uneasily for the next seven months.

Lenin was in exile in Switzerland at the time of the March revolution, and did not manage to get back to Petrograd until April 16, arriving—as documents long suppressed now establish—in a sealed railway car traveling with German assistance. Before his arrival, Bolshevik leaders were cooperating with the new dual power and not seeking to seize power on their own. Thus they were shocked when he informed them that the first stage of the revolution had already been completed and that the time was ripe for the establishment of the dictatorship of the proletariat. This entailed repudiation of the Provisional Government ("all power to the soviets"); seizure of power by the proletariat and poor peasants; and abolition of the institutions of police, army, and bureaucracy. Lenin's plan, initially rejected by the party's Petrograd Committee, was adopted in May.

A July demonstration against the government, now headed by Alexander Kerensky, started spontaneously but was subsequently directed by the Bolsheviks. However, it soon passed out of their control, and Lenin fled the capital to escape arrest. The threat of a Bolshevik takeover contributed to the attempt of the conservative aristocracy and military forces, under the leadership of General Lavr Kornilov, to stage a coup—the failure of which only strengthened Bolshevik popularity and helped the Bolsheviks to win majorities in the Petrograd and Moscow soviets.

This gain in strength, together with rising peasant unrest precipitated by Kerensky's refusal to allow the peasantry to seize land from its owners, produced what Lenin perceived as a "revolutionary situation." By late September, he began to urge the Bolsheviks to seize power without waiting for scheduled elections to the Constituent Assembly. Again, there was resistance in the party, and only on October 23 did Lenin's plan command a majority. The Bolsheviks' military muscle was centered in the Military Revolutionary Committee of the Petrograd Soviet, under Trotsky's command, together with several strategically placed units of sailors and soldiers loyal to the Bolsheviks. On November 6–7 these forces managed to capture Petrograd, meeting with surprisingly little resistance.

Having gained a majority in the Second All-Russian Congress of Soviets (after their conduct provoked a walkout of more moderate delegates), the

Bolsheviks proceeded to establish as the new governing body of Russia a Council of People's Commissars (known by the acronym Sovnarkom), which was nominally responsible to the Congress of Soviets. Lenin was appointed chairman of the council (equivalent to prime minister); Trotsky, commissar of foreign affairs; and Joseph Stalin, commissar of nationalities.

The true extent of Bolshevik popularity outside the largest cities was revealed in December, when elections to the Constituent Assembly were held. The Bolsheviks obtained only 25 percent of the votes, and when the assembly convened in January, it was dissolved after only one session. The soviets were turned into organs controlled by the Bolshevik Party and withered into insignificance, and by 1922 all competing political parties had been formally proscribed.

As one of their "campaign promises," which had proved especially effective in hastening the demoralization of the armed forces, the Bolsheviks had promised to end Russia's involvement in World War I. Accordingly, the first act of the Soviet state—taken on November 8, just one day after the Bolsheviks' seizure of power—was the issuance of the Decree on Peace, approved by the Second All-Russian Congress of Soviets. Addressed to "all warring peoples and governments," it proposed the conclusion of a just and democratic peace, without annexations or indemnities. The intended targets of the document were the mass publics of the "imperialist powers"; one section appealed particularly to the "class-conscious workers" of England, France, and Germany to liberate humanity from the horrors of war and to liberate the masses from all exploitation.

The decree failed to produce either peace or revolution. Having received no reply from other governments, Trotsky appealed to Germany for a cease-fire. Negotiations began November 27 in the eastern front headquarters of the German army in Brest-Litovsk.[12] The Germans offered a cease-fire of twenty-eight days, to be automatically renewed unless either side gave a week's notice, with an agreement that both armies would stand in position. (In fact, many German troops had already been transferred to the western front.) They acceded to a Bolshevik request for fraternization of troops and mutual dissemination of newspapers.

The armistice was signed on December 15, and five days later a conference was assembled to draft a treaty of peace. The initial German position agreed to the principles of no annexations and no indemnities as the basis for a general peace, if Russia's allies would agree. The Russians were elated, thinking that this meant that Poland and Lithuania would be returned to them, and they were crushed when a German draft revealed Berlin's position that the people of these territories had already expressed their will to withdraw voluntarily from the Russian Empire and accept a protected status within the

German empire. While brandishing the threat of a separate peace with the Central Powers, Lenin and Trotsky were trying to persuade the entente to accept a general peace, urging the workers to take the initiative if their governments failed to do so. At the same time, in secret discussions, unofficial emissaries of Britain, France, and the United States considered the possibility that Russia would get Allied support to break off its talks and renew war with the Germans—who had now made it clear that the price of peace, cloaked as "self-determination" rather than annexation, included Poland and much of the Baltic states.

The dissolution of the Constituent Assembly and Lenin's proclamation of the "public liquidation of formal democracy in the name of revolutionary dictatorship" had done further damage to the Bolsheviks' image in Western Europe, where they were already suspected of being German agents. Trotsky devised a plan to demonstrate to the proletariat of Europe the fundamental enmity between Germany and the Bolsheviks. His proposed formula—"we shall stop the war, but we shall not sign the peace treaty"—would put to the test Germany's willingness to resume the war. If they failed to do so, it would be a victory for Russia; if they did, the Bolsheviks would demonstrably capitulate at the point of a bayonet rather than willingly. Lenin argued for accepting the German terms in order to buy time for the Bolsheviks to consolidate their position in Russia, while allowing the two imperialist blocs to destroy each other in continued war. The majority of his colleagues, led by Bukharin, were persuaded by their own propaganda into believing that Europe's workers were ripe for revolution, and they pressed for the Russians to take up arms in the name of revolutionary war. Believing that the dangers in such a war exceeded the risk of harsher peace terms that Trotsky's plan entailed, Lenin agreed to give Trotsky's formula a try, in return for his promise not to later argue for revolutionary war.

On February 10, Trotsky, conducting the peace talks for the Russian side as a public prosecution of German imperialism, unveiled to his unbelieving audience his "no war, no peace" position and withdrew the Bolshevik delegation from the talks. Eight days later, portraying themselves as the saviors of civilization from Bolshevism, the Germans resumed their offensive. Meeting no resistance, their armies crossed 150 miles in five days. Lenin's acceptance of Germany's original peace terms was ignored; new and harsher terms were demanded on February 23. By these terms, the line of Russian noncontrol was shifted eastward, to include Poland, Lithuania, Latvia, Estonia, Finland, and Ukraine. Russia was to renounce interference in these territories, whose future would be determined by Germany and Austria in agreement with their populations. Additional territories in the Caucasus were to be ceded to Turkey. Together, the lost territories included 34 percent of the population of the

Russian Empire, 32 percent of its agricultural land, and 54 percent of its industry. In addition to these losses, Russia was to pay a large indemnity to Germany for the costs of caring for its prisoners of war.

Outraged, most of the Bolshevik leaders again called for revolutionary war against Germany. Threatening resignation, Lenin argued that either the regime must sign the German terms or it would be signing its own death warrant. The only way to save the world revolution was to hold onto its only foothold, Soviet Russia, even under such shameful conditions. The Russian proletariat had triumphed with relative ease, because it had confronted a rotten regime. The victory of the European proletariat would be harder to achieve, because its internal enemies were stronger, but that victory would come—and must come, if the Russian revolution was to be saved. In the meantime, Lenin told the Congress of Soviets, survival of the revolution required signing the peace: "No matter how brief, harsh and humiliating the peace may be, it is better than war, because it gives the masses a breathing space. . . . Everybody who looks reality in the face and does not deceive himself with a revolutionary phrase will agree with this."[13]

To the consternation of the diplomats of the Central Powers, who preferred not to appear to be dictating terms, a Russian delegate returned to Brest-Litovsk on March 3 and signed the treaty without discussion. Although the Congress of Soviets gave its approval, Lenin and his colleagues were denounced as traitors. The German ambassador was assassinated by members of the Left Socialist Revolutionary Party, who later tried to shoot Lenin himself—an incident that led to the unleashing of the Red Terror.

Although Lenin had agreed that the Soviet government would desist from propaganda among the German troops, he later declared that he could not be held responsible for what the Bolshevik Party chose to do. Indeed, propaganda was so widespread that the German eastern front commander complained that his army had become "rotten with Bolshevism." This factor, together with the need to utilize large numbers of troops to keep control of areas taken from Russia, prevented the Germans from transferring troops that might have turned the tide on the western front. On the home front, the new Soviet Embassy in Berlin became the headquarters for German revolutionary forces—not the last time that Soviet diplomats were plotting to overthrow the government to which they were accredited. On November 5 the "accidental" opening in the Berlin railway station of a Soviet trunk containing insurrectionary documents led to the expulsion of the Russian ambassador and his staff. Four days later, the Bolsheviks annulled the Treaty of Brest-Litovsk, which the Germans were also required to renounce in their surrender at Compiegne on November 11.

This episode in early Soviet foreign policy tells a great deal about what was to come. It marked an end to the age of innocence for the Bolsheviks in the international arena, and it constituted the first step in the establishment of the "socialism in one country" doctrine—the belief that Soviet socialism could be constructed even without the assistance of the European proletariat. For Lenin, signing the Treaty of Brest-Litovsk was not a betrayal of world revolution in favor of the Russian state, nor was it a choice between ideology and national interest. In his mind, these two were so interlinked that they could not be viewed as mutually exclusive. The flexibility of Leninism was revealed in Lenin's belief that power relations would change and losses could be undone; a temporary capitulation, buying time to exploit contradictions in the enemy's camp, could have the result that the Soviets would later be in a stronger position to promote their objectives. The case also illustrates the Bolshevik diplomatic style, which has been termed "demonstrative diplomacy"— using negotiations as a propaganda forum, to appeal over the heads of diplomats and directly to their peoples.

The collapse of the Brest-Litovsk arrangement and of the German threat did not, however, ensure the survival of the Bolshevik regime. A new threat of civil war, complicated by the intervention of Allied forces, continued to call it into question. The initial Allied intervention, designed to keep eastern front pressure on the Germans and safeguard Allied military supplies, received the tacit assent of the Bolsheviks. But in the summer of 1918 the intervention assumed an anti-Bolshevik tinge, as the larger Allied forces began to support rival parties who pledged to bring Russia back into the war. By the spring of 1919, British, French, U.S., and Japanese troops were openly cooperating with the White armies in the civil war, in hopes of putting an end to Bolshevism altogether. To make matters worse, an attempted proletarian revolution in Germany was crushed and its communist leaders were murdered, while short-lived Soviet-style regimes in Bavaria and Hungary were put down.

In the midst of these events, Lenin reported to the Eighth Party Congress on the prospects facing the new Soviet state. Consistent with the operational code's certainty that one side or the other must triumph, Lenin made a statement on the inevitability of war between Soviet Russia and the imperialists that was to be often quoted by his successors:

> We are living not merely in a state but *in a system of states* and the existence of the Soviet Republic side by side with imperialist states for a long time is unthinkable. One or the other must triumph in the end. And before that end supervenes, a series of frightful collisions between the Soviet Republic and the bourgeois states will be inevitable. That means that if the ruling class, the proletariat, wants to hold sway it must prove its capacity to do so by its military organization.[14]

In 1920 Polish efforts to intervene in Ukraine in quest of territory led to war between Poland and Russia. Early successes of the Red Army brought it to the gates of Warsaw, again raising hopes that European revolution would result. But military disaster befell the Russians, and they were forced, in the Treaty of Riga in March 1921, to cede parts of Ukraine and Belorussia to Poland. The same month witnessed the March Action in Germany—another failed attempt at revolution. Nevertheless, by the end of 1921—despite the absence of outside assistance and due in part to the disunity of their opponents—the civil war had ended, the Allied intervention had been liquidated, and the Bolsheviks had managed to establish their control over most of the tsarist patrimony. While their survival in isolation was a result they could never have imagined in 1917, the continuous experience of threats, both from internal "counterrevolutionaries" and from outside "imperialist" powers, amply confirmed preexisting expectations on the part of the Bolsheviks regarding the need for vigilance and caution in dealing with the omnipresent enemy.

Russia and the West in the 1920s

Although the Russian communist regime had survived, the situation in which it found itself in 1921 was by no means comforting. In March, sailors at the Kronstadt naval base had demonstrated in favor of democratization. The rebellion was crushed, and the dictatorship was further tightened, as all organized factions within the Communist Party were banned. Political and social unrest were exacerbated by severe economic dislocation. Large parts of the country were experiencing famine, resulting from civil war policies of forced requisition of grain from the peasantry. Industry was disorganized and badly in need of capital equipment.

Lenin's answer to this crisis was the New Economic Policy, which represented a retreat from socialist economics. The peasants were given greater freedom, and private trade and private ownership of small business were again legalized. But economic recovery could not be accomplished without obtaining capital and trade from the outside world—that is, the capitalists. This, in turn, required that the Soviet regime overcome its virtually complete diplomatic isolation. In response to the logical question, "Why should the capitalists help the recovery of the Russian economy?" Lenin argued that, while the capitalists had not changed their stripes and could resume hostile intervention at any time, they were so economically bound up with Russia that they could not properly calculate their own interests. As Bolshevik leader Lev Kamenev so graphically expressed it, "We are convinced that the foreign capitalists, who will be obliged to work on the terms we offer them, will dig their own grave."[15]

The search for peaceful businesslike relations with the outside world—
the assigned priority of the People's Commissariat of Foreign Affairs
(Narkomindel)—was made more difficult by the parallel existence of the
Communist International (Comintern), which was appealing to the revolutionary masses to overthrow the very governments with which Soviet diplomats were attempting to deal. Although the Soviets tried to maintain the
fiction that the Comintern was simply housed in Moscow and operated independently of the Soviet government, in fact from its beginning in 1919 it was
tightly controlled by the Soviet Communist Party. Trotsky (who had resigned
as foreign minister just prior to the signing of the Treaty of Brest-Litovsk)
had been succeeded by Georgii Chicherin. Chicherin was handicapped by
the fact that his rank in the party was much lower than that of Grigorii Zinoviev,
the head of the Comintern and one of Lenin's closest associates. Indicators
of the lowly stature of the Narkomindel in the 1920s could be found not only
in its constant conflict with the Comintern over control of Soviet embassies,
but also in the fact that on occasion the party Politburo would deal directly
with foreign affairs, bypassing Chicherin's foreign office altogether.

Foreign policy during this period was further complicated by the internal
political struggle over the succession to Lenin, who suffered a stroke in 1922
and died in 1924. Of special significance was the dispute between Stalin and
Trotsky on the possibility of building "socialism in one country"—a debate
often misunderstood as posing an extreme choice between concentration of
all resources on promoting the world revolution or abandonment of world
revolution in favor of the narrow pursuit of national interests. In fact, both
agreed that the building of socialism could begin in Russia alone. But Stalin
was insisting that the process could be completed in one country, whereas
Trotsky argued that it could not be completed without the aid of the world
revolution. In effect, there were two differing meanings of "socialism," with
Stalin using Lenin's definition ("Soviet state power plus electrification"),
and Trotsky adding qualities of refinement and civilization. Trotsky's followers tended to be more cosmopolitan and to have greater international
experience, whereas Stalin was making a calculated appeal to the party and
state bureaucracy, which had a vested interest in consolidating domestic power.

Stalin's formula did not amount to casting out world revolution altogether;
he averred that the construction of socialism could not be "final" as long as
the Soviet Union remained encircled by capitalism. The building of Soviet
state power, he argued, was in the ultimate interest of world revolution. As
Stalin expressed it in his report to the Fourteenth Party Congress in December 1925: "our struggle in our country, the struggle for the victory of the
socialist elements in our country over the capitalist elements, our struggle in
the work of construction, is also of international significance, for our coun-

try is the base of the international revolution, for our country is the principal lever for expanding the international revolutionary movement."[16] By 1929 Stalin was able to carry this perspective to its inevitable conclusion: that the world revolutionary movement in fact now existed primarily as an aid to the achievement of Soviet foreign policy requirements: "An internationalist is one who unreservedly, unhesitatingly, and unconditionally is prepared to defend the USSR, because the USSR is the base of the world revolutionary movement, and it is impossible to defend or advance the world revolutionary movement without defending the USSR."[17]

The strains in Soviet policy were fully evidenced in the regime's relations with the West in the 1920s. The first country to accept Lenin's offer of trade was Britain, and the Anglo-Soviet Trade Agreement of 1921 included Britain's de facto recognition of the Soviet regime. The major impediment in expansion of Soviet economic relations with Western Europe was the issue of tsarist debts, which the Soviets were willing to honor only in part and only in return for credits. The Genoa Economic Conference in 1922 constituted an effort on the part of the major powers to present a united front to the Soviets on the issue of debts and to the Germans on the issue of reparations. At the conference, Chicherin brilliantly played the Germans against the British and French. The resulting Treaty of Rapallo, between Soviet Russia and Germany, as a combination of the two outcasts on the European stage, included a mutual renunciation of claims and de jure recognition of the Soviet regime. In fact, the treaty only strengthened a relationship that had begun in 1920, with a secret pact by which the Germans were allowed to circumvent Versailles Treaty restrictions by testing weapons on Soviet soil, in return for assisting in Soviet military development.

The Narkomindel's efforts to develop relationships with Germany and Britain were seriously threatened by Comintern activities, including its support of an armed uprising instigated by German communists in 1923 and its conduct of anti-imperialist propaganda in the British colonies. The atmosphere was such that the discovery of an alleged (and probably forged) letter from Zinoviev to the British communists calling for revolutionary actions led to the defeat of a new Anglo-Russian trade treaty and to the fall of the Labour government. A raid by British authorities in 1927 on the Soviet trade delegation led to a total break in diplomatic relations between the two states. In the meantime, Soviet efforts to forestall a united capitalist front against them were frustrated by the Dawes Plan for easing Germany's reparations burden and the Locarno Treaty, which guaranteed Germany's western borders and allowed her entry into the League of Nations. Consequently, by 1927 the Soviet Union was again experiencing general isolation in Europe.

The Soviets Turn to the East

Unlike its policies in Europe, the Soviet regime's diplomatic and revolutionary activities in Asia in the 1920s were coordinated, as it allied itself with nationalist forces in the struggle against imperialism. In part, this was a continuation of the old Anglo-Russian rivalry in Asia, though it had been restated by Lenin in ideological terms. But the Soviets faced a practical problem in attempting to formulate an operational strategy based on Lenin's sensitivity to the community of interests between the peoples of the oppressed countries and the international proletariat. The difficulty arose in part because of the intractability of Asian social forces to the Marxist categories of analysis, and in part because of the intrusion of the succession struggle into Soviet policymaking.

The Soviets briefly flirted in 1919–20 with the notion of an assault on British-held India, through Afghanistan, reminiscent of three abortive plans during the tsarist period. In the fall of 1920, Lenin approved the plan of Indian communist M.N. Roy to train an army of Indian revolutionaries at Tashkent, where they would form a joint force with Soviet troops, passing through Afghanistan to the Indian frontier and declaring a revolutionary government. Two trainloads of arms and bullion were supplied, and a number of Indians were trained, but the plan was torpedoed by British pressure, both on the Afghan king and on the Soviets, who were threatened with a rupture of trade relations unless the Tashkent school was disbanded.

This same M.N. Roy had been a major participant in a discussion, at the Second Comintern Congress in July 1920, about communist strategy in the East. He had argued against Lenin that the first priority of the Comintern should be liberation of the colonies and semicolonies, since these were the mainstay of the imperialist system. And he had challenged Lenin's thesis that a class-based revolutionary struggle would fail, and that Asian communists needed to subordinate the struggle for socialism and instead cooperate in a united front with "bourgeois nationalists," such as Mohandas Gandhi and Sun Yat-sen, who were leading the independence movements in their countries. Lenin and Roy had agreed that once Asian, African, and Latin American countries had achieved their independence, and were given the support of the proletariat of more advanced countries, they could bypass the capitalist stage of development and move rapidly toward socialism.[18]

The Soviets were active in the early 1920s in supporting nationalist and anti-British tendencies among three Muslim states on their southern border: Turkey, Iran, and Afghanistan. Under a treaty of friendship signed with Ataturk's Turkey in 1921, they extended military aid to the nationalist regime, even though it was persecuting Turkish communists. Treaties of friendship were also concluded in 1921 with Iran and Afghanistan, as those countries were able to subordinate their longstanding border rivalries and their irritation with activities of the Comintern to the need for Soviet support against the British. In 1925 a neutrality pact with Turkey was the first instance in which the Soviet Union extended technical and economic assistance to a less developed country. Relations with Turkey continued to be reasonably good until 1939, when the Soviets rekindled the traditional Russian ambitions toward the straits.

The most extensive Soviet anti-imperialist investment in Asia in the 1920s was in China, whose internal political weakness made it a tempting target for European and Japanese designs, thereby posing a threat to the Soviet Far East. This traditional Russian interest in excluding hostile powers from a weak China converged with the Marxist-Leninist impulse to strike a blow at imperialism by liberating China from its control. The dilemma for Moscow again lay in the potential contradiction between the dual objectives of national liberation and internal socialist revolution, for it was precisely the feudal and bourgeois "oppressing classes" who headed the anti-imperialist movement in China. The strategy by which the Soviets proposed to overcome the dilemma called for supporting the nationalist movement (Kuomintang) against the imperialists and their puppet government in Beijing, while assisting the Chinese communists in penetrating and assuming control over the Kuomintang. The strategy was further complicated by the fact that the Soviets were also dealing with the Beijing government, signing a treaty in 1924 that established diplomatic relations, joint management of the Chinese Eastern Railway, and Soviet withdrawal from Outer Mongolia (where they were quickly replaced by pro-Soviet Mongolian forces).

The Chinese Communist Party (CCP), founded in 1921, was regarded by the Comintern leadership as too weak to lead the anti-imperialist and antifeudal revolution in China. Its members were instructed to join the Kuomintang but to preserve their freedom of action, exposing the compromises of its leadership, even while the Soviet government and the Comintern supported the Kuomintang in its struggle against imperialism. Once it had served its purpose, Stalin reasoned, the Kuomintang "would be squeezed out like a lemon and then thrown away."[19]

In accord with an agreement in 1923 between the Soviet diplomat Adolf Joffe and Sun Yat-sen, the Kuomintang leadership was trained by the Soviets in political organization and military tactics. After Sun's death in 1925, one of the products of Soviet training, General Chiang Kai-shek, took over the Kuomintang leadership, and by the following year was ousting communists from key positions they had won in the organization. Despite the Chinese communists' pleas that they be allowed to withdraw, Stalin ordered them to stay in the Kuomintang, while seeking to achieve control over it. Chiang Kai-shek's northern expedition in 1926–27 brought his forces to the gates of Shanghai, a communist stronghold. The communists rose up and defeated the anti-Kuomintang forces controlling the city. Chiang waited until this was completed and then marched into the city and slaughtered the communists.

Stalin's strategy in China was under heavy fire from Trotsky, who had advocated that the CCP abandon the Kuomintang and form revolutionary soviets. Loath to admit that his policy was mistaken, Stalin still did not allow a total break, ordering the CCP to seek hegemony over the left wing of the Kuomintang, centered in Wuhan. When these forces also turned on the communists, Stalin refused to allow the CCP to concentrate on building up its support among the peasantry, arguing that they must instead prepare for an uprising of the industrial proletariat. In December 1927, needing a victory to display to the crucial Fifteenth Party Congress, Stalin ordered an uprising in Canton. It lasted long enough for Stalin to be able to claim success for his strategy, but then it collapsed, and with it, the urban base of the Chinese communists.

This experience not only destroyed the prospect of friendly relations between the USSR and the government of Chiang Kai-shek, but it also left a residue of bitterness between Stalin and Chinese communist leader Mao Zedong. No less important was the effect of Stalin's failure in China on his future perception of Asian revolutions. Having so focused his energies on the Chinese revolution, to the exclusion of other national-liberation movements, Stalin reacted to his defeat by refusing to reinvest Soviet energies and resources in another Asian revolution. For him, the "lessons of China" precluded cooperation with unreliable Asian nationalists, leaving the Soviets relatively inactive just at the time when anti-imperialist movements were heating up in India and Southeast Asia.

Changing Soviet Policy, 1928–38

The relative isolation of the Soviet regime in the late 1920s and early 1930s was a result not only of diplomatic rebuffs in Europe and revolutionary failures in China, but of internal developments as well—the decision to embark upon the "third revolution," featuring rapid industrialization and collectivization of the peasantry. Concentration on development of the economy, perceived in part as necessary for building military power, required a period of relative peace in Soviet foreign relations. For one thing, the Soviets needed to expand foreign trade and short-term credits. They sought to increase exports sharply, selling anything for which there was a foreign market, without regard to internal demand, in order to get the currency necessary to import heavy machinery. For another, they needed to avoid external adventures at a time of severe internal strain and weakness, when the regime was conducting a virtual war on the peasant majority of its population.

The militant tone of Soviet policy during this period, and the assessment of the international situation that lay behind it, bore the distinctive imprint of Joseph Stalin. In 1928 he announced that the "temporary stabilization of capitalism," which Lenin had declared in 1921, had come to an end, to be replaced by a period of revolutionary upheaval in the capitalist countries and their colonies. Moreover, the capitalists were said to be preparing a new offensive against the USSR. To help ward off this attack, the proletariat of the world must strike a blow against imperialism by concentrating its fire on the social democrats and on the national bourgeoisie in the colonies, and by taking the place of these elements in the leadership of mass movements. This militant isolationism was understandable only in terms of Stalin's perceptions of his domestic political needs. Having defeated Trotsky and his allies, he was now seeking to discredit Nikolai Bukharin, who had become identified with the policy of cooperating with European socialist parties. The Sixth Congress of the Comintern in 1928 issued the directive to foreign communists to switch from a "united front from above" strategy, in which the Communist Party was organizationally allied with socialist and nationalist parties, to a "united front from below," in which cooperation ended and efforts were made to win over the followers of these parties. In this strategy, the "main enemy" was said to be the erstwhile allies on the left.

The most dramatic illustration of the effect of this policy is in the equanimity with which the Comintern and the Communist Party of Germany (KPD) viewed the paralysis of the Weimar Republic and the rise of Hitler. They saw no immediate dangers, but rather thought the Nazis would be useful in helping to destroy the parliamentary illusions of the German masses. Initiated with the collapse of the empire and cursed with the stigma of national shame in defeat, Weimar never acquired legitimacy with the German public. With 6 million unemployed by 1931, Germany's lower middle class was dispossessed by the Great Depression, creating an antiregime majority of rightists and leftists. As a member of the governing coalition, the German Social Democratic Party (SPD) was appealing to the communists for common action against the Nazis. But the KPD tactics, set by the Sixth Comintern Congress, portrayed the SPD as the real fascist beast. The communists celebrated every Nazi gain, believing that Hitler's victory would close the chapter on capitalism and social democracy and would open the way to communist rule.

The Nazi victory in March 1933 led to Hitler's appointment as German chancellor. Even after the Reichstag fire resulted in the banning of the KPD and arrest of its leaders, the Comintern continued to declare that the proletarian revolution was drawing nearer. Soviet foreign policy called for a continuation of military and political cooperation, in the spirit of Rapallo. In December 1933 the new Soviet foreign minister, Maksim Litvinov, said that Hitler's anti-Soviet speeches and his attacks on German communists would not deter the USSR: "We are, of course, sensitive to the sufferings of our German comrades, but we Marxists are the last who can be reproached for permitting our feelings to dictate our policy."[20] In his remarks to the Seventeenth Party Congress the following month, Stalin criticized the attitude of the German regime, but he was no friendlier to the Western capitalists, declaring, "Our orientation in the past and our orientation at the present time is toward the USSR, and toward the USSR alone."[21]

Despite the militant isolationism of 1928–33, the USSR had not been totally inactive on the diplomatic front. In 1928 it had signed the Kellogg-Briand Pact outlawing war as an instrument of policy, and the following year it had formulated with its neighbors the Litvinov Protocol—a reaffirmation of the treaty's terms within the specific region of Eastern Europe. In 1932 the Soviets signed nonaggression pacts with Poland, Finland, Latvia, Estonia, and France, and subsequently advertised their search (ultimately unsuccessful) for an "Eastern Locarno"—a guarantee of Germany's eastern borders.

At this point the seemingly greater threat to Soviet security was in the Far East, where Japan had invaded Manchuria in 1931. Trying to keep the Japanese pointed away from Soviet territory, the Soviets offered Tokyo a nonaggression treaty and hinted at their willingness to sell the Chinese Eastern Railway (for the control of which they had fought a war with China in 1929) to the Japanese puppet regime of Manchukuo. The Japanese declaration of war on China in 1932 came as a huge relief to the Soviet Union.

Far from being pleased that their predictions of imminent imperialist collapse and proletarian victory were being borne out as international instability increased and war clouds approached, the Soviets instead perceived danger to their own security. Their greatest fear was that the capitalist powers would encourage rising German and Japanese militarism to turn toward the Soviet Union. To ensure that this would not happen, Litvinov became the most vocal advocate of disarmament and collective security. In May 1935 the Soviet Union signed treaties with both France and Czechoslovakia. The former lacked specific military provisions, such as had been contained in the Franco-Russian entente of 1891, and was intended by Moscow primarily to deny to Hitler French support or neutrality for a move against the Soviets. Likewise, the latter treaty obligated the Soviets to assist Prague only if the French also gave assistance.

This collective security policy was supplemented by a reversal in Comintern policy. The Seventh Comintern Congress in August 1935 prescribed the Popular Front policy, calling for containment of fascism through electoral alliances between communists and bourgeois and socialist parties. It also sanctioned renewed collaboration between the Chinese Communist Party and the Kuomintang in the struggle against Japan.

The failure of the League of Nations to punish aggression in Manchuria or Ethiopia or to prevent Hitler's reoccupation and remilitarization of the Rhineland reawakened Soviet fears of the softness of the Western powers and their suspicions that they would try to turn Nazi aggression in Moscow's direction. When Austria was invaded in March 1938 and incorporated into the Third Reich, the West failed to act. Litvinov warned that Czechoslovakia was next, and he called for an international conference, but the USSR was not even invited to the Munich Conference in September. Although the Soviets claimed that they were willing to help the Czechs, the Poles and Romanians refused passage to Soviet troops, and the French declined to take military action. With appeasement a popular slogan, collective security was effectively dead, and the Soviets became obsessed with the need to stay out of impending conflict. For, in fact, the Soviet Union could not have been more unprepared for war. Bloody purges in 1934–38 had decimated both the party leadership and the top ranks of the military, as Stalin sought to remove all possible internal opposition to his rule. Their unintended effect was to convince both Hitler and the Western powers of the USSR's internal weakness.

Nazi-Soviet Cooperation, 1939–41

This period provides one of the best studies of Stalin's diplomatic style and of his ability to reconcile doctrinal perceptions with the interests of safeguarding the Soviet state. In 1939 he turned a desperate situation into an apparent diplomatic coup, only to have the situation reverse itself two years later.

The negotiations that produced the Nazi-Soviet Pact proceeded in two phases: a protracted period between the Munich Conference and late July 1939, during which the USSR, Britain, France, and Germany were continuously feeling one another out, followed by a dramatic month in which agreement between Hitler and Stalin was rapidly hammered out. At the opening of the first phase, the Soviets sent signals that they were determined not to have to face Hitler alone, and that they were seeking incentives to make a deal with whichever side would offer the greater assurance to their security. In the fall of 1938, the Soviet press dropped its earlier distinctions between the fascists and the Western democracies. The Soviets began referring to the coming conflict as the "second imperialist war"—a clear sign that they had no intention of being a party to it.

Stalin's report to the Eighteenth Party Congress in March 1939 opened the door to the possibility of improved relations with Germany. He characterized the British and French as "egging on and encouraging the aggressor" and warned that he would "not allow our country to be drawn into conflict by warmongers who are accustomed to have others pull the chestnuts out of the fire for them."[22] At the end of that month, the situation changed fundamentally when British Prime Minister Neville Chamberlain followed Hitler's violation of the Munich Accords with a unilateral British guarantee of Polish security. This seemed to remove the risk that Poland would be attacked by Hitler with impunity—a possibility that posed the greatest danger to Moscow, since it could bring an aggressive and unopposed Nazi army to the very borders of the USSR.

Now, after the British action, Stalin was the arbiter of the situation. The British needed his support so that Hitler would be dissuaded from attacking Poland, or to gain an ally if he attacked anyway. But Hitler could now use an agreement with Russia in order to dissuade Britain from honoring its guarantee to Poland, or at least—if the British honored their guarantee—to avoid a two-front war. Stalin's greatest objective was to stay out of war, preferably while Hitler and the West were locked in a protracted battle, but at the least he needed not to have to fight Hitler alone. The British guarantee to Poland indirectly provided a guarantee to the USSR as well, since any German attack on the Soviets would have to pass through Poland. Stalin suspected that if he were to cast his lot in a formal agreement with the British, they would leave Poland in the lurch with another Munich, leaving only the Soviets in danger. Nevertheless, talks proceeded between the Soviets and the British and French, in part to allow Stalin an opportunity to assess the likelihood that the West would indeed fight for Poland.

Stalin's other alternative—a deal with Hitler—would allow the Germans to buy Russia's neutrality at the price of giving Stalin a free hand in Eastern Europe. Stalin's hints of availability included the dismissal of Litvinov, who was not only identified as an advocate of collective security against fascism, but was also a Jew. His replacement was V.M. Molotov, a member of the Politburo, who was known for his absolute subservience to Stalin. This signal, Hitler later told his generals, was decisive—"it came to me like a cannon shot as a sign of change in Moscow."[23]

On July 26, three lower-level officials met in a Berlin restaurant to discuss the specifics of a Nazi-Soviet agreement. The German assured the Russians that "there was no problem between these two countries from the Baltic Sea to the Black Sea or in the Far East that could not be solved."[24] Over the next month, as Hitler's deadline for the attack on Poland neared, Molotov teased the German diplomats, insisting on caution. Finally, on August 20, Hitler telegraphed Stalin urging that Foreign Minister Joachim von Ribbentrop be allowed to proceed to Moscow to complete negotiations. When the German arrived, he found himself negotiating directly with Stalin.

The resulting treaty provided that if either Germany or the Soviet Union were to become involved in a war with a third country, the other would remain neutral. Although it was termed a "pact of nonaggression," the treaty omitted the usual stipulation that if one of the parties should commit an act of aggression against a third party, the other would be entitled to renounce the pact. It also omitted the standard procedures for ratification. These were clear signs that it was in fact intended to be a pact facilitating aggression. A secret protocol delimited the boundary of the two parties' spheres of influence in Eastern Europe "in the event of a territorial and political rearrangement." The northern border of Lithuania was to be the boundary in the Baltic area; Poland was to be partitioned; in southeastern Europe "attention is called by the Soviet side to its interest in Bessarabia. The German side declares its complete political disinterestedness in these areas."[25]

Stalin was evidently pleased with what seemed to be a perfect situation for the USSR: the capitalists would exhaust themselves in a long and bloody war while the Soviets remained aloof, with a free hand in territories long separated from the Russian Empire. Moreover, the pact with Hitler allowed an easing of tensions in the Soviet Far East, where Soviet and Japanese troops had been fighting an undeclared war all summer. Hitler was eager for Japan to concentrate its energies on British and U.S. possessions in Asia and the Pacific, and evidently encouraged an armistice between the USSR and Japan, which was signed in mid-September.

Hitler's armies crushed Poland in a matter of days. Stalin, not wanting to share the blame for the aggression, delayed occupying the assigned Soviet sphere. When Russian troops finally moved into Poland, the Soviet communiqué, devoid of Marxist pretexts, could have been issued by Catherine the Great. It spoke of the disintegration of the Polish state, "now a suitable field for all manner of hazards," creating a "need to aid kindred Ukrainian and Belorussian peoples who are left defenseless."[26] Von Ribbentrop returned to Moscow at the end of September to sign the Treaty of Friendship and to revise the secret protocol, transferring Lithuania to the Soviet sphere and moving the German line of control eastward in Poland. In a significant demonstration of Stalin's willingness to be a useful partner to Hitler, trade agreements were also concluded. They helped Germany to break the British blockade by providing for critical raw materials to be sent from the USSR in return for German manufactured goods and weapons plans. By June 1940, a high proportion of German imports, 22 percent—many of them critical to the war effort—were coming from or through the Soviet Union.

Although the British and French had declared war on Germany, they had launched no offensive, and the German and Soviet diplomats (the latter, with reluctance) issued an appeal for peace. Western communist parties, so recently engaged in vitriolic propaganda against fascism, were directed—at enormous cost to their reputations—to join in praise for the new German "dove of peace." Additional damage was done to the international image of communism and of the Soviet Union by Moscow's bullying behavior toward Finland. In October 1939 Stalin had demanded that Finland trade strategic territories in the area of Leningrad and the Gulf of Finland in return for other Soviet territory. Finnish refusal led to an invasion by the Red Army on November 29 without a declaration of war, disguised as a response to an appeal from the revolutionary "Finnish People's Government." The Soviets were expelled from the League of Nations, and the British made preparations to assist the Finns. Hitler, seeing a potential Allied intervention in Scandinavia as a menace to Germany, rendered diplomatic assistance that resulted in a peace settlement on March 12, with Finland acceding to the original Soviet demands. The cost of this territory to Soviet prestige was enormous, given the startling demonstration during the Winter War of Soviet military weakness and inability to crush a much smaller army.

The Russians found some consolation later in the spring of 1940, when the "phony war" in the West finally ended in a German blitzkrieg, which also ended persisting Soviet fears that the Germans would eventually team up with the British and French against the USSR. Soviet relief was short-lived, however, as French armies behind the vaunted Maginot Line surrendered in a matter of weeks. Almost immediately, the Soviets moved to consolidate the fruits of the secret protocol, annexing the three Baltic states "at the request of" new governments there, and demanding the cession by Romania of Bessarabia and northern Bukovina (the latter not mentioned in the secret protocol).

In the following month, July 1940, Hitler began planning for an attack on the USSR. Convinced that Britain was refusing to surrender because of encouragement from the Russians, and giddy with success, he took the risk of a two-front war out of a conviction that he could defeat the Soviets in five months. No more concessions were made to Stalin in the Balkans. The Germans guaranteed Romania's frontiers, moved troops into Finland, and forced the adherence of Romania, Hungary, and Bulgaria to the Axis. In an effort to cover up his intentions and possibly intimidate the British, Hitler invited Molotov to Berlin in November 1940 to discuss a possible "quadripartite pact" among Germany, Italy, Japan, and the USSR. The Russians drastically overplayed their hand, demanding, as a price of their adhering to the pact, recognition of the area south of Batum and Baku in the general area of the

Persian Gulf as the center of Soviet aspirations; German troop withdrawal from Finland; a mutual assistance pact with Bulgaria; and a base within range of the straits.[27] Hitler never replied, describing Stalin as a "cold-blooded blackmailer" and telling his generals that "Russia must be brought to her knees as soon as possible."[28]

On December 18 Hitler issued the directive for Operation Barbarossa, setting the invasion date for mid-May. Two major blunders doomed his possibility of success. First, he allowed the Japanese to sign a neutrality pact with the Soviets in April, thereby allowing Stalin to avoid a two-front war. Second, he postponed the beginning of the invasion so that he could "destroy Yugoslavia militarily and as a nation" in punishment for its new government's refusal to join the Axis. Meanwhile Stalin was receiving numerous warnings of Hitler's intentions, which he treated as provocations. Convinced that Hitler wanted to strike a deal, Stalin signaled his readiness for talks by various acts of appeasement, as well as by assuming the premiership himself. The Soviets were caught in a complete tactical surprise. As he listened to the German ambassador read the declaration of war on June 22, 1941, a pale Molotov could only say, "Surely we have not deserved that."[29]

Although Stalin later claimed to have used the twenty-two months of Nazi-Soviet partnership to prepare for the German attack, his successor declared, "this is completely untrue." In his secret speech to the Twentieth Party Congress, Nikita Khrushchev said that "the necessary steps were not taken to prepare the country properly for defense and to prevent it from being caught unawares."[30] Not only had the military been seriously wounded by the purges, but Soviet war-fighting doctrine was based on the assumption that the initial attack would be immediately repelled and the bulk of the war fought on enemy territory; Soviet territory contained few tank traps or other fortifications.

Indeed, in the time Stalin had "gained," Germany had acquired all the resources of Western Europe plus vital economic assistance from the Soviet Union itself to strengthen its war machine, while Stalin had not even prepared border defenses. The "buffer zone" acquired by the Nazi-Soviet Pact was crossed by German armies in a matter of days. The result of Stalin's gamble that a long war would destroy the capitalist West was that the second front that might have been available to him against Germany in 1939 was gone in 1941 and would not be reopened for three years. The European communist parties, which had never been so popular as in the days of the Popular Front against fascism, had become demoralized and weakened by the pro-German defeatist line dictated from Moscow, in the most obvious demonstration in Comintern history of the extent to which the goals for international communism were manipulated to fit the Kremlin's interpretation of Soviet security needs. In sum, while Stalin's decision to sign the Nazi-Soviet Pact might have seemed reasonable at the time, the Soviet gains appeared much less impressive two years later.

Soviet Diplomacy During World War II

From the time of the Nazi invasion until the January 1943 victory at Stalingrad, the very survival of the USSR was in grave doubt. Hitler's initial thrust captured lands that were home to more than 40 percent of the population. Soviet losses—by their own estimate, totaling at least 20 million dead—were most severe during this period. The country's industrial production dropped by half. That the Soviet Union not only survived but emerged from the war as Europe's strongest power was a tribute to Soviet military valor and diplomatic skill.

When Stalin finally emerged from an initial gloomy silence to address the nation on July 3, he made several references to Nazi "treachery." In tacit recognition of how little reason the people had to fight for his regime, the speech was full of patriotic and nationalistic imagery; Marxist-Leninist appeals for the defense of socialism were absent.[31] The German drive stalled at the gates of Moscow in November, through a combination of circumstances: the onset of severe winter, Hitler's decision to bog his army down in attacks on Leningrad and Moscow, his failure to force Japan into the war, and the Germans' unwillingness to use humane treatment in order to tap the anti-Soviet sentiment of non-Russian nationalities.

The following month Stalin demonstrated that he was already calculating Russia's postwar political gains. Unsuccessfully pressing British foreign secretary Anthony Eden for a secret protocol to be included in a British-Soviet treaty of alliance, he sought British recognition of the Russian annexations of 1939–40, Soviet bases in Finland and Romania, and agreement on the dismemberment of Germany. In the spring, Molotov made trips to London and Washington to talk about Allied cooperation and press for opening a second front. In the United States, he found Roosevelt focusing on preservation of friendship among the Allies, preferring to postpone decisions on specific political issues.

Although the Soviets were always keenly attuned to postwar power configurations, they did not appear to have a rigid blueprint but preferred to keep their options open. Issues relating to the future of Poland were particularly sensitive, and neither the Polish government-in-exile in London nor its British patrons were willing to agree to the recognition of the boundaries established in the Nazi-Soviet Pact. To create an alternative, Stalin set up a communist-dominated Union of Polish Patriots in Moscow, but he held off recognizing it as the legitimate government. However, the Soviets severed relations with the Polish government in London following their demands for an international investigation into the massacre in the Katyn Forest of thousands of Polish military officers. The Soviets had denied German charges (later proved accurate) that the atrocity had occurred during the Soviet occupation of that section of Poland. The Russians' feigned indignation was a convenient pretext to free their hand and keep open future political options.[32]

Embarrassed at the behavior of the London Poles, the British and Americans had even greater feelings of guilt when they announced to Stalin in mid-1943 that the opening of the second front would have to be postponed for yet another year. Roosevelt eagerly sought a face-to-face meeting to "win over" Stalin and calm his anger, and it was in this context that the Big Three met in Teheran in November 1943. There Stalin was able to take advantage of divisions between Churchill and Roosevelt to achieve important Soviet objectives.

Roosevelt failed to support Churchill's argument that the invasion of France should be postponed in favor of an invasion of southeastern Europe—an operation that would have altered the political fate of Eastern Europe. Roosevelt also declined, for domestic political reasons, to enter into discussions on Poland. Its fate was essentially decided in bilateral conversations in which the British suggested moving Poland westward, compensating for Soviet gains to the Nazi-Soviet line by ceding German lands to Poland. The plan was illustrated by Churchill with the aid of three matches; he and Eden observed that it "pleased Stalin."[33] Well it might, for it guaranteed that no independent Polish government could accept this plan, and thus that a puppet government would have to be installed. Churchill also suggested that Russia deserved warm-water ports, and Stalin replied that "it might be well" to relax the restrictions on the movement of Soviet warships through the Turkish straits. Stalin followed with an inquiry about what might be done for the Soviets in the Far East, and Roosevelt—grateful for Stalin's expressed willingness to enter the war against Japan after the defeat of Germany— suggested the possible availability of the port of Dairen.

Stalin's apparent willingness to cooperate at Teheran so impressed his U.S. and British allies that they were offering up the very prizes he coveted. No display of this attitude was more striking than a discourse by Churchill that appeared to invite Russian imperialism:

> It was important that the nations who would govern the world after the war should be satisfied and have no territorial or other ambitions. If that question could be settled in a manner agreeable to the great powers, he felt then that the world might indeed remain at peace. He said that hungry and am-

bitious nations are dangerous, and he would like to see the leading nations of the world in the position of rich, happy men. The President and Marshal Stalin agreed.[34]

Churchill's and Roosevelt's focus on preserving friendship with Stalin suggests that they were staking Europe's future on their belief that the Soviet regime had changed fundamentally. Their willingness at Teheran to satisfy Stalin's "security needs" by altering the boundaries of Poland and Germany not only ensured Poland's future dependence on the USSR but also made it impossible for Germany to conclude a separate peace with the West.

In the last summer of the war in Europe, following the Allied invasion of Normandy, Stalin showed how his armies could be deployed to advance his political objectives. In Romania, for example, the Red Army was sent to occupy the entire country even after it had renounced its alliance with the Axis powers. Bulgaria, too, had abandoned Germany and was in the midst of suing for peace when the Soviet Union declared war and invaded. In Poland, in late summer 1944, Stalin cynically employed a tactic he learned from Chiang Kai-shek. He halted the advance of the Red Army outside Warsaw while the Polish underground, rising up on command of the London Poles, was slaughtered in battle with the Nazis. Afterward, the Soviets captured the city and turned it over to their communist-dominated puppet regime.

The following month Churchill was in Moscow for a last attempt at forging a compromise between the London Poles and the Soviets. Despite pressure from both the British and the Russians, Polish premier Stanislas Mikolajczyk refused to comply with Soviet demands for territorial adjustments. An exasperated Churchill, showing again how he valued Soviet friendship, declared, "Because of quarrels between Poles we are not going to wreck the peace of Europe."[35] At this same meeting, Churchill cynically proposed a division of the other countries of Eastern Europe into Western and Soviet spheres of influence, stated in percentage terms, and Stalin quickly acquiesced to the proposal.

The fate of Poland was settled by Soviet and Allied military strategy in 1944, though it was discussed again at the last conference among Roosevelt, Churchill, and Stalin, held at the Crimean resort of Yalta in February 1945. After much discussion, Stalin gave his Western partners a small victory by agreeing to take a few London Poles into the communist-dominated "Lublin provisional government," and by promising to hold free elections in Poland "as soon as possible." However, he reserved the right to limit participation to "democratic" parties—a designation that would be made by Soviet authorities alone. A similar unacknowledged difference in interpretation lay behind Stalin's willingness to agree to sign the Declaration on Liberated Europe, which called for democratic elections to be held in all the liberated and former Axis satellite states. Roosevelt put great stock in this document, which was the focus of later Western charges of Soviet bad faith. Similarly, securing agreement on the basic structure of the United Nations was high on the agenda of the Americans, who were haunted by the memory of President Wilson's mistake of failing to build the international organization before making the final political settlement of the war.

Roosevelt was also eager to secure a reaffirmation of Stalin's willingness to bring the Soviet Union into the war against Japan three months after the German surrender. This Stalin was happy to do, in return for a share of the dismantled Japanese empire—in particular, the territories and privileges lost by the Russians in 1905. The Soviets wanted southern Sakhalin and the Kuriles from Japan, and from China they sought recognition of the independence of Outer Mongolia, access to Dairen, a naval base in Port Arthur, and joint ownership of the Chinese Eastern Railway. Roosevelt persuaded Chiang Kai-shek to accede to this territorial rearrangement in a Treaty of Alliance and Friendship, signed between China and the USSR on August 14, 1945.

In the remaining weeks of the war in Europe, the movement of Soviet troops was followed by the imposition of "friendly governments" in Eastern Europe. The role of noncommunist elements in Poland was seriously constricted; a communist government was forced on Romania, and communists assumed leading positions in Bulgaria, Hungary, and Czechoslovakia. In Yugoslavia, where Tito's communist army was the main force fighting the Germans, the coalition with noncommunist elements was abandoned. The Soviets turned a deaf ear to Western complaints about these actions. But following Roosevelt's death in April, the successor administration of Harry Truman appeared to adopt a harder attitude toward Moscow's behavior, and in May it suspended Lend-Lease assistance to the Soviet Union.

President Harry Truman was able to assess the Soviet leader directly at the final wartime conference, which was held in Potsdam, in occupied Germany. (The other participant, Prime Minister Winston Churchill, suffered electoral defeat during the meetings and was replaced by his successor, Clement Atlee.) The opening day of the conference, July 16, was also the birthday of the nuclear age in international politics. Shortly before his first meeting with Stalin, Truman was informed of the first successful test of the atomic bomb. When Stalin was "casually" informed by Truman "that we had a new weapon of unusual destructive force," he apparently "showed no special interest."[36] In fact, the Soviet Union had been actively conducting its own atomic research program, assisted by intelligence agents who were well informed about U.S. progress.

The main focus of discussion at Potsdam was the reorganization and governance of defeated Germany. There was no disagreement about the need to disarm and de-Nazify the country, but the Soviets and their Western allies adopted sharply differing positions on how to demarcate Germany's borders and dispose of its industrial capabilities. Amid heated disagreements about political developments in their respective spheres of influence, Great Britain and the United States showed no receptivity when Stalin restated his claim to a Soviet base in the Turkish straits.

The United States used the atomic bomb on Japan on August 6 and 9, and on the latter day—exactly three months after Germany's surrender—the Soviet Union declared war on Japan. In the week that passed between that date and the Japanese surrender, Soviet armed forces managed to occupy the northern part of Korea and moved rapidly through northern Manchuria to join up with the army of the Chinese communists. Again using his own armies to acquire his postwar political objectives, Stalin quickly occupied the territories that had been conceded to him at the Yalta Conference. However, he was rebuffed when he sought to extend Soviet influence even further by sending troops to share in the occupation of Japan.

As a result of World War II, communism had expanded from its base in the Soviet Union to extend its domain over an additional 100 million people in eleven more states of Europe: Latvia, Estonia, Lithuania (all soon reannexed into the USSR), Poland, the eastern zone of Germany, Czechoslovakia, Hungary, Romania, Bulgaria, Yugoslavia, and Albania. These states were extremely diverse nationally, religiously, and culturally, while they shared a low level of economic development as well as relative inexperience in self-rule. They also varied in the strength of their communist parties, though all were to some extent under Soviet control. The Western leaders were slow to understand that, for Stalin, the control of these governments by communist politicians loyal to him was not simply ideologically desirable, but was essential to the security needs of the Soviet Union. The gradual tightening of political and economic control over the states of the region was a logical consequence of Stalin's conviction, expressed to Yugoslav communist leader Milovan Djilas, that "everyone imposes his own system as far as his army can reach. It cannot be otherwise."[37]

The Beginning of the Cold War

The cause of the breakup of the cooperative alliance between the Soviet Union and its wartime partners has been the subject of considerable debate among American historians of the period. The "revisionists" write of the betrayal of the idealism of Roosevelt by the Truman administration, while the "orthodox" portray an abandonment of naive illusions by politicians more realistic about Soviet intentions. In fact, as the preceding pages have spelled out, the alliance was never more than a marriage of convenience, marked by misperceptions, misunderstandings, and frequent outbursts of suspicion. Despite their efforts to maintain a spirit of friendship and cooperation, Britain and the United States found themselves able to do so only by papering over their divisions with the Soviet Union, and they never succeeded in drawing Stalin into a genuine shared vision of the postwar political order.

Stalin's certainty about the inevitability of conflict after the war was expressed in a speech on February 9, 1946. In it he set forth his interpretation of the nature and meaning of the war, justified his prewar and wartime policies, and voiced his prescriptions for the future. The persistence of his Marxist-Leninist worldview is evident in his analysis of the causes of the war, which he described as an inevitable consequence of capitalism. The Soviet Union found itself in alliance with Britain and the United States for the very limited purpose of defeating fascism—a cause that would not have been achieved without Soviet participation. Far from being unprepared, he asserted, the Communist Party had long ago begun to provide the resources needed for victory through its policies of industrialization and collectivization and through purging its ranks of traitors and saboteurs.

As for the future, Stalin made it clear that there was to be no easing of the forced-pace drive to "organize a new mighty upsurge in the national economy." The reason for continued sacrifice, he implied, was the external threat: "Only under such conditions can we consider that our homeland will be guaranteed against all possible accidents. That will take three more Five-Year Plans, I should think, if not more. But it can be done and we will do it."[38] There would be no near-term Western effort to pry away the fruits of Soviet victory by force of arms, and this allowed a substantial reduction in Soviet armed forces. But it was clear from a remark Stalin made to Djilas in 1945 that he did indeed expect that a few years of respite would be followed by another war: "The war shall soon be over. We shall recover in fifteen or twenty years [three more Five-Year Plans!] and then we'll have another go at it."[39]

Stalin's speech was indicative of a revival of ideological militancy that had taken place in the Soviet Union following the victory at Stalingrad. After Hitler's invasion, the regime's communications with the Soviet people had been laden with patriotic symbols and evoked prerevolutionary Russian traditions. The reappearance of Marxist-Leninist orthodoxy appeared to be a ritual of purification coinciding with the liberation of Soviet territories from Nazi occupation and with the Red Army's penetration into the capitalist world beyond Soviet borders. Stalin's suspicions about ideological contamination and even betrayal fell most heavily on some of the minority nationalities; during and immediately after the war, whole nations—most notably, the Volga

Germans, the Crimean Tatars, and the Chechens—were subjected to mass deportation.

This sense of threat clearly went beyond ideology; it was an expression of Stalin's deep-seated insecurity. This was amply confirmed in his later years not only by the wide-ranging purge of the Leningrad party apparatus but also in the demented "doctors' plot," through which Stalin in his last days was apparently planning to eliminate many of his closest associates. That this paranoia had a profound impact on Soviet foreign policy was documented in Khrushchev's "secret speech" to the Twentieth Party Congress in 1956. As he described it:

> Stalin was a very distrustful man, sickly suspicious. Everywhere and in everything he saw "enemies," "two-facers," and "spies." . . . He had completely lost consciousness of reality; he demonstrated his suspiciousness and haughtiness not only in relation to individuals in the USSR, but in relation to whole parties and nations.[40]

No account of Soviet foreign policy in the postwar years, and no explanation of the origins of the Cold War, can be complete without an awareness of the extent to which Stalin's policies and personality required isolationism, an atmosphere of hostility, and an omnipresent enemy.

Continuity and Change in Soviet Policy Before the Cold War

During the three decades from the Bolshevik Revolution to the beginning of the Cold War, the Soviet regime functioned in an international system that, in certain fundamental respects, more closely resembled the one faced by the tsars in the eighteenth and nineteenth centuries than the one that emerged after World War II. World War I had not changed the multipolar and Eurocentric nature of international politics, nor had it altered the basic "rules" of balance-of-power diplomacy. Although the Soviet regime differed from its tsarist predecessor in some very fundamental respects, these systemic constants—together with the enduring geopolitical realities—helped produce more continuity in Moscow's policy than might have been expected.

In the wake of the diplomatic thunderbolt that was the Nazi-Soviet Pact, Winston Churchill, one of the closest and most astute observers of the diplomacy of Lenin and Stalin, characterized Moscow's policy with an enduring phrase: "It is a riddle wrapped in a mystery inside an enigma." Unfortunately, the balance of Churchill's observation has been less well remembered: "But perhaps there is a key. That key is Russian national interest."[41]

As we pointed out at the beginning of this chapter, Soviet leaders did not act as though the demands of ideology and those of the Russian national interest were in conflict. Lenin, in negotiating the Treaty of Brest-Litovsk, and Stalin, in negotiating the Nazi-Soviet Pact and in the wartime summit conferences, were constantly aware that their first priority was to ensure the survival of the Russian state and to seek ways to enhance its security, whether through acquiring "buffer" territories or through seeking respites in which to build up its economy and defense capabilities. When they had opportunities to expand, the territories that interested them were identical to those that the tsars had sought, for identical strategic reasons. As we have seen, neither Lenin nor Stalin hesitated to equate policies that pursued Russian national interests with the long-term interests of world socialist revolution. Both were adept at employing communist rhetoric to explain and justify strategic moves that served the interests of Russia.

Indeed, especially for Stalin, the primary purpose of the international communist movement was to serve the interests of Soviet foreign policy, as defined in the Kremlin, no matter how it twisted and turned to meet internal economic or political needs. Revolutionary parties or leaders who were not under Stalin's control were not to be trusted, and—as German, Iranian, Turkish, and Chinese communists could testify—even those who were loyal were expendable if Soviet national interests demanded that they be sacrificed.

The Russia inherited by the Bolsheviks in 1917 was considerably weakened and faced powerful adversaries. In such circumstances, it was not surprising that Soviet leaders sought to enhance their security by aligning with other states to promote their interests—that is, to seek to establish a balance of power, so that they were not faced by an overwhelming hostile coalition. This required that they be capable of assessing changes in distributions of power and willing to align with other states—regardless of ideological orientation—that could help preserve the balance, often playing these states off against each other. Lenin's and Stalin's policies toward Germany, from Brest-Litovsk to Rapallo to the Nazi-Soviet Pact, amply illustrate that communist leaders were no less adept than the tsars at playing the balance-of-power "game."

At the same time, we have noted characteristics in Soviet foreign policy during this period that represented significant changes from the tsarist period. One change was in the practice of diplomacy itself—the use of techniques that have been termed "demonstrative diplomacy." These treat the negotiation as an opportunity to gain an international platform from which to proclaim revolutionary principles that will turn the peoples of other states against the very leaders with whom talks are being held. Sometimes agreements are sought and gained, but sometimes the negotiations are conducted primarily for the propaganda opportunities they present. Trotsky's behavior during the Brest-Litovsk negotiations, Chicherin's at the Genoa Conference, and Litvinov's in the League of Nations all provide evidence of the skill with which Soviet foreign ministers have conducted "demonstrative diplomacy." We also have observed numerous instances in which this dual policy—promoting revolution while conducting diplomacy—created difficulties for Soviet foreign policy, or even led, as in Soviet-British relations in 1927, to a total break in diplomatic relations.

Another element in Soviet foreign policy during this period that differentiates it from the balance of power diplomacy practiced during tsarist times was the assumption, voiced by Lenin in his famous statement of 1919 and often repeated by Stalin, of the inevitability of war between the Soviet Union and its capitalist adversaries. While the tsars fought many wars, they also showed themselves adept at avoiding conflicts with powerful rivals. Tsarist diplomacy, unlike that of the Soviets, was not conducted against a backdrop of implacable hostility toward the outside world. Whereas both Lenin and Stalin argued at particular times that peaceful coexistence with the capitalist world was possible, it was not thought to be a permanent prospect. For Stalin, the very existence of the two hostile "camps," though they could coexist with one another under certain conditions, meant that one or the other must triumph. The Soviet Union could proceed with the construction of "socialism in one country," but as long as "capitalist encirclement" prevailed, the people would have to make sacrifices in order to ensure the country's preparedness for the inevitable day of reckoning. As we have seen, this theme—far from disappearing during the years of the Allied coalition of World War II—was voiced again by Stalin in February 1946 as the prevailing prospect for the coming years of what would be termed "Cold War."

—————— 4 ——————

Soviet Foreign Policy:
The Cold War

The Stalinist Approach to Cold War

The Cold War began as a struggle between two major powers, each at the head of an ideologically defined coalition. Yet this initial bipolarity was not a struggle of equals. The United States emerged from World War II with far greater economic and military strength than the Soviet Union. Even after U.S. troops (other than Occupation forces) were withdrawn from Europe and the Pacific and demobilized, the United States retained unchallenged air and naval superiority, and its monopoly of the new atomic weapon gave it a formidable lead in military capability.

While Stalin expected a respite from armed conflict that would enable him to rebuild the Soviet Union's shattered economy, he nevertheless sought to deter the United States from utilizing its military strength. He did this by capitalizing on the Soviet lead in conventional arms and exploiting the perception that Western Europe was vulnerable to an attack by the Red Army. Although both sides had demobilized, U.S. reductions had left ground forces at about one-half the size of the Soviet Union's. About thirty Soviet divisions were deployed in Germany and Eastern Europe in the late 1940s, compared to about ten maintained by the West. While an active program of atomic research was under way in the USSR, Soviet military doctrine played down the significance of nuclear weapons and stressed the importance of conventional forces and superior morale.

Stalin's political strategy combined opportunistic probing with caution about provoking a military reaction. This was demonstrated in the first postwar crisis, which occurred in Iran—a border area that had tempted Russia's rulers for centuries. When the Soviet Union broke its wartime promise to withdraw occupation troops from northern Iran and instead demanded autonomy for two communist-dominated provincial regimes it had set up there, Iran brought the dispute to the newly established UN Security Council. Under strong U.S.-British pressure, including an implicit threat of force, Soviet troops were withdrawn.[1]

Some voices in the West were already warning early in 1946 that a long struggle was in the offing—most notably, Winston Churchill's declaration that an "Iron Curtain" had descended across Europe, and U.S. diplomat George Kennan's pessimistic "long telegram" from Moscow. But not until the first half of 1947 did the words "Cold War" and "containment" enter the American vocabulary, as the bipolar nature of the postwar conflict became clearer. In February, Britain notified U.S. officials that it was no longer able to act as protector of the existing order in the eastern Mediterranean, where the Greek government was under serious pressure from a communist guerrilla movement and the Turkish government was facing an ominous Soviet demand for frontier adjustments and a naval base in the Turkish straits. After an intensive strategic review, President Harry Truman proposed to Congress that the United States assume the burden of leadership, not only through specific (and ultimately successful) assistance to Greece and Turkey, but through a broader commitment "to support free peoples who are resisting attempted subjugation by armed minorities or by outside pressure."[2] The Truman Doctrine was followed by a proposal from Secretary of State George Marshall—responding to a severe economic and political crisis throughout Western Europe—for massive U.S. assistance in the rebuilding of the Continent.

Although the Marshall Plan was deliberately posed in nonideological terms, allowing for Soviet and East European participation, it was denounced by the Soviets as an imperialist plot to undermine the independence of the states of Europe while staving off economic collapse in the United States. In retrospect, the decision by Stalin that the USSR and its East European allies would not participate in the European Recovery Program appears seriously mistaken. As it happened, the Marshall Plan produced an economic miracle that helped to restore stability and reduce the appeal of communism in Western Europe. Had the Soviets participated, they might have shared in the economic benefits; but it is more likely that the U.S. Congress would never have appropriated large sums for a program with communist participation, in which case communist prospects in France and Italy might have mounted. At any rate, Stalin's decision served to confirm the political and economic division of Europe.

In the summer of 1947, an anonymously published article by George Kennan publicly articulated the U.S. strategy of responding to Soviet behavior with a policy aimed at "long-term, patient but firm and vigilant containment of Russian expansive tendencies" and featuring "adroit and vigilant application of counterforce at a series of constantly shifting geographical and political points, corresponding to the shifts and maneuvers of Soviet policy."[3] Almost simultaneously, at the founding conference of the Communist Information Bureau (Cominform), Stalin's lieutenant Andrei Zhdanov described a titanic conflict between two camps—the "imperialist" camp, led by a predatory and expansionist United States, and the "democratic" camp under Soviet leadership, which sought to "resist the threat of new wars and imperialist expansion, to strengthen democracy and to extirpate the vestiges of fascism."[4]

Clearly, both the USSR and the United States perceived themselves as heading coalitions struggling for peace and justice against an evil and determined rival. Thus, they saw the world in terms of "tight bipolarity," such that all states would be forced to choose one side or the other, and in which the struggle of ideologies left no room for compromise. But while both seemed prepared for protracted conflict, neither appeared willing to risk provoking the other into actual warfare.

The chief purpose of the Cominform was to aid in tightening the Soviet coalition by solidifying Moscow's hold over the states of Eastern Europe and shielding them from the temptations that might be posed by U.S. aid and propaganda. The increasing similarity of these regimes was reinforced in February 1948, when the communist coup in Czechoslovakia removed from the East European political scene the last trace of accountable government. At the same time, Stalin sought to assert his authority over Yugoslavia, where Tito and his followers had created a fiercely pro-Soviet but independent communist regime. When they refused Stalin's demands, the Yugoslavs were expelled from the Cominform. Moscow and its allies mounted a campaign of unrelenting pressure, which Tito was able to resist thanks to solid internal support and timely assistance from the West. Though unwilling to risk war to remove Tito, Stalin proceeded to purge potential imitators in the states of the region and to end any deviations of policy from the orthodox Soviet pattern.

One opening remained in the Iron Curtain, because British, French, and U.S. forces continued to occupy the western sectors of Berlin—one hundred miles within the Soviet zone of Germany. In February 1948, the Western Allies decided to proceed, without Soviet participation, toward economic reform in their zones of occupation in Germany, including West Berlin. They announced a currency reform as a first step toward the creation of a federal republic in Germany. The new state would be included in the European Recovery Program and possibly even in a future anti-Soviet military coalition. Seeking to force a Western retreat from this plan, the Soviets mounted a pressure campaign, which climaxed in June with the blockade of all land routes into Berlin.

The United States responded with an airlift of supplies—a continuous shuttle over the next twelve months of more than a quarter-million flights. The dramatic Berlin airlift inspired the American, Canadian, and West European people and their governments to support the creation, in spring 1949, of the Federal Republic of Germany and of the North Atlantic Treaty Organization (NATO). Acknowledging defeat, the Soviet Union ended the blockade of Berlin and sponsored the creation in its own zone of occupation of the communist-ruled German Democratic Republic (GDR). Although the continuing presence of the West in Berlin was a constant irritant that Moscow would again seek to remove, the political and economic division of Europe appeared complete.

As in tsarist times, diplomatic stalemate in Europe was followed by renewed Russian attention to opportunities for expansion in Asia. There indigenous communist forces were on the verge of establishing control over the world's most populous country, and the European colonial empires in South and Southeast Asia were in the process of being toppled by nationalist revolutions. These revolutions had proceeded without Soviet leadership, in part because of preoccupations in Europe, but also because of Stalin's earlier unhappy experience in China in the 1920s. The Soviet media virtually ignored the military successes of the Chinese communists, and—unlike the resurgent communist parties of France and Italy—the Chinese Communist Party (CCP) received no invitation to the founding congress of the Cominform. Mao Zedong's military victory was essentially complete before he obtained Soviet diplomatic recognition in October 1949. Only shortly before that did the Soviets give public endorsement to the armed struggles being conducted by the communist parties in Indochina, Indonesia, India, Burma, Malaya, and the Philippines. In so doing, they claimed that the true inspiration for the "Chinese path to revolution" was to be found in the teachings of Lenin and Stalin.

Even the conclusion in February 1950 of a Sino-Soviet treaty of alliance—after nine weeks of hard bargaining—gave signs of the ambivalence with which the Soviets regarded the Chinese communist victory. Their experiences with Tito had revealed the potential difficulties with a communist neighbor who had won victory without Soviet military assistance or political counsel. Moreover, Moscow had already established a treaty relationship with Chiang Kai-shek's regime that had produced territorial and economic benefits—control of the Chinese Eastern Railway and the base at Port Arthur—which disappeared in the new treaty. Under its terms, the Soviets were to return control of these assets no later than the end of 1952; they also undertook to render economic assistance to China in its (sure to be costly) efforts to build socialism.

That same year, however, a miscalculation on Stalin's part caused China to be diverted from its major objectives and plunged into an undeclared war with the United States in Korea. That country had been divided into U.S. and

Soviet zones of occupation following the surrender of Japan. In ending the Occupation in 1949, each side had turned over its zone to like-minded political forces. The North Korean regime, run by Soviet-trained communists, was militarily and politically stronger than South Korea, which seemed vulnerable to attack. The United States, which had taken no military action to prevent a communist triumph in China, had failed to include its Korean client within its announced "defense perimeter" in Asia. For Moscow, the situation presented an opportunity to unify the peninsula under a single communist regime, while demonstrating to Japan that it would be unwise to form closer security ties with the United States, which was of uncertain will.

When North Korea invaded the South on June 25, 1950, the Truman administration responded swiftly and boldly. With the United States leading, the UN Security Council—boycotted since January by the Soviet delegate, in protest of the continuing representation of China by Chiang's government—condemned the aggression and appealed to member states to come to the aid of South Korea. U.S. forces stationed in Japan were ordered to Korea by President Truman. He reassured Stalin that the United States sought no direct conflict with the USSR—which in 1949 had broken the U.S. monopoly and become an atomic power. Disavowing responsibility for the conflict and denying that they intended to intervene, the Russians were content to watch the spectacular initial military success of their client.

When the tide of battle in Korea turned in October, however, and United Nations forces were driving the North Koreans all the way back toward the Yalu River border with Manchuria, both the Soviets and the Chinese faced unacceptable prospects. For the Soviets, the defeat of a communist government by U.S. arms was a dangerous precedent; for China, the establishment of a hostile state on its border—or even a possible invasion of Manchuria—had to be prevented. After several fruitless warnings to the United States, and after having received assurances of Soviet aid, China sent "volunteer" forces into the fighting at the side of the North Koreans. Several months of fierce combat were followed by a bloody stalemate at the original boundary of the two occupation zones. Armistice talks commenced in July 1951, but Stalin found it advantageous to prolong a situation in which U.S. forces were tied down in endless conflict with Moscow's proxy. Moreover, China, fighting with arms purchased from the USSR, found itself diplomatically isolated and increasingly dependent on the Soviet Union.

Although Stalin was willing to experiment with new tactics in his latter years, a major reorientation of Soviet policy would have to await new leadership, which came with Stalin's death in March 1953.[5] While the Soviet Union had achieved major successes in the postwar years and had become one of the world's two nuclear superpowers, it confronted equally large challenges.

The Iron Curtain dividing East from West seemed higher and more impenetrable than ever, and behind it, in Moscow's sphere, nationalist tensions and popular dissatisfaction simmered beneath the facade of socialist unity. Stalin's record in foreign policy was decidedly mixed; gains achieved through shrewd bargaining existed alongside opportunities missed because of stubborn inflexibility. Attacked by his successors as a ruthless paranoid whose policies were often divorced from reality, he was again praised by his lieutenants' heirs for his strong and single-minded leadership in building an industrial power capable of awesome military successes. Nearly a half-century after his death, the "genius leader of all mankind" continued to be a dominant, controversial, and unsettling figure both for his own people and for the entire communist world.

The Khrushchev Strategy

Although Stalin's policy had built the Soviet Union into an industrial and military superpower, it had exacted an enormous price in loss of life, human suffering, unmet needs, and personal insecurity for the elite and masses alike. It was evident to the country's new leaders that a continuation of this approach would be counterproductive. The legitimacy of their own rule depended upon restoring the authority of the Communist Party of the Soviet Union, without surrendering its monopoly of political power. Further strengthening the country's economic and military capabilities required motivating the population through material incentives rather than terror. But if they were to achieve domestic stability and improve living standards, the new leaders would need to avoid confrontation with external enemies. They also would need to lessen tensions within the socialist camp—a point that was brought home only three months after Stalin's death, when demonstrations erupted in East Germany and had to be quelled with Soviet tanks.

While persuading the other members of the socialist camp to adopt a "new course" that relaxed the harsher features of the Stalinist system, the new Soviet leaders sought to improve relations in other areas of conflict as well. They resumed diplomatic relations with Greece and Israel, withdrew their territorial claims against Turkey, and—most significantly—took steps to break the stalemate and allow the conclusion of an armistice in Korea. Prime Minister Georgii Malenkov, in a speech to the Supreme Soviet on August 8, 1953, declared that "there are no disputed or outstanding issues which cannot be settled peacefully by mutual agreement." At the same time, he warned those who perceived the new Soviet policy as a sign of weakness that the United States now had "no monopoly on the hydrogen weapon."[6]

The following year Malenkov voiced the previously heretical view that the existence of nuclear weapons meant that war between imperialism and communism would destroy world civilization. He evidently meant to use this doctrine as the basis for cutting the Soviet defense budget, but within a month he was forced by a majority of his colleagues in the collective leadership to modify his thesis to state that only capitalism would be annihilated by nuclear war.

Basking in its new status as a thermonuclear power, the Soviet Union called for a conference of foreign ministers to be held in Geneva in the spring of 1954 to consider Korean reunification and a solution to the conflict in Indochina. The Korean phase of the conference ended in deadlock, but the Indochina phase produced an agreement for a truce between France and the Vietminh National Liberation Committee, led by Ho Chi Minh and a nucleus of communists, which had been fighting French colonial forces since 1946. The Geneva agreement called for France to withdraw its troops, recognize the independence of Laos and Cambodia, and partition Vietnam pending national elections in 1956. Although both sides regarded it not as a final solution but as a springboard to further struggle, the agreement represented a victory for Asian communism.

The adroit diplomacy of Zhou Enlai at the Geneva conference signaled the reemergence of China on the world stage, and its elevated status was confirmed later in 1954 by a renegotiation of its partnership with the USSR. A delegation of Soviet leaders traveled to Beijing to conclude a new treaty that freed China from some of the more humiliating terms imposed by Stalin. The Soviets agreed to withdraw from Port Arthur, to eliminate the joint stock companies set up in 1950, and to increase the level of credits and technical assistance to Chinese industry.

An area of conflict on which no progress was made was Germany. Soviet hopes that disunity in the West would prevent German rearmament were dashed in 1954, when the NATO allies agreed to admit the Federal Republic of Germany, bringing an army of half million under integrated NATO command. In response, the Soviet Union assembled its East European allies in Warsaw and adopted the Pact of Mutual Assistance and Unified Command (the Warsaw Pact), which gave a symbolic symmetry to European defense arrangements.

Despite this setback, the Soviets continued to focus attention on security arrangements in central Europe. In May 1955 the Austrian State Treaty provided for withdrawal of Soviet and Western troops from their respective zones of occupation and for the permanent neutralization of the Austrian state. The cost for the Soviets was relatively low, since no communist state had been set up in the Soviet zone, and they may have hoped to provide neighboring West Germany with another lesson on the advantages of neutrality.

The Austrian treaty helped clear the way for the first big-power summit meeting since Potsdam—the Geneva Summit of 1955. The major Soviet proposal was for the mutual disbandment of NATO and the Warsaw Pact, the withdrawal of non-European (i.e., American) forces from the continent, and conclusion of a European security treaty. Neither this nor the major Western initiative—President Eisenhower's proposal to open the defense installations of each side to aerial surveillance by the other ("open skies")—produced any agreement. But the conference did bring a marked reduction in international tension (the "spirit of Geneva"), fostering the impression that the Soviet leaders (first secretary of the CPSU Nikita Khrushchev and new prime minister Nikolai Bulganin) were reasonable men, with whom it was possible to negotiate.

Later in 1955, the Soviets made another attempt to "exploit the contradictions" in the Western camp by enticing its West European allies away from the United States. Their target was the West German chancellor, Konrad Adenauer, who visited Moscow in September for talks on establishing diplomatic relations and commercial ties. Using the time-honored technique of appealing to capitalist greed, the Soviets hoped to use the bait of renewed commercial relations to gain Adenauer's formal renunciation of the goal of German reunification. But Adenauer had his own initiative to pursue—offering German financial assistance in return for reunification or, as the Soviets saw it, buying the German Democratic Republic from Moscow in return for West German credits and reparations. Although the temptation must have been great, the Soviets were unwilling to deal away "their" part of Germany. Khrushchev later wrote about it in terms similar to the Western "domino theory"—the abandonment of socialism in the GDR would only have encouraged more Western pressure and set off a chain reaction: "Once you start retreating, it's difficult to stop."[7] (As we shall see, Chancellor Helmut Kohl had much better luck making the same proposal to President Gorbachev thirty-five years later, when other dominoes around the GDR had already fallen.)

When the Twentieth Congress of the CPSU convened in February 1956, the new direction in Soviet foreign policy was already evident, but the congress played a significant role by articulating and approving the changes in interpretation of Marxist-Leninist doctrine that supported a relaxation of tensions. This necessitated a turn away from Stalin's rigid two-camp worldview, which left no room for Soviet cooperation with movements and states that were noncommunist but anti-imperialist. The task was not to invent an entirely new approach but to return to Lenin's concept of a temporary strategic alliance between the USSR and various "neutralist" or "nationalist" forces against the imperialist powers.

Khrushchev justified his approach by declaring that the balance of forces in the international arena had shifted as a result of the transition from "socialism in one country" to a powerful socialist world system. This made it possible for Marxism-Leninism to triumph both in individual states and worldwide without war or violence, but through peaceful competition. In his major public address to the Twentieth Congress, Khrushchev proclaimed the major tasks of Soviet foreign policy: (1) pursuing a policy of peaceful coexistence; (2) building stronger relations among the socialist states, including Yugoslavia; (3) strengthening friendship and cooperation with neutralist and peace-loving states in Europe and the Third World; (4) pursuing closer relations with the United States and its allies; and (5) strengthening the USSR's defense potential and exposing the activities of the enemies of peace.[8]

Although these pronouncements at the Twentieth Party Congress represented a significant departure for Soviet foreign policy, Khrushchev's lengthy and controversial secret speech attacking Stalin had an even greater effect, particularly within the socialist camp. Khrushchev's explicit comments in the realm of foreign policy included criticism of Stalin's failure to prepare Soviet defenses for the German attack in 1941; Stalin's "lack of faith in the Chinese comrades," which delayed the establishment of the communist regime in Beijing; his "shameful role" in relating to Tito; his misunderstanding of the nature of the national liberation movement in India; and his "unrealistic" assessment of the situation in Korea, leading to the creation of a "risky situation" there.[9]

Apart from its enormous impact on political, social, and cultural life in the USSR, Khrushchev's de-Stalinization campaign had dramatic consequences for Eastern Europe as well. Khrushchev's denunciation of Stalin, together with his public acknowledgment that "many roads to socialism" were permissible, was intended to help the USSR mend fences with Tito and bring him back into the Soviet camp. The Yugoslav leader traveled to Moscow in June for a "fraternal visit," during which relations between his party and the CPSU were reestablished. Pleasing as they were to Tito, Khrushchev's revelations about Stalin had a shattering effect elsewhere in the socialist bloc, where Soviet authority was linked closely to Stalin's personality and policies. On Soviet initiative, the "little Stalins" ruling in Poland, Hungary, and Bulgaria had been replaced in the first half of 1956 by more reform-minded leaders, and—in another concession to Tito—the Cominform had been abolished. Khrushchev evidently thought that the bonds of Marxism-Leninism and the institutional ties to the Warsaw Treaty Organization and the Council for Mutual Economic Assistance (CMEA) were strong enough to substitute for the late dictator's fearsome iron grip. Clearly, he overestimated how solid these ties were, particularly in the face of revelations that the "genius leader of all mankind" who had presided over the establishment of socialist regimes in Eastern Europe had in fact been a criminal and a madman for most of his career. The "posthumous rehabilitation" of the victims of blood purges in the USSR and Eastern Europe had the effect of stimulating even more searching questions about the nature of a political system that could allow such suffering and injustice.

The most profound reverberations were felt in Poland and Hungary. Strikes and demonstrations began in Poznan, Poland, in June, setting off a chain of events that culminated in October with the election of a new party leader, Wladyslaw Gomulka. Gomulka, who previously had been suspected of "Titoist" sympathies, immediately declared Poland's intention of following its own national path toward communism. A Soviet delegation headed by Khrushchev rushed to Warsaw, and there were strong hints of possible action by the Red Army. The Poles were able to reassure the Soviets that the Communist Party remained in firm control and that it was committed to maintain Poland's alliance with the USSR.

This challenge was followed the same month with an even more serious rebellion on the part of the Hungarian population. This led to an attempt by the new premier, Imre Nagy, to restore multiparty politics and free elections and to withdraw Hungary from the Warsaw Pact. In the first few days of November, Soviet tanks were sent to crush the Hungarian revolution. In a coincidence that was fortunate for the Soviets, the potential negative reaction in some parts of the world to their bloody invasion of Hungary was reduced by the simultaneous invasion by Western forces of a prominent Third World neutralist state. In the eyes of many African, Asian, and Latin American nationalists, Moscow's action to prevent a defection from its East European security zone was less offensive than the British-French-Israeli invasion of Egypt in response to President Gamal Abdel Nasser's nationalization of the Suez Canal and to attacks on Israel by *fedayeen* guerrilla (Arab) terrorists in the Sinai peninsula.

While taking care not to become militarily involved, the Soviet Union championed Nasser's cause and claimed that its noisy threats had forced the retreat of imperialism. The outcome of the Suez crisis seemed to further the USSR's two chief objectives in the Middle East: hastening the decline of British and French influence in the area and combating the Western-sponsored anticommunist alliance—the Baghdad Pact of Britain, Turkey, Iran, Iraq, and Pakistan. The fact that the United States was not a party to the Suez intervention, and in fact harshly condemned it, gained little credit in the region for Washington. In fact, it produced an additional benefit of the crisis for Moscow—the weakening of Western unity.

While the Suez crisis helped to mitigate the international impact of Soviet intervention in Hungary, it did not forestall the weakening of

Khrushchev's domestic political position. His rivals claimed that he had undermined Soviet authority in Eastern Europe with his unwise revelations about Stalin and his concessions to Tito. In June 1957 Khrushchev was faced with a "so-called arithmetical majority" in the Party Presidium that demanded that he step down as first secretary. The resourceful Khrushchev, with the help of Defense Minister Georgii Zhukov, turned the tables on his adversaries by summoning the Central Committee to Moscow to override the Presidium's action and remove his chief opponents (the "anti-Party group") from their positions.

As he set about repairing the damage to his own position, Khrushchev was also engaged in an effort to reconstruct the socialist bloc. This culminated in November 1957 in a meeting in Moscow of the leaders of twelve ruling communist parties. Tito was not present, since the Hungarian events had produced another rupture in Soviet-Yugoslav relations. The Moscow meeting widened the reopened breach by condemning "revisionism" in the communist movement. Mao Zedong, on the other hand, played a prominent role at the meeting, freely giving advice to the Soviets even as he acknowledged (in return for Khrushchev's promise to aid China in developing nuclear weapons) that the CPSU was at the "head" of the socialist camp. But China was clearly beginning to question the validity of Khrushchev's doctrinal interpretations and his ability to lead the socialist bloc to further successes. Under growing pressure, he needed a dramatic breakthrough.

The successful launch by the USSR of an artificial space satellite (Sputnik) in October 1957 provided the key ingredient in Khrushchev's plan—parlaying the Soviet lead in the "space race" with the United States into an assertion of Soviet strategic superiority. In fact, the strategic military balance was quite unfavorable to the USSR, given the U.S. lead in bombers and the fact that the Soviets were not investing in missile production. Khrushchev sought to create the opposite impression by making a series of exaggerated claims regarding Soviet rocket development. Using a combination of threats and proposals for disengagement, he sought to pressure European members of NATO into refusing an expansion of American nuclear capability on the Continent and in Germany in particular.

The purpose of this elaborate missile deception was to extract political concessions from the West, particularly regarding Berlin, which had been divided into zones of occupation since 1945.[10] The three Western zones had de facto linkages to the Federal Republic and shared in its economic prosperity. East Berlin, occupied by Soviet forces, was a depressing study in contrast. Located one hundred miles inside the GDR, Berlin was an easily accessible escape route for East Germans, about 3 million of whom by 1961 had traveled from East Berlin to West Berlin and then on to West Germany.

This outpouring of refugees was a dramatic and embarrassing manifestation of the side-by-side comparison of the achievements of the two economic systems. Together with the GDR's virtual diplomatic isolation, the refugee flow clearly threatened the long-term viability of the German communist regime. Khrushchev hoped to use the missile deception and a carefully deployed combination of enticements and threats to force a change in the status of Berlin. He calculated that this would shake the confidence of West Germans in their NATO partners, while producing formal recognition of Germany's division, neutralization of the two states, and a permanent ban on West German access to nuclear weapons.

Khrushchev sought to achieve a diplomatic triumph in Europe "on the cheap." His ambitious seven-year plan for the Soviet economy, unveiled at the Twenty-First Congress of the CPSU in January 1959, was designed to propel the Soviet economy to a level past that of the United States. Its fulfillment required a further diversion of resources "from guns to butter," and in January 1960 Khrushchev announced a reduction of about one-third in the size of the Soviet armed forces. Adopting ideas expounded by Malenkov in 1954, he acknowledged that nuclear war would destroy both capitalism and communism, and concluded that it was thus no longer necessary for Soviet forces to be of a size and diversity that would allow them to survive an initial nuclear attack and then to win a conventional war with the West.

Khrushchev's strategy was posited on the achievement of favorable results in negotiations on Berlin and a concomitant relaxation of international tensions. He was encouraged by a meeting of the Big Four foreign ministers (of the United States, the USSR, Great Britain, and France) in the spring of 1959, a summit meeting with President Dwight Eisenhower in the United States that autumn, and Western agreement to a Big Four summit on European security issues to be held in Paris in May 1960. As it turned out, however, the Paris summit ended in disaster. A few days before it was to open, the Soviets shot down a piloted U-2 high-altitude plane belonging to the United States, part of an ongoing series of photographic espionage flights over Soviet territory in search of the allegedly numerous (but actually fictitious) Soviet missile emplacements. When President Eisenhower, whom Khrushchev had recently hailed as a peace-loving statesman, took personal responsibility for the spy mission, the Soviets decided that the summit conference could not begin without a personal apology. To be sure, the Soviets were aware that their missile deception had probably been exposed and realized that the Paris negotiations were indeed not likely to produce Western concessions on Germany. An opposition faction in the Soviet leadership, composed of heavy-industry and defense lobbyists and hard-line ideologists, dissatisfied with Khrushchev's defense cuts, apparently took advantage of the situation to force a harder line in Soviet policy. After the breakup of the Paris summit, the remainder of 1960 saw a lingering chill in East-West relations, climaxed by Khrushchev's belligerent performance at the United Nations, in which he banged his shoe on a desk in protest of a speech he found offensive.

The Kennedy administration, which came to power in 1961, pledged an activist response to the Soviet challenge in Europe and the Third World. However, its first foreign policy crisis—an ill-fated U.S.-supported invasion of Cuba by anti-Castro forces at the Bay of Pigs—aroused doubts about Kennedy's resoluteness. A meeting between Kennedy and Khrushchev in Vienna in June, held in a somber atmosphere, was followed by Khrushchev's reinstatement of a deadline for a settlement on Berlin, an announced increase in the Soviet defense budget, and a suspension of the planned reduction in the size of the Soviet armed forces. Kennedy parried with increases in the U.S. defense budget and troop strength.

Khrushchev's next move caught the West by surprise. The Soviets succeeded in August 1961 in solving their immediate problem in Berlin, closing off the escape route by building a wall between the western and eastern sectors of the city. This was followed two months later by an ominous confrontation between Soviet and U.S. tanks at the border of their respective sectors, but Khrushchev again defused the crisis by withdrawing his deadline.

Khrushchev grew increasingly frustrated with the lack of movement toward his longer-range goal of changing the status of Berlin and stabilizing the situation in Germany. The longstanding Soviet fear that West Germany would gain access to nuclear weapons was now multiplied by visions of an aggressive and nuclear China. Not only was the Soviet Union's prestige at stake, but its relative strategic position was worsening. The United States had discovered that the presumed missile gap in favor of the Soviets had never existed—but only after their own strategic buildup had resulted in an actual gap favoring the United States. Khrushchev lacked the economic resources to satisfy both civilian and military needs, and he was under increasing pressure from a hard-line faction to produce a foreign policy victory. At the beginning of 1962, he was desperately seeking a way to demonstrate Soviet military might, thereby impressing the United States and China and impelling them to the negotiating table to resolve pressing political issues. His thoughts led him to a solution that was both unorthodox and bold, as he later recounted in his memoirs:

> I had the idea of installing missiles with nuclear warheads in Cuba without letting the United States find out they were there until it was too late to do anything about them. In addition to protecting Cuba, our missiles would

have equalized what the West likes to call the "balance of power." Now they would learn just what it feels like to have enemy missiles pointing at you; we'd be doing nothing more than giving them a little of their own medicine.[11]

In addition to their military uses, the missiles probably also represented a bargaining chip that Khrushchev could employ to force the West to abandon its positions on key issues. In either context, their effectiveness depended on their being deployed without the knowledge of the United States. On October 14 a U-2 overflight of Cuba produced photographic evidence of the construction of missile installations. Eight days later President Kennedy shared it with the American public and the world. He declared that the United States would consider an attack from Cuba the equivalent of an attack by the USSR, and he announced the imposition of a naval blockade to halt further Soviet shipments. Thus seizing the strategic initiative, in full knowledge of superior U.S. conventional and nuclear power, Kennedy forced Khrushchev to dismantle and remove the Cuban missiles under UN supervision, in return for a face-saving pledge that the United States would not invade Cuba.[12]

In the months following the Cuban missile crisis, Khrushchev's efforts seem to have been focused on restoring an atmosphere of peaceful coexistence, with an eye to negotiating the best solutions he could reach. A treaty banning nuclear tests in the atmosphere was agreed upon in 1963; although the Chinese and the French refused to sign, the Federal Republic of Germany was among the signatories. The following year, there were signs that Khrushchev was planning a trip to Bonn for direct negotiations with the West Germans; but domestic opposition to his policies was growing, and he was forced to backtrack on de-Stalinization and to scrap plans for economic liberalization. Just two years after his humiliation in Cuba, and with the split with China moving to the point of open break, Khrushchev was forced to resign on October 14, 1964.

The Cold War in the Third World

One of Khrushchev's most important foreign policy legacies was the Soviet rediscovery of the Third World as the "vital strategic reserve of imperialism." He saw it as an arena in which the Soviets could compete with the West with high likelihood of success, but with less risk than would result from a direct challenge in the "main arena" of the bipolar struggle. Several significant events in 1955 signaled Soviet priorities and the techniques they were willing to employ in this new arena: the sale of arms (ostensibly from Czechoslovakia) to Egypt, gaining a foothold for Soviet influence in the Middle

East; high-level diplomacy in South Asia, starting with a June visit to Moscow by Prime Minister Jawaharlal Nehru of India and a return trip at the end of the year by Khrushchev and Bulganin to India, Afghanistan, and Burma; and economic assistance to the state sector of developing countries, inaugurated during the Soviet leaders' trip to India with the announcement that the Soviets would finance and construct the giant Bhilai steel mill. Although some were nominally "socialist," most of these countries were not leaning toward communism; rather, they interested Moscow for strategic and geopolitical reasons.

Adopting Lenin's perspective, Khrushchev perceived that Soviet interests were advanced by joining with nationalist and neutralist Third World states in the struggle against imperialism—a temporary alliance he called the "zone of peace." He confidently asserted that Soviet aid to state-owned industries in these countries would help to liberate them from their economic dependence on the West, while simultaneously stimulating the growth of a communist-oriented industrial proletariat.

However, it did not take long for the Soviets to lose their optimistic outlook on the prospects for socialist development in Asia and Africa. In only a few countries were communist parties even allowed to function; rarer still was one with healthy political prospects. The call for the application of "creative Marxism" in further research by Soviet scholars led to a great deal of doctrinal experimentation—a search for alternative paths by which the new states could make the transition to noncapitalist development, and thus be deemed worthy of Soviet support. This produced concepts so pliable that even the most backward economies were said to be capable of socialist development. Indeed, Soviet analysts argued, given a mutually supportive relationship with the Soviet Union, the transition to socialism could occur even without the leadership of the proletariat or of a communist party.

Certain Third World leaders found satisfaction in having their countries proclaimed as candidates for rapid development toward socialism. Khrushchev surely was eager to seize on the new concepts to justify his claims that Soviet policies could produce victories for socialism. The Chinese, on the other hand, objected sharply to the ideological sleight of hand, as did Third World communists whose historical role was thereby eliminated. The most fundamental problem with Khrushchev's approach, however, was that it largely ignored the realities—that Third World countries confronted tremendous obstacles to economic development.

A wide variety of techniques were employed by Moscow in its opportunistic search for influence in the Third World. In addition to diplomatic contacts, the Soviets developed ties with a variety of political parties; promoted exchanges with labor, student, and cultural groups; disseminated massive quantities of print and radio propaganda; and employed tens of thousands of civilian and military technicians and advisors. The Soviet program of foreign aid (totaling just over $47 billion through 1988), though dwarfed in absolute terms by that of the United States, was highly selective, with four countries (India, Iraq, Afghanistan, and Turkey) receiving just under half of the total amount. Disbursed in the form of long-term credits strictly tied to the purchase of Soviet goods, economic aid was closely linked with Soviet foreign trade.

Far greater in volume was the military aid program of the Soviet Union; indeed, weapons were the chief export of the USSR to the Third World. Its military aid relationships presented Moscow with opportunities not only to extend its own political influence in strategic areas while strengthening its clients against local and regional challengers, but, more concretely, to extend its military reach in ways that could alter the international balance of power. However, the program was not without its costs; Moscow did not always find itself on the prevailing side in regional conflicts, and even when it did, it did not always experience gratitude from its allies.

Soviet achievements in the Third World under Khrushchev's leadership may have been far less impressive than he had promised, but he did lay the ideological and operational foundations for long-range Soviet involvement. Although his ambition greatly exceeded Moscow's reach, Khrushchev plunged the USSR into global involvement; he extended the bipolar struggle into the "imperialist reserve" and left the United States unchallenged in no area of the world. He forged active ties with the more radical states of the Third World, for which Moscow represented an alternative source of economic and military capabilities. But lavish Soviet aid and the encouragement of radical socioeconomic change often left economic and political chaos in its wake. Khrushchev's most promising clients—Indonesia's Sukarno, Algeria's Ben Bella, and Ghana's Nkrumah—were toppled shortly after Khrushchev himself.

Despite the failures, Khrushchev's lasting accomplishment was to expand the horizons of Soviet foreign policy beyond the narrow parameters to which Stalin had confined it and to renew the appeal of Soviet doctrine beyond the rigid formulations of his predecessor. In so doing, Khrushchev won for the Soviets some valuable footholds in strategically prized and previously uncharted territories.

As in other spheres, the successor leadership continued the basic objectives of this strategy, while shifting tactics and adopting a more cautious and pragmatic style. In the face of an explicit recognition of the complex and extended nature of social change in the Third World, the emphasis in Soviet pronouncements was soon on the lengthy timetable that would be required for the new states to build socialism. As a leading Soviet analyst phrased his criticism of leaders who pushed social change too quickly, "Proclaiming socialism is not the same thing as building it."[13] The new Soviet approach to economic assistance placed greater stress on the economic feasibility of aid projects, and motivations for Soviet aid and trade were increasingly expressed in terms of mutual economic benefit. More than ever, Moscow's targets in the Third World were chosen according to the degree of Chinese or Western interest in the country, its importance to Soviet security, or its ability to provide support facilities—including airports, harbors, or sites for communications stations—for Soviet military activities.

These factors grew in significance during the years of Leonid Brezhnev's rule, as the Soviet Union deployed its sizable and growing navy in the waters surrounding the Third World. The Soviets sought to use this new capability not merely for military defense but for the political purpose of "protecting state interests in time of peace" or "showing the flag." In the Indian Ocean, for example, by the mid-1980s the Soviets were maintaining a permanent squadron of at least twenty vessels, with occasional "surges" in times of crisis to more than thirty. By expanding its navy in this fashion, Moscow showed its determination to achieve the status of a global superpower—not confined to the Eurasian land mass but capable of projecting its power far beyond its own borders.[14]

As the Soviet Union's investment in strategic Third World resources and facilities grew, its involvement in "national-liberation struggles" and regional conflicts became an issue of greater contentiousness in its relationship with the United States. At times when the Soviets were seeking "détente" or relaxation of tensions with the West in order to widen access to trade and technology or pursue negotiated settlements, their Third World involvements worked at cross purposes, despite Soviet efforts to keep the two arenas separate. Moreover, the strong forces of nationalism and the volatility of regional conflicts in Asia, Africa, and Latin America made it difficult for the USSR to establish reliable patron-client relationships. Among the high-profile reversals were some that resulted when "clients" switched sides in search of a better deal (most notably, Somalia and Egypt), and some that resulted when pro-Soviet regimes were overthrown (such as Chile's Allende and Ethiopia's Mengistu).[15] In fact, Soviet influence seemed to peak in the mid-1970s, with the coming to power of pro-Soviet regimes in Angola, Ethiopia, Nicaragua, and Afghanistan, and the spread of communism to Laos and Cambodia. Afterward, there were no new Third World successes. In the Gorbachev era, the costs of the USSR's investments in the Third World were reassessed, and class struggle and the two-camps thesis were explicitly abandoned in favor of more cooperative relationships with the West, which facilitated a scaling back of Soviet commitments and negotiated solutions to some of the more dangerous regional conflicts in the Third World.

The Sino-Soviet Conflict

In the Third World, as in all other arenas of the Cold War, no development so profoundly affected the foreign policy of the Soviet Union in the 1960s, 1970s, and 1980s as its conflict with China. The challenge to the notion that Moscow was the single center of the international communist movement, initiated by Tito, was raised to shattering heights by Mao Zedong. Yugoslavia in 1948 demonstrated that a communist regime could remain independent of the USSR, and Poland in 1956 showed the possibilities of pursuing home-grown domestic policies within the context of Soviet military control. China in the 1960s became the USSR's chief enemy and thereby forever destroyed the Marxist myth that proletarian forces engage in "international relations of a new type."

At least in part, the schism between the Soviet Union and China was a consequence of a larger change in the international system—the decline of rigid bipolarity and rise of multipolarity, as new power centers emerged in global politics. But China's challenge was not simply that of an emergent great power. Its significance and intensity were magnified by other factors, including a conflict in ideology, a personality clash between Khrushchev and Mao Zedong, longstanding national rivalries, differing levels of economic development, and a rivalry for leadership of the socialist camp. Differences that were expressed confidentially in the late 1950s were more openly communicated in the early 1960s, and by 1964 the split in the socialist system was an acknowledged reality.

Although they had no reason for devotion to Stalin, the Chinese voiced dissatisfaction with Soviet policy only with the accession of Khrushchev to the leadership of the USSR. They were disturbed by the events of the Twentieth Congress of the CPSU in 1956—not only the doctrinal revisions unilaterally announced by Khrushchev, but also his secret speech attacking Stalin. Having been persuaded (in part by the promise of assistance in their nuclear development) to refrain from an open challenge to Soviet leadership at the conference of eastern bloc states in 1957, the Chinese found Soviet behavior in the next two years intolerable. Specifically, they objected during the Middle East crisis of 1958 when Khrushchev proposed a summit conference of the traditional Big Four plus India; later that year, when the Soviet Union was thought to be insufficiently forthcoming on behalf of Chinese claims to the offshore islands of Quemoy and Matsu; and in the following year, when Moscow adopted a stance of neutrality in the border clashes between communist China and "bourgeois" India. Why, in the wake of the launch of Sputnik, the Soviets appeared more interested in peaceful coexistence with the United States and in friendship with India than in aggressively pressing the demands of their socialist ally was a point of bitter frustration with the leaders in Beijing.

For their part, the Soviets were alarmed by the bold policies adopted by China both domestically and externally. In 1958 the Chinese adopted a radical industrialization policy (the "Great Leap Forward") and a system of agrarian communes as methods of moving quickly toward the stage of full communism. Implied in their claims was a challenge to Soviet ideological preeminence. Khrushchev's response was the hastily summoned Twenty-First Party Congress in January 1959—the "Congress of the Builders of Communism"—which adopted an ambitious seven-year plan. In the foreign policy realm, China's quest for control of Taiwan and the offshore islands, its brutal repression in Tibet, and its campaign to force adjustments on the Sino-Indian border escalated global tensions at a time when Khrushchev was emphasizing peaceful coexistence and the potential fruitfulness of negotiations. In an unmistakable sign of their distrust, the Soviets in June 1959 abrogated the 1957 military aid agreement in which they had promised to give China technical data for the manufacture of the atomic bomb. At about the same time, Khrushchev was evidently supporting an unsuccessful challenge to Mao's leadership by the Chinese defense minister.[16] When these moves failed to change China's course, the Soviets curtailed their economic assistance, withdrawing between 2,000 and 3,000 specialists and removing or destroying the blueprints of their projects.

In 1960 Sino-Soviet differences resurfaced, with the publication by the Chinese of a lengthy critique of the Russians under the title "Long Live Leninism."[17] In November of the same year, a conference of eighty-one communist parties in Moscow saw a dozen parties—with Albania foremost among them—support the Chinese positions. Although the overwhelming majority supported the Soviets, and a statement maintaining a facade of unity was published, the Soviets were undoubtedly humiliated by the need to lobby for support in the international communist movement. The Moscow conference proved to be the last meeting of its kind.

The Sino-Soviet conflict escalated further in the early 1960s as a result of incidents along their long border. The Chinese cited nine "unequal treaties" that had been forced on China by the tsars, and they laid claim to some 580,000 square miles of Soviet territory in the Far East. Tension also arose periodically along the Central Asian frontier, which divided the Chinese province of Xinjiang from the Soviet republics of Tajikistan, Kyrgyzstan, and Kazakhstan. Border incidents worsened in the latter half of the decade, during China's Cultural Revolution, and the two countries seemed close to open warfare in the spring of 1969, when armed clashes, involving large troop concentrations and artillery, occurred at their Far Eastern frontier along the Ussuri River. With both sides maintaining massive forces at the border, rumors circulated during the summer of 1969 that the Soviet Union might be considering a preemptive nuclear strike against China.[18] By then, each party clearly regarded the other—and no longer the United States—as its primary security threat. From the perspective of balance-of-power politics, the logic of the situation called for both sides to turn to the United States for assistance against the other. Triangular politics was to become a distinctive feature of the Cold War in the 1970s.

Brezhnev and the Policies of Détente

As a result of the massive build-up of Soviet strategic forces following the Cuban missile crisis, by 1970 the military strength of the two superpowers was approximately equal. While the United States continued to lead in many categories, the USSR pulled ahead in numbers of intercontinental ballistic missiles (ICBMs). However, the military expansion had put tremendous strain on the economy of the Soviet Union, whose rate of growth was rapidly dropping. Hesitant efforts at structural reform, led by Aleksei Kosygin, Khrushchev's successor as premier, challenged too many vested interests and were abandoned. Curtailment of military budgets was apparently not even seriously considered, given the considerable political power of military commanders and the defense industry lobbyists. Facing increasing pressures to improve the quantity and quality of consumer goods available to the Soviet population, Kosygin and Leonid Brezhnev, who had succeeded Khrushchev as head of the CPSU Secretariat, agreed that importing Western technology was their best available means of increasing economic productivity.

The new political landscape of the 1970s—emerging global tripolarity, Soviet-American military parity, and stagnation of the Soviet economy—necessitated a rethinking of Soviet foreign policy. The policy adopted by Brezhnev and his colleagues went beyond earlier practices of "peaceful coexistence"—avoidance of war and relaxation of tensions with the West—to include active collaboration in such areas as arms control, trade, crisis management, and science and technology. In the West, the resulting relationship was labeled "détente" (French for "relaxation"), but in the USSR there was never a connotation that all forms of struggle between opposing social systems had come to an end or that genuine partnership had been established. As Georgii Arbatov, a leading foreign policy advisor to Brezhnev, put it, "these relations will never become relations of an alliance between two su-

perpowers who have divided up the world." Rather, "no matter how successful the process of normalization and détente is, in the historical sense [they]
will remain relations of struggle."[19] Indeed, on both sides of the ideological
divide, influential politicians voiced skepticism about the adversary's intentions and about the wisdom of cooperative agreements.

During its first quarter-century, the main battlefield of the Cold War had
been Europe, and especially divided Germany, and so it was predictable that
the first tests of the new policy would take place there. The Soviet Union's
chief objective was to gain the West's acceptance of the division of Germany
and its recognition of the legitimacy of the postwar territorial and political
changes in Eastern Europe. The election of Social Democratic leader Willy
Brandt as West German chancellor late in 1969 set change in motion. Brandt's
Ostpolitik abandoned the long-held Christian Democratic goal of German
reunification, substituting for it the more conciliatory formula of two German states within one German nation. A Soviet–West German treaty, signed
in August 1970, provided for mutual renunciation of force and recognized
the frontiers "of all states in Europe" as inviolable, including the East German border with Poland. Thus, West Germany confirmed the division of that
nation into two states and the loss of prewar German lands in the east to
Poland. These commitments were confirmed in a separate treaty between the
Federal Republic and Poland later in the year.

Chancellor Brandt's price for ratification of these treaties was a satisfactory
four-power agreement on West Berlin. The West deemed it to be part of the
Federal Republic, while the Soviets still wanted West Berlin to be an independent political entity, access to which would be controlled by East Germany.
Long and difficult negotiations produced a compromise agreement only after
the replacement of hard-liner Walter Ulbricht as East German leader. The Final
Quadripartite Protocol, signed by the Big Four in June 1972, effectively removed Berlin as a source of East-West tension. It stated that West Berlin was
not a constituent part of the Federal Republic, but it acknowledged Soviet responsibility to ensure unimpeded access to the city. This was followed at the
end of the year by a treaty between the two German states that allowed them to
establish mutual diplomatic representation and to gain admission to the United
Nations, without definitively settling their permanent status.[20]

The USSR had long proposed an all-European conference on collective
security as a means of gaining recognition of the postwar territorial and political status quo while reducing U.S. influence on the continent. During the
late 1960s, the campaign for a European security conference took maximum
advantage of the growing strains between the United States and its European
allies, many of whom felt anxious about the escalating dimensions of
Washington's involvement in Vietnam—an area thought by the NATO allies

to be of distinctly secondary importance. The strong antiwar movement in the United States was paralleled by violent student unrest in Western Europe, the sharply anti-American tone of which was exploited by the Soviet Union and its various front organizations.

With the conclusion of the agreements on Germany and the Soviet consent to U.S. and Canadian participation, the Conference on Security and Cooperation in Europe opened in Helsinki in July 1973. The Final Act, known as the Helsinki Declaration, was signed on August 1, 1975, in a summit meeting of thirty-five states that approximated a peace conference for the war that had ended thirty years before. Brezhnev achieved his objective of gaining acknowledgment of the inviolability of the frontiers of all the states of Europe: but during the long negotiations the Soviets had to accede to the Western demand to include provisions ("Basket Three") recognizing and pledging the signatories to respect such human rights as freedom of thought, conscience, and religion; freer movement, contact among individuals, and travel; and free and wider dissemination of information. Brezhnev, who had put an end to the limited experimentation with freer expression that had been allowed in the Soviet Union during the Khrushchev period, and who had presided over a partial rehabilitation of Stalin's record, stated clearly that no such "interference in internal affairs" of the USSR would be accepted.

For U.S. president Richard Nixon and his national security advisor (later, secretary of state), Henry Kissinger, the chief benefit of détente with the USSR was to be found in securing Soviet assistance in extricating the United States from the war in Vietnam under conditions that would not constitute a defeat. Concessions on Soviet priorities would be linked to this. As the major source of aid to North Vietnam, ensuring against Hanoi's defeat, the Soviet Union had been content since the mid-1960s to see Washington tied down in an unpopular war it could not win, so long as the conflict did not escalate to the point that it threatened to draw in Moscow. To put additional pressure on Moscow, Nixon and Kissinger forged a new relationship with China, hoping to enlist Beijing's assistance toward the same objective.

Vietnam was a major topic of discussion in the summit meeting between Nixon and Brezhnev in May 1972. The United States apparently succeeded in gaining the help that it sought; a Vietnam truce agreement was signed in Paris the following January. Equally important at the summit were discussions on the limitation of strategic arms, aimed at countering developments in the arms race that threatened the strategic balance. The talks resulted in the signing of a treaty that would prohibit both sides from building a nationwide defense against ballistic missiles, by limiting the number of antiballistic missile (ABM) sites each side could have. The summit also produced an interim strategic arms limitation agreement (SALT I) establishing a five-year freeze on the number of offensive ballistic missiles possessed by each side, though allowing some replacements for older missiles.

A new, cooperative sphere in the Soviet-U.S. relationship was addressed in agreements on medicine, public health, the environment, space, and the prevention of naval incidents. In the commercial sphere, the two sides established a commission to discuss extension by the United States of most-favored-nation (MFN) trading status to the Soviet Union. This action was necessary to make it possible for the Soviets to pay for the technology and grain they sought to import from the United States, by giving their exports competitive access to the American market. A trade agreement in October 1972 opened the way for granting MFN status and credits in return for partial Soviet payment of the Lend-Lease debt from World War II. A separate agreement arranged for the Soviets to purchase $750 million worth of American grain over a three-year period on extremely favorable terms.

A second Nixon-Brezhnev summit was held in the United States in June 1973. With Vietnam no longer an irritant in the relationship, the two powers seemed closer than at any time since their wartime alliance. In the joint communiqué, they pledged "to turn the development of friendship and cooperation between their peoples into a permanent factor for worldwide peace."[21] Eleven agreements were signed during the summit, including a framework for the next stage in strategic arms limitations (SALT II) and an agreement on cooperation on the peaceful uses of atomic energy. The most important of the measures signed at the summit was the "Agreement on the Prevention of Nuclear War," which contained the following language:

> If at any time relations between the Parties or between either Party and other countries appear to involve the risk of a nuclear conflict, or if relations between countries not parties to this Agreement appear to involve the risk of nuclear war between the United States of America and the Union of Soviet Socialist Republics or between either Party and other countries, the United States and the Soviet Union, acting in accordance with the provisions of this Agreement, shall immediately enter into urgent consultations with each other and make every effort to avert this risk.[22]

Throughout the Cold War, the superpowers had faced the risk that they could be dragged into conflict by allies they could not control. Such crises had occurred numerous times in the conflict in Indochina, as well as in the 1971 Bangladesh War, in which the United States had supported Pakistan and the USSR had backed India. In this accord the superpowers agreed that the need to cooperate with each other would override the interests of their allies, if necessary. Within a few months, the agreement was put to its first test—in the 1973 Yom Kippur War in the Middle East—and it proved wanting.

The war between Egypt and Syria on one side and Israel on the other began with an attack by Egypt's forces across the Suez Canal on October 6. Although the attack was a surprise to Israel and the United States, the Soviets had advance warning, but they did not act to prevent it or to consult the United States. The United States sought an immediate cease-fire, but the Soviets—having launched a massive resupply of arms to the Arabs—urged restraint only after the tide of battle had turned against their clients. Before a United Nations peacekeeping force could be organized, the Soviets had threatened unilateral intervention on behalf of the Arabs, and both superpowers had put their own military forces on high alert. Not only did the crisis raise even stronger doubts about the depth of détente, but it led to the virtual bankruptcy of Moscow's policy in the region, thanks to Henry Kissinger's brilliant "shuttle diplomacy." Realizing that, whereas Moscow could supply the arms for war, apparently only the United States could achieve the peaceful return of Arab territories, Egyptian President Sadat broke with Moscow and agreed to a separate peace treaty with Israel, brokered by the United States.

From the high point of the Washington summit, Soviet-U.S. relations rapidly worsened. The Soviet Union's suppression of dissenters and its harassment of Jews who sought to emigrate weighed heavily with American public opinion, and led to congressional action making MFN or trade credits dependent upon changes in Soviet policy. Angry about such interference, the Soviets eventually canceled the 1972 trade agreement. Likewise, negotiations for SALT II were stalled by U.S. concerns over the growing numbers of heavy Soviet missiles and by disagreements over how to deal with the new technology allowing for multiple independently targeted reentry vehicles (MIRVs). Weakened by the Watergate scandal, President Richard M. Nixon nonetheless journeyed to Moscow in June 1974 for his final summit with Brezhnev, which produced no breakthroughs on the growing list of issues between the two superpowers. Nixon's successor, Gerald Ford, did manage to work out an agreement on further guidelines for a more far-reaching strategic arms limitation treaty during a meeting with Brezhnev in Vladivostok in November 1974. But mounting political discord in the ensuing months again put SALT II on the back burner.

While détente produced a marked change in the security environment of Europe, it was in the Third World that Brezhnev's policy ran aground. The Soviets had never understood détente as obligating them to pass up opportunities to reduce Western influence in the Third World; indeed, in their view, one of the benefits of the relaxation of tensions was that it created more favorable conditions for the pursuit of national liberation and revolutionary struggles. In addition to continuing tensions over Cuba and the crises in the Middle East, developments in Indochina presented an even greater challenge to détente. Not long after the signing of the Paris peace treaty, the United States began to complain to the Soviets about infiltration of North Vietnamese troops into the south. The Soviets chose not to restrain their ally, and the United States was unable to strengthen the resistance of the noncommunist government in Saigon. In the spring of 1975 Vietnam was forcibly reunified under communist rule.

The fall of the right-wing dictatorship in Portugal in 1974 and the dissolution of Lisbon's empire in Africa further illustrated the differing understandings of détente. Whereas U.S. warnings to Moscow to refrain from direct support of procommunist forces in the new government in Portugal—a NATO ally—were apparently heeded, no such caution was demonstrated by the Soviet Union in Portugal's former colonies in Africa. Soviet military aid to the Marxist faction, the Popular Movement for the Liberation of Angola, in Angola's civil war was sharply increased in 1975, and Moscow introduced a new—and to Washington, even more disturbing—element when it tipped the military balance decisively by airlifting some 17,000 Cuban troops to fight on the side of the MPLA. Prevented from intervening by the action of a U.S. Congress still reeling from the Vietnam defeat, the Ford administration could only denounce the Soviet action, with the president even declaring that détente was no longer in his political vocabulary. The Soviets continued to insist that they had never promised to abandon the ideological and revolutionary struggles. As one Russian remarked to his U.S. counterpart, "You Americans tried to sell détente like detergent and claimed it would do everything a detergent could do."[23]

The Soviet-Cuban victory in Angola coincided with the conclusion of the Twenty-Fifth Party congress in March 1976. General Secretary Brezhnev used this Congress to tighten his grip on party leadership and to proclaim the success of Soviet foreign policy. Citing the victory in Vietnam, treaties of friendship with Iraq and India, and normalization of relations with Germany, among other successes, Brezhnev declared that "the international position of the Soviet Union has never been more stable."[24] As we have already noted, however, this proved to be the high-water mark for Soviet influence in the Third World. The CPSU Congress had barely adjourned when Anwar Sadat unilaterally terminated the Soviet-Egyptian treaty. A year later Sudan, a long-time recipient of Soviet aid, also reversed its position and expelled all Soviet technicians and military advisors. Also in 1977, Somalia, angered at Moscow's aid to its antagonist, Ethiopia, followed suit by abrogating its treaty with Moscow, expelling Soviet advisors, and denying its naval facilities at Berbera to the Soviet navy. Even a seemingly contrary example of triumphant Soviet diplomacy and influence in 1978—a twenty-five-year security treaty with Vietnam—soon proved embarrassing. When Vietnam invaded neighboring

Cambodia in support of a rebellion against its pro-Chinese government, China responded by invading Vietnam to punish it for its aggression. Moscow was unwilling to risk war with China by coming to the aid of its ally.

This mixed record of Soviet activism had not prevented the administration of President Jimmy Carter from proceeding with strategic arms negotiations. With great difficulty, a SALT II agreement was hammered out and signed at a summit between Carter and Brezhnev in Vienna in June 1979. The limits set in the treaty froze a status quo that gave the USSR more powerful missiles with a greater throw weight than any possessed by the United States, while leaving the latter with a superiority in the total number of warheads. The main benefit of the treaty was in reducing the risk of war by adding to the stability of the deterrent relationship, making each side's second strike forces more secure. The limits would also permit both sides to reduce their defense budgets.

The SALT II treaty was never ratified, as it and the remaining fragments of détente fell victim to the Brezhnev regime's most dramatic demonstration of lack of restraint—its invasion of Afghanistan in December 1979. The crisis began with a Soviet-instigated coup d'état in which Afghanistan's Marxist president, Hafizullah Amin, was murdered. At the "invitation" of Amin's Soviet-installed successor, Babrak Karmal, Soviet troops entered the country to put down a widespread Islamic insurrection that had been incited by Amin's radical social and economic policies. As the Kremlin saw it, failure to preserve a pro-Soviet government in Afghanistan would have created the specter of a third (with Khomeini's Iran and Zia's Pakistan) anticommunist Islamic republic on the periphery of Soviet Central Asia. Even though Afghanistan was headed by a Marxist government with which a treaty of friendship had been signed, the invasion was the first time Moscow had sent combat forces into a country that was not actually a part of the Soviet bloc. This was the critical distinction that shocked world opinion more than the Soviet invasion of Hungary in 1956 or the Warsaw Pact invasion of Czechoslovakia in 1968. The UN General Assembly in January 1980 voted 104 to 18 to deplore the invasion, and a conference of thirty-six Islamic states later in the month did likewise.

The reaction of the United States was strong. President Carter lamented, "This action of the Soviets has made a more dramatic change in my own opinion of what the Soviets' ultimate goals are than anything they've done in the previous time I've been in office."[25] As punitive measures, he announced the curtailment of U.S. grain sales, suspension of high-technology exports, deferral of cultural and economic exchanges, and a boycott of the 1980 Moscow Olympics. In his State of the Union address, he warned Moscow against pushing further, stating that the United States was prepared to go to war to defend vital oil supply routes in the Persian Gulf. In summary, he said, "The Soviet Union must realize that its decision to use military force in Afghanistan will be costly to every political and economic relationship it values."[26]

The price paid by the Soviet Union for its occupation of Afghanistan was much greater than it anticipated. Like the United States in Vietnam, Moscow learned that conventional military superiority was no guarantee of success against guerrilla forces. By the time of Brezhnev's death in 1982, more than 110,000 Soviet troops were in Afghanistan, but the resistance—using bases in Pakistan, and covertly supplied by the United States—was fiercer than ever. The Afghan government's army had virtually disappeared through defections, and Soviet officials were overseeing almost every function of administration in the country.

Its heavy casualties were not the only costs to the USSR. The collapse of détente had led to a new tension in relations with the West—and especially with the new and stridently anti-Soviet administration of U.S. president Ronald Reagan, which initiated a major build-up in military power. Virtually cut off from Western trade and technology, the Soviet economy continued to decline, deepening the country's social unrest, and the technological development of its weaponry began to slip well behind that of the United States.

Beset with an even deeper economic crisis, communist Poland was faced with a workers' movement led by Lech Walesa, which managed in the fall of 1980 to topple party leader Edward Gierek and achieve recognition of a free trade union, Solidarity. When the crisis threatened to dislodge the communist regime itself, the Soviet Union hinted at invasion. But the immediate danger passed in December 1981 with the declaration of martial law by General Wojciech Jaruzelski, the commander of the Polish armed forces, who also had assumed the posts of party leader and premier. Nevertheless, the experience of neighboring Poland had to serve as a chilling reminder to the aging Soviet leaders of the limits of popular patience with economic and social deprivations.

The Twilight of the "Old Thinking"

In the sixty-five years between the Bolshevik revolution and Leonid Brezhnev's death in November 1982, the Soviet regime had experienced only three real leadership successions: the protracted conflict among Stalin and his various rivals following the illness and death of Vladimir Lenin; the succession to Stalin; and the succession to Khrushchev, which differed from the others in that the incumbent leader was removed not by death but by a coup d'état. In stark contrast, the USSR had three successions during the twenty-eight months (November 1982 to March 1985) that followed Brezhnev's death.

The significance of this brief period goes beyond the fact that three general secretaries of the CPSU died in less than three years, being rooted in a much more profound changing of the aging Kremlin guard. The generation of Brezhnev, Kosygin, Gromyko, and their Politburo colleagues had enjoyed an unusually long tenure in high offices, with most of them rising to positions of command in their thirties as the result of the liquidation of their elders. Thus, the multistage succession to Brezhnev was part of the first thoroughgoing generational change in the Soviet leadership since the Great Purge of the 1930s. The other point that was underscored by the unusual string of successions was that the Soviet Union still had no regular constitutional means by which to replace its top leader. Indeed, even in cases where the top leader had left an heir-apparent, power was inherited by another.

Quite likely, some of the drift and immobility of the latter period of Brezhnev's administration was related to the age and physical condition of the ruling elite. His successor, Yuri Andropov, the long-time head of the security police (KGB), who had only recently moved into the party secretariat, was thought to be intellectually superior to his colleagues. But an initial period of vigorous activity in domestic and foreign affairs came to an early end with the failure of Andropov's health.

Andropov had sought to wake up the stagnant Soviet economy by campaigning against the widespread inefficiency and corruption, but only short-term improvements were possible in the absence of a fundamental restructuring of the system of centralized economic decision making. Although he presided over the removal of some of the oldest and most inept members of the regional party elite, Andropov was either unable or unwilling to introduce radical change into the Soviet system.

During the first part of 1983, the new leader was able to produce modest improvements in Soviet relations with both China and the United States. But Soviet-U.S. relations reentered the deep freeze in September, when the Soviets shot down an unarmed civilian airliner (Korean Airline flight 007) that had strayed over their territory. In the aftermath, the Soviets compounded international outrage by denying responsibility, lying about the facts, refusing to compensate the families of victims, and accusing the United States of using the plane for espionage.

It was also during the final months of Andropov's brief term that Soviet-U.S. arms control negotiations suffered a severe setback. The arms race had intensified, with both sides concerned about weapons developments by the other and worried that they might suffer politically from perceptions that they were falling behind in strength. In order to replace older missiles that had become vulnerable to more accurate U.S. weapons, the Soviets in 1977 had deployed a new intermediate range missile (the SS-20), which was mobile, solid-fueled, accurate, and MIRVed. Perceived by NATO as not only survivable but also a potential first-strike weapon, the missile appeared capable of upsetting the European balance of power unless matched by NATO. Accordingly, in 1979 the alliance had decided to persuade the Soviets to remove the SS-20s or face deployment by 1983 of a modernized intermediate-range nuclear force (INF) of 572 Pershing II and cruise missiles in response. As negotiations bogged down, NATO increasingly saw itself facing a political test of its credibility and cohesion against an adroitly managed Soviet "peace campaign" designed to appeal to a nervous European public.

Paralleling the INF talks and equally stalemated were the negotiations to reduce strategic weapons, now referred to as START. Each side sought to reduce the other's inventory of missiles viewed as capable of destroying their own retaliatory forces in a first strike. After it was announced in March 1983, the Soviets were also intent on forestalling Ronald Reagan's Strategic Defense Initiative (SDI)—a space-based ballistic missile defense ambitiously intended to destroy Soviet missiles before they could reach their targets. Reagan's plans were especially threatening to Moscow, not only because they could destabilize the military balance and force a new round of offensive missile production, but also because the Soviets doubted that they could muster the economic and technological resources to match the U.S. defenses.

When the United States began installing cruise missiles in Britain and Germany in December 1983, as scheduled by NATO, the Soviet reaction was sharp and immediate: it angrily broke off both the INF and the START negotiations. Andropov had calculated that the Soviet walkout would force NATO to halt its deployment, especially in the face of an expected popular outcry in Europe. The tactic backfired, leaving the Soviets with the onus of having cut off all possibilities of curbing the arms race.

Andropov's death in February 1984 did not provoke his colleagues to grasp the opportunity to choose a younger and more vigorous leader. Rather, he was replaced by a seventy-two-year-old, visibly ailing Brezhnev crony, the veteran party bureaucrat Konstantin Chernenko. Domestically, there was not even the pretense of reform of Soviet society or the economy along the lines of Andropov. In foreign policy, there were also no bold initiatives or breakthroughs. However, at the very end of his brief term, Chernenko did retreat from his predecessor's demand that the United States cease deploying INF missiles in Europe as a precondition for the resumption of arms talks. Two days before the negotiations were to recommence, Chernenko died.

This time, the majority of Politburo members could not escape recognizing the necessity of an energetic push toward reform. They elected as general secretary their youngest colleague, Mikhail Gorbachev—at age fifty-four younger than any man to assume the office since Stalin. Gorbachev's colleagues thought that they were electing a tough and earnest reformer, but not a radical. The Soviet system that produced him did not promote to high positions people of unorthodox thought or bold action. Only loyalists advanced in the party apparatus, and nothing in Gorbachev's career suggested that he was anything but a loyal communist.

The Soviet economy that Gorbachev inherited in March 1985 had experienced virtually no real growth in over a decade. It was not even one-half the size of the U.S. economy, and yet it was burdened with the need to support a fully competitive military establishment. Agricultural productivity was less than one-fourth that of the United States, and about one-third of Soviet food production spoiled before reaching the consumer—forcing the USSR to become the world's largest importer of grain. Over 10 percent of the country's gross national product (GNP) was devoted to subsidizing this inefficient agricultural sector, in order to keep food prices artificially low. The housing stock throughout the country was inadequate, especially in the rural areas, where indoor plumbing was still relatively rare. Because of poor diet and low public health standards, the country was experiencing a decline in the average life span of its citizens and an increase in infant mortality. The supply of consumer goods, always irregular, suffered periodic disruptions, resulting in panic buying and in long lines for all shoppers (except the elite, who had access to special stores) whenever goods were available.

During the Brezhnev years, people had been constantly bombarded with the claim that "life is improving," even while they were surrounded with abundant evidence that the country was falling apart. The result of the sharp disjuncture between claim and reality was almost universal cynicism and the search for "private solutions"—which for many citizens meant the black market, and for others meant "dropping out" through alcoholism, drug abuse, or other deviant behavior.

Gorbachev's initial impulse was to continue the approach of his mentor, Andropov, instilling greater discipline into the work force through a combination of exhortation and a law-and-order campaign that included rooting out corruption and drastically cutting down on the availability of alcohol.

The paucity of results brought a recognition that the roots of the problem were deeper, and that what was required was *perestroika* (restructuring)— moderate reform from within the socialist economic system. More resources were to be invested in the domestic infrastructure and in consumer goods, and the military budget was reduced accordingly. In the services sector, some mixing of forms of ownership was allowed. The gigantic state planning mechanism was to be overhauled, the size and power of the central economic ministries reduced, and enterprises throughout the country were gradually to be put on a system of *khozraschet* (an obligation to produce enough value to cover their costs of production). The trouble with this program was that it had all been tried before, in the 1960s, under the sponsorship first of Khrushchev and then of Kosygin, but it had failed to produce the desired results—in part because it had been openly sabotaged by the party and state bureaucracy long enmeshed in Stalinist work habits and the attendant system of perquisites and job security.

Just as the shortcomings of gradual economic reform were not immediately evident to Gorbachev, so also he began his quest for arms control without a fresh (or workable) strategy. His early proposals called for total abolition of nuclear weapons, on which the USSR was less dependent than the West for its security—essentially resurrecting the "ban the bomb" propaganda campaigns of the late 1940s; but his primary emphasis was on derailing Reagan's Strategic Defense Initiative. At his initial summit encounter with Reagan, in Geneva in November 1985, he emerged with nothing to show toward either goal.

After a year of hard campaigning before Western public opinion on behalf of both proposals, Gorbachev met with Reagan again—this time in Reykjavik, Iceland. Agreement seemed near on a number of important issues: a 50 percent reduction in strategic forces; elimination of all INF in Europe and deployment elsewhere of only one hundred by each side; and observance of the ABM treaty for another ten years. But Gorbachev made everything contingent on limiting SDI to laboratory research during the ten-year period. Reagan refused to comply, and the conference collapsed. Even more damaging to Reagan's prestige was the revelation that as the talks progressed he had departed significantly from the prepared U.S. position. First he had proposed, as a condition of the ten-year extension of the ABM treaty, that both sides eliminate all their ballistic missiles by the end of that period, and then he had accepted Gorbachev's counterproposal that not just missiles but all strategic nuclear weapons be eliminated. As a result, the Soviets were able to launch a post-summit propaganda campaign claiming that total strategic nuclear disarmament could have been achieved, had it not been for Reagan's stubborn refusal to abandon SDI.

In Gorbachev's hands, Soviet policy positions were handled more smoothly and energetically in 1985 and 1986, but they were fundamentally the same positions as before. Soviet-U.S. relations continued to be characterized by sharp rhetoric and public posturing on both sides. Tension in Soviet relations with China was slightly reduced under Gorbachev, but could not be eliminated as long as Soviet troops remained in Afghanistan and Vietnamese forces stayed in Cambodia, and as long as the Sino-Soviet border remained heavily militarized. Gorbachev appeared still to be trying to win a military victory in

Afghanistan. Finally, with regard to domestic policies, the Soviet regime's relationship with its own population did not appear to have changed fundamentally under Gorbachev. This was dramatically illustrated by the leaders' failure to give a prompt, full, and honest account of the terrible accident at the Chernobyl nuclear facility in April 1986.

"New Thinking" and the End of the Cold War

Gradually, Gorbachev realized that he must break the power of the bureaucracy in order to accomplish reform of the economy. At a crucial CPSU Central Committee plenum in January 1987, the definition of perestroika was broadened to include democratization of the country, and Gorbachev began to unleash popular forces that he thought would be his allies in the struggle for economic reform. Profound changes such as greater official tolerance for religion, the opening up of new avenues of cultural expression, and the revision of interpretations of prior Soviet history were introduced not as ends in themselves, but as devices intended to mobilize public pressure against the Soviet bureaucracy, so as to break its resistance to the freeing up of economic forces in the country. The intent of the *glasnost* (openness) campaign was not to open up an attack on the legitimacy of the party or its Marxist-Leninist ideology, but to attack the pillars of the Stalinist system. Similarly, the democratization of political institutions was not originally intended to end the Communist Party's monopoly on power. Rather, it was to be guided from above to bring about swifter changes in middle-level party leadership, by forcing unpopular party bureaucrats to face the wrath of the voters, and by utilizing local and national legislatures to put pressure on a conservative party bureaucracy.

The necessary companion to these evolving ideas about domestic reform was a new approach toward changing the confrontational relationship between East and West. What came to be known as the "new thinking" in foreign policy proceeded from the premise of the "interdependence of states and peoples," an idea much discussed in the West, but less familiar in the communist world. In an interdependent world, Gorbachev reasoned, national security could not be based on the use or threat of nuclear weapons. Rather, security for the superpowers must be mutual, and must be ensured by political means. Enormous sums of money and attention had been squandered by prior regimes on the military competition, he acknowledged, to the neglect of possibilities for cooperation.

In the new spirit of glasnost, pointed references to the errors and shortcomings of the Brezhnev-era "old thinking" began to appear in the Soviet press. One writer described the decisions to deploy SS-20 missiles and to introduce Soviet troops into Afghanistan as examples of "solutions of a sub-jectivist nature oriented toward the use of military-force tactics in foreign policy" which did great "moral and material damage" to the USSR.[27] Another condemned the "incompetent approach of the Brezhnev leadership," which had neglected the country's vital national interests by trying to keep up with the United States in an unproductive arms race. "Our true interest," he wrote, was in ensuring an international atmosphere that would allow "profound transformations" in the country's economy and its social and political systems.[28] As the advocates of "new thinking" saw it, economic strength was proving more decisive than military strength in resolving many global issues, and thus only by reversing its precipitous economic slide and establishing linkages to the international economy could the USSR qualify as a true "superpower."

Gorbachev was at pains to stress that the "new thinking" did not amount to an abandonment of the classic principles of Marxist-Leninist doctrine—the "greatest revolutionary worldview." But the ideology had to be adapted to new circumstances: "Loyalty to Marxist-Leninist teaching," he said, "lies in its creative development on the basis of accumulated experience."[29] It was left to Gorbachev's new foreign minister, Eduard Shevardnadze, to announce the most far-reaching change in interpretation of the Marxist-Leninist doctrine—a renunciation of the concept of class struggle as the fundamental guide to foreign policy. At a conference of senior Soviet diplomats and scholars convened in July 1988, he said that in the nuclear age it was no longer justifiable to see peaceful coexistence as a special form of the class struggle. Rather, "the struggle of two opposing systems is no longer the decisive tendency of the contemporary age."[30] A few days later, the Politburo's chief conservative, Egor Ligachev, attempted to rebut this notion. But the last word was given to Gorbachev's close associate, Aleksandr Yakovlev, who wrote in *Pravda*—Lenin's own paper and still the party's authoritative voice—this extraordinary interpretation of Marx's doctrine:

Marxism as such is the interpretation of the common interests of mankind from the point of view of history and the perspective of the development of all mankind, not only that of individual countries or classes, peoples or social groups. In placing in the forefront the interests of the downtrodden and exploited can it be said that the founding fathers of socialism placed the interests of that class against the interests of all the others? Of course not. The thesis of the priority of the common interests of mankind helps us look realistically and soundly at the idea of the coexistence of countries with different political structures as a requirement of history and a manifestation of the internationalist tendencies of global development.[31]

In stark opposition to the positions articulated by Brezhnev and Arbatov during the détente of the 1970s, Gorbachev and his spokesmen were attacking the very foundations of communist ideology.

Simultaneously with this change in doctrine and the movement toward democratization, Gorbachev executed a momentous shift in Soviet foreign policy positions. In February 1987, he made the first of several significant concessions on the INF issue. This quickly led to a treaty, signed at a summit in Washington in December, in which the two sides agreed to eliminate the entire class of Soviet and U.S. medium-range and short-range missiles. The agreement removed a dangerous threat to European security, while resolving a dispute that had poisoned Moscow's relations with Washington for a decade.

The last years of the 1980s witnessed Soviet initiatives to resolve some of the regional conflicts in Asia, Africa, and Latin America that had been so divisive in Soviet-U.S. relations. The American public had been especially concerned about the extent of Soviet assistance to revolutionary movements in Central America. The Sandinista regime in Nicaragua had received massive military and economic aid from the Soviet Union and its allies. In 1989 Gorbachev communicated to President George Bush that the military aid would be terminated. While the Soviets were undoubtedly shocked by the Ortega government's overwhelming electoral defeat early in 1990, Gorbachev was probably pleased to be rid of this burdensome Third World conflict. The longstanding Soviet-Cuban involvement in Angola was terminated through negotiations that were concluded in 1988. In the Middle East, the Soviets joined with the United States in sponsoring a 1987 UN resolution seeking a cease-fire in the lengthy war between Iran and Iraq; when the war finally ended the following year, Moscow moved quickly to improve relations with Iran. At the same time, the Soviet Union adopted a higher profile in urging that international peace talks be initiated, toward resolving the conflict between Israel and the Palestine Liberation Organization (PLO).

Most significant, however, was Gorbachev's decision early in 1988 to liquidate the Soviet Union's costly war in Afghanistan. Gorbachev committed the USSR to a phased withdrawal of its troops without assurances that a communist-dominated government would remain in Afghanistan. By January 1989, after suffering casualties in excess of 13,000 killed and 35,000 wounded, all forces of the USSR had been withdrawn, but the disunity of the anticommunist guerrilla forces helped to extend the life of the pro-Soviet government.

Having thereby removed an irritant in relations not just with Washington but also with Beijing, Gorbachev proceeded to encourage Vietnam to withdraw its remaining troops from Cambodia in 1989. With two of China's three conditions for a normalization in relations thus realized, Gorbachev traveled to Beijing in May 1989 for the first Sino-Soviet summit in twenty years. There he addressed the third condition for normalization, announcing a substantial unilateral cutback of about 200,000 troops in the Soviet Far East and proposing demilitarization of the entire Sino-Soviet border. The rapprochement with China was sealed the following year when Premier Li Peng went to Moscow to conclude a ten-year pact for increased economic and scientific cooperation.

Also improving relations on Moscow's other major front, Gorbachev participated in three summit meetings with American presidents—with Reagan in May 1988, with Reagan and President-elect Bush in December 1988, and with Bush again in December 1989. The fruit of relaxed tensions—benefiting not only world peace but also the Soviet defense budget—was evident in December 1988, when Gorbachev announced in a dramatic speech at the United Nations General Assembly that the Soviet Union would make a unilateral reduction of 500,000 troops and would remove 10,000 tanks, 8,500 artillery pieces, and 800 combat aircraft from the European theater.

As Gorbachev and his reform-minded colleagues began to introduce perestroika, glasnost, and democratization into Soviet domestic politics and "new thinking" into Soviet foreign policy, they were encouraging their communist colleagues in Eastern Europe to join them in the reform program. When they informed the "little Brezhnevs" of Eastern Europe—as early as 1987—that Soviet troops would no longer protect them from their peoples, the Soviet leaders were not anticipating the total repudiation of communism there. Rather, they were hoping that the socialist system in Eastern Europe would be salvaged through the reformist activities of "little Gorbachevs" who would come to power. Justifying Soviet actions in the wake of the dramatic changes of 1989 and 1990, Shevardnadze told the Twenty-Eighth CPSU Congress: "We sensed that unless serious changes and reforms were made, matters would reach the point of tragic events. But, proceeding from the principles of the new political thinking, we couldn't interfere in others' affairs. I think that we acted correctly."[32] However, the attempt to save the socialist system in Eastern Europe by reforming it never got off the ground. Throughout the region, spontaneous mass movements, arising out of depressed living standards and widespread alienation and disillusionment, challenged governments that lacked legitimacy.

The movement began in the spring of 1989 in Poland, where negotiations between President Jaruzelski and Lech Walesa produced in June the first partially free elections since the communist takeover. Solidarity won virtually every contested seat. In August, with Poland pledging to stay in the Warsaw Pact, the Soviet Union consented to a noncommunist prime minister there, and in December, Jaruzelski was replaced as president by Walesa. Also in the spring of 1989, a reformist communist regime in Hungary, having accepted with Gorbachev's approval the creation of independent political parties, negotiated with the opposition to schedule free elections for the following spring—elections that it then lost overwhelmingly. In the meantime, the Hungarian communists startled the world by tearing down the country's barbed-wire border with Austria. Thousands of East Germans, disillusioned with the lack of opportunities in the "workers' paradise," streamed into Hungary and were allowed in September to cross to freedom in West Germany. Hoping to stem the flow, a desperate East German communist regime received Gorbachev's implicit agreement to replacing its aging dictator. Responding to massive demonstrations across the country, the new leaders announced that travel restrictions to the West would be lifted. As hundreds of thousands of East Berliners poured into the streets, a frightened local communist leader felt he had no choice but to open the hated wall. The delirious citizens of Berlin had a weekend party the likes of which the world never expected to see.

A few days later, more than 200,000 people demonstrated in Prague, where the hard-line communist regime—in a striking reversal of the situation in 1968—had been criticized by the Soviet press as insufficiently reformist. A general strike, organized by students, forced an end to the communist monopoly of power in Czechoslovakia and an agreement on free elections. Emerging as the new leader was dissident playwright Vaclav Havel, just released from a Prague prison, who reluctantly accepted the presidency when old-line communist Gustav Husak was forced to resign. In Sofia, Bulgaria, in early December, 50,000 people marched for democracy. In January, the parliament revoked the Communist Party's monopoly of power, and talks began to prepare the way for free elections in June. Changing its name to the Bulgarian Socialist Party, the former Communist Party managed to prevail in the elections, though under new leadership.

Romania's revolt under communism was the last in the Soviet bloc, and the only one that became violent. Iron-fisted dictator Nicolae Ceausescu ordered his security police (the Securitate) to fire on demonstrators in Timisoara on December 15. Staging a rally in Bucharest a few days later to condemn "foreign conspirators" for subverting his regime, Ceausescu was loudly booed by students in the crowd. Some demonstrators were killed and others arrested by police. When violence broke out in the capital, Ceausescu and his wife fled. On December 25 they were apprehended, tried, and executed. A provisional government, the National Salvation Front, was formed, headed by Ion Iliescu, a former high-ranking communist who had been ousted by Ceausescu. This government's assumption of power was forcibly resisted by the Securitate, which was defeated only after much bloodshed. Iliescu's forces were able to win a landslide victory over anticommunist parties in free elections in May.

Ever since the fall of the Berlin Wall in November 1989, the possibility of German reunification had reappeared as a focal point of East-West negotiations. After Gorbachev publicly accepted the principle of unification at the end of January, NATO and the Warsaw Pact discussed for the next several months what political structure would best guarantee Europe's security: a neutral Germany, a unified Germany in NATO, or a unified Germany in both security systems. These discussions were formalized in the "two plus four" talks among the two Germanys and the USSR, Britain, France, and the United States. Apparently, Gorbachev's initial opposition to the membership of a unified Germany in NATO was a bargaining device, and it succeeded in winning him a good price from West German Chancellor Helmut Kohl: a credit of 5 billion German marks, together with an agreement that Soviet troops could remain in eastern Germany through 1994, and that NATO forces would not be moved into the former GDR. Moreover, Germany's army would be limited to 370,000 troops, and Germany would be prohibited from possessing nuclear, biological, or chemical weapons. The Final Settlement with Respect to Germany was signed on September 12, 1990, by the two-plus-four powers, followed the next day by the Treaty of Friendship between Germany and the USSR. The official reunification of Germany took place on October 3.

East Germany's withdrawal from the Warsaw Pact, together with Hungarian and Czech demands for the removal of Soviet troops from their territories, raised the question of the future utility of the alliance. In June 1990, its members declared that the West was no longer an "ideological enemy"—a statement answered the following month by a declaration from NATO that the Warsaw Pact countries were no longer adversaries. The following February, the members of the Warsaw Pact formally voted to disband the military components of the alliance by March 31, 1991.

The reunification of Germany and the end of the system of hostile military alliances in Europe essentially brought the Cold War to an end. A symbolic "peace conference" took place in November 1990, at the summit meeting of the Conference on Security and Cooperation in Europe (CSCE) in Paris, where the Treaty on Conventional Forces in Europe (CFE) was signed. In the CFE Treaty, the countries of NATO and the Warsaw Pact agreed to maintain equal levels of conventional forces in Europe, thus formalizing the removal of the decades-long fear that the Soviet Union could overwhelm the Continent with its conventional superiority. A few weeks prior to the conference, it was announced that Mikhail Gorbachev had been awarded the Nobel Peace Prize for his contributions toward ending the Cold War.

As the Cold War was ending in Europe, a new crisis broke out in the

Middle East. This crisis tested the notion, articulated by both the Soviet and American presidents, of a "new world order" in which the powers would cooperate to defend the principle of the nonuse of force to achieve national objectives. Soviet-American cooperation was especially tested by Iraq's invasion of Kuwait in August 1990 because of Moscow's longstanding alliance with Baghdad. Gorbachev was subjected to cross pressures from his advisors, some of whom stressed the need for the Soviets to join the emerging global coalition against Iraq, and others of whom counseled against the loss of a position of influence in the Middle East. While condemning Iraq's invasion and suspending arms shipments, as well as supporting the UN resolution for an economic and military embargo of Iraq, Moscow refused to withdraw its advisors there and sought to restrain the coalition from using force against Saddam Hussein. Gorbachev sent his special envoy Evgenii Primakov, who had personal ties to Saddam, on missions to Baghdad twice in October and again in February, seeking to persuade Saddam to withdraw from Kuwait. As the deadline neared for President George Bush's ultimatum demanding that Saddam withdraw or face ground war, Gorbachev was desperately telephoning world leaders, seeking support for a compromise solution. Although Soviet prestige suffered when these mediation efforts failed, Moscow and Washington both agreed that their cooperative relationship had survived the Gulf War intact.

During the months of the Persian Gulf crisis, Gorbachev was involved in mounting political difficulties at home. Having achieved constitutional changes in March 1990 that ended the CPSU's monopoly of power and established a new executive presidency, he employed the Twenty-Eighth Congress of the CPSU in July 1990 to change the party statutes to allow for direct election of the general secretary by the congress, to expand the Politburo to include representatives of each of the USSR republics, and in general to shift responsibility for direct management of the economy from the party to new government bodies. Perestroika had become a hollow slogan as the Soviet economy entered a period of negative growth, and democratization and glasnost—intended to weaken the conservative forces of resistance—had spurred revelations and discussions of unsolved problems, heightening frustrations and stimulating further dissension. The dissent, increasingly targeted toward Gorbachev himself, came primarily from three as yet unorganized sources: (1) the working masses—stolidly conservative proletarian and peasant forces, longing for the relative security and patriotic achievement of the Stalin and Brezhnev eras, angered by growing shortages, and opposing measures that threatened the national "safety net" by introducing unemployment, increased prices, and reduced welfare subsidies; (2) the liberal opposition, grouped around Boris Yeltsin, that sought a radical shortening of the time frame of reforms, more concessions to private enterprise and foreign ventures, more radical decentralization of economic decision making, virtual elimination of the residual powers of the party, and drastic reduction in the executive powers now concentrated in Gorbachev's hands; (3) secessionist nationality groups, especially in the Baltic states, the Transcaucasus, and Ukraine, emboldened by glasnost, tempted by the spectacle of even greater freedoms newly enjoyed in the neighboring lands of Eastern Europe, and threatening to break up the multinational Soviet state.

In September 1990, Gorbachev backed away from a political compromise with Yeltsin that would have adopted a "500-day plan" for radical decentralization and market socialism. One by one, his more progressive advisors walked away, in sadness or disgust. The last to leave was Shevardnadze, who resigned as foreign minister in December with a dramatic warning that the country was headed toward dictatorship. In picking a new team, Gorbachev found ministers who appeared to be only younger versions of the gray bureaucrats who had run the Soviet system into the ground for the previous three decades. In January, his new team dispatched military forces to the Baltics, ostensibly to enforce Soviet laws on military conscription, but in fact to bludgeon the defiant secessionists into submitting to Moscow's authority. When demonstrators were killed in both Lithuania and Latvia, there was a storm of international protest.

Yet again, the acrobat tilted his political orientation. Gorbachev concluded a surprise agreement in April with Yeltsin and the leaders of nine union republics, establishing a framework for the new Union Treaty, which would provide considerable autonomy for the republics. Seeking to regain lost international support, Gorbachev signaled his support for an economic reform plan that would utilize large-scale Western aid to assist a move to a market economy in the USSR, but the West was understandably reluctant to make commitments until details of the plan were in place. Gorbachev pleaded his case for aid at the annual summit of the leading industrial nations (the Group of Seven, or G-7) in London in mid-July, and again with President George Bush at a summit in Moscow at the end of that month. The other major feature of the Soviet-American summit was the signing of the long-awaited Strategic Arms Reduction Talks (START) treaty—the first arms control agreement to undertake substantial reductions in the size of the strategic nuclear arsenals of the two countries. Under its terms, the United States agreed to reduce its inventory of warheads from 11,602 to 8,592, and the Soviet Union agreed to reduce its inventory from 10,877 to 6,940.

Although Gorbachev had assumed the presidency of his country, he had rejected advice that he seek a popular mandate through national elections. The enormity of this error became clearer in June 1991, when his reformist rival, Boris Yeltsin, won election as president of the Russian Republic, drawing 57.3 percent of the vote against several conservative candidates. Yeltsin thus eclipsed Gorbachev by becoming the first popularly elected Russian leader in Russian and Soviet history. A few days after the election, key members of Gorbachev's government—led by KGB chief Vladimir Kriuchkov, interior minister Boris Pugo, defense minister Dimitrii Yazov, and prime minister Valentin Pavlov—attempted a constitutional coup by harshly criticizing Gorbachev's policies before the national legislature and asking it to cede many of his powers to them. Oddly, a victorious Gorbachev took no action against them.

Two months later, the same individuals, joined by four others (including Gorbachev's hand-picked vice president), constituted themselves as the State Committee for the State of Emergency, placing the president under house arrest at his Black Sea dacha and usurping his powers. Ineptly led, the coup collapsed after three days, when important units of the military failed to obey orders to dispel large crowds of resisters who were under Yeltsin's leadership. In the wake of the failure of this effort to resurrect the essential features of the old Soviet political order, the entire system unraveled. The weeks after the coup saw Gorbachev's resignation as CPSU general secretary and the suspension of the party's activities, declarations of independence by the republics, and abandonment of many of the institutions of the central government. As in 1917, the country was ruled for the next several months by a "dual power" consisting of Gorbachev on the one hand and Yeltsin and other key republic leaders on the other. They were ostensibly cooperating to adopt a much-revised Union Treaty that would have preserved most of the former Soviet Union (minus the three Baltic republics, whose independence was recognized in September) as the confederated Union of Sovereign States. However, Yeltsin and the leaders of Ukraine and Belorussia, meeting at the Belovezhskaia forest on December 8, decided instead to create the Commonwealth of Independent States (CIS), with Minsk as its capital—leaving no role for a reconstituted USSR or its president. The three leaders telephoned their decision to President Bush before they told the Soviet president. Gorbachev's frantic efforts to save his country and his job went virtually without support. On December 25, 1991, he resigned as president, and on the last day of the year the Union of Soviet Socialist Republics officially went out of existence. In his final television broadcast as president, Gorbachev told his people:

> Our society has attained freedom, has liberated itself politically and spiritually. And that is the major victory, of which we are not yet fully cognizant, undoubtedly because we have not yet learned how to use it. . . .

We live in a new world: the Cold War is over, the threat of a world war has been averted; the arms race and the insane militarization that distorted our economy, our social consciousness, and our morality have been halted. . . .

I am certain that, sooner or later, our joint efforts will bear fruit, and that our peoples will live in a democratic and prosperous society.[33]

"The Cold War Is Over"

For decades, as hostile armies stared at each other across the chasm of divided Europe, most observers' estimates of the Soviet Union's strength and its resolve to hold on to its hard-won security zone in Eastern Europe left them firmly persuaded that Moscow would not voluntarily abandon its empire. This assessment seemed credible in light of images from East Germany in 1953, when Soviet armies fired on striking East German workers; or from Budapest in 1956, when Soviet tanks crushed freedom fighters armed only with Molotov cocktails; or from Prague in 1968, when the combined forces of the USSR, East Germany, Poland, Hungary, and Bulgaria squeezed the life out of Alexander Dubcek's effort to build "socialism with a human face." Thus it seemed inconceivable to observers not only in the West but in Eastern Europe itself that communism would crumble in East Germany, Poland, Czechoslovakia, and Hungary without a shot being fired.

For over forty years the United States had led a coalition of Western nations in pursuit of a policy of containment of the spread of Soviet power through the application not only of firm diplomacy but also of enormous and expensive military deterrent forces. In George Kennan's original formulation of the policy in 1947 he had forecast that the steady application of Western resolve and pressure would someday result in the liberalizing transformation of the countries of the Soviet empire. Though Kennan himself felt that the military expression of containment was at times overused, there is no doubt that the events of 1989–90 would not have occurred but for the Western military deterrent that produced an uneasy stability in Europe throughout the long night of the Cold War.

Another key ingredient in producing the transformation of Eastern Europe was the insistence by Western diplomats—led by the United States, during the long years of bargaining that became known as the "Helsinki process"—on the inclusion of a "basket" of human rights principles in any collective treaty that reaffirmed the postwar borders in Europe. When the Soviet Union and its East European allies signed an agreement at Helsinki called the Final Act of the Conference on Security and Cooperation in Europe, which contained a statement of the fundamental human rights of all the peoples of Europe, their communist dictators probably reckoned that the agreement's ringing phrases were as flimsy as the paper they were written on. To their everlasting consternation, however, human rights groups sprang up throughout the Soviet bloc, seizing on the Helsinki declaration for their moral authority.

In a real sense, however, the seeds of the dissolution of the Soviet empire in Eastern Europe were sown in the very process of its establishment. For the political and economic system that was created there was a virtual replication of the Stalinist totalitarian system that had been imposed on the USSR itself decades before. As an alien system, backed up by the force of the Red Army and managed by puppet regimes, communism throughout most of Eastern Europe lacked the deep roots of legitimacy. Only the determination of Stalin and his successors to hold on to their empire by force kept the system in place despite its manifest unpopularity and its embarrassing economic failures.

Clearly, the indispensable and decisive element in bringing about the swift collapse of these regimes was a changed attitude in the USSR—an unwillingness to continue to support unreformed and unresponsive communist dictatorships. Not even twenty years after it had been brutally articulated, the Brezhnev Doctrine, which justified the use of force to protect the "socialist commonwealth" from the wrath of its own people, had been unmistakably repudiated by Mikhail Gorbachev. Indeed, when asked in 1987, during the Soviet president's trip to Prague, what was the principal difference between the policies of Gorbachev and those of Dubcek, spokesman Gennadii Gerasimov answered with just two words: "Nineteen years."

But explaining the fall of communism in Eastern Europe does not answer the questions why it collapsed in the Soviet Union as well, or why the USSR itself was then unable to survive the demise of the Marxist-Leninist system. Much has already been written on this subject, both in the former Soviet Union and elsewhere, and much more research and analysis will undoubtedly follow. An able summary of the explanations that have been put forward was compiled by Jack F. Matlock, Jr., who served as U.S. ambassador to the USSR during much of the Gorbachev period. In his aptly named study, *Autopsy on an Empire,* Matlock suggests several individuals and key events that might be held responsible for the collapse of Soviet communism and the USSR.[34]

The possibly decisive events, as Matlock enumerates them, include the fall of the Berlin Wall (Boris Yeltsin's own suggestion); several events that helped to create a more powerful Russian entity within the USSR (the Russian parliament's declaration of sovereignty in June 1990, the creation of the separate Russian Communist Party later that summer, and Yeltsin's election as Russia's president in June 1991); actions by Gorbachev that caused him to lose the support of the democratic opposition and much of world opinion (his turn to the right in the fall of 1990, and the use of force against Lithuanian and Latvian protesters in January 1991); the August 1991 coup d'état; the Ukrainian declaration of independence in December 1991; and the Belovezhskaia agreement among Ukraine, Belorussia, and Russia, which itself seemed to have been in part a product of the personal feud between Yeltsin and Gorbachev.

The individuals whom Matlock cites as possibly most responsible include Leonid Brezhnev, whose long inertial reign over the "period of stagnation" saw the USSR lose both internal morale and economic capabilities; Ukrainian president Leonid Kravchuk, whose strong opposition to Gorbachev's proposed treaty may have doomed the effort to create a federal or confederal union; and Russian president Boris Yeltsin, who led both the democratic opposition to the rightist coup in August 1991 and the effort by the republican presidents to create the Commonwealth of Independent States as the successor to the USSR.

Matlock's own conclusion, however, is that Mikhail Gorbachev bore the greatest responsibility for the fall of the communist system in the USSR, both because of his various initiatives that allowed independent opposition forces to bring an end to the CPSU monopoly of power and because of his unwillingness—unique among Russian or Soviet rulers—to employ force to save his own regime. It is probable that most of Gorbachev's countrymen would agree with this verdict. More surprising is Matlock's contention that KGB director Vladimir Kriuchkov, as the organizer of the August 1991 coup attempt, was most responsible for the demise of the USSR, since the coup was timed to block the signing of the Union Treaty (scheduled for August 20), and since, in the wake of the failure of this treaty, it became virtually impossible for Gorbachev again to persuade the republics to unite in a voluntary federation. Of the two, history will devote much more attention to Mikhail Gorbachev, who—though reviled by many in his own country for having surrendered the East European empire and for having failed to preserve the unity of the USSR—was hailed throughout much of the world for having played the decisive part in the third, and even more important, dramatic event of this era: bringing about an end to the Cold War.

The Cold War was a state of relations between opposing states or social systems with a constant policy of reciprocated hostility which, nonetheless, was not allowed to escalate to the level of military force. It was a revolutionary era, with conflict between the hostile powers extended to the realms of ideas and economics, with threats a daily fact of life, and with propaganda and subversion omnipresent. Yet there was also moderation, in that there was no use of nuclear weapons after 1945, and there was no direct military clash between the two main opponents—although crises in Berlin and Cuba threatened to boil over into "hot war." There was even on occasion some joint interest by Moscow and Washington in restraining their junior partners and in using the United Nations to extinguish certain dangerous conflicts. Each exercised a degree of prudence in the other's backyard.

The two faces of the Cold War existed alongside each other because of the increased costs of the use of force. Both superpowers came to recognize that nuclear war would be mutual suicide. The very weapons that marked their strength were the least usable. Each could deny gains to the other, but could not achieve its own offensive objectives through the use of force. Ironically, smaller powers seemed freer to act than did superpowers.

Although the East-West conflict that dominated the world scene for forty-five years stopped short of war, these years were nevertheless rife with war and violence. Most notable for the United States were the two protracted wars in which it participated—Korea and Vietnam, in which the USSR was involved only through surrogate communist regimes; but also there were numerous regional conflicts in the Middle East, South Asia, and Africa that threatened to drag in the superpowers. There were also innumerable Third World civil conflicts, as well as over a dozen "wars of national liberation" in colonial areas, in which the United States and the USSR were supporting rival contenders. On several occasions, the United States and the Soviet Union resorted to the use of force to quell disturbances in their own neighborhoods: the United States in Central America and the Caribbean, the Soviet Union in Eastern Europe and Afghanistan. Finally, there were several major wars between regional powers in which both superpowers were relatively uninvolved but that they were unable to stop, including the bloodiest of all wars in this era—the Iran-Iraq War of the 1980s.

Although the normalization of the relationship between Washington and Moscow and the disappearance of the Warsaw Pact were of enormous significance, most areas of regional tension, and many root causes of civil conflict and revolution, remained. Ironically, while the prospects of a general war in Europe seemed more remote than at any time in the twentieth century, the ending of the Cold War actually increased the chance of certain forms of ethnic or civil conflict on that continent, as witnessed in both the former Yugoslavia and the former USSR. The Middle East and South Asia also remained volatile.

The end of the Cold War actually seemed to have an adverse impact on the Third World. Moscow's foreign aid programs were cut to the bone, and the U.S. Congress seemed in no mood, absent the Soviet threat, to sustain large programs of economic assistance. On the other hand, Washington and Moscow did not cease sales of military hardware to Third World regimes. Prospects of continuing and escalating economic hardship combined with increasing levels of military force did not bode well for orderly peace and development in these regions.

Despite the ending of the Cold War, there remained dozens of unresolved conflicts, with a variety of causes and with great potential for violence, throughout the world. There also remained enormous arsenals of nuclear and conventional weaponry. And despite rhetoric about a "new world order," the world was in fact no closer to constructing an alternative security system to replace the Cold War alliances—security pacts that did after all bring a certain stability to the postwar world.

——— 5 ———

Domestic Factors in the Making of Russia's Foreign Policy

External and Internal Influences on Foreign Policy

When it inherited many of the international rights and responsibilities of the USSR on January 1, 1992, the government of the Russian Federation faced an international system that differed markedly from the one confronted by prior tsarist and Soviet rulers of Russia. The previous chapters have shown how changes in the structure of the international system have influenced the foreign policy of Russia. Such factors as revolutionary developments in military technology, boundary alterations resulting from war or treaty, and shifts in the global distribution of power resulting from changes in states' relative economic and military capabilities have at times produced distinct modifications in Russian policy.

To recapitulate, there were several such changes during the period of the Cold War that had significant impact on the policies pursued by Stalin, Khrushchev, Brezhnev, Gorbachev, and their colleagues. The tight bipolarity of the late 1940s gave way to a multipolar system, as the relative strength of Japan, China, and the states of Western Europe grew during the 1950s and 1960s, and as the United States and the USSR found themselves competing for favors from relatively powerless Third World regimes. Political conflicts between the Soviet Union and other communist states, beginning in Eastern Europe in 1948 and climaxing in China in the late 1960s, doomed the monolithic communist subsystem to fractious polycentrism and finally to disintegration. Thermonuclear weapons and intercontinental ballistic missiles raised the costs of "hot war" between the chief adversaries to unacceptable levels; but once it had achieved a state of military parity with the United States in the 1970s, the Soviet Union, increasingly hobbled by economic shortcomings, was able to keep up the pace of the arms race only at a cost that proved suicidal. Because the Soviet Union was largely isolated from the global economic system, its superpower status was called into question as military prowess became less and less relevant to international issues in the 1980s and 1990s.

By the time the Soviet Union ceased to exist, at the end of 1991, Mikhail Gorbachev had significantly altered the foreign policy of the USSR, in part as a response to these changes in the international environment. He had played a significant role in bringing about an end to the Cold War and the virtual disappearance of the communist international subsystem. As he hastened to move into Gorbachev's former Kremlin office, Russian Federation president Boris Yeltsin inherited these features of a changed international system, as well as territorial boundaries radically different not only from those of the USSR but also from those of any prior independent Russian state. Coastal territories near the Baltic Sea and the Black Sea, acquired by Peter I and Catherine II through costly warfare, now belonged to units of the former USSR that were no longer under Moscow's control. Except for the province of Kaliningrad (formerly Königsberg), separated from the rest of Russia by independent Lithuania, the Russian Federation had no border with the East European states that had been part of Stalin's postwar empire. Thus pushed back from Europe, a Russia shorn of the Transcaucasian and Central Asian republics was also more distant from the Middle East and South Asia, where nineteenth-century tsars had played the "great game" with Britain and other powers. Although the United States had emerged from the Cold War as the globe's only surviving superpower, the leaders of the new Russia, unlike many people outside the new government, nevertheless perceived no threat from it. Indeed, Russia's rulers faced a more benign environment beyond the borders of the former empire than had been the case for centuries. Far more troublesome for Yeltsin and his colleagues were Russia's newly independent neighbors, the former Soviet republics, relations with which were now matters for foreign—rather than domestic—policy.

It is this last change in the external environment that is largely responsible for producing the tightest mixture of foreign policy and domestic politics that Russia has seen since the earliest months of Soviet power. The bureaucratic structures and personnel that were involved with the foreign policy of the new Russian state, many of which were simply inherited from the Soviet Union, had not been tasked to treat the former Soviet republics as objects of foreign policy. Neither the mechanisms nor the expertise were present in the foreign policy structure—rather, they were spread throughout the domestic bureaucracies. Moreover, these new neighbors encompassed many areas of instability and ethnic conflict, and the resulting military and political concerns for the Russian government were magnified by the fact that 25 million ethnic Russians resided in these new states.

In spite of the increased difficulty of untangling external and internal influences on Russia's foreign policy decision making, we will attempt in this chapter to examine the domestic factors and to describe the institutional and conceptual environment in which the foreign policy of the Russian Federation is being formulated. In so doing, we shall demonstrate that, far from being simply a calculated response to external stimuli on the part of a monolithic state, Russian foreign policy emerges from the interaction of decision makers representing a variety of personal and institutional perspectives and involved in the simultaneous resolution of a large number of domestic and foreign issues.

In today's Russia, as in the preceding Soviet state, domestic factors constrain and help to determine foreign behavior in two ways. First, internal economic, social, and political plans and policies can rival foreign and defense policies as claimants on limited resources, creating the constant necessity of choosing whether to spend resources on guns or butter, as well as whether to allocate energies and attention to foreign or domestic pursuits. Second, foreign policy decisions can be shaped by the contests for influence among groups and individuals, thus raising to the fore in Yeltsin's or Putin's Kremlin, not wholly unlike Khrushchev's or Gorbachev's before, the question of *Kto–Kovo* (Who is prevailing over whom?). Although regular competitive elections became part of the institutional landscape in Russia during the 1990s, within the Kremlin struggles over competing policies and struggles for power remain closely linked.

The continuity in the operation of these two domestic constraints is heightened by the similarity in Gorbachev's, Yeltsin's, and Putin's views of the role of foreign policy. For all three presidents, the domestic challenges of economic and political development were clearly paramount. The primary purpose of foreign policy in the late Soviet and early democratic periods of Russian history has been to create a nonthreatening external environment that would be most conducive to this internal development. As was the case in the early decades of Soviet rule, this concentration on domestic development, together with relative shortcomings in military strength, produced a foreign policy of accommodation, retrenchment, and risk avoidance—at least, in Russia's relations with states beyond the borders of the former USSR.

It has certainly not always been the case that Russian rulers have responded to domestic challenges by maintaining a low profile in their external relationships. Our study of the history of the tsarist period, as well as of episodes of Soviet history under Stalin, Khrushchev, and Brezhnev, has revealed ample instances of the contrasting situation, when activist and expansionist foreign policies have been used to strengthen the capabilities of the Russian state at the expense of competing powers. We can learn from this history that simply categorizing the type of regime ruling in Russia—whether imperial, communist, or democratizing—is not a sufficient basis on which to judge how high a priority policymakers will give to foreign policy or what direction it will take. Rather, to gain a full understanding of the impact of internal factors, we must consider specific features of the ideas and institutions that are dominant at a given time.

Continuity and Change in Russian Ideas on Foreign Policy

In the opening chapters, we have already encountered the impact of ideas on the formulation of tsarist and Soviet foreign policy. Only during the Soviet period have the prevailing ideas been encompassed in an official ideology—Marxism-Leninism, which we defined and discussed in chapter 3. In prerevolutionary times, as well as in the post-Soviet period, we encounter not an ideology but ideas, understood as broad concepts or paradigms that help both to shape the way that policymakers view the world around them and to choose policies appropriate to their objectives.

In the late tsarist period, messianic pan-Slavism was such an idea, originating among the intelligentsia but adopted at times by the regime not only as an organizing principle but also as a way of mobilizing popular support for expansionist policies. For the Bolsheviks, Marxism-Leninism provided a different understanding of Russia's international mission, although we have seen that its adherents interpreted it with sufficient flexibility to avoid violating what both they and the tsars perceived to be Russia's national interests. The key precepts of this ideology, as it applied to foreign policy, were rejected before the fall of the Soviet Union, when Mikhail Gorbachev introduced "new thinking." Essentially a variant of liberal internationalism, Gorbachev's foreign policy ideas centered on interdependence, mutual security, cooperative solutions to global problems, the primacy of nonclass values, and an understanding of capitalism that rejected the notion of its inherent militarism and the inevitability of war.

Although it was abandoned as a guide to action by Soviet foreign policymakers before it was officially jettisoned, Marxism-Leninism continues to have some degree of influence on the foreign policy of Russia, not as official ideology but as one of several contending conceptual approaches. This influence is felt not only through the activities of the Communist Party of the Russian Federation—in the 1990s, the largest of Russia's political parties—but also through the role that the doctrine had in the political socialization of many members of the current political elite. Accordingly, some elements of Russia's political culture—especially in such conservative strongholds as the armed forces and certain large economic enterprises related to the former "military-industrial complex"—demonstrate significant continuity with the Soviet era.

Nevertheless, the loss of the ideology's official standing, combined with the fall of the CPSU and the disintegration of the USSR itself, left a conceptual void in the foreign policy of the newly independent Russian Federation that raised to the forefront the question of Russia's national identity. Russia had never existed as a nation-state; rather, during both the tsarist and the Soviet periods it had been a multinational empire with messianic ambitions. Unlike other European imperial states, the modern Russian nation was not formed prior to the period of colonial expansion. Moreover, the tsars, unlike the rulers of Britain or France, colonized lands that bordered on their home territories, thus producing an unusual intermixing of Russian and non-Russian peoples.[1] The Russian Federation remains multinational, but now the proportion of ethnic Russians in the total population exceeds 80 percent, whereas they composed just over half the population of the USSR, as recorded in its last census in 1989. Further complicating the definition of Russia's national identity is the fact that, at the time the USSR disappeared, 25 million ethnic Russians lived outside the Russian Federation, in the other newly independent states (NIS) of the former Soviet Union.

Not only are the people of the Russian Federation experiencing new geopolitical confines, but they are also acutely aware of the relative weakness of their state, in comparison to the superpower status enjoyed by the USSR at the height of its power. The dizzying economic decline of the early 1990s produced a profound sense of national humiliation, as Russia's leaders—first Gorbachev, then Yeltsin—were perceived as meeting with Western leaders in the role of supplicant for foreign aid. The combination of a loss of national mission, a wounded national pride, and a confused national identity has rendered more acute the need for a definition of national purpose in the foreign policy of the new Russia. As presidential advisor Sergei Stankevich wrote in March 1992: "Foreign policy with us does not proceed from the directions and priorities of a developed statehood. On the contrary, the practice of our foreign policy will help Russia become Russia."[2]

The task of articulating the basic principles of Russian foreign policy in the early months of 1992 fell to Foreign Minister Andrei Kozyrev, a young professional diplomat who had spent sixteen years in the Department of International Organizations of the Soviet Ministry of Foreign Affairs. On the foundations of the liberal internationalism of "new thinking," Kozyrev—not surprisingly, given his background—constructed a heavy reliance on Russian participation in international institutions.[3] Determined to liberate Russia from the burdens of empire, the messianism, and the overreliance on military instruments that had characterized both the tsarist and the Soviet periods, Kozyrev developed foreign policy ideas centered on the promotion of human rights and the universal values of global economic, environmental, and nuclear security, realized through a community of democratic states. Since democracies do not attack other democracies, a democratic Russia would have nothing to fear from the West. If the purpose of Russian foreign policy was the creation of the conditions in which the new nation could prosper, Kozyrev reasoned, it would be necessary for Russia to gain membership in the club of developed democratic states and their economic institutions, thus assuming the "fitting place that has been predetermined for us by history and geography."[4] During these early months of 1992, not only Kozyrev but also President Yeltsin and Deputy Prime Minister Egor Gaidar, who was responsible for economic reform, consistently voiced these "liberal Westernizing" views of Russia's national interests.[5]

The tradition of expressing the basic principles of policy in a programmatic and officially endorsed statement still runs strong in post-Soviet Russia. Accordingly, Kozyrev was urged to develop a "foreign policy concept" that would be discussed in the government and adopted by the Supreme Soviet and the president, to serve as the expression of a national consensus as well as guidance for diplomats, parliamentarians, and others. The foreign minister was under attack from a growing number of critics, who perceived that the quest for Western economic assistance had produced a servile Russian imitation of U.S. positions on such issues as arms control and the war in Bosnia. The drafting of a concept became the occasion for a highly political debate over alternatives to Kozyrev's ideas. Further impetus for the expression of competing ideas was given in the spring of 1992 by the organization of two new foreign policy institutions—the Russian Ministry of Defense and the Security Council, a consultative body of key government officials to advise the president on security policy. At the initial meeting of the latter body on May 20, a draft of a document called "Program for the National Security of Russia" was reportedly circulated (but not adopted), stating that the Russian military must be capable of deploying forces "in any region of the world" in order to counteract "possible attempts by the United States to achieve unilaterally advantageous conditions in any region of the world."[6]

As competing ideas such as these began to be heard within the Russian government in the spring and summer of 1992, they quickly focused the question of Russia's identity. For Kozyrev, Gaidar, and other liberals, the Western democracies were the ideal model and partner for Russia. Russia must shed its tradition of distinctiveness and its illusions of serving a "special role" as a "bridge" between Europe and Asia. It must also avoid the temptations of assuming a leading role in the Commonwealth of Independent States, not only because reintegration of Russia's economy with those of the other former Soviet republics would slow market-oriented reforms and integration with Atlantic and European economic institutions, but also because Russia's assumption of a peacekeeping role in the troubled bordering states would restore the privileged status of the military and thereby threaten the tender shoots of democracy in Russia.

Juxtaposed to this Westernizing or "Atlanticist" orientation of the foreign ministry was a "pragmatic nationalist" or "Eurasianist" viewpoint that was expressed by officials in a variety of government and academic institutions. From this perspective, articulated forcefully by presidential advisor Sergei Stankevich, Russia was indeed separate and distinct from the West—even more so with its new boundaries—and did have a special mission to serve as a bridge between Western and Eastern civilizations. Foreign policy must be more than pragmatic opportunism; without displaying messianism, Russia needed a mission—in Stankevich's words, "to initiate and maintain a multilateral dialogue of cultures, civilizations and states. Russia the conciliator, Russia the unifier, Russia the harmonizer. A country that takes in West and East, North and South, and thus is uniquely capable of harmoniously unifying many different elements, of achieving a historic symphony." For Stankevich, Eurasianism was not a rejection of the West, but a balanced policy, although the immediate requirements of balance were to heighten emphasis on the East. With the West, Russia at best could aspire to a role as junior partner, "not worth accepting," but opportunities for displaying great-power leadership were greater among "second-echelon" states such as Mexico, Brazil, South Africa, Greece, Turkey, India, and China. The very first priority for Soviet diplomacy, however, was "to talk in tougher tones"—to defend the Russian population and Russian heritage in the other states of the former Soviet Union from any form of discrimination or attack.[7]

In the first few months after the dissolution of the USSR, it became clear that the CIS was not going to maintain unified security forces, and that regional instability—including threats to the rights and status of ethnic Russians in the "near abroad"—was growing. In response, the "pragmatic nationalists" were increasingly vocal in their insistence that Russia exercise hegemony in the region. In August, another advisor to Yeltsin, Presidential Council member Andranik Migranian, wrote, "Russia should declare to the world that the entire geopolitical space of the former USSR is a space of its vital interests." This declaration should not come in the form of a threat to solve problems by the use of force, Professor Migranian added, but rather an announced intention to act as the guarantor of stability in the region.[8] At about the same time, in a paper he wrote for Evgenii Ambartsumov, the chairman of the Supreme Soviet Joint Committee on International Affairs and Foreign Economic Relations, Migranian likened this proposed declaration to the Monroe Doctrine, and he urged Russia to seek international recognition of its special role in the region, including "special provision for Russia's right to defend the lives and dignity of Russians in the nearby foreign countries."[9]

Although the "pragmatic nationalists" did not go so far as to advocate forcible revision of the boundaries of the Russian Federation, they clearly disagreed with Kozyrev and Gaidar in arguing that Russia should be prepared to make economic, political, and diplomatic sacrifices in order to promote tighter integration of the Commonwealth of Independent States. This point of view—labeled "an enlightened post-imperial integrationist course"—was prominently displayed in a report issued in August 1992 by the new Council on Foreign and Defense Policy. Entitled "A Strategy for Russia," the report had a clear influence on the development of the official foreign policy concept.[10] Among the group's members were Stankevich, Ambartsumov, First Deputy Minister of Defense Andrei Kokoshin, and economist Grigorii Yavlinskii. Another member, Russia's ambassador to the United States, Vladimir Lukin, published a sharp attack on his superior's policies, arguing that preserving friendship with America did not require servile imitation of its policies and "the atrophy of independent thought and action," and advocating the achievement of greater balance in Russian policy than Kozyrev had shown by making "more active use of the potential of other sectors besides the West."[11]

By the end of 1992, this internal criticism was combining with external events—including the disappointing Western response to Russia's requests for economic assistance—to bring to an end the "romantic" phase of Russian foreign policy, and the movement of Russian liberals closer toward the centrist foreign policy views of the "pragmatic nationalists." Another factor contributing to this coalescence was the growing political strength of the "red-brown coalition" of communists and extreme nationalists, whose members voiced an even more sharply critical "fundamentalist nationalist" point of view. Most of the attention given to this orientation was generated by Vladimir Zhirinovskii, leader of the misleadingly named Liberal Democratic Party, a neo-fascist party that showed surprising strength in the parliamentary elections of December 1993. Other proponents included Gennadii Zyuganov, leader of the Communist Party of the Russian Federation, Aleksandr Prokhanov, editor of the extremist newspaper *Den,* and Colonel Viktor Alksnis, leader of the reactionary Soiuz faction in the Congress of People's Deputies. Simply stated, the foreign policy idea expressed by this group sought to re-create the Russian empire—up to and even surpassing the borders of the former USSR—by the use of force, if necessary. Unlike the "pragmatic nationalists," the "fundamentalists" were openly anti-Western, professing to see Western aid as a conspiracy to weaken the Russian economy, and opposing any further moves to integrate Russia into the world economy.

They defined the Russian nation in ethnic rather than civic terms, with some chauvinists openly voicing anti-Jewish and anti-Islamic sentiments. Appealing to many disaffected elements in the military and security establishments, politicians of this orientation advocated the restoration of a strong, authoritarian, imperial state in Russia. More than their "pragmatic" counterparts, these extreme nationalists were the late-twentieth-century heirs of the Slavophiles, contemptuously denouncing "Westernizers" for thinking that Western culture or political institutions were worthy of imitation, and depicting Russian civilization as distinctive and superior.

In the face of growing criticism in parliament from both centrists and "red-brown" extremists, Kozyrev brought Russia's internal debate on foreign policy to international notice in dramatic fashion. Speaking at a meeting of foreign ministers of the Conference on Security and Cooperation in Europe in Stockholm on December 14, the Russian foreign minister declared: "I must amend the conception of Russian foreign policy." He proceeded to assert that Russia, as a Eurasian power, saw limits on its convergence with Western Europe, especially in the face of threatening NATO plans in Bosnia and in the Baltic states. First, he demanded that sanctions against Serbia be rescinded, and he pledged Russian support to Belgrade. Second, he described the space of the former USSR as exempt from CSCE norms and insisted that the former Soviet republics join Russia in a new federation. Third and last, he warned those who were hoping for the further disintegration of Russia that "they [were] dealing with a state that [was] able to stand up for itself and its friends."

Having shocked the delegates into stunned silence, Kozyrev soon returned to the podium to declare that his speech had been an "oratorical tactic," and that President Yeltsin and he had no intention of implementing its ideas. Indeed, he explained, "the text that I read out before is a rather thorough compilation of the demands that are being made by what is by no means the most extreme opposition in Russia," and the purpose of his extraordinary hoax had been "to show the danger that would be posed if events were to develop differently."[12]

Ironically, within a few hours of Kozyrev's speech, and evidently unforeseen by him, pressure from the Congress of People's Deputies forced Yeltsin to replace Egor Gaidar as acting prime minister, appointing veteran industrial manager Viktor Chernomyrdin in his place. Simultaneously, he demoted his chief advisor, Gennadii Burbulis, who had played an active role in developing the "liberal Westernizing" ideas of Russia's foreign policy in 1992. There was widespread expectation that the foreign minister would resign rather than implement the "pragmatic nationalist" policies that were clearly intended to be adopted in the wake of Yeltsin's turn toward the center. Not only did Kozyrev remain in office, but he became a forceful spokesman for the policies he had denounced in Stockholm, eventually explaining that "as a democrat he felt constrained to take into account public opinion on foreign policy matters."[13]

As might be expected from these harbingers, the official foreign policy concept approved by President Yeltsin in April 1993 reflected the complete abandonment of the "liberal Westernizing" idea and the convergence of "establishment" thinking around the "pragmatic nationalist" viewpoint. Even more than the foreign ministry drafts circulated in November 1992 and January 1993, the final document—reportedly written by Security Council Secretary Yuri Skokov—emphasized Russia's rights and responsibilities in the states of the former USSR (in this period, generally referred to as *blizhnee zarubezhe,* or "near abroad").[14]

Of the nine "vitally important interests" listed in the document, only the third pertained to the world outside the borders of the former USSR. In referring to this domain, the authorized summary of the document mentioned the countries of Eastern Europe ("which are in our historical sphere of interests") and of Western Europe (whose "integration without Russia could do serious damage to the Russian Federation's vital interests") before it referred to Russia's relations with the United States. Evidently seeking to correct the perceived earlier imbalance in this relationship, the summary spoke of common interests that create the preconditions for developing a partnership, but it stressed that U.S.-Russian interests did not always coincide, while complaining about "discriminatory restrictions in the commercial, economic, scientific, and technological spheres."

In the Asian-Pacific region, priority was given to "urgent consolidation of the breakthrough" in relations with China ("from our standpoint, the region's most important state") over "normalizing" relations with Japan, where "the expediency of continuing to search for a solution to the territorial problem" was qualified by the caveat, "but not to the detriment of Russia's interests." The document expressed concern over the threat of nuclear proliferation on the Korean peninsula and on the Indian subcontinent, and it deplored the tensions in South and West Asia, given their harmful influence on the former Soviet states of Central Asia and the Transcaucasus. In the Middle East, it called for settlement of the Arab-Israeli conflict, while also envisioning a greater Russian role "in resolving the problems in and around Iraq" and a "stronger Russian presence in the regional arms and raw materials market." Clearly reflecting a reduced global involvement on Moscow's part, the concept document mentioned Central and South America, Africa, and Australia only in the context of "the world community's common efforts to settle regional conflicts."

"Top priority" and "fundamental importance" in Russian foreign policy were reserved to the area of the former Soviet Union. Asserting that Russia remained a great power, the concept document stressed its special responsibility "for the creation of a new system of positive relations among the states that used to make up the Soviet Union," serving as "the guarantor of the stability of these relations." In these relations, Russia sought "the greatest possible degree of integration" based on the principle of "strictly voluntary participation and reciprocity." If certain states chose not to cooperate in some spheres, then it was essential to move ahead in developing arrangements "with the interested countries alone." Specific tasks in this realm included the creation of an effective collective security system, ensuring Russia's status as the only nuclear state in the CIS, securing the external borders of the commonwealth, and developing and improving the peacekeeping mechanism "on the basis of a mandate from the UN or the Conference on Security and Cooperation in Europe." Special urgency was assigned to the "problems of ensuring military security that have arisen as a result of the Soviet Union's disintegration."

Judging from the published summary, the tone of the concept statement fell short of the open hostility toward the external world that was typical of Marxist-Leninist pronouncements and that is still evident in the expressions of "fundamentalist nationalist" politicians. Nevertheless, the concept bore an uncanny resemblance to the positions sketched out in Kozyrev's "shock therapy" in Stockholm, containing far more references to external threats and discriminatory practices than was common in Russian statements when "liberal Westernizing" views prevailed. Clearly, the official statement of guiding policy ideas was less oriented toward participation in multilateral institutions and more forcefully assertive in its enunciation of Russia's objectives than Moscow's foreign policy had been during the previous year.

Andrei Kozyrev remained the target of hostile criticism from parliament and the press—and even, on occasion, from President Yeltsin himself—until after the December 1995 elections, when he resigned as foreign minister to take a seat in the new Duma. His replacement was Evgenii Primakov, an academician whose political career had benefited from the patronage of Aleksandr Yakovlev. Trained as an Arabist, he spent five years as a *Pravda* correspondent (with presumed connections to the KGB) in the Middle East. He defended his dissertation while still with the newspaper and moved into two positions with leading foreign policy research centers: first, as deputy director of the Institute of World Economy and International Relations, and then, as director of the Institute of Oriental Studies. With Yakovlev's sponsorship, he became a close aide to Gorbachev, serving on his Presidential Council and Security Council. After the August coup, he had been appointed as chief of the reorganized Foreign Intelligence Service, and he retained this post in Yeltsin's government.

Expressing his foreign policy ideas in his first press conference as foreign minister in January 1996, Primakov unmistakably allied himself with the "pragmatic nationalist" and "Eurasianist" viewpoints. He declared that "Russia has been and remains a great power, and its policy toward the outside world should correspond to that status," while echoing his predecessor in saying that Russia's policy should create "an environment that would, to the greatest extent possible, be favorable to the development of the economy and the continuation of democratic processes in Russian society."

Russia's relations with its Cold War adversaries, he emphasized, must be "an equitable and mutually advantageous partnership that takes each other's interests into account." Expressing the need to "diversify" Russia's foreign ties, he made special mention of the Middle East and the key states of Asia (not coincidentally, the subjects of his academic specialization). Hailing the stabilization of the global conflict, he sought to salve Russia's wounded pride by asserting that the United States and Russia "jointly won—I want to put special emphasis on the point that there were no victors or vanquished here— jointly won the Cold War." Finally, Primakov enumerated four foreign policy tasks that would be given top priority: (1) creating external conditions conducive to strengthening the country's territorial integrity; (2) strengthening the processes of reintegration, especially in the economy, in the former USSR, though "this does not and cannot mean the rebirth of the Soviet Union in the form in which it used to exist"; (3) settling regional and interethnic conflicts, first of all in the CIS and former Yugoslavia; and (4) preventing the creation of new "hotbeds of tension, and especially the proliferation of means or weapons of mass destruction."[15] In a later interview, Primakov, repeating the formula that "Russia doesn't have permanent enemies, but it does have permanent interests," described these four tenets as Russia's "permanent interests."[16]

A generation older than Kozyrev, Primakov proved a more experienced manager of the foreign ministry and a more adept politician. The liberal press characterized him as a "moderate reformer," with a steady style and immense organizational talent, who "appears to personify a relative foreign policy consensus." One article quoted Yakovlev's declaration that Primakov, though "not a conservative," would pursue a policy that "will constantly remind the Americans of Russia's existence."[17] Primakov's relative immunity from the sharp criticism that had plagued Kozyrev was due in no small part to the fact that the foreign policy ideas he expressed found support among broad segments of the Russian political elite, while his assertiveness in promoting Russia's national interests seemed to restore a measure of pride in Russian foreign policy. In the wake of Primakov's successful intervention in the Iraq crisis in November 1997,

Andrei Grachev, Gorbachev's last press secretary, wrote admiringly of the change in policy, using an especially vivid metaphor:

> During the Kozyrev stage, Russian diplomacy, like a bruised, disoriented boxer who has been knocked down, clung helplessly to its American partner, compelling the rest of the world to applaud the single victor. Therefore, Russia's return to the world ring today is being loudly welcomed by everyone who missed the bouts between genuine professionals. Especially since, under the new rules of play, what we are seeing is not the previous brawl between the superpowers, but something like "fair play" between gentlemen, in which Russia plays a role that is new for it: a referee urging everyone to show restraint.[18]

As shown in Jeffrey Checkel's study of Soviet and Russian foreign policy behavior at the end of the Cold War, the degree of success enjoyed by the promoters of particular foreign policy ideas in a highly politicized setting can depend significantly upon their political skill. Checkel points to Evgenii Primakov and Aleksandr Yakovlev as exemplars of the politically savvy policy entrepreneur, while he attributes Kozyrev's relative lack of success to his "lack of political acuity."[19]

Only after labored attempts did Boris Yeltsin approve "Concept" documents on Russian foreign policy (1993), military doctrine (1993), and national security (1997). Vladimir Putin approved new versions of each of these within the first six months of 2000. First in time and importance—since the other two were essentially derived from it—was the Concept of National Security, the drafting of which was begun during the Kosovo crisis in spring 1999 (when Putin was secretary of the Security Council). The draft was approved by Yeltsin in October 1999, and final approval was given by then acting president Putin in January 2000.[20]

Revealing its origins in the Kosovo crisis, the document begins by describing two mutually exclusive trends in the world: the search for improved means of multilateral management of international affairs, and attempts to create a global structure "based on domination by developed Western countries . . . under U.S. leadership and designed for unilateral solutions (including the use of military force) to key issues in world politics in circumvention of the fundamental rules of international law." It asserts that there are positive prospects for Russia's broader integration and expanded cooperation in the world, but that "a number of states are stepping up efforts to weaken Russia politically, economically, militarily, and in other ways." This theme contrasts with the 1997 concept statement, which emphasized "partnership" with the West.

Next, Russia's national interests are defined as "the combined and balanced interests of the individual, society and the state in economic, domestic political, social, international, informational, military, border, and ecological security." These interests "may be assured only on the basis of sustainable economic development. Therefore, Russia's national interests in economics are of key importance." A broad range of threats to Russia's national security are then described. A long list of economic threats is followed by discussion of demographic and social threats. Underplayed in the 1997 version, a catalogue of external threats follows. Among these are the desire of "some states" to weaken UN and Organization for Security and Cooperation in Europe (OSCE) regimes for international security, the "danger of a weakening of Russia's political, economic, and military influence in the world," NATO expansion, the possible emergence of foreign military bases or presence near Russia's borders, the proliferation of weapons of mass destruction and their delivery vehicles, "the weakening of integrative processes in the Commonwealth of Independent States," the "outbreak and escalation of conflicts near the state border of the Russian Federation and the external borders of CIS member states," and territorial claims on Russia itself. Terrorism and information warfare are singled out for discussion, as is NATO's willingness to use force outside "its zone of responsibility." These adverse trends are exacerbated by the delays in reforming the Russian military and defense industry and by inadequate defense budgets.

The core of the document is a long list of "principal tasks for ensuring the Russian Federation's national security," most of which deal with internal priorities. However, considerable press attention was given to the statement of principles governing the employment of military force: "use of all available forces and assets, including nuclear, in the event of need to repulse armed aggression, if all other measures of resolving the crisis situation have been exhausted and have proven ineffective." Some commentators mistakenly termed this an abandonment of Gorbachev's pledge on "no first use" of nuclear weapons, even though that formulation had in fact been abandoned in the 1993 military doctrine. A number of Western analysts called attention to the loosening of conditions in which nuclear force would be used, although in fact the distinction between this formulation and the 1997 language (which spoke of the use of nuclear weapons against any armed aggression that might threaten Russia's existence as an independent state) was extremely subtle. Indeed, the U.S. State Department spokesman dismissed the change as insignificant.[21] Less noticed in the West but even more striking as a departure from the earlier draft was the next sentence: "use of military force inside the country"—earlier described as "not permitted"—is now "allowed in strict conformity with the Constitution . . . in the event of emergence of a threat to citizens' lives and also of violent change to the constitutional system." A final theme emphasized in the latest version was the need for more attention to fighting terrorism, the trade in drugs, and organized crime.

Consistent with the tone of the national security concept, the foreign policy concept published in July 2000 discussed the need to combat the trend toward creation of a unipolar world, primarily through cooperative efforts at strengthening international institutions. The document noted that threats Russia faced were "aggravated by the restricted resources provided for foreign policy," but claimed that, nevertheless, "the Russian Federation has a real potential for securing a worthy place in the world." The distinctive feature of Russia's foreign policy was said to be its "well-balanced" nature, "conditioned by the geopolitical position of Russia as the largest Eurasian power."

In its discussion of regional priorities, the document echoed the 1993 version in giving first place to the development of good neighborly relations and strategic partnership with all the CIS member states, although it recognized the limitations of the CIS framework by speaking also of "narrower formats" such as the Customs Union and the Treaty on Collective Security, in which only a few of the CIS members participated. A "top-priority" task is to strengthen the Union of Belarus and Russia.

A lengthy section on relations with European states—a "traditional priority direction" for Russia—pays particular attention to developing cooperative relations with the European Union (EU), although it notes that "the military and political dimension of the EU which is being formed must become a matter of special attention." With respect to NATO, cooperation with it is important, although the intensity of that will depend on NATO's fulfillment of key provisions of the 1997 Fundamental Act signed with Russia. Frank acknowledgment is given to the fact that certain of NATO's political and military guidelines "do not coincide with the interests of security of the Russian Federation and sometimes directly contradict them." In particular, Russia takes issue with NATO's new strategic concept, which contemplates out-of-area operations without prior authorization of the UN Security Council. Moreover, "Russia continues to have a negative attitude to NATO enlargement."

No longer is Eastern Europe referred to as "within our historical sphere of interests," as it had been in the 1993 version; and relations with Lithuania, Latvia, and Estonia are for the first time treated in the section on Europe, rather than in conjunction with the other states of the former Soviet Union. Reference is made to the "good prospects" for relations in the Baltic states, with the "indispensable condition" that these states "show respect for Russian interests, including in such a key issue as the observance of the rights of the Russian-speaking population."

As in 1993, relations with the United States are treated after the section on Europe, and in briefer form than in the discussion of the EU. Russia is said to be ready to overcome "considerable difficulties which have emerged of late" in these relations. "Despite the presence of serious and, in a number of cases, essential disagreements, Russian-US interaction is a necessary condition for improving the international situation and ensuring global strategic security," especially in the realms of disarmament, arms control, and nonproliferation. No mention is made in this context of the American plan to build a national missile defense.

Considerable attention is devoted to Asia, which "is acquiring great and ever increasing significance" in Russia's foreign policy. Emphasis is given to increasing Russia's participation in the Asian-Pacific Economic Cooperation forum, in the Association of Southeast Asian Nations (ASEAN) security forum, and in what was then known as the "Shanghai Five" (Russia, China, Kazakhstan, Kyrgyzstan, and Tajikistan). In an interesting alteration of the 1993 document, India now shares with China the "first place" for further development of friendly state-to-state relations.

The concept document refers specifically to several areas of conflict in which Russian participation is necessary: the "Korean problem"; the situation in the Middle East; and the "lingering conflict" in Afghanistan, which "creates a real threat to the security of the southern borders of the CIS," with particular attention to the need for "preventing the export of terrorism and extremism from that country." Specific reference is also made to the need for promoting Russia's economic interests in the Caspian Sea and Black Sea region, "including in the issue of choosing the routes of the passage of important flows of energy products." Finally, as in the 1993 document, only the barest attention is paid to Africa and to Latin America.[22]

In the opinion of Foreign Minister Igor Ivanov, the "chief innovation" of the 2000 foreign policy concept was its "realism." Priorities were more closely based on Russia's long-term goals for domestic development and were more consistent with its actual capabilities and resources. The document gave more attention than did its predecessor to the need to protect the interests of Russian enterprises and "Russian compatriots" abroad. In sum, Ivanov declared, "our policy is predicated on continuity, predictability, and mutually beneficial pragmatism."[23]

The third of these revised concept documents, the military doctrine, was approved by the Security Council in April 2000. One Russian press report attributed the changes from the 1993 version to increases in external threats and further deterioration in Russia's general-purpose forces. The approved version was apparently toned down from an earlier draft, described as "anti-American." References in the 1993 version to "defense security" were replaced with the term "military security," indicating, by this account, "a reassessment of the threats Russia faces: a considerable number of domestic threats have been added to the traditional foreign ones." This commentator approvingly noted that, in general, the tasks envisioned for the military had been toned down: "Russia has no plans to confront the entire world; it merely intends to be capable of coping with direct threats to its own security."[24]

In October 2002, only six days after Chechen terrorists had seized a Moscow theater, holding its occupants hostage until a deadly rescue assault was launched by Russian security forces, Putin called his top security chiefs together to consider revising Russia's National Security Concept. Putin's emphasis was understandably on terrorism, but he was also quite aware that the Bush administration had just released a new National Security Strategy document that explicitly asserted that the United States had the right to use preemptive force in the face of certain threats from terrorists or "rogue" regimes. Putin directed that within a month drafts of a new version of the concept document should be prepared that would authorize the launching of preemptive strikes, in light of the increasing threats of terrorism and the use of weapons of mass destruction. Following this, the military doctrine, which currently lacked any specific guidance regarding the use of the armed forces against terrorists, would also be revised.[25]

While agreeing that these concept documents were now outdated, one analyst complained that the process of formally revising a whole series of documents was an enormous and wasteful bureaucratic enterprise. A more efficient method, he argued, would be for the president to make an address on national security to the Russian parliament, in which new guidance could be given to government agencies.[26] Whether for this reason or some other, there is no evidence that Putin's project for revising the concept documents was in fact carried forward.

The president did, however, make statements in the succeeding years that appeared to serve the purpose of setting priorities for Russian defense policy. In an address to the top military leadership in October 2003, Putin described the features of what was called a new "military doctrine" for Russia. He stressed that a global nuclear war or large-scale conventional war with the United States was no longer probable, and he urged that the military give more of its attention to preparing troops for peacekeeping and peacemaking missions, special operations, antiterrorist operations, and local wars. He described five basic trends in the external environment: (1) new challenges stimulated by globalization, including proliferation of WMD, terrorism, religious and ethnic instability, drug trafficking, and organized crime; (2) the use of force on the basis of temporary coalitions, outside traditional organizations, in which Russia would participate only when these accorded with its national interests and rested on international law; (3) states pursuing their own economic interests, sometimes cynically using armed force as an instrument thereof; (4) a fusion of domestic and international terrorism; and (5) the growth in significance of international nongovernmental organizations and movements.[27]

In July 2004 Putin made another programmatic statement, this time to the Russian ambassador corps. He had addressed the group two years earlier, when he had ranked as Russia's top priority its "trust-based" partnership with the United States, followed by the creation of a single economic space in Europe and relations with the states of the CIS. In 2004, the order was exactly reversed: first priority went to supporting integration processes and protecting the rights of Russian citizens in the CIS, with a caution that in the absence of an effective Russian policy, "other more energetic states" would fill the vacuum. Europe was again second priority, with challenges in forging cooperation with both the EU and NATO. Lastly, Putin said that "relations with the U.S. likewise call for constant attention," and he warned that contacts of trust at the level of leaders was not enough for sustaining a strategic partnership: He exhorted Russia's diplomats to be more effective in helping to shape positive ("unbiased and commendatory") perceptions of Russia among foreign audiences.[28]

Foreign Policy Decision Making: The Institutional Context

During both the tsarist and the Soviet periods of Russian history, foreign policy was conducted by a highly centralized and authoritarian state. The absolute power of the tsar was exercised through a powerful central bureaucracy, which tightly controlled the Russian economy and society at large. The secret police and the state censors combined to restrict political participation and political expression. Until the introduction of limited parliamentarism following the 1905 revolution, there were no regularized channels through which countervailing pressures could be brought to bear on policymakers. The politics of foreign policymaking was largely confined to the imperial court.

After the October Revolution, the Communist Party played the primary role in making foreign policy decisions and exercising control over their implementation. For almost three-quarters of a century, until constitutional changes were made in 1990, the party was "the leading core of all public and state organizations" and the guardian of the purity of Marxist-Leninist doctrine. Throughout most of its history, the Communist Party of the Soviet

Union (CPSU) was a tightly organized hierarchy under strong central direction. In theory—and, as late as 1930, in practice as well—policy on foreign relations, international revolutionary strategy, and domestic issues was debated and decided by the party congress, to which delegates were elected by party organizations throughout the country. Under Stalin, as the party congress grew larger and met less frequently (only three times between 1930 and 1952), it became more and more a creature of its executive organs, which technically were responsible to it. The Central Committee of the CPSU, charged with directing policy between sessions of the congress, was also diluted in authority during Stalin's rule. It became a sounding board and a legitimizer of the policies and personnel decisions offered for its unanimous approval by its executive committee, the Politburo.

Throughout most of Soviet history, it was the Politburo that functioned as the chief decision-making body of the CPSU—and thus, of the USSR itself. The chief exception was during the period that Stalin exercised true one-man rule, personally making all major decisions. After Stalin's death, the Politburo (called the Presidium from 1952 to 1966) again functioned as a collective body—the one political organization in the country in which a vote really decided something. Composed of between twelve and sixteen voting members and six to eight nonvoting members, from 1973 until 1990 it included the prime minister and the ministers of foreign affairs and defense and the director of the secret police (KGB), as well as the most important functionaries of the party apparatus. Not all members were equally involved in foreign policy matters; often, these were referred to subcommittees, of which the most important was the Defense Council. In 1990, as part of the creation of the executive presidency in the USSR, Gorbachev introduced changes in the party rules that changed the composition and reduced the importance of the Politburo. The functions of its Defense Council were largely preempted by the new USSR Security Council.

The other top organ of the CPSU was the Secretariat, which was responsible for formulating the issues and alternatives that constituted the agenda of the Politburo, overseeing the implementation of its decisions, and (with the Politburo) controlling appointments in the party bureaucracy, the government, and the key institutions in society. Since Stalin's time, the general secretary had been able to translate his dominance of the Secretariat into a role as *primus inter pares* in the Politburo itself and, ultimately, as the top Soviet spokesman on both foreign and domestic policy. Among the staff agencies of the Secretariat (the "central apparatus") were several with foreign policy responsibilities. Chief among them were the Department for Liaison with Communist and Workers Parties of the Socialist Countries, which conducted Soviet relations with other communist states; and the International

Department, which was responsible for CPSU relations with nonruling communist parties.

In the last three years of his regime, Gorbachev sponsored changes that reduced the authority of these agencies—and of the Communist Party itself—and invigorated the foreign policy role of the institutions of the government of the USSR. In the eyes of the would-be coup makers of August 1991 (as well as of many outside observers), these changes in longstanding party institutions prepared the way not only for the fall of communism in the USSR, but for the disintegration of the USSR itself.

When the Communist Party, even in its diminished state, was banned in Russia by Yeltsin's decree the week after the attempted coup, there was no longer an effective mechanism at the center for coordinating foreign policy. Indeed, the two institutions of government that had been created in 1990 to assume the responsibility for implementing Soviet foreign and defense policies—the Security Council and the Cabinet of Ministers—were also abolished in the wake of the failed coup, because their leading members had participated in the plot or tacitly supported it. In their place, Gorbachev formed the State Council, composed of himself and the presidents of all the republics, which had the responsibility for overseeing foreign policy and national defense during the remaining months of the Soviet Union's existence. Finding an effective substitute for the party as a coordinating mechanism continued to be a major challenge also for the Yeltsin administration.

The other major change in the conduct of foreign policy that began in the latter period of Gorbachev's rule and continued in the Yeltsin years was the opening of the policy process to wider participation and greater public visibility. Prior to the initiation of glasnost by Gorbachev, extreme secrecy was the norm in the decision-making processes of the USSR, and sensitive foreign policy issues were discussed and decided by a relatively few high-ranking officials within the top leadership. Public discussion, even in parliamentary forums, took the form of after-the-fact justification and ratification of decisions, the basis for which was rarely if ever discussed with completeness and candor. To a limited extent during Gorbachev's last year or two in office, and to a much greater degree in Yeltsin's democratizing Russia, the foreign policy debate became more public, and more open to the participation of a variety of groups representing more diverse viewpoints.

However, during the first term of Putin's presidency, it appeared to many observers that participation was again narrowing and secrecy increasing. Although he himself denied it, Putin seemed to be attempting to rein in the independent mass media. An ominous signal of what might be in store appeared in June 2000, when Putin approved the National Security Information Doctrine, the major theme of which was the need to increase government control over the flow of information.[29] Soon thereafter, Putin's government was engaged in conflicts with two wealthy businessmen ("oligarchs" Vladimir Gusinskii and Boris Berezovskii) whose extensive media holdings included television networks that had taken a critical stance toward the Kremlin. When the dust settled, the two oligarchs were living in exile and their television outlets had been placed under one form or another of state control. Although many Russian newspapers and other media outlets continued to voice independent messages, most Russians (like Americans) get their news from television. By 2003 reporting or opinion not favorable to the Kremlin was seldom being heard by the public through that medium.

The Presidency, Its Advisory Councils, and the Coordination of Foreign Policy

Since the creation of the executive presidency in the USSR in 1990, and continuing in independent Russia, the office of the president has been the institutional centerpiece of Moscow's foreign policy decision making. Prior to 1990, the Soviet "presidency" was a ceremonial position—head of state but not of the government. Formally, the title was Chairman of the Presidium of the Supreme Soviet of the USSR, and only after Brezhnev assumed it in 1976 was it customarily paired with the top position in the party (general secretary of the CPSU). With the changes in 1990, Gorbachev's presidency resembled that of France, with constitutional powers to head "the country's entire system of bodies of state administration." Although the office was intended to be popularly elected, Gorbachev chose not to subject himself to an electoral test and was instead selected by the Congress of People's Deputies. The Soviet president also headed two new institutions with foreign policy responsibilities: the Council of the Federation, which included the presidents of the union republics and gave them a voice in issues of all-union significance, and the Security Council.

This presidential dominance of foreign policy has been even more pronounced in the Russian Federation, especially since the adoption of the new constitution in 1993: Articles 80 and 86 of this document give the president the power to exercise "leadership of the foreign policy of the Russian Federation," within the framework of the constitution and laws of the country.[30] The earlier, Soviet-era constitution of the Russian republic (written in 1978 and—though much amended in its last years—continuing in force until 1993) gave the Russian parliament the formal right to determine the main lines of foreign policy and approve ministerial appointments, but efforts by the legislative body in 1992 and 1993 to turn this formal power into reality were stubbornly resisted by Yeltsin.

The formal or official powers of the Russian president under the new constitution are greater than those of any previous Russian leader since the tsar. Of course, unlike the tsar's powers, those of the president have been granted by a vote of the Russian people. However, while the constitution was approved by a 58 to 42 percent margin, only 54 percent of the eligible voters participated in the December 1993 vote.

Unlike its predecessor, the 1993 constitution clearly gives the president control of the government. The president nominates the prime minister, and if the lower house of the parliament, the State Duma, rejects the nomination three times, the president may dissolve the Duma and call for new elections. The State Duma may vote no confidence in the government, but the president is entitled to reject this vote rather than call for the government's resignation. A second vote of no confidence within a three-month period will lead either to resignation of the government or to new elections of the Duma. On the other hand, the president may demand the government's resignation without the Duma's approval, as Yeltsin did in March 1998—and then on three more occasions in the next eighteen months. In accordance with the constitution and federal laws, the president determines the basic guidelines of domestic and foreign policy; serves as commander-in-chief, and appoints and dismisses top commanders of the armed forces; approves military doctrine; may declare martial law and states of emergency (with the approval of the parliament's upper house, the Federation Council); and may issue binding decrees and directives (providing they do not contradict the constitution or federal law).

Given these considerable powers, it is not surprising that the president has a large staff, directed by the head of administration. Vladimir Putin inherited Yeltsin's chief of staff, Aleksandr Voloshin, who was a member of the departing president's inner circle (the "Family"). Putin reportedly had promised Yeltsin that he would not make changes in the leadership of the presidential administration or the government until his first term ended, and it was not until October 2003 that Voloshin departed (apparently in protest over the arrest of "oligarch" Mikhail Khodorkovskii). He was succeeded by one of his former senior deputies, Putin loyalist Dmitri Medvedev. At the beginning of Putin's second term in 2004, the size of the presidential administration was reduced from 1,500 to 1,200—still a bureaucracy of considerable size, which some analysts compared to the former CPSU Central Committee apparatus.

The president appoints several advisory bodies composed of experts from inside and outside the government. Initially, the most notable of these bodies was the Presidential Council, which included a number of foreign policy specialists. However, following the military invasion of Chechnya in December

1994, when a large number of its members voiced their public protest of the action, the Presidential Council virtually ceased to function.

The presidential staff also includes an assistant to the president for international affairs. This position was filled during Yeltsin's first years in office by a career diplomat, Dmitri Riurikov. An expert on international law and former head of the Soviet foreign ministry's Middle East department, Riurikov was dismissed in April 1997, reportedly for poor staff work on the Russia-Belarus Treaty. He was replaced by another career diplomat, Sergei Prikhodko. With the reorganization of the presidential administration at the beginning of 2004, Prikhodko's title became "presidential aide," but he remained responsible for supervising the work of the foreign policy directorate of the staff.

The president's direct role in foreign policy making is further enhanced by the fact that the foreign minister and the "power ministers" of Russia—the ministers of defense and interior, and the heads of the intelligence and security services—report to the president directly rather than through the prime minister. With so many responsible officials having direct access to the president—and given that Yeltsin's style (a style that was unsurprising for the former provincial party secretary that he was) was to keep his hands directly in so many matters—it is not surprising that there was an endemic messiness in Russian foreign policy during the Yeltsin years. Vladimir Putin, with the more disciplined style of a former KGB officer, brought a significant dose of much needed orderliness to the Kremlin.

The creation of the Security Council in April 1992 was intended to bring the top foreign policy and national security officials together to deliberate and prepare decisions for the president to implement by decree. Its permanent (voting) members initially included the president, the vice president (until 1993), the prime minister, the Security Council secretary, and (as of January 1995) the speakers of the State Duma and the Federation Council. Its nonvoting members included the remaining "power ministers."[31] A reorganization in August 1996 added the foreign minister, defense minister, and director of the Federal Security Service as permanent members. Much of the work of the Security Council is conducted by interagency commissions, on which each relevant ministry is represented by a deputy minister.

Twelve men—several of them prominent political figures—held the position of secretary of the Security Council during its first dozen years of existence. The initial occupant of the position, Yuri Skokov, was a conservative stalwart of the defense industry, identified in the liberal press as the "undisputed leader of the anti-market lobby," and the new council was at first suspected of being an "alternative state structure or shadow cabinet" modeled on the Politburo. Growing doubts about Skokov's loyalty evidently led to his dismissal in April.[32]

In June, Yeltsin appointed Marshal Evgenii Shaposhnikov as Skokov's replacement. Shaposhnikov had become USSR minister of defense in August 1991 after the failure of the attempted coup, and he had been appointed commander-in-chief of the Commonwealth of Independent States after the USSR dissolved. It had been apparent for many months that this was a position without a function, given the failure of the CIS members to create unified armed forces, and so Shaposhnikov's appointment as Security Council secretary helped Yeltsin solve an awkward problem. The hapless marshal resigned only two months later, complaining that he had had virtually nothing to do and no access to Yeltsin.[33]

In filling the vacancy, Yeltsin again turned to a loyal supporter whom he was removing from another position for political reasons. The new secretary, Oleg Lobov, was being ousted from the positions of first deputy prime minister and minister of economics, which he had held for less than six months. Like Skokov, Lobov was a conservative and a close associate of defense industry enterprise directors, but he was of undoubted loyalty to the president—having spent twenty-seven years working with Yeltsin in Sverdlovsk—and was said to be his "oldest friend and comrade-in-arms." Lobov brought his interest in economic matters to his new position, but at the end of 1994 the council's attention was dramatically refocused on a pressing matter of internal security—the threatened secession of Chechnya. Lobov was named in August 1995 as Yeltsin's personal representative to Chechnya—making him, in effect, the top Russian official there. The liberal press again began to write about the Security Council as a shadowy body wielding "inordinate power," acting like "a junta that came to power without a military coup. For several months now, real power in Russia has been in the hands of a small group—politicians, generals, or bureaucrats—whom no one elected and who are under no one's control."[34]

The Security Council's profile loomed even larger on the Russian political scene in the summer of 1996, when Aleksandr Lebed became its secretary. Having finished third in the first round of the presidential elections in June, the former paratroops general was brought into the government by Yeltsin, who was evidently seeking the support of Lebed voters to provide him the margin of victory in the runoff election with Communist candidate Gennadii Zyuganov. Born in 1950, Lebed was a career soldier, having been educated in military institutions, and he had commanded a battalion in Afghanistan and later conducted highly visible (and highly independent) actions in the secessionist Trans-Dniester region of Moldova. A charismatic and supremely self-confident candidate for the presidency, the general swaggered into Yeltsin's administration with the attitude of presumed heir apparent. When Yeltsin suffered a heart attack just prior to the July voting and lapsed into seclusion thereafter, Lebed quickly became the dominant figure in Russian politics, clearly impatient for the top position.

Lebed's appointment as Security Council secretary coincided with the removal of General Pavel Grachev as minister of defense, and it was followed quickly by the dismissal of a powerful troika of Kremlin "hawks"— General Aleksandr Korzhakov, director of the presidential bodyguards; General Mikhail Barsukov, director of the Federal Security Service; and First Deputy Prime Minister Oleg Soskovets.[35] Lebed was highly visible in these maneuvers, and he claimed that the dismissed officials had been preparing to forestall the second round of elections, even by staging a military coup. Lebed immediately began a highly public lobbying campaign to expand the role of the Security Council. Yeltsin obliged, issuing decrees on July 10 that expanded both the powers of its secretary and the council's functions—broadly redefining national security to include questions of "domestic, foreign, and military policy in the area of ensuring the security of the individual, society, and state."

As the summer of 1996 progressed, and Yeltsin's precarious state of health was publicly acknowledged, Lebed became embroiled in more struggles with his rivals in the government. He scored a highly visible success in his mission to engineer a peace settlement in Chechnya—helping to propel him to the top of public popularity polls—but he was highly critical of the performance of interior ministry troops and commanders there. At one point, he ostentatiously offered Yeltsin his resignation, but the president refused to accept it, instructing him to try harder to get along with his colleagues. Finally, in the midst of public accusations of coup plotting between Lebed and interior minister Anatolii Kulikov, Yeltsin's patience was exhausted, and he appeared on television on October 17 to affix his signature to a decree dismissing Lebed.

Lebed's successor as secretary of the Security Council was Ivan Rybkin, the former speaker of the State Duma, who had lent his support to Yeltsin during difficult times in October 1993 and thereafter. In the eyes of the liberal press, whereas Lebed had tried to turn the Security Council into an unconstitutional military-police agency, Rybkin would demilitarize it and restore it to its constitutional place, overseeing a complex of problems in the realm of "economic, ecological, agricultural, and industrial security."[36] One of Rybkin's last achievements as secretary of the Security Council was issuing the long-awaited National Security Concept. Drafting of this document had begun in the late Soviet period. Following discussions in the Security Council, the government, the Duma, and the Federation Council, it emerged for Yeltsin's approval only in December 1997.[37]

In March 1998 Rybkin was appointed deputy prime minister in charge of relations with the Commonwealth of Independent States. In his place as secretary of the Security Council, Yeltsin appointed Andrei Kokoshin, a defense intellectual who, unlike his predecessors, possessed neither military experience nor an independent political base. Evidently, however, Kokoshin could not resist the temptation, shared by so many of his predecessors, to use his position to promote his own political fortunes. During the government crisis of August–September 1998, he backed the "wrong horse"— Moscow mayor Yuri Luzhkov—as the successor to Prime Minister Kirienko, and was unceremoniously dismissed. The new secretary was General Nikolai Bordiuzha, a career security official, most recently head of the Federal Border Service, who was allied with the ultimate victor in the race for prime minister, Evgenii Primakov. By this time, the Security Council had grown to include nineteen voting members—encompassing the power-wielding inner core of the government.[38]

Bordiuzha's political fortunes turned briefly upward when he simultaneously became head of the presidential administration in December 1998. He fell just as rapidly, dismissed by Yeltsin just weeks in advance of Primakov's own firing in the spring of 1999. It was at this juncture, in March 1999, that Yeltsin appointed the still relatively unknown head of the Federal Security Service (FSB), Vladimir Putin, to fill the Security Council vacancy, while keeping his considerable responsibilities for internal security and counterintelligence. Obviously, Putin was able to vault from the Security Council to a position higher than any of his predecessors, becoming prime minister in August 1999; acting president in January 2000; and president of the Russian Federation on March 26, 2000. It was during Putin's brief tenure in the Security Council that the drafting of the new National Security Concept was begun. More importantly, during the summer of 1999 turmoil again arose in the North Caucasus. Following raids by armed Chechen bands into Dagestan, Yeltsin elevated Putin to the position of prime minister, from which he launched the second Chechen war. The attention of the Russian public became riveted on matters of internal security, as mysterious bomb blasts, attributed by the authorities to Chechen terrorists, ripped apart apartment houses, first in Dagestan (in Buinaksk), and then in Rostov province (in Volgodonsk) and in Moscow itself. In an atmosphere of near-panic, Putin's tough talk about "wiping out" the Chechen terrorists rapidly made him Russia's most popular politician.

In November, Sergei Ivanov, a career intelligence officer with the rank of lieutenant general whom Putin has described as his most trusted associate, succeeded the new prime minister in his Security Council post. During Ivanov's roughly 500-day tenure, the council became a beehive of activity, occupying the spotlight not only because of the importance of the tasks assigned to it by

Putin, but also because of the evident closeness between Russia's new leader and his trusted colleague.[39] About 90 percent of the council's 176 staff members under Ivanov were reported to be former KGB personnel.

Working through standing and ad hoc interdepartmental commissions, Ivanov's Security Council involved itself in a host of domestic and foreign issues. Critics again feared the revival of a modern-day Politburo; these fears were fed by rumors heard in Moscow during the last half of 2000, claiming that legislation was in the works to give the Security Council special powers during a declared state of emergency. This concern was not new with Putin; as we noted above, similar fears and rumors about the Security Council were heard in 1994–96, when its members composed the so-called party of war that was conducting the first phase of the war in Chechnya. In a press interview, Ivanov denied that the council duplicated the work of the "power ministries"; rather, he said, it was "designed to prepare the decisions of the president in questions of ensuring the protection of vital interests of the individual, society, and the state from internal and external threats and pursue an integrated state policy in the sphere of security." In 2000 the Security Council adopted revised "concepts" in the realms of national security, military policy, and defense policy, as well as a new document concerned with "information security," and it played the major role in coordinating the preparation of a new round of military reform.[40]

Long rumored to be destined for higher office, perhaps even to the post of prime minister, Ivanov—who had resigned his military commission in November 2000—was Putin's choice to become Russia's first civilian minister of defense in March 2001. As the president put it, since his friend had headed the group that had worked out the main parameters of the military reform, it was only fair to entrust him with its implementation. The appointment was greeted with approval by prominent journalist Pavel Felgengauer, who dubbed Ivanov "the most powerful political figure to occupy the post of defense minister" since Dmitri Ustinov held the post in the 1970s. "Ivanov can make decisions and can make things happen," he predicted.[41]

Completing the first cabinet shake-up of his presidency, Putin removed Vladimir Rushailo from the post of minister of internal affairs, making him Ivanov's successor at the Security Council. Since Rushailo was thought to be linked to Boris Berezovskii, who had become a Putin opponent, it was rumored that the Security Council job was his way station on the road out of power.[42] In fact, however, Rushailo remained in the job until March 2004, though during his tenure the Security Council again lost much of its clout and visibility. The new occupant—the twelfth to hold the job—was Igor Ivanov, who was leaving the post of foreign minister after almost six years. In that position, Ivanov had functioned largely as an implementer rather than initiator of policy, and it was not considered likely that he would raise the Security Council's profile.

The many twists and turns in the short history of the Security Council make clear that some of its more politically ambitious secretaries have sought to inflate its authority, turning it into a powerful decision-making body with broadly defined operational responsibilities. Boris Yeltsin clearly resisted these efforts, evidently sensing that such a body—reminiscent of the post-Stalinist Politburo—would dilute his own power. Vladimir Putin, a former occupant of the position, has followed the pattern of enlarging the council's role only at times that he fully trusts its leadership. Nevertheless, it remains significant if only because of the important positions that are represented on the council. As enumerated in a presidential decree of April 2004, these were: the president, as chairman; the secretary; the prime minister; speakers of the two houses of the Federal Assembly; the foreign, defense, and interior ministers; the heads of both the domestic and foreign intelligence services; the chief of staff of the presidential administration; the head of the Russian Academy of Sciences; and the seven presidential representatives to the "super-regions" of Russia.

Nevertheless, the concurrent existence for a while of the Security Council, the Defense Council (created in 1996), and a Foreign Policy Council (named in December 1995) spoke to the persisting problem of lack of coordination in Russian foreign and defense policy. According to a well-informed journalist, Yeltsin remarked privately, at the time he was asked to approve the creation of the Foreign Policy Council, "I'm already up to here in these councils." As Pavel Felgengauer described it, "He laughed then, and approved it all with a decree."[43]

Contrary to his willingness to approve new coordinating councils in the realms of foreign and defense policy, Yeltsin on several occasions decreed that the Ministry of Foreign Affairs should play the leading role in the coordination of Russian foreign policy. The first such occasion was in November 1992, when the Ministry of Defense and the Security Council had emerged as major competitors of the foreign ministry, and Yeltsin decreed that the foreign ministry "will be entrusted with the function of coordinating and monitoring work by other Russian ministries, committees, and departments to ensure a unified political line" for Russian foreign policy.[44]

Despite Yeltsin's decree, Kozyrev's ministry continued to have problems asserting its primacy, especially on issues relating to foreign economic relations, which were handled by a separate ministry and were often a concern of the prime minister's as well. In March 1995, Yeltsin—hearing the complaints in a meeting with foreign ministry officials—again offered assistance, approving by decree the new Statute on the Russian Ministry of Foreign

Affairs. This decree made the ministry accountable directly to the president, who would henceforth also appoint its deputy ministers (bypassing the prime minister). The statute declared that the foreign ministry determines the overall strategy of foreign policy and implements policy, coordinating and monitoring the relevant activities of other agencies "to ensure the conduct of a uniform Russian policy line." The press reported that the decree "dispelled once and for all" rumors of the possible creation within the president's staff of a new interagency coordinating body, and concluded, "not since World War II have we had a Foreign Minister who has wielded such broad power." Yet, at a press conference barely half a year later, the president was complaining that Kozyrev "can't deal with other ministers," and again spoke of the need to "step up the work of coordinating international and foreign-economic activity at the level of the President."[45]

Soon thereafter, Kozyrev resigned and was replaced by Primakov, and the president issued yet another decree stating that, within the executive branch, the Ministry of Foreign Affairs "shall be the principal agency" in foreign policy "and shall exercise overall supervision of the fulfillment of Russia's international obligations." The decree added that, in Russian embassies, the ambassadors were to assume responsibility for coordinating the activities of all government offices represented in the embassy. Finally, and most specifically, the decree prohibited the presidential staff from accepting for consideration any proposal from an agency regarding foreign economic relations unless the proposal had first been cleared with the foreign ministry, and it declared that official statements on foreign policy might be made only by the president, the prime minister, and the foreign minister (or by others only when instructed by one of these officials). One commentator, noting that this decree resembled the one of the previous year, and that it failed to make any structural changes that might ensure the subordination of foreign economic activity to the foreign ministry, observed that what Yeltsin was attempting "is the coordination of not so much foreign policy as foreign policy rhetoric."[46]

Whether caused by the repeated decrees or, more likely, by the improvement in top-level organizational and political skill, the foreign ministry's ability to achieve a coordinating role over Russian foreign policy increased markedly under Evgenii Primakov. In September 1996, with Lebed still in office at the Security Council and with the new Defense Council in existence, Primakov spoke confidently in an interview of the primacy of his ministry over the making of foreign policy. As he described it, the basic parameters of policy were set by the president, on the basis of which the ministry prepared proposals for his approval. The ministry also could initiate certain concepts and formulate policy, subject to "correction" by the president. The military, Primakov said, had influence on foreign policy, although "interdepartmental accommodation" was more effective now (presumably meaning after Grachev's removal) than before, and the March decree had also helped in this regard. As for the Security Council, "it is not dealing with foreign policy issues at this time, for all practical purposes."[47]

Further evidence of Primakov's dominant role appeared in the last half of 1997. In September, he was named head of a Security Council commission on international security. Shortly thereafter, Yeltsin decreed the elimination of ten consultative bodies in his office, including the potentially troublesome Foreign Policy Council. The number of officials responsible for foreign policy on the presidential staff was reduced from twenty-five to fifteen. A new structure, the President's Foreign Policy Administration, was created, but according to Yeltsin's assistant for international affairs, Sergei Prikhodko, its functions were limited to such roles as polishing Yeltsin's speeches. Contrary to rumors, he said, it was decidedly not a re-creation of the CPSU Central Committee Secretariat's International Department. The responsibility for formulating foreign policy, according to Prikhodko, rested with the foreign minister, who had unimpeded and regular access to the president, and who "confers with the president by telephone more than I do."[48]

The Ministry of Foreign Affairs

From the time of the Bolshevik Revolution until the dissolution of the USSR, only ten men held the position of Soviet foreign minister, and they were widely varied in their influence and personalities. The original occupant, Leon Trotsky, held the position from the time of the revolution until April 1918; he surrendered it gladly, regarding it as beneath his talents. Like Trotsky, four others—Viacheslav Molotov, Andrei Vyshinsky, Dmitri Shepilov, and Eduard Shevardnadze—were high-ranking members of the CPSU leadership at the time they took over the foreign affairs portfolio. Two (Georgii Chicherin and Maksim Litvinov) acquired membership in the Central Committee only after serving for a while as foreign minister, and they never rose above that level.

The longest-serving Soviet foreign minister, Andrei Gromyko—a product of the career foreign affairs bureaucracy—was initially regarded as a technician. He became a member of the Central Committee in 1956 and of the Politburo in 1973, after which he assumed a more prominent role in policy-making—eventually playing a critical role in the selection of Gorbachev as general secretary in 1985. A few months later, Gromyko was "kicked upstairs" to the then ceremonial position of president (formally, chairman of the Presidium of the Supreme Soviet), clearing the way for Gorbachev to place his close ally, Shevardnadze, in charge of the foreign ministry. Under his direction, the entrenched "old guard" of the Gromyko generation was eliminated from the foreign policy bureaucracy. A massive overhaul of the foreign ministry structure and personnel accompanied the introduction of "new thinking" into Soviet foreign policy.

From the time of Chicherin, it was clear that the Soviet foreign minister was not the chief foreign policy maker; he advised and implemented, but unless he held a job in the top councils of the party, his decision making was relegated to secondary matters. Also from the time of Chicherin, it was clear that the Soviet foreign ministry was by no means the sole instrument employed in the foreign affairs realm by the Soviet Union. As we have seen, there was a long rivalry and tension between the foreign ministry, as the instrument of more traditional diplomacy, and the Communist International (Comintern) and its successor agency, the International Department of the Central Committee Secretariat, as instruments of world revolution. Indeed, from the establishment of communist regimes in Eastern Europe after World War II until their collapse in 1989, the primary responsibility for conduct of Soviet relations with other communist states was not even lodged in the foreign ministry, but rather in the CPSU Secretariat's Department for Liaison with Communist and Workers Parties of the Socialist Countries.

An example of the traditional tension within Soviet foreign policy and the lack of integration of various instruments under the Ministry of Foreign Affairs was the Soviet Mission Abroad. The Soviet Embassy housed not only the overseas presence of the foreign ministry itself, but also the foreign representatives of numerous other agencies. A great many of these—often between one-half and two-thirds of the total embassy staff—were intelligence agents, not accountable to the ambassador or the ministries in Moscow, who used their official titles only as cover for espionage activities on behalf of the KGB or GRU (the separate intelligence service within the armed forces). Only in the context of this longstanding Soviet practice is it possible to understand the significance of the inclusion, in the March 1995 Statute on the Russian Ministry of Foreign Affairs, of the provision making the ambassador responsible for all personnel in the Russian embassy.

By no means was this change the only alteration in the organization or practice of Moscow's diplomacy in the post-Soviet period. Although Gorbachev and Shevardnadze already had initiated many changes in foreign ministry structure and personnel, Yeltsin and Kozyrev oversaw an even more thorough housecleaning at the Smolensk Square headquarters of the ministry, which was taken over in its entirety by the Russian Federation. Under the Soviet constitution, a foreign ministry had existed in each of the republics. Kozyrev was appointed as Russian foreign minister by Yeltsin in 1990, and by August 1991 had dismantled the party organization in the Russian ministry and staffed the top echelon with recent graduates of the Moscow Institute of International Relations, together with a few transfers from the Soviet ministry, like himself. When the Soviet ministry was taken over, its "de-ideologization" (and consequent rejuvenation) followed a similar course; all Shevardnadze's deputies were replaced, and many other experienced diplomats either resigned or were removed. Some of the non-Russian personnel left to join the foreign ministries of the other post-Soviet states.

But the new Russian foreign ministry was not a streamlined operation; whereas at the end of 1991 the Soviet ministry had employed 3,700 persons and the Russian ministry 240, by October 1992 the size of the reorganized Russian ministry was 3,200 employees.[49] Initially, there were thirteen departments, including seven dealing with geographic regions, and nine functional administrations. One of the new departments handled relations with other members of the Commonwealth of Independent States—a task for which trained or experienced personnel were mostly unavailable. In November 1993, bilateral relations with the post-Soviet states were shifted to the established regional bureaus, where the level of staff talent was deeper. By mid-1995, there were twenty-seven departments. In addition to these departments, there were the Executive Secretariat, which included the Coordination and Analysis Group, and various ambassadors-at-large with special responsibilities in the realm of conflict resolution.[50]

A government-wide reorganization in 2004, intended to reduce the size of the central bureaucracy and make it less top-heavy, exempted the foreign ministry from the general limitation on the number of deputy ministers—on the grounds that officials of other foreign ministries at the sub-ministerial level would usually expect that their Russian counterpart would hold such a rank. In addition to the senior deputy minister, Valerii Loshchinin, and the general-director of the diplomatic corps, newly appointed foreign minister Sergei Lavrov was allowed to have another five deputy ministers. The number of departments, which had grown to 40, was reduced to 35, and a ceiling of 3,028 was placed on the number of ministry employees.[51]

With the establishment of a direct reporting link from the foreign minister to the president, the formal foreign policy role of the prime minister and his government has been reduced. From the time of Lenin until 1990, when the executive presidency was introduced in the USSR, the prime minister, or head of government, typically played a prominent role in the conduct of Soviet diplomacy. Occupants of this position were members of the CPSU Politburo, usually with significant power bases of their own. Stalin, from 1941 until his death, and Khrushchev, from 1958 until his ouster in 1964, held the post of chairman of the Council of Ministers simultaneously with the leading position in the party Secretariat. Formally responsible to the legislature (the Supreme Soviet) for the administration of affairs of state, the Council of Ministers had among its formal powers the prerogatives to grant and withdraw recognition of foreign states; to establish or break diplomatic relations; to order acts of reprisal; to appoint negotiators and supervise the conduct of negotiations; and to appoint, supervise, and direct Soviet diplomatic representatives abroad. Even after Gorbachev assumed greater executive powers in 1990, the new Cabinet of Ministers retained constitutional powers to "safeguard the country's defense and state security" and to implement its foreign policy. The new constitution of the Russian Federation grants these responsibilities directly to the president.

Nevertheless, the Russian prime minister and his government—and not the Ministry of Foreign Affairs—have been delegated the executive responsibility for the increasingly important function of overseeing Russia's foreign economic relations. Reversing a consolidation that Shevardnadze had accomplished in the fall of 1991, Yeltsin's government created the Ministry of Foreign Economic Relations outside the Ministry of Foreign Affairs, and gave it the primary responsibility for negotiating trade agreements, establishing tariffs and import controls, and promoting exports. The large and sensitive sphere of economic relations with the other former Soviet republics was assigned to yet another body, the Ministry for Economic Cooperation with the Member States of the CIS. In April 1998 both ministries were abolished, their duties split between the foreign ministry and the new Trade and Industries Ministry.

The close relationship of the foreign and defense ministries to the president and their relative insulation from the prime minister and the rest of the government were demonstrated in March 1998. Almost immediately after his dramatic announcement that he was dismissing Prime Minister Viktor Chernomyrdin and his government, President Yeltsin let it be known that his foreign and defense ministers would not be affected by the action. The performance of these ministries thus proceeded relatively smoothly during the lengthy interval in which Yeltsin sought and finally obtained Duma approval of Sergei Kirienko—the young and inexperienced minister of fuels and energy—as Chernomyrdin's successor.

This pattern was disrupted the next time Yeltsin fired a prime minister, but only because the new head of government was Evgenii Primakov, previously the foreign minister. In fact, when Kirienko's government was dismissed in August 1998, in the wake of a major financial crisis that saw both a devaluation of the ruble and a default on government debt, Yeltsin had initially decided to bring Chernomyrdin back as prime minister. But it was clear that the Duma would not accept the man who was widely blamed for the sad state of Russia's economy, and politicians from both wings of the spectrum urged the president to appoint the widely respected Primakov in his stead.

Primakov's deputy, Igor Ivanov, a career diplomat who had been the USSR's last ambassador to Spain, was named to succeed him, but it was evident that the foreign ministry's role during the time of Primakov's premiership (September 1998–May 1999) was merely to implement the policies that Primakov would continue to direct. Nor did the essence of Russian foreign policy change after Primakov's dismissal, which seemed to result not so much from dissatisfaction with his policies as from Yeltsin's jealousy of his growing popularity and irritation at his inability to stave off moves in the Duma for the president's impeachment. Indeed, throughout much of the rest of 1999, Primakov's popularity stayed high, and he was thought for a time to be the most likely successor to Yeltsin. Primakov's successor as prime minister, Sergei Stapashin—a career security official who had served Yeltsin as head of the federal counterintelligence service and as minister of both justice and interior—was himself dismissed in August 1999. In the wake of terrorist attacks in Moscow and the renewal of the war in Chechnya, the sudden rise in popularity of the new prime minister (Yeltsin's fourth in eighteen months), Vladimir Putin, combined with a flurry of negative press evidently orchestrated by the Kremlin and its supporters, eclipsed Primakov and led him to withdraw from presidential politics. But Primakov maintained a cordial relationship with the new president, and the foreign policy line that he had set, still implemented by Ivanov from the foreign ministry, continued to prevail into the first year or so of Putin's presidency.

Putin's first prime minister, Mikhail Kasianov, was—like his chief of the presidential administration—closely associated with Yeltsin's "Family." Experienced as a negotiator on Russia's external debt, he played little role in foreign policy, and his occasional foreign travel was usually associated with promotion of trade relations and foreign investment. Despite regular complaints issuing from the president and his staff about the performance of Kasianov's government, he was left in place until just before Putin's reelection to a second term.

Given the certainty of Putin's reelection, some analysts speculated that Putin might select as the new prime minister one of his strong associates, such as Sergei Ivanov, Dmitri Kozak, or Alexei Kudrin, whose selection would position him as Putin's likely successor at the end of the president's second (and—according to the constitution—last) term. Instead, Putin's choice as new prime minister was the relatively unknown Mikhail Fradkov, most of whose career had been spent in the realm of foreign trade, and whose most recent post had been as Russia's envoy to the European Union.

However, there were other features of Fradkov's biography that suggested ties to the *siloviki*—the members of Putin's entourage whose backgrounds were primarily with the security services. Upon emerging from his university studies in the early 1970s, Fradkov had been posted to the economic affairs staff of the Soviet embassy in India—a posting that often provided cover for an agent of the KGB. In the 1990s, after serving as both minister of foreign trade and minister of trade (both of which were disbanded during his tenure) he briefly held a post as deputy secretary of the Security Council under Putin's closest associate among the *siloviki,* Sergei Ivanov. He had left that position to serve as head of the tax police—yet another post that the seemingly luckless Fradkov lost due to its abolition. The choice of Fradkov seemed to give Putin the opportunity to place in the premiership a man who had proved to be an obedient executor of policy, who had ties to both factions of the president's administration (the *siloviki* and the economic reformers), and who was clearly not considered strong enough to be mistaken as Putin's possible successor—thus allowing the president to defer that choice.

Unlike previous occasions in which the head of government was replaced, the president included the foreign ministry in the 2004 changes. Although he had evidently performed his duties as minister faithfully, Igor Ivanov had never been considered a particularly strong occupant of the post. He had tried in 2002 to deal with suspicions that he was excluded from the inner circle of foreign policy decision making, asserting that, "Not a single fundamental decision on matters of Russian foreign policy has been made in the past several years without my involvement or without regard for the views of the Ministry of Foreign Affairs . . ."[52]

And while Ivanov was handed the potentially significant post of Security Council secretary upon leaving the ministry, his successor—Sergei Lavrov, who had rendered impressive service for ten years as Russia's ambassador to the United Nations—was generally regarded as a stronger and more assertive figure. In an article written shortly after his appointment, Lavrov discussed the priorities of a Russia that was now stronger and more confident in its capabilities, and he seemed to emphasize opportunities to put past differences with the United States aside and to aim for closer cooperation. He saw "no alternative" to the "rational policy" of alliance with the United States in the war on terrorism, improved relations with NATO, and "strategic partnership" with the European Union. Putin's ambitious economic objectives required Russia's integration into the global economy and left no room for "the 'imperial ambitions' of which certain circles accuse Moscow." Lavrov alluded to unilateral actions taken by Washington in Iraq against UN Security Council wishes, but he insisted that "tactical discord" should not impede "rapprochement between the strategic interests of Russia and the United States. . . . We are facing too many problems to waste our time on debates over the past." In the states of the former Soviet Union, he said, Russia's assertion of its vital interests did not imply "putting pressure on other countries." Talk of battles over "spheres of influence" in the CIS was "an odd anachronism."[53]

The Military, the Intelligence Services, and the Making of Foreign Policy

As we have already noted, the creation of the Russian Ministry of Defense in the spring of 1992 reintroduced a powerful rival to the foreign ministry. Especially during the Brezhnev years, the Soviet defense ministry had established itself as a major player in the making of Soviet foreign policy, reflecting the tremendous upsurge in military capabilities in the 1960s and 1970s as well as the growing technical sophistication of weaponry and strategy in the nuclear age. On matters of military strategy and force posture, the judgment of military professionals went unchallenged. Through the minister of defense, these professionals had regular access to the party Politburo. The combination of expertise and access produced a high degree of influence on such issues as budgetary allocations, arms control negotiations, and the use of military capabilities as an instrument of foreign policy.[54]

Nevertheless, the role of the professional military establishment remained restrained and subordinated to the political control of the CPSU. Although the minister of defense was himself a member of the party Politburo and its Defense Council, political supervision of the military was reinforced through the Main Political Administration of the defense ministry, which reported directly to the Central Committee Secretariat. In fact, however, during the period between Khrushchev and Gorbachev, there were such close personal ties and similarities of outlook among the top party and military leaders that the differences of opinion that occasionally came into view paled into insignificance against the backdrop of broad programmatic consensus on Soviet national security policy. In other words, military interests were so well regarded by the civilian leadership that the defense establishment did not need to mount a challenge to party dominance.

In the post-Brezhnev succession, the military sought to maintain this symbiotic relationship. Minister of Defense Dmitri Ustinov played a major role in the selection of Yuri Andropov and Konstantin Chernenko as successors to Brezhnev, and had he not died before Chernenko, it is possible that he could have blocked Gorbachev's rise to the top. There were signs in 1985 and 1986 that the new political leadership was seeking to reduce the foreign policy influence of the military elite. The opening for a dramatic change came in May 1987, when West German teenager Matthias Rust flew his small single-engine plane past vaunted Soviet air defenses to land in Red Square in Moscow (ironically, on Border Guards Day). A furious Gorbachev immediately sacked Minister of Defense Sergei Sokolev and an air defense chief, and he advanced to the top job his own candidate, Colonel General Dmitri Yazov, over more senior claimants. Politically weaker than his predecessors, Yazov nevertheless grew concerned about the deep cuts Gorbachev was making in Soviet defense budgets, partly as a result of arms control agreements that stirred unease among the armed forces, and about the collapse of the Soviet security system in Eastern Europe. The armed forces chief of staff, Marshal Sergei Akhromeev, engaged in a dramatic protest by resigning in December 1988, on the same day that Gorbachev announced unilateral cuts in Soviet military strength. Other military figures, such as General Boris Gromov, the last Soviet commander during the war in Afghanistan, ventured into electoral politics, using the democratization initiated by Gorbachev to gain a platform to condemn his policies. The military was also increasingly involved in the suppression of nationalist and separatist movements within the USSR.

Thus it is not surprising that Yazov was among the coup plotters in August 1991, but his inability to maintain unity in the armed forces contributed significantly to the coup's collapse. Two generals who were close to Yeltsin and had rendered critical aid to coup opponents, air force commander Evgenii Shaposhnikov and paratroops commander Pavel Grachev, became USSR minister and deputy minister of defense after the collapse of the coup. In November, Yeltsin banned activities of the CPSU and the Russian Communist Party within the territory of the Russian Republic, leading to the "de-partification" of the defense ministry and the armed forces. The collapse of Marxist-Leninist ideology, with its strong prohibitions against overt military interference in politics, and the demise of the Main Political Administration as the instrument of party control in the armed forces, removed important restraints on freewheeling political activity in the Soviet military. At the beginning of December 1991, there were widespread rumors that top-ranking military officers were plotting a coup to prevent the collapse of the Soviet Union.

Yeltsin moved quickly to try to reassure the military and gain its support. On December 5 he announced a 90 percent pay increase for all officers, and—in light of the virtual bankruptcy of the USSR—he promised that Russia would pay the salaries. Two days later, he met with the Ukrainian and Belorussian presidents to form the Commonwealth of Independent States. The haste with which this action was taken might well have resulted from the presidents' desire to reassure the Soviet military that a new security structure would be created to replace the USSR. On December 10, in a desperate attempt to save the USSR, Gorbachev met with a group of high-ranking military officials and asked them to support him as commander-in-chief and to endorse his plans to preserve the union. The following day, Yeltsin met with the same group, asking their support of the CIS, and he clearly prevailed in this critical contest with Gorbachev.

At the first summit meeting of the CIS heads of state, on December 30, Yeltsin's plan to retain unified armed forces was set back by the demands of Ukraine, Azerbaijan, and Moldova to form their own national armies. But at the February CIS summit, a joint command was established, responsible for control over strategic nuclear arms, coordination of military doctrines, and resolution of armed conflicts within the CIS and along its borders. Shaposhnikov was named commander-in-chief of the joint forces. However, efforts to create a common security system proved unsuccessful. In March 1992, Yeltsin created a Russian defense ministry, naming himself the acting minister, and in May he created an independent Russian army, with General Grachev as minister of defense. In September, the parliament passed the Law on Defense, which imposed strict state control over the Russian military, but reformers failed to gain approval for a provision that would require a civilian minister of defense.

Despite the principles contained in the new law, imposing control on the military proved extremely difficult, now that prior constraints had been removed and a number of the military's leaders had plunged into political activity. The opinions of military professionals were significantly out of step with the country's civilian leadership, as shown by a January 1992 survey indicating that 71 percent of officers favored restoration of the Soviet state, and a summer 1992 poll that showed that two-thirds would prefer a military-based regime. Ironically, a rallying point for much of this discontent was to be found in Russia's vice president, Major General Aleksandr Rutskoi, whom Yeltsin had handpicked as his running mate in June 1991, in an effort to secure military support for his election. Rutskoi had played an important role in defeating the August coup, personally piloting the air force plane that returned Gorbachev to Moscow. His ambitions ignited, he demanded in October that Yeltsin name him as Russian prime minister, and in December he bitterly criticized Gaidar and the other young reformers on Yeltsin's new team, calling them "young boys in pink shorts, red shirts, and yellow boots." He was also sharply critical of Kozyrev's "liberal Westernizing" policies, voicing statist and interventionist views that apparently were widely shared by his former military colleagues. As Yeltsin's conflict with the Russian parliament escalated in 1993, Rutskoi openly allied himself with the speaker of the Supreme Soviet, Ruslan Khasbulatov, in opposing Yeltsin, and in the October 1993 confrontation he appealed to the Russian military to support the anti-Yeltsin forces.

Initially, Minister of Defense Grachev was hesitant to commit Russian troops to support Yeltsin against the armed parliamentary supporters who stormed the main television station and the municipal administration building. But Grachev yielded to pressure, and Rutskoi, Khasbulatov, and their supporters were forcibly ousted from the Russian White House after bloody fighting that left 145 persons dead and 733 wounded. More than ever before, Yeltsin was in the debt of the military leadership; after the "October events," Grachev seemed to enjoy an expanded influence on Russian policy on such issues as the CFE treaty, NATO enlargement, and peacekeeping activities in the CIS. However, the military did not succeed in fulfilling all its wishes and was notably disappointed in its budget allocations. Nor was Grachev himself a popular political figure, as he became the scapegoat of critics of widespread corruption in the armed forces.

The evident results of Grachev's performance as defense minister—the miserable performance of the armed forces in Chechnya, the high-level corruption and widespread theft of weapons and equipment for resale, and the wretched living conditions of vast numbers of troops—were a favorite target of Lebed's during his presidential campaign, and thus it was not surprising that the minister's dismissal was the first fruit of Lebed's temporary alliance with Yeltsin. The new defense minister, General Igor Rodionov, had been closely associated with Lebed, having once been his commander and having become his political supporter. Since 1989, Rodionov had been commander of the General Staff Academy, where his professional and intellectual strengths were much admired by the top officers who studied under him. He had been sent to the academy with his brilliant military career seemingly in ruins, because it was General Rodionov—as commander of the Transcaucasus Military District—who had been blamed, as "the butcher of Tbilisi," for the massacre of civilians at a separatist rally in the Georgian capital in 1989.[55]

It was not long before Rodionov suffered the same fate as Lebed. He proved to be too slow for Yeltsin's taste in implementing a military reform that would allow further reductions in Russia's defense spending. Yeltsin voiced his outrage on May 22, 1997, at the televised opening session of a meeting of the Defense Council. He fired both Rodionov and the chief of the General Staff, General Viktor Samsonov, replacing Rodionov with General Igor Sergeev, commander of the Strategic Missile Forces since 1992.

The issue of the use of the military to quell internal political disturbances—increasingly sensitive during the Gorbachev years—became acutely controversial in the period surrounding the October 1993 confrontation between Yeltsin and the parliament. Although Grachev and his colleagues had reportedly resisted, the acceptability of this practice was incorporated in the new military doctrine that was adopted by the Security Council and the president in November 1993. Although the document "Basic Provisions of Russian

Military Doctrine" remained classified, it was discussed with the press on November 3 by General Grachev and Oleg Lobov.[56] According to the Security Council secretary, the document spelled out the circumstances under which the military could be activated in internal conflicts: "Proceeding from the premise that the security of Russian Federation citizens and the state as a whole is paramount, the doctrine provides for the use of Army units, Ministry of Internal Affairs internal troops, border troops and other forces in situations in which all other means and capabilities have been exhausted." (As we have seen above, the revised National Security Doctrine further broadened the circumstances under which military force could be used inside the country, to allow it "in the event of emergence of a threat to citizens' lives and also of violent changes to the constitutional system.")

In addition to the "traditional missions" of the armed forces in "deterring and repulsing aggression," the doctrine envisioned an additional mission—"conducting peacekeeping operations within the CIS and, by decision of the UN Security Council and other international bodies, outside the Commonwealth provided they are not in conflict with Russian's interests and Russian law." The possibility of maintaining Russian troops and bases on the territory of other countries was not ruled out, "on the basis, of course, of bilateral and multilateral agreements with the countries in which they would be located." Seeing the chief danger to peace in local wars, the doctrine emphasized the need to create mobile forces that could be dispatched quickly to danger spots. As for the danger of nuclear war, it was said to be considerably reduced, and nuclear weapons were viewed, in Grachev's words, "primarily as a political means of deterring aggression, not as a means to conduct military operations." Accordingly, the military doctrine reversed Gorbachev's earlier pledge that the country would not be the first to use nuclear weapons. That declaration, now identified as mainly a "propaganda thesis," was said to have justified enormous conventional forces and a quest for attaining a superior nuclear potential. These military attributes were no longer necessary in the new circumstances, in which Russia "does not regard any country as its adversary." However, in order to discourage other CIS members from retaining or acquiring nuclear weapons, the Russian doctrine extended the "nuclear umbrella" to all members of the Commonwealth's Collective Security Treaty "and guarantees their territories against any invasion by any country that is an ally of any nuclear power."

As we described above, Putin enunciated a "new military doctrine" when he spoke to the top military brass in October 2003. He expressed confidence that Russia had sufficient strategic missile strength—pressing into service previously stockpiled SS-19 missiles with multiple warheads to replace older missiles—to overcome any potential American anti-missile system. But the defense ministry document warned that Russia would have to ratchet up its strategic forces and change its plans to cut the size of the total armed forces if NATO failed to change its own offensive military doctrine, with its "anti-Russian orientation" and plans to "lower the threshold of using nuclear weapons." At the same time, Putin and Minister of Defense Ivanov stressed that Russia's military command would be paying far more attention in its troop training to peace operations, special operations, anti-terrorist actions, and local wars.[57] On the whole, in its emphasis on mobile units and peacekeeping responsibilities, especially in the CIS, the new Russian military doctrine clearly envisaged the armed forces as an instrument of the country's foreign policy.

By giving the professional military leaders a major role in developing the political element of the doctrine—as he did in a well-publicized meeting of the Security Council in February 1993—Boris Yeltsin had underscored the military's significant influence on the formulation of national security policy.[58] As the internal crisis in the military worsened in the latter part of the 1990s, exacerbated by the memory of its inept and demoralizing performance in Chechnya, General Sergeev played a highly visible role in the intensifying national debate on the critical questions of further refining the military doctrine, funding the armed forces budget, and taking steps toward "military reform"—a goal that would be prominent for years to come.

Only two months after Sergeev's appointment, Yeltsin issued the first decrees describing the proposed military reform. The total size of the armed forces was to be cut by half a million, to 1.2 million; conscription was eventually to be abolished, but not by Yeltsin's original target date of 2000. Future annual military spending was to be limited to 3.5 percent of GNP, down from a 1991 level of 7.2 percent. In the first stage of reductions, 300,000 civilian jobs were to be cut, and various activities not directly related to defense (such as road construction) were to be transferred to civilian agencies. Expenses of the administrative apparatus of the defense ministry were to be limited to 1 percent of the total defense budget. There was no announced plan, however, to reduce the ratio of officers to enlisted men from its current level of 1:1.

Given Sergeev's prior position as commander of the Strategic Missile Forces (SMF), it was not surprising that he recommended merging into it the Military Space Forces and Antimissile Defense Forces, to create the unified Missile Forces. In 1998, the Air Force and the Air Defense Force were to be combined, leaving a total of four branches in the armed forces. Also reflecting Sergeev's background was the proposal to abolish the high command of the Ground Forces and replace it with an administration within the ministry, transferring the function of territorial management to military districts (which were to be reduced in number from eight to six). Moreover, the Ground Forces would take the deepest cuts. Most controversial of all was the proposal to put all troops, including the sizable forces of the border guards and the interior ministry, under the command of a single, general-purpose troop commander within each military district. Costs of providing for discharged servicemen and of the proposed doubling in officer pay were to be provided from funds received from the sale of surplus military equipment to foreign buyers.[59]

Yeltsin rewarded Sergeev's reform initiatives by promoting him to the rank of marshal, but in light of the heavy political opposition—including that of the powerful heads of the Interior Ministry and the Border Guards—and the declining prospect of needed funds in the wake of the 1998 financial crisis, it did not prove possible during the remainder of Yeltsin's presidency to implement all aspects of the proposed military reform. Whereas a successful reform could at best have brought stability to a risky and unpredictable situation in Russia's military, a failure could have had drastic consequences—with possible scenarios including not only the breakup of Russia's military into semiautonomous regional units or its cooptation by criminal gangs, but also an outright attempt to seize political power.

Nevertheless, in the absence of thoroughgoing reform, the state of Russia's military at the end of the 1990s was alarming. As one American expert described it, "Discipline has collapsed, equipment is becoming antiquated, morale has sunk to an all-time low, good officers and non-commissioned officers are leaving the service, the country's generals have been politicized, and Moscow's ability to ensure the military's obedience in a crisis is doubtful."[60] Nothing in its performance in the war in Chechnya belied this pessimistic appraisal of Russian military capability.

Measuring annual military spending in Russia is a complex undertaking, since many categories of expenditure—amounting to up to one-half of the total—are not contained in published defense budgets, appearing in other parts of the state budget or coming from nonbudgeted sources. Moreover, during Yeltsin's tenure, the military rarely received the full amount actually budgeted. One British specialist has estimated that Russia's true defense spending fell in 1998 to $42 billion, a level only one-third of 1992 expenditures, if constant 2000 prices are used. Afterward, he noted, spending probably increased another 20 percent as a result of Russia's improved revenue situation. This amounts to 5 percent of Russia's gross domestic product—still below 1991 Soviet levels but far above Yeltsin's target of 3.5 percent. Two-thirds of the total went to the regular armed forces, with the rest devoted to civilian personnel and paramilitary units.[61]

Another measure reported in the West during the first year of Putin's presidency put the total of Russia's military and law-enforcement expenditures at 35 percent of the entire federal budget. This same report quoted Sergei Ivanov as complaining that "about 70 percent of the military budget is being spent merely to maintain troops and bureaucrats, leaving precious little to maintaining and upgrading equipment."[62] At the same time, the leading Russian military journalist, Pavel Felgengauer, reported manpower figures (previously secret but newly released by the Security Council) of just over 2 million servicemen and 966,000 civilians in the dozen or so military-related ministries. Omitted from this figure are regional police and paramilitary units; "if they are included in the count, the true figure is not 3 million, but . . . closer to 5 million." Felgengauer concluded: "The general figure seems to have remained static during the last decade. . . . The bottom line of the Security Council Statement is this: There has been no genuine military reform in this country, nor any real attempt to demilitarize the country since the demise of the Soviet Union. Many observers knew this all along, but today the ugly fact is official."[63]

President Putin, reportedly frustrated with the failure of numerous efforts to achieve meaningful cuts in military manpower and corresponding increases in efficiency, devoted three meetings of the Security Council to the subject during the second half of 2000. The issue was complicated by a major split in the military leadership over whether cuts should fall primarily on strategic or conventional forces. The minister of defense, Marshal Sergeev, as former commander of the Strategic Missile Forces, had evidently devoted virtually all procurement funds since 1997 to new-generation SS-25 and SS-27 missiles. The armed forces chief of staff, General Anatolii Kvashnin, on the heels of the embarrassing military performance in Chechnya and the perceived threat following the NATO attack in Kosovo, submitted a "sensational" plan to senior ministry officials in July 2000. Kvashnin's plan called for shifting resources to conventional forces and sharply reducing the numbers of strategic warheads (from about 6,000 to 1,500), while altogether eliminating the Strategic Missile Forces as a separate branch of the armed forces and subordinating its assets to the air force. Not surprisingly, Sergeev labeled this plan "criminal stupidity." When the controversy exploded in the press, Putin ordered a truce.

Security Council meetings in August, September, and November did not seem fully to resolve the conflict. Manpower reduction allocations announced to the State Duma in November seemed to favor Kvashnin's side of the argument. By 2010, the regular armed forces were to be cut from 1.2 million to about 850,000. In 2001 the Strategic Missile Forces would lose the missile space defense and military space commands, which would be subordinated to the General Staff, and the SMF would be downgraded from a service to an arm in 2002 and incorporated into the air force in 2006.[64]

Felgengauer, however, was reporting that many of the positions targeted for cuts were currently unoccupied, and that reports coming from commanders in the field suggested that "the announced draconian cutbacks in military personnel are in fact superficial." Nor was the presumed fate of the Strategic Missile Forces being taken by its commander as final. In the face of reports that his branch would lose up to 50 percent of its present strength and be downgraded, General Vladimir Yakovlev told Felgengauer, "'the international situation may change,' and the planned cuts may be reversed. If the United States begins to build a national missile defense in violation of the 1972 ABM treaty, Russia may be compensated by Washington allowing it to retain multiple-warhead land-based ICBMs that are banned by the START II arms control treaty, said Yakovlev." President Putin, however, immediately signaled his disagreement with Yakovlev. He renewed the Russian offer to cut the number of Russian and U.S. strategic warheads in a START III agreement to 1,500 each, but he insisted that the United States should not build the National Missile Defense (NMD).[65]

Despite the Russian protests, President Bush proceeded with notification of U.S. withdrawal from the ABM Treaty and its intention to build NMD, as we describe more fully in chapter 9. Labeling the action a "mistake," Putin nevertheless expressed his continuing interests in further cuts in offensive weapons systems. The agreement, signed in June 2003, called for substantial reductions in deployed forces over a ten-year period, but it removed the START II prohibition on land-based missiles with multiple warheads. This enabled Putin to slow down the schedule of production of new Topol missiles—the extremely expensive alternative the Russians had faced if START II prohibitions had remained—and to replace aging missiles with SS-19 land-based missiles with multiple warheads that had been stockpiled without fuel and were said to be capable of defeating any missile defense system.[66]

Early in 2004 Putin was making even bolder claims about Russian strategic weaponry, declaring that Russia had a cutting-edge intercontinental "hypersonic" maneuverable weapons system that "no other country on earth" possesses. However, the credibility of claims of Russian strategic capability had already been weakened by the tragic sinking of the *Kursk*, a submarine of the most advanced design in the Russian fleet, in August 2000. They were further undermined in February 2004, during a large strategic command-and-staff training exercise, when—with Putin looking on—an SS-23 missile failed to launch from a nuclear submarine. The naval commander tried to cover up the embarrassing failure by claiming that only a "virtual launch" had actually been intended in the first place.[67]

Amidst all the pressure for building new strategic weaponry, Pavel Felgengauer, decrying the evident desire of Russian generals to replay the Cold War, gloomily concluded that Russia had still not opted for a professional military, but was simply engaged in propping up the old one. The generals, he concluded, did not want genuine reform but, rather, still sought restoration of their former status.[68] Evidently sharing that pessimistic assessment, Putin in March 2001 took a dramatic step toward ensuring the implementation of reform by replacing Marshal Sergeev with a (newly minted) civilian, his trusted colleague Sergei Ivanov. To assist the new minister in gaining control of defense ministry finances, he assigned the former deputy finance minister, Liubov Kudelina, as deputy minister of defense—the first female to hold such a high post in the military hierarchy.

Ivanov's progress in advancing the cause of military reform during the rest of Putin's first term was barely discernable. Declaring that the "current level of direct military danger for Russia can be rated as low," he sought to reduce the total level of troop strength, which stood at 1.16 million in 2003, to one million by 2005. More ambitiously, he sought to implement a program—promised by Yeltsin to be in place by 2000—to replace the unpopular and unfair system of military conscription with a "contract" (i.e., volunteer) military force capable of much greater professionalism.[69] But the minister's goals were clearly being resisted by the General Staff of the Armed Forces, and especially by its chief, General Kvashnin. Earlier, the Russian press had reported the General Staff's opposition to the positioning of U.S. troops in Central Asia, the abandonment of Russian facilities in Cuba and Vietnam, and the accommodation with NATO, which Kvashnin had publicly labeled "a public relations smoke screen."[70] Ivanov fired back by declaring that the General Staff had become bogged down in "administrative routine." Weary of the public quarrelling, Putin in June 2004 pushed through the Duma an amendment to the 1996 Law on Defense that stripped the General Staff of its responsibility for operational control of the Russian armed forces, limiting its role to strategic planning.[71]

Shortly thereafter, in the wake of a successful attack by Chechen guerrillas on Nazran, the capital of neighboring Ingushetia, Kvashnin was removed from his post (together with three other officials from the Interior Ministry and FSB). He was replaced by his deputy, General Yuri Baluyevskii, a soldier known as a good theoretician, but lacking in high-level command experience. When the reorganization of the Ministry of Defense was announced in August, it reportedly left the General Staff "almost an empty shell." Its chief was now to be appointed by the minister rather than by the president, and its role was to be focused on "situational analysis and development of troop deployment plans." With the military's power to resist reform now presumably limited, it was expected that Ivanov would be freer to accomplish reform, beginning with a planned reduction of conscript service to one year by 2008, and implementation of a plan to provide mortgage-financed housing as an incentive for recruitment of contract soldiers.[72]

Recovery of Russia's military capabilities was certainly being aided by the recovery of its economy, fueled by soaring revenues from petroleum exports. The defense budget proposed for 2005 amounted to $18 billion, an increase of 28 percent from the 2004 allocation. However, the increase was smaller once it was adjusted for inflation, and Kvashnin had publicly derided it as inadequate shortly before his dismissal. At 2.8 percent of GDP, it remained below the level (3.5 percent) once targeted by Yeltsin. Although, as we noted above, the declared defense budget is somewhat misleading, given the existence of large numbers of armed personnel in other government agencies, it remains at less than 5 percent of the U.S. budget and far below the level of expenditure in the Soviet years. However, the increase did allow a certain amount of catch-up, especially in expenditures on research and development and acquisition of military weaponry—but there was much more catching up required if Russia's declared needs were to be satisfied. Military expert Aleksei Arbatov noted that "less than twenty percent of the weapons that troops now have are relatively new—purchased less than ten years ago." And he complained that real progress in reequipping the armed forces and sustaining the Russian defense industry would not come until the size of the military had been reduced to a level well below Ivanov's announced target of one million. In Arbatov's words, "no reasonable budget can sustain an army consisting of 1.2 million men. And there is no need for such an army. After all, we are not going to start another Great Patriotic War."[73]

Together with the military, the intelligence service was another "power-wielding" institutional actor that regularly found a place at the table when foreign policy decisions were made in the Soviet Union. It continues to do so, without having undergone significant reform, in democratizing Russia. In the USSR, the Committee for State Security (KGB) played an important role not only in conducting intelligence activity in support of foreign policy but also in the policymaking process. Almost continuously since 1973, the director of the KGB had been a member of the key decision-making body, the CPSU Politburo. Indeed, Yuri Andropov, who held this position from 1967 to 1982, managed to succeed Brezhnev as general secretary of the CPSU—a mark of the prestige and importance attained by the KGB in the post-Khrushchev period. Vladimir Kriuchkov, whom Gorbachev appointed director in 1988, again underscored the key role of his agency by leading the attempted coup of August 1991.

In the implementation of foreign policy, the first chief directorate of the KGB had primary responsibility for espionage, including the collection and dissemination of intelligence, the surveillance of Soviet citizens abroad, penetration of "anti-Soviet agencies" abroad, and the coordination of the intelligence efforts of other agencies. As we have seen, it frequently used diplomatic and journalistic "covers" for its agents, and some Soviet embassies were reported to have had two-thirds of the members of their staffs on the KGB payroll. The other components of the KGB were responsible for counterintelligence, military counterintelligence, transportation security, antiterrorism, economic crime and corruption, surveillance, communications, security guards, and border guards.

The best available evidence on the role of the intelligence and security services in post-Soviet Russia demonstrates that Yeltsin did not truly curb the powers of these agencies, but rather chose to coopt their support, not only to perform foreign intelligence functions, but also to assist him in his struggle against his political opponents.[74] The price he paid for these services is that the successors to the KGB continued to play a significant policymaking role. No longer do intelligence personnel perform their functions as a single agency, however. Largely in response to public pressure after the August coup, Gorbachev placed the KGB under the direction of one of his reformist colleagues, Vladimir Bakatin, who presided over a reorganization that split it into three separate agencies. As was the case with the post-coup Soviet foreign ministry and military, this institution was simply transferred to Russian control. After further reorganization, by the end of January 1992 there were five agencies: the Ministry of Security, which absorbed the six KGB directorates responsible for internal security and counterintelligence; the Federal Agency for Government Communications and Information (FAPSI); the Foreign Intelligence Service (SVR); the Main Guard Directorate, later renamed the Federal Protection Service (out of which the Presidential Security Service was created as a separate agency from November 1993 through June 1996); and the Committee for the Protection of the Russian Border. This last agency, responsible for the border guards, was soon put under the command of the Ministry of Security, but in December 1993 it again became a separate agency, called the Federal Border Service (FPS). The Ministry of Security itself was renamed at the same time, becoming the Federal Counterintelligence Service; its name changed again, after April 1995, when it became the Federal Security Service (FSB).

The dispersal of KGB functions into five agencies and the dizzying succession of different names did not really diminish the power of the security apparatus or disguise the fact that most of its personnel were inherited from the KGB. Under the prior constitution, the agencies were subject to parliamentary oversight through the Supreme Soviet Committee on Defense and Security, but the deputy who headed the committee was himself a security official—a situation that created a watchdog mechanism that was hardly effective. A law on the powers of the security services, passed in July 1992, was strikingly similar to the law on the KGB that had been passed by the USSR Supreme Soviet the previous year.

The vacillating behavior of the "power ministries" during the "October days" of 1993 led to another reorganization, but the new constitution provided for even less legislative oversight than before. Yeltsin's emphasis in 1994 on combating crime, together with the invasion of Chechnya at the end of that year, produced a situation in which the investigative powers of security agencies were expanded and safeguards of individual liberties were further constrained. A new law on the security services, passed in April 1995, confirmed this broadened authority, under the president's direct control, and resulted, in the opinion of a Western scholar, in "a security apparatus whose legal powers more than matched those of the KGB."[75]

The directors of all five of the security agencies were made members of the Security Council, and three were also members of the short-lived Defense Council and Foreign Policy Council. On these councils, they clearly played a role in advising the president on issues of foreign and defense policy. Indeed, from the time the Security Council decided upon military action in Chechnya in December 1994 until their dismissal in June 1996, two of these officials—General Aleksandr Korzhakov, the chief of Yeltsin's bodyguards, and General Mikhail Barsukov, head of the Main Guard Directorate and then of the Federal Security Service—seemed to exert especially strong and wide-ranging influence upon Yeltsin.

Subsequently, however, Yeltsin's preference for personnel appointments from the ranks of the security services became even more pronounced. His last three Security Council secretaries (Bordiuzha, Putin, and Ivanov) and his last three prime ministers (Primakov, Stepashin, and Putin) had spent most of their careers in the security or intelligence services. His ultimate successor as president, Vladimir Putin, whose name appears in both lists, was hardly the most politically prominent of these individuals, having risen only to the rank of lieutenant colonel in the KGB, and having had no ministerial experience prior to 1998. Rising quickly in the presidential administration following his move from St. Petersburg to Moscow in 1996, Putin soon caught Yeltsin's eye.

In the third volume of his memoirs, Yeltsin commented on the qualities that commended Putin to him: "a person who was intellectual, democratic, and who could think anew, but who was firm in the military manner." Yeltsin reported that he debated the comparative assets of Stepashin and Putin, concluding that the former was "soft and he liked to pose a bit," while Putin "had the will and the resolve" but did not try to impose himself on the president: "Unlike other deputies, who were always trying to lay out their visions of Russia and the world, Putin did not try to strike up conversations with me."[76] Given his background, it is not surprising that Putin appointed former colleagues from the KGB to key positions (Sergei Ivanov and Sergei Lebedev, and two of the presidential administrators of the super-regions, for example), or that he continued Yeltsin's practice of consulting the security agencies on foreign policy questions.

The security agency that has had the most direct operational impact on foreign policy is the Foreign Intelligence Service, which was headed first by Evgenii Primakov and then—after he became foreign minister—by his former deputy, General Viacheslav Trubnikov. In May 2000 Trubnikov became a deputy foreign minister and was replaced by Putin's former colleague, Sergei Lebedev. All three had previously been employed overseas as Soviet intelligence operatives under cover—Primakov in the Middle East, Trubnikov in South Asia, and Lebedev (like Putin himself) in East Germany—thereby achieving a degree of professional respect that helped their agency remain less controversial than the other security services. Under the Law on Foreign Intelligence, passed in August 1992, the agency reports directly to the president, with little parliamentary oversight. Under Primakov's guidance, the SVR produced major assessments that took strong positions on three important foreign policy issues: warning about the dangers of nuclear proliferation, pointing out the likely adverse effects of NATO enlargement on Russia's security, and warning against Western opposition to efforts to promote CIS economic and political integration.

In April 1994, Yeltsin made an unusual appearance at the headquarters of the SVR at Yasenevo, giving the agency a strong endorsement and making it clear that it would play a key role in designing and implementing foreign policy. At a time when the military budget was being cut, he told the SVR staff, their agency had become the most important guarantee of the country's security. He made special mention of its role in achieving economic security, in combating organized crime, and in cooperating in the international efforts to curb terrorism, nuclear proliferation, and drug trafficking. Not least important was the objective of acquiring "preemptive information" on the plans and intentions of the West toward the states of the CIS, and of monitoring the situation along the country's borders.[77]

The Federal Border Service also played an important foreign policy role, since it assumed responsibility for guarding the outside borders of the entire Commonwealth of Independent States. Russia alone shares borders with eighteen countries, five of which are in the CIS, and has over 60,000 kilometers of borders to protect; but Russian security doctrine is based on the premise that it is the outer borders of the CIS that are most vital to Russia's security, and since most CIS countries lack the manpower or resources to secure their own borders, the Russian Federal Border Service—which was taken over from the KGB Border Guards—assumed the function. With respect to the borders it shared with CIS countries, Moscow sought to establish a minimal border regime—"transparent borders"—with Belarus, Kazakhstan, Ukraine, Georgia, and Azerbaijan. This proved to be more manageable with the former two states than with the others. Ukraine created its own border troops and has disagreed with the Russians on the extent of patrolling on their common border, and conflict in the Caucasus, especially after the outbreak of war in Chechnya, has required tighter border controls on the movement of personnel and goods on the borders with Georgia and Azerbaijan. In March 2003 the FPS was again merged with the Federal Security Service (FSB); and at the same time, FAPSI was abolished and its functions were divided between the FSB and the Ministry of Defense. There were persisting rumors that the two remaining independent agencies of the former KGB, the Foreign Intelligence Service and the Federal Protective Service, would meet the same fate, allowing the FSB finally to assume to full range of functions that once belonged to the KGB. However, when the reorganization of the security services was announced in July 2004, as part of the government-wide "streamlining" process, the FSB was given the new status of ministry but the anticipated merger (though still possibly in the cards) did not take place.

Parliament, Political Parties, and Public Opinion

For most of the Soviet period, the form of government prescribed in the constitution was parliamentary, with the administrative organs of the Soviet state responsible to the USSR Supreme Soviet. Until changes were made in 1989, this bicameral national legislature, comprising a total of 1,500 deputies elected to four-year terms, met for only a few days each year. Between sessions, the Supreme Soviet's powers were exercised by its Presidium, a body of some three dozen members that served as a collective head of state for the USSR and that was empowered to receive foreign ambassadors, ratify or abrogate treaties, and declare war.

The changes made under Gorbachev created the 2,250-member Congress of People's Deputies, which met in a brief annual session to approve the state plan and budget and to consider constitutional amendments. More routine legislative functions were performed by a permanently sitting bicameral inner parliament—the Supreme Soviet—with 542 deputies, chosen from the Congress membership. Sitting in two sessions per year, of three to four months each, the Supreme Soviet became a forum of genuine debate and legislative power. Standing joint committees had responsibilities for the oversight of government ministries, including those that dealt with foreign and defense policy. Gorbachev chaired the new legislature in its initial year, but with the creation of the executive presidency, the government assumed a presidential rather than a parliamentary form. Following the August coup, the Congress of People's

Deputies was summoned to Moscow and virtually ordered by Gorbachev and Yeltsin to dissolve itself, in favor of the interim State Council.

The legislatures of the republics, including Russia, were modeled on the USSR legislature. Thus, when the Russian Federation became independent, its legislative branch consisted of the Congress of People's Deputies, which had the power to determine the general lines of foreign and domestic policy, to impeach the president, or to amend the constitution; and a two-chamber Supreme Soviet—often meeting as a single unit—which considered legislation and controlled the government. The congress met only a few times a year and had more than one thousand members, but the Supreme Soviet sat from six to eight months and had 250 members. The legislature was elected in 1990—when the CPSU still dominated Soviet politics—for a five-year term, and thus seemed destined to clash with Yeltsin's policies. Nevertheless, Yeltsin was granted emergency powers in August and October 1991, and on November 2 the congress gave him the power for one year to bypass the legislature in appointing ministers and passing economic decrees. Yeltsin appointed himself as prime minister and formed a "reform cabinet" whose "shock therapy" on the economy soon aroused parliamentary opposition.

There ensued a titanic struggle between legislature and executive that dominated Russian politics in 1992 and 1993. Ruslan Khasbulatov, an ethnic Chechen handpicked by Yeltsin to succeed him as chairman ("speaker") of the Presidium of the Supreme Soviet at the time of his election to the Russian presidency, utilized the presidium's right to issue decrees to establish a strong power base in opposition to Yeltsin, and he urged the establishment of a parliamentary republic with a weak presidency. The parliament's obstructionist tactics occasionally extended beyond questions of domestic politics and economic reform and into the realm of foreign policy—both on issues relating to the near abroad, such as disputes with Ukraine over the Crimea and the Black Sea fleet, and those connected with the "far abroad," such as the START II treaty and the conflict in Yugoslavia; but for the most part, the International Affairs Committee of the Supreme Soviet—chaired by centrist politicians Vladimir Lukin and Evgenii Ambartsumov—while critical of Kozyrev's foreign ministry, was more moderate and less confrontational in its behavior.

Yeltsin convened the Constitutional Assembly in the summer of 1993, hoping that adoption of a new constitution would force new parliamentary elections; but he did not succeed in pushing the draft through to adoption. On September 21, he issued a decree dissolving the Supreme Soviet and the congress. The resistance mounted by Khasbulatov and his ally, Vice President Rutskoi, was defeated in a bloody confrontation, badly damaging Yeltsin's reputation in the process.

The constitution adopted in the December 1993 referendum created the bicameral Federal Assembly: an upper house, the Federation Council, with 178 representatives chosen from the eighty-nine units of the federation; and a lower chamber, the State Duma, with 450 deputies. The Federation Council, which at first included many regional and republican political officials, has special powers on matters affecting the regions and republics, but it also is given sole power to approve the use of the armed forces outside the Russian Federation. The upper house has three committees that deal with foreign policy matters: International Affairs, Security and Defense, and CIS Affairs.

Both houses must pass a bill by majority vote for it to become law, but a two-thirds vote of each house is required to override a presidential veto or to cancel a presidential decree. The Duma, half of whose membership is elected by a proportional party-list method and half from single-member districts, does much of its work in committees. Five of these relate to international issues: the committees for International Affairs, Security, CIS Affairs and Links with Compatriots, Defense, and Geopolitical Questions.

The 1993 constitution, as we have seen, grants most of the foreign-policy–making power to the president. Among the limited formal powers of the Duma and Federation Council in this realm is the power to ratify and denounce treaties. Nevertheless, to the consternation of the president and the occasional confusion of foreign states, the State Duma has been inclined to pass nonbinding resolutions stating positions contrary to those of the government on sensitive foreign policy issues—particularly territorial issues with other post-Soviet states. Yeltsin bluntly addressed this matter at the March 1997 CIS summit:

> I want to stress that Russia's foreign policy, including that with regard to the other CIS countries, is determined by the President. Official foreign policy statements can be made, in addition to myself, by the Chairman of the Government and the Foreign Minister. I beg you to proceed from this fact. It goes without saying that we could raise the issue of the unpleasant remarks made by parliamentarians, governors, politicians, and bureaucratic officials. We do not do this and are not going to do this in the future. We know behind whose words the policy of the state is.[78]

On the whole, parliamentary influence on Russian foreign policy has been quite limited. If anything, its impact is more indirect than direct, for by serving as a forum for the articulation of dissenting opinions that are widely shared among politicians and elements of the public, parliament helps shape the political climate in which executive decisions must be made, and it may thereby influence the tone and tactics, as opposed to the basic directions, of foreign policy.[79]

As we noted earlier, the greater openness of the political process in Russia, and the requirement that political elites engage in genuine electoral competition, has made policymakers pay more attention than ever before to public opinion on international issues; but Russia is still far from being a mature, functioning democracy, and the channels through which public attitudes are transmitted into the political process are in their infancy. Political parties, in particular, remain too undeveloped as organizations to have any major impact on foreign policy. While the opposition parties that dominated the Dumas elected in 1993 and 1995—Zhirinovskii's Liberal Democratic Party and the Communist Party of the Russian Federation—attempted to capitalize on the public's confusion about Russia's national identity and its sense of national humiliation, surveys showed the public to be less nationalistic and less favorable to the use of force than were the party elites. Moreover, election polls have shown that there are a wide variety of foreign policy viewpoints among each party's voters, making it extremely difficult to predict a voter's party choice on the basis of his attitudes about Russia's external relations.[80]

The results of the December 1999 parliamentary elections, which propelled the new pro-Kremlin Unity Party into the controlling role in the State Duma, were clearly a consequence of Prime Minister Putin's own popularity—won largely through his vigorous prosecution of war in Chechnya. But credit must also be given to Putin's tactical skill. The composition of the new Duma and Putin's maneuver in temporarily dividing its leadership posts between the Unity Party and the Communist Party effectively defanged the noncommunist political opposition. Finally, the timing of the presidential election—resulting from Yeltsin's prematurely vacating the office—threw the opposition off balance, both by shortening the campaign and by avoiding a possible change in public mood over the war in Chechnya.

The opposition was even more decimated in the 2003 parliamentary elections. By then the centrist parties created by Primakov and Moscow Mayor Yuri Luzhkov had merged with the Unity Party, forming a pro-Putin centrist bloc called United Russia. In order to split the leftist and ultranationalist vote, the Kremlin stage-managed the creation of a new bloc called motherland. State-controlled television severely limited the access of opposition parties, and their electoral strength was further sapped by some cases of outright fraud. When the results were announced, United Russia commanded a two-thirds majority in the new Duma, allowing it to assume all of the leadership posts and even to initiate amendments of the constitution—sparking rumors that it might even try to engineer a third term for Putin.

Regional governors, many of whom had joined forces with the Primakov-Luzhkov opposition bloc early in the parliamentary election campaign, scrambled to get on board the Putin bandwagon. Putin, determined to gather more power in the central state institutions, skillfully outmaneuvered the regional bosses. The parliament acceded to Putin's proposal to remove regional executives and legislative chairs from the Federation Council. Although regions retained the right to select their representatives, the reform had the effect of replacing regional leaders with full-time senators, thereby reducing their prominence as national political figures and also depriving them of the parliamentary immunity from prosecution. The president also gained the power to remove regional governors for illegal activities.

As a consolation prize for the governors, Putin established the new State Council. This purely consultative body, composed of the heads of the eighty-nine "subjects of the federation," was to be guided by a presidium on which seven regional leaders would serve rotating six-month terms. The interposition of the new layer of presidential representatives in seven super-regions, combined with the likely future effort to consolidate regions, further enhanced central power.

Measures had already been taken to reduce the quasi-autonomous role that the "subjects of the federation"—the regions and republics and the cities of Moscow and St. Petersburg—had gradually assumed in the realms of foreign economic relations and foreign policy. The January 1999 Law on Coordination of the Foreign Relations and International Trade of the Subjects of the Russian Federation required that they submit drafts of proposed international agreements to the foreign ministry for its approval. The law also required advance notice when negotiations were to be conducted with foreign entities, as well as approval for opening offices abroad. If approved by central authorities, agreements made by the "subjects" were not to have the status of treaties, and their offices were not to be accorded diplomatic status.[81]

Interest groups in Russia initially appeared to be poorly organized and fragmented. While it was possible to identify certain economic interests with particular policy preferences—for example, defense industrialists with protectionism and higher defense spending—early research studies of the lobbying activities of interest groups concluded that they had been of limited effectiveness.[82] However, by 1996 several large financial-industrial groups were exerting increasing influence on the policymaking process. Most of these groups had been built on the foundations of large banks, which had prospered through government favoritism, having been authorized to handle (and profit from) deposits of government funds. As participants in the "loans for shares" stage of privatization in 1995, the owners of these banks had parlayed relatively small investments into controlling shares of large enterprises, especially in the fields of energy and metals. Acquisition of major shares of newspapers, magazines, and television networks further enhanced the political power of this small group of Russian businessmen.[83]

Six of the most powerful of these emerging oligarchs had coordinated with Anatolii Chubais to organize and finance Boris Yeltsin's reelection campaign in 1996. By mid-1997, their interests had begun to diverge; not only were the leading "clans" quarreling among themselves, but some were also using their media outlets to attack decisions made by Yeltsin's government. Chubais, now first deputy prime minister and the powerful leader of the government's economic reform program, became embroiled in an especially bitter controversy with Boris Berezovskii, reputedly the wealthiest of the "new Russians." Having himself been appointed deputy secretary of the Security Council, Berezovskii had special responsibilities for economic reconstruction in Chechnya. In November 1997 Chubais apparently persuaded Yeltsin to dismiss him on grounds of conflict of interest. Berezovskii fired back by revealing that a large payment had been made by a rival oligarch to Chubais and four of his associates, in the form of an advance on royalties for a proposed book. Badly weakened by the ensuing scandal, Chubais was singled out for dismissal when Yeltsin fired the entire government in March 1998.

Although it appeared, as the 2000 elections approached, that the major clans had not been able to maintain their unity, it was nevertheless clear that these business oligarchs, who collectively controlled over one-fourth of Russia's economy, would exercise considerable influence on the choice of Yeltsin's successor; but their political power was not limited to the electoral arena. Of equal interest for our purposes is the fact that several of them have in effect developed "foreign policies" in support of their financial interests. Thus, for example, Gazprom—Russia's largest company and largest earner of foreign currency, formerly managed by ex-premier Viktor Chernomyrdin—has clearly sought to influence Russia's dealings with countries with which it has natural gas supply, exploration, or distribution contracts.

The successor to the Soviet Ministry of the Gas Industry, Gazprom has a near monopoly of natural gas production and transport in Russia. With almost 300,000 employees, it accounts for 40 percent of Russia's tax revenues and 7 percent of its GDP. It has about 27 percent of the world gas production, 38 percent of estimated reserves, and 15 percent of the global gas transport network. Almost 40 percent of its ownership has been retained by the Russian state, but a large part of these shares was managed by the chief executive officer (CEO), Rem Viakhirev—one of the most powerful of Russia's "oligarchs."[84] Unable to collect cash payments for gas supplies from other Russian companies, Gazprom has acquired shares in their ownership instead. Among its substantial investments was a large share of Vladimir Gusinskii's media company, Media-Most, which includes Russia's Independent Television Network (NTV). Already in possession of a 37 percent share of the

Public Radio and Television Broadcasting Company (ORT), Russia's largest network, in April 2001 Gazprom's media subsidiary seized control of NTV's board and installed a new management, less critical of the Kremlin.

Gazprom exports more than one-third of its gas production, with about two-thirds going to Europe and the remainder to the states of the Commonwealth of Independent States. Western Europe obtains more than one-quarter of its gas from Gazprom. A major new pipeline network, connecting the Yamal peninsula to Europe, is under construction. The world's deepest undersea pipeline, *Goluboli potok* (Blue Stream)—extending under the Black Sea from Russia to Turkey—was completed in 2003.

As might be expected, Gazprom employs its considerable influence to support Russian policies that bolster its interests in expanding its markets and building new pipelines. Consummation of the Russia-Belarus Union would give Gazprom more direct control over its pipeline routes to Europe; if Ukraine were also to enter the union, that control would be complete. (The May 2001 appointment of Viktor Chernomyrdin, former Gazprom chairman and former premier, as Russia's ambassador to Ukraine prompted further speculation along those lines.) Strong Russian influence in the Central Asian states—and corresponding reduction in American influence—promotes Gazprom's interests in participating in proposed gas pipelines to China and India. Friendly relations with Iran serve the company's interests, given its participation in the joint exploration of the South Persia fields. Sometimes, the company's tactics are heavy-handed, generating hostility toward Russia itself. For example, as described in the Russian press by a source close to the government, Gazprom was "demonized" by Bulgarian interests and portrayed as a tool of Russian imperialism in the Balkans after it demanded that Bulgaria pay for its gas in convertible currency.[85] And Russia's relations with Turkey were strained in 2003 when Turkey halted its gas purchases from Gazprom because of its claims that the company was charging unreasonably high prices.

As we discuss in chapter 8, Russia's foreign policy is also influenced by its strong interest in promoting the sales of its military hardware to foreign countries. The Russian defense industry could not survive on the orders that it receives from the Russian armed forces alone, and defense manufacturers form a potent lobby in favor of cultivating and maintaining relationships with foreign countries who are reliable or potential customers. A recent example of a foreign policy decision that was made with such considerations in mind was the April 2004 veto by Russia of a U.S.-British resolution in the UN Security Council that would have guaranteed the security of Greek and Turkish Cypriots if they had accepted a UN plan for reunification. It was reported that Russia's veto came at the request of Greece, a purchaser of

Russian arms. It also furthered the interests of Russian businesses that have deposited considerable funds in banks and have created numerous "shell corporations" in Cyprus.[86] On the whole, there is substantial evidence that the short-run profit considerations of Russian businesses do on occasion override what would appear to be longer-term considerations of Russian national interest in the development of relationships with other countries. As summarized in a recent conference of Western specialists on this subject, "Although Putin would no doubt like to see business operating as the seamless extension of Russian national interest, this has not yet been realized. The dog is not fully in control of its tail, and sometimes the tail may even wag the dog."[87]

At the close of Yeltsin's second term, there were some attempts to try to curb the power of the oligarchs. Prime Minister Kirienko made some progress in the effort to reduce the autonomy of Gazprom, in particular by requiring it to channel some of its huge profits toward payment of back taxes. During his brief term as prime minister, Evgenii Primakov attempted to tackle the corruption issue by encouraging the investigation and prosecution of Boris Berezovskii for illegally diverting the profits of Aeroflot to foreign accounts. Only after Putin's election as president, however, was there a sustained effort to curb the political power of the oligarchs. In May 2001, Rem Viakhirev, who had served since 1992 as Gazprom's CEO, was removed. He was replaced by the young deputy energy minister, Aleksei Miller, who had been a protégé of Putin's in the St. Petersburg city government. Long criticized for nepotism, asset-stripping, and other forms of illegalities and corruption, Viakhirev symbolized the kind of powerful, independent political force that Putin's Kremlin was seeking to rein in.

Nevertheless, "it was no accident" (to use the old Soviet expression) that the only two powerful businessmen who were hounded by state prosecutors to the point of voluntary exile, Vladimir Gusinskii and Boris Berezovskii, happened to have had the largest holdings in media organs that were notably unfriendly to the new president. This campaign against the owners of independent media, combined with other events—the detention of journalist Andrei Babitskii (an employee of Radio Liberty) in Chechnya, the trials of environmental whistle-blowers Aleksandr Nikitin and Grigorii Pasko, the denial to nongovernmental organizations of the ability to reregister and preserve their legal status, and a new requirement that Academy of Sciences researchers report on their foreign contacts, for example—produced an atmosphere in Russia that was "hostile to civil liberties, to activists, and, in fact, to anyone with opinions that differ considerably from the Kremlin's."[88]

An even greater impact on Russia's external relations resulted from the arrest in October 2003 of Russia's richest "oligarch"—Mikhail Khodorkovskii, who controlled the powerful oil company Yukos. Khodorkovskii was charged with major violations of Russian tax and accounting legislation, and Yukos was presented with several hefty bills for back taxes that forced it to the verge of bankruptcy, seriously jeopardizing its capacity to export oil at a time when global oil supplies were very tight and prices were reaching record highs. It was widely believed that Khodorkovskii's real sin was not that he engaged in shady economic dealings, since all of the oligarchs were thought to have done so. Rather, he had clearly violated Putin's instruction to the oligarchs that they steer clear of politics. He had financed opposition political parties and extended "favors" to members of parliament, as well as openly speculating about a possible run for the presidency in 2008. Equally serious in the Kremlin's eyes was his brazen attempt to usurp from the state authorities the right to shape the country's energy policies. His company—which had managed to transform itself from a "shadowy" enterprise to a firm modeling Western standards of good management and transparency—had attempted to determine the routing of export pipelines from its Siberian fields to the northern port of Murmansk and to the industrial city of Daqing in northern China; it had negotiated a merger with another Russian oil company, Sibneft; and it had invited investment from major Western companies. All of these initiatives apparently threatened the Kremlin's ability to keep control of its valuable petroleum resources, including its determination not to allow the private development of petroleum pipelines. Although he had obtained his considerable wealth in highly questionable fashion, Khodorkovskii managed to gain a great deal of sympathy from Western businesses and the Western press. It was even said that President Bush had expressed to Putin his concern that the oligarch's arrest might signal a hostile turn toward foreign investment on the part of the Russian government.

Russia's history of strong executive leadership—perpetuated in the 1993 constitution, with the extensive powers it gives to the president—together with the rudimentary development of parties and interest groups, makes the personal attitudes and political skills of the top leader and his closest associates of particular importance. This factor should have produced a strong and coherent vision for Russian foreign policy, smoothly and effectively implemented. That it has not done so is, at least in part, the result of several important internal features of Russian politics during Boris Yeltsin's presidency. In a sense, foreign policy became hostage to the two types of bitter political struggles that Russia endured in its first years of independence.

The most visible realm of political struggle—that between Yeltsin and his parliamentary and political opponents—was able to affect foreign policy primarily because of the openings created by the second realm: the messy struggles within the government itself. Clearly, the greatest impact of these influences from outside the executive branch was on those issues of foreign policy relating to the former republics of the USSR that so suddenly became objects of foreign rather than domestic policy. Even in this realm, one major study has concluded that "the fitful incursions of other political forces into foreign policy have accentuated its meanderings more than they have altered its overall direction."[89]

Ironically, it was in the realm of internecine political conflict—the unceasing struggles for power and allegiance within Yeltsin's top entourage—that the greatest impact on foreign policy was felt. Clearly, President Yeltsin's personality and political style encouraged this political infighting. The constant cabinet realignments and bureaucratic reorganizations; the creation of coordinating councils, one after another; and the endless procession of ministers and advisors contributed greatly to the lack of clarity and coherence in Russian foreign policy. While Yeltsin's fragile health and his personal habits accentuated these tendencies, at root was his failure to articulate his own clear and consistent vision of Russia's national interests and to enforce sufficient discipline on his own government team to translate this vision into effective policy.

The foreign policy challenges that Yeltsin had inherited in 1991–92—like those of the economy and the political system—were passed on to his designated heir essentially unresolved. To be sure, there was no foreseeable external threat to Russia's borders, and the ravenous appetites of the defense sector for the lion's share of Russian resources had been curbed. But Yeltsin was unable to overcome the immense sense of frustration that Russia's policymakers and people felt at having been cast down from the heights of superpower and relegated to a role of seeming insignificance. Although this could be attributed in part to occasional Western arrogance and insensitivity, in part it also testified to Yeltsin's failures as a policymaker and diplomat. In our concluding chapter, we shall evaluate the extent to which the change from Yeltsin to Putin has brought either a clearer sense of purpose or a smoother process for implementing the foreign policy of Russia.

6

Russia and the States of the Former Soviet Union

Until the term became "politically incorrect" in the late 1990s, Russia used *blizhnee zarubezhe* (near abroad) to refer to the fourteen non-Russian former Soviet republics which became independent states when the Soviet Union collapsed. After 1991, relations with these states became an increasingly important focus of Russian foreign policy. As we saw in chapter 5, initially there was confusion among Russians regarding their relationship to the "near abroad." For some it was psychologically difficult to think of these countries as independent states. Even many of those who accepted the separation of Russia from its "internal empire" thought of it as temporary. The idea that boundaries that earlier had been interior—and in many cases, quite arbitrarily drawn—would become international borders seemed to Russian nationalists to be unnatural, if not bizarre. Fundamentally the issue involved the nature of the Russian state itself. Thus to many Russians (and non-Russians alike) the relationships among the former fifteen union republics were issues more of domestic policy than of foreign policy.

Gradually, however, the realization took hold that these former vassals of the Kremlin were in fact independent countries and that they had become the concerns of foreign, not domestic, policy. What has yet to be resolved is the nature of the relationship between Russia and the near abroad. More specifically, what has yet to be determined is the degree of hegemony Russia is to exercise over these newly independent states (NIS).

A central fact about the states of the former Soviet Union is their diversity. Each state is unique, though they can usefully be considered in several groups. The Baltic states (Estonia, Latvia, and Lithuania), for example, are in a class of their own because of the intensity of their nationalism and their determination to break as sharply as possible from Russian control. Alone among the Soviet republics, the Baltic states were independent as late as 1940, and they were never reconciled to their status as component parts of the USSR. It is safe to say that among all the former Soviet republics (with the exception of Belarus), there exists a determination to remain independent, but that determination is clearly strongest among the Baltic states. They were the first to break away from the Soviet Union—having their secession formally approved by Gorbachev's State Council in September 1991—and they alone among the fourteen non-Russian states have consistently refused to join the Commonwealth of Independent States (CIS).

Thus we can identify as a second group the eleven states that have affiliated with Russia as members of the CIS. Within that group, there are also subgroups. The first would be Ukraine and Belarus, the two Slavic states that agreed with Russia on December 8, 1991, to form what they initially termed the Commonwealth of Slavic States. Then there are the three Transcaucasian states—Georgia, Armenia, and Azerbaijan—and the five Central Asian states of Kazakhstan, Kyrgyzstan, Uzbekistan, Turkmenistan, and Tajikistan. (One could also group Azerbaijan with the five Central Asian states, because they share a common Muslim heritage.) In a category of its own is Moldova, a territory largely carved out of prewar Romania. No matter how the states are grouped, it must be stressed that, in terms of culture, level of economic development, resources, and history, each of the former Soviet states is unique.

The Commonwealth of Independent States

Eleven of the former Soviet republics are joined with Russia in the Commonwealth of Independent States. The CIS is an organization whose birth was accidental and whose future remains as uncertain now as it did at its birth. Those who founded the CIS really wanted a different type of union.

In the aftermath of the failed August 1991 coup, both Boris Yeltsin and Mikhail Gorbachev recognized that the Soviet Union would have to be replaced by a new type of union. Gorbachev wanted a union that would give its republics more autonomy, particularly in the economic sphere, but one that would retain considerable powers for the center, particularly in the realm of foreign policy and national security. Essentially Gorbachev wanted a redesigned federal system, which he proposed to call the Union of Sovereign States.[1] Boris Yeltsin also wanted a new union, but he wanted a decentralized system that would give the central government only those powers that the component members were willing to cede. In a word, Yeltsin favored some type of confederation.[2]

In late 1991 there was some uncertainty regarding which republics would join a new union, but Gorbachev and Yeltsin were in agreement that Ukraine would have to be included. Ukraine was the birthplace of the Russian state in the ninth century, when several Slavic tribes were united into an independent polity identified as "Kievan Rus."[3] Few in Russia contemplated the idea of an independent, sovereign Ukrainian state. But equally few grasped the strength of Ukrainian nationalism. On December 1, 1991, a referendum in Ukraine sealed the fate of a new union when 90.3 percent of the voters opted for independence.

Boris Yeltsin was forced to improvise quickly. A week after the Ukrainian referendum, the Russian president met with Leonid Kravchuk and Stanislau Shushkevich, his counterparts in Ukraine and Belarus, and on December 8 at Belovezhskaia Pushcha (a forest preserve near Minsk) agreed to create the Commonwealth of Slavic States (CSS). The Commonwealth was less of a union than Yeltsin had wanted, but Leonid Kravchuk insisted that Ukraine would not participate in any kind of a federation. A loose commonwealth was the only arrangement Kravchuk would accept.[4]

The majority of the other republics wanted some form of affiliation with Russia, and accordingly the CSS was expanded and renamed the Commonwealth of Independent States on December 25, 1991, with the signing in Alma-Ata (now Almaty) of a protocol admitting Kazakhstan, Kyrgyzstan, Uzbekistan, Turkmenistan, Tajikistan, Moldova, Armenia, and Azerbaijan. Of the fifteen union republics, only the Baltic states and Georgia chose not to join. Within Azerbaijan and Moldova strong domestic opposition to the Commonwealth prevented their national parliaments from ratifying their membership. Azerbaijan withdrew from the CIS in October 1992. As we shall see, pressure from Russia subsequently forced Georgia to join, Azerbaijan to rejoin, and Moldova to ratify its membership. Of the fifteen union republics, only the Baltic states are not members, and the Russian government has evidenced no intention to force them to join.

The CIS is an instrument of Russian foreign policy in two ways. It serves as a means of coordination of policies among its members. It is also a mechanism for asserting Russian hegemony over the other eleven states. Both goals have been pursued simultaneously. Initially prominence was given to the former, but with the passage of time the latter has become an important feature of Russian policy. According to the text of the original agreement, the members agreed to coordinate foreign policy activities. They specifically committed themselves to creating a "common military-strategic space" under a joint commander, including a unified control over nuclear weapons. That commitment, along with an agreement to create a "common economic space," was abandoned within two years.[5]

Among the many international organizations in existence, the CIS is unique. The CIS is neither a political alliance nor an economic community, though its activities have elements of both. It is a loose federation with no independent powers of governance. There is provision for central institutions—principally the Council of Heads of State and the Council of Heads of

Government—but these councils lack authority to impose CIS decisions on any member. Decisions require the unanimous consent of all those voting. As a matter of practice, most of the decisions reached have not been put into effect. Not infrequently several members fail to appear at scheduled summit meetings. By failing to participate in a CIS decision, a member is free to opt out of compliance, but even those members participating in decisions and agreeing with them are not obliged to comply and often do not. President Nursultan Nazarbaev of Kazakhstan, one of the most ardent supporters of integration, complained in 1994 that of 452 agreements signed within the CIS framework, most were never implemented.

Behind the failure of the CIS to become the integrated system Yeltsin and other Russians wanted it to be lay the determination of each state to preserve its newly acquired independence and sovereignty. This was true of each member without exception, though there were considerable differences in the degree to which some states were determined to maintain their distance from Russia.

Initially, perhaps Ukraine and Belarus represented the poles of sentiment within the CIS regarding a willingness to integrate with Russia. If the Commonwealth was weak, it was because of Ukraine's determination to keep it that way. Leonid Kravchuk wanted no common law, no common citizenship, and no status for the CIS in international law. It is generally believed that he viewed the Commonwealth basically as a step toward complete separation from Russia. Other members who opposed the creation of strong coordinating structures and close cooperation with Russia were Azerbaijan, Moldova, and Turkmenistan. Those favoring more integration and cooperation were Armenia, Belarus, Kazakhstan, Kyrgyzstan, Tajikistan, Uzbekistan, and of course Russia itself.

No issue better illustrated the bitter struggle between those forces pressing for and against integration than the effort to create a unified CIS military command. As noted above, one of the expressed objectives of the commonwealth was the creation of a "military-strategic space under a joint command," and the promise to pursue this goal was probably the necessary price the republic presidents had to pay in order to obtain the acquiescence of the Soviet armed forces in the dissolution of the USSR. But from the very beginning, differences among the new states emerged over the issue of establishing unified armed forces. At the first CIS summit on December 30, 1991, Ukraine claimed the right to create a national army under Ukrainian command. President Leonid Kravchuk also demanded Ukraine's control over military units on its territory, including the Black Sea Fleet, which was headquartered in the Crimean city of Sevastopol. One of Kravchuk's first acts as president was to require all military personnel in Ukraine to take an oath of

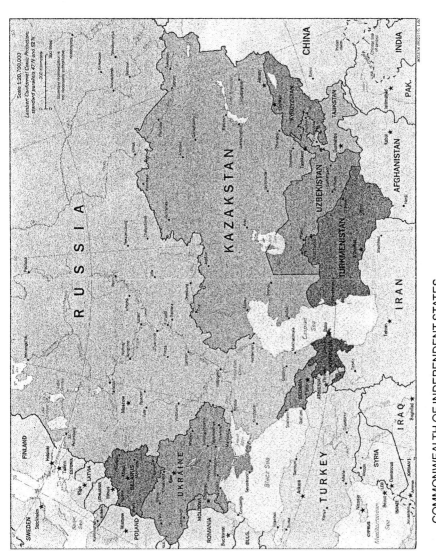

COMMONWEALTH OF INDEPENDENT STATES

allegiance to the Ukrainian state. At the time, the army was only 40 percent ethnically Ukrainian and was commanded by an officer corps that was 75 percent Russian. Clearly, Kravchuk perceived that the lack of control over the armed forces on Ukraine's territory was a serious threat to its sovereignty.

Russia's military leaders opposed the idea of national armies—also being sought by Moldova and Azerbaijan—among CIS members, hoping instead to place the bulk of the former Soviet armed forces under a unified CIS command. The opponents of integration prevailed, however, and the CIS leaders agreed to permit those states that so desired to create their own armies; but they also agreed to establish the Council of Defense Ministers, headquartered in Moscow, and to make Russian General Evgenii Shaposhnikov commander-in-chief of the CIS Joint Armed Forces. While there was no agreement on the size and composition of the so-called Joint Armed Forces, there was no doubt initially that the nuclear forces of the former Soviet Union would be under the CIS Joint Command. It soon became evident, though, that the concept of a joint command—even over nuclear forces—was illusory. Not only Ukraine but also several other members were suspicious that the CIS Joint Command was in effect a surrogate for the Russian High Command. These suspicions were heightened by the close personal relationship between President Yeltsin and General Shaposhnikov.

If Moscow could not unify the armed forces of CIS members, it could take measures to establish control over former Soviet armed forces stationed inside the territory of the Russian Federation. That is what it did on May 7, 1992, when the Russian government announced its decision to create an independent Russian army. Unable to prevent military decentralization, Russia had no choice but to create its own national command. For about a year the CIS Joint Command continued to coexist with the Russian High Command, though the exact responsibilities of the former were unclear. In theory, the CIS Joint Command might have been utilized to control nuclear weapons, but in fact, Yeltsin concurred with the Russian military that all nuclear weapons would be controlled by Russia. By mid-1993, all support for a unified CIS command had dissipated, and on June 15, its abolition was announced in Moscow.[6]

Moscow's decision to take control over nuclear weapons was reached with difficulty and required a period of several years to accomplish. It was made possible in part with the strong support—financial and political—of the United States. When the CIS was created, nuclear weapons were deployed in four states: Russia, Belarus, Kazakhstan, and Ukraine. Those weapons included both tactical and strategic bombs. Tactical bombs are designed for use on the battlefield and held little value for Ukraine, Kazakhstan, and Belarus. Thus agreement was easily reached among the three to remove all tactical stockpiles from their territory. Strategic weapons proved to be a more difficult issue to resolve. All three states committed themselves in principle to ridding their territory of all nuclear weapons, but as Ukraine soon found itself enmeshed in a series of contentious issues with Russia, Leonid Kravchuk balked at the idea of turning strategic nuclear weapons over to Russia. Additionally the question of compensation for the nuclear fuel in these weapons was raised.

With the collapse of the CIS Joint Command, Russia demanded that all nuclear inventories be transferred to Russia. In this Moscow had 'the strong support of the United States, which viewed the problem as a serious nuclear proliferation threat. The United States and other Western governments pressured the three new "nuclear states" to adhere to the Nuclear Nonproliferation Treaty and to ratify the START I Treaty. In pursuit of that goal U.S. Secretary of State James Baker met with the foreign ministers of the four states in Lisbon, Portugal. On May 23, 1992, they signed a protocol to the START I treaty providing that Belarus, Kazakhstan, and Ukraine would ratify the Nonproliferation Treaty "in the shortest possible time."[7]

Russo-Ukrainian relations during 1992–93, however, were frequently antagonistic, and Kravchuk, pressured by domestic forces demanding retention of nuclear weapons, balked at carrying out the terms of the Lisbon Protocol. Ukrainian nationalists clearly saw these weapons as a useful bargaining tool. Kravchuk wanted as a quid pro quo for total nuclear renunciation security guarantees from the United States and financial compensation. During 1992 and 1993, Russia, Belarus, and Kazakhstan ratified the START I treaty, leaving Ukraine as the only holdout. As of late 1993, Ukraine still possessed 1,656 nuclear warheads. In early September Yeltsin met with Kravchuk at Massandra in the Crimea and negotiated an agreement to cancel a portion of Ukraine's huge debt to Russia in exchange for the transfer to Russia of Ukraine's nuclear weapons. That deal collapsed in a firestorm of criticism which Kravchuk encountered on his return to Kiev—so he again reneged. To appease the United States, from which he was seeking financial assistance, Kravchuk promised not to aim Ukraine's nuclear weapons at the United States.[8] This was little consolation to Russia.

In the aftermath of the collapse of the Massandra Accords the new administration in the United States renewed efforts to stop Ukrainian nuclear proliferation. President Bill Clinton, Kravchuk, and Yeltsin met in Moscow on January 14, 1994, to resolve the issue. Concessions were made on all sides. Ukraine, Belarus, and Kazakhstan were promised financial compensation for the highly enriched uranium in the warheads, and Ukraine was given security assurances by both Russia and the United States. The Trilateral Agreement was signed, committing Ukraine to bring START I into force and to "accede to the Nuclear Nonproliferation Treaty as a nonnuclear-weapon state in the shortest possible time."[9] Even this agreement encountered resistance in Kiev. In June 1994 Kravchuk was replaced as president by Leonid Kuchma, who succeeded in November in obtaining overwhelming parliamentary approval of the Non-Proliferation Treaty (NPT). This removed only one of the several problems in Russo-Ukrainian relations.

Russo-Ukrainian Discord

The nuclear problem reflected Ukraine's deep sense of insecurity. Fundamentally Kiev had no need for nuclear weapons and indeed could not even afford the cost of their upkeep, but in Ukrainian public opinion the suspicion was rampant that Russia did not accept the permanence of Ukrainian independence. Two issues that contributed to that fear involved the Black Sea Fleet and the status of Crimea.

The Black Sea Fleet, a naval force of approximately 300 ships, was one of the four fleets of the Soviet Union. It has its headquarters in the Crimean port of Sevastopol, a city under Ukrainian sovereignty but populated largely by ethnic Russians. In a provocative move, in January 1992 the Ukrainian minister of defense laid claim to the bulk of the Black Sea Fleet. Ignoring the existence of the CIS Naval Command, Kravchuk appointed a Ukrainian naval commander for the fleet. Not surprisingly, the Russian response was outrage, particularly from the military, but including the voice of Vice President Aleksandr Rutskoi. President Yeltsin's response was moderate. He rejected the Ukrainian claim out of hand, but nevertheless indicated a willingness to negotiate the issue. Within Russia there was consideration of putting the fleet under CIS control, putting it under Russian control, or sharing control with Ukraine. As the prospects for the CIS command declined in 1992, sentiment in Moscow shifted to the latter two alternatives.

There were nationalist elements in both Kiev and Moscow who took an extreme position on the Black Sea Fleet issue, but Yeltsin was anxious to avoid a rupture with Ukraine, and even Kravchuk understood that in the end he would have to compromise. Over a period of several years the two leaders met often in an attempt to settle the controversy. Four separate agreements were signed between 1992 and 1994, but the issue was not resolved, although the differences were narrowed considerably.[10] Agreements at Dagomys and Yalta in the summer of 1992 provided for division of the fleet and for joint financing until the proportions due for both countries could be established. A year later in Moscow the two presidents agreed on an equal division of the fleet on the condition that agreement could be worked out for the basing of the Russian part of the navy on Ukrainian territory.

This issue of basing rights was the source of bitter exchanges between hard-liners in both countries. On July 9, 1993, the Russian Supreme Soviet resolved that the port of Sevastopol was a Russian city and therefore part of the Russian Federation. This decision, repudiated by Yeltsin, inflamed Ukrainian public opinion and made even more difficult Yeltsin's efforts at compromise. He professed to be "ashamed of the decision."[11]

Another attempt was made at Massandra in September. This meeting sought simultaneously to resolve the issues of Ukraine's nuclear weapons and of the Black Sea Fleet by turning both the nuclear weapons and the fleet over to Russia in exchange for the cancellation of Kiev's debt to Russia (largely incurred by energy imports). It appeared that Moscow had achieved a coup of sorts, but the Massandra deal went the way of earlier agreements when nationalist elements in Kiev forced the government to back down. Kravchuk's last deal before leaving office in 1994 was an agreement in April that the Black Sea Fleet would be divided on an equal basis, after which Ukraine would sell part of its share to Russia.

The Black Sea Fleet issue was never really a security problem, but an expression of the larger political differences between the two states. One of these differences was territorial. Russian authorities, particularly in the legislature, claimed the Crimean peninsula and especially the city of Sevastopol as part of Russian territory. Boris Yeltsin himself never endorsed those territorial claims, but in December 1996 the upper house of the parliament, the Federation Council, called on Yeltsin to impose a moratorium on any agreement on the Black Sea Fleet until a special commission examined the status of Sevastopol. Supporting this position was Moscow's popular mayor, Yuri Luzhkov. President Leonid Kuchma, Leonid Kravchuk's successor, insisted that the loss of Sevastopol would mean the end of Ukrainian independence.

A related and potentially more serious issue is the status of the Crimean peninsula. Crimea was until 1954 a Russian *oblast* (region). According to the last Soviet census in 1989, 67.04 percent of its population were Russians, while Ukrainians composed only 24.75 percent. Almost half of the Ukrainians speak Russian as their native language.[12] In 1954 Nikita Khrushchev arbitrarily transferred Crimea from the Russian SFSR to the Ukrainian SSR to mark the 300th anniversary of the unification of Ukraine with Russia. In the Soviet period the shifting of an oblast from one republic to another meant little, because all political power was concentrated in Moscow. When Ukraine became an independent state, the magnitude of the loss to Russia quickly became apparent. Russia's nationalistic Supreme Soviet voted overwhelmingly to examine the constitutionality of Khrushchev's transfer. On May 21, 1992, the Supreme Soviet went further and resolved that the transfer of Crimea to Ukraine in 1954 "had no legal force from the moment it was adopted."[13] The Russian parliament called for negotiations between Russia and Ukraine and representatives of Crimea. Ukrainians were furious and rejected out of hand the idea of negotiations. Extremist rhetoric was heard from both sides. One Russian member of parliament threatened war between the two countries, to which a Ukrainian legislator replied, "The Crimea will be Ukrainian or it will become totally depopulated."[14]

The presidents of both countries were anxious to prevent this issue from forcing a rupture in relations and took steps to cool passions. Fundamentally, as on the issue of the port of Sevastopol, Yeltsin was not prepared to press Russian territorial claims against Ukraine. At a Russo-Ukrainian summit in Dagomys, Yeltsin and Kravchuk reached agreement on a number of contentious issues including the division of property, the opening of state borders with visa-free access, and the principle of dividing the Black Sea Fleet. Political concessions were made on both sides. Kravchuk affirmed his country's intention not to withdraw from the Commonwealth of Independent States, and both presidents agreed that neither country had a territorial claim on the other. Tacitly Russia acknowledged that Crimea was an integral part of Ukraine.

Boris Yeltsin's administration smothered but did not completely suppress Russian claims to Crimea. In Russian nationalistic circles, the claim to Crimea has been reasserted periodically not only by extremists in the parliaments but even by some liberals, such as the late Anatolii Sobchak, the former mayor of St. Petersburg. Former Russian vice president Aleksandr Rutskoi was a strident defender of Russia's claim to Crimea. Furthermore, within Crimea itself there is a domestic constituency for reuniting Crimea with Russia. In January 1994 the first presidential elections ever held in Crimea resulted in the victory of Yuri Meshkov, a Russian nationalist, who had made reunification with Russia one of the planks in his campaign platform. Pro-Russian sentiment in Crimea remains strong, but the government in Kiev has succeeded in enforcing the Ukrainian claim to sovereignty over Crimea. However, in a concession by Kiev, Crimea has succeeded in acquiring a significant degree of autonomy under the Ukrainian constitution, including the right to establish Crimean citizenship.

Political turmoil within Russia and Ukraine in 1995 and 1996 made impossible a resolution of these differences. Following his reelection in 1996 and the improvement of his health in 1997, Yeltsin was able to reassert his executive authority. Though on many foreign policy issues the hard-line nationalists of the State Duma mirrored their predecessors in the Supreme Soviet, Yeltsin's increased political clout in 1997, together with the strong powers over foreign policy under his tailor-made constitution, permitted the Russian president to override domestic opposition and come to terms with Ukraine. A compelling motive for him to do so was the movement within NATO to expand into Eastern Europe. Russia's leverage against the powerful forces of NATO was meager, but one instrument to bolster its defense was to strengthen the weak bond between the two Slavic states.

This Yeltsin did in the spring of 1997. In late May an accord was finally reached on the Black Sea Fleet. For appropriate compensation Russia was permitted to station its portion of the Black Sea Fleet at the port of Sevastopol for twenty years. This accord set the stage for President Yeltsin to make his first visit to Kiev, where he and Leonid Kuchma signed a treaty of friendship. Moscow agreed to write off most of Ukraine's huge oil debt to Russia. At the ceremony Yeltsin publicly observed, "We respect and honor the territorial integrity of Ukraine."[15]

A resolution of Russian-Ukrainian differences was important to Yeltsin and Kuchma for economic as well as political reasons. Russians were eager to invest in Ukrainian enterprises converted from state to private ownership. Kiev in turn desperately needed Russian assistance for its ailing economy. Ukraine has been plagued since independence with financial and currency problems compounded by a chronic shortage of energy. Early in 1998 Kuchma reciprocated the Kiev summit with a visit to Moscow, where he and Yeltsin signed a ten-year agreement on economic cooperation. A joint statement at the conclusion of the summit proclaimed, "The Presidents reaffirmed that Russian-Ukrainian relations are of a special nature and are a top priority for both states."[16]

Notwithstanding the goodwill shown by the two leaders, suspicions remained strong in both countries. The Ukrainian parliament refused for a year and a half to ratify the Black Sea agreements that gave Russia its much-needed naval base in Sevastopol. In retaliation the Russian upper house waited until 1999 to ratify the May 1997 Treaty of Friendship, Cooperation, and Partnership abandoning territorial claims on Ukraine, and then they did so only upon the condition that the Black Sea Fleet agreements be ratified by Ukraine.

Problems of a nonstrategic nature persisted also. The Russian Duma objected to the requirement that Ukrainian be the sole state language of Crimea, a majority of whose citizens speak Russian. A long-term solution to the problem of Ukraine's debt to Russia for imported natural gas remained elusive. A good expression of the ambivalence in Russo-Ukrainian relations was conveyed by Leonid Kuchma in his second-term inaugural speech: "Although Ukraine will never renounce its independence and will never rejoin a union, Russia is its most important strategic partner."[17]

In fact, some in Ukraine had clearly leaned more toward the anti-Russian side. More heavily aided by the United States than most other former Soviet states, Ukraine had showed considerable interest in cooperating with NATO, signing military cooperation agreements in 1997 and 1998. When the anti-Russian group GUUAM (consisting of Georgia, Ukraine, Uzbekistan, Azerbaijan, and Moldova) was formed among the former Soviet states, Ukraine was one of the "U's" in the pact. Yet it was Leonid Kuchma's own political difficulties that finally seemed to tilt Ukraine toward the side of "strategic partnership" with Russia.

Accused in 2000 of complicity in the brutal murder of muckraking journalist Georgi Gongadze, Kuchma found himself confronted with rising political opposition, including street demonstrations. One of his responses was cracking down on his opponents, including jailing opposition leader Iulia Timoshenko. The other was to turn to a willing "friend in need," Vladimir Putin. During his February 2001 trip to Ukraine, Putin promised the necessary support for Kuchma in return for strengthened political, economic, and military cooperation from Ukraine.[18] As for future gas supply, Moscow was said to be offering a choice of a low price for Ukraine if it joined the Russia-Belarus union, a midlevel price if it rejoined the CIS custom union, or a high price if it chose to "behave like a West European country."[19]

Vladimir Putin, like his predecessor, wanted not just good relations but as much integration with Ukraine as possible. Fundamentally, that meant keeping his Slavic neighbor out of the Western orbit. No single concern was more basic than preventing Ukrainian membership in NATO. Leonid Kuchma's terrible human rights record made Kiev an unlikely NATO candidate, though support for Ukraine did exist in the West.[20] On May 23, 2002, Kuchma chaired a meeting of Ukraine's National Security and Defense Council that voted to initiate the process of Ukrainian membership in NATO. Moscow was displeased with this act of geopolitical disloyalty, but it had its own arsenal of economic and political instruments with which to constrain Kiev. Chief among these was the need for both countries to cooperate in the distribution of Russian natural gas through Ukrainian gas pipelines to markets in Western Europe. In October the prime ministers of the two countries set up an international consortium to manage and develop Ukraine's natural gas system for thirty years. Ukraine was not completely satisfied with the terms of the deal, but Moscow hinted that it was prepared to build a pipeline (through Finland) that would bypass Ukraine together.[21]

President Kuchma was torn between a pro-Western orientation, which he apparently preferred, and a realistic assessment that there were limits on how far he could antagonize his giant neighbor. Kuchma agreed in February that Ukraine would join Russia, Belarus, and Kazakhstan in creating a "single economic space." Like so many of the formal agreements both before and after, this agreement changed very little of substance.

The latent antagonism between Ukraine and Russia became public in late 2003 when Russia started building a dike in the Sea of Azov which threatened to link the Ukrainian island of Tuzla with the Russian coast. Kiev vehemently protested the construction, believing that it would lead Russia to claim the island of

Tuzla. Ultimately, a telephone conversation between Kuchma and Putin led to a resolution of the crisis. Construction of the Russian dike was suspended, and Ukraine reaffirmed its participation in the "single economic space." One consequence of this tempest in a teapot was to strengthen support in Ukraine for membership in NATO. Still, Kuchma could not avoid the geopolitical reality of Ukraine's dependence on Russia. He need only observe the pressure Moscow put on Belarus (see below) to realize his own vulnerability with respect to energy and food. When Putin visited Kiev in January 2004 he was assured by his host that Ukraine "looks east, not west."[22] As the end of the Kuchma era approached, Ukraine appeared to be no closer to union with Russia than it had at the beginning.

Putin's determination to secure Ukraine's continuing orientation toward the east propelled him into a rare diplomatic blunder. The Russian president openly campaigned for Kuchma's chosen successor, Prime Minister Viktor Yanukovich, even appearing at his side prior to both the preliminary and runoff elections in fall 2004. Even before the runoff results were certified in Kiev, and amidst reports from international observers of massive electoral fraud, Putin had declared that the outcome was an "absolute clear" Yanukovich victory. While half a million demonstrators massed in Kiev in support of the opposition candidate, Viktor Yushchenko, and U.S. and European diplomats sought ways of defusing the crisis, Putin summoned Kuchma to Moscow to flatly dismiss the idea that the election should be repeated under stricter supervision.

When the Ukrainian Supreme Court ordered a new runoff, Putin—drawing parallels to recent changes of government in Serbia and Georgia—declared that the demonstrations and election nullification set a dangerous precedent, threatening to destabilize the "post-Soviet space." Nevertheless, he said that he would accept the choice of the Ukrainian people and work with whichever candidate prevailed. A declaration passed by Russia's Duma openly accused the West of having encouraged "chaos" in Ukraine.

A significant compromise was negotiated between Kuchma and the opposition forces, entailing parliamentary ratification of a constitutional amendment to reduce the power of Ukraine's president and increase that of the parliament and cabinet. This cleared the way for the December 26 election, which Yushchenko won decisively. The president-elect, who had earlier been Kuchma's prime minister, and who had not been known for anti-Russian sentiments, reiterated his pledge to make Moscow his first destination as Ukraine's president. Indeed, despite the fact that Western funds aided his campaign, he had promised to withdraw Ukrainian military forces from the U.S. coalition in Iraq. Ironically, Russia's blatant interference on behalf of his opponent probably drove Yushchenko's forces closer to the West than might otherwise have been the case. And although Putin declared that he did not expect the events in Ukraine to set back the "alliance" between the U.S. and Russia, his heavy-handed intervention raised serious doubts in Western capitals about Moscow's commitment to democracy.[23]

CIS Integration

The failure of Ukraine, historically the closest of all the CIS states to Russia, to move toward integration with Russia was paralleled by every other CIS state. Politically the CIS is not a federation, and economically it is not a common market. Even though until 1991 the former Soviet republics were governed as a unitary state with a command economy, as independent states they have achieved far less genuine economic integration than the European Union.

Expectations of economic cooperation were initially high, because as parts of the Soviet Union the former republics were in fact economically interdependent. The non-Russian republics were dependent upon Russia for their supplies of energy, particularly oil and gas. Ukraine provided grain and other foodstuffs and rolled ferrous metal. Central Asia supplied cotton for the clothing industries in the western republics. It made economic sense for the CIS states to agree upon rules to govern the exchange of goods and services among themselves. In addition, at independence the ruble was the common unit of currency for each republic. Russia was in the dominant position, because all the presses for printing rubles were within its domain. If the ruble were to remain a common unit of currency, a central bank and policy-making institution to maintain a uniform fiscal policy would have to be created. But these incentives for economic integration were not strong enough to create workable economic institutions. In the end, each republic chose to create its own currency.

During the early years of the commonwealth, there were unsuccessful attempts to establish a viable economic framework for CIS members. Ironically, it was Russia, the strongest proponent of economic integration, that in practice severely undermined the possibilities. President Yeltsin's top domestic priority was radical economic reform (the so-called shock therapy) that he introduced in January 1992. According to CIS principles, Russia was obligated to consult with its CIS partners regarding economic policy. Yeltsin did not do so, despite the fact that his policy of price decontrol had ruinous impact on all those states using the ruble for their currency. Ukraine, for one, was outraged. But Russia was not alone in its disregard of its neighbors. Several CIS members placed restrictions on the export of goods to the Russian Federation, which in turn led to retaliation by Moscow.

Illustrative of the economic chaos within the CIS was the conflict in the monetary policies of the member states. In 1992 the Russian Central Bank adopted rules governing the settlement of accounts with banks outside Russia that forced Russian enterprises to demand hard-currency payment from buyers in non-Russian republics lacking a positive credit balance with the Central Bank. Non-Russian banks had no control over the amount of rubles in circulation because the presses were in Russia. In this chaotic environment, Russia was often the victim as well as the perpetrator. Inflationary policies pursued by CIS governments had their impact inside Russia.

Russia's unilateral monetary policies created a crisis for the former Soviet states relying on the ruble. In July 1993 the Russian government introduced a currency restriction prohibiting the use of pre-1993 ruble notes in Russia and permitting only Russian citizens and enterprises and foreign visitors to exchange old rubles for new ones. When this reform was introduced, nine of the CIS republics still relied on the ruble. Eventually each state came to the conclusion that national sovereignty required it to abandon the ruble for its own national currency. Ukraine, Belarus, and Kyrgyzstan were among the first to do so.

Notwithstanding the reluctance of the commonwealth members to align their economic policies, their leaders continued to engage in the rhetoric of economic integration. Typical of the gap between rhetoric and behavior was the agreement signed in Bishkek, Kyrgyzstan, on October 9, 1992, creating the Unified Monetary System. Going even further, in May 1993 a declaration of intent was signed calling for an increase in economic integration and envisioning a common market. Later that year Russia, Ukraine, and Belarus announced their intention to integrate their economies into a "single economic space." None of these agreements have been realized.

Early in 1997 the CIS heads of government yet again approved an overall concept for CIS economic integration, but Russian minister for CIS affairs Aman Tuleev admitted that several states would not go along with the concept. The Russian press contemptuously referred to proposals for unified CIS trade, labor, transport, customs, and currency systems as being in the CIS tradition of "paper creativity."[24]

Because the membership of the CIS is so diverse with so many conflicting interests, occasionally smaller groups of CIS states have attempted to organize to achieve specific limited objectives. Thus, in March 1996 Russia signed an agreement with Belarus, Kazakhstan, and Kyrgyzstan to create a customs union. This quartet became a quintet in February 1999, when Tajikistan voted to affiliate with the customs union. To date the union has failed to accomplish very much. Russia apparently has had second thoughts about even a limited free-trade zone that would eliminate the not inconsiderable revenue it earns from transporting energy resources abroad. Nevertheless, the institutionalization of the GUUAM grouping in 2000 apparently led the aforementioned states to formalize their association as the Eurasian Economic Union in October 2000. Voting rights were set up so as to guarantee Russian dominance, with Russia receiving four votes, its close allies Belarus and Kazakhstan, two each, and Kyrgyzstan and Tajikistan, one apiece.[25]

Under Vladimir Putin, Russia has also taken a harder line on border cross-ing by citizens of the commonwealth. In August 2000 Russia withdrew from the Bishkek Agreement on visa-free travel by CIS citizens. Foreign Minister Igor Ivanov gave as a reason the challenges to the country's security from terrorism, organized crime, and drug trafficking. In addition to its desire to reduce illegal immigration, Russia expressed concern about Chechen guer-rillas who were crossing into Russia from former Soviet republics.

Regional Stability and Russian Security

The failure of the CIS to integrate economically or militarily did not prevent Russia from using the organization to establish its dominance over the former Soviet territorial space. During the early period of his administration, Yeltsin was anxious to demonstrate to his new partners in the West that Russia's imperial period was a thing of the past, and Moscow moved slowly and cau-tiously in its relations with the near abroad. As the number and intensity of conflicts among CIS members grew, and as domestic political pressure for asserting Russia's authority increased, the Yeltsin administration increasingly adopted a tougher strategy.

That policy changed yet again in the latter half of the 1990s as Moscow increasingly came to view the use of coercive measures as costly and unpro-ductive. Several factors led to a less coercive strategy. One was the disas-trous experience of the war in Chechnya; another, the economic strain of using military force; and thirdly, the decline in the influence of the Ministry of Defense.[26]

Andrei Kozyrev, Russia's first foreign minister, focused his efforts on de-veloping relations with the West. He did not even bother to make a tour of the near abroad until the spring of 1992. Responsibility for relations with the former Soviet republics was initially entrusted to Fëdor Shelov-Kovediaev, a young first deputy foreign minister. In a report entitled "Strategy and Tac-tics of Russian Foreign Policy in the New Abroad," Shelov-Kovediaev made the case for a more active Russian policy of promoting the integration of the former Soviet republics. While categorically rejecting the use of force in the region, he insisted that Russia had "special interests" that required recog-nition by the international community. One of the most vital of these inter-ests was stability and the prevention of the spread of regional conflicts from bordering states into the Russian Federation itself. Though Shelov-Kovediaev was not to last the year in his post, his ideas were in part embodied in the Russian foreign ministry's "foreign policy concept" published in December 1992 and ultimately adopted by Yeltsin in April 1993. As we have seen in chapter 5, special emphasis in the "concept" was placed on the need to defend the external borders of the CIS. By early 1993 President Yeltsin was firmly committed to an active policy of intervention in the near abroad. In a speech before the politically important Civic Union on February 28, Yeltsin declared:

> Stopping all armed conflicts on the territory of the former USSR is Russia's vital interest. The world community sees more and more clearly Russia's special responsibility in this difficult undertaking. I believe the time has come for distinguished international organizations, including the UN, to grant Russia special powers as a guarantor of peace and stability in the former regions of the USSR.[27]

The problem confronting Russia was how to use the CIS to build an effective mechanism for security. Integration was not working, so other means had to be devised to achieve the desired ends through multilateral cooperation. An attempt toward that end was the Collective Security Treaty. Originally, the idea of a collective security force had been worked out bilaterally between Russia and Kazakhstan. However, the idea appealed to other CIS members, so at a CIS summit in Tashkent on May 15, 1992, a treaty was signed that ultimately brought together Armenia, Kazakhstan, Russia, Tajikistan, Uzbekistan, Azerbaijan, Belarus, Georgia, and Kyrgyzstan.[28] In principle the treaty created a defensive alliance whose ultimate decision-making authority was to be a collective security council.

There were serious limitations with the mechanism for collective security. To begin with, it was never comprehensive. Notably absent were Ukraine and Moldova. In 1999 several members defected. Uzbekistan withdrew in March, giving as its reason Moscow's military activity "in certain CIS states." Azerbaijan and Georgia withdrew later in the year.[29] The Collective Security Treaty also was limited structurally. Essentially a defensive alliance, the treaty could come into force only when one sovereign entity attacked another. It did not cover conflicts that arose between groups within one state, and, with the exception of the war over Nagorno-Karabakh between Armenia and Azerbaijan, the conflicts that plagued the CIS were essentially internal struggles or civil wars. Notwithstanding these limitations, the treaty remained a potentially useful instrument of Russian influence. For one thing it provided a legal foundation for the CIS Unified Air Defense System, which was officially established by an agreement signed on February 10, 1995.[30]

In the aftermath of the terrorist attacks on the United States on September 11, 2001, and the introduction of American forces into Central Asia, Russia sought to use the treaty as an instrument to balance American influence in the region. At a summit meeting of Collective Security members in April 2003, formal steps were begun to transform the alliance into a political-military organization to be known as the Collective Security Treaty Organization (CSTO). Vladimir Putin was chosen as the first CSTO chairman. The CSTO has yet to display any military capability. However, Russia, Kazakhstan, Kyrgyzstan, and Tajikistan agreed to create a Rapid Deployment Force. At its first formal meeting on December 9, 2003, the CSTO Council of Defense Ministers agreed to increase the Rapid Deployment Force by 150 percent.[31]

Russian Peacekeeping

An alternative mechanism that was to prove more efficacious than the collective security approach was peacekeeping. Developed by the United Nations, the institution of peacekeeping involves the use of collective armed force to intervene when invited by the warring parties to monitor a truce or cease-fire. Within the United Nations, peacekeeping developed as an alternative to peacemaking (i.e., the use of armed forces to curb aggression). Originally, peacekeeping by the United Nations was designed to limit interstate conflict, but with the end of the Cold War, peacekeeping operations increasingly dealt with intrastate fighting or civil wars.[32] It was in this kind of conflict—internal wars within states bordering on Russia—that peacekeeping offered the greatest prospects.

Moscow was concerned about the outbreak of ethnic and national conflicts in the newly independent states bordering Russia for several reasons: (1) in several of the regions there were Russians who might need protection; (2) conflict might spread to the Russian Federation; (3) the success of separatist groups outside Russia might encourage separatism within Russia; (4) Islamic fundamentalism might spread to Russia's southern neighbors and then to Russia itself; and (5) there was a belief that its status as a "great power" obligated Russia to assume responsibility for keeping the peace in the region. To these considerations might be added a sixth: hegemonic aspirations—the desire of Russia to reestablish control over the territory once dominated by the Soviet Union.[33]

Interestingly, the initiative for creating a CIS peacekeeping force came from the president of Kazakhstan, Nursultan Nazarbaev, a strong believer in the idea of CIS integration. At a CIS summit in Kiev on March 20, 1992, he proposed to establish a corps of military observers and collective forces to maintain peace among CIS members.[34] Approving the plan were ten CIS states: Armenia, Belarus, Kazakhstan, Kyrgyzstan, Moldova, Russia, Tajikistan, and Uzbekistan, with Azerbaijan and Ukraine signing on the condition that their parliaments must approve. The agreement specified that CIS peacekeeping forces would be used only under the following conditions:

1. Only states not involved in the particular conflict would send troops;
2. Forces would be volunteers recruited on a contractual basis;
3. Command would be joint;
4. Use of peacekeeping forces would require approval of the CIS Council of Heads of States;
5. The belligerent parties had to agree to troop deployment.

Basically, the principles of CIS peacekeeping were modeled on United Nations principles. An attempt was made in July to organize a peacekeeping force in advance that could be called upon in case of a crisis, but no such force ever materialized (as was the case with similar UN efforts in the 1940s).

Peacekeeping operations were organized or planned for five conflicts that developed in the former USSR. Not one of these operations was carried out as specified in the CIS agreement or in accordance with UN principles. The five conflicts were the civil war in Tajikistan, two secessionist movements in Georgia (South Ossetia and Abkhazia), the war over Nagorno-Karabakh in Azerbaijan, and the independence struggle of the Trans-Dniester region in Moldova.

In Central Asia the major conflict was the civil war in Tajikistan. It was a complex war, in which the antagonists differed over political, ideological, ethnic, and regional issues. The war began in late 1991 when a coalition of forces that included groups seeking democracy, Islamic forces, and ethnic Pamirs and Garmis challenged the authority of the government of Rakhmon Nabiev. Bitter fighting during the war took a large toll in lives, produced widespread atrocities, and generated over a half-million refugees. In December 1992 Nabiev was replaced by his communist ally, Imomali Rakhmonov, who appealed to Russia and other CIS states for assistance against the opposing forces. That appeal was received sympathetically in Russia, Kazakhstan, Uzbekistan, and Kyrgyzstan, because of widespread fear that the civil war in Tajikistan would spread instability throughout the region and possibly enhance the prospects of spreading Islamic militancy. Russian involvement was virtually inevitable because of the presence in Tajikistan of Russian (former Soviet) forces, which found themselves caught between warring factions. In 1993 Russian troops were sent to guard the border between Tajikistan and Afghanistan. That same year the leaders of Russia, Kazakhstan, Kyrgyzstan, Tajikistan, and Uzbekistan formally authorized the formation of a CIS peacekeeping force.[35] This operation, controlled by Russia and not invited by the Tajik insurgents, reached a size of approximately 25,000 troops. Russia was accused of using peacekeeping as a pretext for establishing its control over Tajikistan, and indeed, for all practical purposes, while the war lasted, the country was a Russian protectorate. But Moscow made a genuine effort to bring both sides to the negotiating table, and ultimately it succeeded. In June 1997 the presidents of Russia and Tajikistan and the leader of the Tajik insurgency signed a Moscow-brokered pact ending the war.[36] Although intermittent fighting continued for some time, the Russian military presence pacified the country. Tajikistan has become one of Moscow's closest CIS allies, so much so that in September 2003 the study of the Russian language became mandatory in all of Tajikistan's general-education schools.[37]

The Caucasus

No region of the former Soviet Union is more prone to ethnic violence than the Caucasus. All of the conflicts that engulfed the region had their origins during the years of Soviet rule, but they were largely contained by the instruments of state power centered in Moscow. That power was bitterly resented by the diverse nationalities of the region, perhaps nowhere more so than in Georgia. The military suppression of a Georgian nationalist demonstration in Tbilisi in April 1989, which resulted in nineteen deaths and many more casualties, shocked many in Moscow, including the USSR's Georgian-born foreign minister and Gorbachev's ally, Eduard Shevardnadze. The Tbilisi massacre not only spurred Georgian demands for independence, but sparked nationalist emotions throughout the Caucasus.[38]

In October 1990, parliamentary elections in Georgia were won by a nationalist bloc headed by Zviad Gamsakhurdia, and in May 1991 he was elected as Georgia's president. An extreme nationalist who had been repressed as a dissident by Soviet authorities, Gamsakhurdia proved an erratic and repressive leader. He was passionately anti-Soviet and anti-Russian. Georgia joined the Baltics as the only former Soviet republics to reject outright membership in the CIS. Relations with Russia deteriorated under his leadership. Gamsakhurdia even gratuitously offended Moscow by supporting the demands of the Chechens to separate from the Russian Federation. As president, Gamsakhurdia was inept, corrupt, and oppressive. After a brief reign, he was overthrown by domestic opponents who reportedly received weapons from Russian military forces in the region.[39] He was succeeded as Georgia's leader by Eduard Shevardnadze, who was invited by the Georgian parliament in March 1992 to return to his native country. Shevardnadze proved to be a tough leader—not a compliant partner of Moscow—but willing to work with the Yeltsin administration.

Since Georgia attained independence from the USSR, its domestic and foreign politics have been dominated by its struggle with secessionist movements in South Ossetia and Abkhazia. Gamsakhurdia's extreme nationalist policies exacerbated longings for independence among the peoples of these two autonomous republics. Within a month of Gamsakhurdia's parliamentary victory, South Ossetia and Abkhazia both declared themselves sovereign republics.

South Ossetia is a province of Georgia that borders on North Ossetia, an autonomous republic within the Russian Federation. Georgians are Orthodox Christians, while the Ossets are predominantly Muslim. According to the 1989 census, only 14 percent of South Ossetians were fluent in the Georgian language. Because they share ethnicity with the North Ossets, many South Ossets sought political union with their brethren in the north. Fearful that the secessionist movement would spread to its own territory, Moscow refused their demands. President Shevardnadze, though noted as a champion of democracy while serving in the Gorbachev administration, also was sufficiently nationalistic to oppose any measure that would lead to the disintegration of the Georgian state.[40]

Fighting between South Ossetian and Georgian forces broke out late in 1990, intensifying over the next two years. Russia became involved because large numbers of refugees fled north, and because of its concern that the fighting might spread to North Ossetia. Under pressure from Moscow, Shevardnadze agreed to meet with Russian president Boris Yeltsin as well as representatives from North and South Ossetia. In June 1992, at Dagomys near the city of Sochi, the negotiators agreed to a cease-fire and the deployment of a joint peacekeeping force.

This mission in no way involved the Commonwealth of Independent States. It was a first of its kind, organized on a trilateral basis between Georgia, Russia, and South Ossetia. The initial objective was to enforce a cease-fire by separating the warring sides. Nominally under a joint command, the force was effectively subject to Russian authority. This operation was successful in keeping the peace, though it did little to resolve the underlying conflict. The practical effect of the cease-fire was to freeze in place territorial conquests won in battle. Shevardnadze has conceded a degree of autonomy to South Ossetia, but the Ossets wanted more. In view of the unsettled status of Chechnya in the North Caucasus, Russia continues to view outright secession as a bad precedent for the region.

A more serious threat to Georgian territorial integrity is the secessionist struggle of Abkhazia. Located between the Black Sea and the Caucasus mountains, Abkhazia is a province in northwest Georgia. Abkhazians, predominantly Muslims, constitute only 17 percent of the population of the province, although they dominate its government. In August 1990 the Abkhazian Supreme Soviet declared its independence (at the same time as South Ossetia). The brief but repressive administration of Zviad Gamsakhurdia had the same impact on Abkhazia that it did on South Ossetia: it heightened tensions, which ultimately led to bitter fighting. Eduard Shevardnadze was confronted in 1992 and 1993 with a military insurrection by forces loyal to Gamsakhurdia, as well as a war of secession in Abkhazia. The pressure of both forces on his government led to disaster in the fall of 1993. Fierce Abkhaz assaults on Sukhumi, the provincial capital, led to the city's fall and heightened fears that Georgia might disintegrate. In desperation Shevardnadze appealed to Russia for assistance.

Although accounts vary regarding how much responsibility the Russians bore for Shevardnadze's predicament, it is widely believed that Russian forces gave significant aid to Abkhaz leader Vladislav Ardzinba. What is less clear is how much of that assistance was authorized by the Russian president. Ardzinba had important supporters in Moscow, including Vice President Aleksandr Rutskoi and Ruslan Khasbulatov, speaker of the Russian parliament. Furthermore, the Russian military despised Shevardnadze because it held him responsible (along with Mikhail Gorbachev) for the collapse of the Warsaw Pact and the Soviet Union. Shevardnadze's biographers contend that Ardzinba's forces were aided by volunteers from the North Caucasus.[41] Although the evidence is inconclusive, Georgians are certain that Russians were involved in the bombing missions in support of the Abkhaz rebels.[42] Whatever Yeltsin's views, and they were at times apparently ambivalent, he failed to prevent members of the Russian armed forces from helping the separatists. Fearing that the fighting might spread, Yeltsin in late 1992 intervened to mediate a cease-fire. When Abkhazian forces, reinforced with Russian equipment, violated the cease-fire, Russia did nothing to stop the secessionists.

The Georgian military fiasco in 1993 occurred at about the same time that Moscow was in political crisis. Yeltsin's defeat of his political enemies in the parliament—under the leadership of Khasbulatov and Rutskoi—worked to Shevardnadze's advantage, in that it strengthened the Russian president's resolve to stop the fighting in Georgia. But Shevardnadze had to pay a price. In return for Russian assistance against both Abkhazia and the forces of Gamsakhurdia, Shevardnadze had to agree to join the CIS and accept Russian military bases on Georgia soil. "I sent a telegram to Moscow," Shevardnadze said, "saying Georgia will join the Commonwealth of Independent States, which I was against until the last moment."[43] On February 3, 1994, Boris Yeltsin arrived in Tbilisi to conclude the Treaty of Friendship and Cooperation and a status-of-forces agreement with Shevardnadze. Russia received the right to maintain three military bases in Georgia with a troop strength of 23,000. Russia also acquired access to ports on the Black Sea, including Poti, a major terminus of rail lines and roads from Tbilisi.

The initial impact of Russian intervention was to prevent either side from achieving outright victory. Abkhazia could not become independent, but Tbilisi had to concede autonomy for the province. When Moscow rescued Georgia in the fall of 1993, Andrei Kozyrev assured Shevardnadze that Russia opposed the dismemberment of Georgia.[44]

The Abkhaz rebellion was the first conflict in the region to involve the United Nations. While recognizing Georgia's territorial integrity, the United Nations was not prepared to send forces to guarantee it. UN Secretary General Boutros Boutros-Ghali proposed that a CIS peacekeeping force be deployed in Georgia, with UN monitors overseeing the force. On July 2, 1994, the Security Council welcomed the "contribution made by the Russian Federation . . . of a peacekeeping force."[45] At the same time the Security Council authorized 136 UN military observers to monitor the Russian peacekeepers.

Russian peacekeeping in Georgia clearly has served the foreign policy interests of Moscow, but it has failed to achieve all of Russia's objectives. Shevardnadze was forced to accede to a Russian role in the affairs of Georgia. In the face of a persistent deadlock over Abkhazia, the Georgian president sought support from both the United States and the United Nations for a multinational force to replace the Russians. Neither the United States nor the United Nations has been willing to take a stand in opposition to the Russian government. United Nations–sponsored talks in Geneva in 1997 produced direct negotiations between Georgia and Abkhazia, but they failed to achieve a breakthrough.

As efforts to resolve the conflict stalemated, Russian-Georgian relations deteriorated. Shevardnadze assumed that his concessions were a quid pro quo for Russia's commitment to guarantee Georgia's territorial integrity (i.e., forcing Abkhazia to surrender). Yeltsin tried to pressure Georgia and the Abkhzaian separatists to negotiate, but with no success. Beyond that his administration refused to go. Moscow, already deeply involved in a seemingly endless struggle in Chechnya, was not about to get into another war in the Caucasus. Indeed, the Russian military became concerned by the steady number of casualties inflicted on Russian peacekeeping forces.

Georgia's unhappiness with Moscow was reflected in several actions: cooperating with Azerbaijan in building the Baku-Supsa pipeline as an alternative to the Baku-Novorossiisk pipeline through Russia, and with the United States, Azerbaijan, and Turkey in the more ambitious Baku-Tbilisi-Ceyhan pipeline; participating in the pro-Western GUUAM group and expressing a wish to join NATO; permitting a Chechen mission to operate in Tbilisi; and agreeing to enlist the Turkish military in equipping and training Georgian military forces. Russian frustration with Georgia's actions was reflected in a warning made by Defense Minister Sergeev in March 1998 that Russia might altogether withdraw its peacekeeping forces in Georgia.[46]

Although he has not gone as far as Sergeev hinted, Vladimir Putin has certainly stepped up the pressure on Georgia. In December 2000, allegedly in reaction to the infiltration of Chechen fighters across the border and Georgia's refusal to allow Russian troops to pursue them onto Georgian soil, Russia imposed a visa requirement on persons crossing the borders (except from Abkhazia and South Ossetia). This worked a particular hardship on the 500,000–700,000 Georgians living in Russia, whose remittances compose one-fourth of Georgia's income. On January 1, 2001, the Russians stopped the flow of natural gas through their pipeline to Georgia. Although the gas began to flow again after three days, the point of Georgia's total dependence on Russia was driven home in harsh fashion. The Russians were also slowing down measures to close two of their four bases in Georgia and withdraw a number of tanks, artillery pieces, and fighters, as required by the revised Treaty on Conventional Forces in Europe (CFE) signed at an OSCE summit in Istanbul in November 1999. The pressure tactics were intended, at least in part, to reduce support received by Chechen guerrillas in Georgia, but they were also probably aimed at persuading Shevardnadze to back away from his flirtation with NATO and from the Baku-Ceyhan pipeline project.[47] Despite the pressures, Georgia managed to assume control of the Russian base at Vaziani by the July 1 deadline and expected to have the Russians out of the military base in Gudanta soon thereafter. Moreover, far from backing away from NATO, Georgian troops joined NATO forces in the "Cooperative Partner—2000" military exercises held on Georgian soil in June 2001.

Russia's relations with Georgia were further strained in 2002 when Moscow accused Tbilisi of harboring Chechen rebel units in the Pankisi Gorge, a mountainous region bordering the two states. Foreign Minister Igor Ivanov even suggested that Osama bin Laden might be hiding somewhere in the gorge. At Shevardnadze's invitation, a small contingent of United States military forces arrived in Georgia to train the country's special forces in combating terrorism. Adding insult to injury, Shevardnadze failed to consult Russia before inviting the American military presence. Harsh anti-Georgian speeches were made in the Russian Duma, but Putin discouraged any public confrontation with Georgia by remarking, "It's no tragedy."[48]

However, Russo-Georgian relations continued to deteriorate as Shevardnadze doggedly attempted to pursue a pro-Western foreign policy. Russia's Duma continued to grumble about the special privileges Georgia conferred on American servicemen in Georgia. For its part, the Georgian government objected to the visa arrangements Moscow granted to residents of Adzharia, a breakaway territory of Georgia controlled by a local warlord, Aslan Abashidze. Unlike Abkhazia and South Ossetia, this Black Sea region—home of the important port of Batumi, a major oil terminal—shares no border with

Russia, although it is the site of one of the remaining Russian military outposts on Georgia soil.

The political environment in Georgia changed suddenly in November 2003 when a popular revolt (the "rose revolution") forced Shevardnadze to resign the presidency. The objections to the Georgian president were not due to the country's foreign policy but rather to the blatant corruption and economic incompetence of his administration.[49] After the crisis erupted, Vladimir Putin sent Igor Ivanov to help broker a peaceful transition to a new leadership. Shevardnadze's successor was thirty-six-year-old Mikhail Saakashvili, who had studied and practiced law in the United States. Though pro-Western in outlook, he immediately sought to pursue a balancing act similar to that of his predecessor. At his inauguration, he stated, "Today as my first act, I am offering a friendly hand to Russia." Significantly, special honors at the inauguration ceremonies were accorded to U.S. secretary of state Colin Powell.[50] And shortly after assuming the presidency, Saakashvili journeyed to Azerbaijan to reaffirm that Georgia would participate in the Baku-Ceyhan pipeline project.

Yet to be resolved, however, were the problems of the secessionist regions of Adzharia, Abkhazia, and South Ossetia, and the continuing presence of Russian troops on Georgian territory. Saakashvili's first move to restore Georgia's territorial integrity came in March, when he insisted that Adzharia participate in Georgia's forthcoming parliamentary elections. When Abashidze resisted, the Georgia president imposed an economic embargo on the region, forcing its warlord to back down. In the midst of the crisis, Moscow mayor Yuii Luzhkov arrived in Batumi, first to offer his support to "his brother" Abashidze and then to act as an intermediary in resolving the conflict. Following the victory of Saakashvili's party in the March 28 elections, however, Abashidze refused to concede defeat, mobilizing his armed militia as Georgian troops massed on the borders of the province. Violence was averted, and the crisis ended in May when Putin sent Igor Ivanov, now Security Council secretary, to inform Abashidze that his cries for Russian aid would not be heeded. The rebellious warlord resigned his position, and at Saakashvili's request, was granted political asylum in Moscow. Although Putin would no doubt have preferred to keep the pro-Russian Abashidze in place, where he had helped to serve Moscow's economic and security interests, the goal of averting armed conflict was more important. Georgia's president was quick to express his thanks: "I think that President Putin played a very constructive role, and among the things he deserves credit for is the fact that bloodshed and complications were avoided."[51]

Within days, however, Igor Ivanov was back in Georgia to express Russia's concern over Saakashvili's statement that "another revolution" was anticipated in Abkhazia. Georgia was pressing for a resumption of United Nations–

brokered talks with Abkhazia on a plan that would declare the region a "sovereign entity"—but not a subject of international law and not able to conduct its own foreign or defense policy—within a federal Georgia state. The Abkhazian authorities, asserting that they had already won their independence from Georgia, refused to negotiate with Tbilisi. On Georgia's independence day, May 26, 2004, Saakashvili's speech appealed to the peoples of both Abkhazia and South Ossetia, in their native languages, to join in Georgia's democratic revolution, and he reiterated his intention to use peaceful means to reunite the country.

On June 1, however, Georgian special forces troops landed in South Ossetia to guard Georgian police outposts, after the commander of the Russian peacekeeping forces had threatened to dismantle them. The troops withdrew after assurances from the Russian commander, but the Russian foreign ministry complained that the action had been destabilizing, and that it had been carried out by troops that had been trained by the United States for the purpose of combating terrorism, and not for intervening in ethnic conflicts.

At the end of July, Saakashvili met with Putin in Moscow, hoping to agree on terms for a solution in South Ossetia and for the withdrawal of Russian troops from Georgia. Although he professed delight as Putin's "warm attitude toward Georgia," it was clear that he had failed to resolve the issues. Putin promised to "carefully consider" Georgia's proposals, including a plan for a joint counterterrorism center in Georgia, which would employ 500 Russian military personnel (while the remaining 2,500 returned to Russia). While the two presidents did agree on a procedure for simplifying visa regulations, the situation in South Ossetia and Abkhazia remained tense.[52] It became even more so a few days later, when Saakashvili ordered the Georgian coast guard to fire on cargo ships sailing to Abkhazia, warning that all illegal ships (including those carrying Russian vacationers) would be sunk. Russian defense minister Sergei Ivanov immediately denounced the Georgian action as "piracy," vowing to protect Russian citizens—including the large number of Abkhazian residents who had recently taken out citizenship—preferably using "political and diplomatic methods." The United States joined Russia in urging the fiery Georgian leader to disengage his military forces and negotiate a peaceful solution to the reunification conflict. And while Saakashvili pledged to move "in stages" and not to force his country to war,[53] the issue remained one that could conceivably provoke armed conflict between Russian and Georgian troops.

Nagorno-Karabakh

Russia has used the conflict between Armenia and Azerbaijan over the region of Nagorno-Karabakh to exert influence over both countries. Moscow played little role in sparking the initial dispute, but it has sought to monopolize the mediation and peacekeeping efforts to settle the conflict.

Nagorno-Karabakh is an autonomous oblast in Azerbaijan, the inhabitants of which are primarily Armenian. Predominantly Christian, the non-Slavic Armenians have a long history of animosity with the Muslim Azeris. Like many interethnic antagonisms in the former Soviet Union, this one was exacerbated by Soviet nationality policy. Typical of its divide-and-rule practices, the Bolshevik government in 1921 placed Nagorno-Karabakh, whose population was 94 percent Armenian, under the administrative control of Azerbaijan. Even during the height of Soviet rule, political demonstrations between Armenians and Azeris led to violent clashes. The conflict flared up during Gorbachev's rule, defying his efforts at settlement. When Azerbaijan declared its independence in 1991, the government of Nagorno-Karabakh proclaimed itself an independent republic. Fighting again flared up between Nagorno-Karabakh Armenians and Azeris, and when Armenian military forces joined their brethren, an undeclared war between Armenia and Azerbaijan ensued. Militarily the Armenians won on all fronts—within Nagorno-Karabakh itself, taking control of the land between Armenia proper and the oblast, and also occupying territory deep into Azerbaijan east of Nagorno-Karabakh. In the scale of military action and the number of victims, the war over Nagorno-Karabakh was larger than any other conflict in the former Soviet Union, and it was second to none in viciousness. Atrocities were committed by both sides.[54]

The Armenian-Azerbaijani conflict is both an interstate war and a war of secession. Before the Soviet collapse, many in Armenia and Nagorno-Karabakh shared the belief that Nagorno-Karabakh would unify with Armenia. After Armenia and Azerbaijan became independent, the idea of unification declined and was superseded by the notion of an independent Nagorno-Karabakh republic. As the aggressor in the war against Azerbaijan, Armenia found itself under international pressure to withdraw from occupied territory. In April 1993 the UN Security Council demanded the withdrawal of Armenian troops from Azerbaijan.

An earlier and more extended international effort to stop hostilities was made by the Conference on Security and Cooperation in Europe (CSCE—later to become the Organization for Security and Cooperation in Europe, or OSCE). In March 1992 it established the "Minsk Group" (Belarus, France, Germany, Hungary, Italy, Russia, Sweden, and Turkey) to mediate the conflict and plan for a CSCE peacekeeping operation. A CSCE observer group arrived in the region in April 1993.

Russian involvement has complicated the CSCE effort to mediate the conflict or to deploy peacekeepers. Moscow claims the right to play the leading role. Russian mediation succeeded in May 1994 in producing a cease-fire and an agreement for a peacekeeping force. Armenian president Lev Ter-Petrosian sought Russian peacekeepers; Nagorno-Karabakh Armenians wanted no Turkish troops in the force; and Azerbaijani president Gaidar Aliev balked at the idea of a Russian–CIS-dominated force and insisted that only a CSCE-mandate force could operate in his country.

An apparent breakthrough on the principle of an OSCE peacekeeping force was reached at the Budapest summit in December 1994. A force of 3,000 troops was proposed, but the specifics of which countries would contribute were unresolved. To date the force exists in principle only. Meanwhile Armenia continues to occupy Azeri territory, and Nagorno-Karabakh maintains a de facto but unrecognized independence. Nevertheless, the agreement in principle on an OSCE peacekeeping force is more than Russia had previously conceded toward permitting outside forces to engage in peacekeeping and mediation in any of the former Soviet states. No doubt Moscow was especially irritated when the new Bush administration tried its hand at mediating the conflict, bringing the two presidents for a meeting at Key West with Secretary of State Colin Powell in April 2001. Although it pledged to keep trying, the United States—strongly pressured to intervene by domestic oil interests eager to expand their presence in Azerbaijan—was unable to achieve any immediate breakthrough.

Both Yeltsin and Putin have insisted that Russia must play the dominant role in managing conflict in the Transcaucasus. In this sense democratic Russia continues the historic policy of the Soviet Union and Imperial Russia in viewing the Transcaucasus as a "dagger pointed toward the heart of Russia." The issue here, unlike that in the other CIS conflicts, does not involve protecting ethnic Russians, because few live in the region. Instead, Moscow is motivated by a number of economic and geopolitical factors. Of considerable importance is the question of Azerbaijan's cooperation in the exploitation of Caspian Sea oil and the pipelines to bring the oil to Western markets. Russia voiced reservations over the signing in September 1994 of the "deal of the century" to exploit three Caspian Sea oil fields. In the deal, Azerbaijan negotiated a $7.4 billion contract giving eight Western oil companies a 70 percent share in the project. To appease Moscow, Lukoil, the Russian oil giant, was granted 10 percent of Azerbaijan's initial 30 percent stake. Russia has pressed for a larger share. The number and location of the pipelines to deliver the oil to Western markets also remain unresolved.[55]

Azerbaijan's president, the late Gaidar Aliev, a former KGB general and Soviet Politburo member, maneuvered shrewdly in dealing with Russia. Where necessary he made concessions to Moscow, as on the issue of oil production. He also agreed to rejoin the CIS after a brief withdrawal, but alone among the leaders of the former Soviet states, he resisted the stationing of Russian peacekeepers or military bases on Azerbaijan's soil—even going so far as to suggest that he might welcome NATO bases there. Aliev also carefully exploited Russia's concerns about the influence of Turkey, a traditional rival, and Iran, a center of militant Islam, in the region. In 1994 Aliev signed the ten-year Treaty of Friendship and Cooperation with Turkish president Suleyman Demirel. He also concluded several political, economic, and cultural agreements with Iran. Undoubtedly, however, Aliev's politics were constrained by the knowledge that Moscow helped to destabilize the administration of his predecessor, the intensely nationalistic and pro-Turkish leader Abulfez Elchibey. Though potentially one of the richest of the former Soviet states, Azerbaijan remains vulnerable to Russian pressure—which Moscow has not hesitated to exert.[56] While Aliev and Yeltsin reportedly had an intense mutual dislike dating from their days of service together on the Soviet Politburo, Vladimir Putin initiated a rapprochement by making a brief visit to Baku in January 2001. He and Aliev signed a statement of principles governing cooperation in the Caspian, based on the formula (opposed by Iran) "share the water and divide the seabed." Putin agreed to pursue mediation efforts on Karabakh on the basis of strict impartiality; in return, he sought Baku's agreement on Russian participation in the exploration and development of Caspian oil fields.[57]

Azerbaijan's politics entered a new era in December 2003 when Gaidar Aliev died (at a clinic in Cleveland, Ohio) after a long illness. In control to the end, Aliev secured the office of president for his son, Ilkham, who gave every indication of continuing his father's balancing act with regard to relations with Russia and the West. Although Ilkham Aliev's first official trip abroad was to Paris, he followed that up with a visit to Vladimir Putin in Moscow. Both presidents agreed to cooperate further in the economic sphere. As for the Nagorno-Karabakh conflict, Putin promised that Russia's mediation efforts would be "stepped up."[58]

Central Asia

The newly independent states of Central Asia—Kazakhstan, Kyrgyzstan, Uzbekistan, Tajikistan, and Turkmenistan—also lacked a history of independence. Since the eighteenth century the peoples of this vast region have been governed by the tsars, and after them, the Soviets. One scholar described the independence of these states in 1991 as an "unsolicited gift."[59] These countries share a Muslim religious heritage and—with the exception of the Tajiks, who are of Iranian origin—have a common Turkic ethnic origin. National identities in this region were not strongly established. In Gorbachev's 1991 refeiendum on the future of the union, the strongest support in favor of preserving the USSR came from the voters of the five Central Asian republics. One reason was the high degree of economic dependence of the region on Moscow. Both the August coup and the Soviet collapse in 1991 confronted the Central Asians with unpopular choices. They were unprepared for independence, and they welcomed admission to the CIS as founding members.

Another important factor linking the new states to Russia is the large number of Russian minorities living in some of them. According to the 1989 USSR census, in Kyrgyzstan 21.5 percent of the people were Russian. Kazakhstan's population was 37.8 percent ethnic Russian, almost equal in number to the indigenous Kazakh population. It was thus not surprising that Nursultan Nazarbaev, Kazakhstan's president, was an outspoken advocate of keeping the union together and, when that proved impossible, of integrating the CIS as much as possible. Even those regional leaders who advocated independence for their countries acknowledged that close cooperation with Moscow was a necessity for survival. Yet, as weak and dependent as they were, the leaders of Central Asia soon acquired a taste for independence and a determination not to be mere puppets of Moscow.[60]

Russia's vital interests in Central Asia are both political and economic. In a general sense Moscow has sought to maintain a degree of hegemony over the entire region, an equivalent of the U.S. Monroe Doctrine in the Western Hemisphere. Indeed, as we saw in chapter 5, the parallel was made directly in an article by Andranik Migranian, then a member of Yeltsin's Presidential Council.[61] A major consideration behind such thinking was security. Moscow wanted to deploy its troops in the near abroad and to maintain an air defense system that would cover not just Russia but the outer borders of the former Soviet Union. Moscow was also concerned about the growth of Islamic fundamentalism in Central Asia and its possible spread to the Russian Federation itself.

Instability in Central Asia also posed the danger of encouraging the migration of large numbers of Russians back to a country then unprepared to absorb them. According to the 1989 census, some 9.5 million Russians lived in Central Asia. Even though many of these Russians came originally as colonizers, they were not as discriminated against in Central Asia as in some other parts of the former USSR, such as the Baltics. But the fact that on average only 3 percent of the Russians knew the titular language of their country of residence indicated a less than complete level of assimilation and the ever-present possibility of a migration back to the mother country. Indeed, there has been a substantial migration of Russians from Central Asia, notwithstanding that none of the states in the region denied Russians the rights of citizenship. But, with the initial exception of Turkmenistan and

Tajikistan, the Central Asian states rejected the Russian demand that Russian-speaking peoples be given the right to maintain dual citizenship. In April 2003, Turkmenistan's dictator, Saparmurad Niyazov, as part of a general anti-Russian program, revoked dual citizenship for Russian-speaking residents.

Economic objectives also played a role in Russia's relations with Central Asia. For a time an effort was made to keep these countries in a "ruble zone" so as to maintain a measure of fiscal control over them; but a deadlock in negotiations in 1993 forced the states to rely on their own resources and their own currencies. Independence did not bring economic prosperity to Central Asia—just the opposite. For the entire region the post-Soviet period has been one of economic hardship. The reasons are several, including the economic incompetence of Central Asia's governing elites, but adding to their woes were the end of Russian subsidies and Moscow's pursuit of policies almost exclusively to Russia's own advantage. Those countries possessing abundant natural resources, such as Kazakhstan, were pressed to share them with Russia. For example, Russia insisted that the Tengiz oil field in western Kazakhstan be open to Russian participation before the government of Kazakhstan was able to mobilize a consortium of foreign investors. In summary, the relations between Russia and Central Asia in the initial years could be described as "uneasy cooperation."[62]

Petropolitics—or who would control Central Asian oil—became an important factor in Russian–Central Asian relations, as it did in U.S.–Central Asian relations. There were two principal issues: (1) how the oil and gas beneath the Caspian Sea was to be divided, and (2) what routes would be used to transport Caspian Sea oil to markets in the West. Five states bordering the Caspian Sea—Russia, Turkmenistan, Azerbaijan, Kazakhstan, and Iran—laid claim to the oil reserves beneath that body of water.

In the 1990s Moscow unsuccessfully sought to divide up the Caspian Sea so as to give Russia an effective veto over the use of undersea resources by the littoral states.[63] Failing to achieve that end, Russia pressed for a resolution of the legal status of the Caspian Sea that would divide the seabed (and the fossil fuels beneath it) on lines extending from the coast of each state, while keeping the water undivided and accessible to all for fishing and navigation purposes. To date all of the littoral states except Iran have joined in supporting this position.[64] In May 2003 Russia, Azerbaijan, and Kazakhstan divided the northern 64 percent of the Caspian Sea into three unequal parts along this median line principle, giving Kazakhstan 27 percent, Russia 19 percent, and Azerbaijan 18 percent. Turkmenistan and Iran were present at the negotiations but refused to participate in the agreement. While Vladimir Putin remains determined to forge a legal contract that will bind all five states, the fact that agreement has been reached with Kazakhstan and Azerbaijan means that full-fledged exploration can begin in the north section of the Caspian Sea.[65]

A particularly contentious issue in petropolitics is the location of the pipelines that transport the oil from the Caspian Sea basin to markets in Europe and beyond. Under Soviet rule all pipelines from Azerbaijan, Kazakhstan, and Turkmenistan were controlled by Moscow. For both economic and geopolitical reasons, Russia would prefer to maintain that same control. That would mean utilizing its pipelines to transport oil from the Tengiz field in Kazakhstan to the Russian Black Sea port of Novorossisk and from Baku to Novorossisk. But on this issue Moscow has encountered opposition from the United States and Europe, which have sought to minimize the dependence of the Central Asian states upon Russia by having pipelines bypass Russia entirely.

An alternative cheaper route which also bypasses Russia is to ship oil to the Indian Ocean via Iran. This option is politically unacceptable to the United States because of Iranian-American hostility. Consequently, with strong backing from Washington, the Baku-Tbilisi-Ceyhan route to Turkey's Mediterranean coast was approved in 1999 as the main export route for the consortium of oil companies extracting Azerbaijani oil. Another pipeline bypassing Russia, also supported by Washington, is the Trans-Caspian Gas Pipeline, which would take gas from Turkmenistan through Baku and Tbilisi to Erzurum in Turkey. Clearly, these pipeline projects undermine Russian power in the Caucasus and Central Asia, but Moscow cannot stop their construction. In many respects, the maneuvering of the greater and lesser powers to dominate Central Asian and Transcaucasian oil is reminiscent of the nineteenth-century "Great Game."[66]

Oil was only one of the many issues on which the Central Asian states increasingly looked to the West for leadership and assistance. As the second Yeltsin administration showed signs of weakness, Central Asia became bolder in its disregard of Russian policy preferences. Leading the resistance to Moscow was Uzbek president Islam Karimov, who had his own aspirations for regional leadership. Uzbekistan stood alone among the CIS states in refusing completely to accept a Russian military presence on its territory. Karimov withdrew his state from the CIS Collective Security Treaty and affiliated with GUUAM, the group of states friendly to the West and determined to stay independent of Russia. On the other extreme was Tajikistan, where the presence of Russian troops was necessary to prop up the government of Emomali Rakhmonov. Turkmenistan tended to pursue a policy of neutrality, while Kazakhstan and Kyrgyzstan pursued a middle course. They joined with Uzbekistan and Tajikistan to form the Central Asian Economic Community in 1998, but they also affiliated in 2000 with Russia and Belarus to form the Eurasian Economic Union.

There are cross-cutting pressures modifying the foreign policies of all the Central Asian countries. None can afford to earn Russia's outright enmity, nor do any relish a tight embrace by the Russian bear. One issue on which all of the states are in accord with Russia is the threat of Islamic fundamentalism. Islamic extremist rebels have challenged the regimes in Tajikistan, Uzbekistan, and Kyrgyzstan. Joint antiterrorist military exercises were conducted in the region in 1999 and 2000. Code-named "Commonwealth Southern Shield 2000," the second of these maneuvers brought together the troops of Russia and four of the Central Asian states.[67]

President Vladimir Putin took active steps to improve relations with Central Asia, visiting all five states during his first year as president. He warmly congratulated Karimov on his election to a third term as president, stressing "Uzbekistan's close ties with Russia." To Turkmenistan's president Niyazov, he extolled "the dynamic development of relations between Russia and Turkmenistan," and in July 2000 he met with President Askar Akaev in the Kremlin to sign the Declaration of Perpetual Friendship and Partnership Between Russia and Kyrgyzstan.[68] An early fruit of Putin's approach was a rapprochement between Moscow and Tashkent. Uzbek president Karimov visited Moscow in May, declaring that Russia was now his country's "strategic partner."

However, international politics in Central Asia was drastically altered as a result of the attack on the United States by Islamic extremist terrorists on September 11, 2001. The American war on terrorism led directly to a new and unprecedented American intrusion into Central Asia, which initially Moscow accepted, but which soon came to be viewed as a challenge of Russian dominance of the region. As we will see in chapter 9, Vladimir Putin moved quickly and decisively to associate with the United States in its war on terrorism, including his acceptance of U.S. bases in several CIS states.[69] However, uncertainty regarding the duration of these bases and the length of stay of NATO forces in Afghanistan soon gave way to anxiety regarding Russia's regional hegemony. Fear of losing that hegemony led Moscow to become more assertive in its attempts to counter American influence.

Late in 2001 Kyrgyzstan's parliament approved use of its territory for foreign military bases, permitting the United States to build an air base at Manas. At the same time, Uzbekistan concluded an agreement with Washington to operate a military base on its territory. These would be the first American military bases in the Commonwealth of Independent States. The influential Russian newspaper *Nezavisimaia gazeta* reflected the view of many of Russia's political elite in noting, "The U.S. and NATO countries took brilliant advantage of their chance to stage an outwardly 'soft' and 'temporary' but in fact indefinite occupation of Central Asia."[70]

Putin wanted to reassert Moscow's authority in Central Asia and counter American influence without directly challenging the United States. His strategy was complicated by the shifting policies of the region's five states. In various degrees they sought to maneuver between Moscow and Washington, as indeed Moscow itself maneuvered between cooperating with and opposing the United States on a variety of issues. The geopolitical game played by all involved well illustrated the contradictions and paradoxes inherent in international politics.

One result of these contradictions was the proliferation of subgroups within the CIS whose purposes and memberships were constantly shifting. The first CIS subgroup fully independent of Russia was originally formed in 1997 and expanded in the spring of 1999. It was dubbed GUUAM, for the first initials of its members: Georgia, Ukraine, Uzbekistan, Azerbaijan, and Moldova. To Moscow's further irritation, the document creating the organization was signed in conjunction with NATO's fiftieth-anniversary summit in Washington, and its members purportedly sought some sort of partnership with NATO.

Uzbekistan was the only Central Asian state belonging to GUUAM. In March 2002 Uzbek president Islam Karimov visited the United States, where the two countries signed a declaration of strategic partnership. Washington even designated Uzbekistan the United States' chief strategic partner in Central Asia. However, to maintain its freedom to maneuver and to avoid unnecessary provocation of Moscow, Tashkent announced in June 2002 that Uzbekistan was leaving GUUAM, declaring the organization to be ineffective as an instrument for national security.

As a partial counter to GUUAM, Russia initiated the creation of another CIS subgroup, the Eurasian Economic Community (EURASEC), consisting of Russia, Belarus, Kazakhstan, Kyrgyzstan, and Tajikistan. Ostensibly, EURASEC's central mission was to coordinate the economic activities of its members. But political considerations were also important. EURASEC has actually been described by Moscow as a kind of analogue to the European Union, but quite unlike the EU, where each member has the same vote, Russia dominates EURASEC with 40 percent of the vote.[71] Another Central Asian organization came into being in February 2002, when the leaders of Kazakhstan, Tajikistan, Uzbekistan, and Kyrgyzstan met in Almaty, Kazakhstan, to form the Central Asian Cooperation Organization (CACO). This initiative, like GUUAM, was taken completely independently of Moscow. Evolving from an earlier economic cooperation agreement, its purpose was to work with the West to fight terrorism, Islamic militancy, and drug trafficking.[72]

These objectives overlapped those of another organization, the Shanghai Cooperation Organization (SCO), which grew out of the agreements between

China and the three former Soviet states with which it shares a border. Uzbekistan joined the original "Shanghai Five" (China, Russia, Kyrgyzstan, Kazakhstan, and Tajikistan) in June 2001, and the SCO was formally chartered at a summit in June 2002. The following year it became a full-fledged international organization with a budget and structure, including an anti-terrorist center located in Bishkek, Kyrgyzstan. Some observers have described the SCO, which notably includes both Russia and China as members, as a counterweight to NATO, notwithstanding their common struggle against terrorism. Should its relations with NATO or Europe deteriorate, it is possible that Russia could someday see the SCO as a vehicle for closer cooperation with the Asian states.

The formation of these several subgroups of CIS members was clear evidence that the Commonwealth of Independent States was undergoing a steady decline, particularly in Central Asia. Even though some of them served the general interest of fighting terrorism, these organizations in part represented either efforts by Russia to bring Central Asia back into its orbit or efforts by some Central Asian states to escape Moscow's embrace. A good indication of the general state of affairs came at the CIS summit that convened in Kiev in January 2003. The president of every Central Asian state except Tajikistan refused to participate in the summit. As the Russian press noted, "And so the slow extinction of the CIS continues."[73]

Tajikistan is one of the two Central Asian states (along with Kazakhstan) that are most consistently loyal to Moscow. In both cases economic and political factors induce them to cooperate with Russia. Tajikistan is not only weak and dependent on Russia for security, but it is also indebted to Moscow for almost $300 million. During 2003 Russia increased the size of its military force in Tajikistan, in part as a balance to the U.S. presence in the region. Kazakhstan is vulnerable because of the large Russian-speaking population in its regions bordering Russia. The presence of a major missile test site at Baikonur is an important economic asset for Kazakhstan. As for security, its main rival and potential threat is neighboring Uzbekistan. Kazakhstan has responded positively to Russia's proposals for joint military exercises and a common air defense system. Together, Tajikistan and Kazakhstan form the core of Moscow's geopolitical assets in the region.

Although Kyrgyzstan was already host to an American air base, it agreed to permit Russia to open an air base at Kant in 2003. This was the new first military base established by Moscow in another country since the collapse of the Soviet Union. Free use of the airfield facilities was permitted by Kyrgyzstan, but the cost of operating the facility is to be borne entirely by Russia. This military presence was placed in a starker perspective when, in the aftermath of the invasion of Iraq, Russia's defense minister noted that

Russia also reserved the right to assert the principle of "preemptive use of military force in the CIS countries."[74]

Moldova

Moldova is another case of Russian intervention in the near abroad to establish control over territory it believes to be within its sphere of influence. The circumstances of this Russian intervention, however, differ from the others in the degree to which Russian forces have been guided by policy from Moscow. Russian military forces in Moldova were not always completely under Moscow's control, with the result that policy toward the area often had a schizophrenic character.

Moldova is confronted by a secessionist movement in a region referred to by the movement's leaders as the Trans-Dniester Republic. The territory involved is a small strip of land on the eastern bank of the Dniester River between Ukraine and the rest of present-day Moldova. At the time of the 1989 census, the region contained 546,000 people, or 12.6 percent of Moldova's population. Of that number 40 percent are Moldovan, 28.3 percent Ukrainian, and 25.4 percent Russian. Thus the Russians, like the Abkhazians in their territory, are a minority, but they, too, dominate the politics of the region. The Trans-Dniester territory had always been ruled from Moscow; its history was different from that of the west bank, or Bessarabia, which had been a part of the Russian Empire but became a part of Romania after 1917. Bessarabia was returned to Moscow's control as part of the Nazi-Soviet Pact of 1939.

In the period leading up to the collapse of the USSR, the nationalist-minded government in Chisinau adopted laws making Romanian the state language and replacing the Cyrillic with the Latin script. The east bank Russians strongly opposed these measures, believing they would lead to a subordinate status for Russians, and that they heightened the possibility that Moldova would merge with Romania. In addition to the ethnic issues between Chisinau and the east bank capital of Tiraspol, there were sharp political differences. The Trans-Dniester Russians were strong supporters of the Soviet system and welcomed the August 1991 coup in Moscow. Moldova's leaders by contrast opposed the coup and backed Gorbachev. In August 1991 Moldova declared its independence from the Soviet Union, and a week later Trans-Dniester seceded from Moldova, declaring itself a constituent republic of the USSR, with Tiraspol as its capital.

Moldova's efforts to stop the secession and enforce its authority in the Trans-Dniester region led to widespread fighting in 1992. The rebellious Russians were aided by the Fourteenth Army, which as a component of the

Soviet armed forces had been based in Tiraspol. With its active support, the Dniester troops were able to hold off Moldovan forces and establish effective control over the entire east bank of the Dniester River. In the spring of 1992 Boris Yeltsin put the Fourteenth Army under Russian control, and in June he appointed General Aleksandr Lebed to be its commander.

Defeated on the battlefield, Moldova had no choice but to involve Russia in negotiations for a cease-fire.[75] Moldova sought a peacekeeping force under international supervision and requested the OSCE to send such a force. When the OSCE declined, Chisinau had no choice but to accept Russia's proposal for a joint force of Russian, Moldovan, and Trans-Dniester troops to monitor a truce.[76] (Although the contingent was referred to as a CIS peacekeeping force, the CIS members who expressed a willingness to participate ultimately chose not to do so.)

On July 21, 1992, Yeltsin and Moldovan president Mircea Snegur signed an agreement creating the trilateral force and a security zone on both sides of the Dniester. As a step toward a political settlement, the two presidents agreed on the territorial integrity of Moldova and the gradual withdrawal of the Fourteenth Army. As a concession to the Trans-Dniester inhabitants, the region was to be given autonomy, and in the event that Moldova and Romania were to unify, the Trans-Dniester region would have the right to secede.[77]

The joint force successfully kept the peace, but—as so often happens with peacekeeping—little was achieved toward a lasting settlement. Trans-Dniester remains a semisovereign state in all but name. It has a government, passports, and a postal system. While Lebed commanded the Fourteenth Army, he supported Trans-Dniester independence, though he severely criticized the leadership in Tiraspol. He even ran successfully for the Trans-Dniester parliament in 1993. Indeed, during the period of Lebed's command, the Russian government had only partial control over the activities of the Fourteenth Army. Yeltsin's administration was constrained by the fact that the Trans-Dniester cause had attracted strong support among Russian nationalists. However, Yeltsin himself had good reason to oppose the secessionists' cause. The Russians in the region were politically closer to his enemies than to him. During the October 1993 crisis, Moldova supported Yeltsin, while most of the Trans-Dniester leaders sided with Rutskoi and Khasbulatov.[78] And as elsewhere, Yeltsin was sensitive to the implications of Trans-Dniester independence for independence-minded regions within Russia.

In part, the reversals of Russian policy have reflected the tug and pull of diverse domestic political forces. Particularly contentious issues were the timetable and conditions for withdrawal of the Russian Fourteenth Army. On October 2, 1994, Russia and Moldova signed an agreement for these forces to withdraw over a three-year period. The withdrawal, however, was made conditional on a political settlement providing a "special status" for the Trans-Dniester regime.[79] Aleksandr Lebed opposed withdrawal, as did many in the Russian Duma. Yeltsin was pulled in one direction by strong international pressure against Russia's intervention in the internal affairs of a sovereign state, and in another direction by his own military. In April 1995, Yeltsin challenged Lebed, who threatened to resign. Many did not expect Yeltsin to accept the resignation of so popular a military leader, but he did. Lebed went on to challenge Yeltsin in the 1996 presidential election, and then to serve briefly in his administration, but the Trans-Dniester issue has continued to defy resolution.

President Yeltsin was unable to secure parliamentary ratification of the 1994 agreement to withdraw Russian forces from Moldova. At the Istanbul summit of the OSCE in 1999 the issue was elevated to the European regional level when Russia agreed in the revised CFE to withdraw its forces from Moldovan territory by 2002. President Putin has committed himself to doing so, but he has made withdrawal conditional on a mutually acceptable resolution of the conflict. Putin assigned to Evgenii Primakov the task of negotiating a settlement.

Primakov's task was undertaken in the midst of significant political change in Moldova. In February 2001 the Moldovan communists won a solid majority in parliamentary elections. Since Moldova is a parliamentary republic, the communists took control of the executive branch as well. Moldova thus became the first of the former Soviet states in which the people chose to return the Communist Party to power. Their leader, Vladimir Voronin, declared that he would work to give Russian the status of a state language on par with Moldovan. In the opinion of one journalist, however, the elections—which were boycotted by voters in the Trans-Dniester region—did not necessarily presage a solution of the secession crisis: "[D]espite the fact that Communists nostalgic for the USSR are now in power on both sides of the Dniester, no solution to the Dniester region problem is expected anytime soon."[80]

Initially Voronin pursued a cautious policy, so as not to provoke Moscow. Membership in GUUAM complicated Russo-Moldavian relations, prompting Chisinau in 2002 to question whether the organization should continue to exist. Early in 2003 Voronin tackled the Trans-Dniester problem by proposing a federal structure for the country—the first time a Moldovan leader had abandoned the principle of a unitary state. Nothing came of Voronin's initiative at the time because the presence of Russian military forces encouraged intransigence on the part of the separatists. Many Moldovans were suspicious of Moscow's intentions, and during 2003–04 Voronin himself shifted his orientation away from the CIS toward the West. A growing number of Moldovans have come to favor unification with Romania, now that it has become a member of NATO and a candidate for membership in the European Union.

In November 2003, perhaps to forestall that option, Putin seized the initiative to propose a federal system for Moldova. To the Russian president's chagrin, Voronin objected to a provision in Putin's plan that allowed Russian peacekeepers to guarantee the proposed constitutional arrangements. Even more irritating to the Russians was the visit of U.S. Secretary of Defense Donald Rumsfeld to Moldova in June 2004, ostensibly to thank the country for its contribution of a small contingent of forces in Iraq. While there, Rumsfeld expressed his view that Russian forces should be withdrawn from the country.

Moldova's defiance of Moscow was a serious setback for Russian efforts to dominate the states of the former Soviet Union. It revealed clearly that among the members of the CIS there was a powerful urge to be a part of Europe, and that Moscow was losing its struggle to contain that drive.[81]

Russia and the Future of the CIS

The history of the Commonwealth of Independent States has been one of steady decline. Its meetings are only partially attended. Its decisions are largely ignored. The CIS has failed to achieve international recognition as a viable regional organization. During the presidency of Boris Yeltsin, the dominant trend was the drive among the non-Russian members for full national sovereignty and independence. Under Putin this trend has been enhanced, as some members have been inclined toward a pro-Russian orientation and others have been more inclined toward Europe.

Still, no one is proposing the dissolution of the CIS, certainly not the Russians. On occasion the CIS has been useful for coordinating national policies. One issue on which all states agree is that Islamic extremist terrorism is a threat. Putin has persuaded the CIS to establish an antiterrorism center, headquartered in Moscow.

One CIS instrument useful for Russia is peacekeeping. Though Moscow has used peacekeeping to dominate and prevent the extension of outside influence in the CIS region, Russia's peacekeeping has at the same time benefited the states involved by significantly reducing fighting between the parties and in some measure resolving the differences between them.[82]

On issues that are central to Russia, Moscow has relied on bilateral rather than multilateral negotiations. A case in point is the common air defense system between Russia and the CIS states. The Kremlin has succeeded in bringing into the system, one by one, each of the CIS members except for Moldova and Azerbaijan; the first air defense exercise took place in Moscow in April 1998. Similarly, Russia's arrangements for military cooperation with CIS states have been negotiated on a bilateral basis. Ultimately, Putin's preference for bilateral over multilateral relations was evidenced when he abolished the Russian Ministry for CIS Affairs and gave its responsibilities to the Ministry of Foreign Affairs and the Russian Security Council.

Belarus

Belarus is the only former Soviet republic that has moved toward genuine integration with Russia. Belarus is unique because of its closeness to Russia. Ethnically and culturally, the people of Belarus are similar to Russians. Belarus before 1991 had never been an independent state. Its history was one of incorporation into various empires—the Lithuanian domain, the Polish-Lithuanian Commonwealth, the Prussian Empire, the Russian Empire, and finally the Soviet Union. The people of Belarus had a weak sense of national identity. For that reason its leaders were more supportive than those of other republics of Gorbachev's efforts to unite in a new union. Economically Belarus was dependent upon Russia. It relied upon Russia for its security. It was home to a large concentration of military facilities that had been part of the former Soviet Union's defense infrastructure (including nuclear forces). Thus it was natural that Belarus was anxious to participate in the CIS as an original founding member.

Although it was closer to Russia politically and culturally than any other CIS member, Belarus under its first president Stanislau Shushkevich quickly acquired a taste for independence and ruled out any thought of subordinating its sovereignty to Russia. What Shushkevich wanted was close cooperation without merging with Belarus's giant neighbor. In 1992 the parliament of Belarus voted to create a ministry of defense and to subordinate all former Soviet troops on its territory to Belarusian authority. Officially the country defined its foreign and security policies as neutralist. Accordingly, President Shushkevich initially chose not to sign the CIS Collective Security Treaty, discussed above. This decision, however, proved unpopular with the Belarus parliament, which voted in April 1993 to seek entry into the Collective Security Treaty. In June 1994 Shushkevich reversed himself and agreed to affiliation.

Russian pressure had contributed to the change in Belarus's position, as Moscow threatened to charge non-signatories of the Collective Security Treaty for officer training. Shortly after Belarus's adherence the two countries signed a comprehensive military agreement providing for joint training, the maintenance of a joint air defense system, and cooperation in arms development and export.

Belarus's first presidential election, held in 1994, was won in a landslide by pro-Russian Aleksandr Lukashenko. To bolster his program for closer ties to Russia, Lukashenko submitted a referendum asking the public to endorse integration with Russia and recognition of Russian as equal in status to the Belarusian language. Voting on May 14, 1995, the public approved both propositions by a solid 83.3 percent. Immediately thereafter the two countries abolished customs checkpoints along their common border.

Russia's interest in Belarus was not without important qualifications. Security interests were primary. In particular, Moscow wanted legal authorization to station Russian troops on Belarusian territory. This it received in a treaty on cooperation and friendship, signed on April 12, 1994, which the Belarusian parliament ratified in April of the following year. But Lukashenko initially wanted much closer economic relations, to bolster his own weak economy, and on this issue Moscow was hesitant. The Belarusian economy was in such bad shape that integration could only end up as a burden on Russia (as the German Democratic Republic proved to be when it merged with the Federal Republic of Germany). Additionally, under both Shushkevich and Lukashenko, Belarus remained a command economy resistant to economic reform. Lukashenko's ideas on economic reform differed sharply from those of Yeltsin. Consequently Yeltsin resisted the lifting of trade barriers and rejected plans for a monetary or customs union between the two countries.[83] Lukashenko's suppression of the media at home and the increasingly authoritarian nature of his administration, not to mention a mercurial pattern of behavior, put off many in Russia who were trying to nurture a fledgling democracy.

Strong sentiment remains in Russia, particularly among communists and nationalists, for the creation of a union with more teeth than the CIS. During the presidential campaign of 1996, Yeltsin found himself in a bitter struggle with his communist opponent Gennadii Zyuganov. Starting the campaign as an underdog, the incumbent attempted to win over as large a segment of the prounion electorate as possible. As a part of the strategy, Yeltsin signed two agreements pledging integration between Russia and three other CIS members. On April 2, 1996, Russia and Belarus signed a treaty creating the Community of Sovereign Republics, and on May 29, Russia, Belarus, Kazakhstan, and Kyrgyzstan agreed to the "Treaty on the Deepening of Integration in the Economic and Humanitarian Fields." Echoing the goals of the CIS, this new community envisaged the formation of a "single economic space" including a common market. Suggesting that this nucleus of states could expand to include others, Kazakh president Nursultan Nazarbaev—always a proponent of integration—termed the treaty the "$4 + n$" document.

Both treaties were little more than vague commitments to integrate. There was clearly no intention to merge into a new state. The treaties explicitly affirmed that all the parties would retain their national sovereignty. Reference was made to the coordination of foreign policies, synchronization of economic reforms, and a common currency and budget, but no bodies were created to implement these goals nor were any precise timetables established for integration. The treaty between Russia and Belarus permitted either party to opt out with six months' notice.[84] Although no one has opted out of the treaty yet, neither have steps been taken to breathe real life into either agreement. If electoral considerations were paramount to Yeltsin, then the treaties paid off in his success in the June voting and the July runoff. Lukashenko has not wavered in his rhetorical support for the idea of integration, but he has steadfastly avoided taking any measure that would subordinate power in Minsk to that in Moscow. In November 1996, Lukashenko engineered a referendum that greatly expanded presidential powers and gave him virtual control over parliament.

Moscow has waxed hot and cold on the idea of integrating Russia with a Lukashenko-governed Belarus. Union of the two countries is part of a larger vision, shared by nationalists, of uniting all the Slavic peoples into a single state. When Evgenii Primakov became prime minister in 1998, in the aftermath of the Russian financial collapse, the prospects for union appeared to improve. Primakov was known to be sympathetic to integration. On December 25, 1998, Boris Yeltsin and Aleksandr Lukashenko signed a declaration asserting:

> Russia and Belarus have taken a historic step on the path of unifying the two fraternal countries and peoples: on December 25, 1998, in Moscow, we signed a declaration on the creation of a union state in the coming year and a treaty and an agreement on guarantees of equal rights for our states' citizens on the territory of Russia and Belarus.[85]

Though there was discussion that the new "Union State" would have a common budget, common foreign policy, single customs space, and even a single currency, the fact remained that the two states continued to be sovereign and full members of the international community.

During 1999 a joint Belarusian-Russian group worked out the text for a treaty of unification. Resistance to a close embrace was strong within the Kremlin, in part because of the ruthless dictatorship Lukashenko exercised in Minsk, and in part due to the disarray of Belarus's economy. Lukashenko railed at what he considered to be the emerging treaty's lack of radical character, but he nevertheless pushed for its adoption. On December 8, 1999—eight years to the day after the signing of the treaty that created the Commonwealth of Slavic States—Yeltsin and Lukashenko finally signed a document referred to as a Treaty on the Creation of a Union State. Widely understood to be little more than a declaration of intent, the treaty elicited little enthusiasm from the Russian president, who was described in the press as "exhaling heavily with an air of doom, like a bridegroom who had been dragged to the altar by force."[86] Vladimir Putin (who would shortly replace Yeltsin) noted that the integration process would take years. Meanwhile, he said, "the Union of Belarus and Russia will exist only on paper."[87]

Presidents Putin and Lukashenko sparred continuously over the form a union between their countries would take. The central constitutional issue was whether the union would be unitary or confederal. A critical economic issue involved a common currency. The Treaty on the Creation of a Union State specified that the two states would merge their monetary systems by 2005. Unanswered was the question: who would control the ruble? Lukashenko insisted on a union of equals, a position completely unacceptable to the Russian president. Frequent exchanges between the two leaders throughout 2000 resulted in a stalemate. Putin proposed that Belarus be incorporated into the Russian Federation as its ninetieth subject, that it operate with the Russian ruble, and that it be subject to Russian law. It was an offer Lukashenko could not accept. Much was made in the press of a remark allegedly made by Putin that it was necessary "to separate the cutlets from the flies."[88] Both men took care to preserve the outward forms of comity, though Lukashenko's public statements frequently betrayed bitterness. Moscow still wanted to maintain friendly relations with its western neighbor. It continued to provide Minsk with financial assistance including selling natural gas to Belarus at prices well below world market prices.

Wrangling between the two governments over the form of the proposed union and control over the currency continued into Putin's second term. In Belarus the media became increasingly anti-Russian, resulting in a decline in that country for support of a single state.[89] Nevertheless, surveys showed that support for some type of union remained high in both countries.

A bilateral commission worked for six months to draft a constitution acceptable to both sides. In the spring of 2003 a compromise of sorts was worked out providing for a "union of two sovereign states" to be headed by a Supreme State Council (not a president, as Lukashenko wanted). Under no circumstances would Putin agree to be outranked by his mercurial neighbor. While ostensibly narrowing the constitutional differences, the two sides made no headway on the issue of a common currency. Russia insisted that it maintain complete control over ruble emission.[90] Giving Belarus even partial control over the ruble was impossible because Belarus's GDP is no more than three percent of Russia's, and Belarus's unreformed economy still relies on subsidizing industry by printing new money. Inevitably, Russia would be faced with unchecked spiraling inflation.

Another stumbling block in Russo-Belarus relations was the price Russia charged for its natural gas. Lukashenko insisted on the domestic price, not the higher world price, and he made threats to impose charges on Russia for various services provided by Minsk if Moscow failed to agree. Putin was not about to be blackmailed or coerced, yet he was also not inclined to push differences with his fraternal neighbors to the point of crisis. He was, nevertheless, not above applying economic pressure, which he did in February 2004 when Gazprom for the first time completely stopped the flow of natural gas into the Belarusian transport system. That forced Lukashenko to accept Russian terms (i.e., world prices) for natural gas. Bitterly, Lukashenko observed, "our relations with Russia will now be poisoned with gas for a long time to come."[91] This mini-crisis did not impede the continuation into Putin's second term of negotiations toward union. In the long term union is likely, but more on Russian than on Belarusian terms. Before that can happen, Aleksandr Lukashenko will probably have to leave the scene.

The Baltic Republics

Among the states formed from the former Soviet republics, Latvia, Lithuania, and Estonia are the most determined to remain independent of Russia's control. Not only did they reject membership in the CIS, but they vigorously sought political and economic integration with Western Europe. There remains among many of the Baltic peoples a residual bitterness over their forced incorporation into the USSR following the Nazi-Soviet Pact and the brutal treatment inflicted upon them by Stalin. They contend that their incorporation into the Soviet Union was never legally valid, a perspective that permeates their relations with Russia.

Demographics is another factor, and it cuts two ways. Such large percentages of the population of Estonia and Latvia are not of the titular nationality that there is concern over national survival. At independence approximately 40 percent of the population of Estonia consisted of non-Estonians. In Latvia the proportion of non-Latvians was even higher, 48 percent. The situation is different in Lithuania, where according to the 1989 census Lithuanians accounted for almost 80 percent of the total population. In 1994 the percentage of Russians in these three republics was estimated at 29.4 percent for Estonia, 33.5 percent for Latvia, and 8.5 percent for Lithuania.[92] As a consequence of these demographics as well as resentment over a half-century of Soviet (viewed by many Balts as Russian) domination, there was a strong movement in Estonia and Latvia to deny citizenship rights to non-Estonians and non-Latvians and to make the acquisition of citizenship difficult.[93]

From the Russian perspective, the presence of some 1,725,000 ethnic

Russians in the Baltic republics imposed on the Russian government an obligation to protect the civil rights of the diaspora Russians. Indeed, Yeltsin's government was under considerable domestic pressure to act on behalf of the 25.3 million Russians in the "near abroad." Russian refugees from the Baltics were among the organizers of the Congress of Russian Communities, which at its second Congress in 1994 demanded, *inter alia,* "protection of the interests of Russian citizens regardless of their place of residence."[94] The Congress of Russian Communities, with General Aleksandr Lebed among its leaders, became a potent force in Russian politics.

Russo-Balt antagonism did not necessarily mean cooperation among the Baltic states on all foreign policy issues, nor did it preclude considerable accommodation between Russia and the Baltic states. Despite their common struggle for independence, the Baltic republics worked toward common objectives in a very modest way. Close ties were imperiled by preoccupation with domestic problems, competition for Western investments, and often just plain mutual suspicion. Lithuania's relations with Latvia were worse than its relations with Russia, due to an unresolved dispute over the demarcation of Lithuanian and Latvian waters. Latvia and Estonia quarreled over fishing rights. Meetings among leaders of the three states through the Baltic Assembly and the Baltic Council of Ministers were often perfunctory. Though each state has sought admission to NATO, they have never agreed to a mutual assistance alliance among themselves.[95] Politically, Lithuania tends to look toward Poland, while Estonia and Latvia feel stronger ties to Finland and Scandinavia. In terms of economic and security interests, all three are inclined to look to Germany rather than to each other.

Whatever suspicion exists toward Russia is muted by economic dependence and the realization that tiny states must make accommodation with neighbors who happen to be great powers. For decades, noncommunist and democratic Finland illustrated the limits of an independent foreign policy toward the Soviet Union. Baltic military forces are small and poorly armed. The Baltic states are dependent upon Russia for natural gas and other sources of energy. Russia is their largest trading partner, and Russian cooperation is necessary for the transit of goods to any of the other CIS states to the east and south.

Nevertheless, relations have often been contentious. Fundamentally that tension reflects both Moscow's determination to keep the region within Russia's sphere of influence as well as the resistance of the Baltic states to Russian hegemony. The dialectic between the benefits of cooperation and the struggle for power has produced relations that are often fluid and changing. Initially the greatest Baltic concern was the presence of some 130,000 Russian troops in the three countries. Moscow used the issue of withdrawal as a bargaining chip to obtain greater political rights for the Russian minority in the Baltics. Of the three countries, Lithuania's citizenship law was the least restrictive. A combination of pressures (some economic) from Moscow and concessions by Vilnius induced the Yeltsin government to agree to withdraw all Russian forces by August 31, 1993.

Another military problem with political implications for Lithuania involved the transit of Russian military equipment and personnel from the Kaliningrad oblast (a region separate from Russia, on the Baltic Sea south of Lithuania) to Russia. Disagreement over the terms of transit had embittered Russo-Lithuanian relations until a compromise was reached in June 1995 that made it possible for Russian troops to cross Lithuanian territory on terms acceptable to both sides. This agreement illustrated the joint efforts to normalize relations as much as possible. However, in the mid-1990s a new issue arose—NATO expansion—which put the two countries on irreconcilable paths.

Latvian and Estonian relations with Russia have been particularly strained. The slowness of Russian troop withdrawal and the restrictions on Russian citizenship rights were powerful sources of antagonism. Both Latvia and Estonia adopted citizenship and naturalization legislation that the Yeltsin government considered discriminatory. In October 1991 the Latvian Supreme Council ruled that automatic citizenship would be granted only to people who had been citizens of Latvia in June 1940 and their descendants. In November 1993 the citizenship law was modified to include a system of annual naturalization quotas for noncitizens. Russia's position was that all inhabitants of the country should be granted citizenship. Hard-fought negotiations failed to produce an outcome satisfactory to either party. The international community, particularly Europe, exerted pressure on both sides to modify their positions. The OSCE, European Union, and Council of Europe wanted the Baltic states to liberalize their citizenship rules, and the international community wanted Russian forces out of the Baltics.

A partial breakthrough was reached in late 1993, when Russia agreed to withdraw its forces from Latvia by August 1994 if Latvia would permit Russia to retain its radar station at Skrunda for six years and if Russian military pensioners were given social guarantees. These terms, which did not give full satisfaction to either side, were formalized in April 1994 when President Boris Yeltsin and President Guntis Ulmanis signed a treaty in Moscow.[96]

However, problems of citizenship and language continued through the decade to poison relations between Latvia and its giant neighbor. Like its Russian counterpart, the parliament in Latvia is the repository of strong nationalist sentiment. In early 1998 the Latvian parliament considered legislation to make the exclusive use of the Latvian language mandatory in state institutions and in the private sphere. Not only did Moscow condemn the idea as discriminatory to Russian-speakers in Latvia, so did the OSCE's High Commissioner of Human Rights.[97] European and Russian pressure eventually forced the Latvian parliament to make some concessions. The language law, which took effect on September 1, 2000, requires the use of the Latvian language for official functions but permits public events to be conducted in Russian. While it was acceptable to the OSCE, the Russian foreign ministry condemned the law as still discriminatory against Russian speakers.

A few weeks before his dismissal as Russia's prime minister, Viktor Chernomyrdin warned while visiting in Riga that "without a change in the situation of the Russian-speaking populations, and above all, without a fundamental acceleration of the process of granting Latvian citizenship to Russian-speakers, no early progress should be expected in other spheres of bilateral cooperation."[98] His warning failed to deter a downturn in relations in the spring, when, as a result of the forceful suppression of a demonstration of thousands of ethnic Russians in Riga on March 3, Moscow threatened to impose economic sanctions on Latvia. In an effort to ward off a crisis in the region, the Clinton administration pressured Riga to modify its citizenship laws. In April 1998 the Latvian cabinet agreed to grant citizenship to all children born in Latvia after August 21, 1991. Of the 700,000 noncitizens then in Latvia, about 20,000 children would become beneficiaries. Parliament adopted the citizenship law, but nationalist opposition forced a national referendum on the issue. In October 1998 Latvia's voters approved the new citizenship law, thus mollifying feelings in Moscow on that issue, but repeatedly, issues have arisen that reflect the underlying tensions between the peoples of both countries.[99] Latvia has asserted territorial claims against Russia; it has officially endorsed rallies of Waffen-Schutzstaffel (SS) veterans of World II; it has denied renewal of Russia's lease of the radar station at Skrunda; and the president of Latvia has even accused Russia of planning to invade the Baltics.[100]

Estonia's relations with its giant neighbor have also been contentious. It has ignored Russian demands that citizenship be granted to all Estonian residents. Laws adopted in late 1991 and early 1992 granted automatic citizenship only to those who had been citizens of the prewar republic and their descendants. Estonia also angered Moscow by demanding a revision of its border with Russia, based upon the 1920 Treaty of Tartu. This revision would have transferred more than 2,000 square kilometers to Estonia. Russia refused to recognize the validity of the Treaty of Tartu. As in the Latvian-Russian dispute, outside pressure was exerted on both sides to make concessions. The U.S. Senate, much to Moscow's displeasure, threatened to block aid to Russia if Estonia were not freed of foreign troops. On July 26, 1994, Yeltsin and Estonian president Lennart Meri signed agreements providing for the withdrawal of Russian troops by August 31 and committing Estonia to provide some 10,700 military pensioners the same rights as Estonian citizens.[101] Another irritant was removed in March 1999 when Estonia abandoned its demands for the restoration of the prewar boundary lines established by the 1920 Treaty of Tartu. Estonia was motivated in these concessions by the European Union's requirement that prospective members have no unresolved border disputes with their neighbors.

One option that is available to all diaspora Russians is to return to live in Russia as citizens. Relatively few Baltic Russians have chosen to do this, in all likelihood because economic conditions are better in the Baltic states than in Russia, and a move would probably lower their standard of living.

We will see in the following chapter the importance of the issue of NATO expansion in East-West relations. Russia saw NATO expansion from the beginning as a threat to the balance of power and to its prestige as a great power. In the end Moscow was unable to reverse the decision made at Madrid to admit the Czech Republic, Hungary, and Poland to NATO. The issue of the former Soviet states was another matter, and the focus of that struggle was the Baltic states.

It is no exaggeration to describe alignment with Western Europe as the central foreign policy objective of each of the Baltic states. They view being part of Europe as central to their security and sovereignty. That has meant membership in the EU and NATO. On June 9, 1994, the Baltic states were given "associate partner" status in the Western European Union.[102] At the same time several free-trade agreements were signed with the European Union. Although economic reform has taken hold in the economies of the Baltic republics, particularly in Estonia, there was little serious expectation that the Baltic republics would be eligible for full membership for several years, although all of them were included on a December 1997 list of candidates promised eventual membership by the EU. Russia has taken no steps to prevent the expansion of the EU into this region.

NATO is another matter. As determined as the Baltic states were to join NATO, Russia was determined to keep them out. When NATO initiated its Partnership for Peace program in early 1994 as a preliminary step toward possible full membership, the Baltic states quickly joined the bandwagon. Lithuania was the first to join on January 27, 1994, and Estonia and Latvia followed soon thereafter. During the intense debate in 1996 and 1997 over which countries would be among the first to be invited into NATO, there was never any doubt that the Baltics would not be among them. U.S. secretary of defense William Perry warned in September 1996 that the Baltic states were "not yet ready" for NATO, so their exclusion at Madrid in July 1997 came as no surprise.

As we will see in chapter 7, Russia was unable to prevent NATO invitations to three former Warsaw Pact states, but it did attempt to influence the parameters of NATO expansion. One of the limits demanded by Moscow was that NATO not incorporate any of the states of the former Soviet Union. Moscow's greatest concern was the Baltics, which were the only former Soviet states actively seeking admission to NATO. Moscow's policy was formally described in a "conceptual outline" published by the Ministry of Foreign Affairs on February 13, 1997. In it the Russian government acknowledged the inevitability of NATO expansion but insisted that such expansion could not include former USSR republics, "especially the Baltic countries." Admitting the Baltics to NATO would create a "serious barrier" between them and Russia. In compensation Moscow announced its willingness to offer its neighbors some kind of security "guarantees."[103]

Prior to the NATO decision, negotiations were begun in January between Russian foreign minister Evgenii Primakov and NATO secretary general Javier Solana. Primakov took a strong line against Baltic membership in NATO. He publicly warned of the consequences if that were to happen:

> Russia cannot remain indifferent to the factor of distance—the Baltic countries' proximity to our vital centers. Should NATO advance to new staging grounds, the Russian Federation's major cities would be within striking range of not only strategic missiles, but also tactical aircraft. . . .
>
> In other words, as soon as the Balts took such a path our dealings with NATO would be over. There would still be bilateral relations with the Western countries as such, of course, but in other respects Russia's foreign policy would diversify noticeably and be stepped up in the eastern and other sectors. It goes without saying that additional defensive measures would also have to be taken.[104]

This hard line gave way as part of the change in Russia's foreign policy line under Putin, particularly as Russia found it advisable to align with the West in the war against terrorism. As a realist, Putin accepted the incorporation of the Baltic states, not only into the European Union (which took place on May 1, 2004) but also in NATO as well (on March 29, 2004). Their NATO membership further exacerbated Moscow's relations with the Baltic states. NATO's decision to patrol the airspace over its newest members was vigorously condemned by Russia's military as "unfriendly."[105]

Only with Lithuania was there improvement in relations in the spring of 2004. For months Russia and Lithuania had been at loggerheads once again over the rules that would govern the transit of Russians across Lithuania as they traveled to and from Kaliningrad. After May 1, the border being crossed would be not simply Lithuania's, but that of the European Union, and Brussels was reluctant to allow Russian travelers and goods to enter the EU visa-free. By agreeing not to require visas (though issuing instead "facilitated travel documents"), Vilnius met a central objection of Russian negotiators. In return, the Russian parliament, after years of delay, ratified a treaty signed in 1997 that formally established the border between the two countries.

Thus, Russia's relations with the states that formerly comprised the republics of the Soviet Union remain in flux. Russia clearly seeks some form of integration, and the realities of history, economics, and geography guarantee that Moscow's influence will be pronounced for years to come. But the degree of influence desired by Moscow is stymied in some states by the pull of the West and in some by the ambitions of autocratic leaders. Only in the case of the Baltic states is it clear that Moscow's influence is now clearly subordinated to that of the West.

7

Russia and the West in the 1990s

A Changed Orientation

The collapse of the Soviet Union in 1991 changed the structure of the international system. Throughout the Cold War the international system was bipolar. A bipolar system, as contrasted to a multipolar system, is one dominated by two great powers or by two blocs, each led by a great power. Although bipolarity had characterized regions of the world before—for example, Athens and Sparta in the fifth century B.C.—never before had it existed at the global level.

Political science theorists have described a bipolar world as a confrontational one in which each side views the other as a deadly adversary and in which each "pole" views any gain by the other as its own loss. In the language of game theory, the bipolar struggle was a "zero-sum game."[1] It cannot be established with certainty whether bipolarity contributed to the Cold War or whether the dual structure of the international system happened to be dominated by strongly antagonistic states. In either event, by the beginning of the 1990s, the United States was clearly the dominant world power. For the moment, the international system appeared to be "unipolar,"[2] and with the new system came a respite in great power rivalry.

In both Washington and Moscow, a new perception of the other emerged. The two rivals became partners. We observed the beginning of this change in the Gorbachev period, as Gorbachev liquidated one by one the sources of contention between East and West: in the arms race, and in Afghanistan, Africa, Eastern Europe, Germany, Cuba, and elsewhere. But Gorbachev was a man of contradictions. He could never fully divest himself of the spirit of competition between socialism and capitalism. As he expressed it in his book, *Perestroika: New Thinking for Our Country and the World,* "Economic, political, and ideological competition between capitalist and socialist countries is inevitable."[3] We can only speculate how far the rapprochement between East and West would have gone had Gorbachev remained in power.

Gorbachev's successor, Boris Yeltsin, went beyond rapprochement with the United States. He began his administration with a genuine attempt to build a partnership with the United States, even though differences emerged between Moscow and Washington as early as during his first term as president. What explains the transformation in Russian foreign policy? In chapter 5 we noted the shift in the perceptions of the political elite of Russia. Ideology was completely abandoned, ending the worldview of an inherent conflict between political systems. Yeltsin did not just modify communist doctrine, as did Gorbachev; he jettisoned it completely.

In chapter 5 we described the debate in Russian politics between the "Atlanticists" and the "Eurasianists." Yeltsin, and especially his first foreign minister, Andrei Kozyrev, actively trumpeted the Atlanticist position. The Russian president stated his views at a special summit meeting of the UN Security Council on January 31, 1992:

> Russia sees the U.S., the West, and the countries of the East not merely as partners but as allies. This is a highly important prerequisite for, and, I would say, a revolution in, peaceful cooperation among the states of the civilized world.
>
> We rule out any subordination of foreign policy to ideological doctrines or a self-sufficient policy. Our principles are simple and understandable: the supremacy of democracy, human rights and liberties, legality, and morality.[4]

Before a joint session of the U.S. Congress on June 17, 1992, Yeltsin reaffirmed his wish to join "the world community."[5]

Clearly, however, more than ideology or perception was involved. Russia was impelled by its domestic condition to seek outside assistance, and no country was better positioned to aid the new administration than the United States. Yeltsin made the transformation of Russia's economy his number one domestic priority. In the words of Anders Aslund, a Swedish economic advisor to Yeltsin, "When the Soviet Union broke up in December 1991, the Russian economy was in a crisis as complex as it was profound."[6] Foreign help was essential. In an extraordinary speech on October 28, 1991, Boris Yeltsin discussed at length and in detail the need for Western assistance and cooperation, and he even promised to give the West whatever information it would want to facilitate aid.[7]

Western support for Yeltsin had an importance beyond economics. It was also important for him politically. Yeltsin understood that he could count on the support of Washington when he confronted domestic reaction. The value of this support became clearly evident during the failed coup of August 1991.[8] Later, during the parliamentary crisis in October 1993, Yeltsin sought and received support from the West.[9] In sum, the shift in Russian foreign policy toward a pro-Western orientation reflected conviction, necessity, and self-interest.

Arms Control

Russian commitment toward cooperation with the United States began with the issue of arms control and weapons reduction. We have noted in chapter 4 that in the late Soviet period Gorbachev's "new thinking" had redefined the country's national security requirements, placing less emphasis on nuclear weapons and more on arms control. The result was a number of negotiated reductions in weapons, of which the most important were the Intermediate Nuclear Forces (INF) agreement of 1987, the Conventional Forces in Europe (CFE) treaty in 1990, and the Strategic Arms Reduction Talks (START) treaty in 1991.[10] The arms race during the Cold War had been one of the factors that undermined economic growth in the civilian sector. Not surprisingly, Yeltsin immediately pushed for arms cuts, particularly cuts in nuclear weapons. Reducing nuclear weapons, he announced in January 1992, "would make it possible to save substantial amounts of money. This money would be channeled toward civilian objectives and toward implementation of reform."[11]

Cooperation with the United States in arms control offered more than just economic benefits. Yeltsin was attracted to an idea introduced by President George Bush for a scheme known as Global Protection Against Limited Strikes (GPALS). Bush proposed that the United States and Russia jointly deploy a limited number of nonnuclear missile defenses to protect both countries against limited ballistic strikes, whatever their source. Speaking before the United Nations in January 1992, Boris Yeltsin unexpectedly expressed interest in GPALS. Cooperation on missile defense appealed to him because it provided an opportunity to strengthen the foundations of Russian-U.S. cooperation, particularly in a field where Russia would be a genuine partner and not a supplicant. When the two leaders met in a Washington summit in June, they signed a statement in support of the GPALS plan,[12] but nothing ever came of GPALS, because of strong opposition to the plan in both countries. In Russia there was fear, particularly within the military, that GPALS might endanger the Anti-Ballistic Missile (ABM) Treaty and become a stalking horse for the Strategic Defense Initiative (SDI).[13]

A much more important issue confronting Moscow and Washington was a follow-on treaty to the START agreement. Under the terms of the START I treaty, the United States and the Soviet Union had agreed to reduce their strategic nuclear forces from 11,602 to 8,592 for the United States, and from 10,877 to 6,940 for the Soviet Union. Further reductions were to be made in succeeding agreements. Negotiations for START II were begun in the winter of 1992 and completed in the remarkably short time of five months. Two issues dominated the negotiations: the number of strategic nuclear warheads to be permitted each side and which delivery systems were to be destroyed. In January, Boris Yeltsin proposed reducing nuclear warheads on strategic missiles to between 2,000 and 2,500. President George Bush wanted a ceiling of between 4,500 and 5,000.[14] The range ultimately agreed to by both was between 3,000 and 3,500.

From the U.S. perspective, the major benefit of START II was that it prohibited land-based intercontinental ballistic missiles (ICBMs) with multiple warheads. The bulk of the Russian strategic arsenal—the SS-18s, SS-19s, and SS-24s—were of the type outlawed by the START II treaty. For years the United States had sought to prohibit these "MIRVed" missiles because they were considered "first-strike" weapons. A portion of the U.S. strategic inventory did consist of precisely this type of missile (the Minuteman III and MX missiles), but the bulk of the U.S. missiles with multiple warheads are in submarines, deep in the oceans. U.S. doctrine viewed the submarine-launched ballistic missiles as less suitable for use in a "first strike," because they could not be destroyed in a surprise attack and were not accurate enough for a first strike. Thus, there would be no incentive to use them preemptively in a crisis.

The major concession made by Russia in START II was agreement to eliminate all land-based ICBMs armed with multiple warheads—the backbone of its strategic force—while the United States was permitted to retain the heart of its strategic force—multiple-armed warheads in submarines. The date for completing the reduction in warheads and prohibited missiles was 2003.

For the first time since the beginning of the nuclear arms race, Russia abandoned its goal of parity with the United States. "We are departing from the ominous parity," Yeltsin explained, "where each country was exerting every effort to stay in line, which has led to Russia having half of its population living below the poverty line." He acknowledged that Russian concessions were made to give tangible "expression of the fundamental change in the political and economic relations between the United States of America and Russia."[15] START II was agreed upon at the June 1992 summit and signed on January 3, 1993.

Not all Russians were prepared to accept the asymmetrical terms of START II. There was disquiet within the military. *Pravda,* an organ of the opposition, suggested that the treaty could be a "hasty, unwarranted concession to Washington and Russia's final loss of the status and importance of a superpower." It predicted, "This will evoke sharp debates in the Russian Supreme

Soviet during the ratification of the agreement."[16] This prediction was an understatement. Russia did not ratify START II until April 2000.

For almost three years, ratification was linked to the problem of Ukraine's refusal to ratify the START I agreement. START II could not be implemented until all the former Soviet republics possessing nuclear weapons—Russia, Ukraine, Belarus, and Kazakhstan—agreed to ratify the START I treaty and the nonproliferation treaty. We noted in chapter 6 the antagonism in Russian-Ukrainian relations during the early post-Soviet period. Responding to strong domestic opinion, Ukrainian president Leonid Kravchuk resisted giving up the "nuclear card" as a bargaining chip in negotiations with Russia over a variety of issues, including the status of the Crimea, the Black Sea Fleet, and financial compensation for returning its nuclear weapons to Russia. A prolonged effort was made by Russia and the United States, acting in concert, to pressure Ukraine to ratify START I. U.S. secretary of state James Baker negotiated an agreement, concluded on May 23, 1992, in Lisbon, Portugal, that committed Ukraine to START ratification, but the Ukrainian president failed to follow up on his commitment.

The U.S. effort continued under a new administration. At a Moscow summit in January 1994, President Bill Clinton and President Boris Yeltsin induced Leonid Kravchuk to sign a trilateral agreement in which Ukraine would take measures to bring START I into force in return for financial compensation and security guarantees from both Russia and the United States.[17] Even that commitment was stymied because of Ukrainian domestic politics, and final Ukrainian parliamentary approval was not given until later in the year. By that time, Leonid Kravchuk had been succeeded as president by Leonid Kuchma.

Although the accession of Ukraine, Belarus, and Kazakhstan (as well as Russia) to START I legally opened the way to move on Russian ratification of START II, new obstacles developed both in Russian domestic politics and in Russian-U.S. relations. As we will see below, a sharp change in Russian foreign policy resulted from a nationalist surge in Russian politics and the takeover of Russia's legislature in 1993 by nationalist and rightist forces. In 1994, a new issue emerged—NATO expansion—which further deferred ratification.

An issue related to arms control was the problem of the security of nuclear and chemical weapons in the arsenals of some of the newly independent states. Fearful that these weapons might fall into the hands of terrorists or governments supporting terrorism, the U.S. Congress in late 1991 enacted legislation creating the Cooperative Threat Reduction program (CTR), sometimes referred to as the Nunn-Lugar program after its Senate sponsors. The program was intended to give Russia, Belarus, Ukraine, and Kazakhstan financial and technical assistance for dismantling or safely storing nuclear and chemical weapons. Toward that end, projects were financed for defense conversion, housing for former military officers, jobs for scientists, storage of nuclear weapons, improvement of security for transportation of nuclear weapons, and destruction of chemical inventories. The CTR program was scheduled to end in 2001, but the U.S. Congress agreed to continue funding it.

War in the Balkans

At about the same time that the Soviet Union collapsed, the Yugoslav state fell apart, precipitating Europe's first major post–Cold War conflict. The assertion of independence by Croatia and Bosnia-Herzegovina, two of Yugoslavia's constituent republics, led to bitter fighting between Croats, Serbs, and Muslims. The most bitter and prolonged part of the fighting took place in Bosnia-Herzegovina. Each of the three communities fought for control over territory in the newly independent state. The Serbs (who composed 31.3 percent of the Bosnian population) and the Croats (17.3 percent) opposed a unified, independent Bosnian state whose dominant population was Muslim (43.7 percent). The Serbs and Croats wanted instead a loose confederation in which they would be essentially self-governing or free to unite with their brethren in Croatia and Serbia.[18]

Fighting in Bosnia began in the spring of 1992 and continued until a peace agreement brokered by the United States was signed in November 1995. The Bosnian war created a strain in Russian-U.S. relations because the sympathies of the two countries were with different parties to the conflict. Russia was traditionally an ally of Serbia. As we saw in chapter 2, historically Russia had assumed the role of protector of the Orthodox Christian Slavs in the Balkans. This feeling of kinship between Russians and Serbs resonated throughout Russian society. The United States found itself sympathetic to the Bosnian Muslims because they were the victims of widespread Serbian atrocities associated with the policy of "ethnic cleansing" (forcible displacement from territories seized by the Serbs). Both Moscow and Washington were constrained in their support for their respective sides. Russian foreign minister Andrei Kozyrev made no attempt to defend Serbian aggression, and the West recognized that atrocities had been committed, albeit on a lesser scale, by Croats and Muslims also. Nevertheless, throughout the war, Yeltsin found himself having to weigh the benefits of supporting traditional friends with those of cooperation with the West. His dilemma was not unlike that which confronted Mikhail Gorbachev in 1990–91 as a result of Iraq's aggression against Kuwait.[19]

While Yeltsin's policies vacillated over time, reflecting the changing pressures on his administration, he carefully avoided a rupture with the United States. His general strategy was to concede to the United States those points that Washington pressed, while at the same time working to soften the blows inflicted on the Serbs. Thus at a Helsinki meeting of the CSCE in July 1992, Russia joined those governments voting to suspend Yugoslavia's membership because of its aid to Bosnian Serbs who were accused of aggressive actions. Even more important was the debate at the United Nations over the question of imposing economic sanctions against Yugoslavia. Andrei Kozyrev argued that negotiations were preferable to punishing Yugoslavia. Yeltsin was scheduled to meet with President Bush in an upcoming summit, and he was confidentially advised by the Russian ambassador to the United Nations that it was "very important not to oppose on this point the Western countries and the United States, where public opinion is strongly against Milosevic [the president of Yugoslavia]."[20] In the end, Russia—which had the power of the veto—voted with the majority to impose unprecedented, strict sanctions against Yugoslavia.

Yeltsin's Yugoslav policy encountered strong conservative opposition at home. Reminiscent of the USSR Supreme Soviet's condemnation of the UN vote to use force against Iraq, the Russian Supreme Soviet demanded a moratorium on United Nations sanctions against Yugoslavia. Typical of right-wing opinion was the criticism in the newspaper *Sovetskaia Rossiia* that "the consistent antinational policy pursued by the current Russian leadership has found its logical conclusion in the open and unconcealed betrayal of the fraternal people of the allied republic of Yugoslavia." *Pravda* charged, "Moscow does not have a policy course of its own."[21]

Under the leadership of Radovan Karadzic, the Bosnian Serbs ruthlessly pursued their policy of "ethnic cleansing." Though sympathetic to the Serb cause, the Russian government condemned Serb atrocities as well as Yugoslav support for Bosnian Serb aggression. That aggression led to Serb control of approximately 70 percent of the territory of Bosnia-Herzegovina. In August 1992 the issue of using military force to guarantee the delivery of humanitarian aid came before the UN Security Council. Russia, notwithstanding its dislike of coercion against the Serbs, supported resolutions authorizing the use of force if necessary. At the Forty-eighth General Assembly session, the Assembly voted to expel Yugoslavia. Again, the Russian delegate to the Security Council made no effort to use the power of the veto to prevent the expulsion of Yugoslavia from the United Nations.[22] The Yeltsin administration was initially careful to avoid drifting too far from the mainstream of international opinion on Yugoslavia and Bosnia. As the war in Yugoslavia widened during the 1990s, however, relations with the West became seriously strained.

Arms Reductions and Arms Sales

One constituency that Yeltsin could not afford to disregard was the military. He carefully involved the Ministry of Defense in the negotiations for START

II, and, notwithstanding some criticism from the right, was able to secure a degree of political cover with the endorsement of START II by Minister of Defense Pavel Grachev and Chief of the General Staff Mikhail Kolesnikov.[23] Two issues on which the military pressed Yeltsin and received the president's support were revision of the CFE treaty and arms sales abroad. On both issues, Yeltsin pressed the West for accommodation. The CFE treaty, signed in November 1990, established allocations for a variety of conventional weapons in the NATO and Warsaw Pact states. It contained restrictions on the internal distribution of forces in Russia, specifically in the military districts of Leningrad and the North Caucasus, which the Russian military considered too restrictive for post-Soviet Russia. Before the Soviet collapse, these districts were rear-echelon regions, but with the collapse of the Warsaw Pact and the breakup of the USSR, they unexpectedly emerged as part of Russia's first line of defense. Opposition to the CFE within the national security elite was strong even during the Soviet period. The antipathy intensified with the change in Russia's geopolitical position. The limitation in the Leningrad district posed no immediate problems, but instability in Georgia, Armenia, and Azerbaijan, and the use of Russian peacekeeping forces in the Caucasus, required an upward adjustment of limitations. Defense Minister Pavel Grachev first expressed dissatisfaction with the flank ceilings in March 1993. In September Yeltsin formally proposed amending the CFE treaty. There was strong resistance in NATO to this Russian demand, particularly from Turkey, the member of NATO most affected. Russia remained adamant, arguing not only the threat to stability in the region and the long-term danger of Islamic fundamentalism, but also concern for the cohesion of the Russian Federation itself. Facing the possibility of Russian renunciation of the CFE treaty altogether, NATO agreed to negotiate the issue.[24]

Arms exports were another contentious issue. The military wanted government support for arms exports in order to keep munitions and weapons factories in business. The government desperately needed arms exports as a source of hard currency. Yeltsin's arms export policies balanced elements of cooperation with competition with the West. In order not to antagonize Washington, Yeltsin forfeited billions of dollars in arms sales by cooperating with UN sanctions against Libya, Iraq, and Yugoslavia. For this he suffered strident criticism from nationalists at home. On the other hand, Yeltsin was unwilling to abandon the lucrative market in other regions of the world. He pushed his government to expand arms sales in the Middle East and Asia, where for decades the West had been the dominant supplier.

As we will see in detail in the following chapter, some of the larger sales created strains in Russian-U.S. relations. A deal to sell India cryogenic rockets brought protest from Washington and eventually had to be modified to meet some of the U.S. concerns. In 1993 Russia negotiated a large sale to Malaysia of eighteen MiG fighters. The bid overcame competition from the McDonnell-Douglas Company in the United States. As the Russian press noted, "The time has come to acknowledge that where arms exports are concerned, we and the West—particularly the U.S.—are not partners but competitors, both economically and politically."[25]

However, as chapter 8 will describe, the most acute irritant for Washington throughout the 1990s was Russian arms sales to a country where the United States was decidedly not a market competitor—Iran. At first, the United States pressured the new Yeltsin government to cancel deliveries of arms sold to Iran during Gorbachev's last years in office. Then Washington became agitated at Russia's agreement to complete the large nuclear reactor at Bushehr, even though Moscow pointed out that the reactor would be subject to International Atomic Energy Agency (IAEA) inspection. In 1995, a secret agreement between Vice President Al Gore and Prime Minister Viktor Chernomyrdin called for Moscow to conclude by the end of 1999 the delivery of arms already sold to Iran, but to make no further sales. American complaints continued, now centered on the transfer from Russian laboratories of dual-use technology that might assist Teheran to develop its missile program. Then Washington complained, in 2000, that the Russians had not abided by their promise to end the deliveries of conventional arms, and the Gore-Chernomyrdin deal leaked to the press. The Russians responded, to the great distress of the United States, that they were withdrawing from the arrangement and would openly resume the sale of "defensive" conventional weapons to Iran.

Russia's Shift to the Right

For about two years the Yeltsin administration maintained a pro-Western orientation in the conduct of foreign policy. Russian-U.S. summits in 1992 and 1993 demonstrated an unprecedented rapport between the leaderships of the two countries. At the Washington summit of June 1992, Yeltsin and Bush signed the Charter of Russian-American Partnership and Friendship affirming "the indivisibility of the security of North America and Europe" and a common commitment to "democracy, the supremacy of law and support for human rights."[26] In Vancouver, Canada, Yeltsin and President Clinton agreed to create the Russian-American Commission on Questions of Technology (popularly known as the Gore-Chernomyrdin Commission, for its cochairmen). In Canada, Yeltsin received a pledge of an immediate assistance package of $1.6 billion, and the Paris Club granted Russia a ten-year deferral of its debt obligations due in 1993.

As we saw in chapter 5, the "Atlanticist" consensus within Russia's governing elite, led by Foreign Minister Andrei Kozyrev, was by no means universally shared throughout Russian society. Yeltsin was in almost constant conflict with the parliament inherited from the Soviet period. Both in the parliament and in nongovernment circles, Yeltsin was attacked by nationalists for his support of U.S. policy in Yugoslavia, and for such actions as the 1993 U.S. air strike against Iraq. *Pravda* chided Yeltsin, saying, "The role of Washington yes-man is unbecoming of any country, especially Russia, and it inevitably conflicts with national interests."[27] Andrei Kozyrev served as a lightning rod for much of the criticism of the Yeltsin administration. The Supreme Soviet called for his removal, and in 1996 he was replaced by the "pragmatic nationalist" Evgenii Primakov.

Nationalists in Russia held Yeltsin as responsible as Gorbachev for the disintegration of the Soviet Union, and they hated him for it. They had a diffuse agenda ranging from the restoration of the USSR to the protection of Russians throughout former Soviet territories. Other foreign policy issues promoted by nationalists were support for the Trans-Dniester Republic in Moldova, the protection of civil rights of Russians in the Baltic states, retention of the Kurile Islands seized from Japan in 1945, and restoration of Russian sovereignty over the Crimea.

For Boris Yeltsin these pressures imposed a careful balancing strategy. His record as a whole justifies the conclusion that his commitment to partnership with the West reflected a genuine conviction. Indeed, though there were significant swings in Russian foreign policy over the course of Yeltsin's two terms, the underlying rationale never changed. But to understand the swings it is necessary to consider both the political calculations of the governing elite, especially the president, and the evolving political and economic conditions within Russia.

Certainly a factor in the evolution of Russia's policy was popular disillusionment with the fruits of economic reform. "Shock therapy," begun in January 1992, led to severe economic hardship for millions of ordinary people. By virtually every economic index, production declined during the early post-Soviet years. Economic assistance from the United States proved to be disappointingly smaller than most Russians expected. Those who had been critical of Yeltsin to begin with belittled U.S. aid. "For a year and a half," noted *Pravda* after the Vancouver summit, "we have been fed cock-and-bull stories about the inevitable 'rain of gold' from the West to back up Yeltsin's reforms."[28] Nor was disillusionment with U.S. aid limited to hardened anti-Yeltsinites. In late 1993, polls showed that by a 2:1 margin Russians were convinced that the West's economic advice represented a deliberate effort to weaken Russia. This margin increased in 1995 and 1996.[29]

Yeltsin's own views changed with those of the electorate. To say this is not to suggest that Yeltsin shifted with the fluctuating winds of public opinion as measured by polls, but, as president, he felt an obligation to be "comprehensible, controllable, and dependent upon public opinion. He must listen."[30] To many, Yeltsin had the reputation of an authoritarian leader. His repudiation of Mikhail Gorbachev in the waning days of the Soviet Union, his use of force against an intransigent parliament in 1993, and his attempt to suppress the Chechens by military measures sustained that reputation. But there was a different and equally consistent element in his political modus operandi, and that was his willingness to compromise and to find common ground with his critics and opponents. This tendency was evident in his negotiations with Gorbachev before the August coup; it was clear in repeated attempts to find common ground with his enemies in the Supreme Soviet and Congress of People's Deputies; and it revealed itself in his reelection campaign. In short, as the broad contours of public opinion shifted, so did Yeltsin. This could be viewed as political expediency or as the democratic response of a leader to his people.[31]

Vladimir Zhirinovskii's success in the December 1993 parliamentary elections was a bad omen for the president. Although the Liberal Democratic Party lacked a cohesive or comprehensive program, the rhetoric of its leader was that of an extreme nationalist. Many thought of Zhirinovskii as a fascist. Zhirinovskii condemned the dissolution of the USSR and promised to restore Russia to its status as a great power. He offered his leadership as the protector of the 25 million Russians living outside the Russian Federation. Specifically, he promised to recover for Russia lost territories in Ukraine, the Baltic states, Kazakhstan, Turkmenistan, and Finland. In one of his less considered statements, he even suggested the return of Alaska to Russia.[32]

Russia began 1994 with a new constitution and a new parliament. The fact that Yeltsin confronted another antagonistic parliament, as he had prior to the constitutional crisis in 1993, did not mean that he was as constrained as before. As we have noted in chapter 5, the powers of the president were significantly greater under the new constitution. Indeed, with regard to foreign policy Yeltsin had virtually a free hand. He could, should he choose, run roughshod over the parliament, but in so doing he would be going against what appeared to be the popular will.

Russia's new constitutional order shares certain features with that of France. Both nations' constitutions were drafted by strong leaders in times of crisis. In 1958 Charles de Gaulle wrote the constitution for the French Fifth Republic to give himself the power to deal with the crisis caused by war in Algeria. Both constitutions combine elements of presidential and parliamentary systems. As in all parliamentary systems, the government is subordinated to parliament; but in France and Russia, unlike other countries with parliamentary systems, an independently elected president chooses the government. Another similarity is that the potential for stalemate exists in both regimes, if the forces controlling parliament are hostile to the president. That was the situation in Russia in the mid-1990s, as it was with France under François Mitterrand in the 1980s and 1990s.

In France this potential conflict was avoided by a policy of cooperation between the president and parliament that became known as "cohabitation." To the surprise of some, Yeltsin in 1994 engaged in his own form of cohabitation by demonstrating a willingness to compromise with opponents in the State Duma. In domestic politics this meant a slowdown in the economic reform. In foreign policy it meant a shift to the right.[33]

The First War in Chechnya

No issue so dramatized the shift in Russian politics—both domestic and foreign—as the war in Chechnya, which erupted in December 1994. Chechnya is one of the ethnic republics that make up the Russian Federation. It borders on the independent state of Georgia in the Caucasus and has a Muslim population with a long history of resistance to central authority. Some Chechen units collaborated with German forces invading the Caucasus during World War II, provoking Stalin to deport large numbers of Chechens to Central Asia. In 1991 the Chechen Republic declared itself independent, but its independence was recognized neither by the Russian government nor by any other state. During the early years of his administration, Yeltsin avoided a direct confrontation with Chechen forces led by President Dzhokhar Dudaev, but he did give assistance to a dissident force organized as a "provisional council" and headed by Umar Avturkhanov. Its effort to take control in Chechnya failed.

Reports of impending warfare in Chechnya were heard throughout 1994. On December 11, Russia sent armed forces into Chechnya for the purpose of overthrowing President Dudaev and establishing Russian authority in the country. Ostensibly, the reason for the invasion was to establish constitutional order — the Russian constitution denied any of its eighty-nine subjects the right to secede unilaterally—and to suppress widespread crime and corruption in Chechnya. What was not made clear at the time was why Yeltsin had chosen that particular time to act. Why had Yeltsin not attempted to negotiate a special constitutional arrangement with the Dudaev government, permitting a degree of republican autonomy, as he had with other republics?[34]

Russia's opaque political system rendered difficult a clear analysis of whether the decision to invade was made by military leaders not fully responsible to the Russian president, or whether perhaps Yeltsin himself was moving sharply toward a more nationalist, hard-line policy. Either way, the consequences were a significant shift in Russian foreign policy. Yeltsin's political move had some similarities to the rightward move of Mikhail Gorbachev in 1990. As the Soviet president had done that fall, Yeltsin abandoned his political ties with many of his former democratic allies in favor of associates on the political right. The attack on Chechnya was supported by a so-called war party consisting of Defense Minister Pavel Grachev, Interior Minister Viktor Erin, Chief of the Federal Counterintelligence Service Sergei Stepashin, Nationalities Minister Nikolai Egorov, Security Council Secretary Oleg Lobov, and the chief of Yeltsin's bodyguards, Aleksandr Korzhakov.

Evidence that the war in Chechnya was part of a broader change in Russian foreign policy was provided by Yeltsin's dramatic behavior at the Budapest meeting of the OSCE, which convened just days before the outbreak of fighting. Speaking against the expansion of NATO, Yeltsin warned of a new "cold peace" in Europe. His allusion to the United States was unmistakable when he observed, "History proves that it is a dangerous delusion to think that the fates of continents and of the world community as a whole can be controlled from a single capital."[35] Just days earlier, Foreign Minister Andrei Kozyrev had stunned the members of the NATO Council meeting in Brussels with an unexpected announcement that Russia would not join the Partnership for Peace (PFP) program pushed by Washington.

The West did not question the right of Russia to establish, even forcefully, its authority in Chechnya, but it did object to the brutality of Russian forces fighting in the war zones, and particularly to the killing of civilians and indiscriminate bombing of the capital city of Grozny. Russian forces were both wantonly destructive and at the same time totally ineffective in winning the war.

As a result, the prestige of the Russian military declined, and with it the popularity of the Russian president. Chechnya was the first televised war ever viewed by the Russian people, and as the U.S. administration learned in Vietnam, popular viewing of a losing war generates strong domestic opposition. A national poll early in 1995 found a 72 percent disapproval rate of the Kremlin's policy in Chechnya and only a 16 percent approval rating.[36] In February 1995, polls showed that Yeltsin's approval rating had fallen to 8 percent. Particularly significant was the loss of support among many of his former democratic allies. Ironically, Yeltsin's war policy was supported primarily by right-wing nationalist elements, precisely those forces least likely to support his overall foreign or domestic policies.

The war in Chechnya was the most divisive security policy issue in Russian politics during the election years of 1995 and 1996. Its impact was felt in the 1995 parliamentary elections and in the presidential elections the following year. Efforts were made in the State Duma to force an end to the war by legislative means, but they failed because of the refusal of the nationalist parties to attack Yeltsin on that issue. The only parties consistently supporting an antiwar position were Russia's Choice, Yabloko, and Women of Russia, which together could not mobilize a majority in the legislature.[37]

However, in the summer of 1995 a terrorist attack on Russian soil by Chechen forces galvanized public opposition to the war. A gang of 200 guerrillas led by Shamil Basaev seized some 2,000 hostages in the Russian city of Budyonnovsk. Russians were outraged that such a large-scale operation could be undertaken in a city almost a hundred miles from the Chechen border. Compounding the humiliation of the raid was the inept performance of the military effort to rescue the hostages. A desperate attempt to storm the hospital where the hostages were held not only failed, but led to casualties among the hostages. In the end the Russian hostages were saved only by negotiations led by Prime Minister Viktor Chernomyrdin, who had to agree to permit Basaev and his guerrillas to escape. So angered were critics of the war in the legislature that the State Duma voted its first motion of no confidence in the government on June 21, by a vote of 241 to 72 (with twenty abstentions).[38]

Politics in Russia during the second half of 1995 was dominated by the campaign to elect members to a new Duma. The election was scheduled for December 17. Yeltsin's policies were under attack from both the left and right. The principal vehicle for supporting the president's policies was the party Our Home Is Russia, headed by Chernomyrdin. The parliamentary elections turned into a political defeat for the administration. Half the Duma was elected by proportional representation from party lists and half by direct election from districts. Our Home Is Russia garnered only 10.13 percent of the proportional vote. The major parliamentary winner was the Communist Party of the Russian Federation, which won 22.3 percent of the popular vote for the party lists; Zhirinovskii's Liberal Democratic Party was second with 11.18 percent, and Grigorii Yavlinskii's Yabloko Party won 6.39 percent. In the proportional representation vote, no other party among the forty-three registered to participate gained the necessary 5 percent minimum for representation in the Duma. Overall, Yeltsin ended up with a parliament no more sympathetic to him than its predecessor. Those who constituted the opposition—a coalition of leftist and nationalist elements—were potentially in a position to mobilize a majority in the parliament. Thus foreign policy decisions that required the support of the Duma—such as ratification of START II—were problematical at best. However, the fundamental constitutional fact remained that foreign policy was made by the executive branch, not by the parliament.

Almost immediately after the parliamentary elections in December 1995, politics in Russia began to focus on the presidential election scheduled for the following June. As we have seen, one of the casualties of the nationalist upsurge embodied in the new Duma was Foreign Minister Andrei Kozyrev. As one of the longest-serving members of the administration, Kozyrev came to symbolize better than anyone else the liberal, democratic, and pro-Western features of Yeltsin's presidency. As such, he had been for years the point man of bitter criticism from statist, nationalist, and leftist elements in Russian politics. The fact that Gennadii Zyuganov, the head of Russia's Communist Party, welcomed the January 1996 replacement of Kozyrev with Evgenii Primakov meant that Yeltsin would have more clout with the Duma and at the same time not be quite as vulnerable to criticism of his foreign policy from both the left and right. Some saw the Primakov appointment as an indication that Yeltsin intended to run for a second term,[39] and in February, Yeltsin did indeed announce his candidacy for reelection.

Boris Yeltsin's campaign turned out to be a spectacular come-from-behind race. From the beginning his main opponent was Zyuganov, who in January was supported by 20 percent of those who indicated to pollsters their intention to vote, compared to 8 percent who supported Yeltsin.[40] Yeltsin's low rating was due largely to domestic conditions; foreign policy proved not to be an important factor in the campaign, due in part to Primakov's ability to neutralize it as an issue.

Although it was not a campaign issue, the war in Chechnya contributed significantly to popular dissatisfaction with the incumbent. The Russian military simply could not subdue the Chechens. Occasional truces would be signed, only to be violated and followed by renewed fighting. In January, Russia was shocked by another Chechen terrorist assault on Russian territory. Four hundred militants under the command of Salman Raduev, the Chechen president's son-in-law, seized a hospital in the city of Kizlar, taking some 2,000 hostages. Intensive negotiations led to an agreement to permit Raduev to leave the city with 165 hostages in eleven buses. When the convoy reached the town of Pervomaiskoe, they were surrounded by Russian troops who attempted to storm the Chechen positions. After several days of fighting in which dozens were killed on both sides, Raduev managed to escape into Chechnya with some of the hostages. The incident embittered both sides, further dispirited Russia's military, and intensified popular dissatisfaction with the war.

Yeltsin's conundrum was that Russia could neither fight nor negotiate its way out of the war. President Dzhokhar Dudaev never wavered from his demand that Russia unconditionally recognize Chechnya's independence. That Yeltsin was not prepared to do. On March 31, Yeltsin unveiled a new "peace plan" for Chechnya. Admitting that "the Chechen crisis is Russia's gravest problem," Yeltsin proposed an immediate cessation of military operations to be followed by parliamentary elections in the war-torn republic, followed in turn by negotiations to determine "Chechnya's status within the Russian Federation."[41] Though unwilling to meet directly with Dudaev, he offered to enter into talks with the Dudaev side through intermediaries. The problem with this strategy was that it had been tried before without success. Several truces had previously been announced, only to be violated. The Russians sought to better their chances this time by reviving Dudaev and they succeeded in assassinating him in April 1996. Nevertheless, Yeltsin's March peace plan met the same fate as earlier ones, and fighting continued through the summer.

The presidential campaign and the war in Chechnya were closely linked. Like U.S. presidents Lyndon Johnson and Richard Nixon in Vietnam, Yeltsin wanted the political benefits of ending the war but feared the political consequences of paying the price Dudaev had demanded for peace. Chechens, including Aslan Maskhadov, the man who would succeed Dudaev, viewed the March peace initiative as no more than a Russian ploy.

Yeltsin won reelection in spite of the war. In the first round of voting on June 16, he received 35 percent to Zyuganov's 32 percent. Aleksandr Lebed, former commander of Russia's Fourteenth Army in the Trans-Dniester region, came in third with 14.7 percent. In a shrewd political move, Yeltsin made Lebed a member of his administration, appointing him secretary of the Security Council and assistant for national security. Though there was no direct connection between this appointment and the war in Chechnya, Lebed's brief tenure was to significantly influence Russian policy. One of his first accomplishments was to secure the dismissal as defense minister of Pavel Grachev, a strong proponent of military victory in Chechnya. Yeltsin's political strategy paid off with a victory in the second round of voting in July, when he obtained 54 percent of the vote.

Militarily, the situation in Chechnya deteriorated. Within a month of the election, Chechen insurgents had retaken Grozny, the capital. Sent to the scene of battle, Lebed was appalled by the condition of Russian troops, and he concluded that Russia had no choice but to withdraw. Yeltsin, who was in poor health at the time, appointed Lebed as his primary agent to negotiate an end to the fighting. President Clinton and several NATO governments urged Moscow to forgo the option of storming Grozny and to negotiate a settlement with the rebels. Moving swiftly, Lebed did just that. On August 31 he signed an accord with Aslan Maskhadov, Chechen chief of staff, which called for an end to the fighting and the withdrawal of Russian and Chechen forces from Grozny. On the all-important question of the legal status of Chechnya, the agreement deferred the decision for five years.[42]

Thus began a new phase in the Russian-Chechen struggle. Both sides, in agreeing to defer a determination of the final status of Chechnya, had compromised politically. Russia interpreted the agreement to mean that until a decision was made otherwise, Chechnya was a part of Russia; but by agreeing to withdraw its forces from Chechnya, Russia lost de facto control over the republic. The rebel government claimed independence but could not obtain recognition from Russia (or any other government) and was in fact largely dependent upon Russia for economic recovery. But Lebed's agreement did mark the end of active warfare in the country—though only temporarily, as it turned out.

Neither President Yeltsin nor Prime Minister Chernomyrdin was involved in the negotiations of the agreement that ended the war, and it is uncertain whether either approved of what the impetuous Security Council secretary had done. Moscow was in the grip of a political vacuum brought on by a serious deterioration of Boris Yeltsin's health following the strenuous reelection campaign. In late summer Yeltsin announced that he would undergo heart bypass surgery. Through the remainder of the year, as the terms of Lebed's agreement were debated, Yeltsin was forced to delegate much of his authority to others, leaving the government open to the tug and pull of ambitious politicians. In the debate over the Khasaviurt agreement, leftist and nationalist leaders such as Zyuganov and Sergei Baburin condemned the agreement, while liberal spokesmen were more supportive; but, overwhelmingly, Russian spokesmen insisted that Chechnya had to remain a part of the Russian Federation.

Aleksandr Lebed himself did not survive the resolution of the debate as a government official. In October, Yeltsin fired his Security Council secretary because of Lebed's inability to work cooperatively with other members of the administration. Politically ambitious, Lebed had challenged the authority of others in the cabinet and undertaken measures that members of the government considered beyond his authority.

A satisfactory resolution of the Chechen issue has eluded Russian authorities. Yeltsin's decision in November 1996 to withdraw the 101st Brigade of Interior Ministry troops and the Defense Ministry's 205th Brigade from Chechen territory ended any possibility of keeping Chechnya in Russia by force. For all practical purposes, Chechnya operated as an independent state until war resumed in 1999. On November 23, Chernomyrdin and Maskhadov signed an interim agreement on final steps toward peace between Chechnya and Russia, but the language permitted both sides to maintain their previously held positions regarding the republic's constitutional status.

On January 27, 1997, elections were held in Chechnya for a new president. The winner was Aslan Maskhadov. Although he was an ardent nationalist, he was respected by the Kremlin as a relative moderate. Some Russians believed that Maskhadov would prove more tractable on the issue of sovereignty than his unyielding predecessors, but they were mistaken. Indeed, it is unlikely that the Chechen population would have accepted such a concession by their leader. Referring to his country by its ancient name of Ichkeria, Maskhadov promised in his oath of office to "strengthen this independent state."

An attempt to square the circle was made by the two presidents with the signing of a peace treaty on May 12, 1997. Yeltsin officially recognized the independence of the Republic of Ichkeria, while Maskhadov conceded that his country was not seceding from Russia. For the Chechen leader, the central provision of the treaty was Russia's commitment "to build their relations in accordance with generally recognized principles and norms of international law."[43] Both sides also formally renounced the use of force in their relations.

For Russia, Chechnya is important not only because of the constitutional issue and its international prestige. There are vital economic issues at stake, the chief of which concerns oil. A central objective of Russian foreign policy is retention of control of the pipelines transporting the enormous quantities of Caspian Sea oil to the world market. Chechnya has been a vital link in the flow of oil from Baku, Azerbaijan, to the Russian Black Sea port of Novorossiisk. Instability in Chechnya has stimulated among oil producers the prospect of building alternative pipeline routes through Georgia, Turkey, and even Iran. These prospects were profoundly threatening to Russia and were a strong inducement for Moscow to assume control in Grozny.[44]

War and Peace in Bosnia

Russia's shift toward a more nationalistic foreign policy produced in Moscow a stronger defense of the Serbs in their war against the Muslims and Croats in Bosnia. In the face of Western pressure to assist the Muslim-controlled government of Bosnia, Russia successfully blocked efforts in the United Nations to have the arms embargo in Bosnia lifted. It also strenuously opposed military intervention by the West.

Yeltsin's inclination to support the Serbs, however, was curbed by his determination to avoid drifting too far from the mainstream of international opinion. He thus supported Western political initiatives to negotiate a settlement of the war. During 1993, Cyrus Vance and David Owen, on behalf of the United Nations, devised a plan to create a weak confederation in Bosnia-Herzegovina organized around ten ethnically based cantons. Moscow endorsed the plan, as did Milosevic in Belgrade, but the Vance-Owen Plan was rejected by Bosnia's Serbs.

Russian diplomacy in the Balkans was constrained by the fact that its allies were guilty of the larger atrocities committed by the belligerents, and thus the preponderance of world opinion sided with the government of Bosnia. An incident early in 1994 gave Moscow an unexpected opportunity to take the diplomatic initiative. On February 5 a mortar attack on a public market in Sarajevo killed sixty-eight people and wounded two hundred more. Though both sides denied responsibility, the general assumption was that the Serbs had committed the atrocity. Public opinion, especially in the West, was outraged and demanded a military response against the Serbs. NATO, which up to this point had moved cautiously, issued an ultimatum to the Bosnian Serbs, demanding that they remove their heavy weapons twenty kilometers from Sarajevo or place them under UN control. The ultimatum was backed with a threat of air strikes.

The situation posed a dilemma for Moscow. Opinion in Russia overwhelmingly opposed NATO military action against the Serbs. Yet the atrocity in the Sarajevo marketplace seemed to demand a response. However, many in Russia believed that the mortar attack on February 5 was in fact a Muslim provocation. There had been repeated instances of deliberate provocations by the Bosnian government. Foreign Minister Andrei Kozyrev insisted that no military action be unleashed without specific authorization by the UN Security Council, where Russia had the veto. Yeltsin consulted with U.S., German, and British leaders, after which he appealed to the Serbs to withdraw their artillery from Sarajevo, as demanded by NATO. To assuage the Serbs, Yeltsin promised to send a contingent of four hundred Russian soldiers to join UN forces in the combat zone. This was sufficient cover for Slobodan Milosevic and Radovan Karadzic to bow to NATO's ultimatum. Yeltsin's initiative defused the crisis and enhanced Russian prestige all around. Even domestically the Russian president benefited. As a leading newspaper put it, "In this production President Yeltsin collected quite a few foreign policy dividends, both in the West and within our country."[45]

Russia's diplomatic triumph was short-lived. Barely two months after the shelling in Sarajevo, another crisis arose as a consequence of an assault by Serb forces on the Muslim-held city of Gorazde. UN Security Council Resolution 836, which had been adopted unanimously, had declared Gorazde a United Nations–protected safe area. Russian spokesmen insisted that it was the Muslims who had begun combat operations in Gorazde, but the foreign ministry was quick to condemn the Serb assault on a UN-protected city that contained UN and International Red Cross personnel. Russians across the political spectrum, however, were angered that NATO air strikes were carried out on April 10 and 11 against Serb artillery positions without consultations with Moscow. "Trying to make such decisions without Russia is a big mistake and a big risk," warned Andrei Kozyrev. "The bombing of Serbian positions near the city of Gorazde is a slap in the face of Russia's prestige," claimed Deputy Prime Minister Sergei Shakhrai.[46] But Moscow understood the culpability of the Serbs and resented the position in which they had put Russia. Vitalii Churkin, Kozyrev's deputy, vented his spleen to journalists: "The Bosnian Serbs must understand that in Russia they are dealing with a great power, not a banana republic. Russia must decide whether a group of extremists can be allowed to use a great country's policy to achieve its own aims. Our answer is unequivocal: 'never.'"[47]

The crisis in Gorazde illustrated the paradox of the Balkan War for Russian foreign policy. Russia's national interest dictated that NATO forces not be used against the Serbs, so as to prevent NATO from becoming the guarantor of peace in Europe, but Serb war tactics were provoking NATO military strikes, and Moscow was unable to control its nominal allies. The optimal solution for all parties would be a negotiated settlement. Yeltsin proposed a summit meeting that would include Russia, the United States, and the European Union, but nothing came of it. Instead the locus of diplomatic efforts became a group of five nations—Russia, the United States, France, Great Britain, and Germany—known as the "contact group." Their goal was to devise a political solution to the Bosnian civil war.

In July the contact group proposed a new peace plan to the Croats, Muslims, and Serbs. Under the plan, Bosnia-Herzegovina would be divided into two political entities; 51 percent of the country would be governed by a Croat-Muslim Federation, and 49 percent would be governed by Bosnian Serbs. This plan would have required the Serbs to give up part of the 70 percent of the country they controlled. Notwithstanding a personal appeal from Yeltsin to Radovan Karadzic, the Serbs rejected the idea. The Bosnian Serb intransigence led Moscow to abandon relations with the Serb hard-liners in Bosnia and to focus on Milosevic in Belgrade to exert pressure on Karadzic. Although unsuccessful at the time, this plan contained some of the ingredients of the Dayton Accords that ultimately ended the fighting. Meanwhile Russia continued its policy of opposition to lifting the arms embargo against the Muslim-dominated government of Bosnia and the use of NATO forces against the Serbs. Moscow was unsuccessful in persuading the West to lift economic sanctions imposed on Serbia.[48]

As the pace of fighting picked up in Bosnia in late 1994, the pressure on the West to restrain the Serbs increased, undermining Russia's efforts to prevent NATO from becoming involved militarily. In November, NATO planes attacked an airfield in the Serb region of Krajina, in retaliation for a Serb assault on the Muslim city of Bihac, designated by the United Nations as a safe area. Anti-U.S. rallies were held in Moscow, but that did not dissuade Yeltsin and Kozyrev from condemning the Krajina Serbs for provoking the air strikes. Russia's State Duma condemned the NATO action as unwarranted. In December, responding to domestic pressure to provide greater support for the Serbs, Russia vetoed a UN Security Council resolution on the grounds that it was excessively critical of the Bosnian and Krajina Serbs.

By the spring of 1995, Russia's Bosnian policy began to fall apart under its contradictions. Serb military action reached a level of aggressiveness that the West could not ignore. The consequence was an escalation of NATO air strikes against Serb military positions. Moscow could not stop the air strikes or the Bosnian Serb military actions that provoked them. Russia found itself in the humiliating position of being ignored by both sides, each its ostensible friend. In May the Serbs unleashed a massive artillery attack against five UN "safe havens"—Sarajevo, Tuzla, Gorazde, Bihac, and Srebrenica. When NATO, with UN authorization, retaliated against Bosnian Serb positions near the Serb capital of Pale, Serb forces seized more than three hundred UN military observers and peacekeepers (including some Russians) as hostages. Even Belgrade condemned the hostage-taking.

Yeltsin was deeply offended that NATO air strikes were unleashed without any consultation with Moscow. At the same time, in frustration, he publicly acknowledged that the Serbs "got what they deserved."[49] Karadzic's forces eventually released their UN hostages, but that did not prevent the UN from sanctioning the creation of a NATO "rapid reaction force" for use in defense of the Bosnian Muslims. Russia, while criticizing the decision as "overly hasty," abstained (along with China) on the Security Council resolution, which was adopted by a vote of 13 to 0. Boris Yeltsin still believed that the war could be resolved by allowing the Bosnian Serbs to form a confederation with Belgrade. He unsuccessfully pressed that argument with G-7 leaders meeting in Halifax, Nova Scotia.

In August the war in the former Yugoslavia turned decisively against the Serbs. Assaulted by NATO air strikes, Serb positions weakened in both Croatia and Bosnia. A Croatian offensive against Serb-held territory in Krajina led to the occupation of the region by Croatian government forces (and the expulsion of several hundred thousand Serbs). The so-called republic of Serbian Krajina, which had been in existence for four years, collapsed in two days. Moscow protested Croatia's action in vain. Nor could Russia get support from the contact group, because both Washington and Bonn wanted more, not less, pressure put on the Serbs. In desperation, Yeltsin turned toward diplomacy, inviting Croatian president Franjo Tudjman and his Serbian counterpart Slobodan Milosevic to meet in Moscow for talks. That initiative, too, proved to be futile when Tudjman refused to go to Moscow. A follow-on proposal for a trilateral meeting including Alija Izetbegovic, Bosnia's Muslim leader, was no more successful. Finally, Yeltsin proposed a meeting in Moscow of the heads of the "leading states," the opposing sides in Bosnia as well as the presidents of Yugoslavia, Croatia, and Bosnia-Herzegovina. Russia's press blamed the West for sabotaging this idea.[50] Politically Russia's Balkan policies had become bankrupt, giving rise to increased criticism of Yeltsin by his domestic enemies. Combined with the war in Chechnya, the war in Bosnia was pushing Russian foreign policy more than ever before toward an isolated, anti-Western position.

The NATO strikes steadily took their toll on the Bosnian Serb positions on the battlefield. A particularly devastating series of air strikes, the largest conducted by NATO since its formation in 1949, hit Bosnian Serb military installations in late August, in the aftermath of another brutal shelling of civilians in Sarajevo. Nationalists in Russia screamed that NATO was "unleashing a war in the Balkans." Russia's State Duma voted to end participation in the United Nations sanctions against Yugoslavia and called upon Russian volunteers to go to the aid of the "fraternal Serbian people." At the same time it asked Yeltsin to fire Foreign Minister Kozyrev and suspend Russia's participation in the Partnership for Peace program (described below). As in the past, the Russian government protested the NATO air strikes, but Yeltsin vetoed the Duma law seeking to force withdrawal from sanctions against Yugoslavia. (President Clinton, in a symmetrical action, vetoed U.S. congressional moves to force a lifting of the arms embargo on Bosnian Muslims.)

By early fall a combination of military and diplomatic pressure induced the leaders of all the principal parties to agree to a cease-fire, which became effective on October 10. A new stage in Bosnia-Herzegovina's civil war began when presidents Izetbegovic, Milosevic, and Tudjman agreed to meet in the United States to work out a peace settlement. As a sop to Russian prestige, Moscow was given the honor of hosting the ceremonial opening of the talks on October 30, but immediately thereafter the serious business moved to the Wright-Patterson Air Force Base in Dayton, Ohio.

Even before the terms of an agreement could be worked out, a difficult political issue had to be resolved regarding Russia's participation in the peacekeeping operation to enforce the truce in Bosnia. Russia was determined to participate in the force, and NATO agreed that Russian involvement was important to guarantee peace and stability in the Balkans. The problem was that Moscow would not permit Russian troops to be subject to NATO's command, and the United States found unacceptable any arrangement for a dual command. Addressing the General Assembly, Yeltsin proposed a monitoring force that would operate under UN command. Given all the weaknesses that had already been exposed with UN authority over NATO operations in the Bosnian war, there was no possibility that a UN command would be acceptable to Washington. While in the United States for the fiftieth anniversary of the United Nations, Yeltsin met with President Clinton to resolve the issue. This summit convened in Hyde Park, amidst a generally congenial atmosphere. The outcome, finalized days later in Brussels, was a compromise that conceded to Washington the substance of the issue, but offered to Moscow a face-saving appearance. Dubbed by some "Operation Fig Leaf," the plan called for Russian troops participating in Bosnian peacekeeping operations to report to a U.S. general rather than to NATO's commander. For domestic political reasons, both presidents were anxious that their ninth summit be seen as successful. (Russia was in the midst of a parliamentary political campaign, and Clinton was facing a reelection campaign.) At a luncheon, Yeltsin affirmed, "Our partnership is designed to last not for one year, not for a decade, but for centuries, forever."[51]

Under the firm guidance of the United States, in the person of Assistant Secretary of State Richard Holbrooke, the negotiations in Dayton produced an agreement that transformed the military struggle in Bosnia into a political one. The structure of government created by the Dayton Accords was a complex one reflecting a balance—though not necessarily equal—of concerns of the three parties. The principle of a unified, sovereign Bosnian state was maintained in the creation of a central government with a Bosnian parliament and a three-headed presidency. This state would consist of two autonomous parts, a Croat-Muslim confederation occupying 51 percent of the land, and a Serb republic with 49 percent. The Dayton Accords demarcated the territorial lines of the two autonomous regions, with the exception of the corridor around Brcko, which connected the eastern and western parts of the Serb republic. The fate of Brcko was left for later arbitration. Refugees from all parts of Bosnia-Herzegovina were to be permitted to return to their original homes. Those individuals who had been indicted as war criminals by the Special United Nations Tribunal at The Hague were to be turned over to the tribunal.

To ensure compliance with these terms and to enforce the peace, the Accords established a special NATO Implementation Force (IFOR). Originally the IFOR comprised some 60,000 troops. Of these, 1,600 came from the Russian Federation. Russia's participation in the IFOR was approved by the Council of the Federation in January 1966. The IFOR was intended to last only one year, but the ongoing antagonism among all three communities in the country forced NATO to extend its peacekeeping operations.

In one important sense the Dayton Accords were successful. Forty-two months of warfare and brutal atrocities were ended. Daily life for the peoples on all sides became more peaceful, and a semblance of normality returned for many, but peace did not bring national reconciliation. The features of the peace agreement that were intended to establish unified institutions of government have been observed in form but not substance. The parliaments of the two halves of the country are populated largely by intransigent nationalists. In effect Bosnia remained divided, not only between the Serb and Croat-Muslim parts, but also within much of the Croat-Muslim federation. Of the 2 million refugees created by the war, most have not been repatriated because of the opposition of local populations to their return. The ethnic and religious hatreds that gave rise to the war have not been resolved by the Dayton Accords.[52]

In the post-Dayton period, Moscow became preoccupied with a new set of domestic issues, including elections to the parliament in 1995 and presidential elections in 1996. There was still a war going on in Chechnya, as well as the ongoing problems associated with economic reform. For a period of a few years Yugoslavia receded as a source of tension between Russia and the West. Later in the decade it would reemerge with the crisis over the Serbian province of Kosovo. But in the mid-1990s, the focus shifted and a new conflict arose over NATO's plan to expand by incorporating former members of the Warsaw Pact. In time the issue of NATO expansion merged with the crises in the Balkans to pose the larger question of what role Russia would play in European security.

NATO Expansion

The decision by the North Atlantic Treaty Organization to include within its membership some of the countries of Eastern Europe that formerly had been members of the Warsaw Pact became the single most contentious issue in Russian-American relations in the 1990s. Of the many issues related to NATO expansion, the most general and fundamental concerned what type of European security system would replace the alliance structure of the Cold War period. From Russia's perspective, the basic question was how Russia would fit into a system of European security. Would it be accepted as a great power, or simply as another European state? Would it be viewed as a partner or as a potential adversary? And what institutional mechanism would govern decision making for security issues in Europe?

For nearly all Russians, NATO was stigmatized by the history of the Cold War and was viewed as an adversarial organization. Russian political elites much preferred the more politically neutral OSCE as a mechanism for European security. But there was more involved in the expansion of NATO than just vital national interests. National prestige was also an important consideration. Russia had not yet to come to terms with its loss of status as a superpower. Indeed, many Russians questioned whether their country could even be ranked as a "great power." An expansion of the military alliance that played a vital role in the defeat of the Soviet Union was viewed by many as rubbing the Russian nose in the Soviet defeat—a national humiliation.

Besides the questions of foreign policy raised by NATO, there were considerations of domestic politics. One reason the Clinton administration supported the idea was its appeal to many American voters who had close ties to Poland, the Czech Republic, and Hungary. During his campaign for reelection, Bill Clinton delivered a speech in Detroit that called for expanded NATO membership by 1999 and that had the political purpose of attracting the support of some 20 million voters of Central and East European ethnic origin. Presidential candidate Robert Dole was also a strong supporter of NATO enlargement, removing the subject as an issue of debate in the campaign.

Conversely, Russians opposed the admission of former Warsaw Pact members into the Atlantic alliance. As a domestic political issue in Russia, NATO expansion had relatively low salience among the public at large; but among the nation's political elite there was overwhelming opposition, nowhere stronger than in the military. Spokesmen for Russian nationalists used the issue to criticize the Yeltsin administration for not doing enough to block the plan. "Atlanticist" leaders like Andrei Kozyrev were put on the defensive over the issue.

Both sides of the debate over NATO expansion shifted their positions over time. One reason was the abstract and remote rationale for expansion. NATO was a military alliance created to prevent a Soviet invasion of Western Europe. Even if one accepted as valid the glib summary of NATO's purpose offered by its first secretary-general—"to keep the Americans in, the Russians out, and the Germans down"—there seemed little doubt that NATO's objectives either had been achieved or were, after the Cold War, irrelevant. Nobody considered Russia in the 1990s to be a threat. The military arguments for extending the protection of Article V of the treaty to the countries of Eastern Europe were unpersuasive. Conceivably a future Russia might be a threat to Eastern Europe, but that contingency hardly required expanding NATO in the 1990s. By the same token, NATO was no threat to Russia and should not have been perceived as such. There was, in short, a shadow boxing quality to the debate, however serious the issue was in Russian-Western relations.

Two broad considerations moved NATO toward enlargement. One was the need for a new mission and purpose in the aftermath of the Cold War. Some within the alliance came to the conclusion that NATO would survive only by expanding and becoming a security force for all of Europe. This view was strengthened by NATO's decision in June 1992 to move "out of area" and place its military forces at the disposal of the United Nations and the OSCE for peacekeeping operations in the Balkans. Another stimulus to enlargement was the desire of several East European governments, led by the "Visegrad" states (the Czech Republic, Hungary, Poland, and Slovakia) for security guarantees from the West. The December 1993 Russian elections, which led to the spectacular victory of the ultranationalist forces of Vladimir Zhirinovskii, raised concern in Eastern Europe about the long-term dangers of a nationalist regime in Moscow.

Russia responded negatively to the idea of NATO expansion. Although Boris Yeltsin had spoken favorably of Poland's interest in NATO during a visit to Warsaw in the summer of 1993, he quickly reversed himself under pressure from members of his administration, particularly the military. Just before the parliamentary elections in December 1993, Evgenii Primakov, then director of Russia's Foreign Intelligence Service, issued a blistering critique of NATO expansion. He noted that historically NATO and the former Soviet Union had viewed each other as enemies and that "this psychological mind-set cannot be broken painlessly." An expansion of NATO to Russia would create a "new geopolitical situation that is extremely disadvantageous to Russia." This would lead Russia to rethink its defense concepts and restructure its armed forces. He concluded, "If the countries of Central and Eastern Europe join that organization, the objective result will be the emergence of a barrier between Russia and the rest of the continent."[53] Moscow's alternative to NATO expansion was a proposal that NATO and Russia jointly guarantee East European security, an idea that appealed neither to NATO nor to the Visegrad states.

An attempt to satisfy the security interests of Russia and the states of Eastern Europe was a proposal developed by the Clinton administration, known as the Partnership for Peace (PFP). First proposed at a meeting of NATO defense ministers in October 1993, the PFP was designed to be a stepping stone to eventual membership in NATO. It had several objectives: (1) to satisfy the security concerns of the Central and East European states; (2) to avoid destabilization of the delicate political environment in Russia; and (3) to buy time.[54] The PFP was designed to establish cooperative military relations between the members of the partnership through consultation, joint exercises, planning, and training.

The offer of partnership was extended to every member of the OSCE, including Russia. Although they much preferred full membership in NATO, the Visegrad states accepted the offer quickly. By February 1994, agreements to join the Partnership for Peace were also signed by Romania, Lithuania, Estonia, Ukraine, Bulgaria, Latvia, Moldova, and Albania. Moscow's initial response was positive, because it viewed the PFP as an alternative to NATO expansion; but from the beginning there was ambivalence in Moscow. Russians understood only too well that both NATO expansion and the PFP were based upon the fear of Russian aggression, and thus were essentially a continuation of the Cold War policy of containment.

Throughout 1994 the Yeltsin administration wavered in its policy toward the PFP. At a summit meeting with the U.S. president in June, Boris Yeltsin endorsed the PFP initiative. But within the newly elected Russian parliament, opposition to the PFP mounted. Concern within the military intensified as a result of NATO military activity in Bosnia in the winter and spring. Air strikes against the Serbs were made without consulting Russia, giving rise to the feeling in Moscow that Russia was not being accorded the great-power status to which it was entitled. Russia wanted NATO to acknowledge a special strategic partnership, closer than that provided under the PFP. After considerable bargaining, Andrei Kozyrev signed the PFP framework document on June 23, along with a protocol affirming that "Russia and NATO have agreed to prepare a wide-ranging individual program of partnership, in keeping with Russia's size, importance, and potential."[55] The vagueness of the protocol and its lack of a legally binding force failed to satisfy Moscow that Russia was in fact being accorded geopolitical parity with the United States.

If Yeltsin expected the PFP to serve as a barrier to NATO expansion, that hope was dashed in the aftermath of the November 1994 congressional elections in the United States. Republican control of Congress brought renewed demands for NATO expansion, which were endorsed by the Clinton administration. That along with the passage of the Brown Amendment, permitting the Visegrad states privileges in logistics and weapons acquisitions normally reserved for NATO members, increased Russian suspicions.[56] In December Moscow shocked the West with a sharp reversal of the June decision on the PFP. Andrei Kozyrev, the most pro-Western member of the administration, stunned a meeting of the NATO Council in Brussels by postponing Russian participation in the PFP. Boris Yeltsin followed that up with a harsh speech before an OSCE summit in Budapest, warning that pushing NATO up to Russia's borders risked plunging Russia into a "cold peace."[57]

Pressed by his military, Yeltsin sought to persuade the United States and Europe to accept an alternative to NATO for Europe's security. One concept advanced by Kozyrev was to subordinate NATO to the OSCE. Early in 1994 Kozyrev proposed that the North Atlantic Cooperation Council (NACC) be transformed into an independent structure of military-political cooperation, but one that is closely linked to the OSCE. Under this proposal, the OSCE was assigned the role of coordinator of the efforts of NATO, the European

Union, the Council of Europe, the Western European Union, and the CIS in the areas of strengthening stability and security, peacekeeping, and protecting the rights of national minorities in Europe.[58]

NATO flatly rejected the scheme. As it became increasingly evident in 1995 that NATO expansion was inexorable, Moscow focused on the preconditions that it would demand for acquiescing to the inevitable. Among the preconditions advanced were a favorable revision of the CFE Treaty, the nondeployment of military bases and nuclear weapons in the newly admitted countries, exclusion of the former Soviet republics (especially the Baltic states) as candidates for NATO membership, and recognition of Russia's security system with the CIS states.[59]

But Moscow was playing with a weak hand. What Kozyrev was attempting to do was to obtain Western agreement on a European security system that went beyond mere consultation and détente. NATO, while willing to offer some assurances on the deployment of bases and nuclear weapons in Europe, was unprepared to formalize any substantive concessions. Yeltsin relied heavily on Kozyrev's credibility with the West, but the hapless foreign minister was unable to produce the desired results. This failure was not the only reason for Kozyrev's replacement as foreign minister early in 1996, but it was a factor. NATO's leaders tried to soften Moscow's resistance through various diplomatic formulations. President Clinton suggested "a broad, enhanced NATO-Russia dialogue and cooperation going beyond PFP," and France proposed in April a NATO-Russia nonaggression pact, but Moscow remained unappeased.[60] Nevertheless, Moscow signed on to the PFP on May 31, 1995, even as it continued to oppose NATO expansion.

Foreign Minister Evgenii Primakov was, if anything, even more vehement than Kozyrev in his critique of NATO's moving eastward as a military alliance. In April 1996 he proposed that NATO and Russia jointly guarantee the Visegrad states as an alternative to their membership in NATO. Neither Washington nor the states involved were interested. Primakov also objected to NATO membership for Austria, the Baltic states, Finland, and Sweden. Recognizing that Kozyrev's plan for the OSCE to be the structure for Europe's security was not gaining support, Primakov abandoned the idea. Ever the realist, he acknowledged that NATO expansion was inevitable and directed his efforts in 1996 toward securing some concessions for his country, in the form of special arrangements for Russia with regard to NATO decision making. Here also Washington would not budge.

The Clinton administration, mindful of Russian resentment, sought a solution to the impasse that would preserve some measure of prestige for Russia, give support to Yeltsin, and defuse the issue for nationalists. The year 1996 was particularly critical for the Yeltsin administration, beginning with the presidential campaign and concluding with a paralysis of government while the president suffered from a heart ailment. On September 6, Secretary of State Warren Christopher proposed in Stuttgart, Germany, that a "NATO-Russian Charter" be worked out in conjunction with invitations in 1997 for new members in NATO. U.S. policy was to concede to Moscow a voice but not a veto on sensitive security issues. Aleksandr Lebed, then secretary of the Russian Security Council, argued that the NATO-Russian Charter was not sufficient unless it was "very specific in terms of its legal implications" and that it should be embodied in a legally binding treaty. Lebed pressed his argument before NATO Secretary General Javier Solana in Brussels, but he admitted afterward, "We did not come to terms."[61]

President Clinton had determined that NATO expansion would be a centerpiece of his foreign policy. Following his election to a second term, he decided to move rapidly on this issue. He announced that invitations would be formally extended to the first batch of new members at the NATO summit in Madrid in July 1997. Intensive negotiations in the spring of 1997 were conducted to obtain Russian acceptance of the inevitable. On March 12 Moscow dropped its demand that the NATO-Russian Charter take the form of a legally binding treaty, accepting in its place an executive agreement. On May 27, Boris Yeltsin and Javier Solana signed the Founding Act on Mutual Relations, Cooperation, and Security between NATO and the Russian Federation. This act created the NATO-Russian Council, which would meet periodically to consider security problems as they arose in Europe. The Council would operate by consensus, but NATO remained free to act without Council approval. As a concession to the Russians, NATO stated that it had "no intention, no plan, and no reason" to deploy nuclear weapons on the territories of its new members or to significantly increase troop levels on their territories. Evgenii Primakov put the best face possible on the pact, calling it a "big victory for Russia," but in a television interview on the night of the signing Yeltsin acknowledged that Russia was "playing a weak hand."[62] In July, NATO invited the Czech Republic, Poland, and Hungary to apply to become members. Their applications were approved, and the three states were formally admitted as full members in April 1999, the fiftieth anniversary of the founding of NATO.

No event since the end of the Cold War symbolized the new world order more than the expansion of NATO. For Russia it was a major blow to its national prestige. The extension of invitations to Poland, the Czech Republic, and Hungary in the summer of 1997 did not remove this bone of contention between Russia and the West. It marked only a new stage in the Russian struggle to contain NATO. At Madrid, Western spokesmen made clear their intention to go beyond the first three invitations. Madeleine Albright specifically promised

Lithuania, Latvia, and Estonia that they would be future candidates for membership. In reply, a spokesman at Russia's Ministry of Foreign Affairs said, "We are put on guard by the Madrid declaration's mention of the states in the Baltic region, a reference that, although indirect, nevertheless was in the context of prospects for further NATO expansion. I want to emphasize once again that such a decision has been and remains unacceptable to Russia."[63]

Russia and Europe

In the initial period after the collapse of the USSR, President Yeltsin and Foreign Minister Kozyrev pursued the effort to "join the West" as the highest priority of Russian foreign policy, making no particular differentiation among the democratic market societies and associated international institutions whose partnership they sought. Like Gorbachev before them, they knocked on many doors, concluding treaties of friendship and cooperation with individual Western states, seeking membership for Russia in that most exclusive of Western "clubs," the G-7, and pursuing opportunities to cooperate with (and ultimately join) selective organizations such as the European Union, the Council of Europe, the Paris Club, and the London Club, as well as broader financial associations such as the General Agreement on Tariffs and Trade (GATT)—soon to be succeeded by the World Trade Organization (WTO)—the European Bank for Reconstruction and Development (EBRD), and the International Monetary Fund (IMF). In the security realm, the Russian parliament quickly ratified the Treaty on Conventional Forces in Europe, initially concluded in 1990, together with the Charter for a New Europe, which emphasized an undivided "greater Europe" (or, as Gorbachev liked to put it, a "common European home"). Seeking a pan-European security framework, Russia became an enthusiastic participant in the Conference on Security and Cooperation in Europe (CSCE)—later renamed the Organization for Security and Cooperation in Europe (OSCE)—which included the United States and Canada as well as most of the states of Europe.

Heavily criticized by the mounting nationalist opposition for "slavish" imitation of Western policies, stung by the strong showing of Vladimir Zhirinovskii and other "national-patriotic" forces in the December 1993 elections, and disappointed by the lukewarm embrace and hesitant financial support of most of their would-be Western partners, by 1994 Yeltsin and Kozyrev not only had shifted their priorities to the near abroad but also had adopted a more differentiated approach toward the West. Not only political extremists but "establishment" figures were asking whether Russia should be in such a hurry to join the "European-Atlantic" system, thereby binding itself with rules not of its own making and restricting its freedom of action elsewhere.[64]

EUROPE

Quarrels were erupting with the United States over policy in Bosnia, the proposed enlargement of NATO, continuing U.S. trade restrictions, and Russia's planned weapons exports to anti-U.S. regimes, which led to complaints about the United States' "hegemonic" behavior. Particularly after the outbreak of war in Chechnya, Russia's relations with the EU soured and its progress toward membership in the Council of Europe slowed, accentuating Moscow's growing isolation and stimulating tendencies to play Western states off against one another. By the end of 1997, Yeltsin was talking openly in European capitals about the need to reduce U.S. influence in "our Europe."

In its initial enthusiasm for forging links with the countries of Western Europe, Russia during its first year or so of independence clearly neglected its ties with its former Warsaw Pact allies in Eastern Europe. In its new geographical configuration, Russia no longer shared borders with Romania, Hungary, or Czechoslovakia, and only its enclave-province of Kaliningrad had a border with Poland. Some degree of tension in relations resulted from the history of past Soviet offenses against Poland, Czechoslovakia, and Hungary. Yeltsin wrote of "certain psychological difficulties" in relations with Lech Walesa and Vaclav Havel—understandable, he conceded, because "hanging over us is the cursed legacy of the USSR."[65] Further complications arose from Moscow's difficulties in complying promptly with the demand of these countries for a complete withdrawal of Red Army forces.

Another major source of difficulty was in the economic realm. Even before the formal dissolution of the Council for Mutual Economic Assistance in mid-1991, trade between the USSR and Eastern Europe had declined sharply, as a result of the decision in the late 1980s to settle accounts in hard currencies rather than in "transferable rubles." Furthermore, Moscow had begun to demand world prices for the oil and gas it sold to Eastern Europe, hoping thereby to build a trade surplus with the region. However, the collapse of industrial production in the USSR created imbalances in the other direction. Short of hard currency and unable to pay even the interest on the Soviet debt, Russia refused to pay in fuel, for which it could earn hard currency on the world market.[66] The resulting impasse, combined with the eagerness of both the East Europeans and the Russians to reorient their economies to Western Europe, produced further sharp declines in regional trade with Russia; indeed, the total volume dropped by half between 1989 and 1993.

By the end of 1993, the influential political commentator Stanislav Kondrashov was concluding that Eastern Europe now ranked only fourth or fifth in Russia's priorities, having been transformed from a zone under Russian influence to one of "coldness and distrust." Complaining that the potential of the East European "Russian lobby"—established by the Soviet intelligence services and a half-century of ideological coexistence—was being squandered, he asked how Russia could hope to function as a great power if it failed to reestablish friendly relations with these former partners.[67] But in fact relations had probably not yet reached a low point, as the results of the December 1993 elections—the "Zhirinovskii factor"—stimulated fears in Poland and elsewhere of a new security threat. East European leaders began pressing for prompt admission of their states to NATO, much to the displeasure of Russia, with whom relations took on a character—in one journalist's words—of "controlled mutual antipathy."[68]

The concerns of Poland, the largest and most strategically located of Moscow's former allies, illustrate the difficulties in Russia's relations with Eastern Europe. Warsaw's trade with the Soviet Union had almost completely collapsed prior to 1992, and a trade agreement signed with the Russian government in September 1991 failed to halt the decline; annual trade volume dropped from $14 billion in 1989 to $2.7 billion in 1992. The two states were deadlocked for three years on issues related to settlement of mutual debts, finally agreeing early in 1995 to a mutual write-off of indebtedness. President Walesa visited Moscow in May 1992 to sign a treaty on friendship and cooperation, but his trip occurred only after repeated postponements resulting from disagreements on the document's wording, and the atmosphere of the visit was marred by reports that Poland was siding with Ukraine in its territorial conflicts with Russia. Yeltsin's return trip to Poland also was postponed amid the furor over a remark by Kozyrev that all Moscow had lost in Eastern Europe were "false allies we never trusted anyway."[69] It was August 1993 before the Russian president finally journeyed to Warsaw. The visit was marked by several gestures of Russian goodwill: Yeltsin pledged to withdraw the last Russian army units from Poland by October 1, three months early; he handed over to Walesa material from the CPSU Politburo archive that was intended to disprove the suspicion that the Soviets had planned to send troops into Poland prior to General Jaruzelski's declaration of martial law in 1981; and he surprised all observers by inserting into the joint declaration a statement (later reversed) that Poland's decision to join NATO was not in conflict with the interests of Russia.

Despite these gestures and a Russo-Polish agreement on construction of a gas pipeline from the Yamal peninsula to Germany, relations continued to be strained during the following year. A planned visit to Poland by Viktor Chernomyrdin in November 1994 was postponed in protest of alleged mistreatment by Polish police in Warsaw of Russian passengers on a Moscow–Brussels train. The prime minister's visit took place in February 1995, but the Russians were again distressed when Lech Walesa was a notable absentee from celebrations in Moscow in May of the fiftieth anniversary of the

Allied victory in Europe. The Russians were encouraged by former communist Aleksander Kwasniewski's victory over Walesa in the November 1995 presidential elections. Moscow's ambassador to Warsaw noted in a press interview that the new president's professionalism and intelligence "far outstrip" Walesa's and that "he knows us and will refrain from stirring up historical matters that are irritants in Russian-Polish relations."[70] When Yeltsin met with the new Polish president on his first state visit to Moscow in April 1996, he hailed the prospect of improved relations (despite Kwasniewski's persistence in maintaining Poland's earlier stance on NATO), remarking that "lately something hadn't been right between us and Walesa."[71] Poland's relations with Russia did appear to improve in the post-Walesa period, brightened in part by the approaching completion of the first stage of the ambitious pipeline project. This improvement was noted on the occasion of the visit to Moscow in November 1997 of Prime Minister Jerzy Buzek, who pledged that his new government would devote particular attention to building a partnership between Poland and Russia.

As indicated in Yeltsin's memoirs, relations between Russia and Czechoslovakia also were burdened by the legacy of the past, though the presidents of the two countries were evidently able to "break the ice" more successfully (over a beer in a Czech cafe, Yeltsin notes) than were Yeltsin and Walesa. Vaclav Havel visited Moscow in April 1992 to sign a treaty of friendship and cooperation—a document that included a reference to the 1968 Warsaw Pact invasion of Czechoslovakia as an unjustified use of force. The two sides also settled financial issues relating to the withdrawal of Red Army forces, with Havel agreeing to supply materials for building housing in Russia for the demobilized troops, in return for Russia's turning over real estate in Czechoslovakia that had belonged to the Soviet forces.

As was the case with Poland, however, economic relations were slow to recover. The debt issue was still unresolved in August 1993, when Yeltsin visited Prague and Bratislava to sign new bilateral treaties with the now-separated Czech Republic and Slovakia. The new Russian-Czech treaty lacked an apology for the 1968 invasion (a concession to the heightened assertiveness of parliamentary sentiment in Moscow), but Yeltsin and Havel finessed a delicate situation by laying wreaths both at the grave of a Soviet tank crew member killed in the 1945 liberation and at that of a student killed in the 1968 invasion. The atmosphere during Yeltsin's visit to Slovakia was notably warmer, and the trip produced an unexpected agreement on military cooperation between the two countries. Not until May 1994 did Russia and the Czech Republic reach agreement on repayment of Moscow's $3.5 billion debt, partly through transfer of the property of privatized Russian enterprises. In keeping with the direction signaled earlier, Chernomyrdin announced during a two-day visit to Bratislava in February 1995 that the $1.7 billion debt to Slovakia was to be repaid principally with Russian weapons, including six helicopter gunships, and with Russian assistance in the construction of two nuclear power plants.

Issues in Russian-Hungarian relations essentially followed the Polish and Czech patterns, although they were resolved somewhat earlier. Yeltsin visited Budapest in November 1992, where he was able to sign not only a new treaty of friendship and cooperation, but also a financial settlement relating to troop withdrawal and an agreement on repayment of Russia's $1.7 billion debt, half of which was to be paid with weapons (MiG-29s and armored personnel carriers). Prompt settlement of the debt issue allowed Russian trade with Hungary to rebound more quickly than did its trade with Poland or Czechoslovakia. It reached an annual volume of $2.7 billion in 1994, though it was heavily imbalanced in Russia's favor due to Hungary's dependence on imported Russian natural gas. Finally, in the symbolic realm, the Russian president was generous: during his 1992 visit to Budapest, Yeltsin laid a wreath at the grave of Imre Nagy, turned over documents from party and KGB archives relating to the 1956 invasion, and apologized to Hungary for the Soviet intervention. But a paragraph in the bilateral treaty condemning the 1956 invasion caused the Supreme Soviet early in 1993 to withhold ratification.

These four East European states (Poland, the Czech Republic, Slovakia, and Hungary) formed the "Visegrad group," and were thought to be the states most likely to be included in the first round of NATO's expansion. Soon after his appointment as foreign minister, Evgenii Primakov made a point of visiting all four states to discuss Russia's opposition to NATO expansion. As the momentum built toward the Madrid summit of NATO in July 1997, threatening noises were occasionally heard from Russian representatives. Thus, for example, Moscow's ambassador to Prague suggested that Czech participation in NATO could have negative consequences for Russian deliveries of natural gas. Despite a foreign ministry disavowal and direct reassurances from Chernomyrdin during an April 1997 visit, the prudent Czechs hastened to reduce their dependence on Russia by agreeing to import gas from Norway.

Not surprisingly, given its slower progress toward democratic and market reforms (and its notably more pro-Russian policies), Slovakia was not included in the first wave of prospective new members of NATO. Expressing its relief, the Russian newspaper *Segodnia* hailed Slovakia (along with Serbia) as a "bulwark" of Russian policy in Eastern Europe, having resisted temptations to turn westward and instead having made Russia "the main reference point" in its foreign policy. The newspaper noted with favor that trade turnover with Slovakia had climbed to $2.2 billion in 1996, with cooperation at its deepest in the natural gas industry, and that thanks to Slovakia's willingness to take repayment in military hardware rather than hard currency, Russia's debt would be completely repaid within six or seven years.[72]

Romania, another aspiring member of NATO, had distanced itself from the USSR during the long reign of Ceausescu, and relations with Russia after the fall of his regime showed no particular improvement. Not until September 1993 did the Romanian head of government travel to Moscow, where agreements were concluded on restoring economic ties, which had virtually collapsed. Romania continued to be distinguished as the only East European country with which Russia failed to conclude a bilateral political treaty. Reportedly, the primary obstacle was not debt—Romania was the only East European country not owed money by Russia—but rather Bucharest's insistence that such a treaty include a joint condemnation of the Nazi-Soviet Pact, under which the Romanian province of Bessarabia was assigned to the Soviet sphere. Already concerned about a possible future union of Romania and Moldova, Moscow evidently feared that condemning the 1939 treaty would legitimize a possible Romanian claim on former Soviet territory.

Bulgaria, in contrast, had traditionally enjoyed closer relations with Moscow, and its geographical setting made it a less likely military or economic partner for Western Europe. President Zhelyu Zhelev had sensed the shifting political winds earlier than his East European counterparts, having traveled to Moscow in October 1991, pointedly not meeting with Gorbachev, but issuing a joint declaration with Yeltsin on the establishment of diplomatic relations between Russia and Bulgaria. A formal bilateral treaty on friendship and cooperation was concluded during Yeltsin's return visit in August 1992, during which an agreement was reached also on cooperation between the two defense ministries; but economic relations between the two states were anything but cooperative. Not until May 1995, during a visit to Sofia by Chernomyrdin, did they agree on terms for repayment of Russia's $100 million debt, half of which was to be repaid with spare parts for Bulgaria's armed forces. By that time trade between the two had fallen 90 percent since 1990—from $14.4 billion to $1.8 billion—primarily because of disputes over gas prices. Relations warmed following Bulgaria's agreement to participate in a gas pipeline extending from Russia to Greece, and its expression of interest in being part of a future oil pipeline route. Continued sensitivity over economic relations was evident early in 1996, when the government in Sofia officially protested Yeltsin's mention of Bulgaria as a country that might want to join the new economic union among Russia, Belarus, Kazakhstan, and Kyrgyzstan.

For the countries of Eastern Europe, as for Russia itself, the dominant foreign economic concern was not reestablishment of the trade patterns that had prevailed in the region since the end of World War II, but rather the construction of a relationship with Western Europe that would open its enormous markets to their goods, while attracting investment capital to their emerging market economies. The biggest target of these efforts was the European Union, which then comprised fifteen members. Talks between EU representatives and the new Russian government began in the spring of 1992. That this was by no means a negotiation between economic equals was evident later that year, when the EU extended to Russia and the other members of the Commonwealth of Independent States the same tariff preferences it gives to developing countries. President Yeltsin traveled to Brussels in December 1993 to sign a political declaration on partnership and cooperation, but the difficult bargaining on economic relations continued. Whereas the EU had agreed quickly to freer trade with the East European states, a draft partnership agreement with Russia was reached only in the spring of 1994 and signed by Yeltsin in Corfu, Greece, in June of that year, after eight official rounds of talks. The provisional agreement would free the movement of services and capital but only gradually liberalize trade. Restrictions would continue on Russian exports of steel, textiles, and uranium. Though still a nonmember, Russia would obtain the right to demand compliance with GATT practices in its trade with the EU (provided it also complied), and Russia could protect its market through an exemption for five years from strict implementation of most-favored-nation (MFN) status with respect to the EU states, though it would be allowed to extend MFN to the countries of the CIS. Restrictions recently imposed by Russia on the operation of foreign banks in the country would be immediately waived for five major European banks and eventually rescinded altogether.

However, signing of the interim agreement by the EU was postponed after the invasion of Chechnya, which the European parliament harshly condemned. A delegation consisting of the French, German, and Spanish foreign ministers was dispatched to Moscow in March 1995 to explain the EU position. In the words of two *Kommersant-Daily* correspondents, the action signified that Europe was no longer willing to accept Yeltsin's reassurances, "and it appears that Chechnya will become the turning point at which both Europe and the world as a whole will start to regard 'counting on Yeltsin' as an anachronism."[73] Nevertheless, in July the interim agreement was finally signed by the EU, relieving "the unpleasant feeling of isolation" that intensified with the military operation in Chechnya, and paving the way for Russia's further integration with the world economy.[74] When the Agreement on Partnership and Cooperation with the EU was finally ratified by the Duma in October 1996, the influential deputy Vladimir Lukin declared that the agreement was no less important than START II. The treaty would have the effect of lowering EU tariffs on Russian exports by two-thirds, while allowing Russia to maintain considerably higher tariffs on European products; it would thus facilitate Russia's gradual integration into the EU's single market. After further delay, the agreement entered into force only in December 1997, by which time the EU accounted for 40 percent of trade and investment in Russia. However, Russia was still not certified as a "market economy," allowing the EU to retain antidumping restrictions on fifteen products.

Russia's admission to the Council of Europe, an organization of democratic nations focusing on social and political issues, was an even lengthier process. The states of Eastern Europe and the three newly independent Baltic states were admitted with relative ease, but Russia was confronted with a varied and changing list of obstacles to membership. When the initial Russian application was filed in May 1992, the primary obstacle was said to be the continuing presence of Russian troops in the Baltic states of the former Soviet Union. A year later, the list of conditions was expanded to include free parliamentary elections and a new democratic constitution for the Russian Federation. By this point, despite loud complaints from Moscow over Estonia's treatment of its Russian minority, Estonia had been admitted to the Council of Europe—an action that Kozyrev protested by canceling his attendance at the council meeting.

In September 1994, having held elections and adopted a constitution, and having virtually completed all troop withdrawals, Moscow learned from the visiting council secretary-general that it would need to bring its human rights legislation into harmony with European standards. The invasion of Chechnya by Russian troops caused the Council of Europe to "freeze" Russia's application —an action considered insulting by Russian politicians from various camps. Not until January 1996 did the council's parliamentary assembly finally vote to admit Russia, despite a report from its commission on legal and human rights issues, stating that Russia was not yet a law-governed state and was unlikely to become one in the near future. However, even this much-delayed action was not without conditions; the resolution stipulated that Russia must sign the European Convention on Human Rights (an act that would give Russian citizens legal standing before the European human rights court), and must complete the process of adapting its legislation to European standards, including abolishing the death penalty and curbing the powers of the Federal Security Service. The resolution even advised Russia to cease referring to its neighbors as the "near abroad."

In the security sphere, Russia pinned its hopes for becoming part of a pan-European system on the Organization for Security and Cooperation in Europe, a group of fifty-four member countries, spanning the globe from North America to Central Asia. Although the organization sent observers to conflict zones in the former Yugoslavia and USSR, it struggled to achieve consensus for the operation of actual peacekeeping forces on the continent. Yeltsin traveled to Budapest early in December 1994 to address the summit of the OSCE. In the face of mounting discussion about enlarging the membership of NATO, the Russian president warned that Europe was in danger of being plunged into a state of "cold peace," due in part to the "dangerous delusion" that "the fates of the continent and of the world community as a whole can be controlled from a single capital." Creation of an all-European institution with a "reliable legal foundation," which could assume tasks of conflict resolution and peacekeeping, had become a "vital necessity," and plans to expand NATO were at variance with this objective. As for Russia, it sought partnership with the OSCE and the United Nations in the political and material responsibilities of peacekeeping operations in the former Soviet space, though "of course, not to the detriment of effective operations."[75] The summit's decision in principle to create a peacekeeping force of 3,000 for Nagorno-Karabakh was hailed by *Izvestia* as an action that "should go down in history as the birth of a new peacekeeping institution, second in importance only to the United Nations."[76] But Russia failed to gain acceptance of its initiative to change the structure of the OSCE or to obtain a mandate to conduct its own peacekeeping operations in the CIS, leading *Nezavisimaia gazeta* to a far more pessimistic (and ultimately more accurate) conclusion: "Russia, with its claims to OSCE supremacy in peacekeeping in the region, had the unrealizable nature of its hopes pointed out to it in a completely unambiguous way."[77]

Only five days after Yeltsin's return to Moscow from Budapest, he launched the invasion of Chechnya, bringing a hailstorm of European criticism down on his head. The OSCE stiffly reminded Russia of its requirement for a six-week advance notification of major troop movements. The organization sent a three-man delegation to Moscow with an offer to send observers to Chechnya to mediate the conflict. Its chairman, calling for a humanitarian truce and early elections, declared that the use of armed force on such a scale was in violation of OSCE principles and of the principles of human rights. Frostily rejecting such interference in its internal affairs, Russia charged that the violations of human rights were in fact being committed by the Chechen rebels. Clearly, however, the Russian government's actions in Chechnya further damaged its prospects for being accepted into the Western community of nations.

Throughout the 1990s, the primary advocate in regional forums on behalf first of Soviet and then of Russian integration into Europe was Germany. As phrased by Germany's ambassador to Russia, Bonn's role is "somewhat like that of a defense lawyer for Russia in the construction of the new Europe."[78] Antagonists in two world wars and the Cold War, Germany and Russia have come to recognize their mutual stake in preventing conflicts in their common neighborhood that might again cast them in adversarial roles. As we have seen earlier in this volume, since the time of the Treaty of Rapallo in 1922 the two states have engaged in periodic efforts to act as partners in an altered balance of power in Europe.

Bonn had acquired a considerable stake in Gorbachev's success, given the agreements it had forged with him on German reunification and withdrawal of Soviet forces. Yeltsin's initial visit to Bonn as Russian president took place in November 1991, when Gorbachev was still in the Kremlin, and Germany was cautious in discussing diplomatic and economic ties. Kozyrev's follow-up visit in January formalized the understanding that existing treaties between the USSR and Germany would be honored by the Russian Federation. Bonn was particularly interested in the fate of the Russian citizens of German origin whom Stalin had forcibly resettled from the Volga region in 1941, and for whose relocation needs Germany had already committed significant funding. Kohl had no particular wish for large numbers of these "Volga Germans" to emigrate to Germany, and he urged Moscow to establish an autonomous republic for them in the Volgograd region. Given that Germany then accounted for 57 percent of all foreign investment in the CIS economies, and that it has contributed more than half of all foreign economic assistance received by Russia, its wishes carried weight in Moscow.[79]

Chancellor Kohl's first visit to Yeltsin's Russia came in December 1992, at a time when Yeltsin was engaged in a momentous showdown with the Congress of People's Deputies, having been forced to abandon his nomination of Egor Gaidar as premier. In this context, Kohl's reassuring words and actions were viewed in the Russian press as a "life preserver" for Yeltsin, reassuring the "world community of Russian reforms and their continuation." The two leaders signed eight agreements, including a promise by Germany to give an eight-year respite on repayment of Soviet debts to the former German Democratic Republic, and a pledge of an additional 550 million marks (bringing the total to 8.3 billion marks) for construction of housing in Russia for troops withdrawn from Germany. Yeltsin promised in turn to complete the troop withdrawal four months early (by August 1994), and to provide 10 billion rubles in the Russian budget for setting up new "national districts" for the Volga Germans. At the conclusion of his visit, Kohl termed Russia Germany's "major partner in the East."[80]

The harmony between Bonn and Moscow was briefly disturbed in August 1994 by a sensational case of alleged nuclear smuggling, which was played up in the Western press as evidence of lax Russian security. After a German "sting" operation caught a Spaniard and a Colombian carrying 300 grams of plutonium-239 on a plane arriving in Munich from Moscow, the Russian atomic energy ministry hotly denied that the nuclear material was of Russian origin. Discussions between the two nations' security services resulted in an agreement to open offices in each other's capital to facilitate their cooperation in combating illegal trafficking and terrorism.[81]

At the end of August, Yeltsin returned to Germany, accompanied by virtually his entire government team, for a ceremony marking the completion of the withdrawal of Russian troops. Yeltsin drew considerable attention to himself when he seized the conductor's baton and led an army chorus in song; a German magazine reported on his "unsteady gait" at the parade ground. All told, about a half-million troops and more than 100,000 weapons and pieces of equipment were pulled out of Germany within four years. There was considerable grumbling about the pace, since despite Germany's provision of significant funds for housing the forces in Russia, more than 25,000 military families were said still to lack accommodation. On the eve of the fifty-fifth anniversary of the start of World War II in Europe, the Russian president solemnly declared, "This Russia and this Germany will never fight each other again."[82] In an interview with *Izvestia,* he said:

Germany is no longer a threat to peace. The exhausting cold war is over. Therefore the withdrawal of Russian troops is a natural step whose time has come. An era of enmity, distrust, and suspiciousness is ending in the history of Russia and Germany, and in the history of Europe. Russia and Germany have no significant unresolved problems or disagreements. In many spheres we are partners.[83]

The state of Russo-German relations was not entirely insulated from the effects of Moscow's invasion of Chechnya; to cite one example, defense minister Pavel Grachev was uninvited by his German counterpart to a Munich forum on European security scheduled for March 1995.[84] Given the stakes Bonn had in Yeltsin, the estrangement was neither deep nor lasting. Helmut Kohl was back in Moscow at the beginning of the Russian presidential campaign to describe Yeltsin as a "reliable partner," a "tried and true friend of Germany," and the best president for Russia, with "absolutely no reservations."[85] In April 1997, following his reelection and his return to health, Yeltsin journeyed to Germany. The sole major issue then pending between the two states concerned the status of some 200,000 items of "trophy art" removed from Germany by Soviet troops following World War II. Yeltsin had promised Kohl that it would be returned to Germany, but an outraged parliament passed a law declaring it to be Russian state property. Yeltsin's veto was overridden by the Duma just prior to his visit to Germany, but a more diplomatically sensitive Federation Council delayed its vote to override until after the visit had been concluded. As if to soften the impending blow, Yeltsin reminded Kohl that the issue cut two ways, noting that occupying German troops had done $1.3 trillion worth of damage to Russian cultural property. In the end, however, the parliament held firm, refusing to allow Yeltsin to return the property to Germany.

Second only to Germany in Russian priorities in Europe is France. French and Russian diplomats fondly recall the historic Franco-Russian alliance of 1893 and their common struggle against German armies in two world wars. As their Soviet predecessors did from the time of Charles de Gaulle, on occasion Russian leaders have subtly reinforced France's continuing rivalry with Germany and its resentments at Washington's perceived wish to dominate Western Europe. While Yeltsin's personal relations with President François Mitterrand never approached the level of warmth he exhibited with Chancellor Helmut Kohl, the personal dimension in diplomacy has loomed larger since the election in 1995 of Jacques Chirac as France's president.

Although French economic aid to Russia did not approach the level of German assistance, France did grant economic credits in 1992, announced during Yeltsin's February visit to Paris. In 1994, the two countries signed agreements on military cooperation—Moscow's first with a West European state—including projects for joint development and production of weaponry, which were intended in part to allow the two countries to compete more effectively with the United States in the arms export market. By the time of Kozyrev's visit to France in November of the same year, a more explicit anti-American tone was being heard. Neither state was speaking approvingly at this point about NATO expansion, and they pointedly discussed possible initiatives with respect to Bosnia and Iraq that would undercut the perceived unilateralism of Washington's approach to these conflict areas. Mitterrand underscored the need not to isolate Moscow but rather to build Europe with Russian participation, and Kozyrev chimed in, stressing that Russia's cooperation with France, Germany, and Britain "will not be a partnership against the U.S. but a partnership with it, but in such a way that Europe's voice is heard independently, and that Moscow's voice in the European chorus is also sufficiently distinct."[86]

Yeltsin's first direct talks with Chirac, during a stopover on his way to the United Nations in October 1995, again focused on NATO expansion and Bosnia; in the view of a pair of Russian journalists, they displayed a "proximity of views based on a certain anti-Americanism."[87] During the following year, an exchange of visits by the two prime ministers led to closer relations in the economic and technical spheres; a bilateral commission was set up (modeled on the Gore-Chernomyrdin commission), a new French credit was granted, and agreement was reached on Russian repayment of tsarist debts. Further talks between Chirac and Yeltsin in 1997 (with Yeltsin going to Paris once and Chirac traveling three times to Moscow) produced final agreements on questions of debts, clearing the way for Russia's admission to the Paris Club of creditor nations. In September, on the last of these visits, Chirac was accompanied by twenty French businessmen, who engaged in wide-ranging talks on trade expansion. It was noted that while French exports to Russia had increased 30 percent, France still ranked eighth on the list of Russia's trade partners. Political talks between Yeltsin and Chirac again focused on topics on which the two took positions distinct from that of the United States. As if to underscore the warmth of the relationship, Yeltsin presented Chirac with the Order for Services to the Fatherland, First Class (the first time such an award had been presented).[88]

Given its greater geographical distance and the closer proximity of its foreign policy to that of the United States, Britain was a less prominent object of Russian courtship than the two major continental powers of Western Europe. Yeltsin's initial trip to London as Russian president in January 1992 was undertaken with full awareness of the importance to Gorbachev's international reputation of Margaret Thatcher's commendation in 1984: "One can do business with Mr. Gorbachev." Knowing that foreign visits had been an area of triumph for his predecessor, Yeltsin was pleased with his reception. Prime Minister John Major declared that "Yeltsin made a very good impression on me," and the British agreed to increase economic aid to Russia.[89] During a second visit later in the same year, Yeltsin signed a bilateral treaty and an economic agreement, and he was given the opportunity to address the British parliament.

An exchange of visits between Major and Yeltsin in 1994 featured good atmospherics but very little in the way of bilateral accomplishment. In London in September, Yeltsin failed to get British backing for his project to expand peacekeeping responsibilities for the OSCE, but on all other issues the two were reportedly in agreement. The more important trip that year was purely ceremonial—Queen Elizabeth II's visit to Russia in October was the first visit by a British monarch since the Bolshevik revolution. The change of governments in Britain had little effect on the course of Anglo-Russian relations; a visit to Moscow by Prime Minister Blair in October 1997 focused on economic relations, with attention being given to the fact that Britain now ranked second to Germany among foreign investors in Russia.

Other European capitals visited by Yeltsin included three in the south: Rome (December 1991), Athens (June 1993), and Madrid (April 1994). In each case, Russia has signed a bilateral treaty on friendship and cooperation as well as multiple trade and economic agreements, but only in the case of Italy has the economic relationship appeared significant. Indeed, Yeltsin made a second visit to Italy in February 1998, where he signed contracts worth

$3 billion, primarily for oil and gas deliveries and for a joint venture in automobile production. By this time, Italy ranked as Russia's second largest European trading partner.

In contrast, for reasons of geography and history, Russia's relationships with the countries of northern Europe have been more intense. Moscow has participated in the Council of Baltic Sea States established in March 1992 by Russia, Germany, Poland, Sweden, Denmark, Finland, Norway, Lithuania, Latvia, and Estonia. Intended to coordinate policies in the realms of the economy and environment, transportation, energy, law enforcement, and tourism, the council also was a forum in which Russia voiced its complaints about the treatment of Russian minorities in the three Baltic states of the former Soviet Union.

Next to Lithuania, Latvia, and Estonia, whose relations with Moscow were discussed in chapter 6, Finland has been the northern European neighbor most closely tied to Russia. Formerly under the tsar's rule, Finland practiced an anxious neutrality during the Cold War, tilting far enough toward Moscow in its foreign and domestic policies to escape outright incorporation into the Soviet sphere. Echoes of this uneasy past have occasionally been observed in current Russo-Finnish relations. Relations began well, with Finland being the first European state with which Yeltsin's Russia signed a bilateral treaty. On his first visit, Yeltsin laid a wreath at the monument to Finnish soldiers who fell in the Winter War of 1939–40, and documents normalizing economic ties were signed. The approach of Finnish elections the following year brought concerns, however, with the Russian press noting that some presidential candidates were violating the agreement on mutual renunciation of territorial claims by raising the "Karelian question." A considerable stir was raised in Finland when the same Russian ambassador who often lectured the country during the Soviet period issued a harsh protest just days before the election about the behavior of two Finnish nationalist parties. Bilateral economic relations improved following an agreement on repayment of Russia's debt of $1.3 billion, most of which was to be repaid through arms deliveries. By 1997, Russia ranked fifth among Finland's trade partners, with an annual volume of $4.7 billion, much of it in the sphere of energy. Opening a section of a highway in October 1997, Prime Minister Lipponen announced a plan for expanded "northern cooperation" and spoke of Finland as a bridge between Russia and Western Europe.

Yeltsin's last foreign trip of 1997 was a highly publicized visit to Sweden, notable less for its diplomatic achievements than for several embarrassing mistakes made by the Russian president. At one point, Yeltsin evidently believed he was in Finland; on another occasion, he referred to a "Swedish" oil deal that actually had been concluded with Norway. Blurting out a confusing offer for a unilateral reduction in nuclear arms—later disavowed by his staff—he mistakenly identified Germany and Japan as nuclear powers. In this context, observers were uncertain of the status of a declaration he made in a speech to the Swedish parliament—later confirmed by his defense minister and evidently intended to reassure the Baltic states that their membership in NATO would be unnecessary—promising a 40 percent cut in Russian ground and naval forces along the country's northwestern border by 1999. In any event, Yeltsin's strange behavior was later blamed by his staff on fatigue and a developing cold, and he was hospitalized upon his return to Russia.

More diplomatically significant, and symbolic of the growing differentiation that had occurred in Russian policy toward the West, was a trip Yeltsin made a little earlier in the fall of 1997, to a summit meeting of the Council of Europe in Strasbourg. The Russian president seemed at pains to underscore the extent to which Russia regarded itself as part of a Europe that was increasingly resistant to U.S. domination. "We do not need an uncle from somewhere," he declared in an interview before the summit. "We in Europe are capable of uniting ourselves to live normally." In addition to its fears that the United States was seeking to redivide Europe to Russia's disadvantage through expansion of NATO, Moscow resented the continuing U.S. refusal to grant most-favored-nation trade status, Congress's threats to cut off aid (regarded as niggardly in any event) in retaliation for a parliamentary act regulating religious practice in Russia, and Washington's announced intention to retaliate against Russia and France for their cooperative project to develop gas fields in Iran.[90] Within a few weeks, Russia again displayed its independence, joining with France in resisting the tough American stance on UN sanctions on Iraq. In a move clearly aimed at emphasizing that his main Western partners were in Europe, Yeltsin announced at Strasbourg that he would hold annual summits with the French and German leaders to review the state of the European continent.

Yugoslavia Redux

The mix of cooperation and confrontation with the West that characterized Boris Yeltsin's first administration continued through the second (1996–99). As was the case earlier, Yeltsin was forced to moderate his own pro-Western proclivities by pressures from the communist and nationalist forces in the Duma, as well as from elements in the military. On the other hand, Russian foreign policy was unable to pursue a strong position in many arenas because of weakness in the economy, in the military, and in the health of the president. During Yeltsin's second term, two issues that earlier had brought Russia into conflict with the West resurfaced: war in Yugoslavia and in Chechnya.

The 1995 Dayton Accord ended the war in Bosnia, but it did not apply to Kosovo, a province of Serbia about the size of Connecticut. Kosovo had a population of 2 million, of whom 90 percent were ethnic Albanians. Slobodan Milosevic, Serbia's ruler, had revoked Kosovo's autonomy in 1989, imposing a repressive Serbian rule upon its people. A form of resistance to Serbian rule was organized by Ibrahim Rugova, who established a parallel government to administer schools and medical facilities and to levy taxes. Although recognized as the unofficial president of Kosovo, Rugova was too pacifist for a growing number of Albanian Kosovars, who were prepared to use violence against the ruling Serbs. In the early 1990s, a militant guerrilla movement known as the Kosovo Liberation Army (KLA) emerged, determined to break away from Serbia by forceful means.[91] By the spring of 1998 Milosevic confronted a major uprising in Kosovo. He responded to KLA guerrilla warfare with a ruthless policy of "ethnic cleansing" and killings. Approximately 400,000 Muslims were displaced in 1998 and some 2,000 killed.

By early 1999, in response to the growing violence in Kosovo and particularly a massacre by Serbian forces of forty-five people in the village of Racak, a conference was convened in Rambouillet, France, by the Contact Group (Russia, the United States, Britain, France, Germany, and Italy), to set the terms for ending the fighting in Kosovo. The Rambouillet negotiations produced an accord in February, which demanded autonomy for the people of Kosovo, a withdrawal of Yugoslav forces, demilitarization of the KLA forces, a return of refugees, and enforcement of the peace by NATO forces. A future referendum would determine a final settlement. Meanwhile, Yugoslav sovereignty over Kosovo was recognized.

Under Western pressure, the KLA accepted the terms, but Milosevic refused. As a consequence, NATO on March 23 began an air war against Yugoslavia, which lasted for seventy-seven days. Milosevic's immediate response was a massive displacement of Kosovo Albanians from their homes. In June, however, Milosevic capitulated. A NATO contingent known as Kosovo Force (KFOR) entered the territory to enforce the peace and assist in the governance of Kosovo.

Russia, as it had in the Bosnian war earlier, found itself isolated from the Western powers and ineffective with its Yugoslav ally. Even as a friend of Yugoslavia, Russia could not stop Milosevic's suppression of Kosovo's Albanians, let alone persuade Belgrade to restore autonomy to Kosovo. Thus, in March 1998, when the United Nations voted an arms embargo against Yugoslavia, Moscow went along. However, as the Western members of the Contact Group moved closer to military intervention in Kosovo, Moscow took the line that only the United Nations (where Russia has a veto) was empowered to authorize the use of military force against a sovereign state.

Russia's defense minister expressed the hard-line view that launching a NATO assault against Kosovo "would signal the start of a cold war, a break in relations with NATO, and a freezing of the process of START II ratification."[92] Russia's civilian leaders were more subtle, warning of dire consequences if NATO were to use force, without committing to any specific response.

The massacre at Racak in January 1999 complicated Russia's delicate diplomacy. First Deputy Foreign Minister Aleksandr Avdeev rushed to Belgrade where he met with Milosevic behind closed doors. The best the Russians could get from the Yugoslav leader was to reverse his decision to expel the head of the OSCE International Observer Mission, who had publicly condemned the Serbs for the Racak murders. That, however, failed to satisfy NATO, which by then had determined to intervene in Kosovo.

The negotiations at Rambouillet culminated in the ultimatum to Milosevic and led to the air assault in March. Yeltsin's public threat that "We won't let anyone touch Kosovo" turned out to be a bluff. Moscow expressed "outrage" and closed the NATO mission in Moscow. Prime Minister Primakov was on a flight to Washington as the first bombs fell. He was going to negotiate a program of American assistance to Russia, but the requirements of national prestige induced him to reverse course in midflight and return to Moscow.

Russia's diplomacy during the war was as fruitless as were its efforts to prevent NATO's assault. Primakov led a high-level team to persuade Belgrade to make concessions. Yeltsin was compelled to admit that Milosevic was a "difficult negotiating partner." Russia then asked for a special session of the Security Council to demand a stop to the air war. Only two Security Council members—China and Namibia—voted with Russia. A similar appeal to the Parliamentary Assembly of the Council of Europe was rejected. In April, Foreign Minister Ivanov met with U.S. Secretary of State Albright to negotiate the terms for a cessation of fighting, but that effort failed. The main sticking point involved the police force to keep order in Kosovo. Russia was prepared to accept and even participate in a peacekeeping force operating under the flag of the OSCE, but not under NATO.

Finding himself increasingly isolated from world opinion over the Balkan war, in April 1999 Yeltsin switched diplomatic control of the issue away from his hawkish prime minister and foreign minister and made his former prime minister, Viktor Chernomyrdin, Russia's special representative for Yugoslavia. If the Kosovo war were to end without a land invasion by NATO, then Milosevic would have to be persuaded to capitulate. No diplomat was in a better position to press acceptance of Western terms on Milosevic than Chernomyrdin. Some in the Russian media referred contemptuously to Chernomyrdin as NATO's "postman."[93] In May, NATO aircraft bombed the Chinese embassy in Belgrade, provoking a crisis between Washington and

Beijing. Washington insisted the bombing was accidental. Moscow did not publicly endorse the American explanation, but it did agree to send Chernomyrdin to Beijing to help mediate the Sino-American differences.

A more significant mediation took place in early June. Chernomyrdin and Martti Ahtisaari (representing the OSCE) persuaded Milosevic to accept a Western plan for ending the conflict. On all essential points—including a NATO peacekeeping force in Kosovo—the Yugoslav government capitulated to the West. In Moscow, there was a firestorm of criticism from the military, leftists, and nationalists who charged Yeltsin's emissary with betrayal of Yugoslavia's and Russia's interests. Public opinion in Russia, however, tended to favor the Chernomyrdin mission.[94]

In a bizarre postscript to the war in Kosovo, two hundred Russian paratroopers seized the airport at Pristina, Kosovo's capital, before NATO forces could take control. This action apparently was Yeltsin's concession to a military disgruntled about the terms of peace. It was, however brief, an assertion of national honor and a sop to the president's critics, especially in the Duma. Vladimir Lukin, chairman of the Duma's foreign affairs committee, proclaimed: "Russia had lately shown indecision in crisis situations. Now the whole world has seen that we can act brilliantly when all seems lost."[95] It was a daring gesture, but with little consequence. Russia gained the satisfaction of participating in KFOR, but did not get the separate operational sector it wanted, though its military presence was assured in virtually every key area of the province. Over time, Russian forces worked effectively together under overall NATO command, as they did in Bosnia.

The termination of fighting did not end Moscow's differences with NATO. It continuously protested the failure of KFOR to stop ethnic Albanian assaults on Serbs and efforts by former KLA forces to detach Kosovo from Yugoslavia. In principle, the West shared those concerns. A major source of friction between all sides was removed in September 2000 when Milosevic was soundly defeated in his bid for reelection as president of Yugoslavia. Not without initial hesitation, Russia's president recognized Vojislav Kostunica as Yugoslavia's president. In the final analysis, the war in Kosovo revealed the fault lines between Russia and the West, exposed the inability of Russia to challenge the West in the Balkans, and revealed Yeltsin's determination to keep Russia as a partner rather than as an adversary to the United States and Europe.

The Second Chechen War

Barely had peace been restored in the Balkans than a resumption of civil war in the Caucasus brought new strains to Russian-Western relations. Early in August 1999 a second phase of Russia's war with Chechnya began with an invasion of the Russian territory of Dagestan. Led by Chechen warlord Shamil Basaev and his ally Khattab, several thousand guerrillas occupied a number of towns in border districts. Basaev's proclaimed goal was to establish an independent nation, to be called the Islamic State of Dagestan. Almost coinciding with the outbreak of fighting in the North Caucasus was the replacement of Sergei Stepashin with Vladimir Putin as Russia's new prime minister.

Putin's promise to finish off the "bandits" in a fortnight proved to be easier said than done. Russian forces encountered fierce resistance from the guerrillas and often had to give up territory captured from the Chechens. Quickly, the fighting escalated. Russia began bombing villages in Chechnya, which Moscow claimed were support bases for the guerrillas. Basaev responded, "We reserve the right to retaliate anywhere in Russia and at any time."[96] Within a period of weeks in September, terrorist bombers struck several cities in Russia, including two massive bombings in Moscow. Civilian casualties numbered in the hundreds. Although Moscow could not positively identify the perpetrators, Putin's government assumed they were Chechens and used the terrorist attacks as a *casus belli* for a full-scale war on Chechnya.[97] Prime Minister Putin referred to Chechnya as a "huge terrorist camp." He believed that a failure by Russia to destroy the insurgency would ultimately lead to the disintegration of the Russian Federation.[98] On October 1, 1999, Putin gave the order for a full-scale invasion of northern Chechnya. The war that ensued took a large toll in Chechen lives and created hundreds of thousands of refugees.

Unlike the war in 1994–96, the second Chechen war had the support of the majority of the Russian population; but, increasingly, the West became critical—as it had been earlier—of the brutality and destructiveness of the fighting. Europe and the United States, even while acknowledging the principle of Russia's territorial integrity, pressed Moscow to negotiate a political solution with the government of Maskhadov, the elected Chechen president. This Moscow would not do. Putin's government adamantly refused to conduct a dialogue with a member of the Russian Federation in a way that recognized it as an equal partner. When an emissary of Chechnya's government was officially received by the French government in November, the Russian foreign ministry protested vigorously.

Domestically, Putin's ruthless prosecution of the war proved to be popular. Where Yeltsin lost popular support in 1995, Putin gained in 2000. His high approval ratings in March 2000 guaranteed his election as Russia's second president. Even as the war dragged on through 2000, the public's support for Putin's policy in Chechnya remained high. Criticism from the West was deflected in Russia by all except the champions of human rights, who were in a minority. Western criticism remained persistent but restrained. President Clinton warned, "Russia will pay a heavy price for its actions in Chechnya," but Washington never specified what that price would be. In April 2000, the Council of Europe's Parliamentary Assembly initiated procedures for suspending Russia from the Council of Europe, though it did not go so far as actually to expel Russia.[99] Politically, the issue put Russia's critics in a bind: they could not ignore the egregious violations of human rights in Chechnya even as they recognized Moscow's justification (and determination) to suppress the insurgency. Furthermore, there were more important issues between Russia and the West affecting vital interests, which necessitated cooperation from Moscow. In addition, for Russia the same paradox applied: Chechnya had to be subdued, though not at the expense of alienating Europe. "[W]e are," said Putin, "part of Western European culture . . . we are Europeans."[100]

Europe at the End of the Decade

As the decade of the 1990s ended, Russia's relations with Europe declined largely as a result of the war in Kosovo, which Russia opposed, and the war in Chechnya, whose violations of human rights offended Europeans. In the year leading up to those conflicts, the Yeltsin administration had sought with some success to strengthen its relations with Europe.

High on Moscow's priority list was improving economic ties with the EU. Trade with the European Union in 1998 accounted for approximately 45 percent of Russia's foreign trade. If the European Union could be persuaded to grant Russia "market status," the economic benefits would be substantial—at least several billion dollars. Early in 1998, the foreign ministers of Russia and the EU Cooperation Council approved a working program to grant Russia the status of a market economy and to lift discriminatory restrictions on Russian export sectors.

Another road to integration with Europe was the Council of Europe. On February 20, Russia's Duma overcame a major hurdle to Russia's membership in the council by ratifying the European Convention of Human Rights. There still remained the problem of capital punishment in Russia (unacceptable to the European Council) before Moscow would meet all its obligations for membership. By May, however, Russia completed ratification of the required Council of Europe demands and formally joined the council. This meant, among other things, that Russian citizens could for the first time file complaints with the European Court against their own government.

Yeltsin's government also took important steps to improve relations with Europe's major powers. In February, Yeltsin and Italian prime minister Romano Prodi signed a twenty-year action plan for broad economic cooperation. On his visit to Rome, the Russian president had a lengthy and cordial visit with the Pope. In March, Yeltsin hosted a meeting in Moscow with his French and German counterparts, Chirac and Kohl. To Yeltsin, this second summit of Europe's "big three" symbolized a new unity of Europe's leading powers. Kohl obliged his host by observing that "the future of Europe and the European Union will always depend upon close relations with Russia."[101] The three agreed to maintain regular contact.

The reality of Russia's position could not match the rhetoric. The fact remained that 1998 was a bad year for the Russian Federation, both economically and politically. Russia was operating from a position of extreme domestic weakness, which inevitably impaired its diplomatic effectiveness. In August, the economy experienced a financial crisis (a stock market plunge and a collapse of government securities) that forced the government to devalue the ruble and default on its foreign and domestic debts. Europe's confidence in Moscow's capacity to carry through with economic reform noticeably declined. Even Germany, Russia's leading trading partner and source of capital, warned that financial assistance would not be forthcoming so easily as in the past.

Politically, 1998 and 1999 were years of instability as well. In March, Yeltsin fired his longstanding prime minister, Chernomyrdin, replacing him with Sergei Kirienko, a young reformer. The change caused a political crisis when the Duma objected, forcing Yeltsin to nominate his candidate three times. In the aftermath of the financial collapse in August, Yeltsin fired Kirienko and attempted to bring back Chernomyrdin. This time, resistance to Yeltsin was stronger in the Duma, and the deputies faced up to the possibility of dissolution by rejecting Chernomyrdin. Yeltsin was forced to choose a prime minister more acceptable to the conservative Duma. He selected Primakov, who had been foreign minister since 1996 and brought a measure of stability to the government, but Primakov and Yeltsin never overcame their differences. In May 1999, Yeltsin fired Primakov and made Stepashin head of government. In three months, Stepashin was out and Putin became prime minister. Within a period of less than two years, Moscow had functioned under five different prime ministers.

It was not surprising that under conditions of economic weakness and political instability, the prestige of Russia and its president suffered. Yeltsin was seen by many as a spent force. At the Russia-European Union summit in February 1999, the Europeans assumed that Primakov was the man with whom they would be working as a strategic partner; but Primakov was no more successful than Yeltsin in modifying Western policy in the main European conflict in 1999, the war in Kosovo. As Yeltsin prepared to leave office, he had to acknowledge that, in the economic sphere, Europe was moving closer and closer to integration without Russia and in the security area NATO—and not the OSCE—remained the dominant organization. Even before the expiration of his second term, Yeltsin realized that he could no longer effectively carry on the duties of president.

In August, Yeltsin initiated the strategy by which he would choose his own successor. He replaced Stepashin with Putin as prime minister. Six months later, in a surprise move, Yeltsin resigned the presidency, thus making Putin acting president as well as prime minister. In doing so, he embraced Putin as "a strong man worthy of being president." Thus ended the era of Yeltsin and began the era of Putin. In chapter 9 we will assess Russia's foreign policy under its second president.

—————— **8** ——————

Russia and the "Non-West"

As we saw in chapter 4, the international system at the end of World War II was perceived in both the United States and the Soviet Union as rigidly bipolar. In 1947, both the Truman Doctrine and Andrei Zhdanov's speech at the founding conference of the Cominform portrayed a struggle between two camps, each united around its own ideology. As the great colonial empires collapsed in the postwar period, new nations in Asia, the Middle East, Latin America, and Africa joined the few already independent states in those regions, unwillingly cast in the role of an arena for the competition of the two blocs.

During the period of the Cold War the developed states of West and East were depicted as the First World and the Second World, and the less developed countries became known as the Third World. Although the breakup of the Soviet bloc rendered the familiar labels obsolete, Russian foreign policy in the post-Soviet period has continued to differentiate among three "worlds"—the West; the former USSR (the near abroad) and Eastern Europe; and that large grouping of countries in Asia, the Middle East, Africa, and Latin America that we will call (for lack of a better term) the "non-West."

As we have seen, Khrushchev revived the Leninist perception of the developing world as the "vital reserve of imperialism," and he initiated a relatively low-risk Soviet challenge that sought ideological victories for "socialism" as well as strategic benefits in the economic and military spheres. The initial Soviet forays became a broader-based investment under Brezhnev, as the USSR sought to counter Western (and Chinese) influence in all areas of the Third World, establishing in the process facilities that allowed Soviet military power to be projected on a truly global basis. Soviet influence reached its high-water mark in the mid-1970s, after which it lost some of its hard-won beachheads, while also failing to persuade the United States that expansionist and revolutionary activities in the Third World were compatible with superpower détente.

As the Soviet economy faltered, Gorbachev began, even before the end of the Cold War, to liquidate some of the USSR's most costly and unproductive Third World investments. Soviet troops were withdrawn from Afghanistan, and Moscow cooperated in arranging negotiated solutions to longstanding regional conflicts in Asia, Africa, and Latin America. As their global competition ended, both the Soviet Union and the United States sharply cut back their economic and military assistance programs in these regions.

In chapter 5 we examined the domestic political controversy that arose in Russia in 1992 as a result of the initial emphasis given by President Boris Yeltsin and Foreign Minister Andrei Kozyrev to relations with the West, seemingly at the expense of Russia's ties to the near abroad and the non-West. In his critics' eyes, Kozyrev's alleged fixation on the West and slavish imitation of Western positions on international issues came at the expense of specific economic and security interests of Russia. Just as important to the advocates of a more nationalistic foreign policy, Kozyrev's "Atlanticist" policies also permanently relegated the country to a "junior partnership" at best, thereby sacrificing Russia's role as a great power and a global leader—even if only of "second-echelon" countries. The "Eurasianists"—advocates of a more forceful Russian role in the former USSR and in the "East" generally—gained additional ammunition for the campaign to counter a Western-oriented policy when plans for expanding NATO into the former Soviet empire threatened to further isolate Russia from democratic Europe. After Evgenii Primakov, much of whose career had been spent in the Middle East, replaced Kozyrev in 1996, further impetus was given to the reorientation of Russian foreign policy. And when Vladimir Putin returned Russian foreign policy to a more westward-looking orientation in 2001, it was not this time pursued at the expense of other priorities.

At least since the adoption of Russia's official foreign policy concept by President Yeltsin in April 1993—echoed in the revised concept issued in 2000—top priority has been given to relations with the states of the former Soviet Union. Accordingly, the main objective of Russia's policy in the non-West has been to ensure the security of the territories of the former Soviet lands, insulating them from the harmful effects of regional conflicts such as the struggle for control of Afghanistan and from threatening movements such as Islamic extremism. Given the strategic nature of energy resources in the Caucasian and Central Asian republics, Russia has tended to define its security interests in these areas to include preventing outside powers from gaining leverage over these resources. Setting its overall priorities in this way has pointed Russia toward East and South Asia and the Middle East as the zones of greatest concern. These are also the regions where there is the greatest danger of a broader but no less potent threat to Russia's security interests—nuclear proliferation.

With the recent emphasis on the role of foreign policy as a contributor to economic development, it is not surprising that another major objective of

Russia's policy toward the countries of the non-West is economic. These regions constitute an enormous and growing market, where Russian goods— be they raw or semiprocessed materials, lower-quality consumer goods, or the more sophisticated products of Russian science and engineering—have a somewhat better chance of obtaining a competitive advantage than they do in Western marketplaces. Imported products from Asia, Africa, and Latin America have potential benefit for Russian manufacturers and consumers, especially if they are obtained in partial payment of the enormous debts that some countries in these regions have accumulated as a result of their transactions with the former Soviet Union.

The combined total of debt owed to Russia by developing countries was estimated in September 1997 at a staggering $112.7 billion (all but $1 billion of which dated from the Soviet period). Of fifty-one debtor nations, only India was currently repaying its debt in full. The largest debts were owed to Russia by Cuba, Mongolia, India, and Vietnam. Moscow's admission to the Paris Club of creditor nations put international pressure on the debtors to repay. While the Russians agreed to discount the debt, in amounts ranging from 35 to 80 percent, the repayments were to be made in hard currency. Resulting more from debt forgiveness than from repayment, the total debt from the developing countries in 2000 had been reduced to $86.6 billion. Analysts estimated that Russia would eventually receive only $15– $20 billion, spread out over the following twenty to twenty-five years. Nevertheless, Moscow had resumed its earlier practice of extending credits to sweeten its economic dealings. The 2001 budget called for almost $200 million in loans—$58.3 million to Yugoslavia and Bulgaria, $88 million to China, $19.1 million to Cuba, $30 million to India, and small amounts to Morocco and Tunisia.[1]

Whereas, prior to the end of the Cold War, aid and trade transactions between the Soviets and the Third World had been heavily subsidized by Moscow for political reasons, cash-strapped Russia, forced to abandon "soft" credit terms, found its goods far less attractive than they had been. As a consequence, trade with most of the non-West in the immediate post-Soviet period fell sharply. Reflecting these realities, Russia cut back its costly overseas trade-promotion efforts, which were often a front for espionage activities during the Soviet period. Whereas Moscow operated 130 organizationally distinct trade missions abroad in 1991, the number had been cut to 47 by 1996, with trade counselors in Russian embassies taking over the responsibilities in the countries with less promising markets.

As was the case during the Soviet period, Russia's main export to the non-West has been weaponry, and a major beneficiary of renewed activity in these regions has been the underemployed military-industrial complex of

Russia. The depression in Moscow's arms industry actually began in the Gorbachev period, as a result of cuts in Soviet military budgets that accompanied the arms control agreements with the United States, combined with the negotiated settlements of regional conflicts in the Third World.

By 1991, the last year of the Soviet period, the market for arms in the developing countries had dropped to $28.6 billion, down sharply from $61 billion in 1988. It continued to decline in the immediate post-Soviet years, reaching $15.4 billion in 1995, rose again in the second half of the decade, to about $20 billion in 1999, and then declined at the beginning of the 2000s, to $17.7 billion in 2002. The Soviet Union and its allies dominated the Third World arms market until the late 1980s, but their share of a declining market began to plummet in the latter years of Gorbachev's rule and continued to do so in the first post-Soviet years, reflecting Moscow's shrinking political profile as well as the withdrawal of subsidies for arms purchases. Between 1984 and 1994, the world market share of the countries of the former Warsaw Pact dropped from 38 percent to 9 percent, while that of the United States rose from 25 percent to 57 percent. The drop in value of Moscow's arms sales to the Third World was even more precipitous: from $28.8 billion in 1986 to $5.9 billion in 1991 and $1.3 billion in 1992.[2]

As a result of a determined sales effort, Russia reversed the decline, and in 1995 its sales totaled 65 percent higher than the previous year. Although cash receipts in that year were only about $3 billion, Russian sources claimed that this was still twice the amount that actually flowed into state coffers in 1987, when announced sales of $20 billion were almost entirely financed with "soft" credits. As an indicator of the importance of rebounding arms exports to the Russian economy, exports were said in 1995 to constitute half of the industry's total revenues.[3]

The following year, Russia announced figures that would have propelled it to third place in world arms sales, with $4.6 billion (behind the United States at $11.3 billion and Britain at $4.8 billion) in a total world market estimated at $31.8 billion. This growth was announced to have continued in 1997; Russian arms salesmen claimed to have taken $7.3 billion in orders by September, with another $3.25 billion expected by the end of the year.[4] Later reports, however, adjusted these figures downward, to $3.5 billion in 1996 and only $2.5 billion in 1997. The revisions resulted in part from orders being canceled (e.g., Indonesia and Malaysia) or expected sales not materializing (e.g., Ecuador and Bulgaria). In part, however, they resulted from the discovery by the arms export agency's new management that earlier figures had been inflated for political reasons.[5] As actual sales continued to drop in 1998, the chief Russian arms export agency, Rosvooruzhenie, closed fifteen of its thirty-six overseas offices.

In the closing five years of the 1990s, according to calculations of the respected Stockholm International Peace Research Institute, deliveries of Russian arms amounted to $14.6 billion, compared to $53.4 billion for the United States in the same period. In 1999 Moscow was reported to have delivered $2.8 billion, a 6 percent share of the global market, placing it fourth behind the United States (with a 49 percent share).[6] Combat aircraft have accounted for two-thirds of Russia's total sales, with air defense systems composing a large part of the remaining one-third. China and India have accounted for about 70 percent of recent arms sales from Russia. Other researchers, tracking sales rather than deliveries, have reported a steady increase in Russian exports, putting the 1999 Russian total at $3.4 billion, the 2000 sales at $3.9 billion, and projected exports for 2001 at $4.4 billion. With the renewal of conventional arms sales to Iran, Russian exporters had high hopes for continued growth, to an annual level of $6–$7 billion.[7] This level will be difficult to reach, however, given the decline in global demand, from $41 billion in 2000 (in inflation adjusted dollars) to $25.6 billion in 2003. In 2004, Putin reported that Russian exports in the previous year had risen 15 percent, to $5.57 billion—the highest level since the fall of the USSR—and the chief arms export agency was said to have another $12 billion in orders on its books. Leaving aside deliveries from prior orders and focusing on actual signed agreements, however, a respected study conducted by the U.S. government placed the 2003 total for Russia at $4.3 billion, of which $3.9 billion was with the less developed countries.[8]

In spite of the Soviet experience with "soft" credits, the Russians have not moved to a strictly "cash-and-carry" basis for their arms sales. Only about 60 percent of revised 1996 and 1997 revenues were said to have been collected in convertible currencies.[9] The value of Russian arms transfers to some states (including former Warsaw Pact allies Hungary and Slovakia and NATO member Turkey) has been applied toward paying off debts incurred by the USSR as well as those inherited by the Russian Federation. Some customers— prominently including the two largest, China and India—continue to deal with Moscow on a noncash basis. Weapons sales to China include a prominent barter component, and credits extended to India are serviced with payments of Indian goods. As a consequence, Russian arms factories are left—in the words of a leading Russian defense analyst—with the burden of unloading Chinese and Indian "junk" on the domestic market.[10]

The relatively large amount of revenue brought in to the cash-strapped Russian economy by arms exports has sparked a scramble for control of arms sales. Until the practice was ended in 1997, large banks were able to profit from the use of funds deposited from sales, which sometimes never reached the factories that manufactured the weapons. In August 1997, Yeltsin decreed that Rosvooruzhenie would be put under the supervisory control of a commission chaired by the prime minister. In a new division of labor, Rosvooruzhenie was given responsibility to deal with foreign sales of arms and military equipment, while a new agency (Rossiiskie Tekhnologii, or Russian Technologies) was established to sell licenses, and another (Promeksport, or Industrial Exports) to sell obsolete used arms and spare parts. Defense enterprise representatives complained bitterly about the system. Not only did it prevent all but a few of the firms from negotiating their own contracts, but it also reduced their hard currency earnings by allowing a sizable commission to be taken by the state agency.

Continued reports of corruption and inefficiency prompted Putin to reconsolidate arms exports agencies in 2000. The new agency, Rosoboroneksport, was placed under the direction of Andrei Belianinov, a former KGB official. In the future, the president and not the prime minister was to chair the supervisory commission on Military Technical Cooperation with Foreign States (the Russian euphemism for arms sales), although a closer level of scrutiny would be provided by the Ministry of Defense. Putin's decree listed certain types of weaponry approved for export and certain countries eligible to receive them. The Cabinet of Ministers, formerly heavily involved with arms exports, would in the future be consulted only when proposed sales were linked to foreign debts or required government financing. Despite this reorganization, the competition for the lucrative profits of the arms export market continued to be intense. In June 2003 two officials of the Almaz-Antei consortium, the manufacturer of an advanced air-defense system accounting for over $5 billion in export contracts, were murdered, apparently by organized crime elements whose corruption had become the target of their investigations.[11]

As Russia has labored to regain a major share of the shrinking global arms market, it has encountered stiff competition, leading Moscow to complain at times about "unfair" competitive tactics. Not surprisingly, Washington has been regarded as the chief culprit. In recent years, Russia has made incursions into arms markets traditionally dominated by the United States—Latin America (Colombia and Brazil) and South Korea—or into areas regarded by the U.S. government as highly volatile (Cyprus and Iran). As the Russians see it, the U.S. response to being out-hustled in the marketplace has been decidedly heavy-handed.

In addition to Russia's competition with Western arms dealers, another source of vexing rivalry has been the sale of Soviet-designed weapons by the arms factories of former bloc countries such as Bulgaria, Slovakia, and Poland, as well as—most troublesome of all—Ukraine and Belarus. In March 1997 Ukraine delivered the first shipment in a $650 million order from Pakistan for 320 T-80UD tanks. Since India, Pakistan's hostile neighbor, was one of Moscow's best customers, the Russians sought to pressure Ukraine to cancel the order. Key components of the Ukrainian-assembled tank are supplied by Russian plants, and Moscow's minister of foreign trade, Oleg Davydov, threatened to cut deliveries of these parts. Ukraine vowed to obtain alternative supplies from East European sources, and Davydov retreated from his demand, reportedly under heavy pressure from the Russian suppliers, for whom cancellation of Ukraine's orders would mean a $150 million loss. Another reported consideration in the Russian retreat was Ukraine's threat to halt delivery of docking systems that it assembles for the Mir space station.[12] In 1997, Belarus reportedly "grabbed" a Peruvian contract for MiG-29s.[13] The following year Belarus's president visited Syria and Iran in search of further contracts.

Russia's arms dealers also have been on the receiving end of complaints, most notably about the quality of their weapons. Recent combat demonstrations of Russian-made arms—their use by the Iraqi military in the Persian Gulf war and their use by the Russian army in Chechnya—have not inspired confidence in the reliability or technical capacities of certain weapons, and there have been other instances in which purchasers have found numerous cases of defective products or poor servicing of contracts. A detailed account in the Indian press contends that the engines on three-fourths of the MiG-29s purchased from Moscow and put into service by the Indian Air Force in the early 1990s had failed prematurely. Indian engineers discovered a design defect, but India had to shoulder the bill for the lengthy repairs. A 1990 Indo-Soviet agreement to allow overhaul facilities to be established in India took six years to bear fruit. In 1993, a $4.3 million contract for an item of naval hardware produced similar frustrations. When the hardware was delivered, it lacked the cables that allowed it to function. Contending that cables were not part of the contract, the Russian firm refused repeated requests by the Indian Embassy either to supply the cables or to take back the equipment; as of 1997, the equipment reportedly continued to sit in storage with no prospect of use. A final example concerned 1991 and 1992 contracts for R-60 MK air-to-air missiles, supposedly guaranteed for twelve months from the date of delivery and having a shelf life of eight years. Upon their arrival in India, the missiles underwent field tests that found at least twenty-three of them to be unserviceable. When the Indian air force asked that the missiles be replaced, the Russian firm insisted on sending its own team of specialists—at India's expense—to verify the claim. The article concluded: "Even then, at least eleven missiles are currently lying in stock waiting to be repaired. Indian defense planners should now realize that Russia is just one among arms suppliers. No longer the cheapest. Never the best."[14]

Having surveyed some of the general features of Russia's approach to the non-West, we now turn to a region-by-region examination of how Moscow's policy has been implemented.

Russia's Relations in the Far East

As the country with which the Soviet Union shared its longest border, China, not surprisingly, occupied a higher foreign policy priority for Russia than any other non-Western country—all the more so, given the state of high tension on that border in recent decades. As described in chapter 4, Gorbachev took steps in the late 1980s to address the most serious issues in the Sino-Soviet conflict, and his efforts culminated in his May 1989 trip to Beijing, which symbolized the end of the Cold War between the two communist giants. The Chinese were severely displeased with the domestic political changes that Gorbachev was overseeing in the USSR, especially as Soviet democratization became a beacon for Chinese students, whose dissent was crushed on Tiananmen Square just days after Gorbachev's visit. Although the Chinese rulers had reached an accord with Gorbachev's government on 98 percent of their border with the USSR in May 1991, they barely disguised their support for the coup that sought to topple the Soviet president in August.

As the USSR was breaking up in December 1991, Boris Yeltsin sent an emissary to Beijing to reassure China that Russia would abide by the border accords. The following March, Russian foreign minister Andrei Kozyrev was in the Chinese capital for the formal exchange of ratified documents. (However, the validity of the Central Asian sector of the border settlement was now a matter for newly independent Kazakhstan, Tajikistan, and Kyrgyzstan to reaffirm, which they did in October 1992.) Also in March, progress was made in the realms of economic and military cooperation; Russia and China signed a new trade agreement, and the chief of staff of the CIS armed forces concluded an agreement to sell twenty-four SU-27 fighter planes to China. On the ideological front, Kozyrev stated Moscow's wish to avoid confrontation, but signs of tension were not absent during his visit; he expressed Russia's concern for China's human rights behavior, and China brought up the matter of Russia's relations with Taiwan. These relations were complicated in 1992 by the conduct of private diplomacy on the part of Yeltsin's long-time associate Oleg Lobov, who chaired the Moscow-Taipei Coordinating Committee. An exasperated foreign ministry obtained a presidential decree in September that addressed China's concerns by stating that Russian relations with Taiwan would be conducted only on an unofficial level and only with the concurrence of the ministry.

In December 1992 Boris Yeltsin made a state visit to Beijing, and the

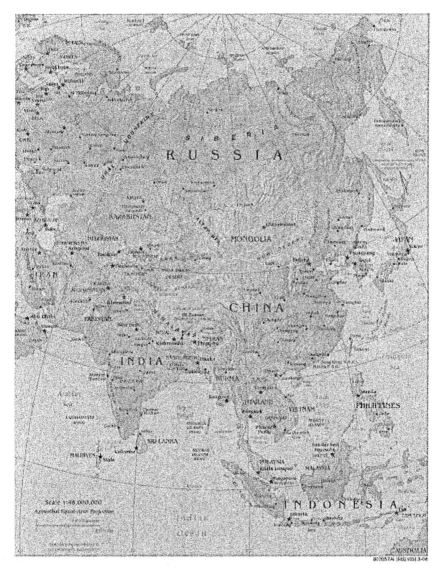

ASIA

Russian delegation signed over twenty documents, among them a mutual promise not to enter into any military-political alliance directed against the other state. The Chinese characterized the atmosphere of talks during Yeltsin's visit as "friendly, open and constructive . . . and in a spirit of mutual respect, understanding and trust." The gradual escalation of such rhetorical descriptions of presidential visits over the next several years serves as a barometer of the changed atmospherics in the Sino-Russian relationship—or, at any rate, of the way in which Moscow and Beijing wanted the world to view it. Thus, Chinese president Jiang Zemin's visit to Moscow in September 1994 was said to signify a "qualitatively new level of relations" of "constructive partnership," although not an alliance and not aimed against any other country. Yeltsin, during his visit to China in April 1996, described a "partnership directed toward the twenty-first century" between nations of which there was "no other such pair in the world." During Jiang's April 1997 visit to Russia, the Russian president reached new rhetorical heights, describing the visit as one of "enormous, and perhaps even historic, significance, inasmuch as we are determining the fate of the twenty-first century." Of the joint declaration signed by the two presidents, Yeltsin declared, "Never before has Russia signed such a document with any other country." Guests at the formal luncheon held during Yeltsin's November 1997 visit to Beijing witnessed not only a warm embrace but singing by the two presidents. Observers could not recall such a cordial atmosphere at prior Sino-Russian summits.[15]

Consistently with the Marxist-Leninist tradition, of which both presidents were well aware, such phrase mongering is not a casual exercise, but is calibrated to carry a distinct message. In this case, the message is not solely or even primarily to be understood as a description of the actual state of relations between the two states, but rather as an indicator of the extent of their mutual concern over the status and behavior of another—the United States—and of their desire to send a warning to its government. Both sides have been explicit in their opposition to "hegemonism"—the effort to build a unipolar international system. As Yeltsin put it in June 1997, "Someone is always dragging us toward a unipolar world and wanting to dictate unilaterally, but we want multipolarity." Such statements on the part of Russia became especially frequent after the United States announced its plans for expansion of NATO. The implied countermeasure—a "pairing" of "great Russia" and "great China," as Yeltsin termed it in 1996—was intended to persuade NATO not to undertake expansion, or at the very least to place limits on it. Although China also denounces NATO expansion as "a policy of blocs," Beijing is less directly affected by it and is more concerned about its differences with the United States on Taiwan, trade, and human rights. Later, both sides harshly condemned as illegitimate the NATO attack on Kosovo, although again the

Russians evidently viewed it as more threatening because of the parallel that could be drawn between Serbian repression in Kosovo and their own policies in Chechnya.

Soon thereafter, Moscow and Beijing were focusing on a third manifestation of attempted "hegemonism"—Washington's announcement of its intention to construct a national missile defense. A joint statement issued in July 2000 during Putin's inaugural trip to Beijing expressed "deep worry" over the U.S. plan, which "boils down to striving for unilateral superiority." Strict compliance with the ABM Treaty was declared to be of "vital significance," and its destruction "would trigger off a new stage of the arms race and turn back positive trends in global politics that appeared after the end of the Cold War." Addressing a particular concern of China's, Putin and Jiang voiced a "resolute protest" over any plan to involve Taiwan in any form of the contemplated missile defense system.

During Putin's July 2000 visit, Jiang sought to retain a modicum of balance in Beijing's ties with Washington by stating that Sino-Russian relations were "not an alliance, not confrontational, and not aimed at any third country." Nevertheless, the two sides reportedly agreed to prepare a new treaty relationship—the Treaty on Good Neighborly Friendship and Cooperation, signed during Jiang's trip to Moscow in 2001—to formalize what Putin liked to call their "strategic partnership," while adhering to China's insistence that it not constitute an "alliance."[16] Nevertheless, the treaty would call the world's attention to how close the relations between the former adversaries (and former allies) had grown. In the estimation of Lu Nanquan, deputy director of the Russian Studies Center of the Chinese Academy of Social Sciences, "now is the best it has ever been. . . . China and Russia have come this far because of the United States."[17]

Doubts about just how far China and Russia had come in their relationship arose soon after the treaty was signed—and again, because of the United States. President Putin decided, in the wake of the September 11, 2001, attacks on the United States, to acquiesce to the movement of American troops over Russian air space to bases in the former Soviet states of Uzbekistan and Kyrgyzstan, and subsequently, not to raise major objections to the U.S. withdrawal from the ABM Treaty, while moving Russia into a closer relationship with NATO. All three of these decisions could easily be interpreted in Beijing as raising serious issues for China's security, and yet there were no indications that any of them were preceded by consultations, as required under their new treaty. As a result, Chinese "Russia experts" were soon asking their Russian colleagues about Russia's motivations and the possible consequences for China, complaining that Putin's actions had put China in a "difficult international situation"—even altering the balance of power in America's favor. Indeed, they reportedly said, "had these changes in the Russian-U.S. relations occurred one year earlier, the treaty would hardly have been signed in its present form."[18]

Bilateral relations between the two neighbors have been normalized on several fronts. Further progress was made in 1994 in demarcating the border, leaving stretches totaling less than ten square miles (two islands near Khabarovsk and another in Chita province) still under dispute. Both presidents confidently predicted during Jiang's June 1997 visit to Moscow that these issues would be resolved in 1997, but Yeltsin faced very strong opposition from local authorities to further concessions. Thus, when it was announced during Yeltsin's November 1997 visit to China—his fifth summit with Jiang Zemin—that the 4,200-kilometer border had been demarcated for the first time in the two nations' histories, the fine print on the agreement revealed continued difficulties. Although Russia and China agreed on joint economic use, the legal status of the islands in the Amur River was still unresolved. Moscow apparently was unwilling to further inflame its already heated relations with regional authorities in Khabarovsk Krai by ceding possession. The work on demarcating the 55-kilometer "western border" at the junction of Kazakhstan, China, and Russia also had not been formalized, though a joint statement issued during Jiang's November 1998 visit to Moscow indicated that the work on it had been completed. A further announcement during Yeltsin's December 1999 visit to Beijing referred to the signing of protocols resolving disagreements on the eastern sector. Curiously, however, no final treaties on the border demarcation were signed when Putin went to Beijing the following July. Even more surprising was the announcement at the time of the signing of the Russia-China Treaty that the dispute over sections of the border was still unresolved.

Jiang's June 1997 visit to Moscow did provide the occasion for signing a significant agreement with Yeltsin and the presidents of the three Central Asian border states (Kazakhstan, Kyrgyzstan, and Tajikistan) on reductions in the military presence along the border. This treaty sets maximum limits on numbers of ground troops, tactical aircraft, and air-defense aircraft within a 100-kilometer-wide zone on either side of the border. In negotiations that had taken place over a five-year period, China had pressed for a 300-kilometer-wide zone, but the extensive Soviet military infrastructure had been built so close to the border that the wider zone would have produced considerable disruption. As the treaty specified, Russia was to reduce the strength of its Transbaikal and Far Eastern border forces over a two-year period by 15 percent—a level reportedly already planned by the general staff as part of overall force reductions. China's forces are deployed further inland, and would not need to be reduced.[19] Subsequent meetings of this group of five countries (which came to be known as the "Shanghai Five") focused on the growing threat of secessionist and Islamic extremist movements in Central Asia, which China feared might spill over into its Xinjiang province. In June 2001 the five became six, with Uzbekistan's entry into what was now called the Shanghai Cooperation Organization (which we described more fully in chapter 6).

A Sino-Russian border issue of considerable sensitivity concerns the extensive Chinese immigration—much of it illegal—into Russian territory. The demographic imbalance along the border, with 150 million Chinese crowded into northeast China and only 7 million Russians in the vast bordering territories of Siberia and the Far East, has been a source of concern for Soviet and Russian citizens, officials, and journalists for many years. As border tensions eased at the beginning of the 1990s, the scale of illegal immigration increased—rising threefold between 1992 and 1993. This prompted Russia to conclude an agreement with Beijing in 1994 to establish formal border-crossing posts and tighten visa restrictions. The immediate impact was a sharp reduction in Sino-Russian trade, much of which was "shuttled" across the border by Chinese traders.[20]

The Russian press continued to provide sensational accounts of illegal immigration (termed in one account an "invasion of Huns"), prompting an advisor to Yeltsin, Emil Pain, to write an article in the government's newspaper stating that "claims about dangerous levels of Chinese immigration and a related real threat to national sovereignty in the Russian Far East are not supported by the actual facts."[21] Nevertheless, Putin himself warned an audience in the Russian Far East that unless steps were taken to develop the region, people there within a few decades would be speaking mostly Chinese, Japanese, and Korean.[22]

As noted above, the reduction in shuttle trade caused the level of Sino-Russian trade, which had reached $7.8 billion in 1993 (second only to the level of Russia's trade with Germany), to fall to $5 billion the following year. It recovered somewhat in 1995, reaching $5.5 billion, and rose to $6.8 billion in 1996—with the Russians enjoying a $3 billion trade surplus. Yeltsin and Jiang set a target of $20 billion by 2000, but the announcement was greeted by skepticism that trade could grow so quickly, and in fact the two sides subsequently backed away from the forecast.

However, several ambitious projects were discussed in high-level visits, most notably a multibillion-dollar gas pipeline from eastern Siberia to the Yellow Sea, which would eventually supply up to 40 billion cubic yards of gas annually, meeting a large part of China's burgeoning energy needs. Additionally, the Russian press has reported agreements for Russian credits to China of $2 billion and $2.5 billion to finance the construction of nuclear power plants in Gansu and Liaoning provinces. While Russia failed to win contracts for engineering work on the huge Three Gorges dam, a $3 billion contract for Russia to develop a nuclear power plant at Lianyungang, left unsigned during Yeltsin's November 1997 visit, was concluded late the following month—and hailed by Russia's atomic energy minister as "the contract of the century." By the end of Yeltsin's term Sino-Russian trade had stagnated at a level just over $6 billion. With the recovery of the Russian economy in the first decade of the new century, trade volume rebounded, reaching almost $12 billion in 2002.[23] Still, whereas China ranked as Russia's sixth-largest trade partner, Russia was only China's eighth largest.

In addition to discussing with Russia projects involving natural gas and nuclear power, China's enormous appetite for energy drove it to seek ways to obtain increased supplies of Russian oil, especially from the largely undeveloped reserves in eastern Siberia near Angarsk. Yukos, the large privatized Russian oil company led by oligarch Mikhail Khodorkovskii, concluded a $1.1 billion deal in 2003 to ship by rail 2 million metric tons of oil over a three-year period. At the same time, Jiang's successor as China's president, Hu Jintao, announced that China and Yukos had reached a general agreement to construct in 2005 a pipeline from Angarsk to the northern industrial city of Daqing. However, the president of Transneft, the state-owned pipeline monopoly, cautioned that no such decision had yet been made by Russia. Indeed, it is likely that it was Khodorkovskii's brazen determination to drive major decisions of energy policy without prior consent of the Kremlin, as much as his widely publicized political activities, that led to his arrest in October 2003, allegedly on tax evasion charges. In any event, Prime Minister Kasianov reportedly received a cool reception that autumn in Beijing when he explained to his Chinese hosts that the fate of the proposed Angarsk-Daqing pipeline was placed in doubt by the objections to its routing by Russia's environment ministry.[24]

In fact, the interest of the Russian government had been piqued by a rival proposal from Japan, calling for a pipeline to be built from Angarsk to the port of Nakhodka on the Sea of Japan. Tokyo was reportedly willing not only to invest $5 billion toward the construction costs of the pipeline, but also to devote another $2 billion to help finance exploration and exploitation of the eastern Siberian oil reserves. A clear advantage of the routing to Nakhodka was the possible access thereby gained not only to the oil-thirsty markets of Japan and South Korea, but also out into the Pacific and on to the United States. The Angarsk-Daqing route, by contrast, locked Russian exports into a single market, depriving Moscow of the advantages of price competition. Public discussion of a possible compromise, involving building a spur pipeline on to Daqing, appeared to be mere window-dressing, given the unlikelihood that the eastern Siberian fields would contain enough oil to justify both routes. Nevertheless, the final announcement on the pipeline route was being withheld until Putin made his scheduled visits to China in the fall of 2004 and to Japan early in 2005.[25]

The Sino-Russian trade relationship is a prime example of one in which armaments constitute the single most important Russian export, accounting for about $5 billion in the last half of the 1990s, and reportedly composing at least one-third of the $7 billion in forward-order sales claimed by Rosvooruzhenie at the beginning of 1997.[26] Combat aircraft have been the chief component of Russian deliveries; China has purchased at least six dozen transcontinental SU-27 fighters, which are capable of making the Beijing-to-Moscow trip in two and one-half hours with one midair refueling. In 1999, China concluded an agreement, valued at more than $2 billion, for forty to sixty SU-30s—two-seat multipurpose fighters capable (with certain modifications) of carrying nuclear weapons. Other categories of purchases that have been concluded or which are being discussed include naval vessels (Sovremennyi-class destroyers equipped with supersonic missiles, two Kilo-636 diesel-powered submarines, and less advanced Varsha-vianka submarines), S-300 surface-to-air missile complexes, T-72 tanks, Smerch multiple rocket launchers, and the technology for advanced gas centrifuges used in uranium enrichment and for MIRVed missiles.

In 1995 China agreed to pay about $1.4 billion for the technology and licenses to manufacture the SU-27 at a factory in Shenyang province, scheduled to begin production in 1999. The Russian press reported concerns that China would thereby free itself of the need to purchase aircraft from Moscow in the future, and that if China made minor modifications to the plane's design, it might even become a competitor in the export market. (Indeed, by 1999 China had already climbed to fourth place in global arms sales.) Russian officials were quoted as saying that Russia needed the contract to save its defense industry, and that profits from the contract would be plowed back into development of new aircraft technology. Another account claimed that there was no prospect of a new generation of Russian-made planes in the foreseeable future, and that officials were simply trying to cover up a major blunder on the part of Russian negotiators, the circumstances of which were even discussed in a special meeting of the Security Council.[27]

Apart from the prospect that Russia could lose control of its most advanced military technology, there have been other concerns raised about the arms trade with China. As noted above, by no means all of the payment comes in the form of cash, and defense factories find themselves needing to dispose of a variety of bartered products in order to realize their profits. Among the most difficult was the case of the Chinese pigs that were traded for an arms shipment and then banned in Russia by the veterinary inspector, who suspected that they might spread hog plague in the country. In another instance, the Chinese bartered 15,000 low-quality radio-cassette players for three Mi-6 helicopters.[28] However, whereas the barter method initially constituted about three-fourths of Chinese payments, China's growing dollar trade surpluses have enabled Russian negotiators to arrange for hard currency payment in recent contracts.[29]

A far more significant issue is whether Russia is endangering its own long-term security by selling to its giant neighbor its most advanced weapons and the know-how to produce them. Russian military sources have expressed envy because Beijing is receiving more modern equipment than their own units possess. Most Russian analysts appear to believe that China's near-term foreign policy ambitions are directed toward Taiwan and the South China Sea, and that her interests in stability in Central Asia parallel those of Russia. Russian-made equipment may indeed enable Beijing to obtain a regional advantage in force-projection capability in a future Taiwan crisis; the Sovremennyi destroyer's cruise missiles have a combat range of 300 miles, are reportedly resistant to U.S. air defense systems, and will allow China to test the naval superiority of the United States in the East China Sea. Nevertheless, the Kremlin appears to perceive no danger to Russia in such contingencies.[30]

Expressing this viewpoint, former defense minister Pavel Grachev declared in 1995 that "China poses no threat to Russian security now and will not in the near future," and he asserted that if Russia did not sell arms to China, some other country would. Indeed, such a prospect seemed nearer to realization in 2004, following Hu Jintao's visit to France, where he was promised by President Chirac that the European Union would soon be reconsidering its long standing embargo on sales of arms to China.[31]

Proponents of the weapons sales have also asserted that China was already engaged in privately hiring Russian scientists and engineers to assist in weapons development, and that Russia only benefits from contractually providing such assistance. As journalist Pavel Felgengauer put it, arms sales to China are "not only a way for our hapless military-industrial complex to preserve jobs and earn money, but also the start of a long-range strategic partnership and a new balance of forces in Asia that would favor Russia." The dissenting view, taking note of the demographic imbalance between Russia and China in the Far East, sees a long-range potential for conflict between the two continental powers. Another trouble spot, China's Xinjiang province, whose population is ethnically kin to that of the neighboring post-Soviet states, is troubled by sporadic anti-Beijing rebellions that could potentially spark a cross-border "liberation war." From the perspective of these observers, even with respect to the nearer term, by closely associating with China and by selling it arms, Russia risks upsetting the delicate military balance in Asia and even being drawn into China's territorial disputes with Taiwan, Vietnam, Japan, and ultimately the United States.[32]

Eighteen months after Grachev stated that he saw no threat, his successor included China on a list of potential enemies of Russia—and was hastily corrected by the foreign ministry; but Rodionov seemed to be voicing what many Russians were thinking. Nevertheless, Yeltsin and Primakov seemed to have calculated that they could keep the relationship with China in check, utilizing it as a way of jointly balancing U.S. influence in Asia, while enlisting Beijing's cooperation in preserving stability in Central Asia. If China's military and economic power continue to grow and her territorial ambitions eventually turn back toward the north and west, Putin and his successors may find greater safety in again tilting the triangular balance by further strengthening Russia's ties with the United States.

Despite the major effort Moscow has made to normalize and strengthen its ties with Beijing, Russia has by no means put all its Far Eastern eggs in the Chinese basket. Following upon Gorbachev's initiatives, Yeltsin also sought to improve Russia's relations with two strong allies of the United States—Japan and South Korea. In both cases, the ideological direction of the new Russian regime gave reason to expect that the two leading East Asian capitalist powers, both relatively poor in natural resources, would be eager investors in the development of Russia's vast Far Eastern mineral reserves. Russia also hoped to play a role in regional security arrangements that would foster stability and promote expanded trade, but neither Tokyo nor Seoul responded to Moscow's overtures with the degree of enthusiasm for which the Russians had hoped.

One reason Japan's investment in the Russian Far East in the 1990s was less than anticipated was undoubtedly the country's political instability, of which Japanese investors are notoriously shy. Japan would rather concentrate Moscow's attention on another factor explaining its reticence: the continuing absence, more than a half-century after World War II, of a peace treaty between Japan and Russia. The obstacle to the conclusion of a treaty is the persisting dispute over the ownership of several small islands—Iturup (called Etorofu by Japan), Kunashir (Kunashiri), Shikotan, and a cluster of tiny islands known as Habomai—which are claimed by the Russians as the southern Kuriles, and by the Japanese as the Northern Territories. First claimed for the tsar by Russian explorers early in the eighteenth century, the Kurile Islands and neighboring (and much larger) Sakhalin Island were the subject of two Russo-Japanese treaties seeking to delineate a territorial boundary between the two countries in the second half of the nineteenth century. The first, signed at Shimoda in 1855, provided for them to share Sakhalin, and it divided the Kurile chain, with Russia getting the islands north of Iturup and

Japan receiving the four southern islands. The second, signed at St. Petersburg twenty years later, gave all of Sakhalin to Russia, in return for which it renounced its claims to the Kuriles, all of which became Japanese territory.

The next alterations in the Russo-Japanese boundary came as a result of war rather than diplomatic compromise. The Treaty of Portsmouth in 1905, at the conclusion of the Russo-Japanese War, again partitioned Sakhalin Island, the southern half of which became Japanese. The Yalta Agreement of February 1945 provided for Moscow to enter the war against Japan three months after Germany's surrender, in return for which the southern half of Sakhalin would be returned to the USSR and the Kurile Islands would be handed over. However, the Potsdam Declaration of July 1945, on the basis of which Japan eventually agreed to surrender, did not specifically mention these territories, and the Japanese claim that they cannot be legally transferred without their consent. At the peace conference in San Francisco in 1951, in which the Soviet Union did not participate, Japan renounced "all right, title, and claim to the Kurile Islands and to that portion of Sakhalin and the islands adjacent to it over which Japan acquired sovereignty as a consequence of the Treaty of Portsmouth." Japan contends, however, that there was no reference made to the geographic definition of the Kurile Islands, to which it says the islands of the "Northern Territories" do not belong—a position to which the United States also stipulated at San Francisco—and, moreover, that it did not in any event cede sovereignty over any of these territories to the Soviet Union.

Nevertheless, the islands remained in the possession of the Soviet Union, and not until after the death of Stalin was their future discussed directly between Tokyo and Moscow. Following the Geneva Summit, Khrushchev was seeking to lure both the West Germans and the Japanese away from their security ties with the United States, and the Soviets were willing to discuss a territorial transfer as a condition of a peace treaty with Japan. In the October 1956 joint declaration between them, the Soviets agreed "to transfer to Japan the Habomai Islands and Shikotan, the actual transfer of these islands to Japan to take place after the conclusion of a peace treaty between the USSR and Japan." After ratification of this declaration by the two parliaments, the Soviet and Japanese foreign ministers exchanged letters expressing readiness to discuss the status of Kunashir and Iturup as well; but the peace treaty was never concluded, and in 1960 Khrushchev used the excuse of the revised U.S.-Japanese Security Treaty to add another condition: The islands would be returned "only on the condition that all foreign troops be withdrawn from Japan."[33] Nevertheless, the offer to return the two southernmost islands following the conclusion of a peace treaty was secretly, but briefly, put back on the table during a visit to Tokyo by Gromyko in 1972, when the Soviets became alarmed at the rapprochement among the United States, Japan, and

China.[34] The Japanese never responded, and the Soviets soon reverted to their position that the territorial issue had been settled at San Francisco.

Contrary to their expectations, the Japanese did not succeed in using the bait of trade and investment to elicit territorial concessions from the proponents of the "new political thinking" in Soviet foreign policy, despite several visits to Tokyo by Shevardnadze and Yakovlev. Indeed, by the time Gorbachev made an official state visit to Tokyo in April 1991, he was politically too weak to be able to deliver such concessions, though he did acknowledge that a territorial issue existed. By this time, however, the Japanese probably thought that they could fare better if Boris Yeltsin were to come to power in Moscow. Yeltsin had traveled to Tokyo in January 1990, when he was still only a member of the Soviet parliament, and during his visit he had proposed the following five-step process of negotiations:

1. Formal recognition of the existence of a territorial dispute;
2. Demilitarization of the four southern islands;
3. Creation of a free enterprise zone with preferential treatment for Japanese investment and a broad cooperation treaty;
4. A formal peace treaty;
5. A formal territorial settlement.

Yeltsin estimated that the process might take a generation to complete, and the Japanese conceded that the islands need not be returned prior to conclusion of a treaty, provided that Japanese sovereignty over them was recognized beforehand.

The dust from the August 1991 coup attempt had barely settled when the Japanese approached the Russian foreign ministry to propose, unsuccessfully, that Yeltsin state his readiness to be guided in a territorial settlement by the 1855 Shimodo Treaty.[35] After the demise of the USSR, Japan continued to show its eagerness to proceed with negotiations, urging an early visit to Tokyo by Yeltsin, but the Russians were in less of a hurry. Thus, in January 1992, when Foreign Minister Watanabe came to Moscow to firm up plans for a Yeltsin visit, the president flew off to the Black Sea without receiving him. In May, however, Yeltsin reconfirmed his commitment to the five-stage resolution of the territorial problem, with a peace treaty to be concluded as early as 1993, and he indicated that all Russian military units on the disputed islands, with the exception of border troops, would be withdrawn.

By this time Yeltsin's foreign policy had become a matter of sharp internal contention in Russia, with critics upset about its excessive softness and unseemly eagerness to please the West. With Yeltsin now scheduled to fly to Tokyo in September, the government's stance on the territorial issue with

Japan became a matter of angry and visible debate. General Pavel Grachev, newly appointed defense minister, stated that Russian army troops would not be withdrawn from the southern Kuriles, prompting a Japanese demand for explanation. The proffered statement from the foreign ministry only deepened the confusion, and a scheduled meeting of the Russo-Japanese working group on a peace treaty was postponed at Moscow's request. On July 28, the Russian parliament held hearings on the territorial issue; these had originally been scheduled for June but were delayed at Yeltsin's request.

At the parliamentary hearings, the inflammatory nature of the issue was evident. A prominent moderate deputy, Oleg Rumiantsev, flatly declared that if Moscow were to make a concession on the territorial issue with Japan, Russia would no longer be an important factor in world politics. The government, obviously sharply divided, refused to state a position prior to Yeltsin's visit. A memorandum from the general staff of the Russian armed forces to the parliament, refuting the notion that the islands were of little importance, pointed out that the most useful straits for passage to the Pacific from Vladivostok and the Sea of Okhotsk, where much of the Russian submarine fleet is based, lie north of the disputed islands. If the southern Kuriles were in Japanese hands, it was argued, they could be turned into a forward military post facing the Russian coastline, giving a significant advantage to the "enemy" in the event of a conflict.[36] Regional authorities also publicly resisted the idea of a territorial concession, with the Sakhalin governor flatly refusing to implement any such action.

On August 25, the official report of the Supreme Soviet Joint Committee on International Affairs and Foreign Economic Relations recommended to Yeltsin that, under present conditions, "unilateral recognition of any form of Japanese sovereignty over any part of Russian territory is extremely dangerous." Committee chairman Evgenii Ambartsumov declared that the Russian people would not accept the idea of territorial changes, and the Supreme Soviet would not ratify any such agreements. Another deputy, giving voice to the "domino theory" that undoubtedly lay behind the concerns of many, warned that if Russia were to make a concession, "others who lay claim to Russian lands, of whom there are quite a few, will immediately pounce on us." Yeltsin himself continued to play his cards close to the vest, noting that he had been presented with twelve options, and that he would reveal his own views only to the Japanese prime minister.

In a stunning reversal, Russia announced on September 10 that Yeltsin's trip to Tokyo, scheduled to begin in four days, had been canceled by the president. *Izvestia* declared that the cancellation—"an insulting demarche which falls outside the bounds of civilized behavior in the international arena"—was a sign of internal weakness and of unreliability in Russia's foreign policy. Kozyrev and the democratic wing of the leadership were seen as having been weakened. The foreign minister seemed to agree with this assessment, denouncing "attempts at unprofessional interference by the bureaucracy in foreign policy" and declaring in an interview that "they" were attempting to shake him up psychologically.[37] The strength of the opponents of territorial concessions must have been truly overwhelming, causing a Russian government that was desperate for financial assistance to turn down what Kozyrev later claimed was a Japanese offer of $28 billion for the southern Kuriles.[38]

The failure to agree on the territorial basis for a peace treaty undoubtedly retarded the development of Russo-Japanese relations in other spheres. Trade between Moscow and Tokyo, which had averaged $5.5 billion a year prior to 1991, fell to $4.8 billion in 1991 and $3.1 billion in 1992. Angry quarrels erupted in 1993 over the Russian practice of dumping nuclear wastes in the Sea of Japan, and in 1994 over incidents in which Russian border guards fired on Japanese fishing vessels that had wandered into waters off the southern Kuriles. Even an October 1994 earthquake on the islands occasioned bilateral tensions, with the Japanese claiming that they had done more than the Russians to provide relief, and accusing the Russians of using the disaster to promote schemes for joint rebuilding efforts that flaunted the premise of Russian ownership.

Contradictory signals on the territorial issue continued to emanate from Russia, to the evident frustration of the Japanese. President Yeltsin finally made his state visit to Tokyo in October 1993, but there were few practical results. The psychological climate was improved by Yeltsin's apology for Stalin's harsh treatment of Japanese prisoners of war in Siberia. Pressured by his hosts to reaffirm the 1956 treaty commitment to return the two southernmost islands, Yeltsin did so only indirectly, by reaffirming that Russia is heir to international agreements signed by the Soviet Union. The president did announce in Tokyo that Russia at an unspecified future time would withdraw military units from the southern Kuriles, with the exception of border troops, in accordance with his five-stage settlement plan, but the effect of this was negated the following year by denials from General Grachev that any Russian troops would be leaving the Kuriles.

With the passage of time and with changes of personnel in key government positions in both Moscow and Tokyo, there were signs of greater flexibility on both sides of the relationship. Perhaps sensing an opening as a result of diminished economic and political stability in Japan, Foreign Minister Primakov journeyed to Tokyo in November 1996 with ideas about promoting a thaw in Russo-Japanese relations. In particular, he proposed that the territorial dispute be set aside while Russia and Japan worked to jointly promote investment in the southern Kuriles; he cited as precedent the joint British-Argentinian prospecting for minerals on the Falkland Islands, or Malvinas Islas as the Argentinians know them, which both countries claim. The Japanese, promising to consider the proposal, offered a goodwill gesture in response, freeing $500 million in soft loans that had been frozen for five years. Although Primakov was trying to break the deadlock while allowing both sides to save face, concrete progress was unlikely given Primakov's statement that any "softening" of Russian sovereignty was out of the question, and given Japan's stance of forbidding its businessmen or officials to engage in any activity on the islands involving permits, licenses, or other actions that would even indirectly affirm Russia's rights.[39]

Further progress was made when Yeltsin hosted Japan's prime minister Ryutaro Hashimoto for an informal "weekend without neckties" in November 1997 in the Siberian city of Krasnoiarsk. The two leaders pledged their "maximum efforts" to conclude a peace treaty by 2000, based on the 1993 Tokyo Declaration in which Yeltsin had acknowledged the existence of a territorial dispute over the southern Kuriles. However, First Deputy Prime Minister Boris Nemtsov downplayed the possibility that the islands might eventually be surrendered, noting that the Russian constitution upholds the territorial integrity of the country, and the president is the guarantor of the constitution.[40] Rather, signs pointed to some sort of joint economic zone in the southern Kuriles, as Primakov had hinted in his visit earlier in 1977. Despite the lingering ambiguities, the "sauna summit" was said by Yeltsin to have helped break the ice and overcome mutual distrust. The two sides discussed initiatives to increase Japanese investment and trade, including joint development of Siberian petroleum reserves and modernization of the trans-Siberian railroad. This atmosphere persisted in a second "weekend without neckties" summit in Japan in April 1998, where hints of further progress continued to be dropped but without tangible signs that a solution was near.

Further confirmation that Japan had abandoned its earlier linkage between a territorial solution and economic cooperation came during the visit to Moscow of Prime Minister Keizo Obuchi in November 1998, when Japan announced an $800 million loan to assist Russia's battered economy. Yeltsin and Obuchi agreed to set up subcommissions to discuss territorial demarcation and joint economic activity in the southern Kuriles, but the details of Russian responses to Japanese proposals were not publicly announced. A subsequent press report, quoting Japanese sources, claimed that the Russians had offered to create a tax-free zone in the territory, administered jointly but under continued Russian sovereignty. Japan would thereby be given complete economic freedom, but would not achieve its objective of gaining ownership of the islands. As the Russian journalist put it, "To each side it is much more important to officially own the wretched, ruined islands, while each is prepared to magnanimously let the other deal with the islands' economic development."[41] The 2000 deadline for a treaty came and went without agreement. When he visited Tokyo in September of that year, Putin let it be known before his departure that he regarded the deadline as unattainable. As an act of goodwill, he did declare his commitment to the 1956 declaration, but the Japanese continued to insist on a return of the entire territory. As a twist on the previous Russian proposal, they reportedly expressed willingness, if Russia would cede sovereignty, to accept continued Russian administrative control. In anticipation of the next round of talks, the Japanese foreign minister visited Moscow in January 2001, only to be bluntly informed by a deputy foreign minister that as far the Russians were concerned, the border is drawn. Deeming the treatment of its chief diplomat impolite, Japan postponed the summit that had been planned for the following month. When it was finally held in March, there was again no apparent breakthrough on the dispute. However, the Japanese press claimed that a secret agreement had been reached at the meeting to negotiate the issue in a "2 + 2" format, discussing the future of Shikotan and Habomai and the associated peace treaty (in the context of the 1956 agreement) separately, but in parallel, with negotiations on the status of the other two islands. Following Foreign Minister Ivanov's visit to Tokyo in February 2002, his Japanese counterpart declared that this agreement was still in place, but Ivanov denied it.[42]

Shortly after this meeting, the Russian press buzzed with speculation about the meaning of a "purge" of Russia experts in the Japanese foreign ministry — allegedly for their association with a scandal involving misappropriation of aid funds designated for the southern Kuriles, but also purportedly for their openness to a compromise on the territorial issue.[43]

The atmosphere improved markedly at the beginning of 2003, with the visit of Prime Minister Yochiro Koizumi to Moscow and the Russian Far East, during which he and Putin agreed to an "action plan" calling for an accelerated effort to resolve the territorial dispute. Not coincidentally, in this improved climate Japanese trade and investment in Russia also increased, with bilateral trade increasing by 25 percent, to $5.5 billion, and Japanese foreign direct investment doubling in an eighteen-month period, to $1 billion, most notably as a result of Japanese involvement in development of gas fields on Sakhalin. During the same year, discussions accelerated on the prospect of the Angarsk-Nakhodka oil pipeline, and the first direct flight between Japan and the Russian Far East was inaugurated. Although the increase in economic activity between Russia and Japan was significant, it is worth noting that even this increased level of trade was dwarfed by the $60 billion in annual trade between Tokyo and Seoul and the $134 billion between Japan and China.[44] Moreover, the Japanese continued to point out that the full potential of bilateral economic relations with Russia would be achieved only with the signing of a peace treaty between the two states. And although Foreign Minister Lavrov pledged to increase the pace of the dialogue on the issue in mid-2004, Russia's ambassador to Tokyo warned that the two sides were still far apart, and that it was by no means certain that a breakthrough would be achieved in time for Putin's scheduled visit early in 2005 to mark the 150th anniversary of the opening of Russo-Japanese diplomatic relations.[45]

In the realm of security relations, a significant departure occurred in May 1997 with the visit to Tokyo of Igor Rodionov—the first ever by a Soviet or Russian defense minister. Aside from agreements to develop confidence-building measures and bilateral defense exchanges, the Russian voiced an especially benign view of the Asian-Pacific security situation, declaring that Moscow no longer viewed any country in the Far East as a potential adversary and no longer objected to the U.S.-Japanese security alliance. For their part, however, the Japanese probably took advantage of this opening to voice a less optimistic view, expressing their concern about the threat to the regional balance arising from China's escalating arms purchases from Russia. In 1999, the Russians became somewhat less complacent as a result of an American-Japanese agreement that allowed Japan to provide support to the United States outside its home territory if an armed conflict should arise in the surrounding region. In February of that year, Foreign Minister Ivanov expressed concern to the Japanese about this development. Nevertheless, in December 2000 Defense Minister Sergeev journeyed to Tokyo to discuss U.S. plans for national missile defense, together with suggestions that Japan might purchase Russian arms. An agreement to establish mechanisms for military consultation was signed, but Moscow subsequently expressed disappointment that no cooperation seemed to be forthcoming.

Whenever they discuss the regional security situation, Russia and Japan undoubtedly voice their mutual concern over the instability on the Korean peninsula. In the waning months of the Cold War, Gorbachev had initiated a balance in Moscow's relations with the two Koreas. In 1988 he allowed Soviet participation in the Seoul Olympics and opened trade relations with South Korea. Two years later Gorbachev realized his hopes for a financial benefit from his initiative; the establishment of diplomatic relations was soon followed by a lavish South Korean credit of $3 billion to Moscow. An exchange of state visits between Gorbachev and President Roh Tae Woo fanned Soviet expectations for additional South Korean investment, but it also further enraged the North Korean regime, which had been heavily dependent on Soviet military and economic aid. In pursuit of greater self-reliance, Pyongyang stepped up its program to develop nuclear capabilities.

Yeltsin and Kozyrev abandoned any pretense of even-handedness in Russia's relations on the Korean peninsula. When the foreign minister traveled to Seoul in March 1992, the South Koreans welcomed Kozyrev's declaration that relations were moving from normalization to "full-fledged cooperation," and they acceded to his request to reinstate credits frozen after the collapse of the USSR. Announcing that Russia had stopped selling offensive weapons to the North, Kozyrev said that not only would Russia not cooperate in the further development of Pyongyang's nuclear program, but it also supported the complete denuclearization of the peninsula. In a meeting with the South Korean foreign minister in June, Yeltsin declared that the 1961 Soviet–North Korean security treaty "has lost its effectiveness and exists in name only." Later in the year, Russia announced that it had prevented sixty-four of its scientists from leaving for North Korea to assist with the latter's missile program.

Yeltsin's first Far Eastern trip as head of state, in November 1992, was made not to Beijing or Tokyo but to Seoul, where he signed a treaty on the basic principles of Russian–South Korean relations and issued a public apology for the 1983 downing of Korean Airlines flight 007. Yeltsin was disappointed when these symbolic acts failed to elicit any additional loans from South Korea. In retrospect, it probably dawned on the Russians that by virtually abandoning their position of influence in Pyongyang, they had made themselves less valuable to Seoul and less necessary as a participant in future security arrangements in Northeast Asia. They set about trying to remedy this situation early in 1993, with a trip to North Korea by Deputy Foreign Minister Georgii Kunadze. Both sides expressed interest in preserving "normal good-neighborly relations," despite the current ideological differences, but the results of the meeting conveyed little sense of neighborliness. Trade between the two had fallen 50 percent in 1992, to 1981 levels, and North Korea owed Moscow $3 billion. However, there was little chance that economically strapped North Korea could pay this down, given Russia's insistence that future trade, including spare parts for Soviet-built weapons, must be on a purely commercial basis. With respect to their security treaty, the terms of which did not permit renunciation prior to 1995, the sides discussed a possible exchange of letters on their different understandings of Article I, which required military assistance in the case of armed conflict. Finally, on the sensitive question of nuclear development, Moscow stiffly reminded North Korea of its international obligations under the Non-Proliferation Treaty (NPT).

Effectively demonstrating Russia's continuing lack of influence, North Korea announced shortly after Kunadze's visit that it planned to abandon its participation in the NPT. Russia called for an international conference on the issue, and threatened to join in sanctions if the threat were carried out. In underscoring Russia's sense of urgency about the security situation in Korea, Kozyrev went so far as to characterize the peninsula as "the near abroad for Russia, if you will."[46] An even sharper display of Russia's seeming loss of relevance came in October 1994, when it was announced that the United States and North Korea had agreed on a new nuclear program for Pyongyang, under which North Korea would freeze its nuclear development, dismantle its graphite-moderated reactors, and replace them with light-water reactors, which were not capable of producing weapons-grade fuel. It was eventually agreed that these would be supplied by an international consortium, in which Russia was pointedly not invited to participate. Moscow's sense of exclusion from discussions of Korean security was later magnified when Washington ignored Russian suggestions for a broader conference and instead promoted quadrilateral talks among the two Koreas, China, and the United States. As one journalist put it, Moscow was being "gently pushed out" of real participation in the Korean peninsula, and—as it now did in the Middle East—would play "only the role of honored guest."[47]

Russia, however, was in no mood to be excluded, and it reasserted its presence on the peninsula in a familiar way—through the sale of arms. This time, Seoul rather than Pyongyang was Moscow's customer. Other aspects of the trade relationship with South Korea had failed to live up to expectations. Total trade in 1994 was up 40 percent over the prior year, but still amounted to only $2.2 billion. The Russians complained that their exports had been primarily raw materials, often sold at below world prices and resold by Seoul. In three years, South Korea had invested only $25 million in Russia, spread over thirty projects. Chernomyrdin, during a September 1995 visit to Seoul, spoke of possible joint development of gas fields in Irkutsk. And Putin, during his February 2001 trip, announced a $4 billion deal for South Korean participation in the building of a gas pipeline from Siberia to China, with a projected extension to Seoul. Given that this project would have to await the dawn of real economic cooperation between North and South Korea, it was clear that the greatest potential for reducing the Russian debt to South Korea was through the sale of arms. The first arms-for-debt-repayment deals were concluded in April and July of 1995, amounting to $650 million worth of T-80U tanks, BMP-3 light infantry vehicles, and S-300 defensive missile systems. In November 1996, Defense Minister Rodionov signed a bilateral cooperation agreement with his South Korean counterpart, calling for military exchanges, naval port visits, and training of some South Korean personnel in Russia; he also expressed hope for future sales of Russian planes. Reports that the Pentagon was objecting to Seoul's purchases from Moscow were met with derision in the Russian press: "In short, the market is the market, and the South Koreans obviously have their own idea about which systems are preferable."[48]

Understandably more strenuous were the North Korean objections to Russia's arms sales. Itself able to obtain only a small number of military spare parts from Moscow, as part of a trade volume that had dropped below $100 million in 1996, Pyongyang's cooperation with Russia was described in the Russian press as "on the brink of extinction." The succession struggle that followed the death of long time leader Kim Il Sung coincided with a severe economic crisis that brought widespread famine to the reclusive country. Tensions on the Korean peninsula rose as some observers predicted that the heavily armed Pyongyang regime might lash out militarily at the South in a final attempt at forcible unification of the country. In this context, it was understandable that Russia was reluctant to associate too closely with its former client state. In reaction to Moscow's tilt toward South Korea, North Korea angrily described Moscow's arms sales to Seoul as a criminal act that showed that "Russia itself is all but in the camp of forces hostile to the DPRK." If Russia continued along this road, Pyongyang warned, "we will have to settle scores with it."[49] However, South Korea's stunning economic collapse at the close of 1997 precluded further purchases by Seoul from the Russian arms industry.

North Korea reminded the world of its potential for threatening the security of its region in 1998, when a three-stage rocket, the Taepo-Dong I, allegedly carrying a space satellite, crash-landed in the seas near Japan. The potential range of this rocket astonished the Americans, causing the Central Intelligence Agency (CIA) to revise forward its estimate of the date when North Korea would be capable of mounting a missile attack on the United States. The changed situation made rebuilding influence in Pyongyang a higher priority for Russia, and the effort to do this made notable progress in February 2000, when foreign minister Igor Ivanov visited North Korea to sign a friendship treaty, replacing the expired mutual assistance treaty. Its terms obligated each party not to join in actions with a third party that would compromise the sovereignty or territorial integrity of the other.

Even more dramatic was the first-ever visit to North Korea by a leader from Moscow—a surprise trip by Vladimir Putin on July 19, 2000. Proceeding to a meeting of the leaders of the G-8 on Okinawa, Putin made the startling announcement that North Korean leader Kim Jong Il had agreed to abandon his missile program—the threat most publicly mentioned by Washington as a justification for its national missile defense—in return for international assistance in launching North Korean space satellites. While it was not clear whether this would entail sharing missile technology with Pyongyang, the effect was to blunt the American case for missile defense. The magnitude of Putin's triumph shrank considerably when the North Koreans let it be known that Kim was only joking with the Russian leader—a revelation that Moscow greeted with frosty denials.

Nevertheless, Putin persisted in seeking to demonstrate that the alleged missile threat from North Korea was a U.S.-authored concoction designed to justify its National Missile Defense program. During his trip to Seoul in February 2001, he elicited a statement from South Korean president Kim Dae Jung that seemed to support Russia's stand on the issue. South Korea backed away from the statement under American pressure, but the cold reception given Kim during a subsequent visit to Washington seemed to demonstrate that Russia's parries on this issue were stinging the new George W. Bush administration, which was far less interested in pursuing talks with North Korea than were either Seoul or Moscow. By summer 2001, the U.S. position had apparently moderated. Bush administration spokesmen welcomed the August 2001 visit of Kim Jong Il to Moscow, where he promised to maintain the moratorium on missile launches until 2003, as a means of restarting the dialogue on cooperative approaches to reducing the threat.

Kim was back in Russia a year later for his third visit with Putin. Russia was clearly using these visits to rebuild its influence with North Korea, thereby winning for itself a place at the table for the discussions of regional security in Northeast Asia. While stressing that they had yet to see evidence that North Korea had restarted a nuclear weapons program, the Russians expressed frustration with the "ambiguity" of Pyongyang's statements on the matter. When North Korea finally admitted in the fall of 2002 that it had indeed restarted its program and then withdrew from the NPT a few months later, Russia's level of concern increased—though not yet to the level displayed by the United States. While they urged North Korea to reverse its decision to withdraw from the NPT, Russian diplomats at the same time expressed their understanding of Kim's desire to be reassured by means of a security guaranty, and they eventually agreed, in the context of the six-power talks brokered by the Chinese in 2003, to be a party to a multilateral security guaranty. Despite initial opposition from the United States, Russia had parlayed its influence with North Korea into a role of full participant in the security talks. While Moscow worked to nudge Kim Jong Il toward concessions in his nuclear ambitions, it was also increasingly concerned that any use of force in the region—including the actual use of nuclear weapons—would be severely destabilizing to the area and an enormous threat to the security of its Far Eastern territories.[50]

Russia and the Middle East

The southward expansion of the Russian Empire in the eighteenth and nineteenth centuries brought it into frequent conflict with the Ottoman Empire and with Persia, as well as with the competing empires of Britain and France. During the Soviet period, Lenin, Stalin, and their successors engaged in active (and occasionally expansionist) diplomacy in the region, as Moscow competed for territory and influence with the countries of the Middle East and with Western "imperialism." Although, after the collapse of the USSR, the Russian Federation now finds itself geographically separated from the Middle East by the buffer states of the Caucasus and Central Asia, Moscow's vital interests in these former Soviet republics and the vast energy reserves they contain—second only to those in the Middle East itself—have made the area high priority for Russian foreign policy.

Accordingly, of highest concern in the region are Turkey and Iran—the two states that share a border with the states of the former Soviet Union and that are thus seen as Russia's potential competitors there. Russia's policies toward them have varied, in part as a result of the shifting political winds in Moscow, with Westernizers and nationalists competing over the direction of foreign policy. There has also been variability in Moscow's perception of the threat that Ankara or Teheran is seeking to extend pan-Turkic or Islamic-fundamentalist influence in the Caucasus and Central Asia at Russia's expense. In both cases, Russian policy has swung back and forth from nervous rivalry to a relationship so cooperative that it has included the sale of arms. As an analyst at the Russian Center for Strategic and International Studies described the policy confusion, "The exchange of blows between the proponents of a pro-Turkish and a pro-Iranian orientation in the Russian establishment is more vigorous than the actual rivalry between those two states in the Central Asian and Transcaucasus regions."[51]

Although Turkey is a member of NATO and was the recipient of some rather brutal threats and territorial demands from Stalin, its relations with the post-Stalinist regimes in Moscow were relatively cooperative. In the wake of the breakup of the USSR, Turkey—a secular, democratic, and market-oriented Islamic state—was widely viewed in the West as a potential model for the development of the newly independent Islamic states of the former Soviet Union, much of the population of which is ethnically and linguistically related to the Turks. Initially, Turkey was cautious in the region, assuring Kozyrev during his February 1992 visit that it did not view itself as competing with Russia for a sphere of influence. Turkey's sympathies were evident, however, in the regional conflict in Nagorno-Karabakh that had embroiled Armenia and Azerbaijan in war since 1988. Turkey was the first country to recognize Azerbaijan's independence, and a visit to Turkey in January 1992 by the strongly nationalist Azeri president, Abulfez Elchibey, aroused Russia's suspicions. During his visit to Moscow to conclude a treaty on principles governing Russo-Turkish relations in May, Prime Minister Suleyman Demirel

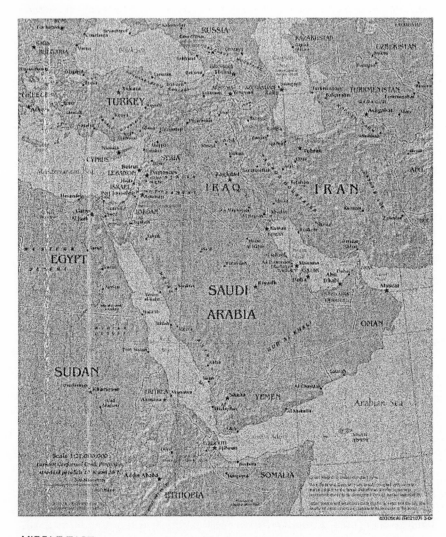

MIDDLE EAST

was pressed for a commitment that Turkey would not intervene militarily in the conflict. Moscow's anxiety was heightened by Azerbaijan's mid-1992 withdrawal from the Commonwealth of Independent States (CIS) in protest of a perceived pro-Armenian stance, together with the marked increase in Azerbaijani-Turkish trade and in the extent of the country's penetration by Turkish media.

These concerns were broadened in October, when the leaders of Kazakhstan, Uzbekistan, Turkmenistan, Kyrgyzstan, and Azerbaijan met with the Turkish head of state in Ankara for discussions of a "Turkic Common Market" featuring cooperation in the economic and security realms. Fears of a burgeoning rivalry for influence were revived when the five Central Asian republics met in May 1993 to form the Central Asian Regional Union, which was encouraged by Turkey, amid talk that their energy resources would be directed away from Russia and through Azerbaijan and Turkey. The second summit of the Turkic-language states in Istanbul in October 1994 occasioned a statement by a Russian foreign ministry spokesman on the "undesirability of a segregation of the Turkic-language countries along national and ethnic lines." In contrast, by the time of the third summit, held in Bishkek in August 1995, there was no official reaction from Moscow. By this time, one journalist noted, it had become evident that the leaders of the former Soviet republics were in no hurry to replace Moscow's patronage with Ankara's, and he wryly observed that three of the six heads of state in attendance spoke not in their native languages, but in Russian.[52]

Moscow's reduced level of anxiety probably resulted from the parallel development of its own economic and security relations with Turkey. In March 1993 the Russians announced a $75 million sale of helicopters and armored personnel carriers to Turkey's national police force, with most of the proceeds to be applied toward Russia's debt. This first-ever Russian arms sale to a NATO member nation was followed in May by the first visit to Turkey by a Russian defense chief in two centuries. A year later Grachev and his Turkish counterpart signed a formal agreement on cooperation between their defense industries, which contemplated joint production of certain weapons systems. An additional sale of Russian military hardware in the summer of 1994, following Germany's suspension of arms sales in protest of Turkish raids on its Kurdish minority, allowed Turkey to demonstrate to the West that it had an alternative source of arms supplies. In December 1995, a package of economic agreements was signed that included a $350 million Turkish credit and a restructuring of the Russian debt. The two sides noted that their trade turnover in 1995 had reached $3 billion, and that Turkish firms had concluded $5 billion in contracts for construction of facilities in Russia—clear signs that Turkey had become one of Russia's leading trade and investment partners.

However, elections in Turkey that same month provided a less favorable portent for Russia. The success at the polls of the Islamic Welfare Party, followed by the accession of its leader, Necmettin Erbakan, to the premiership the following June, aroused new fears in Moscow—understandable in light of Erbakan's stated pan-Islamic goals, which included the "liberation" of Azerbaijan and Chechnya. In the ensuing months there were several signs of growing tension between the two countries. In September, Russian participation in joint Black Sea naval exercises was canceled, amid expressions of concern over Turkey's growing shipbuilding program. In December 1996, Foreign Minister Tansu Ciller's visit to Moscow was marred by a whole list of mutual complaints. On the Russian side, these concerned Turkey's restrictions on the passage of Russian tankers through the Bosporus, allegedly for environmental reasons, and the activities of Turkish groups supporting Chechen separatists. On the Turkish side, there were parallel complaints about activities of Kurdish organizations in Russia, and an expression of sharp anger about Russia's announced plans to sell S-300 surface-to-air missile systems to the Greek-dominated government of Cyprus. These incidents, however, were not likely to permanently mar Russo-Turkish relations, and tensions were expected to again decrease as a result of the military-induced resignation of the Erbakan government in the summer of 1997. Russo-Turkish relations improved after the European Union led in mediating the crisis over the proposed sale of defensive missiles to Cyprus. (It was agreed that the missiles would be deployed on the Greek island of Crete instead.)

Soon thereafter, in December 1997, Chernomyrdin paid a visit to Turkey — the first ever by a Russian prime minister—to celebrate the announcement of a twenty-five-year agreement according to which Turkey would be supplied with 30 billion cubic meters of Russian gas annually, following the completion of the "Blue Stream" pipeline to be built across the Black Sea. Originally scheduled for completion in 2002, the pipeline began deliveries in 2003, with volumes about half of what was originally projected. However, the Turks soon suspended deliveries, claiming that even this reduced volume greatly outstripped their demand. An acrimonious discussion of the price of the gas, originally set at levels high enough to allow Gazprom to recoup its capital investment, finally ended later in 2003, when the Turks resumed their gas purchases at a lower price.

Russo-Turkish relations were again disturbed in 2004, when Russia unexpectedly vetoed a U.S. and British-sponsored UN Security Council resolution calling for a guarantee of the security of both Greek and Turkish Cypriots if they voted to accept a UN-sponsored plan to unify the island. The Greek Cypriot government, backed by Greece, opposed the UN plan, and Russia's veto was seen as a pro-Greek move, unfriendly to Turkey. (Only the Turkish minority voted in favor of the unification referendum, and on May 1 the Greek part of Cyprus alone joined the European Union.) Russia evidently calculated that its strong economic ties to Cyprus, as well as its arms sales relationships with Greece, outweighed the harm that its veto would do to its relationship with Turkey.[53]

The Soviet Union's relations with Iran during the 1980s were not nearly as cordial as those with Turkey, but there may be greater potential for long-term future cooperation between Moscow and Teheran. The ideological tensions that accompanied Ayatollah Khomeini's Islamic revolution have largely disappeared, given Gorbachev's decision to withdraw Soviet troops from Afghanistan, the relative moderation of Iran's revolutionary policies after the ayatollah's death, and the subsequent fall of communism and breakup of the USSR, which nominally removed the yoke of communism from the practice of the Islamic religion there. Initial concerns that Iran would promote "Islamic fundamentalism" among the Muslim minority in Russia or in the buffer zone that has been created between the two countries were clearly overblown. With the exception of the Azerbaijanis, most Muslims in the former Soviet Union do not adhere to the Shiite branch of Islam that predominates in Iran. More to the point, Teheran has seemed willing to conduct its relations in ways that do not threaten the interests of Moscow.

The improvement in relations began during Gorbachev's last years in power. A state visit by President Ali Akbar Hashemi Rafsanjani to Moscow in June 1989 was the occasion for signing several agreements, including an important arms deal, under which the Soviets obtained badly needed hard currency for MiG-29 and SU-24 aircraft, needed by Iran to replace heavy losses during the long Iran-Iraq War. Subsequent sales included T-72 tanks and several Kilo-class submarines, and deliveries were estimated to total $1 billion in 1991 and an even greater sum in 1992. The U.S. government put heavy pressure on the new Yeltsin government to cancel military deliveries to Iran, and Moscow did agree to delay the delivery of some of the submarines; but a Ministry of Foreign Affairs spokesman, in an interview with *Izvestia,* frankly acknowledged Russia's dilemma: "'We understand the U.S.'s concern, and we don't want an arms race to be unleashed in the Persian Gulf, either; but we have our own interests, first of all, our economic interests (convertible currency!). Second, we view Iran as a friendly, neighboring state,' said the Russian diplomat. 'Ignoring its requests in the defense sphere would be unreasonable. Today only enemies are refused deliveries of military equipment.'"[54] When the Yeltsin government followed the American lead, not only was it exposing itself to further ridicule from internal opponents, but it also was ignoring the distinctive security situation Moscow faced. At least at that time, Iran seemed concerned that conflicts within the former Soviet states might spill onto its own territory; it thus appeared to share Russia's desire for good-neighborly cooperation in the interests of stabilizing the region. As long as Iran behaved responsibly in Russia's backyard, Moscow saw no reason to accede to U.S. pressure to cut off arms sales.

These considerations were evident in Kozyrev's March 1993 trip to Teheran. He confirmed Russia's intention to sell arms to Iran and reached agreement on projects in the nuclear field, including the sale of two 440-megawatt nuclear reactors—a deal that he claimed would not put Russia at odds with the United States. Moreover, he discussed a Russian-Iranian "strategic partnership" for ensuring stability in the Caucasus and Central Asia, one immediate fruit of which was Iran's agreement to use its influence over the opposition forces in the Tajikistan civil war to encourage a settlement of the conflict.

Although its primary emphasis was on promoting "cultural Islam" rather than overt political interference in the former Soviet republics, Iran's presence was active enough to keep Moscow on edge. In September 1993, the foreign ministry issued a statement of concern about reports that Iranian troops had crossed into Azerbaijan, and it urged Iran to show restraint in the Nagorno-Karabakh conflict. The following month, a nine-day trip by Rafsanjani to Azerbaijan, Uzbekistan, Kazakhstan, Turkmenistan, and Kyrgyzstan stimulated some alarm in the Russian foreign ministry. In December of the same year, the Turkish prime minister met the Iranian vice president to discuss the possibility of coordinated actions—probably in the form of an energy pipeline—to ease Azerbaijan's economic dependence on Russia.

These concerns were not sufficient, however, to deter Russia from concluding a major deal to assist in the development of Iran's nuclear program. In January 1995, the Russian Ministry of Atomic Power and the Nuclear Industry announced a $1 billion contract—reportedly won despite heavy competition from Western firms—to complete a reactor at Bushehr, the construction of which had been halted by West Germany in 1979. The United States immediately objected, claiming that the reactor would help Iran to build a nuclear weapon, but the Russian ministry said that the project complied with the NPT and would be monitored by the International Atomic Energy Agency. The U.S. Congress prepared legislation that would cut off aid to Russia if the deal went through. A face-saving compromise was announced in May at the Clinton-Yeltsin summit. Gas centrifuges for enriching uranium—supposedly included in the contract without the knowledge of the Kremlin or the Ministry of Foreign Affairs—would be eliminated from the deal, and provisions for training Iranian nuclear physicists in Russia also would be dropped, cutting the value of the deal in half. The other terms of the contract would be analyzed by the Gore-Chernomyrdin commission to verify their conformity with the NPT.[55] The contract for the Bushehr reactor was left in place, but the commission did conclude a secret agreement that Russia would sell no more arms to Iran. Existing sales contracts would be honored, but all shipments would be concluded by the end of 1999.

Despite this embarrassing episode, Russia continued to seek increased trade with Iran, but a worsening economy limited Teheran's attractiveness as a customer. Minister for Foreign Economic Relations Oleg Davydov, visiting Iran late in 1995, said that the main difficulties in Russian-Iranian trade were not political, but were related to problems of payments that followed the 1992 decision to settle accounts only in freely convertible currency. Total trade volume had dropped 29 percent in 1994, to $520 million, and Iran's overdue debt to Russia had climbed to $582 million (two-thirds of which was owed to the state arms trading agency). Nevertheless, Davydov predicted later in the year that the total volume of Russian exports to Iran could reach $5 billion in another decade.[56]

Russia's interest in participating in Iranian energy projects caused another dispute with the United States in the fall of 1997. A joint French-Malaysian-Russian project to develop Iranian gas fields threatened to trigger U.S. sanctions against the participating companies, apparently jeopardizing a plan by the Russian participant (Gazprom) to raise investment capital on the U.S. market. In December 1997, Gazprom announced that it had withdrawn from these financing plans—but not from the proposed deal with Iran.

In his first year in office, Foreign Minister Evgenii Primakov continued the Russian effort to strengthen ties with Iran. Visiting Teheran in December 1996, he declared that relations between the two were "developing along an ascending curve," in part because of Iran's assistance in arranging a cease-fire in Tajikistan. For his part, Primakov's Iranian counterpart told a Russian journalist that Russian-Iranian relations were the best they had been in two hundred years, causing the journalist to conclude that Moscow's way of working with Iran "i.e., trying to bring its behavior into conformity with generally recognized international norms—can be more effective than the ultimatum-based methods of the Americans."[57] Signs of cooperation on regional problems continued into 1997, as the two countries collaborated on their policies toward the Taliban in Afghanistan, and as Russia sought Iran's help in pressuring Turkmenistan and Azerbaijan to cooperate with Moscow in the exploitation of the considerable petroleum reserves in the Caspian Sea. In July 1998, in an agreement with Kazakhstan, Moscow abandoned its common front with Iran and adopted a different standard for division of Caspian oil resources. Whether the Russian-Iranian relationship could remain relatively trouble free was in question, not only because of their ensuing conflict over the Caspian, but also given Iran's expressed interest in acquiring additional arms that would likely upset the regional balance in the Persian Gulf and greatly alarm the United States.[58]

Reports appeared in the Western press in September 1997—"taken very seriously" by the U.S. government—that Russia was supplying missile technology to Iran. Primakov hastily denied the reports, and Yeltsin added a blanket pledge that there would be no deliveries to Iran of missiles or missile technology. Pressed again on the subject the following month by Israeli prime minister Netanyahu, the Russian foreign minister reportedly cited his prior intelligence background as the basis for assuring the Israelis that Iran would not have nuclear weapons or the means to deliver them any time within the next decade. As for the prospect of unauthorized "leakages," Primakov added "that he personally had promoted the adoption of measures to prevent specialists with access to missile and nuclear secrets from having contacts with Iran."[59] As the subject continued to be pressed by the U.S. government in 1998, Primakov acknowledged that some "brain drain" had occurred, but that it was simply not in Russia's interests to assist its neighbor in acquiring long-range missiles.

Despite the Russian government's declared unwillingness to help, Iran succeeded in July 1998 in flight testing a Shahab-3 missile with a range of 1,200–1,500 kilometers—reportedly assisted by China, Pakistan, and North Korea. This development raised new alarms in Washington about possible dual-use technology in the Bushehr project, as well as about illegal transfers of bomb or missile technology from Russia. The United States accused seven Russian enterprises of selling weapons technology to Iran, Libya, and North Korea, and in January 1999 it imposed economic sanctions on three Russian scientific laboratories for alleged assistance to Iran. Although Russian authorities at first denied that such transfers had taken place, nuclear industry minister Evgenii Adamov announced in March that Washington had agreed to lift the sanctions in return for a pledge that the labs' cooperation with Iran would cease.

American unease with Moscow's apparent lack of cooperation increased early in 2000, when Secretary of State Madeleine Albright reportedly complained that, despite the expiration of the grace period, the cessation of arms transfers promised in the secret Gore-Chernomyrdin agreement had not occurred. In October, in the midst of the presidential election campaign in the United States, the existence of the agreement and Russia's violations of its terms was leaked to the American press. Whether this had any effect on Gore's candidacy is unclear, but it did prompt Moscow to denounce the breach of secrecy and to use this as an excuse to withdraw from the agreement. No sooner had this occurred than Marshal Sergeev journeyed to Teheran to inaugurate "a new phase of military-technical cooperation" between Russia and Iran. Although he maintained that only defensive arms would be sold and that no technology transfers would be allowed, the American reaction was expectedly harsh.

Nor was Washington reassured when Iran's president Mohammad Khatami traveled to Moscow in March 2001. Reportedly, his delegation did some shopping for arms, with Mi-17 helicopters, SU-25 attack aircraft, S-300 surface-to-air missiles, and T-90 tanks on the list. Delighted, Russian military sources suggested that Iran, at the time fourth-ranked among Russia's weapons customers, might move into third place, with its arms sales and training expenditures possibly bringing as much as $7 billion in revenues to Moscow during the first half of the decade.[60]

Putin's decision to align Russia more closely with the United States after September 2001 sharpened Moscow's dilemma about how to conduct its nuclear and weapons programs with Iran, especially after Teheran was included as part of Bush's "axis of evil" early in 2002. As Washington stepped up its pressure on Moscow, the issue of Iran's possible acquisition of nuclear weapons became uppermost in U.S.-Russian relations, as we discuss at greater length in the next chapter. Tempted by the prospect of lucrative contracts for both nuclear plants and advanced weaponry, Russia, as one journalist put it, "still wants to have its cake and eat it too."[61] Confirming its pledge to complete the nuclear reactor at Bushehr, and even its willingness to build a second reactor there, Russia announced that it had obtained Iran's agreement that all spent fuel from the Bushehr reactor would be returned to Russia, and it urged Iran to sign a protocol to the NPT that would allow more aggressive inspections of its nuclear program by the IAEA. Russia's voice was added to those of the British, French, and Germans in this effort, and Iran acceded to the pressure in December 2003. However, surprise inspections by the international agency shortly thereafter revealed suspicious activity, and the United States immediately charged that Iran was in violation of its treaty commitments and demanded that international sanctions be applied. The Russians joined the Europeans in insisting on more concrete evidence before asking for sanctions.

In June 2004, the situation became even more complicated when Iran notified the IAEA that it was resuming the production of nuclear centrifuge components—a key element of a weapons program—while continuing to insist that its program was aimed entirely at the peaceful production of nuclear energy. This turn of events caused a commentator for *Kommersant* to complain:

> Over the past decade, Iran's actions have repeatedly put Russian diplomacy in a delicate, if not to say ambiguous, position. . . . A tragicomic situation in which Moscow was attempting to defend Teheran and clear it

of all suspicion, while Iran was doing its utmost to thwart that effort. In the process, it failed to show the least concern for Moscow's image. . . . Under these circumstances, Moscow can, of course, continue to pursue cooperation with Iran while pretending that nothing bad is happening. . . . But that course of action will have increasing political costs.[62]

No less a threat to stability in the Persian Gulf region, and no less undesirable in Washington's eyes as a possible partner for Moscow, was Saddam Hussein's Iraq. We have seen in chapter 4 that Gorbachev and his personal envoy Evgenii Primakov had tried to salvage the longstanding Soviet investment in Baghdad by negotiating a peaceful resolution to the 1990 Iraqi invasion of Kuwait, and how the failure of those mediation efforts had left the Soviet Union trailing unenthusiastically in the wake of the international effort to rein in Saddam Hussein. In the UN Security Council, the representatives of the Soviet Union and Russia have repeatedly voted to support international sanctions on Iraq, but Moscow probably has ranked second only to Baghdad itself in the amount of economic harm it has suffered as a result. Russia has lost a major partner both in energy development and in weapons sales, while holding a debt, estimated as high as $10 billion, that financially strapped Iraq is unable to repay. Given Russia's own economic crisis, Yeltsin's persistence in supporting costly UN sanctions was prominently used by his domestic political opponents as a prime example of Russia's sacrificing its own interests to satisfy the West.

For both Gorbachev and Yeltsin, Kuwait and the other oil-rich moderate states of the Gulf Cooperation Council appeared to offer an alternative market and source of financial support. Kozyrev visited six of these states during a seven-day tour in April and May of 1992, emphasizing Russia's newfound ideological affinity by stating that "now we prefer to deal with stable, moderate regimes" rather than the USSR's previous partners, Libya, Iran, and Iraq. Kozyrev encountered a certain reticence deriving from fresh memories of Moscow's recent friendships in the region; and by the end of his trip, only Oman had offered credits to Russia—a $500 million investment in the oil and gas industry and $100 million for modernization of Russia's oil fields. Nevertheless, the primary importance of strengthening cooperation with the Persian Gulf states was reaffirmed in a foreign ministry "concept"—approved by Yeltsin—that was developed in the fall of 1992 to guide Russia's relations with the Arab world. The chief goals identified in this document were:

1. Ensuring Russia's national security;
2. Preventing the spread of political and military fires in the Middle East to the increasingly unstable regions of the Caucasus and Central Asia;

3. Making use of the potential in the Arab states to help solve Russia's economic problems.[63]

In the longer term, despite Russia's continued support of sanctions—even its dispatch of two ships to the Persian Gulf task force enforcing them—most of the Gulf states remained wary. However, Russia did manage a breakthrough with Saddam Hussein's recent victim, Kuwait, which was busy securing itself against possible future aggression by strengthening economic and military ties with all five permanent members of the Security Council. In December 1993, Russia signed a military cooperation agreement with Kuwait, calling for joint naval maneuvers and an exchange of military delegations. The following November, a visit to the Gulf by Chernomyrdin produced an agreement for a Russian arms sale of $750 million to Kuwait, involving infantry fighting vehicles and rocket launchers, and an agreement (questionably reported in the Russian press at $3 billion) with the United Arab Emirates for joint production of SU-37 fighter-bombers.[64]

For the most part, Russia was disappointed with the size and scope of its economic and military transactions with the states of the Persian Gulf. In April 1993, as Yeltsin's domestic opponents were increasing their pressure on him, parliament speaker Ruslan Khasbulatov sent an emissary to Iraq to explore the possibility of restoring closer relations. The defeat of the parliamentary opposition in October 1993 momentarily eased the domestic criticism of Russia's compliance with the sanctions imposed on Iraq and Serbia, but criticism resumed after the December elections, with Vladimir Zhirinovskii in the forefront. Under the cloak of secrecy, Iraq's deputy prime minister Tariq Aziz visited Russia in July 1994 to enlist Moscow's help in lifting UN sanctions, holding forth the prospect of debt repayment and contracts for Russian firms. Russia lobbied in the Security Council for a gradual lifting of sanctions as a reward for positive steps that Iraq might take, while it urged the Iraqi government to announce recognition of Kuwait's independence and borders.

In October 1994, in the midst of Russia's campaign to champion Iraqi good behavior, Saddam Hussein rekindled the crisis by sending his troops to the Kuwaiti border. As if to heighten Russia's embarrassment and force it into a position counter to that of the West, he simultaneously sent his oil minister to Moscow to discuss future cooperation. Yeltsin sought to salvage the situation by sending Kozyrev to Baghdad in search of a political settlement. His meetings produced a communiqué saying that Iraq was ready to recognize Kuwait's sovereignty and border, in return for which Russia would support a six-month period of monitoring Iraq's compliance with UN requirements, followed by an unconditional end to the sanctions. This initiative was speedily and angrily rejected by the Western powers, who mustered their forces for a military response to Saddam Hussein. Desperately seeking to keep his initiative alive, Kozyrev offered assurances that Saddam had agreed unconditionally to recognize Kuwait's borders, but no high-ranking Iraqi official would confirm his statement, and no other states seemed ready to take Saddam Hussein at his word. Ultimately, once Iraqi forces had been turned back under threat of military reprisal, Kozyrev returned to Baghdad to praise Saddam's wisdom in recognizing Kuwait, and to appeal personally to the Iraqi parliament to ratify the action. Although much of the Russian press praised the initiative as an admirable exercise of independent diplomacy, Vladimir Lukin (the chair of the Duma's foreign affairs committee and former Russian ambassador to the United States) wrote a withering critique of Kozyrev's efforts:

> It is our passion for mere show, the Potemkin village syndrome, that is our undoing. We managed to spoil what we should have been handling with greater care—working relations with the American administration. If our national interest consists in getting Iraq to start paying off its debt as soon as possible while at the same time avoiding any worsening of relations with the West then, as a result of the diplomatic measures we have conducted, the situation has become more difficult on both counts. That's the "bottom line."[65]

Lukin's position was not shared by a majority of his colleagues in the Russian Duma, who continued to chafe under the presumed yoke of Western policy in Iraq. In April 1995, the Duma passed a resolution calling for UN sanctions against Iraq to be lifted, and demanding that the government more actively pursue debt repayment and business investment in Iraq.

The deep rift that had reopened between Russia and the West over the proper response to Iraqi assertiveness appeared again in September 1996, when Saddam Hussein violated UN rules by sending troops into a special Kurdish-inhabited zone in northern Iraq. The United States responded by launching twenty-seven cruise missiles against military targets in Iraq, followed by a second strike with seventeen missiles that completed the destruction of Iraq's air defense system in an expanded "no-fly zone." At the time of the U.S. attack (of which the Russians had advance notification), Deputy Foreign Minister Viktor Posuvaliuk was in Baghdad trying to resolve the crisis. He claimed that he had received assurances from Tariq Aziz that Iraq would withdraw its troops from the special zone, and Posuvaliuk had sought unsuccessfully to forestall U.S. military action. An angry statement from the Russian government—said by Yeltsin's chief of staff to have been fully supported by the ailing president—bitterly denounced the U.S. actions:

Serious concern is prompted by the fact that Washington is essentially laying claim to the role of supreme arbiter, trying, in effect, to supplant the Security Council, which, in accordance with the UN Charter, possesses an exclusive right to authorize the use of force. The decision adopted unilaterally by the U.S. and Britain to expand the "no-fly" zone in southern Iraq should also be viewed in this context. These actions, which set a dangerous precedent, are at variance with international law and are unacceptable. The military actions in and around Iraq must be stopped. Russia insistently urges all parties to abandon the logic of force and to embark on the path of a political settlement of the crisis situation that has arisen.[66]

Responding to what the Russian press termed the low point in U.S.-Russian relations in 1996, the U.S. government expressed its disappointment that Russia had not yet learned that Saddam Hussein responds not to diplomacy but only to force. Nevertheless, with Primakov himself more directly involved in the conversations with his "old comrades" in Iraq, Moscow continued its search for a way to reduce sanctions in return for "good behavior," in the full expectation (avidly encouraged by Baghdad) that when Iraq resumed normal economic activity, Russia would be the major foreign beneficiary.[67]

Saddam Hussein forced the sanctions issue to the forefront again in the fall of 1997, when he ordered the expulsion of American members of the UN inspection team searching for Iraqi weapons of mass destruction. When the entire UN team withdrew in protest, the United States stepped up its military presence in the Persian Gulf region, amid rumors of an impending attack on Iraq. The diplomatic and military coalition that had prevailed in the 1991 war had fallen apart, first of all within the UN Security Council itself, where only Britain among the permanent members gave strong support to the U.S. position. Capitalizing on his personal ties, Foreign Minister Primakov wrested an agreement from the Iraqis to readmit all members of the inspection team. Emerging from a meeting with Yeltsin and Iraqi deputy prime minister Tariq Aziz, Primakov summoned the other "big five" foreign ministers to an extraordinary middle-of-the-night meeting in Geneva to announce his triumph and secure their concurrence.

Insisting to the skeptical Americans that they had made no deal with the Iraqis "behind anyone's backs," the Russians did promise that, on the basis of Iraq's fulfillment of the relevant UN resolutions, Russia would "energetically work for the earliest possible" lifting of UN sanctions. However, the ultimate loophole in the agreement—on the basis of which Saddam Hussein continued to declare "presidential sites" off limits to UN inspectors—was hidden in language that spoke of increasing the effectiveness of the work of the UN special commission "while showing respect for the sovereignty and security of Iraq."

Moscow clearly wanted to push such details to the background, prefer-ring to capitalize on what Primakov termed "a great success for Russian diplomacy . . . achieved without the use of force and without a show of force." In the words of a Russian reporter, the United States was essentially isolated, and Russia strengthened its reputation "as an influential power not only throughout the Middle East but in the world as a whole." Deputy For-eign Minister Viktor Posuvaliuk also saw in the role Russia was playing in the crisis a special significance for broader Russian foreign policy: "The world is increasingly coming to realize that Russia is emerging or has emerged from its period of confusion and major problems, and that it is now oriented toward conducting an energetic and constructive foreign policy. Many coun-tries have confidence in the balanced line we are pursuing." He stressed that Russian diplomats were not acting as "undiscriminating defense attorneys" for Iraq, since they were calling for strict fulfillment of all the UN resolu-tions. "But at the same time we are saying that Iraq must be shown that there is light at the end of the tunnel. Not fire but light."[68]

When the Iraqi conflict flared up again in January 1998 over Saddam Hussein's refusal to allow UN inspectors access to eight "presidential sites," Yeltsin again sought to gain both international and domestic political pres-tige by sending Posuvaliuk to Baghdad in search of a solution. Embarrassed when a "deal" announced in Moscow was immediately denied by the Iraqis, an angry Yeltsin warned that continued U.S. military activities in the Persian Gulf could bring dire consequences: "One must be careful in a world that is saturated with all kinds of weapons. By his actions Clinton might get into a world war. They are acting too loudly." Yeltsin's spokesman sought to ex-plain away the president's inflammatory rhetoric by speculating that foreign reporters might not have adequate command of the Russian language. Mili-tary action was averted when UN Secretary General Kofi Annan's mediation defused the crisis. Claiming a share of the credit, the Russians again saw in the Persian Gulf crisis some hopeful signs that the ability of the United States to dictate its will was waning, and that "the unipolar world is receding into the past."[69]

The rhetorical heights were scaled in Moscow again the following De-cember, when U.S. and British war planes, in an operation termed "Desert Fox," conducted air strikes on Iraq in the wake of the UN arms inspectors' report of continued Iraqi obstruction. Claiming that the chances for a diplo-matic solution to the inspection impasse had not been exhausted, Yeltsin termed the Anglo-American action "senseless," declaring that it "flagrantly violated" the UN Charter and international law and "undermines the entire international security system." Russia's ambassadors to Washington and Lon-don were recalled, the pending vote on ratification of START II was postponed, Vladimir Zhirinovskii called for preemptive strikes against the United States, and Yeltsin was pictured poring over maps of the Middle East amid talk of dispatching Russian warships to the region. Alluding to the pending vote on impeachment in the U.S. Congress, a foreign ministry statement referred to the "true reasons and true motives" for the strikes.[70]

The Russians participated in several efforts in the United Nations to reduce, suspend, or eliminate the sanctions on Iraq, but to no avail. Reportedly, Iraq was pressuring Russia to withdraw unilaterally from the sanctions regime, hinting that prospective Russian contracts for oil exploration in Iraq might depend on Moscow's willingness to do so. Iraqi visitors to Moscow in 2000 included the defense minister and the ubiquitous Tariq Aziz. In November 2000, Foreign Minister Ivanov met Saddam Hussein in Baghdad, but despite charges that Moscow was bending over backward to court "rogue states," Russia held firm to the United Nations sanctions policy. Moscow did not, however, agree to a U.S.-British attempt to move to "smart sanctions," which would tighten the embargo on arms and dual-use goods while easing restriction on imports of civilian goods. Alone among the UN "Big Five," the Russians blocked the plan with their veto threat.

In chapter 9 we consider at some length Russia's policy toward Iraq during the subsequent years, leading up to the American and British invasion of Iraq in March 2003. As in the case of its relations with the other two members of President Bush's "axis of evil," Moscow found it difficult to steer between its newfound alliance with the United States in the "war against terror" and the longstanding relationships it had built up during the Soviet era and beyond with regimes opposed to American policies. After the removal of Saddam Hussein's regime, Russia sought to salvage some of its considerable economic investment. In December 2003, after officials of the Iraqi Governing Council indicated that Russia might be able to reinstate some of the oil contracts that had been negotiated with Saddam, Moscow suggested that it might be willing to forgive about two-thirds of Iraq's $8 billion debt, depending on the outcome of more broad-ranging debt negotiations to be conducted through the Paris Club.[71] Having voted in favor of the lifting of UN sanctions against Iraq, Russia had resumed commercial activity in the country in 2003. However, the wave of hostage taking that erupted in April 2004 prompted Moscow to order all of its workers to leave the country. And while Putin made it clear that he had no reason to wish failure upon the U.S.-led effort to restore stability to the country, he also decided that Russia would not contribute security forces to help in that effort.

A similar, if lower-profile, mix of activities and motives has characterized Russia's diplomacy toward another Middle Eastern pariah state—Libya. The advent of the Yeltsin government had not been welcomed in Tripoli, which refused until 1995 to acknowledge that its $3.8 billion debt to the USSR was now owed to the Russian Federation. When Russia joined with the West in November 1993 in voting for UN sanctions against Libya, in response to the latter's refusal to cooperate against terrorism, Moscow succeeded in obtaining an amendment to the resolution that demanded that Libya repay its debts. Ironically, a Russian trade delegation was discovered to be in Tripoli at that very time, and the embarrassed foreign ministry quickly stated that Russia had every intention of abiding by the sanctions. With the sanctions still in force (and Primakov now in charge at the foreign ministry), a Russian delegation returned to Libya in March 1996 for a discussion of debt repayment and future large-scale economic cooperation. At this point, there were said to be only two hundred Russian specialists remaining in the country—about one-thirtieth the size of the former Soviet contingent. Although Russia claimed that it had suffered at least $7 billion in losses, and though it noted bitterly that some Western companies continued to do business in Libya, Russia nevertheless declared that it would continue to abide by the international sanctions. When the sanctions on Libya were finally lifted in 1999, Moscow was prepared to resume business with Tripoli. A delegation led by Libya's foreign minister was received in Moscow in the summer of 2000 to discuss arms sales, but no deal could be reached in the absence of a mutually acceptable plan for liquidating Libya's Soviet-era debt.

The debt was still an issue when Igor Ivanov went to Libya in May 2001 for talks on trade and economic relations—the first visit by a Russian foreign minister. Libya's full-fledged return to international respectability did not come, however, until the end of 2003, when Qaddafi announced that the country would abandon its weapons of mass destruction programs. With its eye still on the issue of Iraq, Russia hailed Libya's decision as confirmation that the best approach to dealing with the WMD issue is "within the framework of multilateral preventive diplomacy" as opposed to military preemption.[72]

Libya was by no means the only former Soviet arms customer with which the Russian government was reestablishing its contacts. In April 2001 Putin played host to Algerian president Abdelaziz Buteflika. The two presidents signed a declaration of "strategic partnership"—Russia's first with an Arab country—and they discussed Algeria's shopping list for weapons. With about three-fourths of its arsenal Russian-made, Algeria was already one of the top ten customers for the Russian arms exporters. At the time of Buteflika's visit it had purchased $600 million in the previous four years. But the future for Algeria's purchases—like Libya's—was clouded by the issue of debt. Although it acknowledged owing at least $4 billion, Algeria had stopped making payments on the debt in 1998, and difficult negotiations on the settlement still lay ahead.

Yemen was another former Soviet customer that was now purchasing Russian arms. Ten MiG-29 fighter jets were delivered in June 2002—the first installment on a $300 million order, sold by the Russians despite objections from the United States, which feared their possible resale to Iraq. Additional purchases were discussed during the April 2004 visit to Moscow of Yemeni president Ali Abdullah Saleh.

A visitor from the Arabian peninsula with a markedly different agenda had visited Moscow in the fall of 2003. Saudi Arabia's crown prince Abdullah—the first high-level Saudi emissary ever to come to Moscow—discussed the Israeli-Palestinian and Iraqi conflicts with Putin, in an atmosphere clouded with distrust because of Saudi support for Chechen rebels. As if to underscore Saudi Arabia's continuing distress over Chechnya, Prince Abdullah informed Putin that Russia's wish to enter the Organization of Islamic Countries would not be granted because of the continuing conflict there.

As for the longstanding Israeli-Palestinian conflict, Russia was again seeking to play a major role, but with limited success. Evgenii Primakov, a specialist on the Middle East, had seemed determined that during his term as foreign minister Russia would move back onto the center stage of diplomacy in the region. During earlier phases, Moscow had been handicapped by its lack of influence with Israel. This had changed—as did so many other features of Moscow's foreign policy—during the late Gorbachev period. By 1988 Soviet restrictions on Jewish emigration to Israel had eased and consular missions were opened. In October 1991 full diplomatic relations, broken after the Six-Day War in 1967, were restored. At the end of that month Gorbachev attended the Madrid Conference on Middle East peace, which was cochaired by the USSR.

Yeltsin's government moved quickly to further strengthen Russian-Israeli relations. Vice President Aleksandr Rutskoi visited Israel in April 1992, and the following August, Shimon Peres made the first visit to Moscow by an Israeli foreign minister. The following month Peres and Kozyrev signed an agreement calling for closer relations in several spheres. Trade relations between the two countries began to increase at a dizzying speed, moving from only $70 million in 1991 and $280 million in 1993 to about $650 million in 1995. Finally, much to the chagrin of Yeltsin's domestic critics, Moscow demonstrated an unaccustomed even-handedness in the ongoing Arab-Israeli peace process, and Kozyrev was invited to the White House in September 1993 to celebrate the Oslo accords between Israel and the Palestinians.

The strong showing by Zhirinovskii and the nationalist forces in the Duma elections of December 1993 may have motivated Yeltsin initially to play a more independent role in Middle East negotiations, following the disarray caused by the February 1994 massacre of twenty-nine Palestinian worshippers by a Jewish settler in the West Bank town of Hebron. Without consulting Washington, Yeltsin dispatched Kozyrev to Tunis to meet with Palestine Liberation Organization (PLO) leader Yasir Arafat, urged a reconvening of the Madrid conference, and supported the demand of the Arabs for international observers to protect West Bank Palestinians. In April, Arafat and Israeli prime minister Yitzhak Rabin made separate visits to Moscow for consultations with Yeltsin. Although Moscow was not coordinating its initiative with Washington, it nevertheless remained even-handed. Rabin, a former general, was even invited to lecture at the General Staff Academy in Moscow, and he extracted two promises from the Russians—to use their influence with Syria to help in locating captured Israeli soldiers, and to forgo the sale of any new offensive weapons to Syria.

By this point, Moscow had only limited influence in Syria, which had been refusing to negotiate with the Yeltsin government about its substantial debt (more than $10 billion) to the USSR. During an April 1994 visit to Damascus, Deputy Prime Minister Oleg Soskovets opened conversations on debt repayment, while agreeing to resume deliveries of spare parts for Soviet-made weapons. A follow-up visit by Kozyrev in October produced a Syrian agreement on a repayment schedule stretching to 2015. This cleared the way for better relations between Syria and Russia, which still had a Mediterranean naval base in Syria, as well as about 2,000 military and civilian specialists working in the country.

The higher Russian profile in the Middle East occasioned an approving article in the Russian press by Karen Brutents, a veteran academic specialist on the area. Whereas Soviet influence in the Middle East during the Brezhnev period had been comparable to that of Washington, and the Arabs had been Moscow's main economic partners in the Third World, he argued, the early Yeltsin policy had curtailed political ties, wanting to destroy everything "sinful" that had been built up over the years. A legacy had thereby been wasted, and Russia had been relegated to a purely ceremonial role in the peace process. Even though the rise of independent states in the Caucasus had pushed Russia farther away geographically, "in some respects, Russian security is now even more closely connected with the Middle East than it was before," and tremors there could have serious repercussions in the near abroad. The Arab countries remained a promising market for Russia, with possible benefits to stem from coordination of petroleum-exporting policies. Finally, Brutents argued, changes for the better were being seen in Russian policy, with Arafat's visit to Moscow and Kozyrev's trips to the Middle East. The key, he maintained, was pursuing an independent policy that was based on a clear understanding of the importance to Russia of good relations with the Arab world.[73]

By the beginning of 1996, the stage was set for a major effort by Primakov, newly appointed foreign minister, to bring Moscow's diplomacy back to the forefront of the Arab-Israeli relationship. The opportunity came in April, when Israel launched Operation Grapes of Wrath in response to shelling of northern Israeli settlements by Hezbollah guerrillas in southern Lebanon. Primakov traveled to Israel, Lebanon, and Syria, offering himself as mediator in the conflict, and hinting that Russia would be able to exert influence over forces in both Syria and Iran that could assist in normalizing the situation in Lebanon. His meeting with Prime Minister Peres was described as "difficult," and Peres reportedly told him that Israel was interested only in U.S. mediation. A similar message came to Primakov from Washington, in a telephone call from Secretary of State Warren Christopher, who said, "We can handle this without you."[74] The Russian foreign ministry staff bitterly complained to journalists that U.S. "egoism"—a desire to keep a monopoly on diplomatic activity in the area—was the main reason Russia was even being excluded from the international group formed to monitor implementation of the cease-fire in southern Lebanon. One commentator noted that Russia's increasing efforts to develop ties with Iraq, Iran, and Libya probably contributed to the wariness of the United States, though he found an even more basic reason Russia was being left on the sidelines: "Moscow's basic problem is that, unlike the Americans and the West Europeans, it is unable to provide any material backup for its claims to a special role in the region, which is accustomed to massive financial infusions."[75]

Primakov's chief deputy for the Middle East gave a candid interview in which he expressed the foreign minister's frustration with Washington. According to Viktor Posuvaliuk, Russia was proceeding from the premise that the Madrid process needed to be given fresh impetus, and the best way to do this was to assure "a more energetic role for Moscow." However, he told his interviewer, "You are right when you say that an attempt is being made to prevent Russia from taking an active role in the Middle East." Russia's general line was to strengthen ties with all states in the region; paradoxically, Moscow was being accused on the one hand of associating mainly with countries such as Libya, Iraq, or Sudan, but then hindered when it tried to broaden its ties, especially through the sale of arms. In the next five years, he asserted, the countries of the region intended to buy arms worth up to $80 billion. If Russia did not sell to them, then some other country would: "So our task is to find our own niche in these plans."[76]

Primakov did not let his initial disappointment discourage continued efforts in the region. In October 1996 he embarked on another trip to the Middle East, visiting Syria, Lebanon, Jordan, Israel, and the Palestinian Authority. Recognizing that the Arab world's ardor toward Moscow had cooled, partly because its valve of financial and military support had been shut down, partly because of Russia's war in Muslim Chechnya and its support of Bosnian Serbs, but also because Kozyrev had given far more attention to Israel than to its neighbors, Primakov nonetheless persisted in trying to revive former friendships in the Arab world. By the time Arafat came to Moscow in February 1997, on his first visit as elected president of the Palestinian Authority, Primakov had specific suggestions which—in one journalist's words—"left no doubt that Russia's diplomatic train, which had sat on a siding of the Mideast railway for many years, is back on track." These ideas centered on arranging an expanded conference on a comprehensive settlement; the meeting would be held in Moscow and attended by all Middle Eastern countries. In a joint statement with Arafat, Russia declared that Palestinian aspirations to achieve self-determination did not harm Israel's legitimate interests, that the problem of the West Bank settlements must be resolved, and that the outcome of talks on Jerusalem must not infringe on the rights of any religious faith. As this journalist concluded, "The logic of events allows one to assume that in general Moscow will henceforth speak with a more pronounced Arab accent in talks on the subject of a Mideast settlement: Disillusioned with the West's NATO-related ambitions, it will try to charm the Muslim world again."[77]

There is little doubt that Moscow's Arab accent was being heard in Israel as well. In April 1996 the Russian government had revoked the registration of the Jewish Agency in Moscow, which was heavily involved in arranging the emigration of Russian Jews to Israel. Government spokesmen claimed that the agency had violated Russian laws by circumventing visa procedures, but there were widespread complaints in the press about its active inducements toward emigration, especially of talented young people. In a June interview, Posuvaliuk had strongly implied that reregistration would be possible, but he had also stated, with respect to the bilateral relationship, "The 'honeymoon' in our relations with Israel is over, and now they have entered a time of maturity." This was even more evident the following March, when Prime Minister Benjamin Netanyahu visited Moscow. Although he declared that Israel now considered Russia to be a "friendly state," and announced a $50 million loan for Russian agricultural development, there were evidently serious disagreements between him and his Russian hosts, especially about Moscow's arms sales to Syria and Iran. Primakov assured Netanyahu that Russia was not supplying missiles to Iran, and Yeltsin apparently promised him that Moscow would not sell state-of-the-art weapons to Syria.[78] But once again, Russia's active pursuit of opportunities in the weapons market was being regarded as a major obstacle to its acceptance as a responsible partner by all sides in the regional conflict.

Netanyahu reportedly had told the Russians that "there shouldn't be two chefs in the same kitchen"—in other words, that their help was not needed in efforts to settle the Arab-Israeli conflict—but Egypt's president Hosni Mubarak, visiting Moscow a few months later, clearly was encouraging a greater Russian role in the region. Noting with regret the absence of regular high-level visits during the past decade and the 50 percent drop in Russian-Egyptian trade (to an annual level of only $400 million), Mubarak and Yeltsin agreed to set up a bilateral commission to promote trade and economic cooperation.

The following month, following a New York meeting with Secretary of State Madeleine Albright to coordinate U.S. and Russian efforts, Primakov returned to the Middle East for his third tour in less than two years. Visiting Egypt, Jordan, Syria, Lebanon, Israel, and the Palestinian Authority, the Russian foreign minister was well received, but he made no apparent progress in putting the peace process back on track. Not until the election of Ehud Barak as Israeli prime minister in 1999 did prospects for peace talks brighten. Even Syria's president Hafez al Assad signaled his interest in talks during a trip to Moscow in July 1999—his first visit since the end of the Cold War—but Assad may have been primarily interested in purchasing Russian arms to modernize his army, 90 percent of whose equipment was Soviet-made. However, the issue of the unpaid debt—rather than U.S. objections—appeared to be the main stumbling block to a deal. Upon his death the following year, Hafez al Assad was succeeded by his son, Bashar. After the new regime had taken time to settle in, Syria's vice president paid a visit to Moscow in January 2003, again raising the question of arms sales. No agreements were reached, but the Russian press reported that Bashar al Assad was expected to visit Moscow later in 2003. Neither the visit nor the long-anticipated breakthrough on the debt issues or arms sales took place, however. It is probable that the war in Iraq and the attendant emphasis placed by the United States on Syria's weapons programs served to deter further high-level diplomacy of this sort.

The Russian approach to the Israeli-Palestinian conflict during Putin's presidency was decidedly more even-handed than it had been in prior times, as illustrated by Russia's counseling Arafat against a unilateral declaration of Palestinian statehood. Perhaps Moscow's attitude toward the revived *intifada* (uprising) was affected by the realization that one out of four of Israel's citizens was now an ethnic Russian, and that some of the same radical elements spurring conflict in that region were also supporting the rebel forces in Chechnya. Nevertheless, Russia again stood on the sidelines as U.S. president Bill Clinton took the lead in attempting to mediate a solution to the conflict between Israel and the Palestinians. Barak visited Moscow, but the Israelis appeared to be hesitant to concede a larger role to Russia in the face of its warmer relations with Iran. Nevertheless, after the failure of the Camp David talks in the summer of 2000, Moscow again tried to revive its role, only to be humiliated when it failed to get an invitation to an October conference at Sharm el Sheik, where Barak, Arafat, Mubarak, and King Abdullah of Jordan met with President Clinton, UN Secretary-General Kofi Annan, and the European Union's Javier Solana. The conference closed without any visible accomplishment, however, and the subsequent defeat of Barak by Ariel Sharon in the February 2001 elections seemed again to close the door on the chances for a settlement of the conflict.

Sharon and his foreign minister Benjamin Netanyahu were regular visitors to Russia over the next few years, and the statements made by both sides underscored the growing warmth of the relationship, despite disagreements over Russia's aid to Iran. Putin told Sharon in October 2002 that "Russia will never help Israel's enemies."[79] On his visit the following year, Sharon called Putin "a true friend of Israel" and declared that Russia was "one of the key players in the world arena."[80] Russia did not agree with Sharon's policy of isolating Arafat, and Ivanov met with the Palestinian leader at his Ramallah compound in the summer of 2003. Nevertheless, the message the Palestinians were receiving from Moscow about their tolerance of terrorism was sterner than in prior years. Ivanov even reportedly lectured his Palestinian counterpart about his longstanding habit of ending his meetings with declarations that the positions of the two sides coincided completely, and—in a gesture that demonstrated how far Moscow had traveled in its positions since Soviet times—he asked the Palestinian side not to use its contacts with Moscow "for propaganda purposes."[81]

Russian Policy in South Asia

In the hands of Leonid Brezhnev and his immediate successors, the policy of the Soviet Union in South Asia was a function of three conflicts: Moscow's bitter rivalries with Beijing and with Washington, and (after 1979) the Soviet war in Afghanistan. When Mikhail Gorbachev succeeded in 1989 in withdrawing Soviet forces from Afghanistan and achieving a rapprochement with China, and when the Cold War ended in the following year, the Soviet approach to the region changed markedly. The breakup of the USSR increased the geopolitical distance between Moscow and South Asia, just as Yeltsin's and Kozyrev's initial orientation toward the United States and Europe effectively expanded the psychological distance; but, as we have seen, a combination of domestic political pressures and instability in the near abroad—especially in the Muslim-majority states of the Caucasus and Central Asia—heightened Russia's attention to the neighboring Asian states.

In Afghanistan, the communist regime of Najibullah had survived the withdrawal of Soviet troops, largely because of the disunity of the opposition mujahideen forces. Upon assuming control in the Kremlin, Yeltsin cut off military aid and raw material supplies to Najibullah, contributing to the collapse of the Afghan communist government in April 1992. Kozyrev visited Kabul the following month and joined in a statement condemning the imperialistic policy that the USSR had conducted in Afghanistan. The new government in Kabul acknowledged that Moscow's political orientation had changed, but nevertheless asked for reparations from Russia to help in the rebuilding of the devastated country. In no position to comply, Kozyrev did offer to supply spare parts for the Soviet-made weapons found in great abundance in Afghanistan.

Repressive policies by the new regime against members of the former government created a stream of refugees from Afghanistan to Russia, estimated by the late summer to number as many as 15,000. With conflict continuing in the capital, the Russian Embassy was closed and sealed, and embassy personnel were evacuated. When civil war broke out in Tajikistan— the population of which is ethnically similar to a large part of the Afghan population, and which shares a six-hundred-mile border with Afghanistan— Afghan territory became a base for pro-Islamic forces opposing the government of Tajikistan, which was dominated by former communists. Fearing a "domino effect" in Central Asia and parts of the Russian Federation if Tajikistan fell to Muslim extremists, Russia increased its military involvement in the region. By early 1993, an estimated 65,000 Tajiks were in camps in Afghanistan, and many were being actively recruited to guerrilla warfare training centers. Frequent border violations prompted a formal protest from the Tajik foreign ministry, and Russia—whose troops were patrolling the Tajik-Afghan border—was no less alarmed. As one Russian journalist wrote: "[That border] remains Russia's external border. There is no other border, I was told at the Russian Federation Ministry of Security. Events there have a direct bearing on Russian interests."[82]

Border incidents mounted in the summer of 1993, with heavy casualties suffered by Russian troops. When Yeltsin's chief domestic rival, parliament speaker Ruslan Khasbulatov, made direct overtures toward a settlement with the Afghan government—demonstrating again the fractured nature of Russian foreign policy making—the Russian foreign ministry demanded that he break off contact. Meanwhile, the defense ministry was publicly urging that Russian border troops be reinforced, but the government was understandably concerned about public fears of renewed war with Afghanistan. Kozyrev lodged an official protest with Kabul and threatened rocket attacks against rebel bases in the country, and Yeltsin dispatched foreign intelligence director Evgenii Primakov to Kabul and Teheran to seek a resolution to the conflict. In September, Kozyrev himself visited Kabul, where it was announced that Russia and Afghanistan had agreed on the process for talks and eventual elections in Tajikistan.

Although tensions persisted, the immediate crisis on the Tajikistan-Afghanistan border subsided—until alarms were again sounded three years later by the victory of the militant Islamic Taliban faction in Afghanistan. Supported by Pakistan—and initially, at least covertly, by the United States—the Taliban opposition forces burst onto the international scene in the summer and fall of 1996, sweeping through Afghanistan, capturing its capital, and routing the more moderate Gulbuddin Hekmatyar government. One of the Taliban's first actions was to execute the former communist president, Najibullah. Frightened by the prospect that its crusading pan-Islamic zeal would propel the Taliban northward, and ultimately across the Tajikistan and Uzbekistan borders, the leaders of the Commonwealth of Independent States held an emergency meeting at the beginning of October to discuss possible measures for collective defense.

An article published in the Russian press in September by Evgenii Primakov—by then foreign minister, but identified in his capacity as a member of the Russian Academy of Sciences—underscored the particular threat that Russia saw in the Taliban's form of Islam. Noting that "Islamic fundamentalism" was on the rise—even among the 17 million Muslims of the Russian Federation—Primakov distinguished between this movement and "Islamic extremism" of the type exhibited in Afghanistan by the Taliban, which threatened to spill over into Tajikistan.

And not into Tajikistan alone. Many people believed, not without reason, that after Tajikistan such a wave could sweep other Central Asian states as well—an event that would undoubtedly have had an extremely negative impact both on Russia's security and on the prospects for the development of the CIS. Russia does not oppose Islam as a religion; rather, Primakov stressed, it seeks, along with many other states, including Islamic ones, to erect a barrier to Islamic extremism.[83]

Wearing his diplomatic hat, Primakov sent messages to the foreign offices of the United States, Britain, Germany, Italy, and other states, calling for joint action to encourage a political settlement in Afghanistan. Primakov made it clear that Moscow was supporting no specific party in the intra-Afghan conflict, although it had no particular liking for the leaders of the Taliban after their brutal execution of Najibullah. Outside mediation efforts never got off the ground, however, and by May 1997, the Taliban was on the verge of capturing all of Afghanistan. For Pakistan and for oil interests in the United States, the prospect of a unified country spurred talk of a possible gas pipeline to be built from the rich fields of Turkmenistan through Afghanistan and Pakistan to the Indian Ocean. For Russia, this prospect posed not simply the economic threat of competition for the existing pipeline route through Russia, but the more immediate fears of Taliban incursions into Tajik or Uzbek territory. With Afghan refugees streaming into Tajikistan, the Russian government issued a stern warning to the Taliban: "The Russian leadership hereby gives notice that if the borders of Commonwealth countries are violated, the mechanisms of the Treaty on Collective Security of the CIS Member States will be activated immediately. Instructions have been issued to the relevant departments."[84]

The Taliban overreached in the north, alienating local leaders with their harsh policies and suffering military defeats that pushed them back almost to the gates of Kabul by late July 1997. Although the Taliban were still in control of the twenty or so Pashtun-majority provinces, a coalition of other factions dominated the nine provinces inhabited mainly by Tajiks, Uzbeks, and Hazaras. These groups—later dubbed the "Northern Alliance"—were supported by Russia, the Central Asian states, Iran, and India—all united in fear of the Islamic extremism of which Primakov had warned. With no signs of an imminent compromise, however, the fighting continued in this unfortunate country, which had already lost 1.5 million people in more than two decades of war.[85]

By mid-2000, the Taliban had again gained control of virtually the entire country and was increasing its raids into Tajikistan. To the threat of an expansion of Islamic extremism into the former Soviet states of Central Asia the Russians now added their alarm over evidence that the Taliban was assisting some of the "terrorist gangs" active in the renewed war in Chechnya. In April, Security Councsecretary Sergei Ivanov refused to rule out the option of preemptive strikes against "terrorist bases" in Afghanistan, and in July, at the G-8 meetings, President Putin informed his colleagues that "the main hot spot is more and more moving to Afghanistan." Russia assembled the adherents of the Collective Security Treaty of the CIS in Bishkek (capital of Kyrgyzstan) in October to condemn the growing threat from the Taliban. However, a contrary view was voiced by Uzbekistan's representatives, who were said to be suspicious that the threat was being exaggerated by Moscow as a justification for increasing its military presence in the region.[86] A determination to curb the Taliban's support for terrorism and to force it to expel the operations of Osama bin Laden was one goal that found Russia and the United States in accord during this period of troubled relations. In December the two states persuaded the UN Security Council to impose stronger sanctions against Afghanistan. The assassination on September 9, 2001, of Ahmed Shah Massoud, the charismatic leader of the Northern Alliance, appeared to be a serious setback to the anti-Taliban cause. But the terrorist attacks launched two days later against the United States by bin Laden's operatives, and the subsequent refusal of the Taliban to cease its protection of al Qaeda, unleashed the military might of the world's only remaining superpower in the region for the first time. Russia gave important support to the American military strike against the terrorists and their Taliban supporters. We discuss the nature of this support and its consequences in the following chapter.

During the 1980s, the Soviet Union's military involvement in Afghanistan had influenced Moscow's relationships in the decades-long conflict between India and Pakistan. The latter country served as the main base for the Afghan opposition forces, as well as the conduit for American and Chinese aid to the mujahideen, and Pakistan's relations with the USSR during the long war were extremely tense. In the period after the Soviet withdrawal, Pakistan's aid to the Taliban was not particularly motivated by ideological affinity; rather, it was part of its effort to turn Afghanistan into a strategic reserve in its conflict with India, as well as to gain leverage over militant Islamic forces that were conducting struggles in Central Asia and the Caucasus.[87]

As for India, although it had been uncomfortable with the intrusion of superpower military force into the internal struggles of a Third World neighbor, it was sufficiently nervous about the threat of Islamic extremism to keep its concerns muted, especially in light of its unwillingness to jeopardize Soviet support in its conflicts with Pakistan and China. However, the rise of militant Islamic forces in the wake of the Soviet withdrawal placed at risk India's long-term interest in countering Pakistan's strategic ambitions by keeping a more moderate government in power in Kabul.

Nevertheless, it was the Sino-Soviet rapprochement and the end of the Cold War, more than Soviet withdrawal from Afghanistan, that appeared to have the greatest direct impact on Moscow's relations on the subcontinent in the 1990s. Absent the ideological and geopolitical struggles with Beijing and Washington, Moscow's security interests in India were considerably diminished. From the standpoint of trade relations as well, it seemed likely that decline was in prospect. The longstanding problem of a lack of complementarity in their respective economies was exacerbated by a mutual shortage of hard currency and a newly competitive relationship in world capital markets. Even the product that had long been Moscow's chief export to India—weaponry—seemed less appealing to military purchasers in New Delhi after the shortcomings of Soviet-made arms and Soviet war-fighting doctrine had been revealed in the Persian Gulf war.

India had become accustomed to receiving more attention from the Kremlin than any other nonaligned country; it was the only Third World country Brezhnev had ever visited as general secretary (and he went twice), and it also received Gorbachev twice, in 1986 and 1988. Thus the falloff in attentiveness in Gorbachev's last years in office, which continued in Yeltsin's first year and which resulted from Moscow's changing perceptions of its security and economic needs, was acutely felt and perceived as neglect by New Delhi. The major topic of difficult discussions between the two governments in 1992 concerned the financial exchange rates to be used in settling their current trade transactions, and the prospects for repayment of India's $6 billion debt to Russia. The two sides worked out a trade protocol that called for trade volume to be maintained at the 1991 level of $2.2 billion, with India providing tea, coffee, spices, medicines, and raw materials for consumer goods production, and Russia providing oil, metals, copper, newsprint, and arms. India did not have hard currency reserves sufficient to pay in convertible currency, but the credits Russia granted for arms sales were on tougher terms than in the prior period.

The single most troublesome transaction in this period had actually been concluded at the beginning of 1991, when the CPSU Central Committee, against the advice of the Soviet foreign ministry, had approved a deal between the Soviet space agency, Glavkosmos, and the Indian Space Research Organization, for the sale of critical rocket technology. India claimed that it needed the cryogenic engines to launch commercial satellites, but the United States charged that the sale of the engines and the technological information for their manufacture would enable India to assemble ballistic missiles, possession of which would alter the regional military balance. When India was assured by Gennadii Burbulis in May 1992 that the Russian government would honor the $250 million deal, the United States angered both countries by threatening to apply sanctions against them.

President Yeltsin's trip to India in January 1993—said to be characterized by an "extremely warm and cordial atmosphere"—halted the downward slide in relations that had begun in 1990, and among the many reasons it pleased his hosts was his reconfirmation that the rocket deal would go through. A breakthrough was achieved in settling the issue of India's debt; Russia agreed to an exchange rate that automatically subtracted two-thirds of the debt, and the remainder was to be repaid over a period of forty-five years. Russia welcomed a recent thaw in India's relations with China, and India did not object to a replacement of the 1971 Indo-Soviet treaty with a new bilateral treaty lacking security clauses.

Russia's continuing sharp disagreement with the United States over the rocket technology sale reportedly led to cancellation of Chernomyrdin's planned visit to Washington in June 1993. The following month, at the G-7 meeting in Tokyo, Presidents Clinton and Yeltsin worked out a compromise that allowed Russia and India to save face without endangering the South

Asian nuclear balance, while also helping to keep 15,000 Glavkosmos workers employed. Essentially, it provided for Russia to deliver a number of cryogenic booster units and model units for training, but not the technology. India would pledge to use the equipment for peaceful purposes only and not to reexport it.[88]

A few years later, however, the controversy between the United States and Russia over Russian aid to the Indian nuclear program seemed likely to be replayed. Early in 1997 it was revealed that Russia planned to sell two light-water reactors—valued at $1.5 to $2 billion each—for power plants in southern India. Washington protested that the deal would violate a 1992 agreement among nuclear suppliers, which stipulated that nuclear technology could not be sold to nations that are not formally recognized as nuclear weapons states and that do not allow international inspection of all their nuclear facilities. The Russians claimed that the agreement did not apply, since talks about the sale were initiated in 1987. Privately, they argued that the revenues were desperately needed by the atomic energy ministry in order to meet its budget needs.[89]

Indo-Russian trade, despite the ambitious targets that had been set, actually fell to a record low level in 1992, and though it increased more than 40 percent the following year, it still amounted to barely $1 billion. An exchange of visits by the two prime ministers in 1994 produced a series of agreements that sought to revive the commercial relationship, which by then had refocused on the familiar Russian export: armaments. Although India had shopped in the West, and although—as we noted earlier in this chapter—it was not entirely satisfied with the quality of Russian arms, its lack of hard currency limited its options for modernizing its fleet of military aircraft, and the Russians proved willing to accept flexible payment arrangements. Moscow agreed in 1994 to cooperate in building a plant in India that would produce an upgraded version of the MiG-29 fighter. In 1996 India agreed to buy forty of the more advanced SU-30 fighters for $1.8 billion, and the Russians agreed to open talks on licensing its production in India. The SU-30 would replace India's aging British Jaguars as the air force's main strike element through 2015, and would counter Pakistan's squadrons of U.S.-made F-16s and French Mirage 2000s.[90]

By the time of Prime Minister Deve Gowda's visit in March 1997, it was announced that India had purchased $3 billion in arms from Russia in the past two years, and that the two sides were discussing potential contracts of another $7 billion—a level that would move India ahead of China in the ranks of Moscow's arms customers. Tensions between India and Pakistan were on the rise, and the appetite for arms on the subcontinent was enormous. Included on India's shopping list were Russian MiG-31 interceptors and MiG-AT jet trainers, rocket-firing T-72S tanks, "Msta" self-propelled howitzers, Smerch truck-mounted multilaunch rocket systems, Ka-52 "Alligator" helicopter gunships, Kilo-class attack submarines, and antisubmarine frigates. During the visit India agreed in principle to purchase six S-300V air defense systems, and agreement appeared to be close on the sale of the *Admiral Gorshkov,* an aircraft-carrying cruiser. However, Yeltsin was unable to deliver on his promise to Gowda to block the sale to Ukraine of key components for the Soviet-designed T-80UD tanks, 320 of which Pakistan had agreed to purchase from Ukraine.[91] Beyond the commercial attraction, the continued Russian ties to India represented a long-term hedge against a possible downturn in the Sino-Russian relationship. As the Russian ambassador to India put it—perhaps too optimistically—"If we are able to maintain close, friendly ties with India, that will be the best guarantee that China will make no territorial claims on our Far East."[92]

Under Primakov's direction, Russia's emphasis shifted. Rather than seeing India as a possible counterweight to China—the long-held Soviet approach—Primakov began to speak of an alignment joining Moscow, Beijing, and New Delhi as a new "pole" to balance the would-be unipolar power, the United States. In New Delhi in December 1998 as Russian prime minister—and clearly disturbed by the latest U.S.-U.K. bombing campaign against Iraq—he answered affirmatively to a reporter's question as to whether a "new pole in world politics" would be desirable. The Indians were silent on the subject, no doubt aware not only that the project would increase tensions with Washington but also that it was rather unrealistic in the face of the longstanding rivalry between themselves and China. This latter consideration faded somewhat in the opening days of 2001, as a result of a lengthy and apparently cordial visit to India by China's third-ranking leader, Li Peng.

The continuing edginess of the Sino-Indian relationship is not the only factor that has clouded the realization of Primakov's vision of a "strategic triangle." Just as important is the growing warmth in relations between India and the state against which the "triangle" was to have been aimed: the United States. The low point of their relationship had come in 1972, when the United States moved naval forces into the Bay of Bengal in apparent coordination with China and Pakistan during the 1972 Indo-Pakistani war. India's "peaceful nuclear explosion" of 1974 raised nonproliferation concerns to a high level on Washington's radar, and the 1998 nuclear tests brought U.S. economic sanctions down on both India and Pakistan. But Washington had already diminished its security relationship with Pakistan following the Soviet withdrawal from Afghanistan, and India clearly appreciated President Clinton's willingness to pressure Pakistan to back down during the 1999 Indo-Pakistani standoff at Kargil in Kashmir. Several rounds of talks cleared the way for a five-day visit to India by Clinton in 2000 and a return visit to the United States by Prime Minister Vajpayee later that year. In the eyes of one veteran observer, the 1998 nuclear tests had actually "lanced the boil of nonproliferation that previously infected" the Indo-American relationship.[93] In 2001 the Bush administration lifted sanctions against India, and India—delighted that Washington included two Kashmiri organizations on its terrorist list—became an enthusiastic member of the U.S.-sponsored coalition against Islamic extremist terrorism.

India disappointed both Moscow and Beijing by its relatively positive response to Bush's decision to build a national missile defense (which New Delhi correctly gauged to be aimed as much at China's growing arsenal as at any putative missile threat from a "rogue" regime). Finally, the expansion of trade ties between the United States and India since the lifting of sanctions has even extended to the arena of military sales. Much to the distress of Russia,[94] India and the United States have discussed the possible sale of P3 naval surveillance aircraft, sophisticated counterbattery radars, and General Electric engines for India's light combat aircraft. In an unusual three-way deal, the United States also gave Israel permission to include U.S. technology in the Phalcon airborne radar systems that were to be mounted on surveillance planes built under Russian licenses.[95]

In the meantime, Russia under Vladimir Putin continued to develop closer ties with India in parallel with its growing harmonization with China. During Putin's first visit to India, in October 2000, the two sides signed a declaration of "strategic partnership" that had been prepared for the 1998 visit that Boris Yeltsin had canceled. The essence of the partnership continued to be weaponry. About 70 percent of India's arms were of Soviet origin, and the Russians were eager to conclude several major sales. India apparently took advantage of this eagerness to seek further price reductions on the very eve of the signing of the contracts. The largest of these was the sale (for more than $3 billion) of a license allowing India to produce the basic components of 140 SU-30 MKI fighters over a seventeen-year period. The plane, developed by the manufacturer specifically for India's needs, would continue to have about 60 percent of its parts supplied by Russia.[96] Second in size was a contract for India to purchase 310 T-90C main battle tanks. Initially the Russians wanted the tanks to be fully assembled at the factory in Uralvagon Zavod, but India won the right to assemble the parts in its own factory at Avadi.[97] In both cases, India sought and won major price concessions—a sign of how desperately Moscow needed the orders to keep its defense industry alive. Indeed, one Russian journalist, impressed with the number of concessions that Russia was making, concluded that "India is becoming not just an equal partner, but in many ways the senior partner in the bilateral relationship."[98]

Putin's second visit to New Delhi, in December 2002, focused on consolidating the "strategic partnership" and established a joint working group on counterterrorism. Putin's visit followed a year of heightened Indian concern about Pakistani sponsorship of terrorist groups, which had struck both in Kashmir and at the very heart of New Delhi itself. Accordingly, the Indians placed special significance on the joint declaration that "states that abet terrorists or give them haven are guilty of committing terrorist acts to the same degree as the terrorists themselves."

The following spring and summer the two states conducted their first joint exercises in the Arabian Sea in a decade. The Russians delivered the first of three Krivak-III class stealth frigates to India. Designed for antisubmarine warfare and air defense, the frigates are equipped with surface-to-air missiles and cruise missiles and are designed to carry heavy-duty helicopters.

By the beginning of 2004, when Defense Minister Sergei Ivanov traveled to New Delhi, India was accounting for nearly 60 percent of Russia's military exports. Since 1960 it had signed contracts worth $33 billion, including $3.5 billion of weapons currently contracted. This accounted for three-fourths of India's arsenals: 60 percent of the army's weapons, 70 percent of the navy's, and 80 percent of the air force's fleet. Nevertheless, the Russian-Indian arms trade was not without difficulties. The deal on the frigates, signed in 1997, had been marred by controversy; India had dispatched a crew to Russia to train on the first frigate, only to have to withdraw it because the SAM system was not working properly. During his visit Ivanov signed agreements for the delivery (in 2008) of the cruiser *Admiral Gorshkov,* but this $1.5 billion deal had already been in the works for more than ten years. Ivanov confirmed that future arrangements would depart from the buyer-seller pattern of the past and move further toward joint research and development and joint production of weapons. He pointed to the joint project to build the Brahmos antiship cruise missile, as well as existing joint production of tanks and aircraft, as examples. Press accounts acknowledged, however, that India seemed determined to diversify its sources of weaponry.[99]

While Pakistan's importance to Russia has remained relatively high because of Moscow's concerns about the stability of Aghanistan and the states of Central Asia, an exchange of visits by the two countries' foreign ministers in 1993 and 1994, aimed at normalizing relations and increasing trade, bore little fruit. Reports that Pakistan's prime minister would visit Moscow in 1994 proved premature, as the visit fell victim to Russia's renewed "tilt" toward India. Pakistan was not without alternatives, however, and it went shopping for arms in Ukraine while seeking to build its relations with the Muslim states of Central Asia. An October 1996 visit by the Pakistani president to Kazakhstan gained an endorsement from President Nursultan

Nazarbaev for the idea of holding a referendum on the status of Kashmir. To Moscow's evident displeasure, the Pakistani official was also reported to be discussing with the Central Asian states the proposed Afghan-Pakistan pipeline as an alternative to the existing Russian pipeline.

Elections in Pakistan early in 1997 produced a new government, which adopted a less confrontational policy toward Russia. The country's foreign minister visited Moscow in July 1997 for wide-ranging talks, which produced press reports of closer relations. Pakistan invited Russia's assistance in bringing about a resolution of the Kashmir dispute, while Primakov advised his Pakistani counterpart that his country should avoid the Soviet Union's mistake of getting too deeply involved in the Afghan quagmire.[100]

Upon his appointment as foreign minister in January 1996, Primakov had listed nonproliferation of weapons of mass destruction among Russia's priority interests. Nevertheless, Moscow has not been in the forefront of international efforts to this end, and Washington has publicly accused it of assisting both Indian and Iranian nuclear programs. Thus, it was not especially surprising when the Russians failed to heed the U.S. call for G-8 sanctions against India and Pakistan when those countries tested nuclear weapons in May 1998. The Russians expressed regret, and Yeltsin—acknowledging that the Indian explosion had "put us on the spot"—promised to "make every effort to somehow overcome the problem" during his scheduled visit to "our very good friend" India, later in 1998. Although Moscow must have shared the global concern about the heightened risk of nuclear war, it evidently saw no benefit in alienating India in the face of an irreversible reality.

In June 1998, Primakov—reiterating the Russian view that sanctions would only isolate the two newly nuclear states—unveiled a three-point plan for easing relations between India and Pakistan:

1. Putting greater pressure on both to sign the Non proliferation Treaty;
2. Taking steps to persuade India and Pakistan to accede to the Comprehensive Test Ban Treaty;
3. Making an effort to defuse the tensions in the relationship.[101]

Russian efforts failed to produce any evident results, however. Pakistan's prime minister Nawaz Sharif journeyed to Moscow in April 1999—the first visit by a Pakistani leader since 1974—but the atmosphere was soured by Russia's concern over Pakistan's support of the Taliban. After Sharif's ouster in a military coup, Putin's special envoy Sergei Yastrzhembskii was sent to Islamabad late in 2000 to explore prospects for a Kashmir settlement, but he returned empty-handed. By the time Putin visited India in October 2000, the Russians had apparently abandoned the idea of offering a hand in settling the issue. The Russian president altogether rejected the idea of international mediation on Kashmir, declaring that the two sides should resolve the dispute on a strictly bilateral basis.

A further complication in Russo-Pakistani relations was the renewed conflict in Chechnya, amidst rising evidence of the involvement of foreign Islamic extremist forces, clearly supported by the Taliban and al Qaeda, and thus also presumed to have the blessing of Pakistan. Although Chechen president Aslan Maskhadov had been denied entry to Pakistan in 1998, in December 1999 his aide Zelimkhan Yandarbiev was allowed into the country, where he proceeded to raise money for the rebel cause. Moscow treated the visit as "an unfriendly gesture" and a "hostile act"; Islamabad responded by terming the accusations a "gross interference" in its domestic affairs.[102] Pakistan's stance on Chechnya undoubtedly contributed to Russia's unwillingness to facilitate any dialogue with India over Kashmir.

After the events of September 11 changed the strategic calculus both globally and in South Asia, Russia joined with the United States and China to press more urgently for a settlement in Kashmir. Indeed, India and Pakistan came close to full-scale war in the year following the al Qaeda attack on the United States. Borrowing Washington's reasoning, India claimed a right to carry the fight against terrorists into the states that supported them. The Russians —seeing a parallel in their own conflict in Chechnya—showed considerable sympathy for the Indian position. Foreign Minister Igor Ivanov declared in New Delhi that there should be no "double standards" in the fight against terrorism.[103] Nevertheless, Presidents Bush and Putin cooperated in efforts to restrain the Indians, and Bush pushed hard to gain key concessions from Pakistani president Pervez Musharraf. In June, Putin—at the behest of the G-8—sought without evident success to bring Vajpayee and Musharraf together at a meeting they all attended in Kazakhstan. The Russian press proudly noted that this was the first occasion in the long South Asian conflict on which Moscow was speaking "on behalf of all the world's leading countries."[104]

Musharraf's evident willingness to cooperate with the antiterrorist coalition paved the way for his three-day visit to Moscow in February 2003. The results of the trip were said to be "modest": three relatively insignificant agreements on internal security, cultural exchanges, and diplomatic cooperation. Pakistan had hoped to conclude an agreement to participate in a joint gas pipeline with Russia, Iran, and India, but no such pact was signed. Putin was at pains to reassure India about the talks, calling Vajpayee prior to Musharraf's arrival and issuing a statement saying that development of constructive relations with Pakistan would take place "without damage to our traditional partners." Musharraf stressed that he was not asking Russia to mediate the Kashmir dispute. He did, however, offer assurance to the Russians that Pakistani territory would not be used to support terrorist activity, notably adding that Chechnya was a Russian domestic problem.[105] The one surprise was Musharraf's public expression of a desire for Pakistan to join the Shanghai Cooperation Organization. The previous year, the Russians had reacted positively to the prospect of Indian membership in the group, but they refrained from any clear reaction to Pakistan's expression of interest.[106]

Over the past half-century, the one constant hostile relationship in South Asia has been the conflict between India and Pakistan, and the one constant friendship has been that between Moscow and New Delhi. As a consequence, Moscow has been—and probably will continue to be—unable to forge a new, friendlier relationship with Pakistan until the conflict between India and Pakistan is essentially resolved. With all the other states that are involved in the region, Russia enjoys positive relations. As one journalist has stated it, Russia seems to be forging a "triangle of strategic stability, security and suppression of international terrorism with its corners in Moscow, Beijing, and New Delhi."[107] Another, drawing the same conclusion at the end of Putin's 2002 visit to India, declared: "There will be no triple alliance, an idea that likewise remains a relic of a different post-communist but 'pre-September' era. Each country [Russia, India, and China] will be friends with the other, but in pairs"—a combination of three in groups of two.[108]

Beyond the Borders of the CIS: Southeast Asia, Africa, and Latin America

The post–Cold War period witnessed a considerable decline in the level of Moscow's interest and activity in the substantial regions of the "non-West" that are distant from the borders of the former Soviet Union. Facing a greatly reduced threat from the United States and China, and increasingly burdened with the financial costs of trying to maintain its global reach, the USSR under Gorbachev had participated in settling regional conflicts in Southeast Asia, Africa, and Latin America. This had allowed it to cut substantially the level of its involvement in these three regions.

As we noted in chapter 4, Moscow's pressure on Vietnam to withdraw its troops from Cambodia helped to bring about the Sino-Soviet rapprochement, but it also allowed the Soviets to cut back the cost of their presence in Vietnam. Whereas the number of Soviet-Vietnamese summits in the Gorbachev period had averaged two per year prior to his visit to Beijing, there were none in 1990, and there was only one—described in the Russian press as "difficult and complicated"—in 1991. Trade between the two states was moved to a hard currency basis in January 1991, precipitating a fall in Moscow's share of Vietnam's trade from 60 percent in 1990 to 2 percent in 1996. In May 1992 the last Russian military advisors were withdrawn from Vietnam. Vietnam's premier Vo Van Kiet visited Moscow in June 1994 to sign new economic agreements, but the talks did not produce a new "cornerstone" document to replace the 1978 security treaty. Kozyrev journeyed to Hanoi in July 1995 to announce a Russian-Vietnamese agreement to keep the former Soviet naval base at Cam Ranh Bay open through 2004—a decision that was reversed by Putin in October 2001. But little progress was made in settling the issue of Vietnam's $10 billion debt to Russia until 2000. During a visit to Moscow by Vietnam's prime minister, it was announced that 85 percent of the debt had been forgiven by Russia (although part of this cancellation was deemed to be a substitute for Russian rental payments for Cam Ranh Bay). Vietnam agreed to pay the remaining $1.7 billion (later reduced to $1.5 billion) over a twenty-three-year period.

Settlement of the debt issue cleared the way for Putin to visit Vietnam in March 2001—the first official visit ever by a Russian leader. Coming on the heels of a visit by President Clinton the previous autumn, Putin's trip—one. of many he made to Asia in his first year—clearly sought to reassert Moscow's interest in cultivating ties with Vietnam. The two states signed a declaration of "strategic partnership," and discussed Russian participation in oil exploration and electrical power projects. Vietnam's payments on its debt were evidently to be cycled back as Russian investment in such efforts. As for the inevitable discussion of arms sales, it appeared that Vietnam was prepared to pay cash. Although Hanoi accounted for just under 2 percent of Russian arms exports in 2000, it showed interest in purchasing fighter planes, missile attack craft, and air defense systems.

There has been much greater Russian interest in the enormous market potential of the noncommunist countries of Southeast Asia. Russia joined the Pacific Economic Cooperation Council in 1993, and Moscow's representatives attended the annual conferences of the foreign ministers of the Association of Southeast Asian Nations (ASEAN), first as observers and then as official "dialogue partners," as well as the ASEAN forums on regional security. At the 1996 foreign ministers' conference, Primakov described ASEAN as an "influential center of the developing multipolar world" and stated Russia's desire to have open access to the ASEAN free-trade zone scheduled for 2003. But a moratorium that had been placed on new membership in the Asian and Pacific Economic Council (APEC) kept Russia, as a relatively minor trading presence in the region, "on the outside looking in" with respect to the most ambitious of the new regional economic organizations. With Japan's assistance, the Russians finally were admitted to the APEC club late in 1997, and Putin attended the annual APEC summits, though without expectations that Russia's membership would produce "a shower of gold."[109]

When it came to Russia's most competitive product, until recently there was relatively little interest among the ASEAN nations. Until 1997, only Malaysia had concluded a substantial arms deal with Moscow, and this was negotiated with considerable difficulty. A visit from Vice President Aleksandr Rutskoi to Malaysia in March 1993—the first to that country from a Russian leader—underscored Russia's interest in selling MiG-29M fighters. In the ensuing months, arms dealers from several Russian agencies were reported to be practically tripping over one another in Kuala Lumpur, each seeking to be the "lead agency" entitled to a sales commission. In the process, U.S. arms merchants entered the competition, substantially cutting their prices and ultimately dividing the Malaysian order. By the time Deputy Prime Minister Oleg Soskovets concluded the deal in June 1994, it was for only eighteen MiG-29s at a price of $775 million, part of which Russia accepted in palm oil. Nevertheless, the transaction was seen as a breakthrough for Moscow in the lucrative Southeast Asian arms market. Almost ten years later, after Malaysia's recovery from the Asian financial crisis, President Putin was in Malaysia to conclude another arms deal—a $900 million contract for eighteen SU-30 MKM combat aircraft. Again, because of the requirements of Malaysian legislation, one-third of the purchase price was to be paid in palm oil. On this occasion, Malaysia's prime minister Mahathir made a point of referring to Americans as "our former partners," while promising to support Russia's bid for observer status in the Organization of Islamic Countries.[110]

In August 1997 Indonesia—irritated by U.S. criticism of its human rights policies in East Timor—canceled an agreement to purchase F-16 fighters from the United States and signed an agreement with Russia for the purchase of twelve SU-30 warplanes. As talks developed, the deal expanded to include eight Mi-17 helicopters, infantry fighting vehicles, and armored personnel carriers. Originally valued at a half-billion dollars, with payment primarily through barter of palm oil, coffee, and other products, the deal increased to $1 billion, with half to be paid in hard currency. This agreement was canceled in 1998. Together with prospects for further Russian arms sales in Asia, it fell victim to the severe financial crisis that rocked the economies of Indonesia, Malaysia, South Korea, and other prospective customers in 1997. However, Indonesia's recovery brought it back into the arms market; in 2003 Indonesia's president Megawati Sukarnoputri was in Moscow to sign a declaration of "friendly relations and partnership" and to discuss the purchase of four military aircraft and surface-to-air missiles systems.

The civil war in Angola was another conflict in which Gorbachev's consent to a political settlement finally enabled the Soviet Union to extricate itself from a long and costly military involvement. The termination of this conflict, together with the de-escalation of violence in the Horn of Africa, provided an opportunity for Moscow to slash its expensive aid programs in sub-Saharan Africa, from a volume of 12.5 billion rubles in 1989 to 400 million rubles in 1991. To continue making soft loans to countries essentially peripheral to Moscow's interests would be to throw good money after bad, since by the end of 1991 these states already owed 14 billion rubles— 16 percent of the total debt outstanding to the USSR.

Angola alone owed the equivalent of $5 billion—an amount equal to that owed by all the other sub-Saharan African states combined; and like some of the other major debtors to the former Soviet Union, it simply refused to repay the debt to the new Russian government. So the Angolan government informed Foreign Minister Kozyrev, who was visiting the country as part of a five-day tour of Africa in February and March of 1992. There was little the Russians could do about the situation, and in fact they agreed to resume limited shipments of defensive weapons to Angola in 1993, when the civil war resumed. Ten years later there were still about one hundred Russian military advisers in Angola to help with training troops and maintaining costly military hardware.[111]

Kozyrev's trip was intended to demonstrate that Russia was not giving up its global interests, but the facts argued otherwise. In light of the economic difficulties on both ends, there were few trade opportunities; indeed, Africa accounted for only 2 percent of Russia's foreign trade in 1992. Shortly after Kozyrev's trip, the foreign ministry announced that it was closing nine Russian embassies in Africa as an economy measure. Toward the end of the year, four representatives of African ambassadors in Moscow met with acting Russian prime minister Egor Gaidar to express their concern about Russia's apparent lack of interest in the African continent, but there was little that Gaidar could do to reassure them.

South Africa was the one country of sub-Saharan Africa in which the Russian government had initially perceived significant trade and investment possibilities. The primary destination on Kozyrev's 1992 tour was Pretoria, where he participated in ceremonies to establish diplomatic relations with the De Klerk government. President De Klerk paid a state visit to Moscow in June of the same year and announced that South Africa would extend a 100-million-rand credit to Russia. Yeltsin's communist predecessors in the Kremlin had long given support to the African National Congress (ANC), but the change of Moscow's ideological orientation was so dramatic that it was June 1993 before an ANC delegation was even received at the Russian foreign ministry. Thus when ANC leader Nelson Mandela became president of South Africa in May 1994, Moscow found itself in the awkward spot of having to rebuild its relationships with the former revolutionaries who now headed the government. Not surprisingly, the area in which progress was most notable was in the field of "military-technical cooperation." In July 1995, the two governments concluded a military cooperation agreement that called for joint exercises and training, and that provided for Russian aircraft engines to be sold to South Africa for use in its French-made Mirages.

Not until 2001, as Russia hosted another African president—Nigeria's Olusegun Obasanjo, the first high-level visitor from his country since 1974— was there further evidence of a serious interest on Moscow's part in expanding its economic and political ties in Africa. Unlike most other countries on the continent, Nigeria had only a small debt ($50 million) and significant natural resources. Moreover, it had an appetite for arms and an apparent ability to pay for them. Signing the Declaration of Friendly Relations and Partnership, Putin assured his visitor of Russia's interest in "military-technical cooperation," as well in helping to produce and refine Nigerian oil and gas. With a burst of exuberance, one press account declared, "as of yesterday, Nigeria became not only one of Russia's chief partners in Africa, but also a kind of staging area for Russian political and economic expansion on the Africa continent."[112] Even so, Russia's interests and involvement in Africa remained at the lowest level of priority.

Latin America was the other region of low priority for Yeltsin's Russia, and there would have been relatively little activity at all had it not been for the need to look after the very sizable investments Moscow had made over a period of three decades in Cuba. Fidel Castro had enjoyed more success than most other Third World leaders in keeping the Soviet Union involved in his country during the Gorbachev period. Indeed, a friendship treaty between the two countries had been concluded during Gorbachev's April 1989 trip to Havana. Although the treaty made no reference to defense cooperation or to consultations in case of threat, Soviet weapons continued to flow to Cuba.

After August 1991, however, Gorbachev evidently felt that he needed the support of the United States badly enough that—without consulting Castro— he announced that the brigade of Soviet troops that had been stationed in Cuba since 1979 would be withdrawn. Relations between Moscow and Havana deteriorated rapidly on all fronts, especially after the ideological shift in Russia. The level of trade between the two fell in 1992 to 7 percent of the 1991 volume, and Cuba stopped making payments on its debt to Moscow (which was estimated by Russian officials to total $20 billion). Russia made it clear that Cuba would receive no more credits for the purchase of arms, and it demanded that Russian specialists remaining in Cuba be paid in hard currency. Finally, Russia voted in the UN Commission on Human Rights to condemn Cuba for mass violations of human rights. For his part, Castro announced in September 1992 that the nuclear power plant at Juragua, which was being constructed with Soviet assistance at a cost to date of $1.2 billion, would be mothballed. "And so the last beacon of 'fraternal cooperation' in Cuba is being extinguished," wrote a Russian journalist.[113]

However, the shift in Russian policy toward "pragmatic nationalism" soon produced a halt to the deterioration of relations. Moscow evidently decided that it needed to maintain some level of trade relations with Cuba in order to recoup any of its huge debt, and it also was reluctant to lose a key military asset in Cuba—an electronic tracking station and listening post at Lourdes that was capable, among other things, of tracking U.S. missile launches. In November 1992 the two countries concluded an important but limited trade agreement—essentially a bartering of two products—which contemplated the delivery of 1.5 million tons of sugar in return for 3.3 million metric tons of Russian oil and other petroleum products. They also agreed in principle to continue construction of the nuclear plant, contingent on finding a third country to provide financing. Although they failed to resolve the question of the Cuban debt, they did agree that Russia could continue to lease the Lourdes facility. This agreement was supplemented the following summer with a Russian promise of $380 million in credits to Cuba to allow continuation of the construction of a dozen vital projects. Included in this amount was $30 million to pay for the mothballing of the Juragua power plant.

In December 1993 a Cuban delegation led by Deputy Prime Minister Lionel Soto visited Moscow to renew the barter agreement, while seeking to expand trade by establishing direct relationships between Cuban and Russian firms. In principle, the Russians agreed to barter 4 million metric tons of petroleum for 1.5 million tons of sugar; they noted, however, that the numbers were soft, since Cuban sugar production had fallen and less than 1 million tons had actually been delivered to Russia in 1993. There were abundant signs of discord in the conversations. The Cubans reportedly demanded an annual lease payment of $1 billion for the Lourdes station; the Russian Ministry of Defense agreed to pay one-sixth that amount. Soto gave an interview in which he refused to speak of a Cuban debt, but rather referred to "mutual obligations"— a brazen concept according to which Moscow actually owed Cuba considerable sums: "We estimate your country's military presence and the losses Cuba has incurred as a result of the unilateral renunciation of economic obligations at approximately $40 billion."[114]

As domestic political winds in Russia continued to shift toward the hard-liners, the government demonstrated that its foreign policy was not subservient to the United States by making more concessions to Castro. In October 1994 Russia—which had previously abstained on the issue—voted in the UN General Assembly in favor of urging the United States to lift its embargo on Cuba. The following spring, Moscow shifted its vote from "yes" to "abstain" on the question of condemning Cuba for human rights violations. The Russian first deputy minister of defense visited Cuba in November 1994 to conclude an arrangement for paying an annual rent of $200 million on the Lourdes communications facility, to be paid in energy resources, lumber, and military spare parts.

Continuing the pressure on Yeltsin, the Duma held hearings on Russian-Cuban relations in January 1995, with the Cuban ambassador present as an honored guest. The Ministry of Finance reported that in just three years the volume of Russian-Cuban trade had declined 92 percent, from $9 billion to $710 million. Recent barter agreements had not been fulfilled by Cuba, whose sugar production had fallen sharply. The ministry estimated Cuba's debt at 17 billion transferable rubles, which Moscow deemed equivalent to the same number of dollars. Noting that Havana had made no payments since 1991, the official added that Cuba was insisting that the debt should be calculated at a ratio of $1 per 50 transferable rubles. Notwithstanding these adverse economic trends, nationalist legislators called for full restoration of political and economic ties, and for punishment of those responsible for the collapse of the Cuban economy.

As he had to several other key Third World countries with anti-American orientations, Oleg Soskovets, the hard-line deputy prime minister, led a large delegation to Cuba in October 1995. He sought to expand Moscow's once thriving ties with Castro, noting, "Russia regards Cuba as a strategic partner and intends to develop bilateral military-technical cooperation with it." Again, Cuba's unserviced debt was overlooked, and the eager Russian officials— discussing various additional projects, including the Juragua nuclear plant, for which Cuba could pay in sugar—were not deterred by the fact that Cuba had yet to meet its obligations under the sugar-for-oil barter arrangements.[115]

The following May, Evgenii Primakov paid an official visit to Cuba, where he declared that relations with Cuba were now a foreign policy priority for Russia. The Russian foreign minister devoted most of his energies to denouncing the Helms-Burton Act, recently passed by the U.S. Congress, which sought to punish foreign companies that did business with Cuba. In an unusual gesture, Fidel Castro brought a large government entourage to the Russian embassy to meet with Primakov, and he expressed satisfaction with the visit as he saw Primakov off. Nevertheless, there appeared to be little that was achieved, beyond the political showiness; the concrete fruits seemed limited to one agreement on cultural and scientific cooperation. Both sides appeared to play down recent accusations that Cuban foreign trade officials had been lining their own pockets by delaying sugar deliveries to Moscow, while allowing French trading companies to sell Cuban sugar to Russia at inflated prices.

No progress was made during Primakov's visit on the difficult issue of debt repayment. However, a few months later a possible precedent for settlement was negotiated between Russia and Nicaragua on repayment of that country's $3.4 billion debt. After stubborn bargaining, Moscow agreed to write off 90 percent of the debt and schedule repayment of the remainder over a fifteen-year period, with interest at the prevailing market rates. In bitter tones, an *Izvestia* correspondent drew a parallel to Cuba's huge debt:

> This is a major factor, considering that Cuba, a habitual defaulter, would like to revise the whole system of settling debts owed to the former USSR. Now the wily Fidel is demanding that the entire debt be recalculated at the current dollar-ruble exchange rate. Were Moscow to accept such terms, the enormous debt owed it by developing countries—at least $140 billion—would be reduced by at least 5,500 times, to a ludicrous sum less than one-tenth what Nicaragua intends to pay us.[116]

Significantly, Primakov did not confine his Latin American journey to Cuba. His visit extended also to two important oil-producing countries—Mexico and Venezuela—whose economies, though currently depressed, had long-term growth prospects, and whose foreign policies had occasionally demonstrated irritation with Washington. In both countries, Primakov signed agreements on cooperation in economic, scientific-technical, and cultural fields, as well as on joint efforts to combat crime and trafficking in illegal drugs. The following year, the peripatetic foreign minister was back in Latin America, visiting Brazil, Argentina, and Colombia and spreading his message about the necessity of multipolarity in world politics. As he had elsewhere, Primakov won the plaudits of the Russian press for his efforts to demonstrate independence in Russia's foreign policy, and to further its continuing interests in the world beyond the former USSR. As the foreign minister expressed his objective, "As a great power, Russia naturally should have multilateral ties with all continents."[117]

However, the debt problem continued to plague Russian-Cuban relations and even placed a damper on President Putin's attempt to rekindle the relationship with his state visit of December 2000. By this time, Cuba had finally acknowledged a debt of $20 billion but continued to counterclaim $15 billion owed to it as a result of Russia's sudden break in economic and military ties. Amid speeches condemning manifestations of unipolarity by Cuba's neighbor to the north, Putin acknowledged that the break in relations had been a "historic mistake." He said that Moscow was prepared to write off 70 percent of the debt if Havana would agree to repay the balance on the terms utilized by the "Paris Club" of creditor nations. Cuba demanded that 90 percent be written off and that the Paris Club not be involved in the repayment.

Putin hoped to structure Cuba's repayment in a way that would allow Russia to corner the world nickel market. He included in his delegation Vladimir Potanin, the "oligarch" who had obtained a controlling interest in the giant Norilsk Nickel enterprise as a result of the "loans for shares" scheme of 1995. It was expected that Potanin would invest several hundred million dollars in completing the Las Camariocas nickel complex. The Cuban enterprise would then be operated on a joint basis, with the Cuban share of profits devoted to debt repayment. Not only did the two sides fail to agree on this project, but the Cubans also sought yet another loan from Moscow, part of which was to be used for overdue debt payments to which Havana had already agreed. The Russians consented to this arrangement, and Putin apparently left Cuba under the impression that Moscow's terms on the debt repayment had been accepted. Apart from signing a relatively minor set of agreements, the two leaders also toured the Lourdes facility, a vital listening post for the Russians, and they agreed to abandon construction of the Juragua nuclear plant.

After Putin's departure, the Russians experienced what one journalist called the equivalent of "Kim Jong Il's joke." The head of the Cuban parliament's committee on the economy reiterated that Cuba would not agree to discuss its debt to Russia in the framework of the Paris Club. He flatly declared that all of Russia's proposed compromises on the size of the debt write-off and repayment terms were unacceptable to Cuba.[118] The following October, Moscow had the last word. Putin announced that the Russians would pull out of the Lourdes facility—thus removing a major irritant to Washington, while leaving Castro with an additional $200 million annual hole in his budget.

While certain areas have had a higher priority than others, on the whole Moscow's interests in the non-West in the period since the ending of the Cold War have been distinctly more limited than in the prior period. The termination of the global ideological and geopolitical struggle with the United States, together with the significant limitations on Russia's ability to project economic influence, has caused a reorientation of Moscow's priorities to those areas that border the post-Soviet states. As we have noted above, however, the end of the Cold War has not brought peace to the countries of Asia, Africa, and Latin America. Thus, the inescapable fact that billions of dollars in advanced weaponry has been Moscow's dominant export to these regions is a sobering portent that future conflicts could pose even greater dangers to world peace.

——— 9 ———

Russia in the Age of Global Terror

Continuing the Struggle for a "Multipolar World"

Vladimir Putin's two presidential terms coincided with the emergence of global terrorism as one of the dominant issues of international politics. In chapter 1 we identified the international structure as one of the determinants of the foreign policies of states. Political scientists disagree about how to define the international structure or what to deduce from that structure, but there is general agreement that the end of the Cold War witnessed the transformation from a bipolar structure to something else—arguably, unipolar in the military realm and multipolar in diplomacy, in economic interactions, and in transnational relations. Whatever the structure and however dominant its position, the United States was never able to exercise control over world affairs. Nothing illustrated this more than the challenge to the United States posed at the turn of the millennium by the emergence of Islamic terrorism.[1]

Although there had been earlier attacks by al Qaeda against the United States, the destruction of the World Trade Center in New York City and part of the Pentagon in northern Virginia on September 11, 2001, marked the emergence of a full-scale war between Islamic terrorism and the West. That attack had a profound impact on international politics, although it did not fundamentally change the international system. The world remained a state-dominated system with no centralized authority to govern or to protect individual states. But since September 11, terrorism has moved to the top of the agenda for the United States. And, certainly since the horrible events of August and September 2004—the destruction of two civilian airliners by highjackers, an attack on a Moscow subway station, and the unbelievably cruel attack by terrorists on a middle school in Beslan, North Ossetia—it has also been on the top of the agenda for Russia. Terrorism itself is not new in world affairs, but this twenty-first century variant had some special features: (1) it was global in scope and organized not by states but by groups operating independently of states; (2) the terrorists fought in the name of religion and claimed to be motivated by a fundamentalist vision of Islam or a desire for revenge against the claimed oppression of Muslims.

Between his accession to the presidency on January 1, 2000 (first as acting president and then, after March 26, 2000, as elected president) and September 11, 2001, Vladimir Putin pursued a pragmatic, cautious, and nuanced policy that revealed no clear-cut orientations. It revealed a mix of Atlanticist and Eurasianist ("pragmatic nationalist") perspectives. One could have concluded that he was either groping toward a post-Yeltsin direction or that he was testing the waters with several options. In fact there was speculation from the beginning both within Russia and abroad about the direction that Putin would take the country. Was he a liberal or a nationalist? Was he pro-West or anti-West? His career in the KGB and its successor, FSB, suggested a possible hard-liner; but his apprenticeship with the liberal Anatolii Sobchak (now deceased) indicated a more liberal bent. Yeltsin says that he chose Putin in the belief that he was dedicated to democracy and market reform.[2]

It soon became apparent that Putin hewed more toward the policies of Yeltsin's later years rather than to those of his earlier years, i.e., closer to the foreign policy line of Evgenii Primakov than to that of Andrei Kozyrev. Of course, Putin himself had been a part of Yeltsin's foreign policy team, serving as director of the Federal Security Service and Secretary of the Security Council, as well as occupying the office of prime minister during the second half of 1999.

The most visible change that Putin brought to Russia's foreign policy was a heightened level of presidential activism. In his first year as president, he logged two dozen foreign trips. This desire to travel came as a surprise to political observers who reckoned that his major priorities were domestic, and who noted not only that his foreign experience had been limited to his years as an intelligence agent in Germany but also that he had never even traveled extensively within his own country. However, the high volume of Putin's foreign travel appeared less startling in light of the fact that many of these journeys were made to former Soviet states—certainly the area of highest priority for him—and that most of these, as well as many of the ones farther afield, were connected to his search for solutions to pressing economic or security problems at home.

Also evident from the president's own travels was his stated determination to make Russian foreign policy less reactive. A prominent example of Putin's proactive foreign policy was the effort he made to seize the initiative in dealing with the problem of proliferation of weapons of mass destruction and associated missile delivery systems. Rather than simply condemn the American plan to build a national missile defense against such threats, as Yeltsin had done, Putin sought to demonstrate alternative means, both diplomatic and technological, for dealing with the prospect of "rogue" missiles, and he carried his case rather persuasively to the capitals of America's European allies.

Putin also appeared to have a steadier hand on institutional and personnel arrangements related to foreign policy. There was a remarkable contrast with Yeltsin in the continuity in Putin's government. Not only were the frequent ministerial shuffles absent, but also missing was the propensity to create new councils and advisory bodies in the foreign policy realm. Although the size and power of the presidential administration were undiminished, the tendency to involve powerful outsiders (Yeltsin's "family") in key decisions was no longer evident. Early in Putin's term he apparently muscled the oligarchs out of their prominent political role, and he also significantly reversed the creeping regionalism of the Yeltsin years. Governors were removed from the Federation Council and subordinated to supraregional presidential representatives; the new State Council that was created as an evident sop is strictly advisory. Although Putin's predilection for appointing former KGB officials to high positions was frequently cited as a retrogressive move, this trend—as we have noted—actually began during Yeltsin's tenure in office.

The domination of parliament by forces loyal to him and the virtual disappearance of political opposition gave Putin a freer hand in policymaking, but he was also freed at the beginning of his presidency from the necessity to "hold the begging bowl" before the International Monetary Fund (IMF) and its Western supporters. The combination of positive trade effects from the ruble devaluation of August 1998 with the surge in prices for exported oil produced two years of positive economic growth and significant enhancement in Russia's budget revenues. When conditions for further loans from the IMF became too stringent for their liking, Russian officials were able for the first time to walk away.

Early in his administration, Putin outlined a conceptual framework, which highlighted major differences with the West. He described two fundamentally different models of a new world order. One, identified as "unipolar," was a world dominated by a group of highly developed countries and backed by the economic and military might of the United States. Such a world operated by the principle of "might makes right" and substituted for the traditional principles of international law new doctrines of "limited sovereignty" and "humanitarian intervention."

Unipolarity led to wars such as the one in Kosovo and the expansion of military alliances in Europe. The alternative vision—advocated by Russia— was "multipolarity." This model was based upon the reality of globalization, interdependence, and the sovereignty of states. No state or bloc should be hegemonic. In place of NATO, the Russian-preferred model relied on the

United Nations for international security. As for Europe, Russia supported integration and unification, which should include east and west. Again, in place of NATO, Putin argued for the Organization for Security and Cooperation in Europe (OSCE) as the ultimate determiner of continental security.[3]

In reality, the world does not lend itself to a clear dichotomy between unipolar and multipolar. The world is never ordered around pure models of any kind, and governments are forced to confront a recalcitrant reality in contradictory and often ambiguous ways. Thus, Putin's policies were neither purely pro-West nor purely anti-West. He challenged the United States on several important issues, most notably with his opposition to national missile defense and NATO expansion, but at the same time he tried to maintain the partnership with the West begun by Yeltsin.

Putin's Struggle to Preserve the ABM Treaty

Nothing illustrated this duality of purpose better than Putin's initiatives on arms control and disarmament. Within weeks of his presidential victory, Putin successfully mobilized the Duma to ratify the START II treaty. He personally lobbied the deputies on the floor of the Duma. He not only accomplished what Yeltsin was unable to do in eight years, but did so with an overwhelming vote of 288 to 131; however, this "gift" to the United States came with strings. A condition specified in the ratification was that the Anti-Ballistic Missile (ABM) Treaty of 1972 had to be maintained intact. In other words, Washington could have START II or missile defense, but not both.

This diplomatic and parliamentary success was enlarged on April 21 with the ratification by the Duma of the Comprehensive Nuclear Test Ban Treaty (CTBT). Here again, Moscow adroitly secured multiple objectives. Adoption of the CTBT supported Russia's overall policy toward nonproliferation of nuclear weapons. It also put pressure on the United States to do the same. The CTBT was a controversial measure in the United States. President Bill Clinton signed the treaty, but the U.S. Senate refused to give its consent to ratification. This was an issue that Moscow successfully used to put the United States on the defensive before the international community.

No single issue dominated Russian-American relations in the early years of the new millennium as much as the American proposal to build a national defense against a missile attack—dubbed by Russia's Marshal Sergeev as "son of Star Wars." Put on hold by the Clinton administration because of unsuccessful scientific tests to establish its workability, national missile defense had strong support in the U.S. Congress and particularly within the Republican Party. George W. Bush, who became president in January 2001, strongly committed his administration to moving forward on missile defense. The primary rationale was the need to protect the United States from possible future missile attacks by "rogue" states such as Iran, Iraq, and North Korea. On this issue, Moscow was adamant. Russia's military argued that an American defense against missiles would neutralize Russia's ability to retaliate against a nuclear attack. This fear was expressed bluntly in the newspaper *Vremia*:

> If America develops a missile defense umbrella in violation of the 1972 treaty, Russia's nuclear potential will effectively be castrated, and the main external constraint on world domination by the U.S. will be eliminated.[4]

Under the terms of the 1972 ABM Treaty, national ballistic missile defense systems are prohibited. Thus, a major part of the Russian strategy was to persuade the United States not to abrogate that agreement. Putin's campaign on behalf of the ABM Treaty (and against national missile defense) was sophisticated and multipronged. It involved both negative and positive inducements. We have noted above his linkage of ratification of START II with preservation of the ABM Treaty. Putin understood that a negative attack alone would have limited effect. He therefore embarked on a campaign to offer positive inducements as alternatives to the U.S. program.

The first summit between Putin and an American president took place in Moscow in June 2000. He and Clinton discussed missile defense, but could not reconcile their differences. Immediately after the Moscow summit, the Russian president embarked on a European tour. In Italy, he offered an alternative to the U.S. plan. He proposed that Russia, the European Union, and NATO jointly develop a missile defense system for Europe. It was a clever ploy, a good example of political gamesmanship. Capitalizing upon Europe's strong doubts about the American plan to jettison the ABM Treaty in favor of national missile defense, the idea seemed to offer a reasonable alternative. Italy's premier, Giuiliano Amato, did not reject the idea. In Berlin, where Putin pressed his plan, German chancellor Gerhard Schroeder even conceded that the Russian proposal merited attention. In due course, however, Europe could not bring itself to side with Moscow over Washington on an issue vital to Atlantic security.

There were, however, other arrows in Putin's quiver. In November 2000, he launched a new disarmament initiative, proposing a radical reduction in the number of warheads in the U.S. and Russian arsenals. He proposed a reduction to 1,500 warheads for each side by the year 2008, but again only if done within the framework of the ABM Treaty. Putin was known to favor deep cuts in nuclear weapons in order to help finance the modernization of Russia's conventional forces. Russian officials let it be known that Putin was prepared to cut strategic warheads to 1,000.[5]

During the last year of the Clinton administration and the first year of the Bush administration, Putin engaged in a diplomatic offensive to impress on Washington both that a missile defense shield was unnecessary and that building one would be counterproductive. Toward the former end, he met with the leaders of two of the so-called rogue nations to discuss ways to control the spread of ballistic missile technology. In August 2000, he made a surprise visit to North Korea where, among other things, he attempted to persuade Kim Jong Il to abandon his quest to develop missiles capable of hitting Japan or the United States. Putin claimed that Kim offered to forgo ballistic missile development in return for Western assistance in launching civilian satellites. Kim's offer was never formally acknowledged. In March 2001, Putin met with Iranian president Mohammad Khatami to discuss ways to control the spread of ballistic missile technology.

These activities were paralleled by extensive efforts to persuade the European allies of the United States that abandoning the 1972 ABM Treaty would destroy the strategic stability between the great powers and dampen further efforts toward arms control and disarmament. Though Europeans were unwilling to go along with Putin's alternative of a joint European missile shield, they were more receptive to his plea to retain the 1972 ABM Treaty.

In June 2000, when Putin embarked on his European tour to argue for the ABM Treaty, Germany was a particular target because German foreign minister Joschka Fischer was known to be critical of missile defense. In an interview for *Welt am Sonntag,* Putin observed:

> The stance that the Europeans take toward U.S. plans to deploy a national missile defense system is now becoming a matter of great significance to Russia. We view the German leadership's position on this problem as a constructive and sensible one. It is very important that the European nations speak out in favor of preserving the 1972 Russian-American ABM Treaty and thus enhancing strategic stability in the world. We know that Washington cannot carry out its plan on its own, without help from European allies—primarily Great Britain, Denmark and Norway. By letting the United States locate elements of a national missile defense system on their territory, these states risk being drawn into a process that could result in an unpredictable disruption of strategic stability.[6]

While reluctant to endorse Russia's plan outright, many Europeans were sympathetic and wanted Washington to negotiate with Moscow on the issue. Russia's biggest diplomatic success came on November 20, when the UN General Assembly adopted a resolution cosponsored by Russia, China, and Belarus in support of the 1972 ABM Treaty. The resolution was supported by eighty-eight members, with only five in opposition. Additionally, sixty-six members abstained.

While his rhetoric at times could be strident, Putin's strategy never lacked flexibility. In the end, he recognized that the issue might be negotiated, but it could not be forced. One of his last acts of collaboration with the Clinton administration was the signing of the Memorandum of Understanding on Notification of Missile Launches on December 16. In the agreement, the two states agreed to establish a missile-launch notification regime by providing preliminary information no later than twenty-four hours before a planned missile launch. While in substance a positive step in U.S.-Russian relations, this agreement was viewed by Russia as part of an alternative to building a national missile defense system.

Opposition to missile defense was only part of Putin's strategy to counter what Russians perceived to be U.S. global hegemony. Another approach was to build a political coalition to act in concert as strategic partners. The obvious candidates for such a coalition were the states once allied to the former Soviet Union. Toward that end, Putin visited China and North Korea within four months after his election as president. He and Chinese president Jiang Zemin signed a joint declaration expressing concern over U.S. plans to build a national missile defense system. Additionally, they pledged strategic cooperation between Russia and China and joint efforts to establish a multipolar world and the maintenance of a global balance of power. The two leaders did not publicly embrace (à la Soviet leaders), but the Sino-Russian summit was cordial.

Visiting North Korea, Putin became the first Russian leader to set foot in Pyongyang since 1956. The two leaders jointly pledged their friendship. Putin was on his way to a G-8 summit meeting (his first) in Okinawa and was able to use Kim Jong Il's assertion that North Korea's missiles were for peaceful purposes only as a basis for playing the role of peacemaker.

An important component of Putin's global alignment is India. In October, he arrived in New Delhi to court Indian prime minister Atal Bihari Vajpayee. He pleased the Indian leader with his support of India's position on Kashmir and his endorsement of giving India a permanent seat on the UN Security Council (though not with the power of veto). Several agreements were signed, among them a declaration of strategic partnership. In November, Putin visited Mongolia, the country with the distinction of having been the Soviet Union's first satellite.

Among the countries cultivated by Russia in the post-Yeltsin period were several designated by the United States as "rogue" states, supporting terrorism and pursuing a strong anti-American foreign policy. Iraqi deputy prime minister Tariq Aziz visited Moscow in July and was assured by Russian foreign minister Igor Ivanov of Russia's commitment to lifting the economic sanctions against Iraq.

The most publicized of Putin's international travels to former Soviet allies was his visit to Cuba in late 2000. He began his wooing of Fidel Castro by noting that Yeltsin's policy of breaking relations with Havana after the Soviet collapse had been "a historical mistake." The last Russian leader to come to Havana had been Mikhail Gorbachev (in 1989), a man who completely baffled the Cuban leader. Among the several issues on which the Cuban and Russian leaders agreed was that, in the coming millennium, mankind should not have to live under the domination of a single power. Putin was careful not to identify which country that was, but his host had no qualms about naming the United States. Putin, though, was aware of Washington's peculiar sensitivities to Cuba and Castro, and he pointedly signaled his desire not to offend the United States by two specific actions. While in Cuba, he announced that the American Edmond Pope, convicted as a spy, would be released, and he sent his congratulations (from Havana) to president-elect George W. Bush.

The relationship between Putin and the incoming George W. Bush administration began with a confrontational edge. In March 2001 Washington announced the expulsion of some fifty Russian diplomats in retaliation for the revelations about Robert Philip Hanssen (an FBI agent who spied for Moscow). Putin played down the incident, but he expelled an equal number of U.S. diplomats. The same month he agreed with Iranian president Mohammad Khatami to resume the sale of conventional arms to Iran after a hiatus of more than five years. The rhetoric of both Bush and Putin suggested that each would be less accommodating to the other than their predecessors had been.

Washington and Moscow both had powerful incentives to maintain good relations. Neither administration wanted to undermine its domestic goals; in both countries, these had priority over foreign policy. The problem was how to reconcile sharply conflicting positions on several issues, particularly missile defense.

That was the challenge confronting Putin and Bush when they met for their first summit conference on June 18, 2001, in an ancient castle near the Slovenian capital of Ljubljana. To the surprise of some, the two leaders displayed considerable warmth and rapport. "I looked the man in the eyes," said Bush. "I was able to get a sense of his soul." Putin described his satisfaction with his counterpart: "When a president of a great power says that he wants to see Russia as a partner and maybe even as an ally, this is worth so much to us."[7] While none of their differences were resolved at this summit, in this respect their meeting might be compared to the first meeting between President Ronald Reagan and President Mikhail Gorbachev in Geneva. It provided an opportunity for each leader to take the measure of the other.

Within weeks the differences between Moscow and Washington again made headlines. Washington announced plans to accelerate testing for missile defense, even to the point of violating the ABM Treaty. Moscow expressed "dismay." Yet a second Bush-Putin meeting in July produced an agreement that the two sides would explore joint reduction in offensive strategic weapons in a package with talks about missile defenses.

On July 16 President Jiang Zemin and President Vladimir Putin signed in the Kremlin the Treaty on Good Neighborly Friendship and Cooperation. Though the two sides claimed that this was not a military alliance nor overtly directed against any particular country, the treaty constituted a major political act designed to challenge the architecture of global security as articulated by the American president. In the treaty Russia gave full support to China's contention that Taiwan was an integral part of China; opposed the American plan of missile defense; rejected NATO's humanitarian intervention in the Balkans; and pledged military and military technical cooperation with China. Taken as a whole, the Russian-Chinese treaty was Putin's strongest challenge to the world order envisioned by the Bush administration.

Although we are focusing on the geopolitical ramifications of Putin's global diplomacy, we want to point out that economics, too, are an important factor for the new Russian leader. In all of his visits, Putin worked hard to expand Russian markets and to secure, as much as possible, repayment of the debts owed to Russia. Under Putin, Russia has relaxed some of the rules governing the export of arms to Iran. In 1999 and 2000, Russia signed contracts for the sale of ammunition to Libya and for the repair of armored vehicles and air defense systems. With Iraq, sizable contracts were blocked by the UN sanctions. Minister of Foreign Affairs Ivanov vowed that Moscow would work "actively and aggressively" to get them unfrozen. With Cuba, the central economic issue is Cuba's debt to Russia, estimated at $20 billion. Castro would like Moscow to cancel it altogether. Debt cancellation is one of the Cuban leader's main themes in foreign affairs, but Moscow was not singing that song; Putin wanted at least partial repayment.

Russia's Realignment with the United States

The attack on the United States on September 11, 2001, by Islamic terrorists changed the environment of international politics in a fundamental way. On that day nineteen Arab highjackers seized four passenger planes in the United States and with three of them destroyed New York City's World Trade Center and a section of the Pentagon in northern Virginia; a fourth was downed by passengers before it could make its way to attack the U.S. Capitol building or the

White House. In all, 3,021 lives were lost. The human and economic losses were enormous and the psychological impact profound. This attack precipitated a major shift in the foreign policies of both the United States and Russia.[8]

Vladimir Putin's reaction was immediate and unambiguous. He was the first foreign leader to call George W. Bush to offer his sympathy and support. In doing this he had to overcome resistance from within his administration, particularly among the generals. The decision to ally with the United States against terrorism was taken at a meeting of the "power ministries" on September 22 in a session lasting six hours. Two days later Putin appeared on national television to declare his nation's readiness "to make its contribution to the war on terrorism."[9]

In making common cause with the United States against terrorism, Russia hoped to gain some of the benefits that are shared between allies. But there was a deeper motivation. Russia had for years viewed itself as engaged in its own war against Islamic extremism and thus found in the Bush administration a natural and powerful ally against a common enemy. Chechnya was, of course, the most immediate concern to Putin. But the threat of Islamic fundamentalism went well beyond the Caucasus. In the 1990s, as we discussed in chapter 8, Moscow had observed with concern the radical transformation of Afghanistan under the Taliban. Kabul fell to the Taliban in September 1996, only a month after the fall of Grozny to Chechen rebels.[10] Muslim fundamentalists in Afghanistan gave support to the insurgency in Tajikistan. Many Russians feared that Islamic fundamentalists wanted to create a "greater Islamic Caliphate in Central Asia, including parts of Russia itself."[11]

Beyond Central Asia and the Caucasus the Russians saw an Islamic threat in the Balkans. From Moscow's perspective, the Bosnian war and the crisis in Kosovo seriously increased the danger of Islamic extremism. A study by Russian scholars at the Carnegie Moscow Center noted:

> For the public in the West, the story of the Balkans was essentially about Serbian expansionism, but for the Russian government and much of the public, the most serious threat came from Islamists, who Russia believed the United States short-sightedly supported. . . . At the beginning of the turn of the twenty-first century an Islamic strategic triangle emerged that comprised Afghanistan, the North Caucasus and Kosovo.[12]

Russian cooperation with the United States in the war against Islamic terrorism was substantial. An unprecedented sharing of intelligence information took place. American aircraft were permitted to fly over Russian territory. We have already discussed in chapter 7 the building of United States military bases in the CIS countries of Kyrgyzstan, Tajikistan, and Uzbekistan.

Of particular importance was the coordination between the United States military in Afghanistan and the Northern Alliance that Moscow was able to facilitate because of its longtime support to the anti-Taliban struggle. Putin was able to win his suspicious generals over to this policy by pointing out the benefits to Russia of a more secure southern flank.

For about a year after September 11, 2001, Putin remained steadfast in his commitment to the partnership with the United States. It served Moscow's interests as well as Washington's. However, Moscow soon discovered that many of the expected benefits of the partnership were elusive. The hoped-for moratorium on criticizing Russia over its Chechnya policy was slow to materialize. A statement by the United States Department of State spokesman accusing Russian troops in Chechnya of the "disproportionate use of force against civilian installations" and "ongoing human rights violations" was poorly received in Moscow. Equally distressing were meetings in early 2002 between official representatives of Western countries and representatives of Chechen president Aslan Maskhadov. Defense Minister Sergei Ivanov accused his allies of engaging in a policy of "double standards." Nor did George W. Bush's State of the Union address identifying Iraq, Iran and North Korea as an "axis of evil" and the source of world terrorism go over well in Moscow. Russian foreign minister Igor Ivanov argued that other states—indeed U.S. allies—such as Saudi Arabia, Turkey, and Pakistan—were also culpable.

In spring 2002 a brief but bitter fight erupted over trade issues between Washington and Moscow. In March the United States imposed a 30 percent import duty on Russian steel. Exporters in the ferrous metal industry claimed the tax would be a "virtual death blow." The Kremlin (claiming violation of health standards) retaliated with a ban on chicken legs imported from the United States. Good sense and mutual interests in the end prevailed when Russia lifted the ban on American chicken legs and the United States agreed to compensate the Russian steel industry for losses resulting from the prohibitive duties.

There were, however, serious security issues that were not resolved to the satisfaction of Moscow. In December 2001 George W. Bush announced that the United States was unilaterally withdrawing from the Anti-Ballistic Missile Treaty. His intention was to build a limited land and sea-based ballistic missile defense, which could not be done within the confines of the ABM treaty. His decision to do so had been telegraphed from the beginning of his administration, though that did not make it any easier for the Kremlin to accept. Despite rumblings from Russia's military and political elites Putin failed to make an issue of Washington's decision. However, as they had threatened, the Russians subsequently withdrew from the START II Treaty.

Another contentious arms control issue involved the terms of a follow-on treaty to previous agreements reducing nuclear weapons. Under the START II agreement, nuclear weapons were supposed to be limited to 3,500 warheads each. Moscow was anxious to lower that number because it could not afford to maintain so large a force. Realistically the Russians could afford no more than 1,500 warheads. The Bush administration agreed to a reduction, but it wanted the specific number to be spelled out in a bilateral declaration rather than in a formal treaty. When the two presidents met in Moscow in May 2002, they signed a Strategic Offensive Reductions Treaty (SORT) which compromised some of the differences, but which required Moscow to make the most substantive concessions. Putin got the treaty commitment he wanted, but it comprised a meager three pages and permitted either side to withdraw in the relatively short period of three months. The number of warheads permitted ranged from 1,700 to 2,200. What made this new strategic treaty undesirable to many in the Russian military was the provision that the warheads reduced could be stored rather than physically destroyed. While Moscow was free to store as many weapons as Washington, it simply lacked the economic means to keep up with the United States. Everyone understood the asymmetry of the treaty, but it was the best Russia could get from the Bush administration at the time.[13]

George Bush had hoped to offer as a gift to his host at the Moscow summit the repeal of the Jackson-Vanik Amendment, a relic of the Cold War that the United States congress enacted in 1974 to prod the Soviet Union to permit Jewish emigration. A repeal of the amendment would have made it possible to export state-of-the art computers and other high-tech products to Russia. Congressional refusal to comply with Bush's request added to Russia's discomfiture and undermined Russia's hopes to enter the American market with its exports. Even more important to the Russian economy was the formal U.S. recognition of Russia as a market economy. That was important for American investment in Russia as well as for Russian admission to the World Trade Organization (WTO). George W. Bush promised Putin that he would push hard for such recognition, and he delivered on the promise only one month after the summit.

The Moscow summit was proclaimed a success by both leaders. Bush claimed the nuclear pact signaled the end of the Cold War (hardly a new observation), and both presidents proclaimed their states' mutual friendship. Putin displayed the necessary diplomatic tact to conceal his disappointment in the arms agreement. He could do this in part because the arms control issue was not one directly threatening Russia's security. Certainly the concern about terrorist threats trumped worries over a nuclear attack from the United States.

Another security issue of concern to Moscow was Russia's relation to

NATO and the question of NATO expansion. Here too, as with arms control, Russian prestige was an important factor. Because Moscow could not stop the United States from proceeding with enlargement of NATO despite Russian objections, there was widespread resentment among the country's political elite and in public opinion generally.

Moscow's concerns were addressed at a foreign ministers meeting in Reykjavik, Iceland, held at roughly the same time as the Moscow summit, aimed at formulating a new relationship between Russia and NATO. The Russia-NATO Founding Act of 1997 was revised to give Moscow a greater voice in some of NATO's decisions. On specific issues such as terrorism, nuclear nonproliferation, crisis management, and European theater missile defense Russia would have a voice equal to that of the other nineteen members. This was described by some as the "20" format as opposed to "19 vs. 1." Military decisions were excluded from issues of joint consultation, and in no sense was Russia moving toward membership in the alliance. Nevertheless, this concession by the West helped salve some of Moscow's unhappiness with Europe and the United States.[14]

On July 12, 2002, Vladimir Putin made a major foreign policy address to an assemblage of the nation's top foreign policy leadership, including the heads of Russia's diplomatic missions abroad. In that speech he challenged the skeptics around him who doubted the value of having the United States as a partner. "Partnership with the United States," he said, is an "unconditional priority" and "the key elements of our foreign policy must be to counter the threat of terrorism."[15] A seminar of prominent Russian scholars met at the same time to analyze Russia's foreign policy. They inferred the existence of a "Putin Doctrine" whose features were realism, abandonment of goal of pursuing parity with the United States, and integration with the West as the key to economic progress.[16]

War in Iraq

Throughout 2002 the threat of war in Iraq dominated international politics. As a guide to foreign policy the "Putin Doctrine" was too general to predict how Moscow would react to the growing threat of an American military assault on the regime of Saddam Hussein. The crisis began in 1998 with the expulsion by Saddam of the inspectors authorized by the United Nations to find and destroy Iraq's weapons of mass destruction. While the international community clamored for the return of UN inspectors, the Bush administration increasingly came to believe (particularly after September 11) that only the removal of Saddam from power could protect U.S. security and foster peace in the Middle East.

Russia found itself in a dilemma not unlike that faced by Mikhail Gorbachev during the 1990–91 Gulf crisis. Moscow agreed that Saddam had to be divested of weapons of mass destruction, but it believed that that could be accomplished by resuming the inspection process. The Kremlin firmly opposed a military assault on Iraq. To bolster its argument against war, Moscow insisted that only the United Nations could legally sanction the use of force. Of course, with the veto in the Security Council, Russia could always prevent United Nations action.

Moscow's opposition to an attack on Baghdad was partially dictated by economics. Iraq was indebted to Russia by some $8 billion, going back to the days of the Soviet Union. Moreover, Lukoil, the giant Russian oil company, had numerous lucrative contracts with the Iraq government. Russia was Iraq's largest trading partner, with turnover exceeding $2 billion annually. On the other side of the ledger was the importance of American investment in Russia, which Putin valued highly. In January, Tariq Aziz, Iraq's deputy prime minister, went to Moscow to argue Saddam's case—just as he had done years before when Iraq had invaded Kuwait—and Vladimir Putin, not wishing to break ranks with the United States, refused to receive him.

Throughout much of 2002 the United States and its European allies argued over whether inspections (if resumed) or force was the way to deal with Iraq. Russia urged Baghdad to re-admit UN inspectors. In September, making what some believed to be a preemptive move of his own, Saddam agreed to allow inspectors to return to Iraq unconditionally. Russian foreign minister Ivanov voiced his country's enthusiastic approval, "Thanks to concerted efforts, we have succeeded in averting the threat of a military scenario, and in putting the process back on a political track."[17] His enthusiasm was unwarranted. Washington was determined on a regime change, which could be achieved only by war.

On November 6 George Bush obtained congressional approval for war against Iraq. He then sought from the United Nations a resolution authorizing the same. On November 8 the United Nations Security Council resolved unanimously that Iraq disarm within thirty days and permit the United Nations Monitoring, Verification and Inspection Commission (UNMOVIC) unrestricted right to inspect every nook and cranny in the country in order to verify compliance with the demand.[18] In the event that there was any doubt that this was not the authorization for war desired by President Bush, Russia, France, and China issued a joint statement that the Security Council resolution "excludes any automaticity in the use of force."

But automaticity was precisely what the Bush administration had in mind. In the face of mounting global opposition to war, Washington turned to Moscow for assistance. Just as his father had appealed to Gorbachev face-to-face in 1990, George W. Bush went to Russia to obtain what support he could from Vladimir Putin. While Russia's endorsement of war was never in the cards, Bush did hope to soften Moscow's opposition at least publicly. On the surface the brief Putin-Bush summit exuded cordial pleasantries. The American president conveyed his approval of the controversial Russian operation the previous October to free hundreds of Chechen-held hostages in a Moscow theater. For his part Putin took a benevolent attitude toward the NATO decision at the Prague summit in November to enlarge the alliance from nineteen to twenty-six members, including the three Baltic republics. But behind the scenes sharp differences remained. Putin sought—unsuccessfully—American guarantees that a post-Saddam regime would honor Russia's economic interests in Iraq (particularly Iraq's huge debt and Lukoil's numerous contracts).[19] Russia's economic prospects in Iraq after the summit looked bleak. They appeared to diminish even further in December when Iraqi authorities officially informed Lukoil executives that Iraq was canceling an agreement on the development of Iraq's West Kurna-2 site, one of its most promising oil fields. Signed in March 1997, the contract was a production-sharing plan for a period of twenty-three years with the possibility of an extension. On the surface Iraq's action seemed to be an exercise in pressure on Moscow to stand firm against the United States. It is possible that Baghdad objected to Lukoil because that company had American companies as shareholders and worked in collaboration with Americans, or that it was punishing the firm because its executives had sought reassurances on their contracts from Saddam's exiled opponents.

None of the political maneuvering that took place in late 2002 and early 2003 significantly changed the position of any of the great powers involved in the Iraqi crisis. Iraq insisted it possessed no weapons of mass destruction. The United States, supported by Great Britain, was determined to go to war; and Russia, France, China, and Germany continued to oppose war in favor of inspections. On January 27, 2003, Hans Blix, head of UNMOVIC, and Muhammad El-Baradei, IAEA director, reported to the UN Security Council on the results of their inspections of Iraq. It was a mixed message. Hans Blix praised Iraq's cooperation on the process but warned, "Iraq did not appear yet to have come to a genuine acceptance of disarmament."[20] No weapons of mass destruction were found, but neither had Baghdad provided evidence of the destruction of the stocks of prohibited biological and chemical agents or Scud missiles it was thought to have. A story in the Russian press summed up the situation with the byline, "It's clear that nothing is clear."[21]

On the day following Blix and El-Baradei's report, President Bush delivered his State of the Union address to the U.S. Congress. He left no doubt that the United States was preparing for war against Iraq. That policy was opposed by a large preponderance of world opinion. But the opinion with the most significant implications was that of America's European allies. On the issue of going to war with Iraq, eight NATO allies supported the United States: Great Britain, Hungary, Denmark, Spain, Italy, Poland, Portugal, and the Czech Republic. Opposition to the United States was led by France and Germany. Russia, not an ally, but a partner, opposed going to war, but did so in a less strident manner.

Franco-German opposition to war was offensive to the Bush administration in a way that Russian opposition was not. First, the United States expected better from its allies. But more importantly, the rhetoric of the French and Germans conveyed a strong sense of anti-Americanism. Indeed, Gerhard Schroeder's reelection campaign in the fall of 2002 openly appealed to German anti-American sentiment. The French were, if anything, even more strident. Dominique de Villepin, the French foreign minister, became the voice of French hostility, and he made his case with a strong Gallic sting. In January 2003 he angrily told the United States that "nothing justifies military action," thus completely removing the option of war from the table.[22] By contrast, Putin opposed the war but carefully sought to avoid offending the United States. In a speech to students at Kiev University, Vladimir Putin said that good relations with the United States do not mean complete harmony with that country, but "nor do they allow us to slide into confrontation."[23] Of the four great powers involved in this debate, it seems clear that the Russian president displayed the most sophisticated diplomatic skills and achieved greater success than did leaders of the United States, France, or Germany.

A major consequence of the Iraq controversy was the rupture of NATO. At the very time that NATO was expanding its membership, it was becoming divided into pro- and anti-American wings—or, as U.S. Secretary of Defense Donald Rumsfeld put it, into "Old" and "New" Europe. Putin obviously did not cause this rupture, but he took advantage of it. In the end he remained on good terms with all the parties, while relations between Europe and the United States were strained. Diplomatically the crisis over Iraq took its greatest toll on the United States. The Bush administration was widely condemned for what was perceived by its enemies as aggression and by many others as a tendency toward unilateralism, not only regarding Iraq but the environment, arms control, and other issues. Public opinion in Russia in the run up to war was more pro-European than pro-American, though it did endorse Russia's collaboration with the United States in the war on terrorism.[24]

In the early months of 2003 the Bush administration made its final push for UN endorsement of the use of force against Iraq. Secretary of State Colin Powell on February 6 delivered an impassioned appeal before the Security Council. Russian diplomacy was under pressure to maintain some kind of balance between its opposition to war and its unwillingness to break with the United States. A flurry of brief summit meetings of Europe's leaders sought to work out a common position. With Italian prime minister Silvio Berlusconi, a supporter of the United States, Putin intimated that Russia would show flexibility. But with Jacques Chirac and Gerhard Schroeder, Putin reaffirmed the Kremlin's opposition to the use of force. He took the occasion of a visit to Paris to reiterate a theme he had articulated before to justify the Russo-French-German position. He described an emerging European entente as a step toward the building of a multipolar world. "This is," he said, "the first attempt since the time of World War II to find a solution to a serious international crisis outside the framework of [politico-military] blocs."[25] Russia was in effect putting geopolitics before economics.

On February 24 Washington finally introduced a resolution before the Security Council authorizing military action if Saddam failed to disarm. Moscow still hoped to avoid being forced to veto the U.S.-British draft. As a last-ditch effort to persuade Saddam to capitulate, Putin sent Evgenii Primakov to Baghdad. Primakov was the same diplomat used by Mikhail Gorbachev during the crisis over Kuwait more than a decade earlier. He was no more successful in 2003 than he had been in 1990 and 1991.[26] In March, Russian foreign minister Igor Ivanov announced that he would if necessary join France (and likely China) in vetoing the American resolution. In the face of certain defeat the United States and Great Britain withdrew their resolution. When it went to war, Washington would be forced to act without the endorsement of the United Nations and against the overwhelming opinion of the international community.

War began on March 19 with an air strike intended to decapitate the regime by killing Saddam Hussein. The air strike failed, but the military campaign that ensued was successful. Within three weeks Baghdad had fallen to coalition forces. Popular reaction in Russia to the war was initially overwhelmingly hostile. In the State Duma, the most moderate of the resolutions that were debated condemned "U.S. aggression against Iraq." The Communists proposed that Russia withdraw from the partnership with the United States in the fight against terrorism. But Foreign Minister Ivanov helped defeat that measure by warning against letting the antiterror coalition become a casualty of the war. However, he did recommend postponing ratification of the Strategic Offensive Reductions Treaty. While the Russian government confronted a public unsympathetic to the American-led war, Vladimir Putin himself made it clear that "for political and economic reason, Russia does not have an interest in a U.S. defeat."[27]

As the dust of war in Iraq settled—briefly, as it turned out—Putin sought to repair the damage to relations with the United States, while at the same time avoiding a rupture with the leaders of the antiwar coalition in Europe. In mid-April, for example, the Russian president hosted a brief summit in St. Petersburg with Jacques Chirac and Gerhard Schroeder at which the trio agreed that the postwar reconstruction of Iraq must be under the aegis of the United Nations. At the same time, in May a compliant Russian parliament went ahead with ratification of SORT. As a further earnest of its commitment to the Russo-American strategic partnership, Russia supported a UN Security Council resolution in May that lifted the sanctions imposed by the United Nations on Iraq. This was an important step toward legitimizing the American war in Iraq.

We have stressed the balancing act that Putin pursued in his relations with the West. In so doing, he was engaged in what is traditionally referred to as balance-of-power politics. Putin's focus was by no means limited to the great powers in the West. As he balanced the United States and Europe against each other, so also did he balance China against the United States. In May Putin invited Hu Jintao, China's newly chosen president, to a summit meeting in Moscow. Their joint declaration took a relatively moderate position toward the United States. Though they shared a similar geopolitical view of international politics (i.e., preference for a multipolar world), they also found common cause with the United States in opposing Islamic militancy.

China has for years sought to suppress the movement of its Uighur minority in the western province of Xinjiang for autonomy from Beijing's rule. A Turkic people, the Uighurs are Muslims of the Sunni sect and by and large consider themselves to be members of a world Muslim community.

At the Hu-Putin summit, both leaders affirmed the closeness of relations between their countries and their joint commitment to fighting terrorism. One very tangible achievement of the summit was the creation of a formal structure for the Shanghai Cooperation Organization (SCO), uniting Russia, China, Kyrgyzstan, Kazakhstan, Tajikistan, and Uzbekistan. This new structure serves Russia's interest in three important ways: (1) it counterbalances American influence in Central Asia; (2) it adds the weight of Russia and China in the global balance of power; and (3) it provides a vehicle for cooperation with those nations fighting terrorism.

Partnership Frayed

The initial military success of the American-led invasion of Iraq brought neither peace to the victors nor stability to the country. Within a year the coalition found itself engaged in a protracted guerrilla war in which its superior firepower was unable to suppress suicide bombers and kidnappers. The United States was in a quagmire and sought what assistance it could get from the United Nations, its European allies, and its Russian partner. Vladimir Putin in theory never wavered from his commitment to partnership with the United States in the war against Islamic terrorism. But on a wide range of issues the United States and Russia clashed, and neither was prepared to make major concessions to the other simply for the sake of their partnership. Moscow objected to Washington's plans to build a strategic missile defense; to the Pentagon's unwillingness to destroy deactivated nuclear warheads; to the apparent American plans for long-term military presence in Central Asia and Georgia; and to Washington's criticism of Moscow's Chechnya policy, as well as to the Jackson-Vanik Amendment that is still on the American legislative books.

Nor was Moscow in complete harmony with Europe, notwithstanding their common position against the war in Iraq. The European Union and Council of Europe were, if anything, more critical than the United States of Russian human rights violations, particularly in Chechnya. In December an OSCE session criticized Russia for maintaining military bases in Moldova and Georgia. Moscow in turn expressed dismay over British, Danish, and German refusal to extradite Akhmed Zakaiev, a Chechen separatist leader. This, Moscow said, reflected a double standard between the West and Russia in the war on international terrorism. Additionally, Moscow and Brussels were at odds over the terms of Russia's admission to the World Trade Organization and over the question of extending the Partnership and Cooperation Agreement between Russia and the European Union to the ten new EU states admitted in 2004. After tense negotiations and some concessions to Moscow by the EU, agreements were reached in April and May on both of these matters. Russia, however, secured the deal only by including in the "package" an agreement to ratify the Kyoto Protocol on global warming—a subject dear to the hearts of the Europeans. In any event, Moscow's relations with the EU's leading members, France and Germany, remained especially close during this period. Indeed, Putin was hosting President Chirac and Chancellor Schroeder for a summit at his vacation resort on the Black Sea on September 1, 2004, at the very time of the tragic seizure of a school in Beslan, North Ossetia, by pro-Chechen terrorists.

One issue that both united and divided Russia and the West was the proliferation of nuclear weapons. This problem involved particularly Iran and North Korea. As we discussed in chapter 8, Russia's relations with Iran are important to it for economic as well as geopolitical reasons. Moscow has been assisting Iran in the construction of a nuclear power plant at Bushehr. Financially the project involves nearly $1 billion in revenue to Russia and the fate of thousands of jobs in Russia's nuclear power industry. The United States and many Europeans suspect that Iran has a covert aim to build a nuclear weapon. Russia professes to believe that Teheran's interest in nuclear energy is for peaceful purposes only. When the G-8 leaders met in Evian, France, in the summer of 2003, they agreed that countering the proliferation of weapons of mass destruction was a top priority. While agreeing with that objective, Putin still insisted, "Russia is cooperating with Iran and will continue to cooperate with that country."[28] For its part Teheran agreed to return the spent nuclear fuel from the Bushehr reactor to Russia as well as submit to international inspection by the International Atomic Energy Agency (IAEA).

Iran's credibility on this issue was undermined when the IAEA discovered that Iranian scientists had concealed illicit activity (involving uranium enrichment) for almost two decades. In order to obtain assurance about Iran's nuclear program, Great Britain, France, and Germany persuaded the IAEA to press Iran to sign an "additional protocol" to the Nuclear Nonproliferation Treaty that would require it to permit IAEA inspectors to visit nuclear facilities without prior notice. Iran balked at the IAEA demands, threatening even to withdraw from the NPT. The European powers sought Moscow's assistance in obtaining Iranian compliance. Moscow found itself caught in the middle between conflicting parties, all of whom it wanted to accommodate. Washington's position in this struggle differed from that of its European allies and Russia. The Bush administration was convinced that oil-rich Iran had more than enough energy and had embarked on a nuclear program primarily in order to acquire nuclear weapons. Washington wanted the IAEA to declare Iran in violation of the NPT and to have the UN Security Council consider economic sanctions on Iran. Europe and Russia both opposed imposing sanctions on Iran. On October 20 the foreign ministers of Britain, France, and Germany flew to Teheran to persuade the government to accept the IAEA demand to adhere to the additional protocol. Iran agreed to do so and to suspend its enrichment of uranium in return for a promise of Western technological assistance. Vladimir Putin, in Bangkok when this agreement was reached, hailed the outcome as a "great day for Europe."

As a show of support to Russia, the Iranian government chose to announce its acceptance of the IAEA protocol and the temporary suspension of uranium enrichment in Moscow on November 10. At the same time it was announced that Russia would soon begin building a second power-generating unit at Bushehr. Washington continued to insist that Iran had a weapons program. Remembering Israel's 1981 attack destroying the Iraqi Osirak nuclear reactor, Iran has sought Russian assistance in air defense. According to press reports Moscow has agreed to supply $1.6 billion worth of weapons to Teheran —most of it air defense equipment.[29]

What seemed to be progress toward a solution to Iranian nuclear proliferation in 2003 proved illusory. Negotiations by the European powers over technological assistance to Iran broke down in 2004. In July the Iranian government announced that it had restarted building centrifuges that are used to enrich uranium, adding fuel to the American argument that Teheran is seeking an atomic weapon. Although Europeans and Iran again reached agreement on the centrifuges at year's end, Teheran insisted that it was not permanently halting its "peaceful" nuclear programs. Iran's more aggressive posture in 2004 complicates Russia's desire to reconcile its ties to that regime and its commitment to work with the West to stop nuclear proliferation.[30]

North Korea (the Democratic People's Republic of Korea, or DPRK) poses a different set of problems for Russian diplomacy. Kim Jong Il's regime openly acknowledges its nuclear weapons program. On December 31, 2002, the DPRK abrogated the Framework Agreement signed in 1994 with the Clinton administration that froze its nuclear program in exchange for economic assistance. Since then it has used its nuclear program as a bargaining chip to demand direct bilateral negotiations with the United States leading to a non-aggression pact between the two countries. The Bush administration has rejected those demands, agreeing to negotiate with North Korea only in a multilateral context. In 2003, under Chinese initiative, multilateral negotiations were begun that ultimately included South Korea and Japan.

Moscow's objectives were two: (1) to promote de-nuclearization of the Korean peninsula; and (2) to participate in the negotiations to bring that about. Russia, as much as any country, fears the possession by Pyongyang of a nuclear capability, recognizing that this would destabilize the region and likely provoke Japan and South Korea to follow suit. Indeed, according to press reports, the Russian military went so far as to consider the possibility of a preemptive strike against North Korea's nuclear installations in the event of a war between North and South Korea. A nuclear detonation on the Korean peninsula could create a deadly radioactive cloud over much of Russia's Maritime Territory.[31]

Participation in the multilateral negotiations is vital to Russian prestige. Russia, though hardly sympathetic to Kim Jong Il's regime, is a longtime friend of the DPRK, and Putin has a personal relationship with Kim Jong Il that is matched by few other world leaders. Moscow believes that Russia can play a better mediating role than any of the other parties involved. Perhaps as a diplomatic ploy to play the United States and Russia against each other— just as the United States sought to use China to pressure North Korea—Kim Jong Il agreed in July 2003 that Russia should join the talks, enlarging the negotiating group from five to six. As of late 2004 several rounds of talks had failed to stop or even slow the DPRK's efforts to produce nuclear weapons.[32]

As his first term drew to a close, Putin continued to pursue a qualified cooperation with the West. In May 2003 he met with leaders from over forty countries to celebrate the 300th anniversary of the founding of St. Petersburg (his native city). It was a personal triumph for the Russian president. He and George W. Bush reaffirmed their close friendship. That summer brought a painful reminder of terrorism when a Chechen suicide bomber killed fifteen people and wounded fifty-six at a rock concert in Moscow. Washington gave Moscow some satisfaction in August by putting Shamil Basaev on the U.S. terrorist watch list. George W. Bush personally signed the directive. The same measures were taken against the former Chechen president Zelimkhan Yandarbiev (who would be assassinated by Russian agents in Qatar in February 2004).

As the Iraq insurgency dragged on through the year and the United States turned to the United Nations for help, Russia took a moderate position. France and Germany voiced strong objection to sending their troops to Iraq, while Russian defense minister Sergei Ivanov did not rule out the possibility of sending Russian peacekeepers to Iraq (though none were sent). "Russia," he said, "has a vital interest in seeing a legitimate government in place in Iraq and in having order brought to that country."[33] Even while avoiding criticism of U.S. policy, Putin made clear his government's insistence that the United Nations play a decisive role in rebuilding Iraq. On that point he and the Europeans were agreed.

Whoever had control over Iraqi reconstruction would be faced with a daunting financial burden. Accordingly a conference of potential donor states willing to assist in Iraq's reconstruction convened in Madrid in October. Russia participated in the conference but made no offer to contribute. On the other hand, as a member of the Paris Club (of creditors), Russia committed itself to writing off part of Iraq's debt.[34]

One of the strongest criticisms of the Bush administration's foreign policy was its doctrine claiming the right to launch preemptive strikes against states assisting terrorists or developing weapons of mass destruction. Responding to pressures within the Russian military, the Putin administration in the fall of 2003 announced that Russia too would, if necessary, strike preemptively. That doctrine was proclaimed at an expanded conference of the country's military leadership attended by the president himself. Defense Minister Sergei Ivanov stated, "We cannot absolutely rule out even the preemptive use of force if such a measure is dictated by the interests of Russia or by commitment to our allies."[35] This assertion was forcefully reiterated following the terrorist attack on the middle school in Beslan in September 2004.

The Paradox of Putin's Partnership

National elections were held in Russia in late 2003 and early 2004—in December for a new parliament and in March for the presidency. The results gave Putin a second term with a thoroughly compliant parliament. By democratic means Vladimir Putin acquired virtually autocratic powers. Dominating Russia's new parliament was the party endorsed by Putin, United Russia. Altogether the pro-administration forces garnered 325 seats in the Duma, more than enough even to amend the constitution. Paralleling his success in December, Putin won reelection to a second term in a landslide, claiming 71.2 percent of the national vote. Now more than ever, Putin was in a position to pursue his foreign and domestic agendas unconstrained by an internal opposition.

The initial reaction of the West and CIS states to Russia's parliamentary elections was generally negative. A largely critical assessment of the election campaign was issued by the OSCE's International Election Observation Mission, which complained particularly about the unbalanced media coverage. In both Europe and the United States there was talk of a tougher Russian foreign policy, and among many of the CIS states there were fears that the nationalists in Russia would push for a more hegemonic policy.

Indeed, on a range of issues Russian relations with Europe and the United States showed signs of strain. Two were particularly contentious. One involved Russia's relations with its neighbors, and the other, NATO's expansion into the Baltic states. At a meeting of the OSCE in December, Moscow was scolded for keeping military forces in Georgia and Moldova against the wishes of those governments.[36] Moscow resented European efforts to influence the outcome of the conflict between Moldova and Trans-Dniester. Nor was the Kremlin pleased with the closeness of ties between Washington and Georgia. In December, Donald Rumsfeld visited Baku to discuss the possibility of basing U.S. mobile forces in Azerbaijan. Moscow saw this visit as a part of a pattern of expanding American influence in the South Caucasus. Russia's ambassador to Azerbaijan, Nikolai Ryabov, remarked "The Caspian states possess sufficient forces to conduct their own operations against terrorism and smuggling. So there is no need to involve any countries from outside the region."[37] As we noted in Chapter 6, Russia also resented the West's refusal to accept the outcome of fraudulent electons in Ukraine.

NATO's second round of expansion in was more disturbing to Moscow than the first round in 1999 had been. On March 29, 2004, seven new members joined the alliance—Slovakia, Bulgaria, Romania, Slovenia, Lithuania, Latvia, and Estonia. Not only did the alliance now extend close to major Russian cities, but it incorporated three states that had once been united to Russia. Russian prestige was dealt a severe blow. Though NATO was a coalition of states more or less friendly to Russia, the new balance of power would leave Russia more exposed and vulnerable than it had ever been in modern times. Immediately NATO announced its intention to begin aerial surveillance of the airspace over Lithuania, Latvia, and Estonia, a step viewed by the Russian military as "unfriendly." Defense Minister Ivanov complained that combat jets would be a mere "three-minute flight away from St. Petersburg."[38]

Another Russian complaint about NATO enlargement was that it rendered obsolete many of the arrangements worked out in 1990 in the Conventional Forces in Europe Treaty (CFE). To Russia the CFE agreement was important as a protection against the superior military forces in the West and as an instrument for stability in Europe. The CFE had been modified in 1999, but ratification was never completed because of the continuing presence of Russian troops in Moldova and Georgia. With the 2004 enlargement of NATO, the CFE must again be modified to be relevant to Europe's new distribution of military forces.

While the Russian-American partnership seemed on a rocky course at times, the protracted struggle in Iraq continued with no significant impact on Russian relations with the United States or Europe. An announcement by the deputy chief of the Pentagon that firms from countries that had opposed the war in Iraq would not be eligible for contracts for that country's reconstruction was not well received in Moscow. Defense Minister Ivanov parried that announcement with the vow that Moscow would not write off Iraq's debt. However, the lines on these issues were not a sharp as the rhetoric suggested. Vladimir Putin was assured by members of Iraq's Governing Council that Russian firms would in fact participate in the rebuilding of Iraq, and in turn Moscow promised to show flexibility regarding Iraqi debts.

Early in 2004 Moscow announced its refusal to support an initiative on nonproliferation introduced by George W. Bush six months earlier in Krakow, Poland. The U.S. president sought international agreement to seize ships and aircraft in international waters and airspace if there was suspicion that they were transporting weapons of mass destruction or components for them. A particular concern of the United States was trade in such weapons by North Korea and Iran. Moscow, however, changed its position in May, when it voted to support Bush's Proliferation Security Initiative (PSI) in a United Nations Security Council resolution. Moscow's price for its endorsement was the deletion of any specific reference to Iran and North Korea as states guilty of violating the Nonproliferation Treaty.[39]

A turning point in the struggle between Russia, Europe, and the United States over Iraq came in June when the UN Security Council unanimously agreed that the military occupation of Iraq would formally end by June 30 and that power would be transferred to an interim government which would rule the country until elections (no later than January 2005) for a National Assembly.[40] To reach this consensus all sides had to make concessions: the United States, by agreeing to give up its rule in Iraq early, and opponents of the war, by permitting the United Nations to recognize the legitimacy of the changes wrought by the war.

On May 26, 2004, Vladimir Putin delivered his annual message to the nation's parliament. Such messages in all countries are studied as indicators of where the country is going in domestic and foreign policy. This message was notable for its focus on domestic affairs. Nonetheless, in the area of foreign policy a theme stressed by Putin was continuity in the policy of partnership with the United States. "[O]ur line in the struggle against terrorism," he said, "remains unchanged and consistent. . . . I consider the task of strengthening the antiterrorist coalition to be among the most important."[41]

Russia's continuing partnership with the United States was paradoxical, in that Putin maintained it even in the face of United States policies that conflicted with important Russian interests, notably antimissile defense, NATO expansion, the war in Iraq, and NATO intervention in the space of the former USSR. The likely explanation for this paradox is Putin's pragmatism. He reconciled his administration to policies that were inevitable, those he could not prevent. This acquiescence to the inevitable was noted explicitly by Russia's new foreign minister, Sergei Lavrov, at a NATO-Russian summit in Istanbul in the summer of 2004. Referring to the expansion of the alliance's influence in the countries of the Caucasus and Central Asia as "an objective reality," Lavrov was thereby conceding the necessity—in accordance with Russia's larger economic and political interests—of cooperating with the West.[42]

However, there is little doubt that Moscow's declining control in the former Soviet space continues to be troubling both to Russia's political elite and to much of the Russian public. The Baltic states are now part of the West; Moldova has defied Moscow, with EU encouragement; American military advisors are in Georgia; Azerbaijan and Ukraine sent troops to Iraq; the United States has military bases in Central Asia; and Moscow's preferred candidate was not allowed to gain power through a fraudulent election in Ukraine. Taken together, these developments constitute a major geopolitical decline for Russia. On the other hand, the terror attacks of August and September 2004 underscored Russia's continuing inability to resolve the festering conflict in Chechnya or to shut that hapless region off from assistance rendered by foreign extremists. With its vulnerability to internal and external threats thus newly exposed, Moscow needed the cooperation of the West more than ever. How Russia's leaders will accommodate to this dilemma in the years to come remains one of the big issues in Russian foreign policy.

——— Notes ———

Chapter 1: Introduction

1. While communist apologists praised the Nazi-Soviet Pact as a brilliant defensive maneuver, the case that it was a disaster is much stronger. See George Kennan, *Russia and the West Under Lenin and Stalin* (New York: New American Library, 1961), pp. 295–327.

2. For a description of the balance of power, see Hans J. Morgenthau, *Politics Among Nations*, 6th ed. (New York: Alfred Knopf, 1985).

3. For a description of the nineteenth-century "great game," see Peter Hopkirk, *The Great Game: The Struggle for Power in Central Asia* (New York: Kodansha International, 1990).

4. See Kenneth N. Waltz, *Theory of International Politics* (Reading, PA: Addison-Wesley, 1979).

5. Kenneth N. Waltz, *Man, the State and War* (New York: Columbia University Press, 1959), p. 238.

6. Joseph L. Nogee and Robert H. Donaldson, *Soviet Foreign Policy Since World War II*, 4th ed. (New York: Macmillan, 1992), p. 3.

7. The classic analysis of the behavior of states under different conditions of polarity is Morton Kaplan, *System and Process in International Politics* (New York: John Wiley, 1957). A summary of Kaplan's argument is presented in his "Balance of Power, Polarity and Other Models of International Systems," *American Political Science Review*, September 1957, pp. 684–95.

8. Analyses of bipolar and multipolar systems can be found in Kenneth N. Waltz, "The Stability of a Bipolar World," *Daedalus*, Summer 1964, pp. 881–909; Karl W. Deutsch and J. David Singer, "Multipolar Power Systems and International Stability," *World Politics*, April 1964, pp. 390–406; and Joseph L. Nogee, "Polarity: An Ambiguous Concept," *Orbis*, Winter 1975, pp. 1193–1224.

9. A notable exception is Kenneth N. Waltz.

10. An original analysis of bipolarity at the regional level is Peter J. Fliess, *Thucydides and the Politics of Bipolarity* (Baton Rouge: Louisiana State University Press, 1966).

11. *Current Digest of the Post-Soviet Press* (*CDPSP*) 49, no. 17 (1997), p. 2.

12. *CDPSP* 49, no. 21 (1997), p. 1.

13. Anders Aslund, *How Russia Became a Market Economy* (Washington, DC: Brookings Institution Press, 1995).

14. Lee H. Hamilton, "The Debate on Aid to Russia," *Problems of Post-Communism* (May–June 1995), p. 37.

15. Anne Henderson, "The Politics of Foreign Investment in Eastern Europe," *Problems of Post-Communism* (May–June 1995), p. 53.

16. U.S. General Accounting Office (GAO), *Foreign Assistance: International Efforts to Aid Russia's Transition Have Had Mixed Results* (Washington, DC: U.S. GAO, 2000), p. 206.

17. Ernesto Hernandez-Cata, "Russia and the IMF: The Political Economy of Macro-Stabilization," *Problems of Post-Communism* (May–June 1995), pp. 19–26.

18. U.S. GAO, *Foreign Assistance*, p. 202.

19. http://www.russiajournal.com/news/cnews-article.shtml?nd=44268, June 18, 2004.The estimates of the size of the debt given by particular sources vary considerably. The *CIA World Factbook*, for example, estimated Russia's external debt as of September 2003 to be $165.4 billion. See http://www.odci.gov/cia/publications/factbook.

20. http://www.russiajournal.com/news/cnews-article.shtml?nd=44340, June 23, 2004.

21. For more extensive theoretical discussion of the impact of a leader's personality on political situations, see the following: Harold D. Lasswell, *Power and Personality* (New York: W.W. Norton, 1948); Sidney Hook, *The Hero in History* (New York: John Day, 1943); James David Barber, *The Presidential Character: Predicting Performance in the White House*, 4th ed. (Englewood Cliffs, NJ: Prentice Hall, 1992); Fred I. Greenstein, *Personality and Politics* (Chicago: Markham, 1969); Gordon J. DiRenzo, ed., *Personality and Politics* (Garden City, NY: Anchor, 1974); *A Psychological Examination of Political Leaders*, eds. Margaret G. Hermann with Thomas W. Milburn (New York: Free Press, 1977); Barbara Kellerman, *Political Leadership: A Source Book* (Pittsburgh: University of Pittsburgh Press), 1986; and Alexander L. George, "The 'Operational Code': A Neglected Approach to the Study of Political Leaders and Decision-Making," *International Studies Quarterly* 13 (1969), pp. 190–222.

22. Greenstein, *Personality and Politics*, chap. 2, reprinted in Kellerman, *Political Leadership*, p. 43.

23. A persuasive account of Gorbachev's personal impact on Soviet foreign policy can be found in Archie Brown, *The Gorbachev Factor* (Oxford: Oxford University Press, 1996), chap. 7.

24. "Hook's interest, of course, is in lending precision to the notion of the Great Man. Therefore, he is concerned with the individual who, because of especially great talents, is able to alter the course of events. For our purposes, the Great Failure is equally significant: an actor's capabilities may be relevant to an outcome in a negative as well as positive sense." Greenstein, *Personality and Politics*, in Kellerman, *Political Leadership*, pp. 45–46.

25. Boris Yeltsin, *The Struggle for Russia* (New York: Random House, 1994), p. 293.

26. Dimitri Simes, *After the Collapse: Russia Seeks Its Place as a Great Power* (New York: Simon and Schuster, 1999), pp. 128–30.

27. Nataliia Gevorkian, Natalia Timakova, and Andrei Kolesnikov, *First Person: An Astonishingly Frank Self-Portrait by Russia's President Vladimir Putin* (New York: Public Affairs, 2000), p. 169.

Chapter 2: Tsarist Roots

1. Paul Kennedy, *The Rise and Fall of the Great Powers: Economic Change and Military Conflict from 1500 to 2000* (New York: Random House, 1987), pp. 94–95.

2. Ibid., pp. 170–74.

3. Hugh Seton-Watson, *The Decline of Imperial Russia, 1855–1914* (New York: Frederick A. Praeger, 1952), pp. 22–24.

4. Ibid., pp. 90–93.

5. Ibid., p. 102.

6. Quoted in ibid., p. 213.

7. Kennedy, *Rise and Fall of the Great Powers*, p. 233. Much of the following paragraph is drawn from pp. 232–41 of this book.

8. Ibid., p. 240.

9. Henry Kissinger, *Diplomacy* (New York: Simon and Schuster, 1994), p. 140.

10. Ibid., p. 141.

11. Martin Malia, "Tradition, Ideology, and Pragmatism in the Formation of Russian Foreign Policy," in *The Emergence of Russian Foreign Policy*, eds. Leon Aron and Kenneth M. Jensen (Washington, DC: U.S. Institute of Peace Press, 1994), p. 41.

12. Quoted in John P. LeDonne, *The Russian Empire and the World, 1700–1917: The Geopolitics of Expansion and Containment* (New York: Oxford University Press, 1997), p. 368.

13. Kissinger, *Diplomacy*, p. 175.

14. Ibid., pp. 172–73.

15. Malia, "Tradition, Ideology, and Pragmatism," pp. 41, 45.

16. Kissinger, *Diplomacy*, p. 25.

17. Ibid., p. 143.

18. Bruce D. Porter, "Russia and Europe After the Cold War: The Interaction of Domestic and Foreign Policies," in *The Sources of Russian Foreign Policy After the Cold War*, ed. Celeste A. Wallander (Boulder, CO: Westview, 1996), p. 126.

19. Seton-Watson, *Decline of Imperial Russia*, pp. 317–18.

20. Malia, "Tradition, Ideology, and Pragmatism," pp. 40–41, 43.

Chapter 3: From Revolution to Cold War

1. Karl Marx and Friedrich Engels, *The Communist Manifesto*, in *Essential Works of Marxism*, ed. Arthur P. Mendel (New York: Bantam, 1961), p. 44.

2. V.I. Lenin, *Imperialism: The Highest Stage of Capitalism*, in *The Lenin Anthology*, ed. Robert C. Tucker (New York: W.W. Norton, 1975), pp. 204–74.

3. See Alexander L. George, "The 'Operational Code': A Neglected Approach to the Study of Political Leaders and Decision-Making," in *The Conduct of Soviet Foreign Policy*, eds. Erik P. Hoffmann and Frederic J. Fleron, Jr. (Chicago: Aldine-Atherton, 1971), pp. 165–90.

4. Nathan Leites, *A Study of Bolshevism* (Glencoe, IL: Free Press, 1953).

5. Quoted in Alfred G. Meyer, *Leninism* (New York: Frederick A. Praeger, 1962), p. 87.

6. Quoted in ibid., p. 87.

7. Leites, *A Study of Bolshevism*, p. 28.

8. An early and classic version of this debate, with contributions by R.N. Carew Hunt, Samuel Sharp, and Richard Lowenthal, appeared as "Ideology and Power Politics: A Symposium," in *Problems of Communism* 7, no. 2 (March–April 1958), pp. 10–35.

9. See, for example, Adam B. Ulam, "Soviet Ideology and Soviet Foreign Policy," *World Politics* 11, no. 2 (January 1959), pp. 153–72.

10. Vernon Aspaturian, "Soviet Foreign Policy," in *Foreign Policy in World Politics*, 4th ed., ed. Roy C. Macridis (New York: Prentice Hall, 1972), pp. 182–83.

11. Results of a content analysis of speeches of Soviet leaders may be found in Jan Triska and David Finley, *Soviet Foreign Policy* (New York: Macmillan, 1968), chap. 4.

12. The best account of the negotiations at Brest-Litovsk, on which the following paragraphs draw, is John Wheeler-Bennett, *The Forgotten Peace, Brest-Litovsk* (New York: Morrow, 1939).

13. Quoted in *The International Situation and Soviet Foreign Policy*, ed. Myron Rush (Columbus, OH: Charles E. Merrill, 1970), pp. 6–7.

14. Quoted in ibid., p. 12 (emphasis in original).

15. Quoted in *Soviet Russia and the West, 1920–1927*, eds. X.J. Eudin and H.H. Fisher (Stanford, CA: Stanford University Press, 1957), p. 94.

16. Quoted in Rush, *International Situation*, p. 50.

17. Quoted in *Soviet Foreign Policy, 1928–1934: Documents and Materials*, vol. 1, eds. X.J. Eudin and R.M. Slusser (University Park: Pennsylvania State University Press, 1966), p. 21.

18. For a more detailed account of the Lenin-Roy debate, see Robert H. Donaldson, *Soviet Policy Toward India: Ideology and Strategy* (Cambridge, MA: Harvard University Press, 1974), pp. 8–13.

19. Quoted in Robert C. North, *Moscow and the Chinese Communists* (Stanford, CA: Stanford University Press, 1953), p. 96.

20. Quoted in *Soviet Documents on Foreign Policy, III: 1933–41*, ed. Jane Degras (London: Oxford University Press, 1953), p. 56.

21. Quoted in Rush, *International Situation*, p. 82.

22. Quoted in ibid., pp. 93, 96.

23. Quoted in William L. Shirer, *The Rise and Fall of the Third Reich* (New York: Simon and Schuster, 1960), p. 531.

24. Quoted in Alan Bullock, *Hitler and Stalin: Parallel Lives* (New York: Alfred A. Knopf, 1991), p. 614.

25. The text of the treaty is found in *Nazi-Soviet Relations, 1939–1941*, eds. R.J. Sontag and J.S. Beddie (New York: Didier, 1948), pp. 76–78.

26. Ibid., p. 100.

27. Ibid., pp. 235–58.

28. Quoted in Shirer, *Rise and Fall*, p. 810.

29. Quoted in Gustav Hilger and Alfred Meyer, *The Incompatible Allies* (New York: Macmillan, 1953), p. 336.

30. The text of Khrushchev's secret speech to the Twentieth Party Congress may be found in *Khrushchev Remembers*, trans. and ed. Strobe Talbott (Boston: Little, Brown, 1970), app. 4. The quotations are on pp. 587 and 589.

31. For the text of Stalin's radio address, see Joseph Stalin, *The Great Patriotic War of the Soviet Union* (New York: Greenwood, 1969), pp. 9–17.

32. For a full discussion of the circumstances and the evidence relating to the massacre, see Louis Fischer, *The Road to Yalta: Soviet Foreign Relations, 1941–1945* (New York: Harper and Row, 1972), pp. 75–90. When Poland's president Jaruzelski visited Moscow in April 1990, Mikhail Gorbachev presented him with "recently discovered documents" pertaining to the Katyn Forest incident that laid responsibility for the massacre on Lavrentii Beria and his henchmen in the Soviet secret police. A TASS (Soviet press agency) statement was issued expressing "deep regret" over the

tragedy and labeling it "one of the grave crimes of Stalinism" (*Pravda*, April 14, 1990).

33. Winston S. Churchill, *The Second World War: Closing the Ring* (Boston: Houghton Mifflin, 1951), pp. 359–62.

34. U.S. Department of State, *Foreign Relations of the United States: Diplomatic Papers: The Conferences at Cairo and Teheran 1943* (Washington, DC: U.S. Government Printing Office, 1961), pp. 567–68.

35. Quoted in Fischer, *Road to Yalta*, p. 186.

36. Harry S. Truman, *Memoirs*, vol. 1 (Garden City, NY: Doubleday, 1955), p. 416.

37. Milovan Djilas, *Conversations with Stalin* (New York: Harcourt Brace and World, 1962), p. 114.

38. Excerpts from Stalin's speech may be found in Rush, *International Situation*, pp. 117–23.

39. Djilas, *Conversations with Stalin*, p. 115.

40. Quoted in Talbott, *Khrushchev Remembers*, pp. 585, 600.

41. *The Eloquence of Winston Churchill*, ed. F.B. Czarnomski (New York: New American Library, 1957), p. 80.

Chapter 4: The Cold War

1. See Joseph L. Nogee and Robert H. Donaldson, *Soviet Foreign Policy Since World War II*, 4th ed. (New York: Macmillan, 1992), pp. 91–92. Much of the material in this chapter is explicated more fully in this earlier book.

2. Quoted in Joseph M. Jones, *The Fifteen Weeks* (New York: Viking, 1955), p. 22.

3. George Kennan, "The Sources of Soviet Conduct," *American Diplomacy, 1900–1950* (New York: Mentor, 1952), p. 99.

4. Excerpts in Rush, *International Situation*, pp. 125–39.

5. The tactical changes are discussed in Marshall D. Shulman, *Stalin's Foreign Policy Reappraised* (New York: Atheneum, 1965).

6. Quoted in Rush, *International Situation*, pp. 160, 162.

7. Talbott, *Khrushchev Remembers*, p. 358.

8. Rush, *The International Situation*, pp. 166–85.

9. The full text of Khrushchev's "secret speech" is in Talbott, *Khrushchev Remembers*, app. 4, pp. 559–618.

10. For a persuasive statement of the "missile deception" thesis, see Arnold L. Horelick and Myron Rush, *Strategic Power and Soviet Foreign Policy* (Chicago: University of Chicago Press, 1966).

11. Talbott, *Khrushchev Remembers*, pp. 493–94.

12. For a detailed analysis of the Cuban missile crisis, the most famous confrontation of the Cold War, see Graham T. Allison, *Essence of Decision: Explaining the Cuban Missile Crisis* (Boston: Little, Brown, 1971). For updating based on more recent exchanges with the Soviets, see Bruce J. Allyn, James G. Blight, and David A. Welch, "Essence of Revision: Moscow, Havana, and the Cuban Missile Crisis," *International Security* 14, no. 3 (Winter 1989–90), pp. 136–72; and Raymond L. Garthoff, "Cuban Missile Crisis: The Soviet Story," *Foreign Policy* 72 (Fall 1988), pp. 61–80.

13. E.M. Zhukov, "Contemporary Pace of Development of National-Liberation Revolution," *International Affairs* (Moscow), no. 5 (1967), pp. 52–54.

14. A detailed discussion is found in *Soviet Naval Diplomacy*, eds. Bradford Dismukes and James McConnell (New York: Pergamon Press, 1979).

15. For a comprehensive survey, see *The Soviet Union in the Third World: Successes and Failures*, ed. Robert H. Donaldson (Boulder, CO: Westview Press, 1981).

16. See David Floyd, *Mao Against Khrushchev* (New York: Frederick A. Praeger, 1963), p. 66; and William E. Griffith, *The Sino-Soviet Rift* (Cambridge, MA: MIT Press, 1964), p. 18.

17. For the text, see *Essential Works of Marxism*, ed. Arthur P. Mendel (New York: Bantam, 1965), pp. 517–62.

18. Henry A. Kissinger, *White House Years* (Boston: Little, Brown, 1979), pp. 183–86.

19. *Pravda*, July 22, 1973.

20. A firsthand account of these negotiations may be found in James S. Sutterlin and David Klein, *Berlin: From Symbol of Confrontation to Keystone of Stability* (New York: Praeger, 1989).

21. *The Washington Summit: General Secretary Brezhnev's Visit to the United States, June 18–25, 1973* (Washington, DC: U.S. Department of State, 1973), p. 49.

22. Ibid., p. 30.

23. David K. Shipler, "Angola War: Test for American-Soviet Détente," *New York Times*, January 8, 1976.

24. *Documents and Resolutions, 25th Congress of the CPSU* (Moscow, 1976), p. 40.

25. Bernard Gwertzman, "Carter's Russian Lesson Is One in a Long Series," *New York Times*, January 6, 1980.

26. "Transcript of President's State of the Union Address to Joint Session of Congress," *New York Times*, January 24, 1980.

27. Aleksandr Bovin in *Izvestia*, June 16, 1988.

28. Viacheslav Dashichev in *Literaturnaia gazeta*, May 18, 1988.

29. *Pravda*, February 25, 1986.

30. *Pravda*, July 26, 1988.

31. Quoted in Jack F. Matlock, Jr., *Autopsy on an Empire* (New York: Random House, 1995), p. 147. Matlock's analysis of the significance of this issue is particularly enlightening.

32. *Pravda*, July 11, 1990.

33. Quoted in Andrei Grachev, *Final Days: The Inside Story of the Collapse of the Soviet Union* (Boulder, CO: Westview Press, 1995), pp. 204–6.

34. Matlock, *Autopsy on an Empire*, pp. 650–77.

Chapter 5: Domestic Factors

1. For elaboration of this point, see Margot Light, "Foreign Policy Thinking," in Neil Malcolm, Alex Pravda, Roy Allison, and Margot Light, *Internal Factors in Russian Foreign Policy* (Oxford: Oxford University Press, 1996), pp. 35–38; and Karen Dawisha and Bruce Parrott, *Russia and the New States of Eurasia: The Politics of Upheaval* (Cambridge, England: Cambridge University Press, 1994), pp. 26–29.

2. Sergei Stankevich, "A Power in Search of Itself," *Nezavisimaia gazeta*, March 28, 1992, quoted in James Richter, "Russian Foreign Policy and the Politics of National Identity," in *The Sources of Russian Foreign Policy After the Cold War*, ed. Celeste A. Wallander (Boulder, CO: Westview, 1996), p. 69.

3. See the description of Kozyrev's views in Jeffrey T. Checkel, *Ideas and International Political Change: Soviet/Russian Behavior and the End of the Cold War* (New Haven, CT: Yale University Press, 1997), pp. 107–15.

4. Vladimir Abarinov and Vitalii Tretiakov, "The Union Left Russia with a Poor Foreign-Policy Legacy," *Nezavisimaia gazeta*, April 1, 1992, in *Current Digest of the Post-Soviet Press (CDPSP)* 44, no. 13 (1992), pp. 4–6.

5. The terms "liberal Westernizers," "pragmatic nationalists," and "fundamentalist nationalists" are from Malcolm et al., *Internal Factors*. See especially the chapter by Margot Light, pp. 33–100.

6. Sergei Parkhomenko, *Nezavisimaia gazeta*, July 31, 1992, in *CDPSP* 44, no. 31 (1992), pp. 22–23.

7. Sergei Stankevich, "A Power in Search of Itself," in *CDPSP* 44, no. 13 (1992), pp. 1–4. Stankevich's essay bore some resemblance to Stalin's famous article, "Don't Forget the East," published almost three-quarters of a century earlier. Although it notably lacked the Marxist-Leninist terminology, it was similar to the earlier article in seeking to restore balance to Russia's policy. See Robert H. Donaldson, *Soviet Policy Toward India: Ideology and Strategy* (Cambridge, MA: Harvard University Press, 1974), p. 19.

8. Andranik Migranian, "Real and Illusory Guidelines in Foreign Policy," *Rossiiskaia gazeta*, August 4, 1992, in *CDPSP* 44, no. 32 (1992), p. 1.

9. The passage quoted here is taken from Konstantin Eggert, "Russia in the Role of 'Eurasian Gendarme'?" *Izvestia*, August 7, 1992, in *CDPSP* 44, no. 32 (1992), pp. 4–5. Eggert's article attributes the quotations to Evgenii Ambartsumov, who subsequently wrote to the newspaper, naming Andranik Migranian as their author (*Izvestia*, August 25, 1992, in *CDPSP* 44, no. 34 [1992], p. 14). Margot Light, in Malcolm et al., *Internal Factors*, pp. 53–55, repeated this misattribution, apparently having failed to notice the letter and the newspaper's retraction.

10. Council on Foreign and Defense Policy, "A Strategy for Russia," *Nezavisimaia gazeta*, August 19, 1992, quoted in Richard Sakwa, *Russian Politics and Society*, 2d ed. (New York: Routledge, 1996), p. 289.

11. Vladimir Lukin, "America and Our Reforms," *Nezavisimaia gazeta*, September 10, 1992, in *CDPSP* 44, no. 36 (1992), pp. 16–17, 32.

12. Maksim Iusin, "Andrei Kozyrev's 'Shock Therapy,'" *Izvestia*, December 15, 1992, in *CDPSP* 44, no. 50 (1992), pp. 12–13.

13. Quoted in Checkel, *Ideas and International Political Change*, p. 117.

14. Vladislav Chernov, "Russia's National Interests and Threats to Its Security," *Nezavisimaia gazeta*, April 29, 1993, in *CDPSP* 45, no. 17 (1993), pp. 13–15. The quotations that follow are from this account. The final version of the "foreign policy concept" was classified and never published, but this summary, written by a member of the Security Council staff, is widely believed to be authoritative. See Malcolm et al., *Internal Factors*, pp. 69–70, and Leon Aron, "The Emergent Priorities of Russian Foreign Policy," in *The Emergence of Russian Foreign Policy*, eds. Leon Aron and Kenneth M. Jensen (Washington, DC: United States Institute of Peace Press, 1994), pp. 17–34.

15. "Primakov Starts with the CIS," *Moskovskie novosti* 2 (January 14–21, 1996), in *CDPSP* 48, no. 2 (1996), pp. 11–12.

16. "A Minister the Opposition Doesn't Curse," *Obshchaia gazeta* 37 (September 19–25, 1996), in *CDPSP* 48, no. 39 (1996), pp. 22–23.

17. Leonid Mlechin, "The Dark Glasses Keep One from Seeing the Man's True Face," *Izvestia*, May 15, 1996, in *CDPSP* 48, no. 20 (1996), pp. 11–12; see also

Aleksei Pushkov, "Evgenii Primakov Goes Solo," *Moskovskie novosti* 36 (September 8–15, 1996), in *CDPSP* 48, no. 36 (1996), pp. 25–26.

18. Andrei Grachev, "Saddam Is a Time Bomb," *Moskovskie novosti* 47 (November 23–30, 1997), in *CDPSP* 49, no. 47 (1997), pp. 4–5.

19. Checkel, *Ideas and Foreign Policy*, especially pp. 123–32. Checkel's study mobilizes evidence, including interviews of key policymakers and academicians, to support a series of propositions regarding the effect that ideas can have on foreign policy. Under conditions of great international uncertainty or foreign policy crisis, he argues, decision makers are likely to search for information and be more receptive to new ideas. These conditions create "policy windows"—linkages between international events and domestic politics—in which policy entrepreneurs can promote their ideas. The period of perestroika in the USSR and the period just after the Russian Federation achieved independence are identified by Checkel as "policy windows." Centralized states (such as the Soviet Union) have fewer pathways by which ideas can reach decision makers. Adoption of new ideas in such states is thus more difficult, although, once adopted, ideas stand a better chance of being implemented. In less centralized states (such as democratizing Russia), there are more pathways by which ideas can reach elites. Initial adoption of new ideas is easier in these settings, but once adopted, their lasting implementation is problematic. Finally, he argues, policy entrepreneurs will play a critical role in empowering new ideas in centralized states because many of the other pathways for effecting change (parliaments or public opinion, for example) are blocked or less important. In decentralized states, entrepreneurs lose their comparative advantage as the insulation of policy elites diminishes. In such a context, the greater the political skills of the entrepreneur, the greater the chance of success.

20. Mark Kramer, "What Is Driving Russia's New Strategic Concept?" Program on New Approaches to Russian Security (PONARS), Harvard University, January 2000, in *Center for Defense Information (CDI) Russia Weekly*, no. 85. The final version of the concept was published in the military weekly, *Nezavisimoe voennoe obozrenie*, January 14, 2000, in *Johnson's Russia List*, no. 4072. Quotations that follow are taken from this source.

21. David Storey, "U.S. Plays Down Revised Russian Nuclear War Plan," Reuters, January 19, 2000, in *Johnson's Russia List*, no. 4051.

22. "Foreign Policy Concept of the Russian Federation," *Rossiiskaia gazeta*, July 11, 2000, in *Johnson's Russia List*, no. 4403, July 14, 2000.

23. "Predictability and Pragmatism," *Izvestia*, April 11, 2000, in *CDPSP* 52, no. 15 (2000), p. 17.

24. Andrei Shaburkin, "Russia Changes Its Military Doctrine," *Nezavisimaia gazeta*, February 5, 2000, in *CDPSP* 52, no. 6 (2000), pp. 13–14.

25. Nikolai Poroskov and Vladimir Shpak, "A Different Adversary," *Vremia novostei*, October 29, 2002, in *CDPSP* 54, no. 45 (2002), pp. 7–8.

26. Ivan Safranchuk, "A Doctrine in Response to Terrorism," *Nezavisimaia gazeta*, November 6, 2002, in *Johnson's Russia List*, no. 6543, November 9, 2002.

27. Viktor Litovkin, "Security Is Best Achieved through Coalition," *RIA Novosti*; Vladimir Isachenkov, "Putin Says Russian Military Still Mighty"; "Putin Says RF Having Big Amounts of Heavy Missiles," *ITAR-TASS*, in *CDI Weekly*, no. 276, October 2, 2003.

28. "President Putin's Address at the Plenary Session of Ambassadors and Permanent Representatives of Russia," *RIA Novosti*, in *Johnson's Russia List*, no. 8290, July 13, 2004.

29. Oleg Odnokolenko, "Everyone's Free: Security Council Introduces Concept of 'Abuse of Media Freedom,'" *Segodnia*, June 24, 2000, in *CDPSP* 52, no. 26 (2000), pp. 7–8.

30. The text of the constitution can be found in Sakwa, *Russian Politics and Society*, pp. 395–429.

31. Malcolm et al., *Internal Factors*, p. 112. Although the council began to function earlier, a decree forming it was issued by Yeltsin on June 3 (*Rossiiskaia gazeta*, June 11, 1992, in *CDPSP* 44, no. 28 [1992], pp. 4–5), and a second decree on procedures for implementing its decisions was signed on July 7 (Stepan Kiseliov, "Boris Yeltsin's Quiet Coup," *Moskovskie novosti*, July 19, 1992, in *CDPSP* 44, no. 28 [1992], pp. 2–4).

32. V. Prokhvatilov, "In the Corridors of Power: It's Already Noon, but the Shadows Aren't Disappearing," *Komsomolskaia Pravda*, April 29, 1992, in *CDPSP* 44, no. 17 (1992), pp. 22–23; Kiseliov, ibid.; Pëtr Lassavio, "Iurii Skokov—Man of the Year?" *Rossiikie vesti*, December 19, 1992, in *CDPSP* 44, no. 51 (1992), p. 7; Vladimir Orlov, "The Real State of Affairs: Iurii Skokov's Farewell Bow," *Moskovskie novosti*, May 16, 1993, in *CDPSP* 45, no. 19 (1993), pp. 11–12.

33. Pavel Felgengauer, "Evgenii Shaposhnikov—Marshal-Destroyer?" *Segodnia*, June 18, 1993, in *CDPSP* 45, no. 24 (1993), p. 17; Vitalii Marsov, "The Secret Game in the Kremlin Continues," *Nezavisimaia gazeta*, August 12, 1993, in *CDPSP* 45, no. 32 (1993), pp. 12–13.

34. Mikhail Sokolov, "All Power to the Security Council," *Segodnia*, January 12, 1995, in *CDPSP* 47, no. 3 (1995), pp. 19–20.

35. Soskovets's title, first deputy prime minister, was taken by the departing Security Council secretary, Oleg Lobov, but Chernomyrdin clearly was not eager to assign Lobov major duties, and he was left out of the new government formed in March 1997.

36. Mikhail Lantsman, "The Range of Powers of the New Security Council Secretary Is Outlined," *Segodnia*, October 22, 1996; Mikhail Karpov, "The Fifth Secretary of the Security Council Gets Down to Work," *Nezavisimaia gazeta*, October 22, 1996, in *CDPSP* 48, no. 42 (1996), p. 7.

37. "Russian National Security: The Concept," *Prism: A Bi-Weekly on the Post-Soviet States* 4, no. 1, in *Johnson's Russia List*, January 10, 1998. Additional information on the operation of the Security Council may be found in F. Stephen Larrabee and Theodore W. Karasik, *Foreign and Security Policy Decisionmaking Under Yeltsin* (Santa Monica, CA: RAND, 1997), pp. 35–41.

38. In addition to Yeltsin and the Security Council secretary, the members included the prime minister; two deputy prime ministers; the ministers of foreign affairs, defense, finance, interior, atomic energy, emergency situations, and justice; directors of the various bodies that had succeeded the KGB (the Federal Security Service, the Foreign Intelligence Service, the Federal Agency for Government Communications and Information, the Federal Protection Service, and the Federal Border Service); the chief of the Presidential Administration; and (oddly) the president of the Russian Academy of Sciences. *Segodnia*, November 21, 1998, in *CDPSP* 50, no. 47 (2000), p. 16.

39. Asked by journalists, "Who do you trust? . . . Who is on your team?" Putin's immediate response was, "Trust? Sergei Ivanov, Secretary of the Security Council." Gevorkian et al., *First Person*, p. 200.

40. "The Security Strategy of Russia," *Nezavisimaia gazeta*, November 29, 2000,

in *Johnson's Russia List*, no. 4661. The web site of the Security Council may be found at http://www.scrf.gov.ru/default.htm.

41. Pavel Felgengauer, "Hope Glimmers for Reform," *Moscow News*, March 29, 2001, in *Johnson's Russia List*, no. 5176.

42. Paul Klebnikov, *Godfather of the Kremlin: Boris Berezovsky and the Looting of Russia* (New York: Harcourt, 2000), pp. 292–93.

43. Pavel Felgengauer, "The Defense Council as an Advisory Body," *Segodnia*, July 27, 1996, in *CDPSP* 48, no. 30 (1996), p. 5.

44. Quoted in Malcolm et al., *Internal Factors*, pp. 117–18.

45. Ekaterina Akopova, "President Takes Ministry Under His Protection," *Kommersant-Daily*, March 16, 1995; Maksim Iusin, "Three Presidential Decrees that Will Transform the Foreign Ministry," *Izvestia*, March 17, 1995; Mikhail Karpov, "False Alarm," *Nezavisimaia gazeta*, March 17, 1995; Vladimir Abarinov, "Letter and Spirit of the Statute on the Ministry of Foreign Affairs," *Segodnia*, March 24, 1995, all in *CDPSP* 47, no. 11 (1995), pp. 7–9; *Rossiiskie vesti*, October 21, 1995, in *CDPSP* 47, no. 42 (1995), p. 2.

46. Quotations from the decree are found in *Kommersant-Daily*, March 14, 1996; Leonid Velikhov, "Russian Foreign Ministry Named Coordinator of All Russian Foreign Policy for Second Time," *Segodnia*, March 14, 1996, in *CDPSP* 48, no. 11 (1996), pp. 20–21.

47. "A Minister the Opposition Doesn't Curse," p. 23.

48. Denis Babichenko, "The President's Staff Is No CPSU Central Committee Apparat," *Segodnia*, October 17, 1997, in *CDPSP* 49, no. 42 (1997), pp. 22–23.

49. Sakwa, *Russian Politics and Society*, pp. 281–82.

50. Malcolm et al., *Internal Factors*, pp. 122–23.

51. *CDI Weekly*, no. 314, July 15, 2004.

52. "Igor Ivanov Defends Post-September 11 Foreign Policy," in *CDPSP* 54, no. 28, pp. 1–4.

53. Sergei Lavrov, "The Priorities of a Strong Russia," *Vedomosti*, April 6, 2004, in *Johnson's Russia List*, no. 8153, April 6, 2004.

54. For discussion of military influence on Soviet foreign policy, especially during the Brezhnev years, see Edward L. Warner III, *The Military in Contemporary Soviet Politics: An Institutional Analysis* (New York: Praeger, 1977), and Dimitri K. Simes, "The Military and Militarism in Soviet Society," *International Security* 6, no. 3 (Winter 1981–82), pp. 123–43.

55. Pavel Felgengauer, "Igor Rodionov Becomes Minister of Defense," *Segodnia*, July 18, 1996, in *CDPSP* 47, no. 29 (1996), pp. 1–2.

56. Vasili Kononenko, "Russian Military Doctrine Lacks No-First-Use Pledge," *Izvestia*, November 4, 1993; Pavel Felgengauer, "Russia Shifts to Doctrine of Nuclear Deterrence," *Segodnia*, November 4, 1993; Roman Zadunaiski, "Military Doctrine Adopted," *Rossiiskie vesti*, November 5, 1993, in *CDPSP* 45, no. 44 (1993), pp. 11–12.

57. Litovkin; Isachenkov; in *CDI Weekly*, no. 276, October 2, 2003.

58. Roy Allison, "Military Factors in Foreign Policy," in Malcolm et al., *Internal Factors*, p. 255.

59. Pavel Felgengauer, "A Manilov-Style Reorganization of the Army," *Segodnia*, July 21, 1997, in *CDPSP* 49, no. 29 (1997), pp. 4–5. The theoretical underpinnings for the proposed military reform were provided in December 1997, with Yeltsin's approval of the National Security Concept.

60. Dale Herspring, "Russia's Crumbling Military," *Current History*, October 1998, p. 325.

61. Christopher Hill, UK Ministry of Defense, briefing at Center for Strategic and International Studies, Washington, DC, January 31, 2001, summarized in *Johnson's Russia List*, no. 5086.

62. Michael Wines, "Putin Cuts Forces by 600,000, Promising Military Overhaul," *New York Times*, November 10, 2000.

63. Pavel Felgengauer, "Defense Dossier: True Numbers, No Reform," *Moscow Times*, October 5, 2000.

64. Andrei Korbut, "General Staff Assumes Control: The System of Power Departments to Be Overhauled," *RIA Novosti*, November 17, 2000, *Johnson's Russia List*, no. 4640.

65. Pavel Felgengauer, "Defense Dossier: A Reform that Doesn't Hurt," *Moscow Times*, November 16, 2000.

66. Isachenkov, in *CDI Weekly*, no. 276, October 2, 2003.

67. Dmitri Litovkin, "Russia Has a New Weapon," *Izvestia*, February 19, 2004, in *CDPSP* 56, no. 7 (2004), pp. 3–4.

68. Pavel Felgengauer, "Defense Dossier," *Moscow Times*, February 15, 2001, quoted in Center for Defense Information (CDI), *Russia Weekly*, no. 141.

69. "A Combative 'Ivanov Doctrine' for Russian Military?" *CDPSP* 55, no. 40 (2003), pp. 5–7.

70. "Are Putin's Civilian Defense Chief, Military at Odds?" *CDPSP* 54, no. 10 (2002), pp. 8, 20.

71. Simon Saradzhian, "Bill Hands Ivanov Full Control of Army," *Moscow Times*, June 15, 2004.

72. Oleg Odnokolenko, "Decisive Battle," in *CDI Weekly*, no. 317, August 6, 2004.

73. "Inflated Ranks, Tiny Budget and Enduring Paranoia," *Mosnews.ru/Gazeta.ru*, August 24, 2004, in *Johnson's Russia List*, no. 8341, August 24, 2004.

74. Amy Knight, *Spies Without Cloaks: The KGB's Successors* (Princeton, NJ: Princeton University Press, 1996). The following paragraphs draw on Knight's excellent study.

75. Ibid., p. 87.

76. Boris Yeltsin, *Midnight Diaries*, trans. Catherine A. Fitzpatrick (New York: Public Affairs, 2000), pp. 213, 284, 326.

77. Knight, *Spies Without Cloaks*, pp. 128–29.

78. "Text of President Yeltsin's Speech at the CIS Summit Session, Moscow, March 29, 1997," *RIA Novosti*, in *Johnson's Russia List*, March 31, 1997.

79. On this point, see Alex Pravda, "The Public Politics of Foreign Policy," in Malcolm et al., *Internal Factors*, pp. 169–229.

80. Ibid., pp. 188–203; and Jack Snyder, "Democratization, War, and Nationalism in the Post-Communist States," in Wallander, *Sources of Russian Foreign Policy*, p. 36.

81. Mikhail Alekseev, "Russia's Periphery in the Global Arena: Do Regions Matter in the Kremlin's Foreign Policy?" memorandum no. 156, October 2000, Program on New Approaches to Russian Security, at http://www.fas.harvard.edu/~ponars/memos.html.

82. See Wallander, *Sources of Russian Foreign Policy*, especially the chapters by Kimberly Marten Zisk, "The Foreign Policy Preferences of Russian Defense Industrialists: Integration or Isolation?" pp. 95–120, and Matthew Evangelista, "From Each

According to Its Abilities: Competing Theoretical Approaches to the Post-Soviet Energy Sector," pp. 173–205.

83. The interlocking interests of the major financial-industrial groups are described in "The Tycoons Behind the Politicians," *Economist*, April 4, 1998, pp. 56–57.

84. Christian Caryl, "The Empire in Shadows," *Newsweek International*, October 23, 2000. See also Erhan Buyukakinci, "Thinking About the Concept of 'Economic Security': The Importance of Economic Instruments in the Russian Foreign Policy," paper presented at the International Studies Association Forty-First Annual Convention, Los Angeles, March 14–18, 2000.

85. Andranik Migranian, "Russia, Bulgaria, and Gazprom," *Nezavisimaia gazeta* December 30, 1997, in *CDPSP* 50, no. 1 (1998), p. 19. The foreign policy influence of these business lobbies is discussed in Michael McFaul, "A Precarious Peace: Domestic Politics in the Making of Russian Foreign Policy," *International Security* 22, no. 3 (1997–98), pp. 5–35.

86. Pavel Felgengauer, "What Was in It for Russia?" *Moscow Times*, April 27, 2004.

87. Peter Rutland, "Business Influence and Russian Foreign Policy," *Jamestown Foundation Eurasia Daily Monitor*, July 2, 2004, in *Johnson's Russia List*, no. 8282, July 5, 2004.

88. Sarah E. Mendelsohn, "The Putin Path: Civil Liberties and Human Rights in Retreat," *Problems of Post-Communism* 47, no. 5 (September–October 2000), p. 4.

89. Malcolm et al., *Internal Factors*, p. 288.

Chapter 6: Russia and the Former Soviet Union

1. Gorbachev's differences with Yeltsin are described in Mikhail Gorbachev, *Memoirs* (New York: Doubleday, 1995), pp. 651–55.

2. John B. Dunlop, *The Rise of Russia and the Fall of the Soviet Empire* (Princeton, NJ: Princeton University Press, 1993), pp. 266–67.

3. For the origins of the Russian state, see George Vernadsky, *A History of Russia*, 3d ed. (New Haven, CT: Yale University Press, 1961), pp. 14–30.

4. *RFE/RL Research Report* 1, no. 1, March 13, 1992, p. 8.

5. The text of the CIS agreement is in *CDPSP* 43, no. 49 (1992), pp. 10–11.

6. *RFE/RL Research Report* 1, no. 4, January 4, 1992, p. 52. On the military issues, see Stephen Foye, "The CIS Armed Forces," *RFE/RL Research Report* 2, no. 1, January 1, 1993, pp. 41–45; and "End of the CIS Command Heralds New Russian Defense Policy?" *RFE/RL Research Report* 2, no. 27, July 2, 1993, pp. 45–49.

7. For the text of the Lisbon Protocol, see *Arms Control Today*, June 1992, pp. 34–37.

8. "Ukraine Now Says It May Keep Nuclear Weapons," *New York Times*, October 20, 1993.

9. In exchange for its warheads Ukraine was promised money and nuclear fuel. *CDPSP* 46, no. 2 (1994), pp. 6–7.

10. A summary of the agreements between 1992 and 1994 is provided in Mark Webber, *The International Politics of Russia and the Successor States* (New York: Manchester University Press, 1996), pp. 186–87.

11. *Nezavisimaia gazeta*, July 13, 1993, p. 1.

12. Roman Solchanyk, "Ukrainian-Russian Confrontation over the Crimea," *RFE/RL Research Report* 1, no. 8, February 21, 1992, p. 28.

13. *CDPSP* 44, no. 21 (1992), p. 4.

14. Ibid., p. 5.

15. Michael Spector, "Setting Past Aside, Russia and Ukraine Sign Friendship Treaty," *New York Times*, June 1, 1997.

16. *CDPSP* 50, no. 9 (1998), p. 6.

17. Ianina Sokolovskaia, "Leonid Kuchma Delivers 'Coronation Speech' Intended to Please Everyone," *Izvestia*, December 1, 1999, in *CDPSP* 51, no. 48 (1999), p. 22.

18. Charles Clover, "Putin: Good Neighbor or Great-Power Politics?" *Financial Times*, January 23, 2001.

19. Ariel Cohen, "The New Tools of Russian Power: Oil and Gas Pipelines," *Johnson's Russia List*, no. 5003, January 2, 2001.

20. Zbigniew Brzezinski, formerly President Carter's national security advisor, envisioned that Ukraine might make application for NATO and EU membership between 2005 and 2010 if it first undertook domestic reforms. "A Geostrategy for Eurasia," *Foreign Affairs* 76, no. 5 (1997), p. 55.

21. Irina Rybalchenko and Kirill Kazumovskii, "Anatoli Kinakh and Mikhail Kasianov Share Ukrainian Pipeline," *Kommersant*, October 8, 2002, in *CDPSP* 54, no. 41 (2002), p. 15.

22. "Ukraine Looks to the East," *CDPSP* 56, no. 4 (2004), p. 18.

23. The following articles in the *New York Times* provide perspective on this episode: Elisabeth Bumiller, "A Softer Tone from Bush on Ukraine Points to a Quandry for U.S.," November 30, 2004; Steven Lee Myers, "Putin Backs Ukrainian Leader, Dismisses Call for New Run Off," December 3, 2004; C.J. Chivers, "Putin Says He Will Accept Will of the Ukrainian People," December 7, 2004; Steven Lee Myers, "Using Power, Losing Favor," December 19, 2004; C.J. Chivers, "Getting Personal, Putin Voices Defiance of Critics Abroad," December 24, 2004.

24. *Segodnia*, January 18, 1997.

25. Dimitri Kemoklidze, "Has the Commonwealth of Independent States Collapsed?" *Central Asia–Caucasus Analyst*, January 3–10, 2001, in *Johnson's Russia List*, no. 5012.

26. Dov Lynch, *Russian Peacekeeping Strategies in the CIS: The Cases of Moldova, Georgia and Tajikistan* (New York: St. Martin's Press, 2000), pp. 6–11.

27. Quoted in John Lough, "Defining Russia's Relations with Neighboring States," *RFE/RL Research Report* 2, no. 20, May 14, 1993, p. 58.

28. See "Tashkent Summit Signals CIS Realignment," *CDPSP* 44, no. 9 (1992), pp. 1–5.

29. See *CDPSP* 51, no. 5 (1999), p. 11; and ibid., no. 14 (1999), p. 20. States remaining in the Treaty are Armenia, Belarus, Kazakhstan, Kyrgyzstan, Russia, and Tajikistan.

30. Artem Malgin, "The Commonwealth of Independent States," *Russian Politics and Law* 40, no. 5 (September–October 2002), p. 47.

31. Ivan Safronov, "CIS Collective Security Forces Are Eager to Join the U.N. with Their Own Charter," *Kommersant*, December 10, 2003, in *CDPSP* 55, no. 49 (2003), p. 25.

32. The literature on peacekeeping is extensive. Useful analyses are William J. Durch, ed., *The Evolution of UN Peacekeeping: Case Studies and Comparative Analysis* (New York: St. Martin's Press, 1993); *The Blue Helmets: A Review of United Nations Peacekeeping* (New York: United Nations, 1990); William J. Durch, ed. *Peacekeeping, American Policy and the Uncivil Wars of the 1990s* (New York: St. Martin's Press, 1996); and Steven R. Rather, *The New UN Peacekeeping: Building Peace in Lands of Conflict After the Cold War* (New York: St. Martin's Press, 1996).

33. This last contention is controversial and is argued in Suzanne Crow, "Russian

Peacekeeping: Defense, Diplomacy or Imperialism?" *RFE/RL Research Report* 1, no. 17, September 18, 1992, pp. 37–40; Bruce D. Porter and Carol R. Saivetz, "The Once and Future Empire: Russia and the 'Near Abroad,'" *Washington Quarterly*, Summer 1994, pp. 75–90; and Susan L. Clark, "Russia in a Peacekeeping Role," in *The Emergence of Russian Foreign Policy*, eds. Leon Aron and Kenneth M. Jensen (Washington, DC: United States Institute of Peace Press, 1994), p. 120.

34. *CDPSP* 46, no. 12 (1992), p. 11.

35. In November 1992 an earlier and smaller peacekeeping force was formed with Russian and Uzbek troops. A detailed account of Russian peacekeeping in Tajikistan is in Iver B. Neumann and Sergei Solodovnik, "The Case of Tajikistan," in *Peacekeeping and the Role of Russia in Eurasia*, eds. Lena Jonson and Clive Archer (Boulder, CO: Westview Press, 1996), pp. 83–101. See also Kevin P. O'Prey, "Keeping the Peace in the Borderlands of Russia," in Durch, *UN Peacekeeping*, pp. 429–36.

36. "Formal End to War in Tajikistan," *New York Times*, June 28, 1997, p. 2.

37. Anatoli Gordienio, "Rakhmonov Presents an Inexpensive Gift to Putin," *Nezavisimaia gazeta*, September 3, 2003, in *CDPSP* 55, no. 35 (2003), p. 15.

38. Carolyn McGiffert Ekedahl and Melvin A. Goodman, *The Wars of Eduard Shevardnadze* (University Park: Pennsylvania State University Press, 1997), pp. 245–48.

39. Thomas Goltz, "Letter from Eurasia: The Hidden Russian Hand," *Foreign Policy*, no. 92 (Fall 1993), p. 97.

40. See O'Prey, "Keeping the Peace," pp. 420–23. Also Karen Dawisha and Bruce Parrott, *Russia and the New States of Eurasia: The Politics of Upheaval* (Cambridge, England: Cambridge University Press, 1994), pp. 153–54.

41. Ekedahl and Goodman, *The Wars*, p. 265.

42. Goltz, "Letter," pp. 105–7.

43. Serge Schmemann, "In Crushing Blow to Georgia, City Falls to Secessionists," *New York Times*, September 28, 1993. See also Simon Montefiore, "Eduard Shevardnadze," *New York Times Magazine*, December 26, 1993, p. 19.

44. Catherine Dale, "The Case of Abkhazia (Georgia)," in Jonson and Archer, *Peacekeeping*, p. 127.

45. United Nations *Security Council Resolution* 937, July 21, 1994.

46. Lynch, *Russian Peacekeeping Strategies in the CIS*, p. 149.

47. Charles Close, "Putin: Good Neighbour or Great-Power Politics?" *Financial Times*, January 23, 2001; and Douglas Frantz, "Russia's Firm Hand on Heating Gas Worries Its Neighbors," *New York Times*, January 8, 2001. Contrasting views on Russia's gains and losses at the Istanbul summit can be found in "Press Trumpets Russian Victory at Istanbul Summit," *CDPSP* 51, no. 47 (1999), pp. 1–8.

48. "U.S. Military Role in Georgia Has Russia in Uproar," *CDPSP* 54, no. 9 (2002), p. 3.

49. Ilan Greenberg, "The Not-So-Velvet Revolution," *New York Times Magazine*, May 30, 2004, pp. 36–39.

50. Weisman, Steven R. "With Powell on Hand, Georgians Install a New Leader," *New York Times*, January 26, 2004.

51. Gennadi Sysoiev, "Asland Abashidze Outlives His Role as Wise and Loved Leader," *Kommersant*, May 7, 2004, in *CDPSP* 56, no. 18–19 (2004), pp. 6–7.

52. Vladimir Novikov and Aleksandr Gabuev, "Mikhail Saakashvili Takes Little Away from the Negotiating Table," *Kommersant*, July 5, 2004, in *CDPSP* 56, no. 27 (2002), p. 16.

53. C.J. Chivers, "Georgia's New Leader Baffles U.S. and Russia Alike," *New York Times*, August 12, 2004; C.J. Chivers, "Threat of Civil War Is Turning the Abkhazians into Russians," *New York Times*, August 11, 2004.

54. For a description of Armenian-Azeri animosity, see Dimitry Furman and Carl Johan Asenius, "The Case of Nagorno-Karabakh (Azerbaijan)," in Jonson and Archer, *Peacekeeping*, pp. 139–46.

55. See Elizabeth Fuller, "Between Anarchy and Despotism," *Transition* 1, no. 2 (1994), pp. 60–65.

56. See Anthony Richter, "The Perils of 'Sustainable Empire,'" *Transition* 1, no. 3 (March 15, 1995), pp. 14–15, 52; and Elizabeth Fuller, "The 'Near Abroad': Influence and Oil in Russian Diplomacy," *Transition* 2, no. 6 (April 28, 1995), pp. 32–34.

57. Viktoria Sokolova, "They've Reached the Bottom," *Izvestia*, January 10, 2001, in *CDPSP* 53, no. 2 (2001), pp. 15–16.

58. *CDPSP* 56, no. 5 (2004), p. 10.

59. A. Hyman, "Moving Out of Moscow's Orbit: The Outlook for Central Asia," *International Affairs* 69, no. 2 (1993), p. 295.

60. A good introduction to the relations between post-Soviet Russia and the Central Asian states is Martha Brill Olcott, *Central Asia's New States: Independence, Foreign Policy and Regional Security* (Washington, DC: United States Institute of Peace Press, 1996).

61. "Migranian: Near Abroad Is Vital to Russia—I," *CDPSP* 46, no. 7 (1994), p. 4.

62. Bess A. Brown, "Overriding Economics," *Transition* 1, no. 2 (February 15, 1995), p. 53.

63. Stephen Blank, "Every Shark East of Suez: Great Power Interests, Policies and Tactics in the Transcaspian Energy Wars," *Central Asian Survey* 18, no. 2 (1999), p. 155.

64. Nikolai Ivanov, "Legal Status of Caspian Projected," *Segodnia*, February 12, 1998, in *CDPSP* 50, no. 6 (1998), pp. 16–17.

65. See Paul Kubicek, "Russian Energy Policy in the Caspian Basin," *World Affairs* 166, no. 4 (2004), pp. 207–17.

66. Stephen Blank, "American Grand Strategy in the Transcaspian Region," *World Affairs* 163, no. 2 (2000), pp. 65–79.

67. *CDPSP* 52, no. 13 (2000), p. 14.

68. *CDPSP* 52, no. 2 (2000), p. 15; *CDPSP* 52, no. 13 (2000), p. 16; *CDPSP* 52, no. 31 (2000), p. 19.

69. For a description of the dramatic shift in Russian foreign policy after the terrorist attack on the United States on September 11, see Lilia Shevtsova, *Putin's Russia* (Washington, DC: Carnegie Endowment for International Peace, 2003), pp. 204–20.

70. Natalia Airapetova, "How Russia 'Withdrew' from the CIS," *Nezavisimaia gazeta*, December 26, 2001, in *CDPSP* 54, no. 1 (2002), p. 1.

71. Aleksandr Zhelenin, "EURASEC Is No EU," *Vremia MN*, May 14, 2002, in *CDPSP* 54, no. 20 (2002), p. 15.

72. Vasilina Vasileva, "We Write Four. How Many Do We Mean?" *Nezavisimaia gazeta*, March 5, 2002, in *CDPSP* 54, no. 10 (2002), p. 14.

73. Dmitri Glumskov et al., "Whole Region Drops out of Commonwealth," *Kommersant*, January 28, 2003, in *CDPSP* 55, no. 4 (2003), p. 13.

74. Col. Vladimir Mukhin, "Russia Returns to Central Asia," *Nezavisimaia gazeta*, October 24, 2003, in *CDPSP* 55, no. 42 (2003), p. 17.

75. Jeff Chinn, "The Case of Transdniester (Moldova)," in Jonson and Archer, *Peacekeeping*, p. 109.

76. O'Prey, "Keeping the Peace," p. 439.

77. Pal Kolsto and Andrei Edemsky with Natalia Kalashnikova, "The Dniester Conflict: Between Irredentism and Separatism," *Europe-Asia Studies* 45, no. 6 (1993), p. 994.

78. Porter and Saivetz, "Once and Future Empire," p. 84.

79. *CDPSP* 46, no. 32 (2001), p. 16.

80. Oleg Grabovskii, "Intracommunist Conflicts," *Moskovskiie novosti*, no. 9 (2001), in *CDPSP* 53, no. 9, pp. 16–17.

81. See *CDPSP* 55, no. 46 (2003), pp. 11–12 and *CDPSP* 55, no. 47 (2003), pp. 10, 20.

82. Joseph L. Nogee, "Russian Peacekeeping," in *Handbook of Global International Policy*, ed. Stuart S. Nagel (New York: Marcel Dekker, 2000), pp. 222–25.

83. See Ustina Markus, "Business as Usual with Lukashenka," *Transition* 1, no. 8 (May 26, 1995), pp. 57–61; and "Missed Opportunities in Foreign Policy," *Transition* 1, no. 15, August 25, 1995, pp. 62–66.

84. Texts of these treaties are in *CDPSP* 48, no. 14 (1992), pp. 1–8.

85. *CDPSP* 50, no. 52 (1998), p. 1.

86. *CDPSP* 51, no. 49 (2000), p. 13.

87. *CDPSP* 51, no. 47 (2000), p. 23.

88. "Putin Proposes, Lukashenko Rejects, Options for Union," *CDPSP* 54, no. 33 (2002), p. 1.

89. Elena Daneiko and Georgi Ilichov, "Slavophiles and Slovophobes," *Izvestia*, March 18, 2003, in *CDPSP* 55, no. 11 (2003), p. 16.

90. Siuzanna Farizova and Dmitri Kamyshev, "Deputies from Russia and Belarus Complete Work on Draft Constitutional Act on the Union State," *Kommersant*, April 1, 2003, in *CDPSP* 55, no. 13 (2002), pp. 16–17.

91. Aleksei Grivach et al., "Union Poisoned with Gas," *Vremia novostei*, February 20, 2004, in *CDPSP* 56, no. 7 (2004), p. 16.

92. These figures are taken from Martin Klatt, "Russians in the 'Near Abroad,'" *RFE/RL Research Report* 3, no. 32, August 19, 1994, p. 35. The figure of 1,725,000 Russians in the three states is from the 1989 census.

93. See Dzintra Bungs, Saulius Girnius, and Riina Kionka, "Citizenship Legislation in the Baltic States," *RFE/RL Research Report* 1, no. 50, December 18, 1992, pp. 38–40.

94. *Segodnia*, February 1, 1994, p. 3.

95. The highest degree of cooperation between the Baltic states has been in the formation of the Baltic Peacekeeping Battalion (BALTBAT) to serve in UN peacekeeping missions. Saulius Girnius, "Tiny Armed Forces Need Allies," *Transition* 1, no. 2 (December 1, 1995), p. 61.

96. Saulius Girnius, "Relations Between the Baltic States and Russia," *RFE/RL Research Report* 3, no. 33, August 26, 1994, pp. 30–31.

97. See "Russian Language Continues to Suffer Discrimination," *CDPSP* 50, no. 6 (1998), p. 17.

98. *CDPSP* 50, no. 4 (1998), p. 19. See also Steven Erlanger, "U.S. Tries to Defuse Russia-Latvia Dispute," *New York Times*, April 16, 1998.

99. See Nikolai Lashkevich, "Lines for Citizenship Forming in Latvia," *Izvestia*, November 25, 1998, in *CDPSP* 50, no. 47 (1998), p. 20.

100. *CDPSP* 52, no. 18 (2000), p. 16.

101. Girnius, "Relations Between the Baltic States and Russia," p. 32.

102. Full membership is normally granted upon entry to the European Union. The Western European Union is the military arm of the European Union.

103. *Segodnia*, February 14, 1997, p. 7. The full text of the policy document was published in *Rossiiskaia gazeta*, February 13, 1997, p. 7.

104. *CDPSP* 49, no. 9 (1997), p. 19.

105. See Steven Lee Myers, "As NATO Finally Arrives on Its Border, Russia Grumbles," *New York Times*, April 3, 2004.

Chapter 7: Russia and the West in the 1990s

1. For some of the theoretical literature on bipolarity, see Kenneth N. Waltz, "The Stability of a Bipolar World," *Daedalus*, Summer 1964, pp. 881–909; Morton A. Kaplan, "Balance of Power, Bipolarity and Other Models of International Systems," *American Political Science Review*, September 1957, pp. 684–95; Wolfram F. Hanrieder, "The International System: Bipolar or Multibloc?" *Journal of Conflict Resolution*, September 1965, pp. 299–308; Karl W. Deutsch and J. David Singer, "Multipolar Power Systems and International Stability," *World Politics*, April 1964, pp. 390–406; and Richard N. Rosecrance, "Bipolarity, Multipolarity and the Future," *Journal of Conflict Resolution*, September 1966, pp. 314–29. A critique of this literature is given by Joseph L. Nogee in "Polarity—An Ambiguous Concept," *Orbis* 18, no. 4, Winter 1975, pp. 1193–1224.

2. For discussion of the post–Cold War international structure, see Kenneth N. Waltz, "The Emerging Structure of International Politics," *International Security* 18, no. 2 (1993), pp. 44–79; Michael Mastanduno, "Preserving the Unipolar Moment: Realist Theories and U.S. Grand Strategy after the Cold War," *International Security* 21, no. 4 (1997), pp. 49–88; and Christopher Layne, "The Unipolar Illusion: Why New Great Powers Will Arise," *International Security* 17, no. 4 (1993), pp. 5–51.

3. Mikhail Gorbachev, *Perestroika: New Thinking for Our Country and the World* (New York: Harper and Row, 1988), p. 134.

4. *Rossiiskaia gazeta*, February 3, 1992, in *Current Digest of the Post-Soviet Press (CDPSP)* 45, no. 5 (1993), p. 11.

5. Andrew Rosenthal, "Yeltsin Cheered at Capitol as He Pledges Era of Trust and Asks for Action on Aid," *New York Times*, June 18, 1992.

6. Anders Aslund, *How Russia Became a Market Economy* (Washington, DC: Brookings Institution, 1995), p. 41.

7. "B.N. Yeltsin's Speech," *Sovetskaia Rossiia*, October 29, 1991.

8. Andrei Kozyrev claimed that, during the crisis, "the Western embassies in effect began to work for us: through them, we received and passed on information." John Dunlop, *The Rise of Russia and the Fall of the Soviet Empire* (Princeton, NJ: Princeton University Press, 1993), p. 216.

9. In his autobiography Yeltsin acknowledges the support of the West: "[The] unequivocal position from the world community was a heavy blow to the White House occupier." Boris Yeltsin, *The Struggle for Russia* (New York: Times Books, 1994), p. 262.

10. See Michael McGuire, *Perestroika and Soviet National Security* (Washington, DC: Brookings Institution, 1991), pp. 264–72, 371–79.

11. *CDPSP* 44, no. 5 (1992), p. 7.

12. *RFE/RL Research Report* 1, no. 33 (1992), p. 51.

13. In criticizing the antimissile defense system, Aleksei Arbatov, director of the Foreign Policy Association's Center for Disarmament and Strategic Stability, said, "The U.S. government's policy toward our country of late deserves the highest marks. But strengthening relations with America hardly means agreeing with the present administration in everything." *CDPSP* 44, no. 10 (1992), p. 13.

14. See Yeltsin's speech of January 29, 1992, in *CDPSP* 44, no. 4 (1992), p. 7.

15. Thomas L. Friedman, "Reducing the Russian Arms Threat," *New York Times*, June 17, 1992.

16. *Pravda*, June 18, 1992.

17. John W.R. Leppingwell, "The Trilateral Agreement on Nuclear Weapons," *RFE/RL Research Report* 3, no. 4 (1994), p. 14.

18. A good, brief account of the origins of the war in Bosnia is in Warren Zimmerman, "Origins of a Catastrophe," *Foreign Affairs* 74, no. 2 (1995), pp. 2–20. A contrasting account of the responsibilities of the parties to the conflict is in Charles G. Boyd, "Making Peace with the Guilty," *Foreign Affairs* 74, no. 5 (1995), pp. 22–38.

19. The difficult choices confronting Gorbachev as a consequence of the Iraqi invasion of Kuwait in 1990 are described in Joseph L. Nogee and Robert H. Donaldson, *Soviet Foreign Policy Since World War II*, 4th ed. (New York: Macmillan, 1992), pp. 392–96. See also Graham E. Fuller, "Moscow and the Gulf War," *Foreign Affairs* 70, no. 3 (1991), pp. 55–76.

20. Suzanne Crow, "Russia's Response to the Yugoslav Crisis," *RFE/RL Research Report* 1, no. 30, July 24, 1992, p. 32. See also *CDPSP* 44, no. 21 (1992), pp. 19–21, and *CDPSP* 44, no. 22 (1992), pp. 1–6.

21. "Russia's Vote to Punish Belgrade Draws Fire," *CDPSP* 44, no. 22 (1992), pp. 3, 5.

22. Vladislav Drobkov, "Dangerous Precedent: Yugoslavia Expelled from UN," *Pravda*, September 24, 1992, *CDPSP* 44, no. 38 (1992), pp. 20–21. See also Elena Shchedrunova, "Russian Delegation Saves London Conference." *Nezavisimaia gazeta*, August 29, 1992, *CDPSP* 44, no. 35 (1992), pp. 16–17.

23. *Nezavisimaia gazeta*, January 11, 1993, p. 2.

24. For a thorough analysis of the political and military issues involved in the CFE issue, see Richard A. Falkenrath, "The CFE Flank Dispute: Waiting in the Wings," *International Security* 19, no. 4 (1995), pp. 118–44.

25. *Rossiiskaia gazeta*, July 6, 1993, p. 5.

26. *Rossiiskaia gazeta*, June 19, 1992, pp. 1–2.

27. *Pravda*, January 27, 1993, p. 1.

28. *Pravda*, April 6, 1993, p. 3.

29. Jerry F. Hough, *Democratization and Revolution in the USSR, 1985–1991* (Washington, DC: Brookings Institution, 1997), p. 519.

30. Yeltsin, *Struggle for Russia*, p. 288.

31. Leon Aron's biography of Yeltsin makes a strong case for Yeltsin as a democratic leader of Russia. See Leon Aron, *Yeltsin: A Revolutionary Life* (New York: St. Martin's Press, 2000).

32. Zhirinovskii's views are irreverently described by Graham Frazer and George Lancelle in *Absolute Zhirinovskii* (New York: Penguin Books, 1994).

33. Russia's "cohabitation" is described in Joseph L. Nogee and R. Judson Mitchell, *Russian Politics: The Struggle for a New Order* (Boston: Allyn and Bacon, 1997), pp. 121–24.

34. For Yeltsin's policy toward the other republics, see Edward W. Walker, "Federalism—Russia Style: The Federation Provisions in Russia's New Constitution," *Problems of Post-Communism* 42, no. 4 (1995), p. 4. See also Robert Sharlet, "The New Russian Constitution and Its Political Impact," *Problems of Post-Communism* 42, no. 1 (1995), pp. 6–7.

35. "At CSCE Summit, Yeltsin Warns of Cold Peace," *CDPSP* 46, no. 49 (1994), p. 8.

36. The poll was conducted by the Open Media Research Institute (OMRI) and reported by Michael Haney in "Russia's First Televised War: Public Opinion on the Crisis," *Transition* (April 14, 1995), p. 7.

37. "Duma Majority Votes Support of War," *CDPSP* 47, no. 4 (1995), p. 12.

38. This was the first successful vote of no confidence under the new constitution. Michael Specter, "Angry Russian Parliament Votes to Rebuke Yeltsin Government," *New York Times*, January 22, 1995. This action did not bring down the government because it was not followed by a second vote of no confidence within a three-month period, as required by the constitution.

39. "Yeltsin Names Primakov New Foreign Minister," *CDPSP* 48, no. 2 (1996), p. 10.

40. *CDPSP* 48, no. 19 (1996), p. 5.

41. *CDPSP* 48, no. 13 (1996), p. 1.

42. The text of the agreement is in *Izvestia*, September 3, 1996, p. 1.

43. *CDPSP* 49, no. 19 (1997), p. 10.

44. See Andreas Andrianopoulos, "The Long Arm of Oil Interests," *Transition* 4, no. 1 (1997), pp. 36–37.

45. Mikhail Karpov, "The West Asked Russia to Do Everything It Could so That NATO Wouldn't Have to Put Its Ultimatum into Effect," *Nezavisimaia gazeta*, February 19, 1994, *CDPSP* 46, no. 7 (1994), p. 4.

46. *CDPSP* 46, no. 15 (1994), pp. 5–6.

47. Quoted in Maksim Iusin, "Serbs Deal a Cruel Blow to the Prestige of Russian Diplomacy," *Izvestia*, April 20, 1994, *CDPSP* 46, no. 16 (1994), p. 1.

48. Steven Greenhouse, "Year's Effort by 5-Nation Group Accomplishes Little in Bosnia," *New York Times*, March 22, 1995, p. A4.

49. *CDPSP* 47, no. 21 (1995), p. 6.

50. *CDPSP* 47, no. 32 (1995), p. 8.

51. *CDPSP* 47, no. 43 (1995), p. 6.

52. A year after the Dayton Accords, the parties still were unwilling to comply with the agreement. See James A. Schear, "Bosnia's Post-Dayton Traumas," *Foreign Policy*, no. 104 (Fall 1996), pp. 87–101.

53. "Russia Issues a Warning on NATO Expansion," *CDPSP* 45, no. 47 (1993), pp. 11–13.

54. See Allen Lynch, "After Empire: Russia and Its Western Neighbors," in *RFE/RL Research Report* 3, no. 33 (1994); Alfred E. Reisach, "Central Europe's Disappointments and Hopes," *RFE/RL Research Report* 3, no. 33 (1994); and Kjell Engelbrekt, "Southeast European States Seek Equal Treatment," in *RFE/RL Research Report* 3, no. 33 (1994).

55. Michael Mihalka, "European-Russian Security and NATO's Partnership for Peace," *RFE/RL Research Report* 3, no. 33 (1994), p. 44.

56. Hall Gardner, *Dangerous Crossroads: Europe, Russia, and the Future of NATO* (Westport, CT: Praeger, 1997), p. 21.

57. *CDPSP* 46, no. 49 (1994), pp. 8–10.

58. *CDPSP* 46, no. 8 (1994), p. 13.

59. Gardner, *Dangerous Crossroads*, p. 22.

60. Ibid., p. 23.

61. See Almar Latour, "Lebed Warns NATO: Stall Plans to Expand Eastward," *Wall Street Journal*, October 8, 1996. Also see Vladimir Peresada, "Lebed in the Wolves' Den," *Pravda*, October 9, 1996, p. 3.

62. Michael Gordon, "Russia Agrees to NATO Plan Pushed by Clinton to Admit Nations from Eastern Bloc," *New York Times*, May 15, 1997, p. A8.

63. *CDPSP* 49, no. 28 (1997), p. 2.

64. See, for example, the views of Viktor Kalashnikov, director of the Russian Federation Public Policy Center, "Should Russia Be in a Hurry to Join Europe?" *Segodnia*, November 18, 1993, in *CDPSP* 45, no. 46 (1993), pp. 29–30.

65. Yeltsin, *Struggle for Russia*, pp. 138–39.

66. Maksim Iusin, "Paying for Fraternalism," *Izvestia*, February 10, 1995, in *CDPSP* 47, no. 7 (1995), p. 24.

67. Stanislav Kondrashov, "Eastern Europe and Russia's Policy," *Izvestia*, November 6, 1993, in *CDPSP* 45, no. 44 (1993), p. 28.

68. Aleksei Pushkov, "Eastern Europe—A Time for Gathering Stones," *Moskovskie novosti*, no. 51, July 30–August 6, 1995, in *CDPSP* 47, no. 30 (1995), pp. 23–24.

69. Mikhail Tretiakov, "How Do We Answer Warsaw's Trybuna?" *Pravda*, June 23, 1993, in *CDPSP* 45, no. 25 (1993), pp. 20–21.

70. Leonid Kornilov, "People Who Understand Russia Are Back in Power," *Izvestia*, December 14, 1995, in *CDPSP* 47, no. 50 (1995), p. 24.

71. Dmitri Gornostaiev, "Yeltsin and Kwasniewski Get Acquainted," *Nezavisimaia gazeta*, April 10, 1996, in *CDPSP* 48, no. 15 (1996), p. 22.

72. Iana Mirontseva, "Gazprom as Lodestar of Slovak Foreign Policy," *Segodnia*, October 11, 1997, in *CDPSP* 49, no. 41 (1997), pp. 22–23.

73. Georgi Bovt and Natalia Kalashnikova, "Sides Hold to Their Own Opinions," *Kommersant-Daily*, March 10, 1995, in *CDPSP* 47, no. 10 (1995), pp. 18–19.

74. Aleksei Portanski, "Partnership with EU Becomes Reality," *Finansovie izvestia*, no. 51, July 20, 1995, in *CDPSP* 47, no. 29 (1995), p. 23.

75. "A Common Security Space," *Rossiiskaia gazeta*, December 7, 1994, in *CDPSP* 46, no. 49 (1994), pp. 8–9.

76. Boris Vinogradov, "3,000 Peacekeepers Are Supposed to Create Conditions for a Settlement in Karabakh," *Izvestia*, December 9, 1994, in *CDPSP* 46, no. 49 (1994), pp. 10–11.

77. Mikhail Karpov, "Sunrise for NATO, Sunset for the CSCE?" *Nezavisimaia gazeta*, December 7, 1994, in *CDPSP* 46, no. 49 (1994), pp. 11–12.

78. Pavel Shinkarenko, "Russia's Decisive Contribution to the Creation of a New Europe," *Rossiiskie vesti*, August 31, 1994, in *CDPSP* 46, no. 35 (1994), p. 3.

79. Nikolai Pavlov, "Forgotten Germany," *Izvestia*, March 18, 1992, in *CDPSP* 44, no. 11 (1992), pp. 8–9.

80. Leonid Velekhov, "Kohl Comes to Yeltsin's Rescue," *Nezavisimaia gazeta*, December 18, 1992, in *CDPSP* 44, no. 50 (1992), pp. 19–20.

81. The following year, the Russian press, relying on a report in *Der Spiegel*, described the whole incident as a German intelligence operation, designed to trace channels by which dangerous contraband entered Germany, and using agents provocateurs

to test monitoring systems at Russian airports. Igor Korotchenko, "Nuclear Smuggling Case," *Nezavisimaia gazeta*, April 13, 1995, in *CDPSP* 47, no. 15 (1995), p. 23.

82. Dmitri Pogorzhelskii, "Farewell to the Past," *Segodnia*, September 1, 1994, in *CDPSP* 46, no. 35 (1994), p. 2; and Aleksandr Batygin, "Grab Your Greatcoat and Let's Go Home," *Rossiiskaia gazeta*, August 30, 1994, in *CDPSP* 46, no. 35 (1994), p. 5.

83. *Izvestia*, August 31, 1994, in *CDPSP* 46, no. 35 (1994), p. 1.

84. Natalia Kalashnikova, "German Defense Minister Is Not Eager to Meet with Russian Counterpart," *Kommersant-Daily*, January 24, 1995, in *CDPSP* 47, no. 4 (1995), p. 28.

85. Vladimir Abarinov, "Kohl Considers Yeltsin a Tried and True Friend and the Best President for Russia," *Segodnia*, February 21, 1996, in *CDPSP* 48, no. 8 (1996), p. 26.

86. Aleksandr Krausulin, "He Came, He Saw, He Persuaded," *Rossiiskaia gazeta*, November 22, 1994, in *CDPSP* 46, no. 47 (1994), pp. 23–24.

87. Natalia Kalashnikova and Vitali Dymarskii, "Go-for-Broke Diplomacy, but There's Nothing to Ante Up," *Kommersant-Daily*, October 24, 1995, in *CDPSP* 47, no. 43 (1995), pp. 23–24.

88. Gennadii Sisoev, "Russia Likes French Dissidence," *Kommersant-Daily*, September 25, 1997, in *CDPSP* 49, no. 39 (1997), pp. 21–22; Maksim Iusin, "Yeltsin's Friendship with Chirac Developing into a Russian-French Alliance," *Izvestia*, September 27, 1997, in ibid., p. 22.

89. Maksim Iusin, "Yeltsin's Visit to London Was a Complete Success," *Izvestia*, February 11, 1992, in *CDPSP* 44, no. 5 (1992), pp. 10–11.

90. "Kremlin Adopting a New Anti-American Line?" *Jamestown Foundation Monitor*, October 20, 1997, in *Johnson's Russia List*, October 21, 1997.

91. Chris Hedges, "Kosovo's Next Masters," *Foreign Affairs* 78, no. 3 (1999), pp. 24–42.

92. Iulia Berezovskaia, "Conflict in Kosovo Threatens 'Cold War,'" *Izvestia*, October 7, 1998, in *CDPSP* 50, no. 40 (1998), p. 14.

93. Vladimir Mikheev, "Seven Plus One Still Isn't Eight," *Izvestia*, May 7, 1999, in *CDPSP* 51, no. 18 (1999), p. 4.

94. "Balkan Accord Reached, Chernomyrdin Role Disputed," *CDPSP* 51, no. 23 (1999), pp. 1–6.

95. Gennadi Charodeev, "There's Only One Person Who Could Have Given the Order: The President," *Izvestia*, June 15, 1999, *CDPSP* 51, no. 24 (1999), p. 3.

96. Quoted in *Kommersant*, August 27, 1999, in *CDPSP* 51, no. 34 (1999), p. 5.

97. See Rajan Menon and Graham E. Fuller, "Russia's Ruinous Chechen War," *Foreign Affairs* 79, no. 2 (2000), pp. 32–44.

98. In his autobiographical interview, Putin claims responsibility for Russia's Chechnya policy even while Yeltsin was still president. He described his rationale as follows: "They [the Chechens] built up their forces and then attacked a neighboring territory. Why? In order to defend the independence of Chechnya? Of course not. In order to seize additional territories. They would have swallowed up Dagestan, and that would have been the beginning of the end. The entire Caucasus would have followed—Dagestan, Ingushetia, and then up along the Volga River to Bashkortostan and Tatarstan, reaching deep into the country." Nataliia Gevorkian, Natalia Timakova, and Andrei Kolesnikov, *First Person: An Astonishingly Frank Self-Portrait by Russia's President Vladimir Putin* (New York: Public Affairs, 2000), p. 142.

99. For Clinton's position, see Maksim Iusin, "'Russia Will Pay a Heavy Price' for Chechnia," *Izvestia*, December 8, 1999, in *CDPSP* 51, no. 49 (1999), p. 10. On Europe's position, see "Is Russia on the Verge of 'Expulsion' from Europe?" *CDPSP* 52, no. 14 (2000), pp. 1–4.

100. Gevorkian et al., *First Person*, p. 169.

101. Nikolai Paklin, "'Big Three' Draws Europe Toward Unification," *Rossiiskaia gazeta*, April 1, 1998, in *CDPSP* 50, no. 13 (1998), p. 21.

Chapter 8: Russia and the "Non-West"

1. Figures from the U.S. Congressional Research Service, cited in Philip Shenon, "Russia Outstrips U.S. in Sales of Arms to Developing Nations," *New York Times*, August 20, 1996.

2. Congressional Research Service, cited in Eric Schmitt, "Arms Sales to the Third World, Especially by Russia, Drop," *New York Times*, July 19, 1993.

3. Iuri Golotiuk, "Russia Is 'Aggressively' Entering World Arms Market," *Segodnia*, March 29, 1996, in *CDPSP* 48, no. 13 (1996), p. 22; and Pavel Felgengauer, "Arms Trade Is Not as Lucrative for Russia as Russia Claims," *Segodnia*, March 10, 1995, in *CDPSP* 47, no. 10 (1995), pp. 16–17.

4. Andrei Ivanov and Judith Perera, "Unscrupulous Russia May Soon Surpass U.S. in Arms Sales," Interpress Service, in *Johnson's Russia List*, no. 1180, September 7, 1997.

5. Pavel Felgengauer, "Arms Exports Aren't as Lucrative as They're Said to Be," *Segodnia*, December 26, 1997, in *CDPSP* 49, no. 52 (1997), p. 18; Konstantin Makienko, "There Are Fewer Russian Weapons in the World," *Kommersant-Daily*, February 13, 1998, in *CDPSP* 50, no. 8 (1998), pp. 12–13; and Interfax report, quoting Evgenii Ananev, general director, Rosvooruzhenie, in *Johnson's Russia List*, no. 2158, April 21, 1998.

6. Michael R. Gordon, "Russia Is Pushing to Increase Share in Weapons Trade," *New York Times*, July 14, 2000. See also the annual reports from the Stockholm International Peace Research Institute, *SIPRI Yearbook: Armaments, Disarmament, and International Security* (New York and London: Oxford University Press).

7. "Russia's Arms Bazaar," *Jane's Intelligence Review*, April 2001. Somewhat different sales figures are reported in the annual estimates by the Congressional Research Service.

8. *Johnson's Russia List*, no. 8096, March 2, 2004; Thom Shanker, "U.S. and Russia Still Dominate Arms Market, But World Total Falls," *New York Times*, August 30, 2004.

9. Felgengauer, "Arms Exports Aren't as Lucrative"; and Makienko, "There Are Fewer Russian Weapons."

10. Felgengauer, "Arms Exports Aren't as Lucrative," pp. 16–17.

11. Vladimir Isachenkov, "Russian Arms Industry under Siege," *Johnson's Russia List*, no. 7216, June 9, 2003.

12. Matthew Brzezinski, "Rival Arms-Makers Lure Buyers Away from Russia," *Wall Street Journal*, April 1, 1997.

13. Makienko, "There Are Fewer Russian Weapons."

14. Wilson John, "Quality Decides: Russia Is No Longer the Cheapest and Most Quality-Conscious Arms Supplier," *Pioneer* (Delhi), May 28, 1997, in *Johnson's Russia List*, June 1, 1997.

15. Reports of Sino-Russian presidential visits may be found in Vasilii Kononenko and Vladimir Skosyrev, "Russian-Chinese Declaration Is Essentially Tantamount to a Nonaggression Pact," *Izvestia*, December 21, 1992, in *CDPSP* 44, no. 51 (1992), pp. 13–14; Aleksandr Chudodeev, "Partners, but Not Allies," *Segodnia*, September 2, 1994, in *CDPSP* 46, no. 36 (1994), p. 13; Tatiana Malkina, "Boris Yeltsin Sees No One Who Could Stand Against Such a Pair as 'Great Russia' and 'Great China,'" *Segodnia*, April 27, 1996, in *CDPSP* 48, no. 17 (1996), pp. 7–8; "A Breakthrough for Russian Policy on the Asian Front," *Rossiiskie vesti*, April 24, 1997, in *CDPSP* 49, no. 17 (1997), pp. 1–2; Aleksandr Chudodeev, "Boris Yeltsin and Jiang Zemin Find Harmony," *Segodnia*, November 12, 1997, in *CDPSP* 49, no. 45 (1997), p. 6; and "Joint Statement of President Vladimir Putin of the Russian Federation and Chairman Jiang Zemin of the People's Republic of China on ABM," *Krasnaia zvezda*, July 19, 2000, in *CDI Weekly*, no. 111 (2000).

16. For an analysis of the treaty, see Robert H. Donaldson and John A. Donaldson, "The Arms Trade in Russian-Chinese Relations: Identity, Domestic Politics, and Geopolitical Positioning," *International Studies Quarterly* 47 (2003), pp. 709–32.

17. John Pomfret, "Beijing and Moscow to Sign Pact," *Washington Post*, January 13, 2001.

18. Evgenii Berlin, "Challenges and Opportunities," *Vremia MN*, July 16, 2002, in *CDPSP* 54, no. 29 (2002), pp. 16–17.

19. Ilia Bulavinov, "Russia's Boundless Friendship with China," *Kommersant-Daily*, April 25, 1997, in *CDPSP* 49, no. 17 (1997), p. 5.

20. See James Clay Moltz, "Regional Tensions in the Russo-Chinese Rapprochement," *Asian Survey* 35, no. 6 (June 1995).

21. Emil Pain, "'Illegals' on the Banks of the Amur," *Rossiiskie vesti*, May 6, 1997, in *CDPSP* 49, no. 19 (1997), pp. 1–3.

22. Evgenii Berlin, "Russia at Far Eastern Crossroads," *Vremia MN*, July 25, 2000, in *CDPSP* 52, no. 30 (2000), pp. 15–16.

23. For more on Sino-Russian trade and their economic relations, see Jeanne L. Wilson, *Strategic Partners: Russian-Chinese Relations in the Post-Soviet Era* (Armonk, NY: M.E. Sharpe, 2004), chapter 4.

24. "Kasianov Attends to Russia's Relations to the East," *CDPSP* 55, no. 38 (2003), pp. 5–7.

25. James Brooke, "Japan and Russia Working Hard to Build Economic Ties," *New York Times*, January 22, 2004.

26. "Russia and China: Can a Bear Love a Dragon?" *Economist*, April 26, 1997, pp. 19–21.

27. Andrei Bagrov, "In Every Propeller Breathes a Scandal," *Kommersant-Daily*, July 18, 1996, in *CDPSP* 48, no. 30 (1996), pp. 20–21.

28. Boris Barakhta, "Is China's Experience Outdated?" *Pravda*, December 22, 1992, in *CDPSP* 44, no. 51 (1992), pp. 14–15.

29. Pavel Felgengauer, "Russia Too Busy Arming China to Care About Consequences," *St. Petersburg Times*, July 14–20, 1997, *Johnson's Russia List*, July 17, 1997.

30. An extended argument regarding Russia's security concerns in East Asia can be found in Donaldson and Donaldson, "The Arms Trade in Russian-Chinese Relations."

31. For a statement of concern about Russia's ability to stay competitive in the Chinese arms market, see Vitali Mikhailov, "Moscow-Beijing: Arms, Technolo-

gies, and Money," *Russkii kurier*, December 19, 2003, in *CDPSP* 55, no. 51 (2003), p. 17.

32. The juxtaposition of views is found in Pavel Felgengauer, "Russia and the Conflict in the Taiwan Strait," and in Vladimir Abarinov, "Benefits of Alliance with China Are Dubious," *Segodnia*, March 13, 1996, in *CDPSP* 48, no. 11 (1996), pp. 10–12. See also Pavel Ivanov, "Fears that China Will Bite the Hand that Arms It," *Asia Times*, August 1, 1997, *Johnson's Russia List*, no. 1108, August 1, 1997. Scenarios for the future of Russia-China relations can be found in several of the essays in *Rapprochement or Rivalry? Russia-China Relations in a Changing Asia*, ed. Sherman W. Garnett (Washington, DC: Carnegie Endowment for International Peace, 2000).

33. Quoted in Euikon Kim, "The Territorial Dispute Between Moscow and Tokyo: A Historical Perspective," *Asian Perspective* 16, no. 2 (Fall–Winter 1992), p. 145.

34. Robert F. Miller, "Russian Policy Toward Japan," in *Russian Foreign Policy Since 1990*, ed. Peter Shearman (Boulder, CO: Westview, 1995), p. 143.

35. Stanislav Kondrashov, "Trials and Tribulations of Making Peace with Japan," *Izvestia*, August 14, 1992, in *CDPSP* 44, no. 33 (1992), pp. 15–17.

36. Major-General Georgi Mekhov, "Military Aspects of 'Territorial Problem,'" *Kras,iaia zvezda*, July 22, 1992, in *CDPSP* 44, no. 29 (1992), p. 18.

37. Maksim Iusin, "Visit's Cancellation Indicates a Change in the Alignment of Forces in the Russian Leadership," *Izvestia*, September 11, 1992, in *CDPSP* 44, no. 36 (1992), p. 7; an interview with Kozyrev was printed in *Moskovskie novosti*, no. 38, September 20, 1992, in *CDPSP* 44, no. 37 (1992), pp. 18–19.

38. Kozyrev made this claim in his memoirs. See Robert Orttung, "Kozyrev Publishes New Book," *OMRI Daily Digest*, February 28, 1995.

39. Vasili Golovnin, "Evgenii Primakov Invites Japanese to the Southern Kuriles," *Segodnia*, November 19, 1996, in *CDPSP* 48, no. 46 (1996), p. 25.

40. "Argued for 52 Years, Settled in Two Days," *Rossiiskie vesti*, November 4, 1997, in *CDPSP* 49, no. 44 (1997), pp. 1–2.

41. Vasilii Golovnin, "An 'Ingushetia' in the Southern Kuriles?" *Moskovskiie novosti*, no. 45, November 15–22, 1998, in *CDPSP* 50, no. 46 (1998), p. 12.

42. Andrei Ivanov, "Russia and Japan Mount Joint Defense—Against Reporters," *Kommersant*, February 6, 2002, in *CDPSP* 54, no. 6 (2002), p. 19.

43. Vasili Golovnin, "'Black Mark' for Diplomat," *Izvestia*, April 3, 2002, in *CDPSP* 54, no. 14 (2002), pp. 18–19.

44. Brooke, "Japan and Russia Working Hard to Build Economic Ties."

45. "Russia, Japan Fail to Set Timetable for Peace Agreement," AFP, June 25, 2004, in *Johnson's Russia List*, no. 8269, June 25, 2004.

46. "The North Korean Lobby in the Duma Is Acting Against Russia's Interests," *Izvestia*, June 18, 1994, in *CDPSP* 46, no. 24 (1994), pp. 14–15.

47. Natalia Kalashnikova, "In Expectation of Meat Soup and Silk Clothing," *Kommersant-Daily*, April 18, 1996, in *CDPSP* 48, no. 16 (1996), p. 24.

48. Ivan Shomov, "'Patriot' Games: What's Good for American Manufacturers Is Good for Seoul," *Segodnia*, April 8, 1997, in *CDPSP* 49, no. 14 (1997), pp. 21–22.

49. Col.-Gen. Leonid Ivashov, "Old Friends Still Talking," *Asia Times*, May 21, 1997, *Johnson's Russia List*, May 21, 1997; and "North Korea's Final Warning to Moscow," *Kommersant-Daily*, October 1, 1996, in *CDPSP* 48, no. 39 (1996), p. 26.

50. "For Russia, A Key Role in North Korea Talks?" *CDPSP* 55, no. 34 (2003), pp. 1–5.

51. Vitali Naumkin, "Tajikistan: The USSR's Last War or the New Russia's First

War? Moscow Still Has No Unified Policy," *Nezavisimaia gazeta*, July 29, 1993, in *CDPSP* 45, no. 30 (1993), pp. 12–13.

52. Aidyn Mekhtiiev, "Central Asian Commonwealth Could Become Alternative to CIS," *Nezavisimaia gazeta*, October 21, 1994, in *CDPSP* 46, no. 42 (1994), p. 23. See also Georgi Bovt, "Turkic Summit: 'I'm Telling You in Plain Russian,'" *Kommersant-Daily*, August 30, 1995, in *CDPSP* 47, no. 35 (1995), p. 28.

53. Pavel Felgengauer, "What Was in It for Russia?" *Moscow Times*, April 27, 2004, in *Johnson's Russia List*, no. 8183, April 27, 2004.

54. Vladimir Skosyrev, "Iran, Superpower of Persian Gulf, Builds Up Its Military Might with Moscow's Help," *Izvestia*, February 5, 1992, in *CDPSP* 44, no. 5 (1992), pp. 19–20.

55. Vladimir Abarinov, "Moscow and Washington Stick to Their Own Interests," *Segodnia*, May 12, 1995, in *CDPSP* 47, no. 19 (1995), pp. 1–2.

56. Sergei Strokan, "Time to Repay Debts," *Moskovskie novosti*, no. 1, January 1–14, 1996, in *CDPSP* 48, no. 1 (1996), pp. 23–24; "Russia Intends to Drastically Increase Deliveries of Weapons to Iran," *Kommersant-Daily*, November 29, 1996, in *CDPSP* 48, no. 48, p. 22.

57. Georgi Bovt, "Synchronizing Watches: With Accuracy Up to a Century," *Kommersant-Daily*, December 25, 1996, in *CDPSP* 48, no. 52 (1996), pp. 19–20.

58. "Moscow Makes Headway in Iran," *Asia Times*, June 27, 1997, in *Johnson's Russia List*, June 30, 1997.

59. Leonid Gankin, "Primakov Persuades Netanyahu," *Kommersant-Daily*, October 28, 1997, in *CDPSP* 49, no. 43 (1997), p. 21.

60. "Russia's Arms Bazaar."

61. Sergei Strokan, "'Axis of Evil' Passes through Moscow," *Kommersant*, April 6, 2002, in *CDPSP* 54, no. 14 (2002), p. 7.

62. Sergei Strokan, "What's at Stake," *Kommersant*, June 30, 2004, in *CDPSP* 56, no. 26 (2004), pp. 17–18.

63. Sergei Filatov, "Politics Is a Subtle Business, but One Would Like Clarity," *Pravda*, November 11, 1992, in *CDPSP* 44, no. 46 (1992), p. 18.

64. Aleksandr Shumilin, "Why No Breakthrough?" *Moskovskiie novosti*, no. 60, November 27–December 4, 1994, in *CDPSP* 46, no. 47 (1994), p. 23.

65. Vladimir Lukin, "Bengal Light in the Arabian Sands," *Moskovskie novosti*, no. 50, October 23–30, 1994, in *CDPSP* 46, no. 41 (1994), p. 13.

66. "Thinks It Can Do as It Pleases," *Nezavisimaia gazeta*, September 5, 1996, in *CDPSP* 48, no. 36 (1996), p. 8.

67. See, for example, Kirill Dybski, "Oil and Money Will Flow to Russia Through 'Iraqi Pipeline,'" *Segodnia*, December 11, 1996, in *CDPSP* 48, no. 50 (1996), p. 25.

68. "Saddam Is a Time Bomb," *Moskovskie novosti*, no. 47, November 23–30, 1997, in *CDPSP* 49, no. 47 (1997), pp. 3–4.

69. Sergei Markov, "Iraq Intensifies Anti-Americanism the World Over," *Izvestia*, February 26, 1998, in *CDPSP* 50, no. 8 (1998), pp. 8–9.

70. "U.S. Strike on Iraq Draws Angry Outcry in Russia," *CDPSP* 50, no. 51 (1998), pp. 1–6, 16.

71. Andrei Kosesnikov, "Vladimir Putin Plays with Someone Else's Puppets," *Kommersant*, December 23, 2003, in *CDPSP* 55, no. 51 (2003), pp. 16–17.

72. Andrei Zlobin, "Qaddafi Gets Tired of Being a Pariah," *Vremia novostei*, December 22, 2003, in *CDPSP* 55, no. 51 (2003), p. 16.

73. Karen Brutents, "Time to Return," *Nezavisimaia gazeta*, October 5, 1994, in *CDPSP* 46, no. 41 (1994), pp. 13–14.

74. Konstantin Eggert, "Russia Wants to Be the Equal of the U.S. in the Middle East," *Izvestia*, April 26, 1996, in *CDPSP* 48, no. 17 (1996), p. 10.

75. Maksim Iusin, "Washington No Longer Wants to Share the Laurels of Peacemaker with Moscow—Evgenii Primakov's First Defeat," *Izvestia*, April 30, 1996, in *CDPSP* 48, no. 17 (1996), p. 11.

76. Leonid Gankin, "We Have Become Mature Partners," *Moskovskie novosti*, no. 23, June 9–16, 1996, in *CDPSP* 48, no. 23 (1996), pp. 13, 20.

77. Piotr Fedin, "Russians' Friend Arafat Goes Home Satisfied," *Kommersant-Daily*, February 20, 1997, in *CDPSP* 49, no. 8 (1997), pp. 20–21.

78. Aleksei Bausin, "Well, Friends, No Matter How You Sit, for Partnership You're Just Not Fit," *Obshchaia gazeta*, no. 10, March 13–19, 1997, in *CDPSP* 49, no. 11 (1997), p. 26.

79. Aleksei Slobodin, "Monday Is Sharon Day," *Vremia novostei*, October 1, 2002, in *CDPSP* 54, no. 40 (2002), p. 17; Zakhar Gelman, *Rossiiskaia gazeta*, October 2, 2002, in ibid.

80. Katerina Labetskaia and Elena Suponina, "Sharon Asks Putin About 'Arrest of a Jew,'" *Vremia novostei*, November 4, 2003, in *CDPSP* 55, no. 44 (2003), p. 18.

81. Leonid Gankin, "Igor Ivanov Asks Palestinians to Hold Their Tongues," *Kommersant*, January 22, 2004, in *CDPSP* 56, no. 3 (2004), p. 19.

82. Boris Vinogradov, "Conflict Brewing on Afghanistan-Tajikistan Border," *Izvestia*, February 19, 1993, in *CDPSP* 45, no. 7 (1993), pp. 19–20.

83. Evgenii Primakov, "Russia Doesn't Oppose Islam," *Nezavisimaia gazeta*, September 18, 1996, in *CDPSP* 48, no. 40 (1996), p. 32.

84. Galina Sidorova, "Uzbek Soldiers Called Upon to Be Ready to Rebuff Any Incursion," *Kommersant-Daily*, May 27, 1997, in *CDPSP* 49, no. 21 (1997), p. 26.

85. John F. Burns, "Would-Be Afghan Rulers Find Their Islamic Steamroller Halted," *New York Times*, July 27, 1997.

86. Sergei Guly, "Difficult Road to Alliance," *Noviie izvestia*, October 12, 2000, in *CDPSP* 52, no. 41 (2000), p. 9.

87. Anatol Lieven, "The Pressures on Pakistan," *Foreign Affairs* 81, no. 1 (2002), pp. 106–18.

88. Vladimir Naumov, "Fate of 'Space Deal,'" *Rossiiskie vesti*, January 4, 1994, in *CDPSP* 46, no. 1 (1994), p. 18.

89. Michael Gordon, "Russia Selling Atomic Plants to India; U.S. Protests Deal," *New York Times*, February 6, 1997.

90. "India and Russia: Brothers in Arms," *Economist*, November 23, 1996, pp. 38–40; and Aleksandr Sychov, "India to Rely on SU-30," *Izvestia*, December 3, 1996, in *CDPSP* 48, no. 48 (1996), pp. 21–22.

91. Fred Weir for the *Hindustan Times*, March 26, 1997, in *Johnson's Russia List*, March 27, 1997.

92. "Pakistan Will Go Without Russian Weapons," *Kommersant-Daily*, March 30, 1996, in *CDPSP* 48, no. 13 (1996), p. 23; Maksim Iusin, "The Pakistani Titmouse and the Indian Crane," *Izvestia*, December 22, 1995, in *CDPSP* 48, no. 1 (1995), pp. 12–13.

93. Dennis Kux, "India's Fine Balance," *Foreign Affairs* 81, no. 3 (2002), pp. 93–106.

94. Georgi Bovt, "New Friend," *Izvestia*, August 31, 2001, in *CDPSP* 53, no. 35

(2001), pp. 16–17; Ekaterina Grigorieva and Andrei Lebedev, "Potential for Cooperation with India Is Nearly Exhausted," ibid., p. 17.

95. Kux, "India's Fine Balance."

96. Mikhail Kukushkin, "Big Game of Sukhoi," *Vremia novosti*, December 29, 2000, in *CDPSP* 52, no. 52 (2000), p. 22.

97. Iuri Golotuik and Viktor Belimov, "For Us, Money Is No Object," *Vremia novosti*, February 16, 2001, in *CDPSP* 53, no. 7 (2001), pp. 16–17.

98. Boris Volkhonskii, "Victory for Indian Diplomacy," *Kommersant*, October 6, 2000, in *CDPSP* 52, no. 40 (2000), pp. 8, 20.

99. Dmitri Litovkin, "Russia Will Earn $1.5 Billion from Indian Military Contracts," *Izvestia*, January 21, 2004, in *CDPSP* 56, no. 3 (2004), p. 18.

100. Leonid Gankin, "Russia Is Losing Its Enemies," *Kommersant-Daily*, July 9, 1997, in *CDPSP* 49, no. 28 (1997), p. 23.

101. Marat Zubko, "Evgenii Primakov's Three Points," *Izvestia*, June 2, 1998, in *CDPSP* 50, no. 22 (1998), p. 11.

102. Rouben Aziaian and Peter Vasilieff, "Russia and Pakistan: The Difficult Path to Rapprochement," *Asian Affairs: An American Review* 30, no. 1 (2003).

103. Vladimir Skosyrev, "Igor Ivanov in the Line of Fire," *Vremia MN*, February 5, 2002, in *CDPSP* 54, no. 6 (2002), p. 10.

104. Vladislav Vorobiov, "Almaty Hopes to Reconcile Everyone," *Rossiiskaia gazeta*, June 4, 2002, in *CDPSP* 54, no. 23 (2002), pp. 17–18.

105. Olga Berezintseva, "President Musharraf Asks Vladimir Putin to Reconcile India and Pakistan," *Kommersant*, February 6, 2003, in *CDPSP* 55, no. 5 (2003), pp. 17–18.

106. Sergei Blagov, "Musharraf a Small Fish in Putin's Pool," *Asia Times*, February 6, 2003, in *CDI Weekly*, no. 243, February 6, 2003. Whether it resulted from the added pressure emanating from Moscow, Washington, and Beijing, or from the domestic political and strategic calculations of the two parties to the conflict, significant progress did take place in 2003–04 toward the lessening of Indo-Pakistani tensions.

107. Viktor Litovkin, "Nonequilateral Triangle," *Vremia MN*, December 3, 2002, in *CDPSP* 54, no. 49 (2002), pp. 5–6.

108. Arkadi Dubnov, "Not Allies, but Never Enemies," *Vremia novostei*, December 3, 2002, in ibid., p. 5.

109. "No 'Shower of Gold' Expected," *Moskovskie novosti*, no. 48, November 30–December 30, 1997, in *CDPSP* 49, no. 48 (1997), p. 24.

110. Arkadi Dubnov, "Without a Hitch," *Vremia novostei*, August 6, 2003, in *CDPSP* 55, no. 31 (2003), pp. 18–19.

111. Salavat Suleimanov, "Peace Will Come to Angola," *Nezavisimaia gazeta*, April 4, 2002, in *CDPSP* 54, no. 14 (2002), p. 20.

112. Gennadi Sysoiev, "'We Realized How Much We're Alike,'" *Kommersant*, March 7, 2001, in *CDPSP* 53, no. 10 (2001), p. 20.

113. Evgenii Bai, "Russia Concerned by Castro's Unilateral Decision to Stop Construction of Nuclear Power Plant in Cuba," *Izvestia*, September 9, 1992, in *CDPSP* 44, no. 36 (1992), p. 23.

114. Karen Khachaturov, "Russian-Cuban Relations Are Equitable and Mutually Advantageous," *Nezavisimaia gazeta*, December 29, 1993, in *CDPSP* 45, no. 52 (1993), p. 28.

115. Leonid Velekhov, "Russia and Cuba: A Dialogue Between a Poor Man and a Beggar," *Segodnia*, October 13, 1995; Pavel Felgengauer, "Russia Needs the Island of Freedom Again," *Segodnia*, October 17, 1995; and Aleksei Basin, "Russia and Cuba: Back to the Future?" *Moskovskie novosti*, no. 71, October 15–22, 1995, in *CDPSP* 47, no. 42 (1995), pp. 6–7, 24.

116. Evgenii Bai, "Half a Loaf Is Better than None," *Izvestia*, October 10, 1996, in *CDPSP* 48, no. 41 (1996), p. 28.

117. Karen Khachaturov, "Russian Breakthrough in Latin America," *Nezavisimaia gazeta*, May 29, 1996; and Anatoli Sosnovski, "On the Benefit of Routine Professionalism," *Moskovskie novosti*, no. 21, May 26–June 2, 1996, in *CDPSP* 48, no. 21 (1996), p. 27.

118. Georgi Bovt, "Sortie into America's 'Backyard,'" *Izvestia*, December 21, 2000, in *CDPSP* 52, no. 51 (2000), p. 24.

Chapter 9: Russia in the Age of Global Terror

1. Islamic terror was also directed against those Arab governments that were friendly to or allied with the United States.

2. Boris Yeltsin, *Midnight Diaries* (New York: Public Affairs, 2000), p. 327.

3. The text of Russia's foreign policy concept can be found in *CDPSP* 52, no. 28 (2000), pp. 7–9, and *CDPSP* 52, no. 29 (2000), pp. 6–8.

4. Stanislav Kondrashov, "Language of Gestures in Putin's Diplomacy," *Vremia MN*, in *CDPSP* 52, no. 52 (2000), p. 6.

5. Patrick E. Tyler, "With U.S. Missile Defense, Russia Wants Less Offense," *New York Times*, November 15, 2000.

6. "Vladimir Putin: We Will Not Allow Governmental Authority to Be 'Privatized,'—Germany's *Welt am Sonntag* Interviews Russian President," *Rossiiskaia gazeta*, June 15, 2000, in *CDPSP* 52, no. 25 (2000), p. 8.

7. Frank Bruni, "Leaders' Words at First Meeting Are Striking for Warm Tone," *New York Times*, June 17, 2001.

8. Some scholars question the degree to which September 11 changed Russian policy. See, for example, Rick Fawn, ed., *Realignments in Russian Foreign Policy*, London: Frank Cass, 2003, pp.1–8.

9. Lilia Shevtsova, *Putin's Russia* (Washington, DC: Carnegie Endowment for International Peace, 2003), p. 206. Support for Putin's pro-American policy was opposed by some among Russia's political elite. See Andrei P. Tsygankov, *Whose World Order? Russia's Perception of American Ideas after the Cold War* (Notre Dame, IN: University of Notre Dame Press, 2004), pp. 120–24.

10. Ahmed Rashid, *Taliban* (New Haven: Yale University Press, 2001), p. 48.

11. Dmitri Trenin and Aleksei V. Malashenko with Anatol Leiven, *Russia's Restless Frontier, The Chechnya Factor in Post-Soviet Russia* (Washington, DC: Carnegie Endowment for International Peace, 2004), p. 166.

12. Ibid., p. 167.

13. For the terms of the treaty and the Russian reaction see "Russia, U.S. to Sign New Strategic Arms Treaty," *CDPSP* 54, no. 20 (2002), pp. 1–4 and "Putin, Bush Sign Treaty to Cut Weapons," *CDPSP* 54, no. 21 (2002), pp. 1–6.

14. "New Council Will Give Russia Role in NATO," *CDPSP* 54, no. 20 (2002), pp. 4–7 and "Russia-NATO Summit Formalizes New Relationship," *CDPSP* 54, no. 22 (2002), pp. 1–5.

15. "Putin Sets Policy Priorities for Russian Diplomats," *CDPSP* 54, no. 28 (2002), p. 5.

16. "Is There a 'Putin Doctrine' in Foreign Policy?" *CDPSP* 54, no. 31 (2002), p. 1.

17. "Iraq Agrees to Arms Inspections; U.S., Russia at Odds," *CDPSP* 54, no. 38, (2002), p. 4.

18. United Nations Security Council Resolution 1441, November 8, 2002.

19. The most that Bush would commit was to "be respectful" of Russia's economic interests in a new Iraq. Georgi Bovt, "A Gentlemen's Agreement with Specifics," *Izvestia*, November 23, 2002, in *CDPSP* 54, no. 47 (2002), pp. 2–4.

20. Hans Blix, *Disarming Iraq* (New York: Pantheon Books, 2004), p. 148.

21. Evgenia Slutskaya in *Novie Izvestia*, January 29, 2003, p. 3, in *CDPSP* 55, no. 4 (2003), p. 1.

22. Robert Woodward, *Bush at War* (New York: Simon & Schuster, 2002), p. 354.

23. Aleksandr Samokhotkin, "Hurry Up and Turn on the Light," *Vremia novostei*, January 29, 2003, in *CDPSP* 55, no. 4 (2003), p. 2

24. See "Surveys Chart Russians' Views on Foreign Policy," *CDPSP* 54, no. 42 (2002), pp. 1–4. Russian opinion of the United States changed with events. It declined in March 2002 following a bitter controversy over the winter Olympics in Salt Lake City. Later in the summer of 2002, some two-thirds of the Russians had a good opinion of the United States. Vitali Golovachov, "We Understand Each Other Better Now," *Trud*, September 11, 2002, in *CDPSP* 54, no. 37 (2002), p. 18.

25 "Have Russia, 'Old Europe' Formed 'Antiwar Entente'?" *CDPSP* 55, no. 6 (2003), p. 2.

26. For Primakov's earlier missions, see Joseph L. Nogee and Robert H. Donaldson, *Soviet Foreign Policy since World War II*, 4th ed. (New York: Macmillan, 1992), pp. 393–95.

27. Statement made in interview with *Izvestia*, April 4, 2003, in *CDPSP* 55, no. 13, (2003), p. 8.

28. "Iran's Nuclear Aims—a New U.S.-Russian Conflict?" *CDPSP* 55, no. 22 (2003), p. 6. Iran cooperated with Russia to end the civil war in Tajikistan in the 1990s.

29. Aleksandr Reutov, "Iran Gives in to the IAEA," *Kommersant*, December 19, 2003, in *CDPSP* 55, no. 50 (2003), p. 18.

30. "Iran Says It Will Not Give up Uranium Enrichment Program," *New York Times*, August 1, 2004.

31. "Russia to Join Talks on North Korean Nuclear Issue," *CDPSP* 55, no. 30 (2003), p. 1.

32. Dana Sanger, "Diplomacy Fails to Slow Advance of Nuclear Arms," *New York Times*, August 8, 2004, p. 7.

33. Svetlana Babaieva, Dmitri Litovkin, and Maksim Iusin, "We Go to Iraq and They Come to Chechnia?" *Izvestia*, September 5, 2003, in *CDPSP* 55, no. 36 (2003), p. 3.

34. The Paris Club established Iraq's debt to Russia at $3.5 billion, but that did not include interest. With interest, the full debt was closer to $8 billion.

35. "A Combative 'Ivanov Doctrine' for Russian Military?" *CDPSP* 55, no. 40 (2003), p. 5.

36. At a summit meeting of the OSCE in Istanbul in 1999, Russia agreed to withdraw its armed forces from Georgia. See "Is Conflict with U.S. Brewing in Russia's Backyard?" *CDPSP* 55, no. 49 (2003), pp. 13–14.

37. Ibid., p. 13.

38. Thom Shanker, "Russian Faults NATO Opening to Baltic States," *New York Times*, August 15, 2004, p. 10.

39. Natalia Ratiani, "Moscow Finally Supports Bush Initiative," *Izvestia*, June 1, 2004, in *CDPSP* 56, no. 22 (2004), p. 20. See also *CDPSP* 56, no. 5 (2004), p. 19.

40. United Nations Security Council Resolution 1546, January 8, 2004.

41. "Putin Delivers a New Kind of Annual Message," *CDPSP* 56, no. 21 (2004), p. 5.

42. "U.S., Russia Encounter Friction at EU, NATO Summits," *CDPSP* 56, no. 26 (2004), p. 8.

Index

About the Authors

Robert H. Donaldson, educated at Harvard University, is Trustees Professor of Political Science at the University of Tulsa. Past president of both the University of Tulsa and Fairleigh Dickinson University, he also has taught and held administrative positions at Lehman College of the City University of New York and at Vanderbilt University. He has served at the U.S. Department of State as International Affairs Fellow of the Council on Foreign Relations, and at the Strategic Studies Institute of the U.S. Army War College as visiting research professor. Professor Donaldson has written extensively on Soviet and Russian politics and foreign policy and has authored or co-authored five other books.

Joseph L. Nogee, professor emeritus at the University of Houston, was educated at the Georgetown School of Foreign Service, the University of Chicago, and Yale University. Professor Nogee also has taught at Vanderbilt University, New York University, the University of Virginia, Rice University, and the U.S. Army War College. His teaching and research areas are international politics and Soviet and Russian politics. He is the author, co-author, or editor of eight books, including most recently *Russian Politics: The Struggle for a New Order* (1996).